CONSERVATION IN HIGHLY FRAGMENTED LANDSCAPES

JOIN US ON THE INTERNET
WWW: http://www.thomson.com
EMAIL: findit@kiosk.thomson.com

thomson.com is the on-line portal for the products, services and resources available from International Thomson Publishing (ITP). This Internet kiosk gives users immediate access to more than 34 ITP publishers and over 20,000 products. Through *thomson.com* Internet users can search catalogs, examine subject-specific resource centers and subscribe to electronic discussion lists. You can purchase ITP products from your local bookseller, or directly through *thomson.com*.

Visit Chapman & Hall's Internet Resource Center for information on our new publications, links to useful sites on the World Wide Web and an opportunity to join our e-mail mailing list. Point your browser to: **http://www.chaphall.com** or **http://www.thomson.com/chaphall/lifesce.html** for Life Sciences

A service of

CONSERVATION IN HIGHLY FRAGMENTED LANDSCAPES

EDITED BY
MARK W. SCHWARTZ
UNIVERSITY OF CALIFORNIA, DAVIS

CHAPMAN & HALL

I(T)P® International Thomson Publishing
New York • Albany • Bonn • Boston • Cincinnati • Detroit • London • Madrid • Melbourne
Mexico City • Pacific Grove • Paris • San Francisco • Singapore • Tokyo • Toronto • Washington

Cover design: Saïd Sayrafiezadeh, *Emdash Inc.*

Photo credit: Michael Jeffords (Illinois Natural History Survey)

Printed in the United States of America

Chapman & Hall
115 Fifth Avenue
New York, NY 10003

Chapman & Hall
2-6 Boundary Row
London SE1 8HN
England

Thomas Nelson Australia
102 Dodds Street
South Melbourne, 3205
Victoria, Australia

Chapman & Hall GmbH
Postfach 100 263
D-69442 Weinheim
Germany

International Thomson Editores
Campos Eliseos 385, Piso 7
Col. Polanco
11560 Mexico D.F
Mexico

International Thomson Publishing–Japan
Hirakawacho-cho Kyowa Building, 3F
1-2-1 Hirakawacho-cho
Chiyoda-ku, 102 Tokyo
Japan

International Thomson Publishing Asia
221 Henderson Road #05-10
Henderson Building
Singapore 0315

1 2 3 4 5 6 7 8 9 10 XXX 01 00 99 98 97

Library of Congress Cataloging-in-Publication Data

Conservation in highly fragmented landscapes / Mark W. Schwartz,
    editor.
        p.   cm.
    Includes bibliographical references and index.
    ISBN 0-412-07031-6
    (pbk. : alk. paper)
       1. Nature conservation–Middle West.   2. Fragmented landscapes-
    -Middle West.   3. Natural areas–Middle West.   I. Schwartz, Mark W.
    QH76.5.M53C66   1997
    333.95′16′0977–dc20   96-36445
                                                              CIP

British Library Cataloguing in Publication Data available

To order this or any other Chapman & Hall book, please contact **International Thomson Publishing, 7625 Empire Drive, Florence, KY 41042.** Phone: (606) 525-6600 or 1-800-842-3636. Fax: (606) 525-7778. e-mail: order@chaphall.com.

For a complete listing of Chapman & Hall titles, send your request to **Chapman & Hall, Dept. BC, 115 Fifth Avenue, New York, NY 10003.**

Dedication

Conservation in the Midwest has been guided by many luminaries: Aldo Leopold, John Muir, Steven Forbes, Henry Chandler Cowles, Vic Shelford, Charles Kendeigh, and John Curtis, to name but a few. This book is dedicated to the legions of professionals and volunteers, past and present, who are working to save natural habitats in the Midwest. More proximally, I dedicate this to Sharon, Eli, and Ari for their support.

Table of Contents

List of Contributors

Roger C. Anderson
Department of Biology
Illinois State University
Normal, IL USA 61790

Jeffrey D. Brawn
Center for Wildlife Ecology
Illinois Natural History Survey
607 East Peabody Drive
Champaign, IL USA 61820

Kevin S. Cummings
Illinois Natural History Survey
607 E. Peabody Drive
Champaign, IL USA 61820

Ann Dennis
Pacific Southwest Research Station
P.O. Box 245
Berkeley, CA USA 94701

Brian K. Dunphy
Illinois Natural History Survey
607 E. Peabody Drive
Champaign, IL USA 61820

John E. Ebinger
Botany Department
Eastern Illinois University
Charleston, IL USA 61920

James S. Fralish
Department of Forestry
Southern Illinois University
Carbondale, IL 62901

Stephen P. Havera
Illinois Natural History Survey
River Research Laboratory
Havana, IL USA 62644

Tom Heavisides
Illinois Department of Natural Resources
524 S. 2nd Street
Springfield, IL USA 62701

James R. Herkert
Illinois Endangered Species Board
Illinois Department of Natural Resources
524 S. Second Street
Springfield, IL USA 62701

Sharon M. Hermann
Tall Timbers Research Station
Route 1, Box 678
Tallahassee, FL USA 32312

Joyce Hoffman
Illinois Natural History Survey
607 E. Peabody Drive
Champaign, IL 61820

Jeffrey P. Hoover
Center for Wildlife Ecology
Illinois Natural History Survey
607 East Peabody Drive
Champaign, IL USA 61820

Lisa Horth
Department of Biological Sciences
Florida State University
Tallahassee, FL 32306-2043

Susan Kalisz
Department of Biological Sciences
University of Pittsburgh
Pittsburgh, PA USA 15260

Bob Lieberman
Illinois Department of Natural Resources
524 S. 2nd Street
Springfield, IL USA 62701

James O. Luken
Department of Biological Sciences
Northern Kentucky University
Highland Heights, KY USA 41099-0400

Mark A. McPeek
Department of Biological Sciences
Dartmouth College
Hanover, NH USA 03755

Philip C. Mankin
Department of Natural Resources and
   Environmental Sciences
University of Illinois
1102 S. Goodwin
Urbana, IL USA 61801

Paul Matthiae
Bureau of Endangered Resources
Wisconsin Department of Natural
   Resources
Box 7921, Madison, WI 53707

Jeffrey W. Olson
Illinois Natural History Survey
607 E. Peabody Drive
Champaign, IL USA 61820

Lawrence M. Page
Illinois Natural History Survey
607 E. Peabody Drive
Champaign, IL USA 61820

Mark Pyron
Illinois Natural History Survey
607 E. Peabody Drive
Champaign, IL USA 61820

Kenneth R. Robertson
Center for Biodiversity
Illinois Natural History Survey
607 East Peabody Drive
Champaign, IL USA 61820

Scott K. Robinson
Center for Wildlife Ecology
Illinois Natural History Survey
607 East Peabody Drive
Champaign, IL USA 61820

Mark W. Schwartz
Center for Population Biology
University of California
Davis, CA USA 95616

Craig L. Shafer
George Wright Society
P.O. Box 65
Hancock, MI USA 49930

Forest Stearns
University of Wisconsin-Milwaukee
Forestry Science Laboratory
5985 Highway K
Rhinelander, WI 54501

Liane B. Suloway
Illinois Natural History Survey
607 East Peabody Drive
Champaign, IL USA 61820

John B. Taft
Illinois Natural History Survey
607 East Peabody Drive
Champaign, IL USA 61820

Ann Marie Trame
Illinois Natural History Survey
607 E. Peabody Drive
Champaign, IL USA 61820

Phillip J. van Mantgem
Graduate Group in Ecology
University of California
Davis, CA USA 61820

Richard E. Warner
Department of Natural Resources and
  Environmental Sciences
University of Illinois
1102 S. Goodwin
Urbana, IL USA 61801

Introduction

Mark W. Schwartz

> Soon after we came into extensive meadows: and I was assured that those meadows continue for a hundred and fifty miles, being in winter drowned lands and marshes. By the dryness of the season they were now beautiful pastures, and here presented itself one of the most delightful prospects I have ever beheld; all low grounds being meadow, and without wood, and all of the high grounds being covered with trees and appearing like islands: the whole scene seemed an elysium.
>
> Capt. Thomas Morris. 1791

> I am sitting in a 60-mile-an-hour bus sailing over a highway originally laid out for horse and buggy. The ribbon of concrete has been widened and widened until the field fences threaten to topple into the road cuts. In the narrow thread of sod between the shaved banks and the toppling fences grow the relics of what once was Illinois: the prairie.
>
> Aldo Leopold. *Sketches Here and There.* 1949

The 150 years spanned by these quotes saw the complete and wholesale conversion of native prairies east of the Mississippi River to agricultural lands, mostly row crops. More than 85% of the virgin forests in the 48 coterminous states have been logged (Postel and Ryan 1991); over 90% of the grasslands east of the Mississippi are gone, with regional estimates typically exceeding 99% (Noss et al. 1994); and water flow in 77% of the major rivers north of 40° latitude has been moderately to severely altered through dams (Dynesius and Nilsson 1994). Extreme loss of natural habitat is now the typical, rather than the exceptional, condition. In contrast, most of the theoretical underpinnings of conservation biology were developed under a conceptual model of landscapes that are not yet entirely fragmented. The science of designing bioreserves, habitat corridors, and sustainable use preserves assumes an ongoing process of habitat loss. The loss of habitat in urban and agricultural regions, what I call *highly fragmented* regions, differs from this model, which typifies the core of theoretical conservation research. Habitat conversion in these regions is complete, extensive, and typically in the realm of the historical.

Conservation in highly fragmented landscapes requires a different approach with a different science of conservation biology. Preserve design is no longer a choice between many small or few large but between small and intact versus large and degraded. In a highly fragmented region macro-site, or bioreserve, *conservation* means habitat restoration; *metapopulation dynamics* for vertebrates means capture and release programs; *preserve design* means asking what is for sale; and *wildlife management* means convincing the public that more deer isn't necessarily better and that managing a healthy herd may mean increasing the mortality rate. Conservation in highly fragmented regions is living with the harsh reality that we have limited resources and that choosing to work toward saving one thing is choosing to postpone something else; it is the decision to partition few resources between small and large conservation projects. This book focuses on the science behind these tough choices and seeks to encourage the development of conservation biology for regions where small, highly isolated natural habitats are the norm. The audience is intended to include academicians, policymakers, and land managers, as we attempt to link information that is vital to the professional development of all three groups.

Enumerating all of the highly fragmented habitats and regions could fill volumes. Most biomes and regions of the world have examples where habitat loss is virtually complete. The purpose of this book is not to describe the details of biotic losses, but to consider how past chronic habitat loss drives conservation efforts. To focus this effort I have adopted a test-case approach to examine conservation problems in one highly fragmented landscape: the eastern tallgrass prairie–forest border of the midwestern United States. This book presents problems that, while having a specific manifestation within the focal region, are common to highly fragmented landscapes. The goals of this book are to (1) delineate the problems facing this region; (2) delineate the choices that must be made regarding practical conservation strategies when we cannot simultaneously adopt all strategies, protect all habitats, or predict the success of varying conservation strategies; (3) propose ways to allocate and balance conservation efforts between different strategies; (4) discuss the role of concepts such as adaptive management strategies, bioreserve conservation, habitat connectivity, and ecosystem-based management in a highly fragmented region; and (5) describe ways in which these ideas are being implemented in the study region.

The Midwest was chosen as the case study for this book because of its severe habitat loss (e.g., Illinois and Iowa rank 49th and 50th among the 50 states in remaining natural habitats, respectively—Klopatek et al. 1979) in conjunction with active conservation programs. In addition, this region embodies conservation concerns that are of interest to a broad spectrum of conservationists (e.g., non-native species invasions, loss of large vertebrates, and disrupted historical disturbance regimes). Finally, the Midwest provides a good setting for this treatment because of a long history of ecology and conservation. Many of the founders of the field of ecology either got started or conducted their professional careers in the Midwest (McIntosh 1985). Several professional organizations (e.g., the Natural Areas Association and the Society for Restoration Ecology) began in the region. In the 1930s, a fledgling wing of the Ecological Society of America formed on the campus of the University of Illinois to try to address applied ecological problems. This group later split from the Society to become an independent organization, one that we now know as The Nature Conservancy. Similarly, the region boasts several fine local conservation organizations (e.g., Save the Prairie Society, Natural Lands Institute, and Grand Prairie Friends). The Illinois volunteer stewardship network, with over 5,000 people involved, is probably the largest in the country. Illinois and Wisconsin were among the first states to institute state nature preserves systems.

This book has three parts. Part 1 defines the regional context through habitat descriptions. These chapters (1–4) provide critical background information on the region by synthesizing information on habitats in terms of (1) composition and diversity, (2) historical and current distribution and abundance; (3) the degree of habitat fragmentation, and (4) current threats. Part 2 (chapters 5–15) describes general problems of conservation in highly fragmented regions using specific examples. Chapters 5 and 6 discuss the problem of weedy species diminishing the ability of a habitat to sustain natural levels of biodiversity. The problem is considered in terms of both exotic (chapter 5) and native (chapter 6) species. Chapters 7 and 8 focus on how mammals and birds are faring in human-dominated landscapes. Chapter 9 addresses the impact of degradation and loss of natural habitats in flowing water systems. Chapter 10 considers the historical role of fire and how this relates to the application of fire as a management tool and chapters 11 and 12 describe the rapid alteration of natural habitats as a result of fire suppression. Chapter 13 considers the problem of small population size in isolated stands. Chapter 14 examines the role of agricultural grazing in midwestern woodlands. Part 3 (chapters 15–19) links midwestern conservation problems to conservation strategies. Chapters 15 and 16 describe conservation strategies for highly fragmented regions, and chapters 17–19 detail specific conservation programs.

At the heart of conservation biology is the faith that science has the power to affect human policy regarding the use of biotic resources and the maintenance of biological diversity. To bring this about scientists must devote attention to societal goals and values and the perceived cost imposed by conservation activities. How we interact with our environment close to home drives how we choose to restrict our impact on the systems where large blocks of natural habitats persist. Arguing that every dominant society throughout recorded history rose to power through a rich resource base in wood, Perlin (1989) links the depletion of wood resources and environmental degradation to the decline of regionally dominant cultures in Mesopotamia, Crete, Greece, Rome, and Europe. Throughout the deforestation process, these cultures consistently exhibited an increased empathy toward the natural world as resources became scarce; listened impatiently to alarmed calls for conservation as wood became chronically scarce; failed to put constraints on the consumption of resources; and declined in world power once their renewable resource was not renewed. Previous cultures failed to regulate consumption in order to preserve the very processes of the natural environment upon which they depended. While this pattern has slowed as the global community has shifted its energy resource base from wood to fossil fuels, conserving biological diversity in tandem with human land use is a critical key to breaking the pattern of ecological failure. This entails doing an effective job of conservation where people live and interact with their environment: in highly fragmented habitats.

References

Dynesius, M., and C. Nilsson. 1994. Fragmentation and flow regulation of river systems in the northern third of the world. *Science* 266: 753–762.

Klopatek, J.M., R.J. Olson, C.J. Emerson, and J.L. Joness. 1979. Land-use conflicts with natural vegetation in the United States. *Environmental Conservation* 6:191–199.

Leopold, A. 1949. *A Sand County Almanac, and Sketches Here and There.* Oxford University Press, New York.

McIntosh, R.P. 1985. *The Background of Ecology: Concept and Theory.* Cambridge Studies in Ecology. Cambridge University Press, New York.

Noss, R.F., E.T. LaRoe III, and J.M. Scott. 1994. *Endangered Ecosystems of the United States: A Preliminary Assessment of Loss and Degradation.* U.S. Dept. of Interior. National Biological Service. Biological Report no. 28. Washington, DC.

Perlin, J. 1989. *A Forest Journey: The Role of Wood in the Development of Civilization.* W. W. Norton, New York.

Postel, S., and J.C. Ryan. 1991. Reforming forestry. In L. Starke (ed.), *State of the World 1991: A Worldwatch Institute Report on Progress Toward a Sustainable Society.* W. W. Norton, New York, pp. 74–92.

PART I

The Context:
The Highly Fragmented Midwest

1

Forest Communities of the Midwestern United States

John E. Ebinger
Botany Department, Eastern Illinois University, Charleston, IL 61920

Introduction

The deciduous forests of eastern North America have become excessively fragmented as a result of increased human activity during the past four centuries.
Originally deciduous forest extended as an almost unbroken blanket across eastern
North America from just north of the Great Lakes and the Gaspe Peninsula south
to the gulf coast, including eastern Texas and all but the southern third of Florida
(Braun 1950). The western boundary was indistinct, with a mixture of upland
prairies and forests extending along rivers in Minnesota, Iowa, Missouri, Oklahoma, and Texas. These western woodlands became more open, with a dramatic
decrease in canopy cover forming open-woodland communities and savannas,
before giving way to prairie (Taft Chapter 2, this volume). The upland prairie
patches extended eastward on drier sites throughout Illinois, Indiana and Ohio
(Robertson et al., Chapter 3, this volume).

The eastern deciduous forest is dominated by broad-leaved, angiosperm tree
species that are mostly deciduous, generally losing their leaves in the fall. On
mesic sites the canopy is closed, exceeding 90% cover, and trees are in excess
of 30 m in height (Braum 1950). In xeric areas the canopy is commonly more
open and the trees shorter. In these forests a subcanopy layer is well developed,
containing future canopy trees and many understory species that rarely enter the
canopy. Usually a thick woody understory layer is present, composed of numerous
seedlings, saplings, and shrubs. In the spring the forest floor is generally very
colorful because of the many spring-blooming ephemerals, while numerous sum-
mer- and fall-blooming herbs, many without obvious flowers, are also an important component (Wilhelm 1991). Species of ferns are present, particularly on
mesic sites, while mosses are rarely important due to a thick layer of litter. In
the southern parts of this, forest evergreen angiosperms and conifers are common
in the canopy along with the deciduous species. Various species of conifers,
particularly pines (*Pinus* spp.) again become important to the north in the Great
Lakes region and to the south and west in parts of Missouri, Arkansas, eastern
Oklahoma, and Texas (Kuchler 1964).

Throughout the eastern deciduous forest the climate is mild, subtemperate, and humid. Most of this region receives between 80 and 150 cm of precipitation, which is fairly evenly distributed throughout the year. The mean annual snowfall varies from 20 cm in the west to nearly 244 cm in the northeast. This seasonal distribution and amount of precipitation, along with the length of the growing season, favors the formation of deciduous forest. The decrease in precipitation, along with droughts, and a high evaporation/precipitation ratio at the western margin of this forest favors grasslands with the corresponding decrease in forest (Transeau 1935). Average January temperatures range from near −7°C in the north to +4°C at the southern limit, but with distinct seasons throughout. A decrease in summer warmth, the shorter growing season, and low winter temperature extremes appear to limit the extent of deciduous forest to the north, while a combination of high summer temperatures and infrequent frosts are probably the factors controlling the southern limits of this forest.

At present, forests occupy only a small portion of their original area, although some portions of the eastern deciduous forests are increasing in extent. The purpose of this chapter is to review the forces that gave rise to the eastern deciduous forest prior to European contact, the natural composition of these forests, and threats and trends in these forests, most notably the impact on forested habitats by European settlement in the Midwest (Figure 1.1).

The Historical Midwestern Forest

Glacial History and Forest Development

Past glaciation has had a profound effect on the vegetation of North America. At the time of maximum Wisconsin glaciation, approximately 18,000 years before the present (B.P.), the northern half of North America (including Iowa, most of Wisconsin, northeastern Illinois, central Indiana, Ohio, and Pennsylvania) was covered by the Laurentide Ice Sheet (Pielou 1991). Plant fossil records, particularly fossil pollen profiles, have been used to show the major vegetation changes in eastern North America during Wisconsin glaciation (Delcourt and Delcourt 1981, 1993). Tundra communities were situated just south of the ice sheet (Figure 1.2). South of the tundra the boreal forest, dominated by conifers (Table 1.1), extended as a broad band across the Great Plains and the Ozark Mountains to the Atlantic coast, with a narrow extension south in the Mississippi River alluvial valley to the Gulf of Mexico. A narrow band of forest composed of conifers and northern hardwoods existed south of the boreal forest, while a temperate deciduous forest of varying species compositions was restricted to the Gulf and lower Atlantic coastal plains. A mixed mesophytic forest composed of a diverse assemblage of species (Table 1.1) occurred on the loess bluffs east of the Mississippi

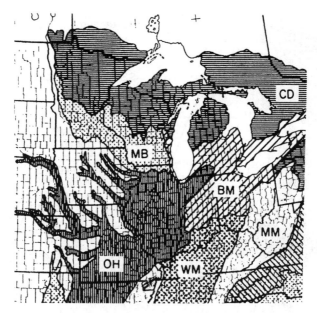

Figure 1.1. Map of the forest associations of the deciduous forests of the northern midwestern United States. Abbreviations of the associations shown are: CD—conifer / northern hardwoods; MB—sugar maple / basswood; BM—beech / sugar maple; OH— oak / hickory; CTO—bald cypress / water tupelo / oak; WM—western mesophytic forest (not discussed); MM—mixed mesophytic forest (not discussed).

From Greller (1988)

River valley and within the dissected valleys of major rivers in the southeast (Delcourt and Delcourt 1981).

By 10000 B.P. the ice sheet had retreated and the pattern of natural vegetation throughout the Midwest was becoming similar to that of today (King 1981). The increased warmth and aridity during this Hypsithermal Interval (8000 to 5000 B.P.) resulted in prairie, oak-savanna, oak-hickory, and southeastern evergreen forests shifting toward the north (Figure 1.2). During this period the growing season was about two weeks longer than it is today and there was a 10–20% decrease in precipitation.

Since 6000 B.P. the Midwest has experienced a slight cooling trend as well as a nominal increase in precipitation. These climatic changes, under normal conditions, would have resulted in an increase in forest at the expense of prairie throughout much of the prairie peninsula. The flat to gently rolling landscape created by the glacier, however, provided an ideal terrain for the movement of fire, an agent that shaped and perpetuated the prairies for the next 6000 years. The presettlement distribution of the major vegetation types (prairie, savanna,

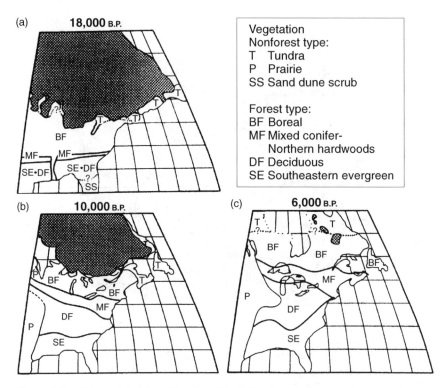

Figure 1.2. Extent of the glacial ice sheet (shaded regions) and vegetation mapped across eastern North America at: (*a*) 18,000 years before present (B.P.), (*b*) 10,000 B.P., and (*c*) 6000 B.P.

From Delcourt and Delcourt (1993)

open woodland, and forest) throughout much of the prairie peninsula was determined largely by firebreaks, such as lakes and rivers, and by topographic relief that controlled the frequency and intensity of fires (Gleason 1913, Wells 1970, Grimm 1984, Anderson 1970, 1983).

Indigenous Forest Use

It is a popular belief that the early European settlers, when they entered North America, found an unbroken forest of giant trees. Until the latter half of this century many botanists dismissed the possibility of any significant disturbance by the Native Americans. We now know that in many parts of North America indigenous people built large cities, farmed extensive areas of ground, and operated far-ranging trading networks (Williams 1989). Though appearing pristine to the casual observer of the 1600s, these primeval forests of eastern North America had been subjected to both human and natural disturbances (Davies

Table 1.1. Dominant woody species of forest communities present in the midwestern United States during the full- to late-glacial period (>10,000 years ago).

Boreal forests	River valley forests
Spruce (*Picea* spp.)	Oak (*Quercus* spp.)
Jack pine (*Pinue banksiana*)	Maple (*Acer* spp.)
Fir (*Abies* spp.)	Beech (*Fagus grandifolia*)
	Basswood (*Tilia* spp.)
	Elm (*Ulmus* spp.)
	Walnut (*Juglans* spp.)
	Hemlock (*Tsuga canadensis*)
	Sweet gum (*Liquidambar styraciflua*)

1994). Native Americans had been living in this deciduous forest for more than 11,000 years. When they arrived in an area they almost immediately began altering their environment, exploiting plant, animal, and mineral resources. Their use of natural resources caused the extinction of some plants and animals, introduction of new species into the forest, and extensive modification of the composition and structure of the forest (Russell 1983, Day 1953, Dorney and Dorney 1989, Davies 1994, McClain and Elzinga 1994).

These early agriculturalists cleared and farmed small patches of land, commonly removing trees. Fires were often used to clear the forest understory to facilitate travel and hunting and to encourage the growth of native food plants (Day 1953, Davies 1994). In the prairie peninsula the Native Americans started fires for a multitude of reasons—to prevent enemies from burning the prairie, to destroy pests, to reduce cover for enemies and predators, to encourage fire-dependent food plants, and to hunt bison by driving them into traps where they could be more easily killed (Day 1953, McClain and Elzinga 1994). These activities had a profound effect on the vegetation, particularly in the Midwest, where fires caused the prairie and savanna to increase at the expense of the forest (Anderson 1983).

Though Native American agricultural activities were usually small and localized, some large Native American settlements did exist in pre-Colombian times. One of the largest was at Cahokia, in the American Bottoms of Illinois, across the Mississippi River from present day St. Louis, Missouri (Fowler 1975, Fowler and Hall 1975, Hall 1975). In A.D. 1100 this Native American settlement covered an area of 9 square km and had an estimated population of 25,500 to 42,700 (Gregg 1975). It is estimated that more than 15,000 acres (6,000 ha) were cultivated to supply Cahokia with food. In 1650, when European settlers entered the region, all that remained were the historical remains of a collapsed culture.

Characterizing the Presettlement Forest

Probably the best source of information available to reconstruct presettlement vegetation is the field notes of the Public Land Surveys (Lutz 1930, Bourdo

1956, Hutchinson 1988). These survey notes contain the most accurate record and scientific description of the structure of presettlement vegetation. Starting with Ohio, a system was developed involving townships six miles square, with lines running due north and south, and others crossing these at right angles. The job of the surveyors was to establish a grid system of townships and range lines by the placement of section and quarter-section posts. The section posts were placed at each mile, and the quarter-section posts at each half mile along north/ south and east/west section lines. In timbered areas two (or four) bearing trees (witness trees) were commonly blazed, and the distance and direction of these trees from the section and quarter-section posts were recorded along with the common name and estimated diameter at breast height of each bearing tree. The surveyors also recorded general information about the character of the land crossed by each of the section lines: points of entry and departure from forest and prairie, topography, water, unusual and artificial features, natural distur- bances, and soil fertility. After surveying a township the surveyors drew a rough map (plat) where the features listed in the survey were shown, including the position of most natural features and the extent and position of forest and prairie (Figure 1.3).

The notes made by these early surveyors are invaluable to our understanding of this relatively undisturbed landscape. They contain the most accurate records and scientific descriptions of the near-presettlement conditions, most being com- pleted before European settlers had greatly altered the landscape. By using these historical records, soil maps, and current field observations, it is possible to reconstruct the composition, and to some extent the structure, of the presettlement vegetation of a particular area (Hutchison 1988).

Many ecologists now believe that these early survey records provide the most reliable and accurate description of presettlement vegetation that is available (Thomas and Anderson 1990). As might be expected, however, some mistakes and shoddy work did occur, but fraudulent surveys are uncommon (Hutchison 1988).

Relatively few studies of the surveys noted have been completed, with most studies involving a county-sized or smaller area. In most Midwest states a few counties have been studied (e.g., Kenoyer 1934, Cottam 1949, Ellarson 1949, Potzger and Potzger 1950, Potzger et al. 1956, Kilburn 1959, Anderson and Anderson 1975, Grimm 1984, Ebinger 1987, Thomas and Anderson 1990). Most of the surveys in the Midwest states indicate extensive prairie, mostly on relatively flat ground; open oak-hickory woodlands on sloping topography of relatively low relief; and closed, mesic forests on protected sites, particularly in areas of rugged topography.

Forest Vegetation Associations of the Midwest

At the time of settlement by Europeans, prairie occupied over 61% of Illinois, with forest, woodlands, and savannas accounting for the remainder (Iverson et

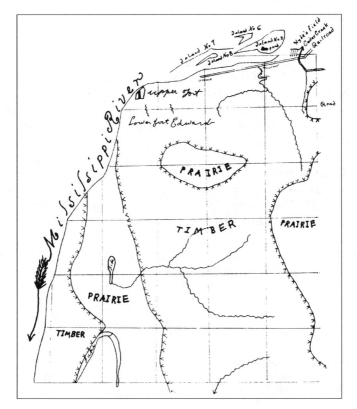

Figure 1.3. Facsimile of public land survey plat of T4N, R9W in Hancock County, Illinois.

From Hutchison (1988)

al. 1991). In the western part of this area in northern Missouri, Iowa, and western Minnesota, prairie was even more extensive, the forest being restricted to areas of rough topography (Kuchler 1964). Toward the east, north, and south, prairie gave way to the eastern deciduous forest. In Indiana, prairie accounted for only about 13% of the land surface (Petty and Jackson 1966), and was reduced to small isolated patches within the predominantly forested landscape of Ohio.

This western part of the eastern deciduous forest, extending from central Ohio to Nebraska and from the Great Lakes to northern Arkansas and Kentucky (Hunt 1974), was variable in composition and structure (Braun 1950, Kuchler 1964). Boundaries between forest associations are rarely exact, with many environmental and anthropogenic factors controlling the vegetation of a particular site. Four major forest associations (oak-hickory, beech-sugar maple, basswood-sugar maple, and the Mississippi River floodplains) are generally considered to exist in this area (Braun 1950, Kuchler 1964; see Figure 1.1).

Oak-Hickory Forests

Oak-hickory–dominated communities are most common in the western part of the eastern deciduous forest, representing an ecotone between the tallgrass prairie to the west and the beech-sugar maple and other mesophytic forests to the east and south. Within this association a distinct transition occurs, from closed forest to open-woodland to savanna and tallgrass prairie. The overstory is typically dominated by any of several oaks or hickories, although under particularly dry and sandy soils any one of a different set of species locally dominate (Table 1.2). Regionally subdominant trees include a variety of hardwood species (Table 1.2). Oak-hickory forests frequently have a less well developed understory than more mesic forests with typically only one or two species occurring as understory trees (Table 1.2). The oak-hickory association in presettlement time contained many edaphically controlled subordinate communities that graded between forest

Table 1.2. Major woody species of midwestern oak-hickory (Quercus–Carya) forests. Many of these observations are derived from Bowles and McBride (1994) and White (1994).

Dominant overstory species	*Locally dominant overstory trees*
White oak (*Quercus alba*)	Bur oak (*Q. macrocarpa*)
Black oak (*Q. velutina*)	Blackjack oak (*Q. marilandica*)
Red oak (*Q. rubra*)	Post oak (*Q. stellata*)
Bitternut hickory (*Carya cordiformis*)	Black hickory (*C. texana*)
Shagbark hickory (*C. ovata*)	Mockernut hickory (*C. tomentosa*)
Pignut hickory (*C. glabra*)	
Other trees	*Common understory trees*
American elm (*Ulmus americana*)	Hop-hornbeam (*Ostrya virginiana*)
Black walnut (*Juglans nigra*)	Flowering dogwood (*Cornus florida*)
Sugar maple (*Acer saccharum*)	Downy serviceberry (*Amelanchier arborea*)
Black cherry (*Prunus serotina*)	Redbud (*Cercis canadensis*)
White ash (*Fraxinus americana*)	
Green Ash (*F. pennsylvanica*)	
Dominant shrubs	*Shrubs of sandy, acid soils*
Dogwood (*Cornus* spp.)	Blueberry (*Vaccinium* spp.)
Coralberry (*Symphoricarpos orbiculatus*)	Huckleberry (*Gaylussacia* spp.)
Squaw-bush (*Rhus aromatica*)	
New Jersey tea (*Ceanothus americanus*)	
Shrubs of mesic sites	*Shrubs of open woodlands*
Bladder-nut (*Staphylea trifolia*)	Hazel (*Corylus americana*)
Spice-bush (*Lindera benzoin*)	New Jersey tea (*Ceanothus americanus*)
Common hop-tree (*Ptelea trifoliata*)	Various berries in the genus *Rubus*
American hydrangea (*Hydrangea arborescens*)	Sumac (*Rhus* spp.)
	Rose (*Rosa* spp.)
	Dogwood (*Cornus* spp.)
	Fire-stunted oak grubs (*Quercus* spp.)

and tallgrass prairie, including barrens, glades, and savannas (Taft, Chapter 2, this volume).

In presettlement times oak-hickory forest dominated southern Indiana, Illinois, Missouri, and Arkansas, with fingerlike extensions along river valleys in Minnesota and Iowa. This forest had its best development in the Ozark Plateau Province of northern Arkansas and southern Missouri, where it dominated the entire landscape (Kuchler 1964, Jenkins and Pallardy 1993). To the northeast in Illinois the forest was more open, varying from savanna to open woodland, determined largely by fire frequency that, in turn, was controlled by topographic relief and the occurrence of firebreaks (Gleason 1913). Dissected landscapes do not readily carry fire; the well-developed drainage systems serve as firebreaks. Because of fires and the prevailing westerly winds, closed forests were usually associated with the east sides of waterways, rough topography, and bodies of water. Reduced fire frequency permitted the establishment of tree species such as bur and white oak (*Quercus macrocarpa, Q. alba*) with their thick fire-resistant bark (Thomas and Anderson 1990). Toward the east (e.g., in Indiana), oak-hickory–dominated forests typically occupied the driest sites.

Few oak-hickory forests remain in an undisturbed condition, having been subjected to at least some cutting, and probably all having been grazed to varying extents since European settlement. Also, during the past century and a half of agricultural development, periodic fires have ceased in the prairie peninsula, and the oak savannas and open oak-hickory forests have become closed-canopy forests (Anderson 1983, 1991; Ebinger and McClain 1991). Most of the remaining woodlots are changing to forests dominated by mesic, shade-tolerant, fire-sensitive species such as sugar maple, (*Acer saccharum*), American and red elm (*Ulmus americana, U. rubra*), and white and green ash (*Fraxinus americana, F. pennsylvanica*) (Fralish, Chapter 11, this volume). In particular, the sugar maple has shown a dramatic increase in importance. Most of our best quality oak-hickory communities are apparently undergoing an irreversible change as sugar maple and other mesic, shade-tolerant species replace the veteran oaks and hickories when they die (Nigh et al. 1985, Ebinger 1986). In these forests, oaks and hickories are found only in the largest size categories, with beech and sugar maple dominating the smaller diameter classes and sugar maple dominating the seedling and sapling layer (Petty and Lindsey 1961, Lindsey and Schmelz 1964).

Beech-Sugar Maple Forests

In the Midwest, at the time of settlement by Europeans, American beech (*Fagus grandifolia*) and sugar maple dominated much of the forest throughout central Indiana, Ohio, and the southern half of Michigan (Gordon 1936, 1969, Fritts and Holowaychuk 1959, Kuchler 1964). Generally, this forest type occurred on soils of Wisconsin aged glacial till (Lindsey et al. 1965). Here beech was usually the dominant canopy tree, while sugar maple was codominant in the canopy and frequently dominated the understory along with several subordinate hardwood species (Table 1.3). To the north in the Greak Lakes region yellow birch (*Betula alleghaniensis*) and eastern hemlock (*Tsuga canadensis*) were important associates with the sugar maple and beech. Presently it is not uncommon for beech and sugar maple to make up 80% of the canopy on relatively moist sites with little topographic relief (Petty and Jackson 1966).

Though sugar maple was the dominant understory species in this region, numerous other woody species were important (Table 1.3). As is typical with closed-canopy temperate forests, the herbaceous layer was well developed, particularly in the spring when there was extremely high diversity due to the early ephemerals. Depending on topography and climate the tree species composition varies extensively in this region. On coarse, dry soils, particularly in areas of rough topography, oaks and hickories were important (DenUyl 1954). Areas of flat topography were commonly dominated by tallgrass prairie, particularly on wet sites and where firebreaks were lacking. In low areas with wet soils, elm-oak-ash forests were important (Table 1.3).

Much of the area historically occupied by beech-maple forests is now farmland. Since this forest region occupied relatively flat, fertile soil, it was some of the first cleared during the mid-1800s. Most of the remaining groves give little indication of the structure and extent of the original forests, though many of the major forest tree species, with their common understory components, are still

Table 1.3.   Major woody species of midwestern beech-maple (Fagus granifolia-Acer saccharum) *forests.*

Common dominant trees	*Common subdominant trees*
Red maple (*Acer rubrum*)	American elm (*Ulmus americana*)
Red oak (*Quercus rubra*)	Ash (*Fraxinus* spp.)
Basswood (*Tilia americana*)	Tulip tree (*Liriodendron tulipifera*)
Black walnut (*Juglans nigra*)	Black cherry (*Prunus serotina*)
Yellow birch (*Betula alleghaniensis*)[1]	Eastern hemlock (*Tsuga canadensis*)[1]
Dominants in low, wet areas[2]	*Subdominants in low, wet areas*[2]
American elm (*Ulmus aremicana*)	Swamp white oak (*Quercus bicolor*)
Green ash (*Fraxinus pennsylvanica*)	Pin oak (*Q. palustris*)
Red maple (*Acer rubrum*)	Red oak (*Q. rubra*)
Sugar maple (*A. saccharum*)	Slippery elm (*Ulmus rubra*)
	Quaking aspen (*Populus tremuloides*)
Common small trees	*Common shrubs*
Redbud (*Cercis canadensis*)	Spice-bush (*Lindera benzoin*)
Flowering dogwood (*Cornus florida*)	Common elderberry (*Sambucus canadensis*)
Blue beech (*Carpinus caroliniana*)	Leatherwood (*Dirca palustris*)
Hop-hornbeam (*Ostrya virginianus*)	Wahoo (*Euonymus atropurpureus*)
Pawpaw (*Asimina triloba*)	Maple-leaved viburnum (*Viburnum acerifolium*)

[1]Northern Great Lakes region only

[2]From Greller (1988)

present. Most of these forests were selectively logged during the late 1800s, and the high-grade species were removed. Beech, and to a lesser extent sugar maple, which are not valuable lumber trees, were left. This selective cutting, as well as the high replacement potential of the two species, has made them overly abundant in our present-day forests (Petty and Jackson 1966).

Sugar Maple-Basswood Forests

This association, in which sugar maple dominates the understory and is a major overstory component, along with basswood, occurred in extreme northwestern Illinois, the southern halves of Wisconsin and Minnesota, and the extreme north-western corner of Iowa (Greller 1988). In extreme northern Illinois the sugar maple-basswood forests occurred in the mesic valleys, while the oak-hickory forests were on drier sites at the prairie/forest boundary. In Wisconsin, basswood (*Tilia* spp.) replaced beech, which occur in the extreme southeastern part of the state (Ward 1958).

Mesic forests, with basswood and sugar maple as dominants, did not occur as a single unit even in presettlement times, but rather as scattered islands (Daubenmire 1936, Grimm 1984). Between these islands of mesic forests were tallgrass prairies, oak savannas, open oak woodlands, and oak forests. Local topography, streams, and other natural features, which afford some protection from fires, undoubtedly determined the boundaries of the sugar maple-basswood forests (Braun 1950, Grimm 1983). The numerous fires in presettlement and early settlement times (Cottam 1949, Curtis 1959) created extensive areas of oak savanna on the more exposed xeric sites of central Minnesota and Wisconsin (Bray 1960, Kline and Cottam 1979). In contrast, sugar maple, basswood, and numerous other thin-barked species (Table 1.4) were commonly top-killed by these fires.

Presently, only small remnants remain of the sugar maple-basswood association. Many of the forests were destroyed or significantly altered by fire, while much of the land has been cleared for agriculture or logged. The fragmented remains give only a slight indication of the structure, composition, and extent of this association.

Bald Cypress-Water Tupelo-Oak Forests

In presettlement times bald cypress (*Taxodium distichum*) was the most character-istic species of the extensive alluvial plains of the Mississippi River, and together with water tupelo (*Nyssa aquatica*), usually made up more than half of the overstory in the swamps and shallow ponds of these forests (Braun 1950, Penfound 1952, Voigt and Mohlenbrock 1964, Robertson 1994). The oak species associated with these wet forests (Table 1.5) varied extensively depending on locality as well as water depth and duration of inundation (Hosner and Boyce 1962. Bedinger 1979, Robertson 1994, Robertson et al. 1978). In deep swamps, sloughs, and

Table 1.4.   Major woody species of midwestern sugar maple-basswood (Acer saccharum-Tilia americana) forests

Codominant trees[1]	Common understory trees
American elm (*Ulmus americana*)	Blue beech (*Carpinus caroliniana*)
Slippery elm (*U. rubra*)	Box elder (*Acer negundo*)
Bur oak (*Querus macrocarpa*)	Hop hornbeam (*Ostrya virginiana*)
Red oak (*Q. rubra*)	Witch hazel (*Hamamelis virginiana*)
White oak (*Q. alba*)	Birch (*Betula* spp.)
Bitternut hickory (*Carya cordiformis*)	
Green ash (*Fraxinus pennsylvanica*)	
Common shrubs	
Bladder-nut (*Staphylea trifolia*)	
Bush honeysuckle (*Diervilla lonicera*)	
Hazel-nut (*Corylus americana*)	
Leatherwood (*Dirca palustris*)	
Maple-leaved viburnum (*Viburnum acerifolium*)	
Prickly ash (*Zanthoxylum americanum*)	
Wahoo (*Euonymus atropurpureus*)	
Dogwood (*Cornus* spp.)	

[1]Data from Daubenmire (1936), Eggler (1938), and McIntosh (1957).

bayous, which are usually permanently inundated, bald cypress and water tupelo dominated, sometimes being the only overstory species present. In areas where the ground was dry for parts of the growing season, hardwood bottoms occurred, with sweet gum, red maple, pecan, and various oak species the important forest components (Table 1.5). Woody vines (Table 1.5) were an important part of this association; many reached large sizes (Voigt and Mohlenbrock 1964). Early reports mentioned that some individuals had stem circumferences of 20 to 40 inches just a few feet above the ground.

At one time these forests extended from extreme southern Illinois to Louisiana, encompassing the arca referred to as the Mississippi Embayment. Though once common, channelization, drainage, and subsequent clearing for agriculture has reduced these forests to scattered local areas, particularly in the central and northern parts of the Mississippi Embayment. It is estimated that the bottomland forests of southern Illinois have been reduced in area by 98% as a result of clearing and drainage (Robertson 1994). In Missouri, of the more than 1,000,000 ha of bottomland forest present in early settlement times, 96% has been lost (Korte and Fredrickson 1977).

Threats and Trends

Habitat Loss

The forests of the Midwest were being utilized and modified by Native Americans long before European cultures entered North America. Low population densities

Table 1.5. Common woody species of midwestern cypress-gum (Taxodium distichum-Nyssa aquatica) *swamp forests.*

Common subdominant trees	**Other associated species**
Basket oak (*Quercus michauxii*)	Black willow (*Salix nigra*)
Cherry-bark oak (*Q. pagoda*)	Red maple (*Acer rubrum*)
Overcup oak (*Q. lyrata*)	Silver maple (*Acer saccharinum*)
Pin oak (*Q. palustris*)	Pecan (*Carya illinoensis*)
Shumard's oak (*Q. shumardii*)	Pumpkin ash (*Fraxinus profunda*)
Spanish oak (*Q. falcata*)	Sweet gum (*Liquidambar styraciflua*)
Water oak (*Q. nigra*)	Sycamore (*Platanus occidentalis*)
Willow oak (*Q. phellos*)	Southern hackberry (*Celtis laevigata*)
	Swamp cotton wood (*Populus heterophylla*)
	Cottonwood (*P. deltoides*)
Vines	**Woody understory species**
Pepper-vine (*Ampelopsis arborea*)	Swamp rose (*Rosa palustris*)[1]
Racoon-grape (*A. cordata*)	Virginia willow (*Itea virginica*)[1]
Poison-ivy (*Toxicodendron radicans*)	Buttonbush (*Cephalanthus occidentalis*)[2]
Supple-jack (*Berchemia scandens*)	Spice bush (*Lindera benzoin*)[3]
Trumpet-creeper (*Campsis radicans*)	Pawpaw (*Asimina triloba*)[3]
Grapes (*Vitis* spp.)	Possum haw (*Ilex decidua*)[3]
	Swamp privet (*Forestiera acuminata*)[3]
	Giant cane (*Arundinaria gigantea*)[4]

[1]Deep swamps on the knees of the bald cypress.

[2]Open area of lowland swamps.

[3]On drier sites, particularly in hardwood bottoms.

[4]On shallow ridges, particularly when the overstory is open or removed.

and primitive technology prevented excessive destruction; the use was significant in localized areas, but the majority of the broad expanse of forests remained intact, and except for the use of fire, the Native Americans had a relatively minor impact (Abrams 1992). With the arrival of European settlers, the rapid destruction of this vast tract of timber started. The largest part of the forest was destroyed; the fragmented remains were highly modified by fire suppression, grazing, and the introduction of exotic and weedy species. Other, more subtle changes were caused by acid rain, chemical pollutants, drainage, and species extinctions.

During the last 200 years much of the original forest has been cut, and the vast majority of the land has been used for crop production. Most of the remaining forests are second growth communities that usually differ significantly from the presettlement forest, not only in size but in species composition. In Illinois it is estimated that in 1820, the time when European settlers were beginning to enter the state, 5.55 million ha (13.8 million acres) were wooded. A little over one century later, only 1.22 million ha (3.02 million acres) of forest remained (Telford 1926). By 1985 forested land had increased to 1.72 million ha (4.26 million acres), mostly due to the reduction in cattle production and the decrease in

Table 1.6.   The total area (hectares) of forest lands at the time of settlement and at the present time in the states of the midwestern United States.

State	Land area	Presettlement forest	Present forest[1]
Illinois	14,399,000	6,000,000	1,726,000
Indiana	9,291,000	8,100,000	1,796,000
Iowa	14,472,000	2,400,000	830,000
Minnesota	20,621,000	13,800,000	6,766,000
Missouri	17,845,000	11,800,000	5,669,000
Ohio	10,607,000	10,100,000	3,182,000
Wisconsin	14,068,000	13,300,000	6,278,000
TOTAL	101,303,000	65,500,000	26,247,000

[1]From Smith et al. (1994).

farming marginal land, with the subsequent conversion of these areas to secondary forests (Iverson and Schwartz 1994). Similar reductions in forest acreages are common for other stages (Table 1.6).

Small Patch Size

In addition to the loss of original forests to agriculture and timber harvesting, many of the remaining forests are highly fragmented. Large, continuous blocks of timber are rare throughout most of the Midwest, commonly occurring only in areas of rough topography and along waterways and in depressional areas where farming is not practical. These fragmented communities have a reduced ability to maintain biological diversity, since many species, particularly birds and large mammals, require large tracts of forest to survive (Robinson 1988, Byers and Montgomery 1991, Robinson et al., Chapter 8, this volume). In addition, the amount of forest edge increases when fragmentation occurs, allowing more exotic and weedy species into the forest interior. Wildlife populations may decline if the species are sensitive to increased isolation and smaller habitat size or are sensitive to the proximity of "edge." Recent studies indicate that forest interior avifauna are particularly sensitive to the decreased size of forest fragments and the configuration of fragments that reduces the core area available to these species (Whitcomb et al. 1981, Wilcove 1987, Brawn and Robinson 1994). Fragmented habitats also inhibit gene flow between isolated populations, increasing the likelihood of inbreeding depression, which then increases the possibility of local extinction.

Fire Suppression

The reduction in fire frequency in the oak-hickory forests of the Midwest has completely changed the structure and composition of these forests, open woodlands, and savannas. During the past century and a half of agricultural development, periodic fires have all but ceased in the prairie peninsula. Savannas and open woodlands have become closed-canopy forests, resulting in an increase in shade-tolerant, fire-sensitive trees and a decrease in oak regeneration (Anderson 1991, Ebinger and McClain 1991). The closed canopy also causes a dramatic change in the species composition and in the structure of the understory and a corresponding loss in the wildlife depending on those species.

Species Introductions

The introduction of exotic and weedy species and their rapid spread into forest communities as a result of fragmentation has had a very significant impact on the biota of the deciduous forests of the Midwest (McKnight 1993). It is estimated that the number of foreign species in the Midwest is between 20% and 30% of the flora (Stuckey and Barkley 1993). In Illinois, 28.7% of the vascular plant species in the flora are exotics (Henry and Scott 1980), in Ohio 23.8% (Weishaupt 1971), in Missouri 23% (Steyermark 1963), and in Minnesota 19.5% (Ownbey and Morley 1991). Many are agricultural and roadside weeds that are rarely problems in forest communities. Some species, however, are major pests in forest communities, and the problem will continue to increase in severity and scope as new species enter the flora. Exotic plant species commonly reduce diversity, decreasing habitat for native plant species and habitat quality for the native fauna.

Exotic insects and pathogens have also become a major problem in forests, sometimes attacking entire communities, in other instances decimating a particular tree species. By the mid-1900s the introduced *Dutch elm disease* fungus and the virus disease, *phloem necrosis,* had eliminated the American elm as an important stand component. Earlier, the introduced *chestnut blight* all but eliminated the American chestnut (*Castanea dentata*), radically altering a major forest association of the eastern deciduous forest and the fauna and flora depending on that species. Gypsy moths, which were imported from Europe in the late 1800s, are capable of causing enormous devastation over large areas. The larvae will feed on the leaves of most native forest trees and shrubs, completely defoliating and eventually killing hardwood forests.

The structural complexity and extent of the deciduous forests has resulted in high species diversity. In presettlement times this diversity was undoubtedly higher, but extinction, range reductions, fragmentation, and the resulting inbreeding depression, as well as introduction of exotic species and other anthropogenic factors have resulted in many species becoming threatened and endangered (Herkert 1994). The greatest threats to native species diversity are the destruction of habitat and the competition from non-native species.

Conclusions

During the latter half of the nineteenth century the American conservation movement gained momentum. Since that time efforts have been made in most parts of the United States to protect representative samples of many biotic community types. As people became increasingly aware of the loss of natural vegetation and species extinction, more and more individuals felt that something needed to be done. During much of the twentieth century, efforts involved protecting small units of vegetation with their complement of species, the general policy being to try to secure the highest quality sites. Presently all midwestern states have a system of nature preserves; most of these preserves are relatively small. In Illinois, of the 214 high-quality forest sites discovered by the Illinois Natural Areas Inventory, only 11% are larger than 40 ha (100 acres) in size (White 1978, Iverson and Schwartz 1994). Many of these preserves are so small and isolated that they may experience severe problems in maintaining biological diversity, and the excessive edge adversely affects many animals, particularly forest-interior avifauna.

The current trend in most midwestern states is to secure and develop the largest possible sites, where much of the land is highly degraded, retaining little, if any, of its original natural character. On these sites the overall goal is to restore and maintain a network of native ecosystems large enough and diverse enough to ensure the perpetuation of native biological diversity characteristic to each ecosystem, and to maintain other crucial ecosystem functions (Leach and Ross, 1995).

References

Abrams, M.D. 1992. Fire and the development of oak forests. *BioScience* 42:346–353.

Anderson, R.C. 1970. Prairies in the prairie state. *Transactions of the Illinois State Academy of Science* 63:214–221.

Anderson, R.C. 1983. The eastern prairie-forest transition—an overview. In R. Brewer, ed. *Proceedings of the Eighth North American Prairie Conference.* Western Michigan University, Kalamazoo, 86–92.

Anderson, R.C. 1991. Presettlement forest of Illinois. In G.V. Burger, J.E. Ebinger, and G.S. Wilhelm, eds. *Proceedings of the Oak Woods Management Workshop,* Eastern Illinois University, Charleston, IL, 9–19.

Anderson, R.C., and M.R. Anderson. 1975. The presettlement vegetation of Williamson County, Illinois. *Castanea* 40:345–363.

Bedinger, M.S. 1979. Relation between forest species and flooding. In P.E. Greesen, J.R. Clark, and J.E. Clark, eds. *Wetland functions and values: the state of our understanding.* American Water Resources Association, Minneapolis, Minn., 427–435.

Bourdo, E.A., Jr. 1956. A review of the General Land Office Survey and of its use in quantitative studies of former forests. *Ecology* 37:754–768.

Bowles, M.L., and J.L. McBride. 1994. Presettlement barrens in the glaciated prairie region of Illinois. In J.S. Fralish, R.C. Anderson, J.E. Ebinger, and R. Szafoni, eds. *Proceedings of the North American Conference on Savannas and Barrens,* Illinois State University, Normal, 75–83.

Braun, E.L. 1950. *Deciduous Forests of Eastern North America.* Blakiston, Philadelphia, PA.

Brawn, J.D., and S.K. Robinson. 1994. Forest birds in Illinois: changes in abundances and breeding ecology. *Erigenia* 13:109–116.

Bray, J.R. 1960. The composition of savanna vegetation in Wisconsin. *Ecology* 41:721–732.

Byers, S.M., and R.A. Montgomery. 1991. Diversity and ecological relationships of oak woodland wildlife. Pages 91–101. in G.V. Burger, J.E., Ebinger, and G.S. Wilhelm, eds. *Proceedings of the Oak Woods Management Workshop.* Eastern Illinois University, Charleston.

Cottam, G. 1949. The phytosociology of an oak woods in southwestern Wisconsin. *Ecology* 30:271–287.

Curtis, J.T. 1959. *The Vegetation of Wisconsin: An Ordination of Plant Communities.* University of Wisconsin Press, Madison.

Daubenmire, R.F. 1936. The "Big Woods" of Minnesota: its structure, and relation to climate, fire, and soils. *Ecological Monographs* 6:233–268.

Davies, K.M., Jr. 1994. Some ecological aspects of northeastern American Indian agroforestry practices. *Northern Nut Growers' Association Annual Report* 85:25–37.

Day, G.M. 1953. The Indian as an ecological factor in the northeastern forest. *Ecology* 34:329–346.

Delcourt, P.A., and H.R. Delcourt. 1981. Vegetating maps for eastern North America: 40,000 yr B.P. to the present. *Geobotany* II:123–165.

Delcourt, P.A., and H.R. Delcourt. 1993. Paleoclimates, paleovegetation, and paleofloras during the Late Quaternary. *Flora of North America* 1:71–94.

DenUyl, D. 1954. Indiana's old growth forests. *Proceedings of the Indiana Academy of Science* 63:73–79.

Dorney, C.H., and J.R. Dorney. 1989. An unusual oak savanna in northeastern Wisconsin: The effect of Indian-caused fire. *American Midland Naturalist* 122:103–113.

Ebinger, J.E. 1986. Sugar maple, a management problem in Illinois forests? *Transactions of the Illinois State Academy of Science* 79:25–30.

Ebinger, J.E. 1987. Presettlement vegetation of Coles County, Illinois. *Transactions of the Illinois State Academy of Science* 80:15–24.

Ebinger, J.E., and W.E. McClain. 1991. Forest succession in the prairie peninsula of Illinois. *Illinois Natural History Survey Bulletin* 34:375–381.

Eggler, W.A. 1938. The maple-basswood forest type in Washburn County, Wisconsin. *Ecology* 19:243–263.

Ellarson, R.S. 1949. The vegetation of Dane County Wisconsin in 1835. *Transactions of the Wisconsin Academy of Science, Arts and Letters* 39:21–45.

Fowler, M.L. 1975. A pre-columbia urban center on the Mississippi. *Scientific American* 233(2):93–101.

Fowler, M.L., and R.L. Hall, 1975. Archaeological phases at Cahokia. Perspectives in Cahokia Archeology. *Illinois Archaeological Survey, Inc. Bulletin* 10:1–14.

Fritts, H.C. and N. Holowaychuk. 1959. Some soil factors affecting the distribution of beech in a central Ohio forest. *Ohio Journal of Science* 59:167–186.

Gleason, H.A. 1913. The relation of forest distribution and prairie fires in the middle west. *Torreya* 13:173–181.

Gordon, R.B. 1936. A preliminary vegetation map of Indiana. *American Midland Naturalist* 17:866–877.

Gordon, R.B. 1969. The natural vegetation of Ohio in pioneer days. *Bulletin of the Ohio Biological Survey,* N.S. 3(2).

Gregg, M.L. 1975. A population estimate for Cahokia. Perspectives in Cahokia Archaeology. *Illinois Archaeological Survey, Inc. Bulletin* 10:126–136.

Greller, A.M. 1988. Deciduous forests. In M.G. Barbour and W.D. Billings, ed. *North American Terrestrial Vegetation.* Cambridge University Press, Cambridge, England.

Grimm, E.C. 1983. Chronology and dynamics of vegetation change in the prairie-woodland region of southern Minnesota, USA. *New Phytologist* 93:311–350.

Grimm, E.C. 1984. Fire and other factors controlling the Big Woods vegetation of Minnesota in the mid-nineteenth century. *Ecological Monographs* 54:291–311.

Hall, R.L. 1975. Chronology and phases at Cahokia. Perspectives in Cahokia Archaeology. *Illinois Archaeological Survey, Inc. Bulletin* 10:15–31.

Henry, R.D., and A.R. Scott. 1980. Some aspects of the alien component of the spontaneous Illinois vascular flora. *Transactions of the Illinois State Academy of Science* 73(4):35–39.

Herkert, J.R. 1994. Endangered and threatened animal species of Illinois forests. *Erigenia* 13:122–28.

Hosner, J.F., and S.G. Boyce. 1962. Tolerance to water saturated soil of various bottomland hardwoods. *Forest Science* 8:180–186.

Hunt, C.B. 1974. *Natural Regions of the United States and Canada.* Freeman and Company. San Francisco, Calif.

Hutchison, M. 1988. A guide to understanding, interpreting, and using the public land survey field notes in Illinois. *Natural Areas Journal* 8:245–255.

Iverson, L.R., G.L. Rolfe, T.J. Jacob, A.S. Hodgins, and M.R. Jeffords. 1991. *Forests of Illinois.* Illinois Council on Forest Development, Urbana, and Illinois Natural History Survey, Champaign, IL.

Iverson, L.R., and M.W. Schwartz. 1994. Forests. In J.P. Ballenot, ed. *The Changing Illinois Environment: Critical Trends.* Technical report of the critical trends assessment project, vol. 3: Ecological resources, 33–66.

Jenkins, M.A., and S.G. Pallardy. 1993. A comparison of forest dynamics at two sites in the southeastern Ozark Mountains of Missouri. In A.R. Gillespie, G.R. Parker, P.E. Pope, and G. Rink, eds. *9th Central Hardwood Forest Conference.* Purdue University, West Lafayette, Ind., 327–341.

Kenoyer, L.A. 1934. Forest distribution in southwestern Michigan as interpreted from the original land survey (1826–1832). *Papers of the Michigan Academy of Science, Arts and Letters* 19:107–111.

Kilburn, P.D. 1959. The forest-prairie ecotone in northeastern Illinois. *American Midland Naturalist* 62:206–217.

King, J.E. 1981. Late Quaternary vegetational history of Illinois. *Ecological Monographs* 51:43–62.

Kline, V.M., and G. Cottam. 1979. Vegetation response to climate and fire in the driftless area of Wisconsin. *Ecology* 60:861–868.

Korte, P.A., and L.H. Frederickson. 1977. Loss of Missouri's lowland hardwood ecosystems. *Transactions of the 42nd North American Wildlife and Natural Resources Conference* 42:31–41.

Kuchler, A.W. 1964. *Potential Natural Vegetation of the Coterminous United States.* American Geographical Society Special Publication 36.

Leach, M.K., and L. Ross, eds. 1995. Midwest oak ecosystems recovery plan: a call to action. Paper presented at the Midwest Oak Savanna and Woodland Ecosystem Conference, Springfield, MI.

Lindsey, A.A., W.B. Crankshaw, and S.A. Qadir. 1965. Soil relations and distribution map of the vegetation of presettlement Indiana. *Botanical Gazette* 126:155–163.

Lindsey, A.A., and D.V. Schmelz. 1964. Composition of Donaldson's Woods in 1964 with its 1954 forest map of 20 acres. *Proceedings of the Indiana Academy of Science* 74:169–177.

Lutz, H.J. 1930. Original forest composition in northwestern Pennsylvania as indicated by early land survey notes. *Journal of Forestry* 28:1098–1103.

McClain, W.E., and S.L. Elzinga. 1994. The occurrence of prairie and forest fires in Illinois and other midwestern states, 1679 to 1854. *Erigenia* 13:79–90.

McIntosh, R.P. 1957. The York Woods: a case history of forest succession in southern Wisconsin. *Ecology* 38:29–37.

McKnight, B.N., ed. 1993. *Biological Pollution: The Control and Impact of Invasive Exotic Species.* Indiana Academy of Science, Indianapolis.

Nigh, T.A., S.G. Pallardy, and H.E. Garrett. 1985. Sugar maple-environment relationships in the River Hills and central Ozark Mountains of Missouri. *American Midland Naturalist* 114:235–251.

Ownbey, G.B., and T. Morley. 1991. *Vascular Plants of Minnesota: A Checklist and Atlas.* University of Minnesota, Minneapolis.

Penfound, W.T. 1952. Southern swamps and marshes. *Botanical Review* 18:413–446.

Petty, R.O., and M.T. Jackson. 1966. Plant communities. In A.A. Lindsey, ed. *Natural Features of Indiana.* Indiana Academy of Science. Indianapolis, 265–296.

Petty, R.O., and A.A. Lindsey. 1961. Hoot Woods, a remnant of virgin timber, Owen County, Indiana. *Proceedings of the Indiana Academy of Science* 71:320–326.

Pielou, E.C. 1991. *After the Ice Age: The Return of Life to Glaciated North America.* University of Chicago Press, Ill.

Potzger, J.E., and M.E. Potzger. 1950. Composition of the forest primeval from Hendricks County southward to Lawrence County, Indiana. *Proceedings of the Indiana Academy of Science* 60:109–113.

Potzger, J.E., M.E. Potzger, and J. McCormick. 1956. The forest primeval of Indiana as recorded in the original U.S. land surveys and an evaluation of previous interpretations of Indiana vegetation. *Butler University Botanical Studies* 13:95–111.

Robertson, P.A. 1994. Overstory vegetation along an upland to swamp gradient in southern Illinois. *Erigenia* 13:91–105.

Robertson, P.A., G.T. Weaver, and J.A. Cavanaugh. 1978. Vegetation and tree species patterns near the northern terminus of the Southern Floodplain Forest. *Ecological Monographs* 48:249–267.

Robinson, S.K. 1988. Reappraisal of the costs and benefits of habitat heterogeneity for nongame wildlife. *Transactions of the 53rd North American Wildlife and Natural Resources Conference* 53:145–155.

Russell, E.W.B. 1983. Indian-set fires in the forests of the northeastern United States. *Ecology* 64:78–88.

Smith, W.B., J.L. Faulkner, and D.S. Powell. 1994. *Forest Statistics of the United States, 1992.* Metric units. U.S. Forest Service General Technical Report NC-168. St. Paul, Minn.

Steyermark, J.A. 1963. *Flora of Missouri.* Iowa State University Press, Ames.

Stuckey, R.L., and T.M. Barkley. 1993. Weeds. *Flora of North America* 1:193–199.

Telford, C.J. 1926. Third report on a forest survey of Illinois. *Illinois Natural History Survey Bulletin* 16.

Thomas, R., and R.C. Anderson. 1990. Presettlement vegetation of the Mackinaw River valley, central Illinois. Transactions of the Illinois State Academy of Science 83:10–22.

Transeau, E.N. 1935. The prairie peninsula. *Ecology* 16:423–437.

Voigt, J.W., and R.H. Mohlenbrock. 1964. *Plant Communities of Southern Illinois.* Southern Illinois University Press, Carbondale.

Ward, R.T. 1958. The beech forests of Wisconsin–their phytosociology and relationships to forests of the state without beech. *Ecology* 39:444–457.

Weishaupt, C.G. 1971. *Vascular Plants of Ohio: A Manual for Use in Field and Laboratory.* 3rd ed. Kendall/Hunt, Dubuque, Iowa.

Wells, P.V. 1970. Historical factors controlling vegetation patterns and floristic distribution in the Central Plains region of North America. In W. Dort, Jr., and J. K. Jones, Jr., eds. *Pleistocene and Recent Environments of the Central Great Plains.* University Press of Kansas, Lawrence, 211–221.

Whitcomb, R.F., C.S. Robbins, J.F. Lynch, B.L. Whitcomb, M.K. Klimkiewicz, and D. Bystrak. 1981. Effects of forest fragmentation on avifauna of the eastern deciduous forest. In R.L. Burgess and D.M. Sharpe, eds. *Forest Island Dynamics in Man-Dominated Landscapes.* Springer-Verlag, New York, 125–205.

White, J. 1978. Illinois Natural Areas Inventory Technical Report, vol. 1. *Survey Methods and Results.* Illinois Department of Conservation, Department of Landscape Architecture, Springfield, Ill.

White, J. 1994. How the terms *savannah, barrens,* and *oak openings* were used in early Illinois. In J.S. Fralish, R.C. Anderson, J.E. Ebinger and R. Szafoni, eds., Proceedings of the North American Conference on Savannas and Barrens. Illinois State University, Normal, Ill, 25–63.

Wilcove, D.S. 1987. From fragmentation to extinction. Natural Areas Journal 7:23–29.

Wilhelm, G.S. 1971. Implications of changes in floristic composition of the Morton Arboretum's east woods. In G.V. Burger, J.E. Ebinger and G.S. Wilhelm, eds. *Proceedings of the Oak Woods Management Workshop.* Eastern Illinois University, Charleston, Ill. 31–54.

Williams, M. 1989. Americans and their forests: a historical geography. Cambridge University Press, New York.

2

Savanna and Open-Woodland Communities

John B. Taft
Illinois Natural History Survey, Champaign, IL 61820

> Among the 'oak-openings' you find some of the most lovely landscapes of the West, and travel for miles and miles through varied park scenery of natural growth, with all the diversity of gently swelling hill and dale—here, trees grouped, or standing single—and there, arranged in long avenues as though by human hands, with slips of open meadow between. Whenever a few years elapse without the conflagration [fire] touching a district, the thick sown seeds of the slumbering forest, with which the rich vegetable mould seems to be laden, spring up from the green sod of the country. The surface is first covered with brushwood composed of sumac, hazel, wild cherry, and oak; and if the fire be still kept out, other forest trees follow.
>
> C. J. Latrobe, traveling in the Midwest, *The Rambler in North America,* 1835

Introduction

Vegetation maps including the upper Midwest generally show two basic vegetation formations: prairie and forest (Vestal 1936, Shelford 1963, Anderson 1970, Iverson et al. 1991). The sharp dividing boundaries implied are more a matter of convenience of scale and difficulties in mapping variable boundaries than a reflection of reality. Of course, the fires that contributed largely to the maintenance of the tallgrass prairies of this region (Risser et al. 1981, Axelrod 1985) usually did not stop abruptly at a forest border. These fires penetrated beyond the open grassland, often forming structural gradients from open prairie to closed forest. The kinetic quality of the prairie-forest transition zone has challenged our spatial- and temporal-scale ecological understanding, yielding variable interpretations of vegetational history (Bielmann and Brenner 1951, Steyermark 1959), distribution (Braun 1950, Anderson 1983, Nuzzo 1986), and classification (White and Madany 1978; Nelson 1985; Faber-Langendoen 1994). A mixture of climatic and landscape conditions, fire history, and biotic interactions results in a mosaic pattern of forest, savanna, and prairie in the Midwest (Kilburn 1959, Anderson 1983) that is considered a prairie-forest ecotone (Barbour et al. 1980).

Tropical savannas in Africa with herds of large herbivores have been called stable *ecosystems* (Noy-Meir 1975, Walker and Noy-Meir 1982, Dublin et al. 1990), with concepts of stability largely a scale-dependent phenomenon (Skarpe 1992). In contrast, the rapid conversion of open savanna to closed woodland upon settlement and fragmentation of the midwestern landscape, and thus the apparent instability of North American prairie-forest transition zones, has been cited frequently (e.g., Gleason 1913, Cottam 1949, Rice and Penfound 1959, Abrams 1986). In a period of a few decades of fire absence, many plant communities in the Midwest were altered through vegetational changes and habitat destruction. The once widespread oak savannas have become among the rarest plant communities (e.g., Curtis 1959, White 1978, Nelson 1985).

The goals of this chapter are to describe savanna and open woodland habitats in the Midwest and to discuss their biology and conservation in the context of a highly fragmented landscape; thus, the chapter is organized into two sections. Section 1 provides an overview of the historical and contemporary distribution of these systems and their general character. Specifically noted is the structural and compositional variability along spatial and temporal gradients. Despite considerable habitat loss, there is a general paucity of globally rare species of savanna-like habitats though many taxa have become regionally rare. Section 2 examines the challenges of reaching a consensus on savanna classification, the consequences of fragmentation on composition and structure, pattern and process in midwestern savanna and open woodland habitats in regard to fire history, and the role of habitat restoration in savanna conservation. These topics will stress diversity relationships and conservation strategies. A general objective is to emphasize the need for community-level conservation while acknowledging that the constraints of highly fragmented landscapes may limit the complete restoration of ecotonal function and presettlement savanna heterogeneity.

Section 1

General Characteristics of Savanna and Open Woodland Habitats

Savannas often are depicted only in tropical regions of the world (Frost et al. 1986); however, the application of the term to temperate regions is not new (Dyksterhuis 1957). A generally accepted definition of savanna is scattered, open-grown trees with or without shrubs and a continuous herbaceous ground cover characterized by graminoid species (modified from Eiten 1986). Woodland generally refers to a partially closed canopy (e.g., up to about 80%), with or without a shrub stratum, and a ground cover including dominance of forbs, woody plants, (seedlings and vines), and graminoid species. Because savannas and open woodlands often are (were) part of a continuum from prairie to forest, for convenience they are referred to jointly as savanna-like habitats.

Midwestern savanna-like habitats have several unifying characteristics. These include an open-canopied structure (relative to closed forest), canopy dominance by a few species of oaks, a ground cover usually rich in species associated with tallgrass prairie, a majority of floristic diversity contained in the ground cover, and a dependence on disturbance (landscape-scale perturbations) for maintenance of diversity and stability. Oak-dominated systems particularly appear dependent on periodic fire for persistence (Lorimer 1985, Abrams 1992).

Contrary to popular belief, midwestern landscapes are spatially heterogeneous. Edaphic characteristics like soil depth, permeability, available moisture, and parent materials are highly variable. In some regions, there are also considerable topographic differences. Climate widely varies throughout the region. Consequently, fire frequencies and intensities varied on the presettlement landscape producing the diverse vegetation (e.g., brushy prairie, barrens, scrub savanna, open savanna, oak openings, open woodland) reported by the earliest chroniclers of the landscape.

Distribution

The presettlement distribution has been estimated for deep-soil, tallgrass savannas (Nuzzo 1986) and the Eastern Prairie-Forest Transition zone (Anderson 1983). A total area of about 12 million ha of tallgrass oak savanna was estimated for the Midwest (Nuzzo 1986). However, neither estimate includes the region of the Ozark Plateau, the southern portion of the Illinoian till plain, or the Shawnee Hills region. Considering the vegetation documented in these regions (Engelmann 1863, Vestal 1936, Bielmann and Brenner 1951, Ladd 1991), which consist of open woodlands and local inclusions of a prairie-like flora, the extent of savanna-like communities considered here expands somewhat beyond the region of tallgrass savanna and transition zone (Figure 2.1). Like the prairie-forest transition zone described by Anderson (1983), this region is intermediate between predominantly grasslands of the Great Plains and forests of eastern North America.

The contemporary status of tallgrass savannas in several midwestern states has been reviewed by Nuzzo (1986), who notes the occurrence of 113 noteworthy sites throughout the tallgrass savanna region totaling a mere 2,607 ha (0.02% of previous extent) of relatively high-quality tallgrass savanna habitat remaining. At the present time in the Midwest we are at a threshold where we can still recognize former savanna and open-woodland areas by the form and density of the oldest trees in closed woodland and also identify sites where vegetational changes in oak savanna-like communities have been retarded (though not stopped) in the absence of fire by droughty edaphic conditions. In addition, many savanna-like areas have ben structurally maintained or formed by livestock grazing; however, the ground cover has been replaced mostly by adventive species.

Temporal Scale

Post-Pleistocene vegetational trends have been described for the Midwest (e.g., Wright 1968, King 1981, Grimm 1983). These trends included a phase, possibly brief, of tundra, followed by boreal spruce-fir forests beginning about 14,000 to

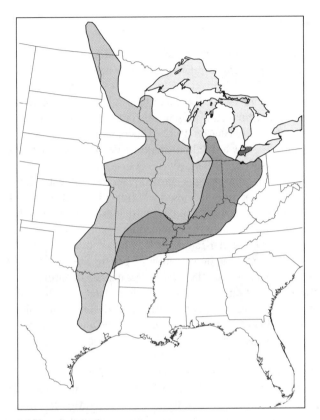

Figure 2.1. Generalized distribution of midwestern savanna and open-woodland communities. The map combines distributions from Anderson (1983) for the prairie-forest transition zone, Nuzzo (1986) for tallgrass savanna (light shading), and Ladd (1995), who mapped areas characterized by savanna and open woodland mixed with other, primarily forest, vegetation types (darkest shading). Scale = 1:2.160,000; 1 inch = 340 miles.

12,000 B.P. The boreal forest yielded to deciduous forest from 9000 to 8000 B.P. With the development of the hypsithermal climatic interval about 8300 B.P., prairie species began to invade deciduous forest. The resulting prairie peninsula formed a wedge extending into western Ohio. Palynological evidence suggests that oak-dominated communities were probably established in Illinois about 8000 B.P. An increase in graminoid pollen (Poaceae and Cyperaceae) about 5000 B.P., together with the prominence of oak pollen, suggests oak savannas may have been present at that time. The maintenance of most oak-savanna-like areas subsequent to climatic periods of increased moisture and cooling is attributable primarily to increased use of fire on the landscape by Native Americans (Curtis 1959, Anderson 1983).

Spatial Distribution

The distribution of trees into the prairie peninsula was constrained by a complex of site and landscape factors related to soil water-holding capacity and fire frequency and intensity (Kaminski and Jackson 1978, Rogers and Anderson 1979, Anderson 1982, Grimm 1984). Exposure to wind, solar radiation, frequent fire, drought, disease, and browsing pressure in prairies created challenges for tree survival (Sampson 1921, Hanson 1922, Anderson 1983). The greater predominance of trees on the leeward side of major waterways was noted to be due to fire protection (Gleason 1913). These water courses, as well as moraines protected from fires by surrounding sloughs, provided portals of entry into the prairie peninsula for the major tree species, including oaks (Gleason 1912). Lateral dispersal into ravines from these sources, particularly by the fire tolerant bur oak (*Quercus macrocarpa*) explains the colonization patterns for trees into the prairie (Gleason 1912, Weaver and Kramer 1932, McComb and Loomis 1944). This expansion was accelerated upon cessation of prairie fires (Abrams 1986).

Thus, within the region of the prairie peninsula, dendritic and centrifugal patterns of woody plant encroachment prevailed (Gleason 1912, Abrams 1986). In prairie border regions and where the landscape sloped (usually greater than 4–7%—Anderson 1991a), where savanna, woodland, and forest were more dominant, a centripetal pattern of closure appears to have been prevalent (McClain 1983, Robertson and Schwartz 1994). In Wisconsin, oak openings (dominated by bur oak) and scrub savannas (dominated by black and other oak species) have been perceived to be distinct from each other and true prairie (Bray 1955). Oak openings are proposed to have formed from fire-affected mesic forests that subsequently were invaded by bur oak. Scrub savannas are proposed to have formed from fire-affected woodland dominated by sprout-forming oak species (Bray 1955). Both savanna types converge toward closed woodland and forest in the absence of fire. It is most likely that savannas were formed both by trees invading prairie with periodic periods of fire absence and prairie invading woodland and forest during periods of greater fire frequency. In this context, "unstable" savanna requires association with equally unstable prairie and forest, at least in transitional zones.

Superimposed on these dynamic patterns are features in the surface geology that have promoted the persistence of savanna-like habitats. Droughty conditions found at inland deep sand deposits and where bedrock is near the surface (often associated with bluffs along the major rivers and in unglaciated portions of the region) appear to have retarded vegatational changes characterized on silt-loam soils generally by the encroachment of woody species in the absence of fire. Due to the agricultural limitations imposed by these edaphic conditions, these areas are disproportionately represented among natural savanna remnants. For example, the Illinois Natural Areas Inventory (INAI) has delineated a mere 4.5 ha of relatively undisturbed savanna on silt-loam soils compared with 499 ha found on sandy soils (White 1978). The INAI also has identified 32 ha of dry-to-mesic barrens. Barrens, as defined by the INAI, include shallow-soil habitats that support an assemblage of prairie species and scattered, open-grown trees within a generally forested landscape (White and Madany 1978). Savanna-like habitats were observed throughout the Ozark plateau at the time of early settlement (Beilmann and Brenner 1951, Ladd 1991) particularly on shallow-soil ridge crests (Steyermark 1959). However, in the absence of fire, regardless of disputes on the vegetational history of the Ozarks, these habitats have converted to closed woodlands. Some open flatwoods on the Illinoian till plain occur where the surface soil horizons contained relatively more sand above the claypan compared with typical silt-loam sites; these conditions appear to have promoted a degree of inertia to change (Taft et al. 1995).

Floristic Composition

Floristic surveys in midwestern savanna-like communities that comprehensively describe the composition of all strata have been only infrequently published. The descriptions of savanna-like systems in Wisconsin are among the most comprehensive efforts (e.g., Bray 1958, 1960; Curtis 1959).

Floristic composition of savanna-like habitats is dependent on a complex of factors including phytogeography, physiography (parent material, soil chemistry, texture, and soil moisture), shade (% canopy cover), and disturbance history. Consequently, composition gradually changes, and many remnants apparently do not have high degrees (>~60%) of floristic similarity when common and rare species are included (Curtis 1959, Taft et al. 1995). Because of the rapid, widespread loss of many savanna-like habitats, determining the floristic composition at the local level often requires speculation. We can be somewhat more confident about the composition of dry-to-xeric sites, which appear to be slower to change without fire. Nonetheless, field botanists in the Midwest have empirical knowledge of what some characteristic savanna species are/were (Table 2.1). In addition, a composite species list of barrens (savannas) for Hancock County, Illinois (Mead 1846), containing only partial similarity with the list in Table 2.1, has become central to many restoration and reconstruction efforts in the Chicago region (Packard 1991). Most of these taxa are not restricted to savanna-like habitats but also can be found in prairies and/or woodlands and occasionally forests. The fact that Curtis (1959) identified few (six) modal oak opening (savanna) species (i.e., taxa that reach their maximum presence in oak openings) does not suggest that savannas did not exist or were unimportant on the landscape (see final section).

Tree Stratum

The major tree species of savanna-like habitats, in general, are widely distributed throughout the Midwest. Abrams (1992) indicated the regional distribution

Table 2.1. Select list of characteristic savanna and open-woodland species in the Midwest. Though many may be found currently in prairie and closed-woodland habitats, these species often signal savanna and open-woodland habitats. Many important savanna species (e.g., prairie grasses) are not listed because their presence does not necessarily suggest savanna. Regionally rare species (most listed as threatened or endangered in Illinois) are shown in **bold**. Species indicated by S are characteristic on sandy soils. Nomenclature follows Mohlenbrock (1986).

Angelica venenosa	*Liatris x niewlandii*
Apocynum androsaemifolium	Liatris scabra
Asclepias purpurescens	Liatris squarrosa
Asclepias quadrifolia	Lithospermum caroliniense—S
Aster patens	Lupinus perennis—S
Astragalus canadensis	Moehringa lateriflora
Aureolaria grandiflora	Monarda bradburiana
Besseya bullii—S	Paronychia canadensis
Bromus purgans	Paronychia fastigiata
Cacalia atriplicifolia	Parthenium integrifolium
Callirhoe triangulata—S	Perideridia americana
Camassia scilloides	**Phlox pilosa subsp. sangamonensis**
Carex hirsutella	**Poa wolfii**
Carex muhlenbergii—S	Polygala polygama
Carex pensylvanica	Polygala senega
Carya texana	Porteranthus stipulaceus
Ceanothus americanus	Psoralea onobrychis
Convolvulus spithameus	Psoralea psoralioides
Corylus americana	Pteridium aquilinum—S
Dichanthelium laxiflorum	Pycnanthemum pilosum
Dichanthelium linearifolium	Quercus ellipsoidalis
Dichanthelium perlongum	Quercus macrocarpa
Dichanthelium depauperatum	Quercus marilandica
Dichanthelium sphaerocarpon	Quercus stellata
Dodecatheon meadia	Scleria triglomerata—S
Echinacea purpurea	Seymeria macrophylla
Eupatorium sessilifolium	Silene stellata
Galium pilosum	Taenidia integerrima
Gentiana alba	**Talinum rugospermum—S**
Helianthemum bicknellii—S	Tephrosia virginiana—S
Helianthemum canadense—S	Thaspium barbinode
Helianthus divaricatus	Tradescantia virginiana
Heliopsis helianthoides	**Trifolium reflexum**
Heuchera americana	**Trifolium stoloniferum**
Krigia biflora	Veronicastrum virginicum
Lathyrus ochroleucus	Viola pedata—S
Lechea villosa—S	

of important upland oak species for the Central Plains eastward. The distribution of *Quercus macrocarpa* is nearly identical to the distribution of savanna-like habitats (Figure 2.1). *Quercus alba* and *Q. velutina* are widespread throughout eastern North America, overlapping with much of the transition zone. *Quercus stellata* and *Q. marilandica* are not present in the northern states. *Quercus palus-*

Table 2.2.   Characteristic oak (Quercus) species for midwestern savanna and open-woodland habitats. X = dominant; O = occasional to local. Modified from Haney and Apfelbaum (1990).

Species	Tallgrass Savanna	Mesic Savanna	Sand Savanna	Dry-Xeric Woodland	Flatwoods
Q. alba		X	O	O	O
Q. ellipsoidalis			X (WI. MN)		
Q. macrocarpa	X	X			
Q. marilandica			X	X	O
Q. palustris			O		O
Q. stellata	O-X		X	X	X
Q. velutina		O	O	X	O

tris is centrally distributed while *Q. ellipsoidalis* is found in the northern states. The important oak species by savanna/open woodland type for the Midwest are shown in Table 2.2.

Fire exerts a strong selective force on the composition of woodlands and savannas favoring fire-resistant oak species (Rogers and Anderson 1979, Anderson and Brown 1986), particularly larger trees with thicker bark (Harmon 1984). *Quercus alba* and *Q. macrocarpa* dominance has been correlated to differences in species response to environmental variables. While *Q. macrocarpa* demonstrates a relatively broad amplitude, *Q. alba* is sometimes more common on steeper, more north-facing slopes with lower fire intensity (Will-Wolf and Montague 1994). The dominant trees over claypans in open flatwoods, *Quercus stellata* and *Q. marilandica,* are most common on drier sites. *Quercus stellata* is inversely correlated with A-horizon calcium content whereas *Q. marilandica* is strongly correlated to sand and magnesium content (Taft et al. 1995). *Quercus velutina* and *Q. marilandica* are often the dominant species within their ranges on sandy soils; *Q. ellipsoidalis* replaces *Q. marilandica* to the north (Whitford and Whitford 1971).

Shrub Stratum

The presence or absence of a shrub stratum or shrub zone is due to landscape and physiographic factors that influence composition and fire frequencies (Curtis 1959). Many early descriptions of savanna-like areas report open understory structure (summarized in Ladd 1991 and White 1994). Following a period of fire absence, resprouting oaks (e.g., *Quercus ellipsoidalis, Q. imbricaria, Q. macrocarpa, Q. marilandica,* and *Q. velutina*) contributed to a brushy stratum together with shrub and possibly bramble species. One common historic application of the term *barrens* refers to oak grub and shrub-dominated zones. These sometimes occurred as part of the prairie-woodland continuum and sometimes as isolated islands within prairie (Bowles and McBride 1994, White 1994). Extensive shrub-dominated zones were present at the time of Euro-American settlement, sometimes over a mile in width (Bowles and McBride 1994). Important shrubs included *Corylus americana, Ceanothus americanus, Rhus* spp., *Rubus* spp., *Cornus* spp., *Rosa* spp., and *Salix* spp. Non-native species (e.g., *Rhamnus cathartica*) currently infest many woodlands and former savannas.

Ground Cover

Generally, the compositional changes from open prairie to closed woodland are gradual as individual species increase or decrease in abundance along this gradient (*sensu* Gleason 1926). The greatest species richness in savanna-like habitats is contained in the ground cover (Haney and Apfelbaum 1990, Taft et al. 1995). The ground cover of open savannas (grasslands with scattered trees) usually is similar to tallgrass prairie (Curtis 1959). Prairies from the shortgrass to tallgrass zones have been characterized as dominated by several graminoid species and forbs (Robertson et al., chapter 3 this volume). The relative importance of these species varies with intensity and frequency of fire, grazing, haying (Collins and Gibson 1990, Norman and Nigh 1993), and soil disturbances. The importance of graminoid species tends to decline and woody plant seedlings and vines increase along the gradient from open prairie to closed forest (Bray 1960). A principal difference between tallgrass savanna and open-woodland communities is the composition of matrix graminoid species. While the dominant prairie grasses (e.g., *Andropogon gerardii, Sorghastrum nutans, Schizachyrium scoparium, Panicum virgatum, Stipa spartea*) are important in open savannas, woodlands are characterized by the presence of somewhat more shade-tolerant grasses (e.g., *Cinna arundinacea, Elymus hystrix, Diarrhena americana,* and several *Dichanthelium [Panicum]* spp.) and sedges (e.g., *Carex pensylvanica. C. artitecta, C. umbellata, C. muhlenbergii, C. hirsutella*). The transition from prairie-grass dominance to woodland-grass/sedge dominance can be abrupt, suggesting prairie grasses share a common threshold of shade (in)tolerance (Bray 1958). The accumulation of litter with increasing tree density is known to reduce shoot yield and favor rhizomatous mid grasses compared with bunch grasses dominant in prairies (Coupland 1974). Fire can reverse this trend by reducing woody plant stem density and litter. Savanna-like habitats on different parent materials can have a distinctive herb layer. Typical sand savanna species are listed in Table 2.1.

Rare Savanna Species

Several species noted as characteristic savanna species (Table 2.1) are also rare within the Midwest and a few are rare throughout their ranges. However, despite the general and widespread loss of savanna-like habitats, it is possible that no "savanna" plant species yet have been extirpated from the region. In

Illinois, posthumously known as the "Prairie State," where the tallgrass prairie has been reduced to several small and isolated fragments (Robertson et al., this volume), only about five prairie taxa have been extirpated from the state (Taft 1995). All of these taxa were apparently infrequent at the time of European settlement. Relatively few species of mesic black-soil prairies are listed as endangered in Illinois. In contrast, about 100 taxa from less widespread prairie communities are very rare in Illinois. These trends are suggestive of a once-resistant species pool that may begin to lose species rapidly (Wilcove et al. 1986). The relatively small number of "modal" savanna species and the somewhat broad amplitude of several of the characteristic species (Table 2.1) suggests that savanna-like habitats also may possess a resistant species pool.

Animal Composition of Savanna-like Habitats

Faunal composition of savanna-like habitats is less well known than floristic composition. Fauna adapted to savanna-like habitats have had to adapt to either the small, isolated fragments that remain, degraded habitats that structurally mimic savanna-like conditions, radiate into new habitats, or become rare. As in the African savannas described by Pellew (1983) and Skarpe (1992), certain mammal species in North American savannas are presumed to have had influence on the structure of savanna-like habitats (e.g., bison, elk, wolf). As in African savannas, there may have been positive feedback mechanisms between grazers, browsers, predators, humans, and fire. However, bison appear to have been recent in Illinois, and these grazers, browsers, and their predators now have been eliminated from the region. A portion of the browsing/grazing role may have been replaced by the region's burgeoning deer herds. Extirpation of large herbivores from grasslands may result in a loss of nutrients from the surface soil (Skarpe 1992).

Coyote and red and gray foxes were probably common in savanna-like habitats. Small mammals in midwestern savanna-like habitats include the woodland jumping mouse, plains pocket gopher, prairie vole, short-tailed shrew, masked shrew, white-footed mouse, least weasel, raccoon, eastern spotted skunk, badger, fox squirrel, gray squirrel, and Franklin's ground squirrel. Other species that are regionally rare or extirpated include the eastern spotted skunk, badger, and white-tailed jack rabbit (Appendix D in Botts et al. 1994). Small mammals have been shown to be important in community structure in a desert grassland (Brown and Heske 1990) and may operate similarly in midwestern savanna-like habitats.

Recent work with birds (Braun 1994, Robinson 1994, Sample and Mossman 1994) is contributing to the development of a concept of what a savanna/barrens avifauna is. These studies are helping identify the critical habitat components and how individual species in the community are affected by fire. While some savanna birds have become rare, others appear to have adopted surrogate habitats that in ways mimic savanna conditions and either have prospered or, at least, not declined. Examples include the American robin, mourning dove, common grackle, American crow, northern bobwhite, song sparrow, chipping sparrow, field sparrow, common yellowthroat, indigo bunting, northern cardinal, blue jay, and American goldfinch (Herkert 1994). Numerous bird species (>100) are associated with savanna-like habitats in the Midwest and about 83 species breed in these habitats; many are declining in abundance (Braun 1994, Herkert 1994, Sample and Mossman 1994). Nest parasitism by cowbirds is suspected to be high in forest openings in southern Illinois (Robinson 1994, Robinson et al., in press. Transition-zone breeding bird species considered threatened or endangered in at least one midwestern state include Backman's sparrow, Bell's vireo, Bewick's wren, the golden-winged warbler, lark sparrow, loggerhead shrike, long-eared owl, merlin, prairie warbler, and Swainson's hawk (Herkert 1994).

The savanna herpetofauna has been described for northeastern Illinois by Mierzwa (1994). All species are dependent on water for reproduction, with hydroperiod influencing community composition. Vegetation structure within wetlands influences predation rates. Open wetlands with less emergent vegetation were characterized by greater predation and lower species richness (Mierzwa 1994). Increased heterogeneity in savanna structure, hydroperiodicity, and wetland type appear to increase herpetofauna species diversity. The influence of spatial dynamics of glades and savanna-like openings on the genetic diversity of the collard lizard in the Missouri Ozarks has been examined (Templeton et al. 1990). A determination of what species are rare savanna species has not been made. The massasauga rattlesnake is known from savanna and former savanna habitats in northeastern Illinois (Mierzwa 1994). Other species considered rare throughout their ranges or within the Midwest that occur in savannas or associated habitats include the slender glass lizard, Illinois chorus frog, mole salamander, many-ribbed salamander, Oklahoma salamander, crayfish frog, Kirtland's snake, plainbelly water snake, and copperbelly water snake (Appendix D in Botts et al. 1994).

Savanna invertebrates are poorly known. Species and population-level responses to post-settlement impacts including fire absence, fire reintroduction, and fragmentation are even less understood. Most work appears to be with Lepidoptera, particularly rare species. Certain rare arthropod species (e.g., butterflies) appear to be unsuited to frequent fire and are best maintained under a spatially heterogenous disturbance regime with patchiness within and between preserves offering the best metapopulation development (Swengel 1994). Several rare butterfly species (e.g., the Karner blue, regal fritillary and Dakota skipper) have shown a decline in local population levels with frequent fire (Swengel 1993a, 1993b). Paradoxically, the host plant for the Karner blue, *Lupinus perennis,* is a species of sand savanna ultimately dependent on fire. These butterfly species apparently were maintained in the pre-Eurosettlement landscape by metapopulation dynamics characterized by local extinctions and colonizations (Bleser and Leach 1994). However, the metapopulation structure of the Karner blue, and presumably other species, has been destroyed by habitat (and host plant) destruction and degradation resulting in increasing distances between habitat patches (Shuey 1994).

Section 2

Given that there appear to be relatively few endangered species restricted to savanna/open woodland habitats, one might argue that conservation of midwestern savanna/open-woodland populations, species, communities, and ecosystems is best accomplished at the community level or higher. However, conservation at the community level poses several difficulties, particularly with dynamic systems in highly fragmented landscapes.

Classification and Structure

Community classification, though an essential conservation tool (e.g., White 1978), is fraught with challenges similar to those imposed by taxonomic species concepts (Ehrlich and Raven 1969, Levin 1979). The debate as to whether plant communities actually exist (Wilson 1991, 1994; Keddy 1993) becomes more complex as knowledge of the spatial and temporal dynamic nature of individual species and vegetation is gained (Gleason 1926, van der Maarel and Sykes 1993). The physiognomic variation characteristic of prairie-to-forest gradients undermines the general requirements of classification, which are dependent on homogeneity and recognizable boundaries (Palmer and White 1994). The plausibility of the classification of remnant vegetation, however, is enhanced in a severely fragmented landscape such as that found throughout much of the Midwest, particularly in Illinois.

The composition, diversity, and abundance patterns of woody species in savanna/open woodland system is strongly influenced by available soil moisture and fire frequency and intensity. Increased density and diversity of woody plants is positively correlated with available soil water-holding capacity (AWC) in savanna/woodland communities (Adams and Anderson 1980, Anderson 1983, Taft et al. 1995). Comparison of basal area and density measurements for trees in oak-savanna and woodland communities throughout the region yield a wide variety of structural characteristics (Table 2.3) crossing precipitation and AWC gradients. Most of these examples are representative of post-settlement artifacts of altered fire regimes and most sites are characterized by long fire-free intervals.

Many vegetation classification schemes in the Midwest overlay vegetative structure on parent material (Nelson 1985, Homoya 1994) and soil moisture gradients (White and Madany 1978), achieving many objectives of classification. However, efforts at oak-savanna/woodland classification at times have been constrained by terms originally used to describe the pre- and early-settlement landscape. For example, *prairie* is relatively unambiguous and refers to a grassland,

Table 2.3. Comparison of basal area and density between various woodlands, savannas, and barrens. Unless otherwise noted, trees include stems > 10 cm. Data demonstrate considerable variability within and among regions and habitat, but show general trends of decreasing basal area and stem density across perceived gradients of lower available soil moisture and regional precipitation.

Region	Habitat	Basal area (m²/ha)	Density (stems/ha)	Reference
Southern Indiana	Post oak flatwoods	22.5	1384	Dolan and Menges 1989[1]
	Barrens	17.7	820	
Southern Illinois	Post oak flatwoods (mean of six sites)	22.9	456.4	Taft et al. 1995[2]
Southern Illinois	Dry woodland/barrens	18.2	1040	Taft, unpublished data[2]
	Dry woodlands/barrens	17.8	945	
Southern Illinois	Xeric woodland	15.2	650	Fralish et al. 1991
Central Illinois	Terrace savanna	25.2	280.4	McClain et al. 1993
	Terrace savanna	21.3	301.3	
Central Illinois	Sand savanna	3.0	117	Anderson and Brown 1986
	Sand forest	17.5	630	
Oklahoma	Woodlands/savanna	11.3	NA	Rice and Penfound 1959
Missouri	Oak savanna	7.7	184	TNC—MO Field Office data
Minnesota	Oak woodland	28.7	636	Tester 1989
	Oak savanna	4.5	165	

[1]Stems > 1.0 cm dbh

[2]Stems > 6.0 cm dbh

though sedge and forb species may be abundant. Conversely, *barrens* is an example of a term used repeatedly over wide physiographic space and environmental conditions to describe distinctly different vegetation (Hutchison 1994, White 1994, Faber-Langendoen 1994). The ambiguity of barrens requires a separate definition for each application (White and Madany 1978, Aldrich and Homoya 1984, Bowles and McBride 1994). The historic and contemporary use of the term *barrens* has received extensive review (Hutchison 1994, White 1994).

Schematic representations of various classification methods have been summarized (Botts et al. 1994) and are repeated here (Figure 2.2). The variation is primarily due to differences in percent tree canopy cover for each class, a measure often not recorded in vegetation sampling. Despite the sharp community boundaries implied, vegetation community boundaries often are indistinct. Though abrupt transitions from prairie to forest were occasional (Hanson 1922, Grimm 1984), the transition from open prairie to closed forest was probably more often gradual. However, abrupt, anthropogenically produced vegetation boundaries are now common.

A recovery plan for oak ecosystems has been developed which contains a proposed classification system for the Midwest region (Faber-Langendoen 1994). In general, this classification follows *Bailey's Ecoregions of the United States* (1976) and is based on community gross physiognomy. The general physiognomic levels that define the major classes of savanna/woodlands are shown in Table

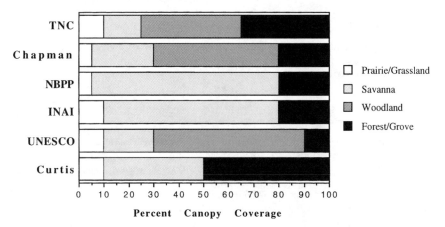

Figure 2.2. Comparison of definition parameters based on tree canopy coverage for community classes in the prairie-to-forest structural gradient. TNC = Faber-Langendoen (Attachment 1 in Botts et al., eds. 1994; Chapman = Crosswalk Classification of Terrestrial and Palustrine Community Types; NBPP = North Branch Prairie Project (TNC Chicago area volunteer stewards); INAI = Illinois Natural Areas Inventory (White and Madany 1978); UNESCO = Mueller-Dombois and Ellenberg. *Aims and Methods of Vegetation Ecology;* Curtis = Curtis (1959)

2.4. This classification effort is a first step toward recovery of the savanna ecosystem. However, similar to conflicts between taxonomic splitters and lumpers, classifications which rely on few characteristics (e.g., only physiognomy or composition) risk incompletely accounting for the variation of the vegetation under consideration. Since an important goal of classification is use as a conservation and prioritization tool, too much reductionism can result in failure to "protect" unaccounted for variants in the classification scheme. The limited consideration of parent material and soil moisture class (although accounted for somewhat by characteristic species) could be problematic in any comprehensive conservation effort. Further, because classification is typically designed for present rather

Table 2.4. Physiognomic groups with floristic associations for savanna, shrubland, and woodland in the upper Midwest. Modified from proposed classification system by Don Faber-Langendoen (Attachment 2 in Botts et al., eds. 1994). Used by permission of the author.

Formation	Series
I.A.1. Wooded tall grasslands with broad-leaved deciduous trees (tree savannas, barrens)	*Populus deltoides* Wooded grassland series *Populus tremuloides* Wooded grassland series *Quercus macrocarpa (Q. alba-Q. velutina-Q. stellata)* Wooded grassland series *Quercus stellata-Q. marilandica* Wooded grassland series *Quercus ellipsoidalis-Q. velutina* Wooded grassland series *Quercus palustris-Q. macrocarpa* Wooded grassland series
I.A.2 Wooded tall grasslands with broad-leaved deciduous and needle-leaved evergreen trees	*Pinus* spp.-*Quercus* spp. Wooded grassland series
II.A.1. Shrubby tall grassland with broad-leaved deciduous shrubs (shrub savannas, scrub barrens)	*Corylus americana* Shrub grassland series *Populus tremuloides-Quercus* spp. Shrub grassland series
III.A.1. Temperate deciduous woodland with evergreen needle-leaved trees	*Juniperus virginiana-Quercus muehlenbergii-Quercus* spp. Woodland series *Pinus banksiana-Quercus velutina-Q. ellipsoidalis* Woodland series *Pinus echinata-Quercus* spp. (*Q. velutina-Q. stellata-Q. coccinea*) Woodland series
III.A.2 Temperate deciduous woodland without evergreen trees	*Quercus alba* Woodland series *Quercus alba-Q. coccinea-Q. falcata-Carya* spp. Woodland series *Quercus macrocarpa* Mixed oak woodland series *Quercus macrocarpa-Q. muehlenbergii* Woodland series *Quercus stellata-Q. marilandica* Woodland series
III.A.3 Temperate alluvial woodland without evergreen trees	*Quercus macrocarpa* Alluvial woodland series *Quercus palustris-Q. bicolor* Woodland series

than past vegetation, remnants in a state of vegetative change that could, with management, be restored might not be recognized.

(In)Stability and Fire

Fire has long been a major landscape-scale ecological force in North America (Pyne 1982) and the Midwest is no exception. Fire sources have been primarily anthropogenic, though lightening-caused fires also have been reported (McClain and Elzinga 1994). The frequency of fire during the Holocene has been variable, with climate (Swetnam 1993) and probably human population densities explaining much of the variation. The season of midwestern fires also was variable but were common during the period of dry, relatively warm weather that typically occurs in October and early November (Pyne 1982, Ladd 1991, McClain and Elzinga 1994). One particularly salient consequence of fragmentation is altered fire regimes. Though fire frequency is projected to increase with climatic warming and drying (Sandenburgh et al. 1987), predictive models that indicate an increased probability of fire with time since the last fire (Clark 1989) lose validity where habitats occur as isolated fragments. The contemporary midwestern landscape is dominated by an inflammable matrix or is so frequently punctuated with other fire breaks (e.g., roadways) that presettlement fire regimes are difficult to reproduce.

Numerous models relating woodland compositional and structural stability have been proposed that indicate oak recruitment on medium to good sites is primarily dependent on some form of stochastic perturbation (Loucks 1970, Adams and Anderson 1980, Abrams 1986, Pallardy et al. 1988, Fralish 1994). The evolution and maintenance of oak woodlands in eastern North America is largely dependent on a recurrent fire history and/or edaphic conditions that limit the encroachment of shade-tolerant species without preventing establishment of oak recruitment (Abrams 1992). That most savannas were maintained by frequent fires has been widely recognized (e.g., Gleason 1913, Stewart 1951, Curtis 1959, Rogers and Anderson 1979). In such a dynamic and complex pattern of change, stability may have little practical meaning (Christensen 1991), at least on the local scale. The general developmental trends with and without fire are schematically illustrated in Figure 2.3.

Tree Stratum

Trends Without Fire

Changes in savanna composition and structure can be inferred from existing closed oak woodlands with scattered, open-grown large oaks (Curtis 1959, Kline and Cottam 1979, Tester 1989), though the estimated age of some large oaks with "presettlement" open-structure often may be exaggerated (Szafoni et al. 1994). Without frequent fire, oak grubs (resprouts from fire-pruned oaks like *Q. macrocarpa*) quickly develop into trees. Compositional changes in mesic to dry-

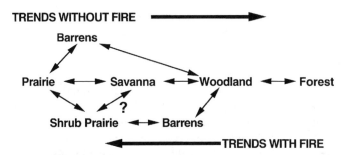

Figure 2.3. Schematic diagram of developmental trends and pathways with and without fire for midwestern plant communities.

mesic woodlands (including former savannas), presently characterized in the canopy by oak dominance, have been reported in many areas (Cottam 1949, McIntosh 1957, Boggess and Bailey 1964, Boggess and Geis 1966, Auclair and Cottam 1971, Grimm 1983, Pallardy et al. 1988). These changes typically include invasion of numerous woody-plant species not represented in the canopy stratum and poor recruitment of important canopy oak species (McCune and Cottam 1985, Lorimer 1985, Apfelbaum and Haney 1991, Abrams 1992, Taft et al. 1995). There is a general shift of vascular plant diversity from primarily the ground-cover stratum to woody species in the subcanopy and canopy strata, resulting in a net loss of species richness (Taft et al. 1995).

Oak woodlands on xeric sites, however, are compositionally relatively stable without fire since environmental conditions (e.g., high sand content, shallow soil, extreme exposure, and overall reduced available water-holding capacity) limit invasion by mesophytes (Rice and Penfound 1959, Reich and Hinckley 1980, Adams and Anderson 1980, Anderson and Brown 1986, Fralish et al. 1991). However, they can be structurally unstable as stem density can increase. Likewise, there is an inverse relationship between woody-stem density and ground-cover species richness, density, and cover (Taft et al. 1995, Taft unpub. data). Compositional and structural patterns found with flatwoods characterized by sandy soils over the claypan, compared with silt-loam sites, appear more stable (Taft et al. 1995).

Trends with Fire

Anderson and Brown (1986) reported that fire had a stabilizing influence on an Illinois sand savanna and a destabilizing effect in an adjacent closed forest (i.e., fire had little effect on the open-grown savanna trees; considerable mortality occurred among forest trees, particularly small-diameter stems as well as larger trees). Stability, in this sense, is a relative term since the forest (dominated by *Quercus marilandica. Q. velutina,* and *Carya texana*) apparently was former savanna destabilized by fire absence. Differential available fuel load between savanna and forest was considered an important factor in the variation in mortality rates. Very little of the ground cover within one meter of the base of savanna trees was burned, while leaf litter accumulation beneath the forest trees resulted in nearly complete burn coverage (Anderson and Brown 1986). Following two burns in a southern Illinois dry barrens, few trees in the most open portion of the barrens have external fire scars, while most of the visible fire damage and mortality is in the smaller size classes within an area of former barrens that is now closed woodland (Taft unpub. data). Similarly, in a Minnesota *Q. ellipsoidalis* savanna no trees > 25 cm dbh were killed following 14 years of annual fire (White 1983). These results suggest that fire-scar frequency in wood may under-represent fire history in open systems, since low-intensity fires generated by low fuel loads, either because of fuel absence (Anderson and Brown 1986) or fuel limited by frequent fire (White 1983), would not result in injury (Ladd 1991). On the other hand, Guyette and McGinnes (1982) have shown that fire scars on *Juniperus virginiana* (a thin-barked species) in a Missouri glade provide a record of frequent fire. Further, describing results from Oklahoma, Johnson and Risser (1975) reported that fires produced greater mortality in savannas than forests, though the mortality was among small-diameter stems that perhaps had little shading effect on the surrounding fuel matrix (Anderson 1983). Fires in savannas and woodlands can induce selective mortality on smaller-diameter stems since cambium layers in larger trees are more protected by thick bark (Irving and Alsamit 1983, Harmon 1984). Fires also exert selective forces favoring species with fire resistance particularly *Q. macrocarpa. Q. velutina,* and *Q. alba* (Rogers and Anderson 1979, Lorimer 1985, Reich et al. 1990, Russel and Dawson 1994).

Shrub Stratum

Trends without Fire

As noted previously, observations of the structural changes in prairie, savanna, and open woodland following the cessation of fire were recorded frequently (summarized in Ladd 1991 and White 1994). The woodland or savanna often was bordered by a brushy thicket (e.g., *Corylus americana, Rhus glabra, Cornus* spp., *Quercus* spp. sprouts). The terms *barrens* (Bowles and McBride 1994) and *shrub prairie* (White and Madany 1978) have been applied to this zone. Due to apparent fire dependence, few extensive remnants have persisted. *Corylus americana* (hazel) has been described as an immobile species (Gleason 1912) and an invader (Apfelbaum and Haney 1991); it is considered very tolerant of fire (Stearns 1974). Though hazel is a common species in closed oak woodlands throughout Illinois, no reproduction occurs in dense shade. These stems may be remnants from past hazel thickets overtaken by the "slumbering forest" or vegetatively sustained individuals dispersed into woodland interiors. In presettlement northeastern Illinois hazel was most abundant where there was some form of fire protection (Bowles et al. 1994); in a Minnesota savanna, hazel was more abundant in unburned compared with burned areas (White 1983). A shrub/sapling stratum within savannas and open woodlands also typically formed including *C. americana, Prunus* spp., *Rhus* spp., *Populus* spp., and *Quercus* spp. (Engelmann 1863, Bowles et al. 1994).

Trends with Fire

Post-fire effects on shrubs in the transition zone between prairie and forest are species dependent. In a Minnesota study, true prairie shrubs tended to increase with fire, while non-prairie shrubs tended to decline (Tester 1989). Fires did not reduce the stem number of most shrubs. Hazel stem density increased, though biomass and cover was reduced (Axelrod and Irving 1978, White 1983). *Rubus allegheniensis* is a Wisconsin woodland (Reich et al. 1990) and the closely related *R. pensylvanicus* in an Illinois flatwoods (Taft unpub. data) increased greatly in cover following fires. Shrub and small tree species in a southern Illinois dry upland barrens declined following each of two fires. However, *Ulmus alata*, a species believed to be controlled by fire in xeric woodlands (Fralish et al. 1991), has been reduced only slightly compared with control vegetation following the two fires (Taft unpub. data). Most studies of post-fire effects suggest that when fire management is used alone, persistence will be needed to reduce the density of some fire-resistant species and larger, more fire-resistant size classes.

Ground Cover

Trends without Fire

As shade increases with increasing woody stem density, ground-cover species with high light requirements gradually decline in cover, while more shade-tolerant species, if present, increase. Tree seedlings and woody vines become more common. Total species density, richness, and cover declines, while percent bare ground increases (Taft et al. 1995). Competition and resource allocation patterns among vascular plants along the gradient from full sun to light-limited communities (e.g., prairie to forest) shift from primarily below ground (roots) to primarily above ground (Tilman 1994). In woodland fragments, prairie-savanna-open-woodland species often are found only near the edges suggesting selective persistence along gradients of available light (pers. obs.); immigration into woodland edges of most of these taxa usually is not plausible, since the mostly agricultural matrix areas often do not provide suitable habitat.

Trends with Fire

The response of prairie vegetation to fire has been relatively well documented (e.g., Kucera and Koelling 1964, Vogl 1974, Risser et al. 1981, Gibson 1988,

Hulbert 1988, Collins and Gibson 1990). Considerably less is known of the response of savanna and open-woodland ground cover to fire (DeSelm et al. 1973, Apfelbaum and Haney 1991, DeSelm and Clebsch 1991, Heikens et al. 1994). The general trends are an increase in species richness, density, and cover of ground-cover species, and a reduction in density and cover of woody plants (White 1983, Haney and Apfelbaum 1990, Taft et al. 1995). Ongoing research indicates maximum vascular plant diversity may be maintained by fires at least every two or three years (Taft unpub. data). The response of increased species richness, density, and cover at a dry upland barrens and a flatwoods in southern Illinois were consistent across a range of tree densities indicating the presence of viable seed banks in relatively recently closed woodlands.

General trends with a mixed prairie-woodland ground-cover flora have included an increase in prairie grasses, especially *Schizachyrium scoparium* (DeSelm and Clebsch 1991, Heikens et al. 1994). However, there are exceptions. All C-4 prairie grasses at a southern Illinois barrens (e.g., *S. scoparium, Andropogon gerardii,* and *Sorghastrum nutans*) have declined in both frequency and cover, while several *Dichanthelium* spp. (C-3 taxa), particularly *D. laxiflorum,* have shown significant increases (Taft, unpub. data). These trends were consistent with both a fall and a spring burn. Cyclical patterns of percent cover independent of fire periodicity seems to occur with some taxa (including *Schizachyrium scoparium*) that only emerge following long-term (>20 years) monitoring (DeSelm and Clebsch 1991). These findings highlight the need for long-term monitoring of vegetational trends in managed natural areas in order to assess change and adapt management strategies accordingly.

Species density at a frequently burned post oak flatwoods on the Illinoian till plain was over four times greater than species density at five other unburned sites (Taft et al. 1995). The burned site contained significantly greater ground-cover species richness, cover, and diversity compared with unburned sites. The burn site was characterized by numerous dry-habitat species (32), about twice the number found at five other sites combined. This abundance of dry-habitat species suggested that either the fire management history had influenced a change in floristic composition favoring species of drier habitats, or more likely, these generally shade-intolerant taxa were the floristic elements lost from fire-suppressed sites (Taft et al. 1995).

Physiognomic group responses vary over time. In an ongoing study of post-fire effects in a southern Illinois barrens, some annual and biennial species responded dramatically following a single dormant-season fire, but quickly returned to pre-burn conditions during the second post-burn growing season. In contrast, graminoid and perennial forb species both showed significant increases ($0.005 > P > 0.001$) by the second year following a fire.

Preservation and Restoration of Midwestern Savanna-like Communities

You may know the story of Grandfather's axe "got a new handle, and years ago lost the original head." Are we sometimes prescribing burns for Grandfather's axe? The debate concerning the preservation value of savanna-like remnants hinges on two main points: (1) What do we attempt to protect? What is, what was, and what could be restored with management? Or, what will be without intensive management? and (2) Do savanna-like systems (ecotonal vegetation complexes bordering broad, relatively well-defined communities) contribute uniquely to the maintenance of regional biodiversity?

The wide recognition of the savanna as a rare and endangered element in our landscape (Curtis 1959; Nuzzo 1986; Packard 1988, 1993) has fostered considerable effort toward their conservation, restoration, and even reconstruction (e.g., the Oak Ecosystem Recovery Plan [Botts et al. 1994]). However, capturing and preserving the dynamic spatial heterogeneity of savanna-like systems within set preserve boundaries is particularly challenging in a highly fragmented landscape. Small reserves of fire-dependent savanna-like systems are at great risk of disfranchising species dependent on a particular serial stage in the dynamic continuum (Noss and Cooperrider 1994). They are likely to require intensive management activities that maintain or enhance population sizes and existing levels of diversity and prevent vegetational changes from altering the preserve target species or community (White and Bratton 1980).

Landscape-scale fires are naturally more spatially heterogenous than the action of prescribed fires in microsites (Stritch 1990) and preserves ideally should be large enough to contain a shifting mosaic of natural disturbance regimes. A general guideline of protecting 50% of the landscape as "wilderness," or the minimum dynamic area (Pickett and Thompson 1978), has been suggested to include functional disturbance regimes that allow for a shifting mosaic of "recovery" (Noss 1991, 1992). Adding perspective, in much of Illinois we are ceaselessly engaged in battles to prevent the destruction of prairie remnants in 10-meter-wide railroad-highway rights-of-way. Even the slightly more realistic, for our region, recommendation of reserve sizes for oak systems of 300–400 acres (121–162 ha) in the Oak Ecosystem Recovery Plan (Botts et al. 1994) requires massive infusions of money, time, and effort to protect one area, much less a functioning, interconnected landscape.

A recent shift in preserve priorities toward macrosites in Illinois has yielded the acquisition of one central Illinois site 15,000 acres (6,070 ha) in size, containing mostly cropland, forest, and hill prairie degraded by a long, destructive history of cattle grazing. Even the most optimistic projection holds little hope for recovery to presettlement conditions of more than perhaps 20% of the area. Further, even large preserve boundaries can occur as landscape islands or within a matrix of degraded lands. The maintenance of a species pool is dependent on a balance of emigration and extirpation rates with immigration and speciation (Eriksson 1993). However, immigration potential for many species of limited dispersal capabilities or other taxa eliminated by the disturbance history appears low. Missing species do not preclude preservation value for a reserve (Shafer 1995). When species have been lost from the pool, the general goals of conserving biodiversity in a savanna will depend usually on community-level restoration activities, though for certain cases, species-level restoration also may be appropriate.

Reservations about the use of fire in the contemporary landscape for ecological management occasionally emerge (Mendelson et al. 1992, summarized by Denny 1993). Although Pyne (1982) stated that "the evidence for aboriginal burning in nearly every landscape of North America is so conclusive, and the consequences of fire suppression so visible, that it seems fantastic that a debate about whether Native Americans used broadcast fire or not should ever have taken place," the historic role of fire even has been questioned (Stannard 1984). It is the contemporary use of fire, a force not likely to occur at presettlement frequencies without intensive intervention, that draws the question, Are we making an arbitrary decision to manage lands toward the perceived presettlement condition? The unambiguous response to this concern is to be found in the loss of community and species diversity with fire absence and the critical role preserves have in the long-term maintenance of regional biodiversity.

One of the central questions facing UNESCO's Man and the Biosphere Program was, "What is the importance of ecotones in maintaining local, regional, and global biodiversity?" (Naiman et al. 1988). Curtis (1959), Anderson (1991b), and others consider few vascular plant species to be dependent on savanna-like areas (the prairie-forest ecotone) and Anderson (1991b) notes that separation of savanna from forest and prairie requires arbitrary criteria since savanna-like areas often merge gradually and imperceptibly with prairie and forest. Packard (1988, 1991, 1993) promotes the idea that numerous taxa reach their peak frequencies in savannas and that this in turn implies ecosystem rather than ecotonal status for midwestern savannas. Under the Packard hypothesis, this community modality has been disguised by artifacts of disturbances (i.e., fire absence, grazing) and the small databases available. Anderson (1991b), in contrast, points to individualistic species responses to landscape and geographic variables (Gleason 1926) and the relatively broad amplitudes of most species of prairies and open woodlands, some of which may reach their peak frequencies in savannas. This assessment signifies an important role for ecotonal habitats in plant species/community conservation, particularly in a highly fragmented landscape and a region where habitat loss has been extensive. Whether ecotone or ecosystem, the rich assortment of species found in savanna-like habitats makes remnant identification, preservation, and management a critical aspect of conserving biodiversity in the region of the prairie-forest transition.

Acknowledgments

I wish to thank J. White for sharing the historical quote of Latrobe. Thanks to K. Hunter for preparing the map. Thanks to M. Bowles, M. Schwartz, J. White, D. Ladd and M. K. Solecki for discussion about savanna ecology. K. Kramer and M. Schwartz provided valuable comments on a draft of this chapter.

References

Abrams, M.D. 1986. Historical development of gallery forests in northeast Kansas. *Vegetatio* 65:29–37.

Abrams, M.D. 1992. Fire and the development of oak forests. *BioScience* 42(5):346–353.

Adams, D.E. and R.C. Anderson. 1980. Species response to a moisture gradient in central Illinois forests. *American Journal of Botany* 67:381–392.

Aldrich, J.R. and M.A. Homoya. 1984. Natural barrens and post oak flatwoods in Posey and Spencer Counties, Indiana. *Proceedings of the Indiana Academy of Science* 93:291–301.

Anderson, R.C. 1970. Prairies in the prairie state. *Transactions of the Illinois State Academy of Science* 63(2):214–221.

Anderson, R.C. 1982. An evolutionary model summarizing the roles of fire, climate, and grazing animals in the origin and maintenance of grasslands. In J. Estes, R. Tyrl, and J. Brunken, eds. *Grasses and Grasslands: Systematics and Ecology.* University of Oklahoma Press, Norman, 297–308.

Anderson, R.C. 1983. The eastern prairie-forest transition—an overview. In R. Brewer, ed. *Proceedings of the Eighth North American Prairie Conference.* Western Michigan University, Kalamazoo, 86–92.

Anderson, R.C. 1991a. Presettlement forests of Illinois. In G.V. Burger, J.E. Ebinger and G.S. Wilhelm, (eds.) *Proceedings of the Oak Woods Management Workshop,* Eastern Illinois University, Charleston, Ill., 9–19.

Anderson, R.C. 1991b. Savanna concepts revisited. *BioScience* 41:371.

Anderson, R.C., and L.E. Brown. 1986. Stability and instability in plant communities following fire. *American Journal of Botany* 73:364–368.

Apfelbaum, S., and A. Haney. 1991. Management of degraded oak savanna remnants in the upper Midwest: preliminary results from three years of study. In G.V. Burger, J.E. Ebinger, and G.S. Wilhelm, eds. *Proceedings of the Oak Woods Management Workshop.* Eastern Illinois University, Charleston, Ill. 81–89.

Auclair, A.N., and G. Cottam. 1971. The dynamics of black cherry (*Prunus serotina* Ehrh.) in the understories of southern Wisconsin oak forests. *Ecological Monographs* 41:153–177.

Axelrod, D.I. 1985. Rise of the grassland biome, central North America. *Botanical Review* 51:163–202.

Axelrod, A.N., and F.D. Irving. 1978. Some effects of prescribed fire at Cedar Creek Natural History Area. *Journal of the Minnesota Academy of Science* 44:9–11.

Bailey, R.G. 1976. *Ecoregions of the United States.* U.S. Forest Service, Ogden, Utah.

Barbour, M.G., J.H. Burk, and W.D. Pitts. 1980. *Terrestrial Plant Ecology.* Benjamin/Cummings, Menlo Park, CA.

Beilmann, A.P., and L.G. Brenner. 1951. The recent intrusion of forests in the Ozarks. *Annals of the Missouri Botanical Garden* 38:261–282.

Bleser, C., and M.K. Leach. 1994. Protecting the Karner Blue Butterfly in Wisconsin: shifting focus from individuals to populations and processes. In J.S. Fralish, R.C.

Anderson, J.E. Ebinger, and R. Szafoni, eds. *Proceedings of the North American Conference on Barrens and Savannas.* Illinois State University, Normal, 139–144.

Boggess, W.R., and L.W. Bailey. 1964. Brownfield Woods, Illinois: woody vegetation and changes since 1925. *American Midland Naturalist* 71:392–401.

Boggess, W.R., and J.W. Geis. 1966. The Funk Forest Natural Area, McLean County, Illinois: woody vegetation and ecological trends *Transactions of the Illinois Academy of Science* 59:123–133.

Botts, P., A. Haney, K. Holland, and S. Packard, eds. 1994. Midwest oak ecosystems recovery plan (draft of 30 September 1994). Results of working sessions prior to the Midwest Oak Savanna Conference, Chicago, Ill., February 1993.

Bowles, M.L., M.D. Hutchison, and J.L. McBride. 1994. Landscape pattern and structure of oak savanna, woodland, and barrens in northeastern Illinois at the time of European settlement. In J.S. Fralish, R.C. Anderson, J.E. Ebinger, and R. Szafoni, eds. *Proceedings of the North American Conference on Barrens and Savannas.* Illinois State University, Normal, 65–74.

Bowles, M.L., and J.L. McBride. 1994. Presettlement barrens in the glaciated prairie region of Illinois. In J.S. Fralish, R.C. Anderson, J.E. Ebinger, and R. Szafoni, eds. *Proceedings of the North American Conference on Barrens and Savannas.* Illinois State University, Normal, 75–86.

Braun, E.L. 1950. *Deciduous forests of eastern North America.* Hafner, New York.

Braun, J.D. 1994. An overview of avian communities in North American savanna habitats: current knowledge and conservation needs. In J.S. Fralish, R.C. Anderson, J. E. Ebinger, and R. Szafoni, eds. *Proceedings of the North American Conference on Barrens and Savannas.* Illinois State University, Normal, 145–146.

Bray, J.R. 1955. The savanna vegetation of Wisconsin and an application of the concepts order and complexity to the field of ecology. Ph.D. thesis, University of Wisconsin, Madison.

Bray, J.R. 1958. The distribution of savanna species in relation to light intensity. *Canadian Journal of Botany* 36:671–681.

Bray, J.R. 1960. The composition of savanna vegetation in Wisconsin. *Ecology* 41:721–732.

Brown, J.H., and E.J. Heske. 1990. Control of a desert-grassland transition by a keystone rodent guild. *Science* 250:1705–1707.

Christensen, Jr., N.L. 1991. Variable fire regimes on complex landscapes: ecological consequences, policy implications, and management strategies. Keynote address. In Nodvin, S.C., and T.A. Waldrop, eds. *Fire and the environment: Ecological and cultural perspectives.* Proceedings of an international symposium. Knoxville, Tenn. General Technical Report SE-69. Asheville, N.C.: U.S. Department of Agriculture, Forest Service, Southeastern Forest Experiment Station, ix–xiii.

Clark, J.S. 1989. Ecological disturbance as a renewal process: theory and application to fire history. *Oikos* 56:17–30.

Collins, S.L., and D.J. Gibson. 1990. Effects of fire on community structure in tallgrass and mixed-grass prairie. In S.L. Collins and L.L. Wallace, eds. *Fire in North American Tallgrass Prairies.* University of Oklahoma Press, Norman and London.

Cottam, G. 1949. Phytosociology of an oak woods in southwestern Wisconsin. *Ecology* 30:271–287.

Coupland, R.T. 1974. Fluctuations in North American grassland vegetation. In R. Tüxen, ed. *Handbook of Vegetation Science.* Part VIII. *Vegetation Dynamics* (R. Knapp, ed.). Dr. W. Junk, The Hague, Netherlands, 235–241.

Curtis, J.T. 1959. *The Vegetation of Wisconsin.* University of Wisconsin Press, Madison.

Denny, J. 1993. The new ecology, the search for presettlement. In *Biodiversity,* Missouri Department of Natural Resources Institute 1992–1993, 25–43.

DeSelm, H.R., and E.E.C. Clebsch. 1991. Response types to prescribed fire in oak forest understory. In S.C. Nodvin and T.A. Waldrop, eds. *Fire and Environment: Ecological and Cultural Perspectives.* Proceedings of an international symposium, Knoxville, Tenn., March 20–24, 1990. Southeastern Forest Experiment Station Technical Report SE-69, Asheville, N.C., 22–33.

DeSelm, H.R., E.E.C. Clebsch, G.M. Nichols, and E. Thor. 1973. Response of herbs, shrubs, and tree sprouts in prescribed-burn hardwoods in Tennessee. *Proceedings of the Annual Tall Timbers Fire Ecology Conference,* Tallahassee, Fla., 13:331–334.

Dolan, R.W., and E.S. Menges. 1989. Vegetation and environment in adjacent post oak (*Quercus stellata*) flatwoods and barrens in Indiana. *American Midland Naturalist* 122:329–338.

Dublin, H.T., A.R.E. Sinclair, and J. McGlade. 1990. Elephants and fire as causes of multiple stable states in the Serengeti-Mara woodlands. *Journal Animal Ecology* 59:1147–1164.

Dyksterhuis, E.J. 1957. The savannah concept and its use. *Ecology* 38:435–442.

Ehrlich, P.R., and P.H. Raven. 1969. Differentiation of populations. *Science* 165:1228–1232.

Eiten, G. 1986. The use of the term "savanna." *Tropical Ecology* 27:10–23.

Englemann, H. 1863. Remarks upon the causes producing the different characters of vegetation known as prairies, flats, and barrens in southern Illinois, with special reference to observations made in Perry and Jackson counties. *The American Journal of Science and Arts* 108:384–396.

Eriksson, O. 1993. The species-pool hypothesis and plant community diversity. *Oikos* 68(2):371–374.

Faber-Langendoen, D. 1994. A proposed classification for savannas and woodlands in the midwest. Attachment 2. In P. Botts, A. Haney, K. Holland, and S. Packard, eds. *Midwest Oak Ecosystems Recovery Plan* (draft of September 1994), The Nature Conservancy, Minneapolis, Minnesota.

Fralish, J.S. 1994. The effect of site environment on forest productivity in the Illinois Shawnee Hills. *Ecological Applications* 4:134–143.

Fralish, J.S., F.B. Crooks, J.L. Chambers, and F.M. Harty. 1991. Comparison of presettlement, second-growth and old-growth forest on six site types in the Illinois Shawnee Hills. *American Midland Naturalist* 125:294–309.

Frost, P., E. Medina, J.-C. Menaut, O. Solbrig, M. Swift, and B. Walker. 1986. Responses of savannas to stress and disturbance. *Biology International* 10:1–82.

Gibson, D.J. 1988. Regeneration and fluctuation in tallgrass prairie vegetation in response to burning frequency. *Bulletin of the Torrey Botanical Club* 115:1–12.

Gleason, H.A. 1912. An isolated prairie grove and its phytogeographical significance. *Botanical Gazette* 53:38–49.

Gleason, H.A. 1913. The relation of forest distribution and prairie fires in the middle west. *Torreya* 13:173–181.

Gleason, H.A. 1926. The individualistic concept of the plant association. *Bulletin of the Torrey Botanical Club* 53:7–26.

Grimm, E.C. 1983. Chronology and dynamics of vegetation change in the prairie woodland region of southern Minnesota. *New Phytologist* 93:311–350.

Grimm, E.C. 1984. Fire and other factors controlling the big woods vegetation of Minnesota in the mid-nineteenth century. *Ecological Monographs* 53:291–311.

Guyette, R., and E.A. McGinnes. 1982. Fire history of an Ozark glade in Missouri. *Transactions of the Missouri Academy of Science* 16:85–93.

Haney, A., and J.I. Apfelbaum. 1990. Structure and dynamics of midwest oak savannas. In J.M. Sweeney, ed. *Management of Dynamic Ecosystems.* North Central Section, the Wildlife Society, West Lafayette, Ind. 19–30.

Hanson, H.C. 1922. Prairie inclusions in the deciduous forest climax. *American Journal of Botany* 9:330–337.

Harmon, M.E. 1984. Survival of trees after low-intensity surface fires in Great Smoky Mountains National Park. *Ecology* 65:796–802.

Heikens, A.L., K.A. West, and P.A. Robertson. 1994. Short-term response of chert and shale barrens vegetation to fire in southwestern Illinois. *Castenea* 59:274–285.

Herkert, J.R. 1994. Breeding birds of the midwestern grassland-forest transition zone: who were they and where are they now? In J.S. Fralish, R.C. Anderson, J.E. Ebinger, and R. Szafoni, eds. *Proceedings of the North American Conference on Barrens and Savannas.* Illinois State University, Normal, 151–154.

Homoya, M.A. 1994. Indiana barrens: classification and description. *Castanea* 59:204–225.

Hulbert, L.C. 1988. Causes of fire effects in tallgrass prairie. *Ecology* 69:46–58.

Hutchison, M.D. 1994. The barrens of the midwest: an historical perspective. *Castanea* 59:195–203.

Irving, F.D., and S.E. Aksamit. 1983. Tree mortality by fire in oak savanna restoration (Minnesota). *Restoration and Management Notes* 1:18–19.

Iverson, L.R., G.L. Rolfe, T.J. Acob, A.S. Hodgins, and M.R. Jeffords. 1991. *Forests of Illinois.* Illinois Council on Forestry Development, Urbana, and Illinois Natural History Survey, Champaign.

Johnson, F., and P. Risser. 1975. A quantitative comparison between an oak forest and an oak savanna in central Oklahoma. *Southwestern Naturalist* 20:75–84.

Kaminski, D.A., and M.T. Jackson. 1978. A light and moisture continuum analysis of the presettlement prairie-forest border region of eastern Illinois. *American Midland Naturalist* 99:280–289.

Keddy, P. 1993. Do ecological communities exist? A reply to Bastow Wilson. *Journal Vegetation Science* 4:135–136.

Kilburn, P.D. 1959. The forest-prairie ecotone in northeastern Illinois. *American Midland Naturalist* 62:206–217.

King, J.E. 1981. Late-quaternary vegetational history of Illinois. *Ecological Monographs* 51:43–62.

Kline, V.M., and G. Cottam. 1979. Vegetation response to climate and fire in the driftless area of Wisconsin. *Ecology* 60:861–868.

Kucera, C.L. and M. Koeliing. 1964. The influence of fire on composition of central Missouri prairie. *American Midland Naturalist* 72:142–147.

Ladd, D. 1991. Reexamination of the role of fire in Missouri oak woodlands. In G.V. Burger, J.E. Ebinger, and G.S. Wilhelm, eds. *Proceedings of the Oak Woods Management Workshop.* Eastern Illinois University, Charleston, 67–80.

Ladd, D. 1995. *Tallgrass Prairie Wildflowers: A Field Guide.* Falcon Press, Helena, Mont.

Latrobe, C.J. 1835. *The Rambler in North America.* R.B. Seeley and W. Burnside, London.

Levin, D.A. 1979. The nature of plant species. *Science* 204:381–384.

Lorimer, C.G. 1985. The role of fire in the perpetuation of oak forests. In J.E. Johnson (ed.). *Challenges in Oak Management and Utilization.* Cooperative Extension Service, University of Wisconsin, Madison, 8–25.

Loucks, O.L. 1970. Evolution of diversity, efficiency, and community stability. *American Zoologist* 10:17–25.

McClain, W.E. 1983. Photodocumentation of the loss of hill prairie within Pere Marquette State Park, Jersey County, Illinois. *Transactions of the Illinois State Academy of Science* 76:343–346.

McClain, W.E., and S.L. Elzinga. 1994. The occurrence of prairie and forest fires in Illinois and other midwestern states, 1679–1854. *Erigenia* 13:79–90.

McComb, A.L., and W.E. Loomis. 1944. Subclimax prairie. *Bulletin of the Torrey Botanical Club* 71:46–76.

McCune, B., and G. Cottam. 1985. The successional status of a southern Wisconsin oak woods. *Ecology* 66:1270–1278.

McIntosh, R.P. 1957. The York Woods, a case history of forest succession in southern Wisconsin. *Ecology* 38:29–37.

Mead, S.B. 1846. Catalogue of plants growing spontaneously in the State of Illinois, the principal part near Augusta, Hancock County. *Prairie Farmer* 6:35–36, 60, 93, 119–122.

Mendelson, J., Aultz, S.P., and Mendelson, J.D. 1992. Carving up the woods. Savanna restoration in northeastern Illinois. *Restoration and Management Notes* 10:127–131.

Mierzwa, K.S. 1994. Patch dynamics of amphibians and reptiles in northeastern Illinois savanna ecosystems. In J.S. Fralish, R.C. Anderson, J.E. Ebinger, and R. Szafoni, eds. *Proceedings of the North American Conference on Barrens and Savannas.* Illinois State University, Normal, 161–166.

Mohlenbrock, R.H. 1986. *Guide to the Vascular Flora of Illinois.* Southern Illinois University Press, Carbondale and Edwardsville.

Naiman, R.J., M.M. Holland, H. Décamps, and P.G. Risser. 1988. A new UNESCO Programme: research and management of land/inland water ecotones. *Biology International,* Special Issue 17:107–136.

Nelson, P.W. 1985. *The Terrestrial Natural Communities of Missouri.* Missouri Department of Natural Resources and Missouri Department of Conservation, Jefferson City.

Norman, F., and T.A. Nigh. 1993. *Changes in the Composition of a Missouri Tallgrass Prairie in Relation to Eight Management Treatments.* Natural History Division, Missouri Department of Conservation, Jefferson City.

Noss, R.F. 1991. Sustainability and wilderness. *Conservation Biology* 5:120–121.

Noss, R.F. 1992. The Wildlands Project: Land conservation strategy. *Wild Earth,* Special Issue:10–25.

Noss, R.F., and A.Y. Cooperrider. 1994. *Saving Nature's Legacy: Protecting and Restoring Biodiversity.* Defenders of Wildlife. Island Press, Washington, D.C.

Noy-Meir, I. 1975. Stability of grazing systems: an application of predator-prey graphs. *Journal of Ecology* 63:459–481.

Nuzzo, V.A. 1986. Extent and status of Midwest oak savanna: presettlement and 1985. *Natural Areas Journal* 6:6–36.

Packard, S. 1988. Just a few oddball species: restoration and rediscovery of the tallgrass savanna. *Restoration and Management Notes* 6:13–22.

Packard, S. 1991. Rediscovering the tallgrass savanna of Illinois. In G.V. Burger, J.E. Ebinger, and G.S. Wilhelm, eds. *Proceedings of the Oak Woods Management Workshop.* Eastern Illinois University, Charleston, 55–66.

Packard, S. 1993. Restoring oak ecosystems. *Restoration and Management Notes* 11:5–16.

Pallardy, S.G., T.A. Nigh, and H.E. Garrett. 1988. Changes in forest composition in central Missouri: 1968–1982. *American Midland Naturalist* 120:380–390.

Palmer, M.W., and P.S. White. 1994. On the existence of ecological communities. *Journal of Vegetation Science* 5:279–282.

Pellew, R.A.P. 1983. The impacts of elephant, giraffe, and fire upon the *Acacia tortilis* woodlands of the Serengeti. *African Journal of Ecology* 21:41–74.

Pickett, S.T.A., and J.N. Thompson. 1978. Patch dynamics and the design of nature reserves. *Biological Conservation* 13:27–37.

Pyne, S.J. 1982. *Fire in America: A Cultural History of Wildland and Rural Fire.* Princeton University Press, Princeton, N.J.

Reich, P.B., M.D. Abrams, D.S. Ellsworth, E.L. Kruger, and T.J. Tabone. 1990. Fire affects ecophysiology and community dynamics of central Wisconsin oak forest regeneration. *Ecology* 71:2179–2190.

Reich, P.B., and T.M. Hinckley. 1980. Water relations, soil fertility, and plant nutrient composition of a pigmy oak ecosystem. *Ecology* 61:400–416.

Rice, E.L., and W.T. Penfound. 1959. The upland forests of Oklahoma. *Ecology* 40:593–608.

Risser, P.G., E.C. Birney, H.D. Blocker, S.W. May, W.J. Parton, and J.A. Wiens. 1981. *The True Prairie Ecosystem.* US/IBP Synthesis Series Volume 16. Hutchinson Ross, Stroudsburg, PA.

Robertson, K.R., and M.W. Schwartz. 1994. Prairies. In J.P. Ballenot. *The Changing Illinois Environment: Critical Trends.* Vol. 3: Ecological Resources, Illinois Department of Energy and Natural Resources, Springfield, 1–32.

Robinson, S.K. 1994. Bird communities of restored barrens and savannas of southern Illinois. In J.S. Fralish, R.C. Anderson, J.E. Ebinger, and R. Szafoni, eds. *Proceedings of the North American Conference on Barrens and Savannas.* Illinois State University, Normal, 147–150.

Robinson, S.K., J.P. Hoover, and R. Jack. In press. Effects of tract size, habitat, nesting stratum, and life history on levels of cowbird parasitism in a fragmented midwestern landscape. In T. Cook, S.K. Robinson, S.I. Rothstein, S.G. Sealy, and U.N.M. Smith, eds. *Ecology and Management of Cowbirds.* University of Texas Press, Austin.

Rogers, C., and R.C. Anderson. 1979. Presettlement vegetation of two prairie counties. *Botanical Gazette* 140:232–240.

Russell, M.S., and J.O. Dawson. 1994. The effects of artificial burning on cambial tissue of selected tree species of the central hardwood region of North America. In J. S.F Fralish, R.C. Anderson, J.E. Ebinger, and R. Szafoni, eds. *Proceedings of the North American Conference on Barrens and Savannas.* Illinois State University, Normal, 385–390.

Sample, D.W., and M.J. Mossman. 1994. Birds of Wisconsin oak savannas: past, present, and future. In J.S. Fralish, R.C. Anderson, J.E. Ebinger, and R. Szafoni, eds. *Proceedings of the North American Conference on Barrens and Savannas.* Illinois State University, Normal, 155–160.

Sampson, H.C. 1921. An ecological survey of the prairie vegetation of Illinois. *Illinois Natural History Survey Bulletin* 13:523–577.

Sandenburgh, R., C. Taylor, and J.S. Hoffman. 1987. Rising carbon dioxide, climate change, and forest management: an overview. In W.E. Shands and J.S. Hoffman, ed. *The Greenhouse Effect, Climate Change, and United States Forests.* Conservation Foundation, Washington, D.C., 113–121.

Shafer, C.L. 1995. Values and shortcomings of small reserves. *BioScience* 45:80–88.

Shelford, V.E. 1963. *The Ecology of North America.* University of Illinois Press, Urbana.

Shuey, J.A. 1994. Dancing with fire: oak barrens/savanna patch dynamics, management and the Karner blue butterfly. In J.S. Fralish, R.C. Anderson, J.E. Ebinger, and R. Szafoni, eds. *Proceedings of the North American Conference on Barrens and Savannas.* Illinois State University, Normal, 185–189.

Skarpe, C. 1992. Dynamics of savanna ecosystems. *Journal of Vegetation Science* 3:293–300.

Stannard, L.J. 1984. On the origin and maintenance of La Grande prairie of Illinois. *Erigenia* 4:31–36.

Stearns, F.W. 1974. Hazels. In J.D. Gill and W.M. Healy, eds. *Shrubs and Vines for*

Northeastern Wildlife. General Technical Report NE-90. U.S. Forest Service Northeastern Experiment Station, 65–70.

Stewart, O. 1951. Burning and natural vegetation in the United States. *Geographical Review* 41:317–320.

Steyermark, J.A. 1959. Vegetational history of the Ozark forest. *University of Missouri Studies* 31:1–138.

Stritch, L.R. 1990. Landscape-scale restoration of barrens-woodland within the oak-hickory mosaic. *Restoration and Management Notes* 8:73–77.

Swengel, A.B. 1993a. *Observations of Karner Blues and the Barrens Butterfly Community in Wisconsin 1987–1993.* Report to National Biological Survey and U.S. Fish and Wildlife Service, Baraboo, Wis.

Swengel, A.B. 1993b. *Research on the Community of Tallgrass Prairie Butterflies 1988–1993.* Report to National Biological Survey, The Nature Conservancy and U.S. Fish and Wildlife Service.

Swengel, A.B. 1994. Conservation of the prairie-savanna butterfly community. In J.S. Fralish, R.C. Anderson, J.E. Ebinger, and R. Szafoni, eds. *Proceedings of the North American Conference on Barrens and Savannas.* Illinois State University, Normal, 133–138.

Swetnam, T.W. 1993. Fire history and climate change in giant sequoia groves. *Science* 262:885–889.

Szafoni, R.E., R.L. Phipps, and F.M. Harty. 1994. Large, open-grown trees as indicators of presettlement savanna. *Natural Areas Journal* 14:107–112.

Taft, J.B. 1995. Ecology, distribution, and rareness patterns of threatened and endangered prairie plants in Illinois. In T.E. Rice, ed. *Proceedings of the Fourth Central Illinois Prairie Conference.* Milliken University, Decatur, Ill., 21–31.

Taft, J.B., M.W. Schwartz, and L.R. Phillippe. 1995. Vegetation ecology of flatwoods on the Illinoian till plain. *Journal of Vegetation Science* 6(5):647–666.

Templeton, A.R., K. Shaw, E. Routman, and S.K. Davis. 1990. The genetic consequences of habitat fragmentation. *Annals of the Missouri Botanical Garden* 77:13–27.

Tester, J.R. 1989. Effects of fire frequency on oak savanna in east-central Minnesota. *Bulletin of the Torrey Botanical Club* 116:134–144.

Tilman, D. 1994. Competition and biodiversity in spatially structured habitats. *Ecology* 75:2–16.

van der Maarel, E., and M.T. Sykes. 1993. Small-scale plant species turnover in a limestone grassland: the carousel model and some comments on the niche concept. *Journal of Vegetation Science* 4:179–188.

Vestal, A.G. 1936. Barrens vegetation in Illinois. Transactions of the Illinois Academy of Science 29:29–80.

Vogl, R.J. 1974. Effects of fire on grasslands. In T.T. Kozlowski and C.E. Ahlgren, eds. *Fire and Ecosystems.* Academic Press, New York, 139–194.

Walker, B.H., and I. Noy-Meir. 1982. Aspects of the stability and resilience of savanna ecosystems. In B.J. Huntley and B.H. Walker, eds. *Ecology of Tropical Savannas.* Springer-Verlag, Berlin, 556–590.

Weaver, J.E., and J. Kramer. 1932. Root system of *Quercus macrocarpa* in relation to invasion of the prairie. *Botanical Gazette* 94:51–85.

White, A.S. 1983. The effects of thirteen years of annual prescribed burning on a *Quercus ellipsoidalis* community in Minnesota. *Ecology* 64:1081–1085.

White, J. 1978. *Illinois Natural Areas Technical Report, Volume 1. Survey Methods and Results.* Illinois Natural Areas Inventory, Urbana.

White, J. 1994. How the terms savanna, barrens, and oak openings were used in early Illinois. In J.S. Fralish, R.C. Anderson, J.E. Ebinger, and R. Szafoni, eds. *Proceedings of the North American Conference on Barrens and Savannas.* Illinois State University, Normal, 25–64.

White, J. and M.H. Madany. 1978. Classification of natural communities in Illinois. In J. White, *Illinois Natural Areas Technical Report. Volume 1. Survey Methods and Results.* Illinois Natural Areas Inventory, Urbana, 310–405 (App. 30).

White, P.S., and S.P. Bratton. 1980. After preservation: Philosophical and practical problems of change. *Biological Conservation* 18:241–255.

Whitford, P.B., and K. Whitford. 1971. Savanna in central Wisconsin. U.S.A. *Vegetatio* 23:77–79.

Wilcove, D.S., C.H. McLellan, and A.P. Dobson. 1986. Habitat fragmentation in the temperate zone. In M.E. Soule, ed. *Conservation Biology: The Science of Scarcity and Diversity.* Sinaruer Associates. Sunderland, Massachusetts, 237–256.

Will-Wolf, S., and T.C. Montague. 1994. Landscape and environmental constraints on the distribution of presettlement savannas and prairies in southern Wisconsin. In J.S. Fralish, R.C. Anderson, J.E. Ebinger, and R. Szafoni, eds. *Proceedings of the North American Conference on Barrens and Savannas.* Illinois State University, Normal, 97–102.

Wilson, J.B. 1991. Does vegetation science exist? *Journal of Vegetation Science* 2:289–290.

Wilson, J.B. 1994. Who makes the assembly rules? *Journal of Vegetation Science* 5:275–278.

Wright, H.E., Jr. 1968. History of the prairie peninsula. In R.E. Bergstrom, ed. *The Quaternary of Illinois: A Symposium in Observance of the Centennial of the University of Illinois.* University of Illinois College of Agriculture Special Publication No. 14. Urbana.

3

The Tallgrass Prairie Mosaic

Kenneth R. Robertson
Center for Biodiversity, Illinois Natural History Survey, 607 East Peabody
Drive, Champaign, IL 61820

Roger C. Anderson
Department of Biology, Illinois State University, Normal, IL 61790

Mark W. Schwartz
Section of Plant Biology, Robbins Hall, University of California-Davis, Davis,
CA 95616.

Introduction

Grasslands are biological communities in which the landscape is dominated by herbaceous vegetation, especially grasses: they contain few trees or shrubs. An estimated 16 to 40% of the world's land surface is, or was, covered by grasslands (Singh et al. 1983, Burton et al. 1988, Groombridge 1992). Area estimates of current savanna and temperate grasslands are from 16.1% to 23.7% of the world's land area (Groombridge 1992). Notable examples include prairies of North America, llanos of northern South America, cerrados and campos of Brazil, pampas of Argentina, steppes of central Asia, veldt and savannas of Africa, and grasslands of Australia. Grasslands are the largest vegetational unit in North America, covering approximately 20% of the land area, and prairies are the most abundant type of grassland on the continent (Küchler 1964, Risser et al. 1981, Burton et al. 1988). Prior to European settlement, prairies occupied a more or less continuous (except at the fringes), roughly triangular shaped area covering 3.6 million square km. The base extended for 3,900 km along the foothills of the Rocky Mountains from the Canadian provinces of Saskatchewan and Manitoba southward through New Mexico into Texas (Figure 3.1). The apex of the triangle, the prairie peninsula (Transeau 1935), extended 1,600 km eastward into the Midwest and included the prairies of Illinois, Iowa, Indiana, Minnesota, Missouri, and Wisconsin, with scattered outliers in southern Michigan, Ohio, southwestern Ontario, and Kentucky (Risser et al. 1981; Madson 1982; Farney 1980; Weaver 1954, 1968; Whitney and Steiger 1985) (Figure 3.1). This chapter focuses on this eastward projection of tallgrass prairie around what is known as the *prairie peninsula* (Transeau 1935).

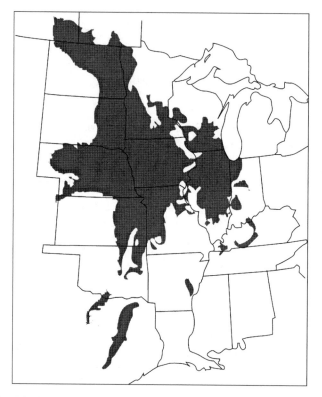

Figure 3.1. Distribution of the tallgrass prairie ecosystem prior to European settlement.
Adapted from Anderson 1991

The Prairie Biome

Prairies are complex ecosystems in which plants, browsing and burrowing mammals, insects and other organisms, fire, and climate interact. In agricultural terms, the tallgrass prairie sustains high productivity while building and maintaining soil (Chapman et al. 1990). Prairies developed and were maintained under the influence of three major disturbance factors: aridity with periodic drought, fire, and grazing (Anderson 1982, 1990, 1991).

Occurring primarily in the central portion of North America, prairies are subject to a continental climate with wide seasonal variability in temperatures—hot summers and severely cold winters. Because of the rain shadow effect of the Rocky Mountains, which intercepts the eastward flow of moist air from the Pacific Ocean, there is a gradual increase in average annual precipitation from west to east, and this is reflected in dominant species and the types of prairies found in central North America (King 1981a,b). From west to east within the central grasslands, average annual precipitation increases from 25–38 cm to 75–100 cm and becomes more reliable, potential evapotranspiration decreases, the number of days with rainfall increases, and periods of low humidity and periodic droughts in July and August decrease (Risser et al. 1981). Droughts, characteristic of North American prairie, may last only one or two months or continue for several years. Based on a study of tree rings, Blasing and Duvick (1984) concluded that severe droughts occurred in the decades of the 1930s, 1890s, 1820s, and 1700s. During severe dry spells, drought-tolerant species shifted their geographical ranges eastward, replacing drought-sensitive species that became locally extirpated, and shifted back as rainfall patterns changed and individual droughts ended (Weaver 1968).

Most ecologists believe that prairie vegetation in the midwestern United States would have largely disappeared during the past 5,000 years had it not been for periodic burning. Presettlement fire return intervals are estimated to have been one to five years (McClain and Elzinga 1994). These fires moved rapidly across the prairie, and damaging heat from the fires did not penetrate the soil more than a few mm below the surface (Anderson 1982, 1990). While a few wildfires were undoubtedly started by lightning, most fires were deliberately set by Native Americans (Moore 1972, Higgins 1986, McClain and Elzinga 1994, White 1995). The role of Native Americans in maintaining the prairies and the reasons they burned these grasslands have been discussed and documented by various authors (e.g., Stewart 1951, 1956; Curtis 1959; Pyne 1986).

Grazing also played a major role in forming the structure of prairies. Grasses generally produce more biomass annually than can be decomposed in a year. This production of excess herbage probably evolved in response to grazing; however, the productivity of grasslands declines when excess plant litter is not removed by fire or grazing (Golley and Golley 1972, Knapp and Seastedt 1986). A considerable portion of the above-ground biomass of a prairie was consumed each year by the grazing of a wide range of browsing animals, such as bison, elk, deer, rabbits, and grasshoppers (Risser et al. 1981). Bison graze selectively both spatially and temporally (Vinton et al. 1993). When conditions are favorable, bison consume grasses almost exclusively. Burning favors grasses; hence, bison use burned areas more than unburned (Fahnestock and Knapp 1993). Grazing by bison and fire interact in determining plant community composition (Vinton et al. 1993).

Deer, on the other hand, browse on prairie forbs rather than grasses. The forb species browsed by deer vary seasonally and from year to year, and deer browsing intensity on forbs varies seasonally, being highest in early to mid-July (Anderson et al. 1995; Anderson, this volume). Deer consume a large portion of the vegetative mass of the plants they browse, and deer browsing can cause a significant reduction in the reproductive output of some forb species. The great wave of late Pleistocene-early Holocene extinction of 35–40 species of large mammals, many herbivorous, from North America occurred before the formation of the tallgrass prairie (Graham et al. 1987, Pielou 1991).

Finally, activities by animals created disturbance patches within prairies. Bison or buffalo wallows can be quite large—several meters to 45 m in diameter (Polley and Collins 1984), and they can persist, used and unused, for many years. Other disturbances were made by smaller mammals, such as badgers, pocket gophers, and prairie voles, as well as arthropods, such as ants (Gibson 1989, Gibson et al. 1990, Platt and Weis 1977, Reichman et al. 1993). Trampling by bison, as well as cattle, also created small open areas. These disturbances added to species richness and spatial heterogeneity in tallgrass prairies. The plant species most often associated with disturbed sites in prairies are pioneer species and include a number of annuals (otherwise rare in tallgrass prairie) as well as perennials. Some species have subsequently become troublesome agricultural weeds. Haver-camp and Whitney (1983) classified prairie forbs into three categories: indicator species, modal species (species that have their maximum presence value in prairies), and weedy species.

Thus, grasslands evolved under conditions of periodic drought, fire, and grazing and are adapted to all three (Owen and Wiegert 1981; McNaughton 1979, 1984; Anderson 1990). Prairie plants thrive under these conditions largely by being herbaceous perennials with underground storage/perennating structures, growing points slightly below ground level, and extensive, deep root systems. The three factors of periodic drought, grazing, and fire are important to keep in mind when formulating management practices for today's prairie remnants. In later discussions in this chapter, grazing is mentioned as being a disturbance factor in prairie remnants, but this refers only to grazing by domestic livestock, which has a quite different impact than the free-ranging grazing of native large mammals, such as bison.

Although many woody species, for example, oaks (*Quercus* spp.), readily resprout after being top-killed by fire, prairie species are generally better adapted to burning than are most woody plants. The adaptation that protects grasses and forbs from fire is their herbaceous growth habit: the plant dies back to its underground organs each year, exposing only dead material above ground (Gleason 1922a). While prairie fires are very hot above ground (up to 680°C—Wright 1974; Rice and Parenti 1978), they move quickly and soil is a good insulator, thus little heat penetrates the soil. The same adaptation that protects prairie plants from fire also protects them from drought and grazing. Growing points beneath the surface of the soil permit regrowth after intense grazing and protect perennating organs from desiccation during periods of drought or from fire at any time of the year (Gleason 1922a; Tainton and Mentis 1984; Anderson 1982, 1990).

The grasslands of North America originated in the Miocene-Pliocene transition, about 7–5 million years before the present (B.P.) in association with the beginning of a global drying trend. In addition, the uplift of the Rocky Mountains created a partial barrier between moist Pacific air masses and the interior portion of the continent. Woody plants are generally less well adapted to drought than most grass species, and the spread of grasslands occurred at the expense of forests. As the grassland expanded, numbers of grazing and browsing animals increased, an indication that the association of grasses and grazers occurred over a long period of time (Stebbins 1981, Axelrod 1985, Webb et al. 1983).

Ecologists traditionally have separated the central grassland into three major west-east divisions: an arid western grass prairie, an intermediate mixed grass prairie, and a relatively moist eastern tallgrass prairie. The dominant grasses of the eastern tallgrass prairie, the focus of this chapter, are big bluestem (*Andropogon gerardii*), Indian grass (*Sorghastrum nutans*), and switchgrass (*Panicum virgatum*)—grasses that reach heights of 1.8 to 3.6m—on mesic tallgrass prairie sites; prairie cordgrass (*Spartina pectinata*) and bluejoint grass (*Calamagrostis canadensis*) on wet prairies; and little bluestem (*Schizacharyum scoparium*) and sideoats grama (*Bouteloua curtipendula*) on dry sites (Figure 3.2. Weaver 1954, Risser et al. 1981, Parrish and Bazzaz 1982, Umbanhowar 1992). The eastern tallgrass prairie was formed following the most recent period of the Pleistocene glaciation (Axelrod 1985). Based on the evidence of fossil pollen grains, tallgrass prairie pushed east of the Mississippi River about 8,300 years ago (King 1981a,b). As the last of the most recent ice sheet retreated, mesic deciduous forests dominated most of the midwestern landscape. A drying and warming trend began about 8700–7900 B.P., and prairie began to replace deciduous forests in the Midwest. Prairie maximized its eastern extent during the Hypsithermal Period (8000–6000 B.P.), which was the hottest and driest part of the Holocene (Pielou 1991), and much of the prairie persisted as the climate became cooler and moister following the Hypsithermal.

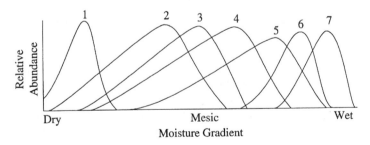

Figure 3.2. Generalized distribution of major grass species across a soil moisture gradient: (1) sideoats grama (*Bouteloua curtipendula*); (2) little bluestem (*Schizachyrium scoparium*); (3) Indian grass (*Sorghastrum nutans*); (4) big bluestem (*Andropogon gerardii*); (5) switchgrass (*Panicum virgatum*); (6) bluejoint grass (*Calamagrostis canadensis*); (7) prairie cordgrass (*Spartina pectinata*).

Adapted from Anderson 1991

The Tallgrass Prairie Mosaic

While the prairie biome was nearly continuous (except at the fringes), it was by no means homogeneous. Prior to European settlement, the landscape of the tallgrass prairie was a complex matrix with specialized communities embedded in the prairie—fens, pannes, sedge meadows, marshes, ponds, kames, sand blowouts, savannas, and prairie groves. Prairie occurs in both glaciated and unglaciated areas, and there is much variation in soil particle size, heterogeneity, texture, organic content, and pH. Some prairies occur where there are outcrops of sandstone, limestone, dolomite, quartzite and chert. All of these foster variation in biotic communities and determine what prairie species occur at a particular place at a particular time. Overlaying this local variation in soils and topography onto a continental moisture gradient in the lee of the rainshadow of the Rocky Mountains, it becomes difficult to divide the long prairie continuum into discrete units of classification.

Prior to European settlement, the vegetation of much of the Midwest was a shifting mosaic of prairie, forest, savanna, and wetlands that was largely controlled by the frequency of fire under climatic conditions that were capable of supporting any of these vegetation types (Gleason 1913, Grimm 1983). The frequency of fire, and hence the distribution of prairie, was largely determined by topography and the occurrence of natural firebreaks (e.g., rivers, streams, and wetlands). Fires carry readily across level to gently rolling landscapes, but is patchy in hilly and dissected landscapes (Wells 1970; Grimm 1984). Fire tends to carry well uphill because rising convection currents encourage its spread. But as fire moves down slopes, the convection currents tend to retard it by rising upward and working against the downward direction of the moving fire. The importance of waterways in determining the distribution of forest and prairie prior to European presettlement was demonstrated for Illinois by Gleason (1913) and Minnesota (Grimm 1983) through the use of the Government Land Office Records. Both authors found that prairies were associated with the west sides of streams and other natural firebreaks. Gleason (1913) attributed this pattern to prevailing westerly winds that carried fires from west to east; the west sides of waterways, therefore, burned more frequently than the east sides.

Using a map showing the distribution of prairies and timber (forest and savanna) for Illinois, based on the Government Land Office Records (Anderson 1970), and a map of the average slope range for the state (Fehrenbacher et al. 1968), Anderson (1991) determined the simultaneous occurrence of slope categories and vegetation. Most of the prairie vegetation (82.3%) occurred on landscapes with slopes of 2–4%; only 23.0% of the timbered land, usually on floodplains, was associated with this slope category. In contrast, 77% of the timbered land occurred on sites that had slopes greater than 4% (4–7% slope = 35.2% timber and >7% slope = 41.8% timber—Figure 3.3). Iverson (1988) also showed that presettlement forests were positively correlated with sloping landscapes.

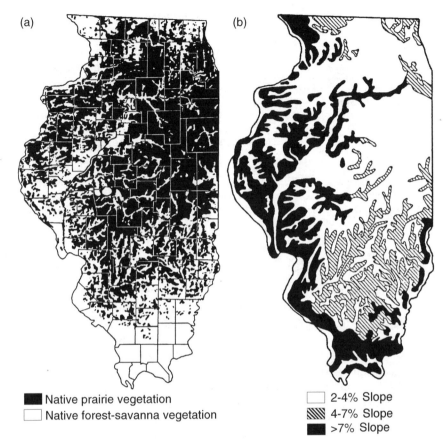

Figure 3.3. The distribution of native forest-savanna vegetation and prairie (a) compared to average slope categories (b) in Illinois.

A number of different classification schemes have been developed to categorize the great variety found in the tallgrass prairie. The systems used in three states are shown in Table 3.1. All three are based on natural community classification. The systems for Illinois and Missouri use soil/substrate as the primary unit and are similar, differing primarily to account for differences in the natural landscape of the states. The scheme for Minnesota is based primarily on water regimes. The Nature Conservancy classification system describes four main types of tallgrass prairie, based primarily on geologic history: Lake Agassiz type, Central Midwest type, Glaciated Lower Midwest type, and Unglaciated Lower Midwest type (Chapman et al. 1990). Often available soil moisture is used to delineate five moisture categories: wet, wet-mesic, mesic, mesic-dry, and dry (Curtis 1959). The moisture categories are often used with other descriptions, e.g., *wet-mesic*

Table 3.1. Comparisons of prairie classifications for three midwestern States. Sources of data: Illinois (White 1978), Missouri (Nelson 1985), and Minnesota (Aaseng et al. 1993).

Illinois	Missouri	Minnesota
(Blacksoil) prairie	(Blacksoil) prairie	Upland prairie
5 moisture categories	5 moisture categories	mesic
		dry
Sand prairie	Limestone/Dolomite prairie	barrens subtype
5 moisture categories	2 moisture categories	sand-gravel subtype
		hill subtype
Gravel prairie	Chert prairie	bedrock bluff subtype
3 moisture categories	2 moisture categories	
Dolomite prairie	Sandstone/Shale prairie	
5 moisture categories	2 moisture categories	Wet prairie
Hill prairie	Sand prairie	
4 substrate categories	2 moisture categories	
Shrub prairie	Handpan prairie	

sand prairie. Today, when used alone these generally refer to "blacksoil" or "typical" prairies of the region that have fine-textured, deep soils derived from loess or glacial till, although some may occur on alluvium (White 1978).

The number of species that occupy a prairie is rather high for a temperate ecosystem. For example, inventories of vascular plants occurring in small (ca. five acre) black-soil prairie remnants typically exceed 100 native species (Robertson unpublished data, Illinois Nature Preserves Commission unpublished data, Robertson et al. 1983). Weaver (1954) placed prairie plants into four phenological categories: prevernal, vernal, aestival, and autumnal. The first two are low in stature and generally die back to the ground after setting seeds. As the season progresses into summer and fall, the plants become progressively taller. The early season grasses generally have the C_3 photosynthetic pathway, while later species are C_4. A useful phenology chart is included in Kirt (1995).

Parish and Bazzaz (1982) propose that coexistence of species in grasslands occurs by (1) alpha-niche differentiation involving coevolution or pre-adaptation to reduce competition for resources among plants sharing the same location, i.e., staggered timing of growth and reproduction or stratification; (2) niche separation on the beta-scale, i.e., among habitats within a landscape, which is governed principally by available soil moisture; and (3) regeneration characteristics that enable species to become established on disturbed sites (Burton et al. 1988).

Original Extent and Recent Loss of Prairie in Midwest

Midwestern prairies, as defined in the context of this book, are all within the tallgrass prairie peninsula region and bounded on the north, east, and south by regions of deciduous forest (Transeau 1935). The original extent of the tallgrass prairie in six midwestern states is given in Table 3.2. At the west end of the region prior to European settlement, prairie occupied about 85% of the land area (12 million ha) of Iowa, and just over 60% (8.5 million ha) of Illinois was tallgrass prairie. Toward the east the tallgrass prairie became patchy, barely reaching Ohio (Lafferty 1979) and Ontario (Bakowsky and Riley 1994), occupying about 2.5% of the land area of each. Most of these area estimates are based on the original land surveys and, unfortunately, surveyors did not consistently distinguish prairie from some types of savannas or open wetlands such as sedge meadows and fens.

The loss of eastern tallgrass prairie has been nearly complete. The Nature Conservancy (Chapman et al. 1990) estimates that more than 99% of the tallgrass prairie east and north of the Missouri River has been destroyed, and only about 15% remains to the west and south of this river. Klopatek et al. (1979) estimated the amount of remaining intact natural habitats and ranked the three states in the heart of the prairie peninsula (Indiana, Illinois, and Iowa) as 48–50th respectively. Further, remaining high-quality prairies tend to be found in very small patches. Of the 253 prairie sites identified as grade A or B by the Illinois Natural Areas Inventory, 83% are smaller than ten acres and 30% are less than one acre (Figure 3.4). Three examples from Illinois counties illustrate these drastic changes in tallgrass prairie: 158 ha (0.07%) of 211,200 ha, 2 ha (<0.0007%) of 271,100 ha, and 0.4 ha (0.0002%) of 239,700 ha of high-quality remnant prairies remain in Cook, McLean, and Champaign counties, respectively. Using this kind of information, Noss et al. (1995) categorized the tallgrass prairie east of the Missouri as a critically endangered ecosystem.

This staggering amount of habitat loss occurred in an astonishingly short period, roughly between 1840 and 1900. European settlers, emigrating from

Table 3.2. Original extent of the tallgrass prairie and present day remnants for six states in the upper Midwest.

State	Acres of prairie prior to European settlement	% of natural vegetation in prairie	Acres of prairie remaining	% of original prairie remaining
Illinois	21,000,000	60%	2,300	0.01%
Indiana	3,000,000	13%	1,643	0.055%
Iowa	30,000,000	85%	30,000	0.1%
Minnesota	18,000,000	36%	75,000	0.4%
Missouri	15,000,000	34%	70,000	0.47%
Wisconsin	2,100,000	5.5%	2,111	0.1%

Sources of data: Illinois (Anderson 1970, Schwegman 1973, White 1978), Indiana (John Bacone and Robert Petty, Wabash College, via John Bacone), Iowa (Smith and Jacobs 1992, Thompson 1992), Minnesota (Wendt 1984; Robert Dana, personal communication, Aug 1995), Missouri (Greg Gremaud, personal communication, Aug 1995; Nelson 1985, Schroeder 1981), Wisconsin (Eric Epstein, personal communication, Aug 1995).

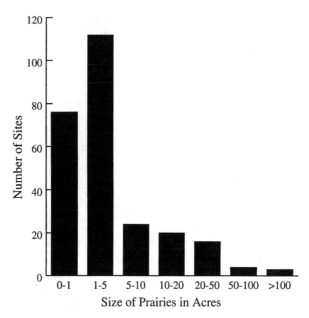

Figure 3.4. Number of grades A and B (high quality) prairies remaining in Illinois classified by size category.

(White 1978) Database updated by the IL Department of Natural Resources, Springfield, Ill

forested regions in Europe and eastern North America, found the prairies to be inhospitable due to the hordes of insects, intense summer heat and high humidity, bleak winters, and periodic fires. As the settlers migrated, they followed the finger-like traces of forest along the major waterways and initially avoided the larger tracts of prairie. Timber was considered such an important commodity on the prairie that counties were not allowed to form as governmental units until residents could demonstrate that they had access to sufficient timber to support development (Prince and Burnham 1908). Another difficulty with settling the prairie was that the prairie sod was deep and dense with tangled roots. Prairie sod could not be broken easily until 1837, when John Deere invented the self-scouring, steel-bladed plow. Finally, many larger tracts of prairie remained unsettled because of the lack of transportation to get crops to distant markets. With the coming of the railroads in the 1850s and 1860s, however, prairies were rapidly converted to cropland (Anderson 1970). Page and Jeffords (1991) estimated that 3.3% of the prairies in Illinois were plowed each year during this period. In Iowa, nearly 12 million ha of prairie was converted to agriculture between 1850 and 1930, for an average of 150,000 ha per year (Thompson 1992). Robert Ridgway (1889), the noted pioneer of ornithology in Illinois, related that in 1871 Fox Prairie (Richland County, Illinois) was a large rolling plain of uninterrupted prairie 10 km by 16 km (16,000 ha), but that by 1883 only 65 ha (0.4%) remained.

As the prairies were converted to agriculture, landscape-scale fires, which had swept nearly annually across the prairie in presettlement times, were actively stopped by settlers who viewed them as a threat to economic security. Cessation of fire furthered the demise of the prairies as many remaining sites were converted to forests or savannas by invading tree species. Mesic black-soil prairies continued to persist in unplowed cemeteries and along railroad rights-of-way. Railroad rights-of-way, extending at least 30 m on either side of the track, were established prior to prairie conversion, fenced to keep out livestock, and often managed with fire. Those fires, along with many accidental fires, prevented the invasion of woody species and exotic weeds. In the last 20 to 30 years, however, many of the remnant prairies along railroads have disappeared because of railroad abandonment and subsequent habitat conversion or herbicide use to manage rights-of-way. Thus, a fully functional tallgrass prairie ecosystem in the Midwest is only a historic phenomenon. Existing remnants lack the full complement of natural processes that operate at large scales (e.g., landscape fires, large grazing mammals, top predators, or interaction with adjacent natural habitats).

Impact of Habitat Loss on Biodiversity

The tallgrass prairie has been called "the most diverse repository of species in the Midwest [and] . . . habitat for some of the Midwest's rarest species" (Chapman et al. 1990). It is difficult to give a total number of species that occur in the tallgrass prairie. While many species maximize their frequency of occurrence in prairies, few species are endemic in the tallgrass prairie ecosystem. For this discussion we define all species that occupy or utilize the types of habitats generally recognized as prairie by natural community classifications of midwestern states as prairie species. Excluded are species restricted to savannas and open grass, sedge, and forb-dominated communities classified as wetlands, such as sedge meadows and fens.

Plants

Using various sources, Widrlechner (1989) compiled a list of 862 species of plants native to prairies of the midwestern United States. Similarly, the Illinois Plant Information Network (ILPIN), a computerized database listing life history, habitat, taxonomic, and distributional information available on the vascular flora of Illinois (Iverson 1992), records 851 species of plants native to Illinois prairies. A general pattern of increasing diversity with size of a habitat patch, referred to as the species/area curve, is commonly observed across a wide range of taxonomic groups and habitat types (Gleason 1992b, MacArthur and Wilson 1967, Simberloff and Gotelli 1984). The species/area curve observed in the flora of prairies suggests that even very small patches, as small as 4 ha, contain most of the local diversity of plants likely to be found on prairies of a much larger size, approximately 100 species (Figure 3.5). Unfortunately, few remaining prairies (e.g., <17% of high-quality prairies in Illinois—Figure 3.4) are above this size threshold. A total of approximately 140 species of native prairie plants occur in three blacksoil prairie remnant nature preserves (Loda, Prospect, and Weston, each about 2 ha) in central Illinois (Robertson, unpublished data). Each prairie individually has 85–90 native species, but the combined total gives a reasonable approximation of the level of plant diversity that might have been observed in large tracts of mesic prairie prior to European settlement. Most plant species are infrequently encountered on individual prairie sites, as demonstrated by two floristic surveys of small prairie fragments in Illinois and Indiana (Betz and Lamp 1989, 1992). In both studies, most species were found in fewer than four sites (Figure 3.6). Therefore, the complement of species found on any given prairie remnant is likely to be individualized and somewhat unique. Any further loss of prairie fragments represents the potential for a serious erosion of the floristic diversity of the state because of the relatively few good habitat patches in which many of these species are currently found. Nonetheless, it is notable that few of the plant species that occur on midwestern tallgrass prairies are so rare as to merit attention on the federal endangered species lists (Taft 1995).

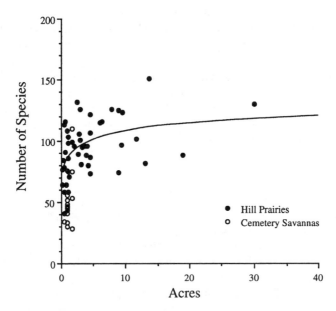

Figure 3.5. Number of plant species censused in prairie remnants of various sizes demonstrating that diversity of prairies increases with size.

Data are from Evers (unpublished data on file at the Illinois Natural History Survey) and Betz and Lamp (1989, 1992)

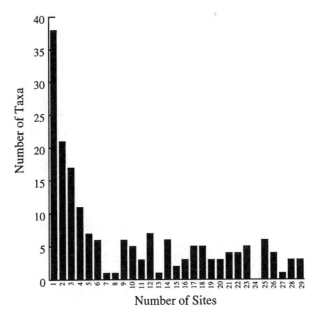

Figure 3.6. Number of sites in which each of 180 native taxa of plants were found in a survey of 29 remnant black soil prairies in Illinois and Indiana.

Data from Betz and Lamp (1989)

Birds

As one might expect, the dramatic change in the landscape after European settlement resulted in equally dramatic changes in bird populations. Several Illinois bird population studies, beginning in the mid-1800s and continuing through 1989, have provided insight into these changes. At first the change from prairie to agricultural land caused an increase in several bird species with the formation of secondary grasslands such as pastures and hayfields. These secondary grassland habitats became acceptable breeding grounds for a majority of prairie birds (Graber and Graber 1963). The prairie chicken especially benefited from this new combination of food and cover as well as the decrease in animal predators. It is thought that the dickcissel preferred secondary grasslands over original prairie (Kendeigh 1941, Graber and Graber 1963, Zimmerman 1971). Despite increased populations of some prairie birds throughout Illinois, however, Graber and Graber (1963) found that population changes were negligible for most species between 1909 and 1956.

Nevertheless, many birds considered very common prior to 1900 decreased during this century (Herkert 1991b). The most dramatic decline in almost all prairie bird populations in Illinois occurred from 1967 to 1989 (United States

Fish and Wildlife Services breeding bird survey, unpublished data—Table 3.3). Although the cause of this recent decline is not fully known, it is thought to be related to the rapid conversion of grazing lands to either crops or forest. A decrease in hay production coupled with pasture reduction has resulted in a loss of secondary grasslands on top of the depletion of the original prairie. This overall loss of grassland habitats is partially responsible for the current fragmented landscape. A reduction in available habitat results in a reduction of individuals, local populations, or perhaps even species. Less obvious, but also important to breeding birds, is that smaller habitats may lack essential resources and provide less of a buffer in the event of natural catastrophes or predation. Although only three species of prairie birds have been eliminated from Illinois, 13 more species are considered threatened or endangered, mainly because of habitat loss (Herkert 1991a,b).

One of the birds included on the endangered species list has experienced an enormous decline in numbers due more to the invasion of its habitat by a nonnative species than to a reduction of habitat. In 1860, the state of Illinois was home to 10 million greater prairie chickens (Westemeier 1983, Westemeier 1990, Westemeier and Edwards 1987), a species that had survived in large numbers over several thousand years despite native predators such as coyotes, skunks, and opossums. Although much of the prairie was gone by 1912, prairie chickens

Table 3.3. *Relative abundance (A = abundant; VC = very common; C = common) of several prairie bird species in Illinois before 1900 and changes in species populations from 1967 to 1989.*

Species	Prior to 1900	1967–1989
Eastern meadowlark	A	−67.0
Dickcissel	A	−46.0
Grasshopper sparrow	A	−56.0
Bobolink	A	−90.4
Henslow's sparrow	A	——[1]
Red-winged blackbird	VC	−18.8
Greater prairie chicken	VC	——[1]
Upland sandpiper	VC	−16.8
Vesper sparrow	C	+12.1
Horned lark	C	0.0
Field sparrow	C	−52.6
Song sparrow	C	−29.3
Savannah sparrow	C	−58.4
American goldfinch	C	−42.8
Common yellowthroat	C	−8.8
Sedge wren	C	−22.5

[1]Too sparse throughout period to determine a trend.

Data prior to 1900 are based on the work of Nelson (1876) and Ridgway (1889, 1895). Population changes from 1967 to 1989 are based on U.S. Fish and Wildlife Service breeding bird survey data as tabulated by Herkert (1991b).

still occupied 92 counties but quickly decreased in numbers with the release and establishment of ring-necked pheasants (Westemeier 1983). Since 1989, there have been fewer than 100 prairie chickens in Illinois (Ron Westemeier, personal communication May 1994). Sanctuaries were established around the state to ensure that suitable habitat for prairie chickens would always exist. Unfortunately, these sanctuaries are also attractive to pheasants, which have become the greatest threat to prairie chickens.

The main problem associated with the coexistence of prairie chickens and pheasants appears to be the result of hen pheasants "parasitizing" or laying eggs in the nests of prairie chickens. Pheasant eggs hatch about two days earlier than those of prairie chickens, sometimes causing the hen to leave the nest before her own chicks have hatched. Even if both eggs are hatched, the problem of harassment of prairie chicks by the larger pheasant chicks can occur. The survival of any species depends on successful reproduction, and the prairie chicken has not been able to effectively coexist with the pheasant.

Insects

Vertebrates constitute a small fraction of the animal species found in terrestrial ecosystems. Most animals are invertebrates, and most invertebrates are insects. An estimated 17,000 species of insects occur in Illinois (Post 1991); several thousand of these must have originally inhabited the vast Illinois prairie. Fortunately, most seem to have survived the near-total destruction of their pre-European settlement habitats. A majority of these animals today inhabit a variety of humanized habitats, such as pastures, hayfields, parks, yards, and fencerows. Some insect species have actually benefited from the alteration of their presettlement plant communities and can often be found in exaggerated numbers in degraded habitats (Ron Panzer, personal communication, Oct. 1996). A smaller but significant number of prairie insect species have not managed to adapt to the modern midwestern landscape. It is not clear what the frequency of remnant-dependency is for prairie insects, but one estimate suggests that probably not more than 25% of species rely specifically on high-quality prairie for habitat (Panzer et al. 1995). These remnant-dependent species are very discriminating in their choice of habitats and are rarely found outside of the context of their native plant communities (Panzer et al. 1995). Isolated as small populations on small, widely scattered prairie remnants, these species must contend with excessive edge effects and the high extinction rates associated with island-dwelling organisms. Having lost more than 99.99% of their presettlement habitats, this group of remnant-requiring animals is clearly vulnerable to the ongoing alteration of the Illinois landscape. Entomologists carry two unique concerns regarding prairie conservation. First, is the commonly used method of evaluating sites by using plants as indicators of habitat quality adequate for identifying sites with high insect diversity (Ron Panzer and Mark Schwartz, unpublished data)? Second, are current habitat management practices having a negative impact on the ability of fire-sensitive insects to survive (Stannard 1984, Panzer 1988)?

Endangered Species

Because 99% of the tallgrass prairies in the Midwest east of the Missouri River have been destroyed, the numbers of individuals of all prairie plants and animals are very small today. For example, the prairie white-fringed orchid (*Platanthera leucophaea*) was once widespread on the blacksoil prairies and has been reported historically from 33 counties in Illinois alone. Today it is known in Illinois from mostly small populations in eight counties, and some of these are under threat by non-native species, unscrupulous collection, and lack of proper management practices (Herkert 1991c, 1994).

Despite the nearly complete habitat loss, we have few instances of global endangerment of species of midwestern prairies. While in 1991 116 prairie species were listed as endangered or threatened within Illinois (Illinois Endangered Species Protection Board 1994), only 7 are sufficiently globally threatened as to appear on the federal list of threatened and endangered species (Table 3.4).

Table 3.4. Federally listed threatened and endangered species of midwestern prairies.

Species	IL	IN	IO	MI	MN	MO	OH	WI	Habitat
A. Plants									
Asclepias meadii	X	X	X			X			dry prairies[1]
Boltonia decurrens	X					X			moist places[1]
Dalea foliosa	X								dolomite prairie[1]
Geocarpon minimum						X			sandstone glades[2]
Hymenoxys acaulis v. glabra	X						X		dry open places[1]
Lespedeza leptostachya	X		X		X			X	dry prairies[1]
Lesquerella filliformis						X			limestone glades[2]
Platanthera leucophaea	X		X	X			X	X	wet prairie[1]
Platanthera praeclara				X		X	X		wet prairies[2]
Trifolium stolonifera		X				X			dry woods and prairies[2]
B. Insects									
Lycaeides melissa samuelis	X			X	X		X		savannas and open woods[3]
Neonympha mitchellii mitchellii		X		X					prairie fens[3]

[1]Mohlenbrock (1986)

[2]Steyermark (1963)

[3]Michigan Department of Natural Resources (1987)

Examining the federal endangered species lists for Indiana, Ohio, Missouri, Michigan, Minnesota, and Wisconsin only expands the list of globally endangered and threatened species found on prairies to 12 species (Table 3.4). As far as we know, only one plant species that occurred in Illinois prairies is both extirpated and extinct. This plant, *Thismia americana*, was last seen in 1914 (Mohlenbrock 1983). Several animals that occurred on the prairies have been extirpated from the Midwest since European settlement, such as the bison, elk, prairie wolf, mountain lion, sharp-tailed grouse, and black bear (Bowles et al. 1980, Hoffmeister 1989, Mankin and Warner Chapter 7, this volume).

Non-native Species

The tallgrass prairie ecosystem has not only been largely destroyed by the conversion of habitat for agricultural and urban uses, but the remaining fragments are threatened by what has been called *biological pollution* (McKnight 1993). A number of species native to non-prairie ecosystems in other geographical regions, often other continents, have become established in natural communities, including the tallgrass prairie. A recent estimate (Post 1991) indicates that there are 2,068 species of native vascular plants in Illinois. The most recent floristic manual (Mohlenbrock 1986) gives the total number of vascular plants known to be native or naturalized as 2,853. Using these figures, about 27.5% of the vascular plants growing spontaneously in Illinois were introduced from other regions. Slightly different estimates have been obtained using other sources of data (Henry and Scott 1980, Reed 1988). The number of non-native species has increased dramatically with European settlement, from 10.2% in 1846 to something around 30%. The impact of non-native species on prairies is large. In a study of 44 pioneer settler cemeteries on silt-loam soil, Betz and Lamp (1989) found a total of 180 native prairie species, 73 non-native herbaceous species, 22 species of both native and non-native woody plants, and 13 species of cultivated forbs. In a subsequent study of 16 old settler savanna and sand-prairie cemeteries, Betz and Lamp (1992) found 238 native prairie or savanna species, 22 species of woody plants, 54 species of weedy native or non-native herbaceous plants, and 14 species of cultivated forbs. A combined species list for three central Illinois blacksoil prairie pioneer cemetery nature preserves—Loda Cemetery, Prospect Cemetery in Paxton, and Weston Cemetery (K. Robertson, Illinois Natural History Survey, unpublished data), each about 2 ha—shows a total of 186 species, of which 46, or 24.7%, are non-native.

Non-native plant species can be divided into three categories: (1) extremely serious weeds that outcompete native species and threaten to destroy natural plant communities in the prairies; (2) species that occur regularly in prairies but are not overly aggressive and are not likely to further significantly change species composition or frequency in prairies; and (3) species that would probably be eliminated with proper management practices (Robertson and Schwartz 1994).

Different prairies have different disturbance and management practices that affect the occurrence of non-native species. For example, black-soil cemetery prairies are different from other prairie remnants in that they often contain species that were planted as ornamentals.

Given that habitat loss was nearly complete a century ago, one might think that the invasion of non-native species is also a thing of the past. This is not the case. For example, the two most serious non-native species at Loda Cemetery (Iroquois County, Illinois) are daylily (*Hemerocallis fulva*) and cut-leaved teasel (*Dipsacus laciniatus*). Since 1978, these species have increased greatly, and one large colony of daylily has nearly divided the prairie in half, crowding out all native vegetation. Cut-leaved teasel, a recent invader, was first recorded in Missouri in 1980 near Kansas City. Vast populations can now be found along midwestern roadsides where there were few or no populations only 5–10 years ago (Glass 1991, Solecki 1989). The expansion of both cut-leaved and common teasel (*D. sylvestris*) appears to have been assisted by two phenomena. First, the location of population centers along interstate highway rights-of-way suggests that cut-leaved teasel moves with highway construction. Second, horticultural use of common teasel in floral displays at gravesites has resulted in numerous colonizations of cemetery prairies (Swink and Wilhem 1994).

In moist prairies, especially in the Chicago region, common buckthorn (*Rhamnus cathartica*), glossy buckthorn (*R. frangula*), and various bush honeysuckles (*Lonicera maackii, L. morrowii, L. tatarica*) can be serious problems (Heidorn 1991, Swink and Wilhelm 1994). Black locust (*Robinia pseudoacacia*) is a problem in the sand prairies of central Illinois. Another troublesome species in some sand prairies is sour dock (*Rumex acetosella*). Most plant species that invade and encroach upon hill prairies are native woody species, although black locust is invasive on some hill prairies.

The second category of non-native species includes widespread but benign species that occur with regularity in prairies. They appear to be adapted to current climate and management practices, are not overly aggressive, and are not likely to dramatically change species composition in the prairies. There are numerous examples of these in blacksoil prairies, including Queen Anne's lace (*Daucus carota*), wild parsnip (*Pastinaca sativa*) (Kennay and Fell 1992), asparagus (*Asparagus officinalis*), ox-eye daisy (*Chrysanthemum leucanthemum*), and moneywort (*Lysimachia nummularia*). Blackberry lily (*Belamcanda chinensis*) is in this category on hill prairies. Kentucky blue grass (*Poa pratensis*) and Canada blue grass (*P. compressa*) occur widely in many types of prairies. They are cool-season grasses and begin to grow before most of the native species break dormancy. Although these are a serious problem in some prairies, they do not generally seem to be as extremely disruptive as species in the first category, and they appear impossible to eliminate from prairies; mid-spring burns may, however, help reduce the frequency of occurrence.

The third category includes species that will probably be eliminated with proper management practices. These are species that either persist from cultivation or are opportunistic in disturbances in the prairies. Examples include flowering almond (*Prunus glandulosa*), lily of the valley (*Convallaria majallis*), cultivated iris (*Iris* species), chicory (*Cichorium intybus*), and Adam's needle (*Yucca filamentosa*).

Prairie Management

Some of the most striking habitat changes, such as conversion to agricultural lands, are beyond our immediate ability to correct. Because of these extensive changes, an appropriate question is, What aspect of natural grassland ecosystems should we, or can we, conserve? Table 3.5 summarizes most of the major factors that have resulted in changes in tallgrass prairie. These extensive anthropogenic changes have eliminated the ability of even the largest of our remaining grasslands to exist as fully functioning ecosystems. Two centuries of change in these grassland habitats, without consideration of the many factors that are working in unison to generate these changes, have left our grasslands quite different from what they probably were prior to European settlement. The challenge is how to manage what remains to maintain as much biological integrity as possible.

The single most important stress affecting the remaining midwestern prairies is human exploitation. Consequently, the primary management strategy for the preservation/restoration of the remaining prairie remnants is a no-loss policy combined with a vigorous restoration program. Currently only 6% of the areas listed on the Illinois Natural Areas Inventory are afforded the maximum protection against future changes in land use as dedicated Illinois Nature Preserves (James Herkert, Jean Kearnes, personal communication, Aug. 1995). Seventy-eight percent of Illinois prairie areas are classified as unprotected. The threats of destruction to these unprotected areas are numerous and include building and highway construction, railroad maintenance, grazing, and cemetery mowing. Seventy-three

Table 3.5. Major anthropogenic changes in Illinois grassland ecosystems

Factor	Ramifications
Destruction of habitat	>99.99% loss of grassland habitats.
Drainage	Decreased growing season water availability.
Nitrogenous pollutants	Increased biomass production and invasibility of non-prairie species.
Fragmentation	Increased probability of local extinction and habitat degradation.
Climate change	Shifts in relative abundances, possible local species losses.
Fire suppression	Increased invasion of woody species, shifts in species abundances.
Non-native species	Displacement of native species.
Extirpation of bison	Loss of grazing disturbance resulting in shifts in species abundances.
Domestick livestock	Increased invasion by non-native grasses, loss of biodiversity.

Adapted from Robertson and Schwartz 1994.

percent of these prairie areas are likely to experience major threats within five years, and 9% are in immediate danger (White 1978). Unfortunately, little conservation acquisition effort has been directed toward small sites (Schwartz and van Mantgem, Chapter 16, this volume).

Current Management Practices

The primary management goals for prairie remnants are to increase species productivity and diversity and to reduce the encroachment of aggressive woody and non-native herbaceous vegetation. In general, these goals are accomplished by three management practices: (1) prescribed burning, (2) selective removal of woody or non-native ground cover species, and (3) habitat restoration through planting.

The tallgrass prairie of Illinois is considered a fire-adapted community (Henderson 1982). Historical records indicate that the prairies of Illinois burned frequently (McClain and Elzinga 1994). Thus, it is not surprising that prescribed fire is the most important tool in the development, maintenance, and management of prairies. Fire can be employed for two purposes in prairie management. In new restorations or neglected remnants, fire is used to directly suppress or kill non-prairie species. When fire serves this function, it is important to time the burn such that it coincides with the most vulnerable period in the target species life history (Illinois Nature Preserves Commission 1990). In a healthy system, fire reduces accumulated litter, allowing the prairie plants to gain a competitive edge on their non-native competitors (Schramm 1992). Fires that serve this purpose are usually started in the early spring (although there is a trend toward more fall burning; see the following discussion).

In small preserves the primary management objective is most often to prevent further habitat loss caused by non-native and woody species invasion. The major tool used to accomplish this goal is fire. When used properly, fire is very effective at reducing populations of non-prairie species. However, in cases in which fire is ineffective [purple loosestrife (*Lythrum salicaria*), autumn olive (*Elaeagnus umbellata*), wild parsnip, black locust], managers need to employ methods that selectively remove undesirable vegetation.

Mechanical control techniques such as mowing, girdling, cutting, and hand-pulling unwanted species are a viable alternative to fire. Hand-pulling is recommended for purple loosestrife, autumn olive, Canada thistle (*Cirsium arvense*), and teasel (Illinois Nature Preserves Commission 1990). The effort to control teasel is a good example of the necessity of understanding the biology of a species before undertaking control measures. Although teasel was introduced from Eurasia prior to this century (Werner 1975), it has only recently become a problem weed in Illinois (Glass 1991, Solecki 1989). Because teasel is a biennial species, initial attempts at control involved hand-cutting the flowering stalks and leaving them in the prairie to add to biomass for burning the following spring.

Unfortunately, enough stored energy remains in the cut stalks for seed to set (Solecki 1989, Glass 1991). Control measures now include transporting the cut stalks off site as well as very early spring burns (late January in 1993) when the winter rosettes are exposed and native plants are dormant. The spot application of herbicides has been found to control several woody species on prairie sites (Illinois Nature Preserves Commission 1990). Herbicides used in conjunction with fire or mechanical measures are very effective in controlling undesirable plant species. For example, fall fire facilitates the control of white sweet clover (*Melilotus alba*) by inducing rapid early sprout growth, thereby allowing the application of a herbicide prior to the emergence of the other forbs (Schwegman and McClain 1985, Cole 1991). In contrast, biennial fire regimes encourage sweet clover because the burn promotes germination of seed while the following burn-free year allows plants to mature and set seed. Regardless of the short-term control methods used to regulate non-native plant populations, the long-term goal of prairie management should be toward the restoration of the natural processes (fire, hydrology, etc.) that originally maintained the health of the system.

Suggested Changes in Management Practice

The two most needed changes for prairie management strategies in the Midwest are the frequency and timing of fire. Surprisingly, considering the importance and cost effectiveness of this management tool, fire is not used enough in prairie management (Peter Schramm, Gerald Wilhelm, Steve Packard, personal communications). New prairie restorations or neglected prairie remnants should be burnt yearly for up to a decade. Once a mature healthy system is established, the prairie plants will prevent most of the encroachment of undesirable species. At this stage fire should be applied on a rotation of one to three years. A conservative manager may wish to burn half of the area each year, providing unburned refugia for insects (Schramm 1992).

Changing the timing of the prescribed burn is also being considered in prairie management. In the past, prescribed burns have usually been conducted in the early spring, but most historical accounts of prairie fires indicate that presettlement burning frequently occurred in the fall (McClain and Elzinga 1994). Proponents argue that fall fires burn hotter and will carry over a larger area, while opponents say early spring fires are important for preserving winter wildlife cover and protecting against soil erosion. Both sides, however, agree that fire in either the fall or the spring is better than no fire at all. For more information on fall versus spring burning, see Whisenant and Uresk (1989), and Henderson (1992, 1995).

Prairie Restoration

Habitat restoration has been heralded as a viable technique for the amelioration of habitat loss caused by human activities. The first attempts at habitat reconstruction involved prairies, and the first of these prairie restorations was started at the

University of Wisconsin-Madison Arboretum (Anderson 1972; Anderson and Cottam 1970; Blewett and Cottam 1984; Cottam 1987; Sperry 1983, 1994). The idea originated with Norman Fassett, and Aldo Leopold and John Curtis provided the early leadership. The two prairie restorations at the University of Wisconsin-Madison Arboretum—Curtis and Greene—now total more than 40 ha making them among the largest prairies now occurring in Wisconsin. More than 300 species of native vascular plants have been recorded from the restorations, and they provide excellent habitat for numerous prairie insects, small mammals, and birds (Reich 1971, Selser 1994).

Early stages of work at the University of Wisconsin-Madison Arboretum prairie restoration utilized crews (about 200 people) and equipment from the Civilian Conservation Corps between 1935 and 1941. Because the process of prairie restoration was considered experimental, in 1937 a series of plots was established using different combinations of soil treatment and planting methods. Using seeds, seedling, and sod, single-species block plantings were made of 42 different species up until 1941. Some additional experimental plantings were made during the 1940s, and most large scale plantings of a total of 156 species were made in the 1950s using a variety of techniques, with stratified seed on disced ground under a cover crop giving the best results (Blewett and Cottam 1984). The use of prescribed fires, mostly biennial, has been an integral part of management at the Arboretum prairies (Anderson 1972). Over time, the plant species have segregated themselves according to their optimum moisture regimes. Careful records and maps were kept, and there have been several quantitative surveys and resurveys of the different restoration plots (Anderson and Cottam 1970; Cottam 1987; Cottam and Wilson 1966; Sperry 1983, 1994). As a result, the first prairie restoration has also been the most completely documented prairie restoration.

Several prairie restorations in Illinois have been successful in establishing high biological, or at least botanical, diversity on formerly agricultural or degraded land. A good example is the Schulenberg Prairie at the Morton Arboretum in Lisle (Schulenberg 1970, Johnson and Rosenthal 1992). Initially, volunteers were used extensively to grow plants from seed in a greenhouse, hand-plant the material on the site, and control non-native species. Some direct seeding has been done on additional parts of the site, and there has been considerable species enrichment through transplanting. A complete phenology of prairie species is found at the Schulenberg Prairie, and emphasis has been given to including prairie sedges, which are often overlooked in restorations. Another diverse restoration is the Doris L. Westfall Prairie in Forest Glen Preserve (Campbell and Westfall 1991). Over 120 species of prairie plants native to Vermilion County are found in this site, and most have been introduced through repeated seeding.

The largest prairie restoration project in Illinois, and perhaps the Midwest, is at Fermilab in Batavia (Betz 1986, Mlot 1990). The goal is to convert the entire area enclosed by the nuclear accelerator ring into prairie. The ring is 2 km (1.2

m) in diameter, 6.4 km (3.9 miles) in circumference, and encloses 314.2 ha (776.3 acres), with an area of 184 ha (455 acres) available for restoration. Additional restorations have been planted outside the ring. As of 1988, over 700 acres of prairie restoration had been planted. Restoration at Fermilab has proceeded by establishing a "prairie matrix" of warm-season grasses together with aggressive prairie forbs to establish a cover of native species that can compete with weedy species. Several years after initial planting, the area is handsown with seed of both forb and grass species that do well after weedy species have been greatly reduced. As this second wave of species becomes established, seedlings are planted of the most conservative prairie species, such as *Gentiana puberulenta, Lilium philadelphicum,* and *Habernaria leucophaea.* About 115 native prairie species have been planted in the restoration. Records have been kept of the variety of restoration techniques used at Fermilab. Most tracts that have been under prairie restoration management for over ten years show only a fraction of the floristic diversity of the native prairie. Likewise, the insect diversity on these restorations tends to be low (Panzer et al. 1995).

In the past quarter century, hundreds of prairie restorations have been planted in the Midwest. The vast majority of these contain at most one-fourth to one-half of the plant species that would be found in a natural prairie remnant of comparable size. Several factors are responsible. Because of cost and labor limitations, most prairie restorations are planted with a one-time seeding. Relatively few species (mostly warm-season grasses and rather aggressive forbs) are included in the seeding mixes, a complete phenology of species is not attempted, a number of species included in the mixes rarely succeed from seed, and follow-up species enrichment does not take place. While many of these restorations are aesthetically pleasing, they are not biological replacements for natural prairies.

The success of prairie restorations seems to depend largely upon the techniques used to restore the prairie. While a great many prairie restorations have been planted, few long-term detailed monitoring studies have been undertaken quantifying different techniques, with the notable exceptions of the examples at the beginning of this section. Nevertheless, a number of useful articles and publications exist that contain a wealth of personal experiences with the process of prairie restoration (Campbell and Westfall 1991, Schramm 1992, McClain 1986, Sperry 1994, Shirley 1994). Restorations can be conducted through a process of seeding, planting seedlings, or transferring sod from intact prairie. It appears that transplating sod increases the likelihood of success in establishing soil microorganisms and a fuller complement of vascular flora. The lack of a full diversity of prairie plants, however, should not discourage the use of restoration techniques to increase the total area of prairie in the Midwest. At present, we do not yet know whether these restored sites will eventually become more diverse. Also, over the short term these restoration sites provide habitat for species that are becoming increasingly rare in the state. The application of ecological theory (Burton et al. 1988a,b), such as niche quantification, mechanisms of succession and community stability, and spatial heterogeneity and landscape ecology, may improve the success of prairie restorations.

Conclusions

In the upper Midwest, the tallgrass prairie is gone—left behind are incomplete ecosystem remnants devoid of the full complement of natural ecological processes. These remnants are today under considerable stress from (1) further habitat loss and fragmentation, (2) continued degradation through invasion of woody and non-native herbaceous species of plants, and (3) potentially inappropriate management practices owing to our lack of understanding of the effects of management on a broad array of taxa. Yet, interest in preserving the remaining remnant prairies is strong, as shown by the national efforts of the Nature Conservancy and the Sierra Club and by regional conservation organizations and governmental agencies. Restoration and enhancement projects provide the only real opportunity to increase the total area of tallgrass prairie and to create large-sized sites. The prairie restoration process is labor intensive and applies methodologies based largely on practitioners' experience rather than on science. Most restorations lack the ecological complexity and diversity of remnant patches.

While the situation regarding midwestern prairies is dire from a landscape perspective, there are still fairly complete communities represented in remnants, and very few species have been extirpated from the region or have become extinct. Efforts need to be made to preserve the remnants and restore natural processes to the extent possible. Recently, there has been a shift in land acquisitions for conservation purposes from small but high-quality prairie remnants to large-sized disturbed sites that have recovery potential. While the high-quality remnants are important, larger recovering sites may have greater long-term potential for preserving the tallgrass ecosystem in the Midwest.

Acknowledgements

Some of the information in this chapter was adapted from Anderson (1991) and Robertson and Schwartz (1994) including information garnered by R. Panzer and R. Phillipe. Jennifer Tate helped with obtaining references and proofreading. P. Schramm, G. Wilhelm, S. Packard, John Bacone, Robert Dana, Greg Gremaud, and Eric Epstein also provided valuable insights.

References

Aaseng, N.E., J.C. Almendinger, R.P. Dana, B.C. Delaney, H.L. Dunevitz, K.A. Rusterholz, N.P. Sather, and D.S. Wovcha. 1993. *Minnesota's Native Vegetation. A Key to Natural Communities.* Version 1.5. Minnesota Department of Natural Resources Biological Report No. 20.

Anderson, M.R., and G. Cottam. 1970. Vegetational change on the Greene Prairie in relation to soil characteristics. In P. Schramm, ed. *Proceedings of a Symposium on Prairie and Prairie Restoration.* Knox College, Galesburg, Illinois, 42–44.

Anderson, R.C. 1970. Prairies in the prairie state. *Transactions of the Illinois State Academy of Science* 63:214–221.

Anderson, R.C. 1972. Prairie history, management, and restoration. In J. Zimmerman, ed. *Proceedings of the Second Midwestern Prairie Conference.* Madison, Wisconsin, 15–21.

Anderson, R.C. 1982. An evolutionary model summarizing the roles of fire, climate, and grazing animals in the origin and maintenance of grasslands: an end paper. In J.R. Estes, R.J. Tyrl, and J.N. Brunken, eds. *Grasses and grasslands: systematics and ecology.* University of Oklahoma Press, Norman, 297–308.

Anderson, R.C. 1990. The historic role of fire in North American grassland. In S.L. Collins and L.L. Wallace, eds. *Fire in North American Tallgrass Prairies.* University of Oklahoma Press, Norman, 8–18.

Anderson, R.C. 1991. Illinois prairies: a historical perspective. In L.M. Page and M.R. Jeffords, eds. Our living heritage: the biological resources of Illinois. Illinois Natural History Survey Bulletin 34(4):384–391.

Anderson, R.C., E. Corbett, M.R. Anderson, G. Corbett, and J. Nelson. 1995. Influence of deer browsing on prairie forbs. In T.E. Rice, ed. *Proceedings of the Fourth Central Illinois Prairie Conference.* Grand Prairie Friends of Illinois in cooperation with Millikin University Biology Department and Macon County Conservation District, Urbana and Decatur, 64–65.

Axelrod, D. 1985. Rise of the grassland biome, central North America. *Botanical Review* 51:163–201.

Bakowsky, W., and J.L. Riley. 1994. A survey of the prairies and savannas of southern Ontario. In R.G. Wickett, P.D. Lewis, A. Woodliffe, and P. Pratt, eds. *Proceedings of the Thirteenth North American Prairie Conference: Spirit of the Land, Our Prairie Legacy.* Department of Parks and Recreation, Windsor, Ontario, Canada, 7–16.

Betz, R.F. 1986. One decade of research in prairie restoration at the Fermi National Accelerator Laboratory (Fermilab) Batavia, Illinois. In G.K. Clambey and R.H. Pemble, eds. *Proceedings of the Ninth North American Prairie Conference: The Prairie: Past, Present and Future.* Tri-College University Center for Environmental Studies, Fargo, North Dakota and Moorhead, Minnesota, 179–185.

Betz, R.F., and H.F. Lamp. 1989. Species composition of old settler silt-loam prairies. In T.B. Bragg and J. Stubbendieck, eds. *Proceedings of the Eleventh North American Prairie Conference: Prairie Pioneers: Ecology, History and Culture.* University of Nebraska, Lincoln, 33–39.

Betz, R.F., and H.F. Lamp. 1992. Species composition of old settler savanna and sand prairie cemeteries in northern Illinois and northwestern Indiana. In D.D. Smith and C.A. Jacobs, eds. *Proceedings of the Twelfth North American Prairie Conference: Recapturing a Vanishing Heritage.* University of Northern Iowa, Cedar Falls, 79–87.

Blasing, T.J., and D. Duvick. 1984. Reconstruction of precipitation history in North American corn belt using tree rings. *Nature* 307:143–145.

Blewett, T.J., and G. Cottam. 1984. History of the University of Wisconsin Arboretum prairies. *Transactions of the Wisconsin Academy of Sciences, Arts, and Letters* 72:130–144.

Bowles, M.L., K. Kerr, R.H. Thom, and D.E. Birkenholz. 1980. Threatened, endangered and extirpated birds of Illinois prairies. *Illinois Audubon Bulletin* 193:2–12.

Burton, P.J., K.R. Robertson, L.R. Iverson, and P.G. Risser. 1988. Use of resource partitioning and disturbance regimes in the design and management of restored prairies. In E.B. Allen, ed. *The Reconstruction of Disturbed Arid Lands. An Ecological Approach.* Westview Press, Boulder, Colo., for the American Association for the Advancement of Science, Washington, D.C., 46–88.

Burton, P.J., K.R. Robertson, L.R. Iverson and P.G. Risser, 1988b. Suggested applications of ecological theory to prairie restoration. Article 01.16 in A. Davis and G. Stanford eds., The prairie: roots of our culture, foundation of our economy. Proceedings of the 10th North American Prairie Conference, Native Prairie Association of Texas, Dallas.

Campbell, M.F., and D.L. Westfall. 1991. *The Prairie in Vermilion County.* Outdoor Heritage Foundation of Vermilion County, Westville, Illinois.

Chapman, K., M. White, R. Johnson, and Z.M. Wong. 1990. *An Approach to Evaluate Long-Term Survival of the Tallgrass Prairie Ecosystem.* The Nature Conservancy, Midwest Regional Office, Minneapolis, Minnesota.

Cole, M.A.R. 1991. Vegetation management guideline: white and yellow sweet clover [*Melilotus alba* Desr. and *Melilotus officinalis* (L.) Lam.]. *Natural Areas Journal* 11:213–214.

Cottam, G. 1987. Community dynamics on an artificial prairie. In W.R. Jordan III, M.E. Gilpin, and J.D. Aber, eds. *Restoration Ecology: A Synthetic Approach to Ecological Research.* Cambridge University Press, New York, 257–270.

Cottam, G., and H.C. Wilson. 1966. Community dynamics on an artificial prairie. *Ecology* 47:88–96.

Curtis, J.T. 1959. *The Vegetation of Wisconsin. An Ordination of Plant Communities.* University of Wisconsin Press, Madison.

Fahnestock, J.T., and A.K. Knapp. 1993. Water relations and growth of tallgrass prairie forbs in response to selective grass herbivory by bison. *International Journal of Plant Science* 154:432–440.

Farney, D. 1980. Can the tallgrass prairie be saved? *National Geographic* 157(1):37–61.

Fehrenbacher, J., B. Ray, and J. Alexander. 1968. Illinois soils and factors in their development. In R.E. Bergstrom, ed. *The Quaternary of Illinois.* Special Publication 14. College of Agriculture, University of Illinois, Urbana, 165–175.

Gibson, D.J. 1989. Effects of animal disturbance on tallgrass prairie vegetation. *American Midland Naturalist* 121:144–154.

Gibson, D.J., C.F. Freeman, and L.C. Hulbert. 1990. Effects of small mammal and invertebrate herbivory on plant species richness and abundance in tallgrass prairie. *Oecologia* 84:169–175.

Glass, W.D. 1991. Vegetation management guideline: cut-leaved teasel (*Dipsacus lacinia-tus* L.) and common teasel (*D. sylvestris* Huds.). *Natural Areas Journal* 11:213–214.

Gleason, H.A. 1913. The relation of forest distribution and prairie fires in the middlewest. *Torreya* 13:173–181.

Gleason, H.A. 1922a. Vegetational history of the middlewest. *Annals of the American Association of Geographers* 12:39–86.

Gleason, H.A. 1922b. On the relation between species and area. *Ecology* 3:158–162.

Golley, P.M., and F.B. Golley, eds. 1972. Papers from symposium on tropical ecology with an emphasis on organic production. Institute of Ecology, University of Georgia, Athens.

Graber, R.R., and J.W. Graber. 1963. A comparative study of bird populations in Illinois, 1906–1909 and 1956–1958. *Illinois Natural History Survey Bulletin* 28(3):382–383.

Graham, R.W., H.A. Semken, Jr., and M.A. Graham, eds. 1987. Late Quaternary mammalian biogeography and environments of the Great Plains and prairies. *Illinois State Museum Scientific Papers* 22.

Grimm, E.C. 1983. Chronology and dynamics of vegetation change in the prairie-woodland region of southern Minnesota, USA. *New Phytologist* 93:311–350.

Grimm, E.C. 1984. Fire and other factors controlling the Big Woods Vegetation of Minnesota in the mid-nineteenth century. *Ecological Monographs* 54:291–311.

Groombridge, B., ed. 1992. *Global-Biodiversity: Status of the Earth's Living Resources.* A report compiled by the World Conservation Monitoring Centre. Chapman & Hall, London.

Havercamp, J., and G.G. Whitney. 1983. The life history characteristics of three ecologically distinct groups of forbs associated with the tallgrass prairie. *American Midland Naturalist* 109:105–119.

Heidorn, R. 1991. Vegetation management guideline: exotic buckthorns. Common buckthorn (*Rhamnus cathartica* L.), glossy buckthorn (*R. frangula* L.) and Duhurian buckthorn (*R. davurica* Pall.). *Natural Areas Journal* 11:216–217.

Henderson, R.A. 1982. Vegetation—fire ecology of tallgrass prairie. *Natural Areas Journal* 2(3):17–26.

Henderson, R.A. 1992. Ten-year response of a Wisconsin prairie remnant to seasonal timing of fire. In D.D. Smith and C.A. Jacobs, eds. *Proceedings of the Twelfth North American Prairie Conference: Recapturing a Vanishing Heritage.* University of Northern Iowa, Cedar Falls, 121–126.

Henderson, R.A. 1995. *Plant Species Composition of Wisconsin Prairies. An Aid to Selecting Species for Plants and Restoration Based upon University of Wisconsin-Madison Plant Ecology Laboratory Data.* Technical Bulletin 188. Wisconsin Department of Natural Resources, Madison.

Henry, R.D., and A.R. Scott. 1980. Some aspects of the spontaneous Illinois vascular flora. *Transactions of the Illinois State Academy of Science* 73:35–40.

Herkert, J.R. 1991a. *An Ecological Study of the Breeding Birds of Grassland Habitats within Illinois.* Ph.D. dissertation, University of Illinois, Urbana.

Herkert, J.R. 1991b. Prairie birds of Illinois: Population response to two centuries of habitat change. In L.M. Page and M.R. Jeffords, eds. Our living heritage: The biological resources of Illinois. *Illinois Natural History Survey Bulletin* 34(4):393–399.

Herkert, J.R., ed. 1991c. *Endangered and Threatened Species of Illinois: Status and Distribution.* Vol. 1: Plants. Illinois Endangered Species Protection Board, Springfield.

Herkert, J.R., ed. 1994. *Endangered and Threatened Species of Illinois: Status and Distribution.* Vol. 3: 1994 changes to the Illinois list of endangered and threatened species. Illinois Endangered Species Protection Board, Springfield.

Higgins, K.F. 1986. *Interpretation and Compendium of Historical Fire Accounts in the Northern Great Plains.* U.S. Dept. of the Interior, Fish and Wildlife Service, Resource Pub. 161. Washington, D.C.

Hoffmeister, D.F. 1989. *Mammals of Illinois.* University of Illinois Press, Urbana and Chicago.

Illinois Endangered Species Protection Board. 1994. *Checklist of Endangered and Threatened Animals and Plants of Illinois.* Illinois Endangered Species Protection Board, Springfield.

Illinois Nature Preserves Commission. 1990. *Vegetation Management Manual.* Vol. 1, No. 1–27. Springfield, Illinois.

Iverson, L.R. 1988. Land-use changes in Illinois, USA: the influence of landscape attributes on current and historic land use. *Landscape Ecology* 2:45–61.

Iverson, L.R. 1992. *Illinois Plant Information Network (ILPIN).* A database on the ecology, biology, distribution, taxonomy, and literature of the 3,200 plant species found in Illinois. Computer database at the Illinois Natural History Survey, Champaign.

Johnson, C.B., and M.W. Rosenthal. 1992. Thirty years of prairie reconstruction. *Morton Arboretum Quarterly* 28:11–15.

Kendeigh, S.C. 1941. Distribution of upland birds in Illinois. *Transactions of the Illinois State Academy of Science* 34:225–226.

Kennay, J., and G. Fell. 1992. Vegetation management guideline: wild parsnip (*Pastinaca sativa* L.). *Natural Areas Journal* 12:42–43.

King, J.E. 1981a. The prairies of Illinois. *The Living Museum* 43:42–45.

King, J.E. 1981b. Late Quaternary vegetational history of Illinois. *Ecological Monographs* 51:43–62.

Kirt, R.R. 1995. *Prairie Plants of the Midwest: Identification and Ecology.* Stipes Publishing, Champaign, Illinois.

Klopatek, J.M., R.J. Olson, C.J. Emerson, and J.L. Joness. 1979. Land-use conflicts with natural vegetation in the United States. *Environmental Conservation* 6:191–199.

Knapp, A.K., and T.R. Seastedt. 1986. Detritus accumulation limits productivity of tallgrass prairie. *BioScience* 36:662–668.

Küchler, A.W. 1964. *Potential Natural Vegetation of the Conterminous United States.* American Geographical Society Special Publication 36.

Lafferty, M.B. 1979. *Ohio's Natural Heritage.* Ohio Academy of Science, Columbus.

MacArthur, R.H., and E.O. Wilson. 1967. *The Theory of Island Biogeography.* Princeton University Press, Princeton, New Jersey.

Madson, J. 1982. *Where the Sky Began: Land of the Tallgrass Prairie.* Houghton Mifflin, Boston.

McClain, W.E. 1986. *Illinois Prairie: Past and Future, a Restoration Guide.* Illinois Department of Conservation. Springfield.

McClain, W.E., and S.L. Elzinga. 1994. The occurrence of prairie and forest fires in Illinois and other Midwestern states, 1679 to 1854. *Erigenia* 13:79–90.

McKnight, B.N. 1993. *Biological Pollution: The Control and Impact of Invasive Exotic Species.* Proceedings of a symposium held at the University Place Conference Center, Indiana. University-Purdue University at Indianapolis, Indiana Academy of Science.

McNaughton, S.J. 1979. Grazing as an optimum process: grass-ungulate relationships in the Serengeti. *Ecological Monographs* 55:259–294.

McNaughton, S.J. 1984. Grazing lawns: animals in herds, plant form, and coevolution. *American Naturalist* 124:863–886.

Michigan Department of Natural Resources. 1987. *Michigan Endangered Threatened and Special Concern Plant and Animal Species.* 3rd ed. Michigan Natural Heritage Program, Lansing.

Mlot, C. 1990. Restoring the prairie. Big bluestem and other native tallgrass plants make a comeback. *BioScience* 40:804–809.

Mohlenbrock, R.H. 1983. *Where Have All the Wildflowers Gone? A Region-to-Region Guide to Threatened or Endangered U.S. Wildflowers.* Macmillan, New York.

Mohlenbrock, R.H. 1986. *Guide to the Vascular Flora of Illinois.* Revised and enlarged ed. Southern Illinois University Press, Carbondale and Edwardsville.

Moore, C.T. 1972. *Man and Fire in the Central North American Grassland 1535–1890: A Documentary Historical Geography.* Ph.D. dissertation, University of California, Los Angeles.

Nelson, E.W. 1876. Birds of northeastern Illinois. *Essex Institute Bulletin* 8:90–155.

Nelson, P.W. 1985. *The Terrestrial Natural Communities of Missouri.* Missouri Natural Areas Committee, Columbia.

Noss, R.F., E.T. LaRoe III, and J.M. Scott. 1995. *Endangered Ecosystems of the United States: A Preliminary Assessment of Loss and Degradation.* National Biological Service, U.S. Department of the Interior. Biological Report 28.

Owen, D., and R. Wiegert. 1981. Mutualism between grasses and grazers: an evolutionary hypothesis. *Oikos* 36:376–378.

Page, L.M., and M.R. Jeffords, eds. 1991. Our living heritage: The biological resources of Illinois. *Illinois Natural History Survey Bulletin* 34(4):vi, 357–477.

Panzer, R. 1988. Management of prairie remnants for insect conservation. *Natural Areas Journal* 8:83–90.

Panzer, R., and M.W. Schwartz, N.d. Assessing the ability of prairie plants to predict insect diversity in the Chicago region. Unpublished.

Panzer, R., D. Stillwaugh, R. Gnaedinger, and G. Derkovitz. 1995. Prevalence of remnant dependence among the prairie- and savanna-inhabiting insects of the Chicago region. *Natural Areas Journal* 15:101–116.

Parrish, J., and F. Bazzaz. 1982. Organization of grassland communities. In J. Estes. R. Tyrl, and J. Brunken, eds. *Grasses and Grasslands: Systematics and Ecology.* University of Oklahoma Press, Norman, 233–254.

Pielou, E.C. 1991. *After the Ice Age: The Return of Life to Glaciated North America.* University of Chicago Press, Chicago, Illinois.

Platt, W.J., and I.M. Weis. 1977. Resource partitioning and competition within a guild of fugitive prairie plants. *American Naturalist* 111:479–513.

Polley, H.W., and S.L. Collins. 1984. Relationships of vegetation and environment in buffalo wallows. *American Midland Naturalist* 112:178–186.

Post, S.L. 1991. Appendix One: Native Illinois species and related bibliography. In L.M. Page and M.R. Jeffords, eds. Our living heritage: The biological resources of Illinois. *Illinois Natural History Survey Bulletin* 34(4):463–475.

Prince, E., and J. Burnham. 1908. *History of McLean County.* Vol. 1. Munsell, Chicago.

Pyne, S.J. 1986. Fire and prairie ecosystems. In G. Clambey and R. Pemble, eds. *Proceedings of the Ninth North American Prairie Conference: The Prairie: Past, Present and Future.* Tricollege University Center for Environmental Studies, North Dakota State University, Fargo, 131–137.

Reed, P.B., Jr. 1988. *National List of Plant Species That Occur in Wetlands in Illinois.* U.S. Fish and Wildlife Service. NERC-88/18.13.

Reich, B. 1971. *Guide to the Arboretum Prairies.* Friends of the University of Wisconsin Arboretum, Madison.

Reichman, O.J., J.H. Benedix, Jr., and T.R. Seastedt. 1993. Distinct animal-generated edge effects in a tallgrass prairie community. *Ecology* 74:1281–1285.

Rice, E., and R. Parenti. 1978. Causes of decrease of productivity in undisturbed tallgrass prairie. *American Journal of Botany* 65:1091–1097.

Ridgway, R. 1889. *The Ornithology of Illinois.* Vol. 1. Illinois State Laboratory of Natural History, Bloomington.

Ridgway, R. 1895. *The Ornithology of Illinois.* Vol. 2. Illinois State Laboratory of Natural History, Bloomington.

Risser, P.G., E.C. Birney, H.D. Blocker, S.W. May, W.J. Parton, and J.A. Wiens. 1981. *The True Prairie Ecosystem.* Hutchinson Ross, Stroudsburg, Pennsylvania.

Robertson, K.R., W.E. McClain, and A.C. Koelling. 1983. First confirmation of *Erythronium mesochoreum* (Liliaceae) east of the Mississippi River. *Castanea* 48:146–150.

Robertson, K.R., and M.W. Schwartz. 1994. Prairies. In Illinois Department of Energy and Natural Resources. *The Changing Illinois Environment: Critical Trends.* Technical Report of the Critical Trends Assessment Project. Vol. 3: Ecological Resources. Illinois Department of Energy and Natural Resources, Springfield, ILENR/RE-EA-94/05.

Schramm, P. 1992. Prairie restoration: a twenty-five year perspective on establishment and management. In D.D. Smith and C.A. Jacobs, eds. *Proceedings of the Twelfth North American Prairie Conference: Recapturing a Vanishing Heritage.* University of Northern Iowa, Cedar Falls, 169–177.

Schroeder, W.A. 1981. *Presettlement Prairie of Missouri.* Missouri Department of Conservation, Natural History Series 2.

Schulenberg, R. 1970. Summary of Morton Arboretum prairie restoration work, 1963–1968. In P. Schramm, ed. *Proceedings of a Symposium on Prairie and Prairie Restoration.* Knox College, Galesburg, Illinois, 45–46.

Schwegman, J. 1973. *Comprehensive Plan for the Illinois Nature Preserves System.* Part 2. The Natural Divisions of Illinois. Illinois Nature Preserves Commission, Rockford.

Schwegman, J.E., and W.E. McClain. 1985. Vegetative effects and management implications of a fall prescribed burn on an Illinois hill prairie. *Natural Areas Journal* 5(3):4–8.

Selser, E.J. 1994. Diversity, abundance and distribution of butterfly species in remnant and tallgrass prairie. In R.G. Wickett, P.D. Lewis, A. Woodliffe, and P. Pratt, eds. *Proceedings of the Thirteenth North American Prairie Conference: Spirit of the Land, Our Prairie Legacy.* Department of Parks and Recreation, Windsor, Ontario, Canada.

Shirley, S. 1994. *Restoring the Tallgrass Prairie: An Illustrated Manual for Iowa and the Upper Midwest.* University of Iowa Press, Iowa City.

Simberloff, D., and N. Gotelli. 1984. Effects of insularisation on plant species richness in the prairie-forest ecotone. *Biological Conservation* 29:27–46.

Singh, J.S., W.K. Lauenroth, and D.G. Milchunas. 1983. Geography of grassland ecosystems. *Progress in Physical Geography* 7:46–80.

Smith, D.D., and C.A. Jacobs, eds. 1992. *Proceedings of the Twelfth North American Prairie Conference: Recapturing a Vanishing Heritage.* University of Northern Iowa, Cedar Falls.

Solecki, M.K. 1989. The viability of cut-leaved teasel (*Dipsacus laciniatus* L.) seed harvested from flowering stems—management implications. *Natural Areas Journal* 9:102–105.

Sperry, T.M. 1983. Analysis of the University of Wisconsin-Madison prairie restoration project. In R. Brewer, ed. *Proceedings of the Eighth North American Prairie Conference.* Western Michigan University, Kalamazoo, 140–147.

Sperry, T.M. 1994. The Curtis Prairie Restoration, using the single-species planting method. *Natural Areas Journal* 14:124–127.

Stannard, L.J. 1984. On the origin and maintenance of La Grande Prairie of Illinois. *Erigenia.* 4:31–36.

Stebbins, G.L. 1981. Coevolution of grasses and herbivores. *Annals of the Missouri Botanical Garden* 68:75–86.

Stewart, O.C. 1951. Burning and natural vegetation in the United States. *Geographical Review* 41:317–320.

Stewart, O.C. 1956. Fire as the first great force employed by man. In W. Thomas, ed. *Man's Role in Changing the Face of the Earth.* University of Chicago Press, Chicago, Illinois, 115–133.

Steyermark, J.A. 1963. *The Flora of Missouri.* Iowa State University Press, Ames.

Swink, F., and G. Wilhelm. 1994. *Plants of the Chicago Region.* 4th ed. The Morton Arboretum, Lisle, Illinois, and the Indiana Academy of Science, Indianapolis.

Taft, J.B. 1995. Ecology, distribution, and rareness patterns of threatened and endangered prairie plants in Illinois. In T.E. Rice, ed. *Proceedings of the Fourth Central Illinois Prairie Conference.* Grand Prairie Friends of Illinois in cooperation with Millikin University Biology Department and Macon County Conservation District, Urbana and Decatur, 21–31.

Tainton, N., and M. Mentis. 1984. Fire in grasslands. In P. de V. Booysen and N. Tainton, eds. *Ecological Effects of Fire in South African Ecosystems.* Springer-Verlag, Boston, 117–147.

Thompson, J.R. 1992. *Prairies, forests, and wetlands: The Restoration of Natural Landscape Communities in Iowa.* University of Iowa Press, Iowa City.

Transeau, E. 1935. The prairie peninsula. *Ecology* 16:423–437.

Umbanhowar, C.E., Jr. 1992. Reanalysis of the Wisconsin prairie continuum. *American Midland Naturalist* 127:268–275.

Vinton, M.A., D.C. Hartnett, E.J. Finck, and J.M. Briggs. 1993. Interactive effects of fire, bison (*Bison bison*) grazing and plant community composition in tallgrass prairie. *American Midland Naturalist* 129:10–18.

Weaver, J.E. 1954. *North American Prairie.* Johnsen, Lincoln, Nebraska.

Weaver, J.E. 1968. *Prairie Plants and Their Environment. A Fifty Year Study in the Midwest.* University of Nebraska Press, Lincoln.

Webb, T., III, E.J. Cushing, and H.E. Wright, Jr. 1983. Holocene changes in the vegetation of the Midwest. In H.E. Wright, Jr., ed. *Late-Quaternary Environments of the United States.* University of Minnesota Press, Minneapolis, 142–165.

Wells, P. 1970. Postglacial vegetational history of the great plains. *Science* 167:1574–1582.

Wendt, K.M. 1984. *A Guide to Minnesota Prairies.* The Natural Heritage Program, Minnesota Department of Natural Resources, St. Paul.

Werner, P.A. 1975. The biology of Canadian weeds. 12. *Dipsacus sylvestris* Huds. *Canadian Journal of Plant Science* 55:783–794.

Westemeier, R.L. 1983. Responses and impact by pheasants on prairie-chicken sanctuaries in Illinois: a synopsis. In R.T. Dumke, R.B. Stiehl, and R.B. Kahl, eds. *PERDIX III: Gray Partridge and Ring-Necked Pheasant Workshop.* Wisconsin Department of Natural Resources, Madison, 117–122.

Westemeier, R.L. 1990. Prairie-chicken responses to management in Illinois before and after pheasant intervention. In *Summaries of Selected Talks from Prairie Chickens at the Crossroads.* Missouri Prairie Foundation and Missouri Department of Conservation, 4–6.

Westemeier, R.L., and W.R. Edwards. 1987. Prairie chickens: survival in the Midwest. In H. Kallman, C.P. Agee, W.R. Goforth, and J.P. Linduska, eds. *Restoring America's Wildlife.* U.S. Fish and Wildlife Service, Washington, D.C., 119–131.

Whisenant, S.G., and D.W. Uresk. 1989. Burning upland, mixed prairie in Badlands National Park. *Prairie Naturalist* 21:221–227.

White, J. 1978. *Illinois Natural Areas Inventory Technical Report.* Vol. 1: Survey methods and results. Illinois Natural Areas Inventory, Urbana.

White, J. 1995. The ecological effects of disturbance on the early Illinois landscape. Unpublished report to the Illinois Department of Natural Resources, Springfield.

Whitney, G. G., and J. R. Steiger. 1985. Site-factor determinants of the presettlement prairie-forest border areas of North-Central Ohio. *Botanical Gazette* 146:421–430.

Widrlechner, M.P. 1989. Germplasm resources information network and ex situ conservation of germplasm. In T.B. Bragg and J. Stubbendieck, eds. *Proceedings of the Eleventh North American Prairie Conference: Prairie Pioneers: Ecology, History, and Culture.* University of Nebraska, Lincoln, 109–114.

Wright, H. 1974. Range burning. *Journal of Range Management* 27:5–11.

Zimmerman, J.L. 1971. The territory and its density dependent effect in *Spiza americana. Auk* 88:591–612.

4

Wetlands in the Midwest with Special Reference to Illinois

Stephen P. Havera, Liane B. Suloway, and Joyce E. Hoffman
Illinois Natural History Survey

Introduction

Wetlands are generally defined as lands where water is a key factor determining both soil development and the plant and animal communities living in the soil as well as on its surface (Wilen and Frayer 1990). Consequently, wetlands are transitional lands between terrestrial and aquatic systems where the land is covered by shallow water or the water table is at or near the surface.

Wetlands ecosystems are characterized by continual change. Water levels may fluctuate daily, seasonally, annually, or over several years. The high degree of biological productivity of wetlands is a result of their dynamic and transitional water levels (Feierabend and Zelazny 1987). The plant and animal species associated with wetlands are adapted to a fluctuating environment. Nevertheless, the quantity and quality of wetlands are sensitive to human disturbances, and our activities have greatly affected their productivity (Feierabend and Zelazny 1987).

Wetlands are among our most important ecosystems (Figure 4.1). The unique and irreplaceable functions of wetlands include storing water, recharging groundwater, regulating the flow of water, filtering and purifying water, trapping sediments, providing habitat for an incredible diversity of plant and animal species, and furnishing recreational opportunities (Wilen and Frayer 1990). Wetlands are an important part of our nation's heritage providing benefits for all citizens (Feierabend and Zelazny 1987).

Until recently, "wetlands have been regarded as nuisances, wastelands, habitats for pests, and threats to public health" in the United States (Wilen and Frayer 1990:182). Wetlands have been "reclaimed" by draining, clearing, and filling in the name of progress. Now, however, wetlands have become more appreciated for their functions and economic values (Farber and Costanza 1987). This chapter describes wetlands of the upper Mississippi River valley using Illinois as a focus. The amounts, associated flora and fauna, and trends of wetland ecosystems are discussed.

Figure 4.1. Wetland complexes, such as Quiver Creek in Mason County, Illinois, are extremely productive systems that host a variety of plants and associated animals.

(Photo by Michelle M. Georgi, Illinois Natural History Survey)

Definition and Description

Water, or *hydrology*, is the dominant force that creates and maintains wetlands. In general, wetlands exhibit the following characteristics:

1. The water table (the upper limit of that portion of the ground that is entirely saturated with water) remains at or near the surface, or water covers the land at least part of the year.
2. The soils are hydric (wet for most of the year and low in oxygen).
3. The wetland plants are adapted to life in water or saturated soil (hydrophytes).

Wetlands typically have two sources of water: surface water from precipitation and groundwater. A depression that is deep enough to extend below the water table forms a wetland fed by groundwater and surface water. A depression that does not extend below the water table receives only surface water, such as precipitation and runoff from the surrounding land. The length of time the area remains saturated depends on the degree of slope, soil characteristics, and the frequency of flooding or runoff from precipitation.

Wetlands range from those in which the soil is saturated for at least part of the year to those with permanently standing water, from wetlands associated with the seasonal changes that occur along a river to those that were formed directly or indirectly by the action of ancient glaciers, from wetlands characterized by organic soils (peat or muck) to those in which inorganic (mineral) soils predominate, and from grassy wetlands to those that are forested. Wetlands formed by rivers are of several types, including oxbow marshes, bottomland forest, and backwater lakes. When a meandering river changes course and leaves a portion of its channel isolated except during flood, an oxbow pond is formed. In time, this pond fills in and becomes an oxbow marsh. Floodplain bottomlands are characterized by periodic flooding and host forest, swamp, and marsh habitats. Backwater (bottomland) lakes are created by soil and sand settling out of river currents and forming long islands along the river.

In the Midwest, wetlands were generally formed by rivers or by the action of glaciers. After the Wisconsonian glaciation, remnant blocks of ice from the main glacier melted and formed lakes. In other areas, glacial action created shallow depressions where water accumulated. Most of Illinois is relatively flat glacial till plain except for small areas of more rugged relief in the unglaciated regions of the northwestern west-central, and extreme southern parts of the state. Northeastern Illinois, the region of most recent glaciation, is characterized by poorly drained soils that support rich and diverse wetland communities. All of the state's glacial lakes and bogs are in this region as well as many of its remaining marshes. Northeastern Illinois is also heavily urbanized because of the Chicago metropolitan area. Central Illinois was historically tallgrass prairie with abundant marshes characterized by very fertile but poorly drained soils; this area was largely converted to agriculture by the early 1900s, with ditches and tile lines draining almost all the marshes. The southern third of Illinois was a combination of prairie and forest. Because of the rugged topography in this region, wetlands are concentrated along its rivers.

Different wetland types have their own unique characteristics leading to differences in their vegetational assemblages. Forested wetlands flood frequently and usually have mineral soils; these factors can result in a lower diversity of tree species than forests located on higher ground. Swamps were once common in the southern Midwest and the soil in swamps can be either organic or mineral, but it usually has a topmost organic layer underlain with mineral soil. Swamps are flooded on a more permanent basis and are often dominated by bald cypress (*Taxodium distichum*). The cypresses may reach prodigious size and are among the oldest living organisms on earth. In southern Illinois, thousand-year-old specimens can still be found. Marshes are extremely productive habitats where hundreds of species live. Two factors account for their high productivity. One factor is the ability of marsh plants to capture large amounts of energy from the sun and transform and store it as chemical energy in the form of plant tissue. The second factor is the efficient recycling of nutrients. Recycling is accomplished as dead plants and animals decompose and become nutrients used by living organisms (thus, the soil is sometimes mineral, but is often covered by muck—organic sediment).

Present Status of Wetlands in Illinois

The wetlands of Illinois were inventoried in the 1980s as part of the National Wetlands Inventory (NWI) program, a nationwide effort by the United States Fish and Wildlife Service to locate and classify wetland and deepwater habitats (Cowardin et al. 1979). The Illinois Wetlands Inventory (IWI), an enhanced version of NWI, was created to facilitate description of the wetlands in the state (Suloway and Hubbell 1994). The IWI is a computerized geographic database that stores spatial data and descriptive information about each wetland including location, area, shape, perimeter, an NWI code describing the ecological and physical characteristics of the feature, and an Illinois Classification code (an alternate description based on the NWI codes). The IWI distinguishes between wetlands that are *natural* and those *modified* or created by human activity (i.e., diked, impounded, dug, or channelized). Natural wetlands generally represent the original or naturally occurring wetlands in the state.

During the 1980s, 917,765 acres (371,414 ha) of natural wetlands (2.6% of the total land in Illinois) were identified using the IWI classification (Table 4.1) (Suloway and Hubbell 1994). Natural wetlands were concentrated in northeastern Illinois and along the rivers (Figure 4.2). All existing wetlands, including those modified and created, occupied 1,253,891 acres (507,443 ha), or 3.5% of the state.

Wetlands were divided into three categories: palustrine, lacustrine and riverine (Figure 4.3) (Cowardin et al. 1979). Palustrine wetlands included forested, open water, emergent, and scrub-shrub habitats. Forested wetlands were separated into two categories, bottomland forest and swamp, based on water regime and vegetation. Emergent wetlands were divided into shallow marsh/wet meadow and deep marsh. According to the IWI in the mid-1980s, bottomland forests encompassed 758,693 acres (307,163 ha) (650,621 natural acres; 263,409 ha) in Illinois (Table 4.1). There were 162,913 acres (65,957 ha) (146,873 natural acres; 59,463 ha) of shallow marsh/wet meadow, which represented 81% of emergent wetlands and 13% of all wetland acreage (Figure 4.4). Three percent of the wetland acreage was deep marsh representing 38,708 acres (15,671 ha) (25,305 natural acres; 10,245 ha). Open water accounted for 11% of wetlands with 143,345 acres (58,034 ha); 89% had been modified or altered by dikes, impoundments, or excavation. Scrub-shrub occupied 50,366 acres (20,391 ha) (38,401 natural acres; 15,547 ha). Lacustrine wetlands represented 55,568 acres (22,488 ha) of which 82% were modified or altered, and riverine wetlands accounted for 29,358 acres (11,886 ha) (19,302 natural acres; 7,815 ha) (Table 4.1).

Table 4.1. Amounts and percent of various wetlands in Illinois (Based on Illinois Wetlands Inventory classification; taken from Suloway and Hubbell 1994).

Wetlands	Acres	Percent of total land	Percent of total wetlands	Natural		Modified/artificial	
				Acres	Percent	Acres	Percent
Palustrine	1,168,964	3.3	93.2	888,155	76	280,809	24
Forested	773,632	2.2	61.7	661,174	86	112,458	15
Swamp	14,939	0.0	1.2	10,553	71	4,386	29
Bottomland forest	758,693	2.1	60.5	650,621	86	108,072	14
Emergent Shallow marsh/	201,621	0.6	16.1	172,178	85	29,443	15
wet meadow	162,913	0.5	13.0	146,873	90	16,040	10
Deep marsh	38,708	0.1	3.1	25,305	65	13,403	35
Open water	143,345	0.4	11.4	16,402	11	126,944	89
Scrub-shrub	50,366	0.1	4.0	38,401	76	11,964	24
Lacustrine	55,568	0.2	4.4	10,307	19	45,261	82
Riverine	29,358	0.1	2.3	19,302	66	10,057	34
Total	1,253,891	3.5	—	917,765	73	336,126	27

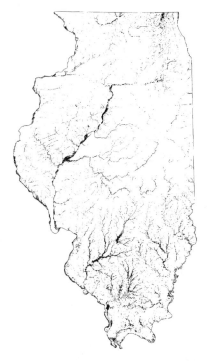

Figure 4.2. The distribution of wetlands in Illinois, 1980–1987.

(From Suloway and Hubbell 1994)

Trends and Impacts from Presettlement to the Present

By the mid-1980s, only about 47% of wetlands present in colonial America remained in the conterminous United States (approximately 103.3 million acres [41.8 million ha] of an estimated 221 million acres [89.5 million ha]) (Dahl and Johnson 1991). Wetlands now occupy approximately 5 percent of the land area in the conterminous United States (Dahl and Johnson 1991). Wetland loss has continued in recent times. Some 11 million acres (4.46 million ha) of wetlands were lost between the mid-1950s and mid-1970s; an estimated 2.6 million acres (1.06 million ha) were lost between the mid-1970s and the mid-1980s (Frayer et al. 1983, Dahl and Johnson 1991). Net wetland loss on nonfederal lands in the conterminous United States declined by approximately 792,600 acres (320,761 ha) from 1982 to 1992 (Stephen J. Brady, personal communication, July 1996).

Indications are that national wetland losses have slowed. The average rate of wetland loss from the mid-1950s to the mid-1970s was 458,000 acres (185,350 ha) per year, an approximate 0.5% annual loss. Between the mid-1970s and the mid-1980s, the average annual loss of wetlands was approximately 290,000 acres per year (117,361 ha). The percentage of wetland destruction due to agriculture

PALUSTRINE WETLANDS

93.3% of both the natural and artificial wetlands. Vegetation usually present. Includes marshes, bogs, fens, sedge meadows, wet prairies, swamps, bottomland forests, and ponds.

Open Water

11.4% of wetlands. Must have area < 20 acres and depth < 6.6 feet. Examples include natural ponds, farm ponds, borrow pits, small reservoirs, and open water areas within a marsh. Typical plants are arrowhead (Sagittaria latifolia), spadderdock (Nuphar luteum), and water lily (Nymphaea spp.).

Forested

61.7% of wetlands. Characterized by vegetation > 20 feet tall. Largely concentrated in southern Illinois, with scattered concentrations along river floodplains.

Bottomland Forest

60.5% of wetlands. Temporarily or seasonally flooded. Typical vegetation includes silver maple (Acer Saccarinum) and eastern cottonwood (Populus deltoides).

Swamp

1.2% of wetlands. Characterized by the presence of a more permanent water regime. Dominated by bald cypress (Taxodium distichum) and water tupelo (Nyssa aquatica).

Emergent

16.1% of wetlands. Dominated by erect, rooted, herbaceous hydrophytic vegetation. Water depth in marshes ranges from zero (saturated soil) to 6.6 feet. In Midwestern marshes, both floating leaf plants (ie. water lily - Nymphaea tuberosa) and submerged aquatic plants (ie. pondweeds - Potamogeton spp.) are frequently associated with emergent species.

Shallow marsh/ Wet meadow

13.0% of wetlands. Standing water or soil saturation is present for brief to moderate periods during the growing season. Often part of larger wetland complexes, such as the edge of ponds or lakes. Common vegetation includes chufa (Cyperus esculentus), and common barnyardgrass (Echinochloa crusgalli).

Deep Marsh

3.1% of wetlands. Standing water is present, or the soil is saturated on a semipermanent to permanent basis during the growing season. Typical vegetation includes bluejoint grass (Calamagrostis canadensis), bulrush (Scirpus atrovirens), and common cattail (Typha latifolia).

Scrub-Shrub

4.0% of wetlands. Characterized by woody vegetation < 20 feet tall. Typical vegetation includes black willow (Salix nigra) and buttonbush (Cephalanthus occidentalis). Successional stage in transition from an emergent wetland to forest.

LACUSTRINE WETLANDS

4.4% of wetlands. Situated in a topographic depression or are dammed river channels; shallow (< 6.6 feet deep), larger than 20 acres, and have less than 30% vegetative cover. Most are created by dikes, impoundments, or excavation. Typical vegetation includes American lotus (Nelumbo lutea), coontail (Ceratophyllum demersum), and common cattail (Typha latifolia).

RIVERINE WETLANDS

2.3% of wetlands. Shallow waters (< 6.6 feet) contained within a channel where water is usually flowing. Not dominated by vegetation and not impounded. Most are intermittent streams. Typical vegetation includes devil's beggarticks (Bidens frondosa), sandbar willow (Salix exigua), and straw-colored sedge (Cyperus strigosus).

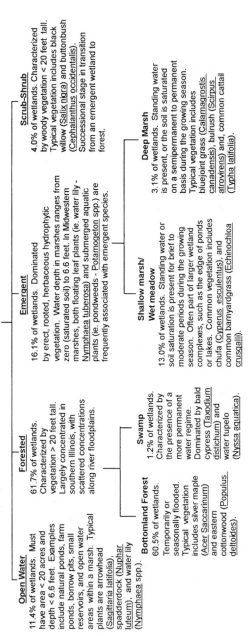

Figure 4.3. Palustrine, lacustrine, and riverine wetlands in Illinois. Percents of the wetland categories are from Suloway and Hubbell (1994).

All Wetlands

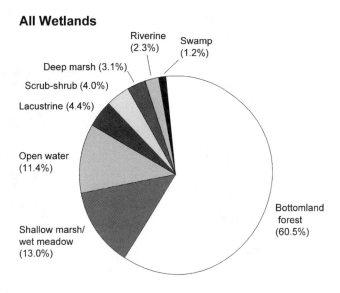

Figure 4.4. Percentage of wetland types in Illinois, 1980–1987.

decreased from 87% for the mid-1950s to the mid-1970s; to 54% during the mid-1970s to the mid-1980s; and to about 20% from 1982 to 1992 (Dahl and Johnson 1991; Stephen J. Brady, personal communication, July 1996). During the latter period urban and industrial development accounted for about 57% of the gross loss of wetlands (Stephen J. Brady, personal communication, July 1996).

Wetland loss in the Midwest has been particularly extensive. Six of the seven states with the highest wetland loss (81% or more) since presettlement times are Illinois, Indiana, Iowa, Missouri, Kentucky, and Ohio (Dahl 1990). Wetland acreage in Illinois prior to settlement by Europeans, based on quantitative analysis of soil types, has been conservatively estimated at 8.3 million acres (3.3 million ha) (Havera 1985), or an area covering approximately 23% of the surface area of the state (Figure 4.5). Preliminary results from a recent hydric soil survey indicate even greater presettlement wetland acreage. The modern soil survey identified about 8.9 million acres (3.6 million ha) of hydric soil in Illinois (John C. Doll, personal communication, Aug 1996).

By the 1980s, Illinois had lost approximately 90% of its original wetland acreage based on the preliminary hydric soil estimate of 8.9 million acres (Figure 4.5). Wetland losses continued at a slower pace in Illinois in recent years with a decline of 33,400 acres (13,517 ha) from 1982 to 1992 (McLeese 1995). Many of the original wetlands were lost in the northern two-thirds of the state, particularly in east-central Illinois. Natural wetlands in Illinois declined from 25% to about 2.6% of the state's surface area. Only about 6,000 acres (2,429 ha; 0.05% of the original total) of wetlands persist in a relatively undisturbed

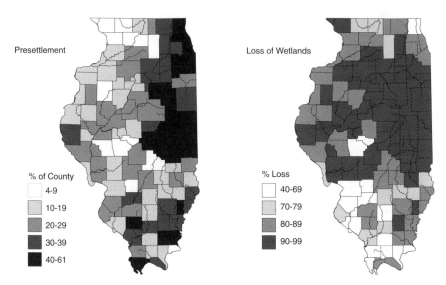

Figure 4.5. The percent of presettlement wetlands and the percent of their loss in the counties of Illinois. Presettlement wetlands were determined from data on hydric soils (Havera 1985). Percent loss of wetlands was determined by comparing the amount of presettlement wetlands with present wetlands as determined from the Illinois Wetlands Inventory (1980–1987).

condition in Illinois (White 1978). The locations of high-quality, relatively undisturbed wetland communities were concentrated along the Fox, Des Plaines, and Kankakee rivers in northeastern Illinois; along the middle Illinois River valley; and in the Gulf Coastal Plain of extreme southern Illinois (White 1978). These relatively undisturbed, high-quality wetlands are the most reliable qualitative indicator of the original structure and composition of the various wetland communities.

An important factor in the demise of wetland resources was the implementation of drainage and levee districts. The passage of a series of Swamp Lands Acts in 1849, 1850, and 1860 resulted in the destruction of many wetlands in the United States. Under these acts, Congress gave 65 million acres (26.3 million ha) of wetlands to 15 states for conversion to agriculture (Steinhart 1990). In Illinois, 5.5 million acres (2.2 million ha) of the state's 35.9 million acres (14.5 million ha) had been drained by organized districts by 1937, and an additional 4 million acres (1.6 million ha) had been drained by private enterprise (Illinois Tax Commission 1941, Sanderson et al. 1979). By 1978, the total area of land drained for agriculture in Illinois was 9.7 million acres (3.9 million ha), or approximately 27% of the state (U.S. Department of Commerce 1978). Nationally, agricultural land artificially drained under organized enterprises totaled approximately 107.5 million acres (43.5 million ha) in 1980 (Dahl 1990).

In Illinois, the majority of wetland complexes, defined here as contiguous wetland units comprised of one or more wetland types, are small and isolated and few are relatively large and diverse. Ninety-nine percent of wetland complexes cover less than 100 acres (40.5 ha) and account for approximately half the total wetland acreage. Ninety-three percent of wetland complexes are less than 10 acres (4.04 ha) and account for approximately one-fifth the total wetland acreage. Nearly two-thirds of the wetland complexes are less than one acre (0.4 ha). How much of the current spatial configuration of wetlands in Illinois is original and how much is a result of fragmentation since presettlement is difficult to assess.

Although the loss of wetlands is of monumental importance, the biological, chemical, and physical degradation and the resultant decline in productivity and diversity of remaining wetlands are also significant. Wetlands have been affected by many factors, including alteration of natural hydrological regimes (i.e., drainage, dams, channelization, reservoirs), agriculture, urbanization, and sedimentation. In the upper Midwest, sedimentation, resulting from soil erosion from cropland and streambanks as well as urban construction and development, has been a major problem. Sedimentation affects wetlands by deposition; by increasing turbidity, which reduces light penetration necessary for photosynthesis in submerged aquatic vegetation; and by creating soft bottoms, which preclude the ability of wetland plants to remain rooted (Bellrose et al. 1979, 1983; Havera and Bellrose 1985). With the loss of aquatic plants as a result of sedimentation and other factors, the integrity of the wetland systems are significantly diminished (Havera and Bellrose 1985). Illinois, Iowa, Minnesota, Missouri, and Wisconsin represent only about 15% of the hydrologic area of the Mississippi River basin but produced about 40% of all the sediment originating from cropland (Peterson 1991). Furthermore, about 55% of the land in these five states was cropland as compared with a national average of 18% (Peterson 1991). Although erosion rates have been reduced in recent years, the rate of erosion in these five states was 32% above the national average (Peterson 1991). Erosion was responsible for removing 201 million tons (182 million metric tons) of soil each year in Illinois (Illinois Department of Agriculture 1992).

Wetland Plants

Water regime is perhaps the most influential physical factor in determining the types of plants that occur at a specific site. Because more plant species are adapted to moist-soil conditions than to open water (strictly aquatic conditions), shallower water supports a potentially greater diversity of species.

Wetland plants typically have one of three basic life histories. Free-floating plants, such as duckweeds (*Lemna* spp.), are not rooted but remain on the surface of the water. Emergent plants, including cattails (*Typha* spp.), arrowheads (*Sagittaria* spp.), and bulrushes (*Scirpus* spp.), grow with their roots in wet soil for all or part of the year and send up leaves that stand erect above the surface of the water. Submergent plants like pondweeds (*Potamogeton* spp.) are also rooted in the soil, but their stems and leaves remain entirely underwater. Other plant types that occupy the drier portions of wetlands include moist-soil herbaceous, shrub, and forest species. Some wetlands contain all of these vegetation types, but others have only one or two.

The majority of wetland plant species in Illinois are forbs with over 500 species representing most of the herbaceous plants except the graminoid monocots, such as sedges, grasses, vines, and ferns. Sedges are the most species-rich family in the wetland vascular flora of Illinois with 163 species, followed by the grass family (*Poaceae*) with 81 species. The most species-rich wetland subfamily is the sedge genus *Carex* with 90 species.

In Illinois, approximately 952 species of vascular plants are wetland species; this constitutes about 32% of the 2,959 vascular plant species (both native and non-native) that occur in the state (Havera and Suloway 1994). Native wetland species constitute 42% of the total native vascular flora. A total of 108 of the 172 families of vascular plants that occur naturally in Illinois contain species that thrive in aquatic or moist-soil habitats. With 163 species, the sedge family (Cyperaceae) is the most species-rich family in the wetland vascular flora of Illinois, followed by the grass family (Poaceae) and sunflower family (Asteracea) with 81 and 65 wetland species, respectively. The most species-rich wetland genus is the sedge genus *Carex* with 90 species.

Non-native plants can have devastating effects in natural wetlands including a decrease in plant and animal diversity (Bratton 1982, Harty 1986). The two non-native species that most seriously affect wetlands in Illinois are purple loosestrife (*Lythrum salicaria*) and glossy buckthorn (*Rhamnus frangula*) (Havera and Suloway 1994).

Wetland-dependent or wetland-related species comprise 26% of the 109 federally listed endangered and threatened plant species in the United States (Feierabend and Zelazny 1987). Approximately 30% of 2,500 plants potentially in need of federal protection depend on wetlands (Feierabend and Zelazny 1987). In Illinois, 162 species of native vascular wetland plants are listed as endangered or threatened; wetland species account for 45% of the plants listed as state endangered or threatened (Bowles et al. 1991; Herkert 1991, 1994). Approximately 34 wetland plant species appear to have become extirpated in Illinois and have been removed from the list of endangered species (Bowles et al. 1991, Post 1991, Sheviak 1974). Most of these extirpated species were confined to wetlands in the heavily urbanized northeastern counties (Herkert 1991).

Wetland Animals

Many amphibians, reptiles, birds, and mammals, as well as a host of invertebrates, utilize or depend on wetlands for survival or successful reproduction, and several of these species are listed as endangered or threatened. Nationally, 94 (45%) of the 209 animal species listed as federally endangered and threatened in 1986 were wetland-dependent or wetland-related (Feierabend and Zelazny 1987). In Illinois, of the 99 species of vertebrates currently listed as endangered or threatened (Illinois Endangered Species Protection Board 1994), 75% either depend on or utilize wetlands during at least one stage of their life cycle (e.g., larval development) or for specific functions (e.g., foraging).

Amphibians

As a vital link in food webs, amphibians are an important component of wetland ecosystems. Amphibians are major consumers of arthropods, mollusks, and annelids and, in turn, are an important source of food for many predatory fishes, reptiles, birds, and mammals. Because the life history of most amphibians includes both aquatic and terrestrial stages, 37 of the 41 amphibian species that occur in Illinois use wetlands at least part of the time (Smith 1961, Conant and Collins 1991). Temporary and seasonal wetlands can be crucial in the life cycle of amphibians because their eggs and larvae are less vulnerable to predation by fishes in such habitats (Environmental Defense Fund and World Wildlife Fund 1992). Nineteen species of amphibians in Illinois depend on ephemeral wetlands, such as vernal woodland ponds, flooded fields, or roadside ditches, for breeding (Morris 1991). Five species of amphibians are listed as endangered or threatened in Illinois (Illinois Endangered Species Protection Board 1994) and four of these (silvery salamander [*Ambystoma platineum*], dusky salamander [*Desmognathus fuscus*], four-toed salamander [*Hemidactylium scutatum*], and Illinois chorus frog [*Pseudacris streckeri*]) depend on wetlands (Smith 1961, Conant and Collins 1991).

Reptiles

Reptiles, as a group, are less dependent on water than are amphibians. Nevertheless, many reptiles are aquatic, including a large proportion of turtles and several snakes. Of the 60 species of reptiles found in Illinois (Morris et al. 1983), at least 46 species utilize or depend on wetlands (Smith 1961, Conant and Collins 1991). Thirteen species of reptiles, four turtles and nine snakes, are listed as endangered or threatened in Illinois (Illinois Endangered Species Protection Board 1994). Ten of these species, the alligator snapping turtle (*Macroclemys temmincki*), spotted turtle (*Clemmys guttata*), Illinois mud turtle (*Kinosternon flavescens*), river cooter (*Pseudemys concinna*), Kirtland's snake (*Clonophis kirtlandi*), green water snake (*Nerodia cyclopion*), broad-banded water snake (*N. fasciata*), eastern ribbon snake (*Thamnophis sauritus*), eastern massasauga (*Sistrurus catenatus*), and timber rattlesnake (*Crotalus horridus*), occur in wetlands (Smith 1961, Conant and Collins 1991).

Birds

Wetlands provide cover and nest sites for birds and an abundance of plants and animals used as food by birds (Benyus 1989). Among the avifauna that depend on wetlands are waterfowl, wading birds, shorebirds, and numerous song birds. Avifauna are unique among wetland inhabitants because many are migratory and rely on widely dispersed wetlands on a seasonal basis. Migrant species use wetlands for foraging and resting during migration and some return to the same wetlands each year to rear their young.

Although more than 439 avian species have been recorded for Illinois, only 274 species are commonly observed, including some endangered or threatened species (Bohlen 1989). The mobility of birds enables them to exploit a variety of habitats to fulfill their life history requirements. Therefore, any of these 274 avian species can use wetlands for nesting, foraging, or resting: twenty-four are dependent on wetlands as nesting or foraging sites, 81 are strongly associated with wetlands during their life cycles, and the remaining 169 may use wetlands opportunistically (Havera and Suloway 1994).

The numbers and distributions of many wetland-dependent avian species have decreased because of the destruction and degradation of wetlands throughout Illinois (Bohlen 1989, Herkert 1992). Forty wetland avian species are now listed as endangered or threatened in the state (Illinois Endangered Species Protection Board 1994); 31 species are strongly associated with wetlands, especially during the breeding season, and 9 use wetlands throughout the year.

Mammals

At least 46 of the 58 species of mammals that occur in Illinois use wetlands (Hoffmeister 1989, Hofmann 1991). Relatively few mammal species are specifically adapted for living in wetlands (Fritzell 1988), but wetlands provide abundant food (e.g., invertebrates, amphibians, eggs, and nestlings) and cover for a variety of mammals. For example, 16 species of rodents can be found in wetlands, although few are limited to such habitats (Mumford and Whitaker 1982, Hoffmeister 1989). The rodents most closely associated with wetlands are the beaver (*Castor canadensis*), muskrat (*Ondatra zibethicus*), and marsh rice rat (*Oryzomys palustris*). Similarly, 10 of Illinois' carnivore species use wetlands; those most strongly associated with wetlands are the raccoon (*Procyon lotor*), mink (*Mustela vison*), and river otter (*Lutra canadensis*). Several of the mammal species that utilize wetlands are of economic importance as furbearers or game animals.

Losses of wetlands have decreased the amount of suitable habitat available to many mammals, with the greatest impacts on species limited to or highly dependent on wetlands. Two such wetland species are the swamp rabbit (*Sylvilagus aquaticus*) and marsh rice rat, which have limited ranges in Illinois and occur in scattered populations that are vulnerable to local extirpation (Kjolhaug et al. 1987, Hofmann et al. 1990). The swamp rabbit inhabits bottomland forests and swamps in southern Illinois (Kjolhaug et al. 1987, Hoffmeister 1989) where destruction and fragmentation of these habitats have adversely affected its numbers (Kjolhaug et al. 1987). Historical records suggest that swamp rabbits were was once widely distributed in eight major river drainages. During extensive searches in 1984 and 1985, swamp rabbits were found at only 22 sites in four drainage systems (Kjolhaug et al. 1987). Similar declines in numbers of swamp rabbits as a result of habitat loss have been noted in Missouri and Indiana (Korte and Fredrickson 1977, Whitaker and Abrell 1986).

Eight of the nine endangered and threatened mammal species in Illinois (Illinois Endangered Species Protection Board 1994) use wetlands: the southeastern bat (*Myotis austroriparius*), Rafinesque's big-eared bat (*Plecotus rafinesquii*), marsh rice rat, golden mouse (*Ochrotomys nuttalli*), river otter, bobcat (*Lynx rufus*), and the federally endangered Indiana bat (*Myotis sodalis*) and gray bat (*M. grisescens*) (U.S. Fish and Wildlife Service 1991).

Invertebrates

Invertebrates, the most abundant but least conspicuous animals in wetlands, are essential in making plant energy available to other animals, including fishes and waterbirds. Among the invertebrates found in midwestern wetlands are sponges, flatworms, worms, crustaceans (isopods, amphipods, and crayfish), mollusks (clams and snails), and insects. Of the 49 species of invertebrates listed as endangered or threatened in Illinois (Illinois Endangered Species Protection Board 1994), one isopod, two amphipods, one crayfish (oxbox crayfish [*Orconectes lancifer*]), and four insects (swamp metalmark [*Calephelis muticum*], Hine's emerald dragonfly [*Somatochlora hineana*], elfin skimmer [*Nannothemis bella*], and redveined prairie leafhopper [*Aflexia rubranura*]) can be considered wetland species (Herkert 1992, 1994).

Summary

Wetlands are among the most important ecosystems on our planet. In the past wetlands have been regarded as nuisances and have been "reclaimed" by draining, clearing, and filling. In recent years, wetlands have become more appreciated for their functions as well as for their economic values. The functions of wetlands include regulating the flow of water, storing water, filtering and purifying water, trapping sediments, recharging ground water, providing habitat for plants and animals, and furnishing recreational opportunities.

Wetlands are generally defined as lands where water saturation is the dominant factor that determines both soil development and the types of plant and animal communities living in the soil and on its surface. They are generally characterized by the presence and duration of water, soil type, and plant communities.

By the mid-1980s, approximately 103 million acres (41.7 million ha) (47%) of the estimated 221 million acres (89.4 million ha) of wetlands present at the time of European settlement remained in the conterminous United States. The remaining wetlands occupy approximately 5% of the land area of the contermi-nous United States. Six midwestern states ranked in the top seven incurring for the greatest loss of wetland acreage, primarily as a result of drainage for agricultural purposes. Approximately 918,000 acres (371,510 ha) of natural wetlands re-mained in Illinois by the 1980s, or about 10% of the original wetland acreage.

Natural wetlands occupied about 2.6% of Illinois in the 1980s and only 6,000 acres (2,428 ha) were high quality and relatively undisturbed.

Wetlands support a diversity of plants and animals. Wetland plants compose 32% (952 of 2,959 species) of the total flora (both native and non-native) of Illinois and 42% (862 of 2,069 species) of the native flora of the state. The majority of the amphibians, reptiles, birds, and mammals in Illinois use wetlands. Overall, 75% of the 99 species of vertebrates listed as endangered or threatened in Illinois utilize wetlands during some part of their life cycle. The numbers of plant and animal species dependent on wetlands are a testimony to the irreplaceable intrinsic functions and values of wetlands ecosystems and their importance to our society.

Acknowledgments

This chapter is an integrated synopsis of recent works on wetlands produced by staff of the Illinois Natural History Survey and is based on the Wetlands Chapter of the Critical Trends Assessment Project Technical Report. Assistance in preparation of the manuscript was provided by Alicia K. Admiraal, Lynn L. Anderson, Michelle M. Georgi, Christopher S. Hine, Patti L. Malmborg, Marilyn J. Morris, Katie E. Roat, John B. Taft, and Aaron P. Yetter.

References

Bellrose, F.C., F.L. Paveglio, Jr., and D.W. Steffeck. 1979. Waterfowl populations and the changing environment of the Illinois River valley. Illinois Natural History Survey Bulletin 32:1–54.

Bellrose, F.C., S.P. Havera, F.L. Paveglio, Jr., and D.W. Steffeck. 1983. The fate of lakes in the Illinois River valley. Illinois Natural History Survey Biological Notes No. 119. 27 p.

Benyus, J.M. 1989. Northwoods wildlife: a watchers guide to habitats. Northword Press, Minoqua, Wisconsin. 453 p.

Bohlen, H.D. 1989. The birds of Illinois. Indiana University Press, Bloomington. 221 p.

Bowles, M.L., J.B. Taft, E.F. Ulaszek, D.M. Ketzner, M.K. Solecki, L.R. Phillippe, A. Dennis, P.J. Burton, and K.R. Robertson. 1991. Rarely seen endangered plants, rediscoveries, and species new to Illinois. Erigenia 11:27–51.

Bratton, S.P. 1982. The effects of exotic plant and animal species on nature preserves. Natural Areas Journal 2:3–13.

Conant, R., and J.T. Collins. 1991. A field guide to reptiles and amphibians (eastern and central North America). Third edition. Houghton Miflin, Boston. 450 p.

Cowardin, L.M., V. Carter, and E.T. LaRoe. 1979. Classification of wetlands and deepwater habitats of the United States. U.S. Fish and Wildlife Service FWS/OBS-79/31, U.S. Government Printing Office. 131 p.

Dahl, T.E. 1990. Wetlands losses in the United States 1780s to 1980s. U.S. Fish and Wildlife Service, Washington, D.C. 21 p.

Dahl, T.E., and C.E. Johnson. 1991. Status and trends of wetlands in the conterminous United States, mid-1970s to mid-1980s. U.S. Fish and Wildlife Service, Washington, D.C. 28 p.

Environmental Defense Fund and World Wildlife Fund. 1992. *How wet is a wetland?: The impacts of the proposed revisions to the federal wetland delineation manual.* 175 p.

Farber, S., and R. Costanza. 1987. The economic value of wetland systems. Journal of Environmental Management 24:41–51.

Feierabend, J.S., and J.M. Zelazny. 1987. Status report on our nation's wetlands. National Wildlife Federation, Washington, D.C. 46 p.

Frayer, W.E., T.J. Monahan, D.C. Bowden, and F.A. Graybill. 1983. Status and trends of wetlands and deepwater habitats in the conterminous United States, 1950s to 1970s. Department of Forestry and Wood Science, Colorado State University, Fort Collins. 32 p.

Fritzell, E.K. 1988. Mammals and wetlands. Pages 213–226 *in* D.D. Hook, W.H. McKee, Jr., H.K. Smith, J. Gregory, V.G. Burrell, Jr., M.R. DeVoe, R.E. Sojka, S. Gilbert, R. Banks, L.H. Stolzy, C. Brooks, T.D. Matthews, and T.H. Shear, eds. The Ecology and management of wetlands. Vol. 1: Ecology of wetlands. Croom Helm, London and Sydney. 592 p.

Harty, F. M. 1986. Exotics and their ecological ramifications. Natural Areas Journal 6:20–26.

Havera, S.P. 1985. Waterfowl of Illinois: status and management. Final Federal Aid Performance Report, 1980–1985. Cooperative Waterfowl Research W-88-R. 785 p.

————, and F.C. Bellrose. 1985. The Illinois River: a lesson to be learned. Wetlands 4:29–41.

————, and L.B. Suloway. 1994. Wetlands. Pages 87–153 *in* Illinois Department of Energy and Natural Resources. *The changing Illinois environment: critical trends.* Vol. 3: Technical Report. Illinois Department of Energy and Natural Resources, Springfield. ILENR/RE-EA-94/05.

Herkert, J.R., ed. 1991. Endangered and threatened species of Illinois: status and distribution. Vol.1: Plants. Illinois Endangered Species Protection Board, Springfield. 158 p.

————, ed. 1992. Endangered and threatened species of Illinois: status and distribution. Vol. 2: Animals. Illinois Endangered Species Protection Board, Springfield. 142 p.

————, ed. 1994. *Endangered and Threatened Species of Illinois: Status and Distribution.* Vol. 3: *1994 Changes to the Illinois List of Endangered and Threatened Species.* Illinois Endangered Species Protection Board, Springfield.

Hoffmeister, D.F. 1989. Mammals of Illinois. University of Illinois Press, Urbana. 348 p.

Hofmann, J.E. 1991. Status and distribution of wetland mammals in Illinois. Illinois Natural History Survey Bulletin 34:409–415.

————, J.E. Gardner, and M.J. Morris. 1990. Distribution, abundance, and habitat of the marsh rice rat (*Oryzomys palustris*) in southern Illinois. Transactions of the Illinois State Academy of Science 83:162–180.

Illinois Department of Agriculture. 1992. Annual progress report. Illinois Department of Agriculture, Division of Natural Resources. 73 p.

Illinois Endangered Species Protection Board. 1994. *Checklist of Endangered and Threatened Animals and Plants of Illinois.* Illinois Endangered Species Protection Board, Springfield.

Illinois Tax Commission. 1941. Drainage district organization and finance, 1879–1937. State of Illinois, Springfield. 213 p.

Kjolhaug, M.S., A. Woolf, and W.D. Klimstra. 1987. Current status and distribution of the swamp rabbit in Illinois. Transactions of the Illinois State Academy of Science 80:299–307.

Korte, P.A., and L.H. Fredrickson. 1977. Swamp rabbit distribution in Missouri. Transactions of the Missouri Academy of Science 10 and 11:72–77.

McLeese, R. 1995. Pages 75–81 *in* Elizabeth D. Wagner, ed. Proceedings of the 1995 Governor's Conference on the Management of the Illinois River System, Special Report No. 22. 197 p.

Morris, M.A. 1991. Breeding biology and larval life history of four species of *Ambystoma* (Amphibia: Caudata) in east-central Illinois. Illinois Natural History Survey Bulletin 34:402 (abstract).

———, R.S. Funk, and P.W. Smith. 1983. An annotated bibliography of the Illinois herpetological literature 1960–1980, and an updated checklist of species of the state. Illinois Natural History Survey Bulletin 33:123–137.

Mumford, R.E., and J.O. Whitaker, Jr. 1982. Mammals of Indiana. Indiana University Press, Bloomington. 537 p.

Peterson, J.W. 1991. Erosion and sediment today's challenge. Proceedings of the Forty-seventh annual meeting of the Upper Mississippi River Conservation Committee. P. 4–11.

Post, S.L. 1991. Appendix one: native Illinois species and related bibliography. Illinois Natural History Survey Bulletin 34(4):463–475.

Sanderson, G.C., F.C. Bellrose, and G.V. Burger. 1979. Wetland habitat in Illinois. Proceedings of the Governor's Wildlife Habitat Conference. P. 101–118.

Sheviak, C.J. 1974. An introduction to the ecology of the Illinois Orchidaceae. Illinois State Museum Scientific Papers XIV. Springfield. 89 p.

Smith, P.W. 1961. The amphibians and reptiles of Illinois. Illinois Natural History Survey Bulletin 28:1–298.

Steinhart, P. 1990. No net loss. Audubon. July:18, 20–21.

Suloway, L., and M. Hubbell. 1994. Wetland resources of Illinois: an analysis and atlas. Illinois Natural History Survey Special Publication 15. 88 p.

U.S. Department of Commerce. 1978. Census of agriculture.

U.S. Fish and Wildlife Service. 1991. Endangered and threatened wildlife and plants; animal candidate review for listing as endangered or threatened species. 21 November 50 CFR Part 17, Federal Register 56(225):58804–58836.

Whitaker, J.O., Jr., and B. Abrell. 1986. The swamp rabbit, *Sylvilagus aquaticus*, in Indiana. Proceedings of the Indiana Academy of Science 95:563–570.

White, J. 1978. Illinois natural areas inventory technical report. Vol. 1: Survey methods and results. Illinois Natural Areas Inventory, Urbana. 426 p.

Wilen, B.O., and W.E. Frayer. 1990. Status and trends of U.S. wetlands and deepwater habitats. Forest Ecology and Management 33/34:181–192.

PART II
Problems and Case Studies

5

Conservation in the Context of Non-Indigenous Species

James O. Luken
Department of Biological Sciences, Northern Kentucky University,
Highland Heights, KY 41099-0400

Introduction

There is currently worldwide concern regarding the invasion of natural areas by non-indigenous species. Several recently published books have addressed this issue in terms of ecological interactions (Mooney and Drake 1986), resource management problems (McKnight 1993), and regulatory impact (OTA 1993). Furthermore, specific regions of the United States have been analyzed relative to invasion pressure and the threat that non-indigenous species pose to biological communities [e.g., the Pacific Northwest (Mack 1986), California (Rejmánek and Randall 1994), and Hawaii (Stone et al. 1992)]. Relatively little effort has been devoted to understanding biological invasions of natural areas in the midwestern United States.

Natural areas in the Midwest, like most natural areas in human-disturbed landscapes, are susceptible in varying degrees to invasions by non-indigenous species. Nature stewards and natural resource managers are currently investing much time and effort in development of strategies that, it is hoped, will eliminate existing populations of non-indigenous species, limit the introduction of additional non-indigenous species, and make natural areas more resistant to invasion. In the future, biological invasions will likely become even more widespread as human influence and disturbance intensify at the margins of natural areas and preserves.

Funds for conservation activities are limited. As such, private, state, and federal agencies are faced with difficult choices regarding the balance between acquiring new land for conservation purposes and managing lands already acquired. Here, the problem of invasion by non-indigenous species assumes even greater importance because it is clear in many situations that eradication efforts could consume entire resource management budgets—and even more if funds were available. It is imperative that resource managers be able to identify those problems associated with non-indigenous species that threaten the ecological integrity (i.e., conservation value) of natural areas as compared to situations where biological invasion is relatively benign.

This chapter will examine the issue of biological invasion and the following questions will be addressed: (1) What non-indigenous species are found in natural areas of the Midwest? (2) What conservation dilemmas are raised by these biological invaders? (3) What types of strategies have been developed to combat these organisms? and (4) Have these strategies been successful in achieving conservation goals?

Defining Problems Linked to Non-Indigenous Species

While it is clear that 20–30% of the plant species now occurring in the Midwest are indeed considered non-indigenous (e.g., Myers and Henry 1979), it is important to assess which of these numerous introduced species are actually causing resource management problems. Such problems can be defined only if resource management goals are also well-defined. Generally, conservation efforts in the Midwest focus on two types of terrestrial communities: prairies and forests. Prairies may be remnants (i.e., original communities that escaped destruction by agricultural activity) or restored (i.e., communities assembled by various management activities). Regardless of prairie origin, non-indigenous species capable of outcompeting indigenous prairie species and those that speed succession to a shrub- or forest-dominated community would be considered management problems.

Forests of conservation value can exist as old-growth remnants or may be communities that escaped disturbance long enough so that a forest community has developed via succession. Here, non-indigenous species working against management goals would be those that change the physiognomy of the forest in general (e.g., large shrubs), that can successfully compete with understory seedlings and saplings, or that retard succession (see e.g., Hiebert 1990).

Presently, there are a few of the many hundreds of non-indigenous plants that are widely considered to be management problems, at least as defined in the preceding paragraphs (Table 5.1). However, as subsequent sections of this chapter demonstrate, this distinction applied to various species may be based more on their wide distribution, ability to invade natural areas (DeMars 1994; Ebinger and McClain 1991), and apparency rather than on the actual thwarting of management goals. [See, for example, Anderson (1995) for a critical review of presumed ecological effects associated with invasion by purple loose-strife (*Lythrum salicaria*).] Still, it is becoming clear that populations of organisms in small, isolated natural areas are subject to unique stresses that may lead to local extinction. Interactions (overt and covert) with invasive non-indigenous species must be considered as another ecological factor that may influence biodiversity in these areas.

*Table 5.1. Invasive plant species of natural areas in the
Midwest. Group 1 includes species that invade prairies and
savannas. Group 2 includes species that invade forests.*

Common name (Scientific name)	Growth form
Group 1	
Canada thistle (*Cirsium arvense*)	herb
fescue (*Festuca pratensis*)	grass
leafy spurge (*Euphorbia esula*)	herb
smooth brome (*Bromus inermis*)	grass
sweet clovers (*Melilotus* spp.)	herb
wild parsnip (*Pastinaca sativa*)	herb
crown vetch (*Coronilla varia*)	vine
Japanese honeysuckle (*Lonicera laponica*)	vine
Amur honeysuckle (*Lonicera maackii*)	shrub
autumn olive (*Elaeagnus umbellata*)	shrub
buckthorns (*Rhamnus* spp.)	shrub
multiflora rose (*Rosa multiflora*)	shrub
red-osier dogwood (*Cornus stolonifera*)	shrub
black locust (*Robinia pseudoacacia*)	tree
osage orange (*Maclura pomifera*)	tree
quaking aspen (*Populus tremuloides*)	tree
Siberian elm (*Ulmus pumila*)	tree
Group 2	
garlic mustard (*Alliaria petiolata*)	herb
moneywort (*Lysimachia nummularia*)	herb
Japanese honeysuckle (*Lonicera japonica*)	vine
round-leaved bittersweet (*Celastrus orbiculatus*)	vine
wintercreeper (*Euonymus fortunei*)	vine
Amur honeysuckle (*Lonicera maackii*)	shrub
buckthorns (*Rhamnus* spp.)	shrub
multiflora rose (*Rosa multiflora*)	shrub

Invasion of Remnant or Restored Prairies

The single most important factor influencing the invasion of remnant prairie communities by non-indigenous plants is species availability. To understand this factor one need only review research conducted by Myers and Henry (1979). They showed that two counties in Illinois lost 16% of indigenous plant species with a corresponding increase in non-indigenous plants. This change, occurring from 1833 to 1976, was presumably linked to agricultural activities and high rates of species introductions. Animals such as the ring-necked pheasant (*Phasianus colchicus*) also have been introduced into midwestern regions, primarily in efforts to develop huntable populations of novel game species (Harty 1993). Other introductions (e.g., earthworms) were unintentional and often go largely unnoticed. Such species introductions may change system attributes of entire landscapes primarily because new species may modify ecological interactions, community development and structure, ecosystem processes, and disturbance regimens.

Remnant prairies in the Midwest are commonly invaded by non-indigenous grasses and herbs. Interestingly, most of the problem invaders are not the traditional weeds of agricultural fields [e.g., cocklebur (*Xanthium strumarium*) or giant foxtail (*Setaria faberi*)], perhaps because these require large-scale frequent soil disturbance for persistence. Instead, prairies are invaded by plants such as herbs and grasses that thrive in more stable sites (i.e., roadsides, fencerows, and rights-of-way) where disturbances are small and random in pattern. Many of these represent species that were originally introduced for ornamental or functional reasons.

Solecki (1993) described two herbs, cut-leaved teasel (*Dipsacus laciniatus*) and common teasel (*D. sylvestris*), as potential invaders of natural areas in Illinois. Although data were presented primarily on species biology, she maintained that these plants can "quickly form large monocultures excluding most native vegetation," page 85.

Non-indigenous grasses introduced as forage for livestock can also invade prairies. For example, smooth brome (*Bromus inermis*) has invaded preserved prairies in the Great Plains region, prompting a search for management techniques that will eliminate this species while increasing populations of indigenous prairie grasses (Blankespoor and Larson 1994; Grilz and Romo 1995). Seeding experiments conducted in southwest Manitoba to determine how best to reestablish prairie communities on disturbed sites suggested that non-indigenous grasses may outcompete indigenous grasses and that the best approach is to avoid seeding of the non-indigenous species (Wilson 1989). Strong competition from non-indigenous grasses is a perpetual problem for those attempting to restore species-rich prairie, especially when nitrogen availability is high due to residual fertilizer or atmospheric pollution (Luken 1990).

In the Midwest a large variety of non-indigenous shrubs and small trees have been introduced to roadsides and wildlife management areas primarily to control erosion or to provide wildlife habitat. These woody plants may escape and invade the prairies, quickly converting them to scrub or shrub communities. Dispersal of seeds is facilitated by birds (White and Stiles 1992). Zimmerman et al. (1993) observed that a restored tallgrass prairie in Illinois was invaded by seven non-indigenous woody plants. The most important of these (Table 5.1) were autumn olive (*Elaeagnus umbellata*), red-osier dogwood (*Cornus stolonifera*), and multiflora rose (*Rosa multiflora*). These plants had escaped from nearby wildlife areas, presumably via bird activity. Similarly, hill prairie at Pere Marquette State Park in Illinois (McClain and Anderson 1990) was invaded by a non-indigenous shrub. Amur honeysuckle (*Lonicera maackii*). In both of these situations (restored tallgrass prairie and hill prairie), indigenous woody plants invaded in tandem with the non-indigenous woody plants. Clearly, in the absence of management (e.g., periodic prescribed burning) woody plants will convert prairies to shrub communities; however it is unclear whether non-indigenous plants are speeding the conversion or are simply participating in succession much like indigenous species.

In addition to the previously described invaders, the Illinois Nature Preserves Commission (INPC 1990) listed several other plants as potential problems in prairie reserves (Table 5.1). For all of these species, their classification as weeds has been based on the observation that they can and do invade prairies. Few, if any studies exist demonstrating direct effects on indigenous species, community dynamics, or ecosystem processes.

Direct negative effects of an introduced bird, the ring-necked pheasant (*Phasianus colchicus*) on the indigenous greater prairie chicken (*Tympanuchus cupido*) have been demonstrated in Illinois (Vance and Westemeier 1979). However, near extirpation of the greater prairie chicken in Illinois is likely linked to habitat destruction rather than introduction of the ring-necked pheasant.

Invasions of Remnant Forests

Although it is often assumed that mature forests are more resistant to invasions than early-successional sites, recent evidence suggests that forests also can be readily invaded even in the absence of overt disturbance. Perhaps the best-studied invader of midwestern forest reserves is garlic mustard (*Alliaria petiolata*), a biennial herb native to Europe. Nuzzo (1993) traced the introduction and spread of this species. It was first introduced to New York in 1868 and by 1991 it was naturalized in 30 states. The majority of garlic mustard collections are made in forests and it is here where it presumably achieves greatest population densities (Nuzzo 1993). Entrance to forests is facilitated by disturbance, but such disturbance is apparently not a prerequisite for invasion; the plant is tolerant of deep shade and populations may persist for many years.

Low light availability in forest interiors is likely the most important factor that limits invasion of remnant forests by many non-indigenous species. Higher numbers of non-indigenous species may be found at forest edges where light levels are enhanced, but plant densities decline with increasing distance into forest interiors. For example, Brothers and Spingarn (1992) studied forest remnants in Indiana and found that only *Rosa multiflora* and *Solanum nigrum* maintained sizable populations in forest interiors. Most of the invaders in this study were plants from gardens or pastures rather than weeds of cropland; they were limited to the relatively well-lighted forest edges (Brothers and Spingarn 1992).

Amur honeysuckle also can invade forest remnants, but its performance and reproduction are closely linked to light levels. Disturbances that create canopy gaps likely increase growth (Luken et al. 1995) and seedling densities decline with distance from forest edges (Luken and Goessling 1995). Clearly, very small remnant forests (high edge-to-interior ratios) and those experiencing canopy disturbances are most susceptible to invasions by non-indigenous plants.

In addition to the previously mentioned species, INPC (1990) listed several other species as potential problems in forests (Table 5.1). Here again, these plants have been observed invading forest communities, but little information exists on community- or ecosystem-level effects.

Kalisz (1993) found that remnant forests in the Bluegrass region of Kentucky were all invaded by non-indigenous earthworms. He hypothesized that indigenous species were eliminated by disturbance and that non-indigenous species occupied vacant niches. It is unknown how this change in the below-ground community has affected ecosystem-level processes.

Control of Non-Indigenous Species and Conservation Dilemmas

The presence of non-indigenous plants in nature reserves has prompted many resource managers to search for direct methods of plant control. Indeed, various control methods have been developed and tested for many of the species described in previous sections (Blankespoor and Larson 1994; Grilz and Romo 1995; INPC 1990; Luken and Mattimiro 1991; Nuzzo 1991; Solecki 1993). Unfortunately, there have been few successes in eradication of non-indigenous species because in most situations the invasive plant regenerates new populations soon after management activities. This occurs as a result of new plants establishing from the propagule bank (i.e., seeds, roots, or fragments) or from long-distance seed dispersal.

McCarthy (1997) presented results of a three-year study where garlic mustard was hand-weeded from permanent plots established in a Maryland forest. Removal of garlic mustard resulted in rapid release of indigenous species (primarily species of *Impatiens*) but by the end of the experiment species richness in control and removal plots was not significantly different. He concluded that such removal might at best serve as a temporary window of opportunity for release of indigenous understory plants. Luken and Mattimiro (1991) repeatedly cut adult shrubs of Amur honeysuckle in the understory of Kentucky forests. Although repeated cutting proved to be a successful method of killing adult shrubs, the resulting gaps were quickly colonized by Amur honeysuckle seedlings, garlic mustard, and several other non-indigenous plants!

The preceding examples support the contention of Hobbs and Huenneke (1992) that when fundamental system attributes (e.g., the seed bank) are changed by plant invasions, it is possible that either natural disturbance or management activities will facilitate invasions. Even when natural areas are large and relatively removed from human influence, various management practices may have both positive and negative effects on the invasion and establishment of non-indigenous species (Gibson et al. 1993).

A further dilemma is presented to managers of natural areas when apparent positive interactions emerge between indigenous animals and non-indigenous plants. It is now well-established that many indigenous birds utilize fruits of non-indigenous woody plants (Ingold and Craycraft 1983; White and Stiles 1992). Furthermore, the structure provided by these shrubs may in some instances serve as nesting habitat (Whelan and Dilger 1992). Such interactions may emerge because non-indigenous species provide superior resources or because indigenous plants were extirpated and the non-indigenous species are occupying unfilled niches. Regardless of the fundamental cause of emerging ecological interactions, it is possible that shrub eradication efforts could have a negative impact on indigenous animals. Whelan and Dilger (1992) suggested that if shrub control efforts are initiated, they should be phased so that some habitat remains while indigenous species are becoming established.

Whenever the failures of direct management activities targeting non-indigenous plants are discussed and debated, the conversation inevitably turns to biological control as the ultimate solution. Unfortunately, discovering, testing, developing, and releasing a biological control agent is a costly and lengthy enterprise. Such efforts will not likely be funded by government agencies unless the non-indigenous plant is widespread and is causing identified damage (in terms of dollars or human health and safety). To date, no attempts have been made to assess the economic impacts of non-indigenous plants in midwestern terrestrial natural areas. At best, costs of traditional control efforts have been tallied.

Conservation Practice and Biological Invasions

It is unlikely that the fundamental attributes of natural areas in the Midwest will change during the next century. They will remain small, remnant patches of vegetation radically different from the surrounding landscape in terms of community structure and ecosystem function. Future invasion of these remnant natural areas by non-indigenous species may depend equally on processes occurring in the natural area and on processes occurring in the surrounding landscape.

Intra-system processes that may contribute to invasion are (1) increased degrees of fragmentation, (2) soil disturbance, (3) extirpation of indigenous species thus creating unfilled niches, (4) natural disturbances creating canopy openings, and (5) management activities. Linked to these processes are other inter-system processes that may influence the arrival and success of non-indigenous species, e.g., dispersal of seeds by birds, transport of nutrients in air and water, and activities of people in the surrounding landscape that bring more non-indigenous species into close contact with natural areas. To understand the future direction of natural areas under these many natural and anthropogenic processes requires a landscape perspective that includes the activities of people. Pickett et al. (1992) suggested that conservation efforts should assume a nonequilibrium condition of biological systems with research efforts aimed at understanding the processes governing a system, the context of a system, the historical change in a system, the historical and extant impacts of humans in a system, and the limits of organisms now comprising the system. Along these same lines, Hobbs and Humphries (1995) suggested that any attempt to manage invasive plants must consider characteristics of the invading species, attributes of the invaded system, and human activities that may influence both system attributes and species availability.

As a first step, resource managers should begin long-term monitoring of biological communities using permanent plots; data should be stored on publicly accessible media. Plots should be established along both natural environmental gradients and along gradients of human impact. This will allow managers to record, and if need be, eradicate initial populations of invaders. Long-term monitoring will provide information on critical points of species entry. It will also help determine the types of human activities most conducive to import and establishment of non-indigenous species. Finally, permanent plots, when established within the context of a paired (removal vs. control) design, can provide valuable information on community level impacts of invaders. Information derived from permanent plots will form the basis of prioritizing species in terms of impact and feasibility of control.

Even when a non-indigenous plant is recorded as an expanding component of the preserved system, managers should not rush to eradicate without first determining if the species is filling a vacant niche or if the species has developed a positive interaction with indigenous animals. Such benefits must be balanced against competitive exclusion of indigenous plants.

It is ironic that the best-intentioned conservation efforts throughout the Midwest have created natural areas that are now changing as a result of biological invasions. Often there is no one person or entity to blame; it is simply the result of small natural areas being placed in the context of abundant non-indigenous species. The challenge facing resource managers is twofold: identifying and formalizing realistic conservation goals for preserved nature in the context of a disturbed landscape, and assessment of these biological invasions so that management practices can push biological communities in a direction that satisfies these goals (see, e.g., Luken 1994; Schwartz 1994)

References

Anderson, M.G. 1995. Interactions between *Lythrum salicaria* and native organisms: a critical review. *Environmental Management* 19:225–231.

Blankespoor, G.W., and E.A. Larson. 1994. Response of smooth brome (*Bromus inermis* Leyss.) to burning under varying soil moisture conditions. *American Midland Naturalist* 131:266–272.

Brothers, R.S., and A. Spingarn. 1992. Forest fragmentation and alien plant invasion of central Indiana old-growth forests. *Conservation Biology* 6:91–100.

DeMars, B.G. 1994. Star-of-Behlehem. *Ornithogalum umbellatum* L. (Liliaceae): an invasive naturalized plant in woodlands of Ohio. *Natural Areas Journal* 14:306–307.

Ebinger, J.E., and W.E. McClain. 1991. Natualized Amur maple (*Acer grinnala* Maxim.) in Illinois. *Natural Areas Journal* 11:170–171.

Gibson, D.J., T.R. Seastedt, and J.M. Briggs. 1993. Management practices in tallgrass prairie: large- and small-scale experimental effects on species composition. *Journal of Applied Ecology* 30:247–255.

Grilz, P.L., and J.T. Romo. 1995. Management considerations for controlling smooth brome in fescue prairie. *Natural Areas Journal* 15:148–156.

Harty, F.M. 1993. How Illinois kicked the exotic habit. In B.M. McKnight, ed. *Biological Pollution: The Control and Impact of Invasive Exotic Species.* Indiana Academy of Science, Indianapolis, 195–209.

Hiebert, R.D. 1990. An ecological restoration model: application to razed residential sites. *Natural Areas Journal* 10:181–186.

Hobbs, R.J., and L.F. Huenneke. 1992. Disturbance, diversity, and invasion: implications for conservation. *Conservation Biology* 6:324–337.

Hobbs, R.J., and S.E. Humphries. 1995. An integrated approach to the ecology and management of plant invasions. *Conservation Biology* 9:761–770.

Ingold, J.L., and M.J. Craycraft. 1983. Avian frugivory on honeysuckle (*Lonicera*) in southwestern Ohio U.S.A. *Ohio Journal of Science* 83:256–258.

Illinois Nature Preserves Commission (INPC). 1990. *Vegetation Management Manual.* Vol. 1, nos. 2–27, Springfield, Ill.

Kalisz, P.J. 1993. Native and exotic earthworms in deciduous forest soils of eastern North America. In B.N. McKnight, ed. *Biological Pollution: The Control and Impact of Invasive Exotic Species.* Indiana Academy of Science, Indianapolis, 93–100.

Luken, J.O. 1990. *Directing Ecological Succession.* Chapman and Hall, London.

Luken, J.O. 1994. Valuing plants in natural areas. *Natural Areas Journal* 14:295–299.

Luken, J.O., and N. Goessling. 1995. Seedling distribution and potential persistence of the exotic shrub *Lonicera maackii* in fragmented forests. *American Midland Naturalist* 133:124–130.

Luken, J.O., and D.T. Mattimiro. 1991. Habitat-specific resilience of the invasive shrub Amur honeysuckle (*Lonicera maackii*) during repeated clipping. *Ecological Applications* 1:104–109.

Luken, J.O., T.C. Tholemeier, B.A. Kunkel, and L.M. Kuddes. 1995. Branch architecture plasticity of Amur honeysuckle (*Lonicera maackii* (Rupr.) Herder): initial response in extreme light environments. *Bulletin of the Torrey Botanical Club* 122:190–195.

Mack, R.N. 1986. Alien plant invasion into the intermountain west: a case history. In H.A. Mooney and J.A. Drake, eds. *Ecology of Biological Invasions of North America and Hawaii.* Springer-Verlag, New York, 191–213.

McCarthy, B.C. 1997. Response of a forest community to experimental removal of an invasive non-indigenous plant (*Alliaria petiolata*, Brassicaceae). In J.O. Luken and J.W. Thieret, eds. *Assessment and Management of Plant Invasions.* Springer-Verlag, New York.

McClain, W.E., and E.A. Anderson. 1990. Loss of hill prairie through woody plant invasion at Pere Marquette State Park, Jersey County, Illinois. *Natural Areas Journal* 10:69–75.

McKnight, B.N., ed. 1993. *Biological Pollution: The Control and Impact of Invasive Exotic Plants.* Indiana Academy of Sciences, Indianapolis.

Mooney, H.A., and J.A. Drake, eds. 1986. *Ecology of Biological Invasions of North America and Hawaii.* Springer-Verlag, New York.

Myers, R.M., and R.D. Henry. 1979. Changes in the alien flora in two west-central Illinois counties during the past 140 years. *American Midland Naturalist* 101:226–230.

Nuzzo, V. 1993. Distribution and spread of the invasive biennial *Alliaria petiolata* (garlic mustard) in North America. In B.N. McKnight, ed. *Biological Pollution: The Control and Impact of Invasive Exotic Species.* Indiana Academy of Science, Indianapolis, 137–145.

Nuzzo, V.A. 1991. Experimental control of Garlic mustard (*Alliaria petiolata* (Bieb.) Cavara & Grande) in northern Illinois using fire, herbicide, and cutting. *Natural Areas Journal* 11:158–167.

Office of Technology Assessment (OTA), U.S. Congress. 1993. *Harmful Non-Indigenous Species in the United States.* OTA-F-565. U.S. Government Printing Office, Washington, D.C.

Pickett, S.T.A., V.T. Parker, and P.L. Fiedler. 1992. The new paradigm in ecology: Implications for conservation biology above the species level. In P.L. Fiedler and S.K. Jain, eds. *Conservation Biology: The Theory and Practice of Nature Conservation, Preservation and Management.* Chapman and Hall, New York, 65–88.

Rejmánek, M., and J.M. Randall. 1994. Invasive alien plants in California: 1993 summary and comparison with other areas in North America. *Madrono* 41:161–177.

Schwartz, M.W. 1994. Conflicting goals for preserving biodiversity: issues of scale and value. *Natural Areas Journal* 14:213–216.

Solecki, M.K. 1993. Cut-leaved and common teasel (*Dipsacus laciniatus* L. and *D. sylvestris* Huds.): profile of two invasive aliens. In B.N. McKnight, ed. *Biological Pollution: The Control and Impact of Invasive Exotic Species.* Indiana Academy of Science, Indianapolis, 85–92.

Stone, C.P., C.W. Smith, and J.T. Tunison, eds. 1992. *Alien Plant Invasions in Native Ecosystems of Hawaii: Management and Research.* University of Hawaii, Cooperative National Park Resources Studies Unit, Honolulu.

Vance, D.R., and R.L. Westemeier. 1979. Interactions of pheasants and prairie chickens in Illinois. *Wildlife Society Bulletin* 7:221–225.

Whelan, C.J., and M.L. Dilger. 1992. Invasive, exotic shrubs: a paradox for natural area managers? *Natural Areas Journal* 12:109–110.

White, D.W., and E.W. Stiles. 1992. Bird dispersal of fruits of species introduced into eastern North America. *Canadian Journal of Botany* 70:1689–1696.

Wilson, S.D. 1989. The suppression of native prairie by alien species introduced for revegetation. *Landscape and Urban Planning* 17:113–119.

Zimmerman, U.D., J.E. Ebinger, and K.C. Diekroeger. 1993. Alien and native woody species invasion of abandoned crop land and reestablished tallgrass prairie in east-central Illinois. *Transactions of the Illinois Academy of Science* 86:111–118.

6

Native Pests: The Impact of Deer in Highly Fragmented Habitats

Roger C. Anderson
Department of Biological Sciences Campus Box 4120, Illinois State
University, Normal, Illinois 61790-4120, e-mail rcander@rs6000.cmp.ilstu.edu

Destruction of native habitat due to conversion to agriculture, logging, and urbanization, and subsequent fragmentation of the remaining habitat, has affected many species negatively (Guttenspergen 1983). Affected organisms include those dependent upon large blocks of habitat such as forest interior birds (Robbins 1980, Robbins et al. 1989), and large predators including the gray wolf (Fritts and Carbyn 1995) and grizzly bear. Other species like the North American bison required large blocks of habitat (Risser 1990), and they also may have migrated from summer to winter ranges (Dary 1974). Such migration would have been disrupted by habitat fragmentation. Even populations of perennial plant species persisting and reproducing in fragmented habitats can experience decline in genetic heterozygosity. These isolated populations, with limited gene flow, are threatened with local extirpation (White et al. 1983).

In this chapter, I focus on the role of white-tailed deer in modifying fragmented environments to the detriment of species whose success has been constrained by habitat fragmentation. The selected examples focus on northern Wisconsin forests and the urbanized and agricultural landscapes of Illinois. These three systems provide the white-tailed deer with different resources. Nevertheless, they share the common features of fragmented habitats where insufficient biological control, or management by humans, has allowed the white-tailed deer population to expand such that herbivory threatens the continued success of other species.

In contrast to species that decline with habitat fragmentation, the white-tailed deer in eastern North America has recovered from habitat modification and population declines, and flourishes in the presence of habitat fragmentation and, under some conditions, conversion of native habitat to agricultural lands. When Europeans first arrived in North America it is estimated that there were about 40 million deer on the continent. However, in the middle of the 19th century large numbers of deer were killed by settlers, sportsmen, and commercial hunters. In Wisconsin, for example, "enormous amounts of saddles, hams, and carcasses . . ." of deer were shipped to Chicago and Milwaukee markets in the 1870s. At the same time in

Eau Claire, Wisconsin, venison was being sold for as little as five to six cents per pound (Bersing 1966). There was also massive loss of natural habitat by conversion to agricultural lands and repeated wildfires. In northeastern Wisconsin, the Peshtigo fire of 1871, fueled by logging slash, is estimated to have burned over 5.6 million ha. This fire, and other recurring and widespread fires, reduced deer habitat by converting shrubs and second growth forests to grasslands (Dahlberg and Guettinger 1956, Bersing 1966).

According to Nixon et al. (1991), Illinois may have been near the center of deer abundance in North America prior to European settlement. There are no estimates for pre-Columbian deer densities in the state, but the prairie-forest transition zone of the Midwest and islands on the Atlantic Gulf Coast may have supported the highest deer densities prior to European settlement. Deer numbers increased in Illinois, and some adjacent states, between the 1820s and 1850s as populations of indigenous peoples were reduced or eliminated (Nixon et al. 1991). As in other areas, year-round market hunting and habitat destruction in the middle 1800s caused a rapid decline in the deer herd. In Illinois, deer were probably extirpated throughout most of the state by the end of the 19th century (Nixon et al. 1991), although deer may have persisted in southern Illinois until 1910 (Pietsch 1954). Deer numbers were reduced to about one-half million animals on the continent at about the same time (Trefethen 1975, Clutton-Brock and Albon 1992).

Massive declines in deer populations caused several states to enact protective deer legislation beginning in the early part of this century. Restrictions ranged from a complete ban on hunting in 1901 in Illinois (Pietsch 1954), to limiting areas and seasons available for hunting, and the hunting of bucks only, in Wisconsin and other states (Dahlberg and Guettinger 1956, Bersing 1966). Elimination of major predators, restriction of hunting, and restoration of habitats caused a rapid increase in deer abundance. Deer were well adapted to the large amount of edge resulting from agricultural activities and the development of second growth forests. Brush lands and secondary forests developed as wide-spread fires were contained. In addition, farm lands with low agricultural potential were abandoned.

In some areas, deer densities recovered in the altered habitats to levels that are currently in excess of those thought to have occurred in pre-Columbian times. Prior to logging in northern Wisconsin, for example, extensive areas (75–83%) of virgin forest (Canham and Loucks 1984) lacking understory growth and severe winters produced marginal deer habitat that probably supported few deer (< 4 per square km) (Alverson et al. 1988). Logging began in the 1800s and most of the virgin timber was harvested prior to 1920. However, as noted earlier, frequent severe wild fires reduced suitable habitat for deer. Following fire suppression and the passage of protective deer legislation, however, deer populations grew rapidly. By the 1930s in Wisconsin, over twice as many bucks were harvested by legal hunters as during the deer seasons of the 1920s. The continued growth of the deer herd was indicated by annual harvests of over one-half million deer in the 1940s. This was more than twice the combined harvest of the 1920s and 1930s (Bersing 1966).

Deer densities in northern Wisconsin peaked at about 14 deer per square km in the 1930s and 1940s. However, subsequent maturation of forests, loss of understory species, and breakup of mature aspen stands reduced deer densities in the last 25 years to between 5 and 12 per square km (Dahlberg and Guettinger 1956, Bersing 1966, McCaffery 1986, Alverson et al. 1988).

As early as the 1940s, browsing deer were damaging selected woody species including Canadian yew (*Taxus canadensis*), eastern hemlock (*Tsuga canadensis*), and white cedar (*Thuja occidentalis*) in portions of Wisconsin (Swift 1948, Dahlberg and Guettinger 1956). In the late 1960s and early 1970s, Orie Loucks and I (Anderson and Loucks 1979) demonstrated that, in areas of high deer density in northwestern Wisconsin, shade-tolerant eastern hemlock was not replacing itself in stands where it was a canopy dominant. This lack of replacement occurred despite several studies reporting that hemlock is capable of maintaining itself in closed-canopy, mixed conifer-hardwood forests (Martin 1959, Hett and Loucks 1976, Frelich and Lorimer 1985). Hemlock is a preferred winter browse species (Dahlberg and Guettinger 1956) which frequently does not recover when its terminal shoots are browsed by deer, or at a minimum, its potential for regrowth is limited. In areas of heavy deer browsing in northern Wisconsin, some hemlock seedlings less than 15 cm tall were found because they were covered with snow during the winter and escaped browsing. However, larger seedlings that would protrude above the snow cover were essentially absent. In many of these forests, sugar maple was the most common species in the seedling, sapling, and smallest tree size classes, even though it was poorly represented in the larger tree classes.

Sugar maple is browsed by deer, but it is able to recover from browsing because it readily resprouts. If sugar maple, which may be the most shade tolerant of the eastern deciduous forest trees, is not browsed for a few years, its terminal shoots may grow beyond the reach of deer. This differential response to deer browsing by the two species of trees encourages the replacement of hemlock as the dominant tree by sugar maple. However, even sugar maple can be killed by extensive and persistent deer browsing. Basswood and black ash, two low-use browse species that are less shade tolerant than hemlock, were also important in the reproductive strata in intensely-browsed hemlock forests (Anderson and Loucks 1979, Anderson and Katz 1993).

Using data from deer exclosures in hemlock stands, Alan Katz and I (Anderson and Katz 1993) found that, after 12 years of protection from deer browsing, hemlock was well-represented in the seedling stratum (2,721/ha), but it was not present as a sapling. In an exclosure established in 1949, seedlings (2,346/ha) and saplings (148/ha) were present after 27 years of deer exclusion, and hemlock had a diameter distribution characteristic of shade-tolerant species in all-aged forests. Deer do not eliminate hemlock trees. However, they eliminate seedlings and saplings and prevent recruitment into larger size classes. We suggested that in hemlock-dominated forests subjected to continuous and intensive browsing pressure since the early part of this century, it may take as long as 70 years of protection for browse-sensitive tree species to achieve a size class distribution characteristic of all-aged forests.

In contrast to our conclusion (Anderson and Loucks 1979, Anderson and Katz 1993) that failure of hemlock recruitment is due to deer browsing pressure, Mladenoff and Stearns (1993) proposed that deer browsing is only a site-specific factor preventing successful hemlock regeneration. They concluded that hemlock reproduction on a regional scale is affected by a large number of variables. These variables include appropriate climatic and disturbance regimes, suitable seed beds for germination, and availability of seeds. They do not refute the importance of deer in limiting hemlock regeneration. However, they think that other factors provide restraints on hemlock regeneration before deer browsing limits hemlock reproduction. The plethora of factors proposed by Mladenoff and Stearns (1993) may be important in preventing hemlock regeneration. However, their ideas remain untested because of the influence of deer browsing on hemlock generation. It is only in the absence of deer browsing on a regional scale that the effect of other factors on hemlock regeneration can be examined. However, the occurrence of hemlock seedlings less than 15 cm tall, so they are hidden beneath winter snows and escape deer browsing, and successful regeneration of hemlock in deer exclosures, suggest that appropriate conditions for hemlock recruitment may exist in the absence of deer browsing pressure.

Alverson et al. (1988) reported that in northern Wisconsin small patches of old- and mature-growth forest occupy less than 5% of the forested areas and occur as islands within a matrix of younger successional forests. This reverses the pattern of old-growth and mature forest and successional forests that supported low deer densities prior to the logging era. Trembling aspen, which resprouts vigorously after cutting or browsing, and initially provides browse and cover for deer, is the dominant tree species in these successional forests. For example, in National Forests in the region (Chequamegon and Nicolet) aspen increased in abundance from about 1% in the European presettlement forests to about 26% in recent times (Alverson et al. 1988).

Alverson et al. (1988) proposed that even large continuous blocks of relatively undisturbed forest, such as the National Forests of the Great Lakes region, can be profoundly affected by deer browsing because of the ability of large herbivores to wander widely. Moreover, the beneficial effects of edge on game species has encouraged management of forests through timber harvests to enhance the ratio of edge to interior. To maintain biological diversity in old-growth forest, they suggested that deer densities should be less than four deer per square km, and perhaps as low as one to two per square km. According to Alverson et al. (1988), because of the reluctance of hunters to utilize areas of relatively low deer density, hunting will not reduce deer numbers to the suggested level. Only large blocks of unsuitable habitat (e.g., mature forest), as much as eight km in radius, will achieve this recommendation. This sort of management would require a large shift in the philosophy of forest managers who strive for multiple use forests, including maintenance of deer densities that maximize hunter success. Deer densities (about four to nine deer per square km) that would be sufficiently low to permit regeneration of most tree species in northern forests, maintain a healthy deer herd, and provide an acceptable level of hunter success, would not be low enough to satisfy conservationists who are concerned with maximizing biological diversity (Alverson et al. 1988). This diversity includes many species of under-story herbs and shrubs, such as Canadian yew (*Taxus canadensis*), large-leafed aster (*Aster macrophyllus*), wild sarsaparilla (*Aralia nudicaulis*), bluebead lily (*Clintonia borealis*), false Solomon's seal (*Smilacina racemosa*), nodding trillium (*Trillium cernuum*), white trillium (*T. grandiflorum*), and others (Balgooyen and Waller 1995), as well as species of forest trees.

In northern Wisconsin during the winter, deer often congregate in restricted areas called deer yards, especially when deep snow impedes their movements (Dahlberg and Guettinger 1956). This results in trails being cut in the deep snow, and deer may focus their activities on these trails. Deer commonly yard in white cedar swamps, and white cedar, like eastern hemlock, is a preferred winter browse species. High deer densities result in heavy browsing occurring on white cedar and other species of plants in swamps used as winter yards (Habeck 1960). The cessation of repeated wild fires and abandonment of farm lands in the 1920s and 30s, which resulted in the expansion of summer deer range, probably had little effect on increasing winter range. Cedar swamps probably experienced a substantial increase in browsing pressure at this time as a result of the rapid increase in the size of the deer herd.

Following extirpation of deer in Illinois, deer were reintroduced beginning in the northern part of the state in 1903 (Pietsch 1954, Nixon et al. 1991). Deer probably also entered the state by migrating from Wisconsin down the Rock River valley and from Missouri in the southwest. The growth of the Illinois deer herd generally mirrored that of Wisconsin's during this century. Presently, in Illinois there are few habitat constraints on the continued growth of the deer herd in agricultural areas with fragments of forest available for winter cover (Nixon et al. 1991).

Deer reached nuisance numbers in the Rock River area in northern Illinois and near Horseshoe Lake in the southern portion of the state by the 1940s (Leopold 1943, Leopold et al. 1947). By 1957, the herd had expanded sufficiently that hunting was permitted in selected counties in Illinois. With the continued growth of the deer herd, hunting deer with firearms now is allowed in all but four highly urbanized counties (Cook, DuPage, Kane, and Lake) in the extreme northeastern part of the state. There are presently about 600,000–800,000 white-tailed deer in Illinois (Kelley 1994) and about 20 million on the continent (Clutton-Brock and Albon 1992).

Some of the most serious impacts of deer on fragmented habitats occurs in the highly urbanized northeastern portion of the state where control of deer by hunting with firearms is not permitted. Several of these northeastern counties have Forest Preserve systems that consist of isolated patches of natural vegetation surrounded by intensive urban development. In Cook County alone, the 30 Forest Preserves comprise 11% (27,080 ha) of the land area and range in size from 16–6,070 ha (Witham and Jones 1987). Once deer enter these preserves there is little resistance to rapid population growth and deer numbers soon become excessive.

The Ned Brown Forest Preserve, a 12 square km Cook County Forest Preserve, is typical of urban natural areas that have experienced excessive expansion of the deer populations. The Ned Brown Preserve is located about 5.5 km from O'Hare International Airport, and in 1985 it supported deer densities of about 28–38 deer per square km (Witham and Jones 1990). It is completely surrounded by urban development and interstate highways from its northern and western boundaries.

Formerly, the white-flowered trillium (*Trillium grandiflorum*) was a prominent understory species in a portion of the preserve known as Busse Woods, and provided remarkable displays of flowers in the spring. The presence of the trillium was one of the factors influencing the dedication of Busse Woods as an Illinois State Nature Preserve in 1965 (McFall 1991). By 1985, the trillium was nearly eliminated from the site by deer browsing (Witham and Jones 1992). Browse lines were visible on trees and shrubs. In the forest understory, overbrowsing had greatly reduced the abundance of most of the understory species, except for unpalatable species such as wild garlic (*Allium canadense*) and wild leek (*A. tricoccum*) (Witham and Jones 1992). When I visited the site in 1985, only scattered patches of a sedge (*Carex pensylvanica*) were prominent on the forest floor by late summer. Concomitantly, studies by the Illinois Natural History Survey demonstrated that deer were in poor condition, exhibiting classic signs of malnutrition and experiencing low reproductive rates. Efforts to reduce the herd's size were impeded initially by concern over potential adverse public reaction. Eventually, deer were removed from the site with a goal of maintaining a density of about eight deep per square km (Witham and Jones 1987).

Management of deer herds in urban settings is often much more difficult than in rural areas because of public opposition to killing deer or even reducing deer numbers by trapping (Girard et al. 1993). Because of sufficient or excessive numbers of deer in nearly all areas of Wisconsin and Illinois, trapping and relocating deer is prohibited in these states by law. In rural areas, a tradition of hunting and harvesting deer to maintain the herd in balance with other resources, as well as to provide hunters the opportunity to hunt deer, is readily accepted.

However, some urban dwellers often are unable to accept deer removal and view it as being cruel, inhumane, and disruptive of the balance of nature.

Vigorous public reaction to proposed or actual deer management by trapping or shooting occurred in several urban areas in the Midwest and the eastern United States (Girard et al. 1993). This has made maintaining deer numbers at levels appropriate for maintenance of habitat conditions and biological diversity difficult. This problem is illustrated by the efforts of the Lake County Forest Preserve District to manage the deer herd in the 223 ha Edward Ryerson Conservation Area.

In the 1980s, excessive deer were indicated by the appearance of distinct browse lines at Ryerson. As in Busse Woods, displays of white-flowered trillium, which were spectacular in several locations (including an area adjacent to the Ryerson Visitors' Center), were reduced to colonies with few flowering plants, and vegetative plants of short stature. In 1989, wildlife biologists proposed reducing the deer herd (by shooting) to 16 individuals from an existing population of about 77 animals. This proposal resulted in the formation of a citizen group called "Concerned Veterinarians and Citizens Committee to Save the Ryerson Deer," which sought a court injunction to prevent the shooting of deer. Eventually, 39 deer were shot by sharpshooters at a cost of $179 per animal. The 2,513 pounds of venison was ground and given to local charities. Additionally, 25 animals were trapped at a cost of $637 per animal not including transportation. Of these animals, five died as a result of being traumatized during trapping, and one was killed because it tested positive for Lyme disease. Eighteen trapped deer were transported to the Wildlife Prairie Park near Peoria, Illinois, where several eventually died from diseases. Two deer escaped and were shot by hunters (Girard et al. 1993).

In the spring of 1989, I developed a procedure to monitor the influence of deer browsing on vegetation in Lake County Forest Preserves. The goal was a relatively rapid, but reliable, index of assessing browsing intensity using key ecosystem components to characterize the influence of browsing on the vegetation as a whole (Anderson 1994).

In a deer exclosure constructed near the Ryerson Visitors' Center in 1987, the extent of flowering and the height of unbrowsed trillium stems were much greater inside the exclosure than outside. Deer select trillium for browse and appear to favor flowering plants, which are the largest plants, over non-flowering plants. Once a plant is browsed it does not resprout until the following year, but because carbon resources have not been restored, the resprouted plant is smaller. As browsing intensity increases, the height of the unbrowsed trillium plant becomes progressively smaller. I was able to demonstrate that change in unbrowsed trillium stem heights was a good indicator of browsing intensity on the understory as a whole (Figure 6.1).

To determine a stem height that would indicate acceptable levels of browsing, I compared trillium stem heights in Ryerson and other sites in Lake County subjected to varying degrees of deer browsing intensity. Using this information,

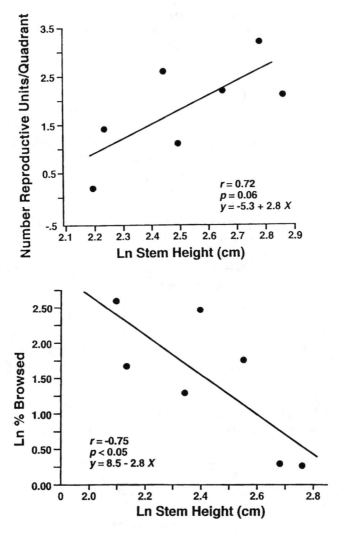

Figure 6.1. The relationship between logn trillium stem height and the number of reproductive units (buds, flowers, and fruits) in the upper panel and the logn percent of understory species browsed in the lower panel. Adapted from Anderson, 1994.

I recommended that deer population density should be managed so that a stem height of 12–14 cm is maintained in Lake County Forests. This height was chosen because two of the six unprotected areas studied had trillium populations with stable stem heights in this range. For these two populations, flowering plants comprised 21 and 34% of the individuals. This stem height was associated with deer density of about 5 deer per square km, based on an aerial count made during the winter. In contrast, three areas that had trillium stem height (8.0–8.8 cm) below the recommended level had deer density of 23–24 deer per square km.

Lake County has continued to monitor trillium stem height in Ryerson and at three other sites to assist in making decisions regarding the management of the deer herd. The stem height, coupled with the percentage of trillium plants in flower, has been a useful tool in assessing deer browsing intensity. In the deer exclosure at Ryerson, mean stem height increased from 1989 to 1993 and then declined in the next two years. The decline in stem height was due to the recruitment of trillium seedlings.

In agricultural areas in Illinois, habitat fragmentation has produced conditions in which food limitations on deer herd growth are essentially nonexistent, migration and dispersal of deer is high, and deer impact on remaining native habitats is strongly seasonal and often extensive (Nixon et al. 1991).

Production of agricultural crops, mainly corn and soybeans, provides deer with sufficient food to permit the continued expansion of the deer herd (Nixon et al. 1991). Deer eat developing corn plants beginning in late May or early June, when young seedlings apparently have an especially high concentration of nitrogen. In late July, deer eat developing kernels in the "milk stage." Later, mature grain is used heavily by deer. Soybeans provide forage during the summer months and mature beans in the fall. Fall plowing, a common practice, further depletes the availability of food from farm fields, but developing winter wheat compensates as an additional resource. Nixon et al. (1991) reported that in central Illinois deer obtained 60% of their food by volume from agricultural crops from December through February (38% corn, 18.1% wheat, 3.8% soybeans, and 0.1% clover).

Even though food may be available in agricultural fields, the lack of cover after corn harvest causes deer to concentrate in fragments of forest that occur as isolated patches of a few to several hundred ha, or as linear strips following the major waterways (Nixon et al. 1991, Strole and Anderson 1992). Typically, these fragmented forest habitats are subjected to intensive deer browsing from late January to the middle of May. Woody species are browsed most heavily from January to April, and forest herbs from April through the middle of May (Strole and Anderson 1992, Kelley 1994).

Nixon et al. (1991) reported that woody browse represents a smaller component of the white-tailed deer energy needs than crop residues even during the winter months. However, deer browse selectively so the influence of browsing does not affect all woody species equally. If population density is high, the impact of browsing on woody species can be a major factor in diminishing tree and shrub recruitment of palatable species (Beals and Cottam 1960, Ross et al. 1970, Horsley and Marquis 1983, Frelich and Lorimer, 1985). In central Illinois forests, Todd Strole and I (Strole and Anderson 1992) reported 13.7% of woody twigs available to deer were browsed. However, the four most preferred species, choke cherry

(*Prunus americana*), gray dogwood (*Cornus racemosa*), multiflora rose (*Rosa multiflora*) and white oak (*Quercus alba*), had more than 50% of their available twigs browsed.

In upland forests in central Illinois, replacement of white oak by sugar maple (*Acer saccharum*) is common. This species replacement may be due largely to elimination of periodic fires (Adams and Anderson 1980) which apparently were common prior to European settlement. Fire exclusion permitted shade-tolerant but fire-sensitive species like sugar maple to invade and replace the less shade-tolerant but more fire-resistant oak and hickories (*Carya* spp.). Sugar maple and white oak constitute a similar percentage of browse utilized by deer (white oak = 4.7% and sugar maple = 5.4%). However, white oak constitute only 1.3 percent of the twigs available to be browsed, whereas sugar maple was 18.8% of the available browse. The differential way deer browse white oak and sugar maple may result in oak being more negatively affected by browsing than sugar maple. Sugar maple and white oak resprout after browsing, but deer tend to browse the tips of sugar maple twigs and often leave some buds on the shoot, whereas white oak is often browsed close to the ground and may have to send up new shoots from root stocks. The high preference deer have for white oak and their low preference for sugar maple, and the differential browsing pattern on the two species, along with fire exclusion and competition from other low-use, browse-tolerant species, may add to the decline of reproduction in oak forests (Strole and Anderson 1992).

Acorns are a favored food of white-tailed deer, and extensive use of this resource can further reduce recruitment of white oak seedlings. Because of the importance of oak mast to many species of wildlife, the impact of deer on the oak community may extend beyond the autotrophic level in ways that have not been fully appreciated.

As deer browsing intensity increases there is a notable increase in the abundance of understory gooseberry (*Ribes* spp.). Gooseberry is among the least browsed of the available woody browse species (Strole and Anderson 1992). Deer apparently browse gooseberry very little during the dormant period when mature stems are protected by spines. My observations indicate that browsing of gooseberry occurs mostly in the spring when the new growth has not yet developed protective structures. Even this species, however, declines in abundance under intensive deer browsing pressure. This ability of deer to shift resource use depending on availability of resources may be one of the reasons deer are so successful and also so potentially damaging to vegetation.

The effect of deer browsing on forest herbs is generally concentrated in the spring of the year (April and May) when many of the understory plants including the spring ephemerals (Curtis 1959) are available, and before new crops provide adequate forage (Kelley 1994). Kelley (1994) studied browsing impact at the Illinois Power Company nuclear facility at Clinton, Illinois. When the cooling lake for the power plant was constructed, a peninsula was formed which extended into Clinton Lake. The inner portion of the peninsula was composed of approximately 243 ha of agricultural cropland and 324 ha of second growth oak-hickory forest and plantations of red alder (*Alnus rubra*) and pine (*Pinus strobus* and *P. resinosa*). Because of the close proximity (five km) to the power plant, hunting was prohibited on the peninsula for a period of 15 years. Aerial census of the deer herd in January of 1991 indicated a minimum count of 546 deer (94 per square km). In 1991, crop depredation damage of $40,000 was paid to tenant farmers. Beginning in the winter of 1991, two-month bow hunts (Nov. 1–Jan 1) were authorized to reduce the herd size. Over the next three years, bow hunts reduced the size of the herd to 187 deer (32 deer per square km).

To document changes in deer browsing intensity as herd size was being reduced, Kelley (1994) sampled understory vegetation in two deer exclosures and in an unprotected control area adjacent to the exclosures. Samples of the above-ground herbaceous biomass were taken in the spring (April, May), mid-summer (July), and late summer (August). The results showed that generally significant differences in biomass between the exclosures and control area occurred in the spring samples but not during July and August. Reducing the deer herd size might have allowed some recovery of herbaceous plants in the unprotected area.

Kelley (1994) concluded that deer browsing was more intense in woodlands in early spring than in summer. Deer move out of wooded areas in late spring as agricultural crops begin to provide food and cover, and the amounts of forage deer obtain from forests decreases (Nixon et al. 1991). Consequently, plants maximizing biomass production in spring suffer more negative impacts from deer browsing than species that grow and maximize biomass production later in the growing season when availability of food resources in crop fields increase. Changes in the food quality of the herbaceous plants available in the spring and summer also influence seasonal browsing patterns. Spring herbaceous species may be more palatable than species that dominate the woodlands later in the growing season.

Deer readily change browsing patterns as preferred food items are eliminated or reduced in abundance. For example, in my study of deer browsing in Lake County, Illinois (Anderson 1994), wild leek (*Allium tricoccum*) was a low-use species in two of seven study sites. However, leek was a preferred species in MacArthur Woods which had the highest level of browsing and the highest density of deer. Similarly, on the 5,968 ha North Manitou Island in northern Lake Michigan, a pre-winter population of 2,080 deer (0.35/ha) in 1981 foraged heavily on wild leeks, and in some areas dug up the bulbs (Case and McCullough 1987). The excessively large deer population had developed over a period of years, before the island was acquired by the National Park Service in 1980, when hunting and winter feeding was administered by the previous owners. Because of the high deer density, winter browse was essentially eliminated on the island, except for the unpalatable American beech. From spring through fall, food supply was favorable and included the alewife fish, which die in annual cycles in Lake Michigan and wash up on the shore where they were eaten by the deer.

The sometimes disparate lists of preferred browse species that appear in the literature (LaGory et al. 1985, Case and McCullough 1987, Tilghman 1989, Strole and Anderson 1992) are likely the result of the ability of deer to shift browsing preferences as a function of what food resource is available. This adaptability in food utilization may be due in part to the continual production of a tannin-binding protein that is present in the saliva of the white-tailed deer (Robbins et al. 1987, Austin et al. 1989). Items that are readily eaten by deer and that contain high levels of tannins include black walnut twigs (Strole 1988) and red oak acorns. The ability to shift browsing patterns is of great adaptive value to the white-tail deer. However, this ability results in deer continuing to browse the remaining vegetation after the most preferred items are eliminated from a site, but with a reordered browse preference. This can continue until only unpalatable species that provide little or no nutrition to the deer remain. Thus, it is possible for ecosystems to be seriously impacted and species lost before the deer population begins to show signs of malnutrition. Furthermore, in agricultural areas in Illinois, because of the availability of food from crop fields throughout the year, woodland plant food resources can be drastically reduced. This reduction of forest resources can occur without the corresponding stabilizing reduction in the deer herd that would occur in wholly forested areas because of diminishing browse quality and quantity.

In the Midwest, prairies as well as forests are fragmented habitats. In Illinois, the size of the 200 remnant prairies ranges from a few acres to over a thousand acres. In most instances, prairies are surrounded by agricultural fields or forests. A survey of the published literature on deer browsing on tallgrass prairies yielded only a single reference reporting the browsing of prairie forbs in a restored prairie (Englund and Meyer 1984). However, from 1992 through 1994, I studied the influence of deer browsing on prairie forbs at Goose Lake Prairie State Park in Grundy County, Illinois (unpublished data). Near the study area deer density during the winter varied from 25–27 deer per square km between 1989 and 1994.

During the growing season, the intensity of browsing varied. Browsing intensity increased from May into mid- to late June and then decreased into August. Deer selectively browsed on forbs and did not use grasses during the months of my study (May through August). Preferred browse species varied from year to year. Of the 100 species of forbs sampled, 26 were selected species (browsed in significantly greater proportion than the population of forbs as a whole) in at least one of the seven samples that were taken. The selected species included Culver's root (*Veronicastrum virginicum*), lead plant (*Amorpha canescens*), ver-vain (*Verbena stricta*), wild bean (*Vicia americana*), spiderwort (*Tradescantia ohiensis*), rattle-snake master (*Eryngium yuccifolium*—usually only the tips of leaves are browsed early in the growing season), purple prairie clover (*Petalos-*

temum purpureum), Illinois tickseed (*Desmodium illinonense*), and others. Legumes seem to be preferred browse items, although some of them, *Baptisia leucantha* and *Petalostemum candidum*, were not represented with sufficient abundance in the study area to statistically demonstrate this pattern. Comparing flowering in exclosures and unprotected adjacent areas revealed that deer browsing significantly reduced the number of flowering stems of several species of forbs. For example, in an exclosure the density of lead plant was 6.0 stems per square m, while in an adjacent unprotected area stem density was not significantly different at 4.6 per square m. However, more than one-half of the stems in the exclosure flowered (3.2 per square m), whereas in the unprotected area there were no flowering stems and more than 50% of the stems (2.5 per square m) were browsed by deer.

Deer are most likely to influence the prairie vegetation by causing a shift in plant species' abundances and competitive abilities. By browsing selectively, deer reduce the competitive abilities and reproductive output of selected species, and this indirectly favors non-browsed and low-use species. As in the forest, the average percentage of stems browsed does not provide a good representation of the influence of the deer on the vegetation. During the growing season, deer browsed from 3.5% to 18.9% of the standing crop of forb stems. However, for individual species the percentage browsed ranged from 0 to 100%. For example, in July of 1992, the average percentage of the forb stems browsed was 18.9%. Of the 55 species of forbs sampled, about one-half (27) experienced browsing, ten species (18.2%) had more than 50% of their stems browsed, and three species had all of their stems browsed.

The net effect of intensive deer browsing on prairies is to reduce forb diversity and, because deer do not browse on prairie grasses, favor the abundance of grass. Historically, there may have been niche separation on the prairie between bison and deer. Bison consume much more graminoid (grasses and sedges) than forb biomass (McCullough 1980, Larson and Murdock 1989), whereas deer, and perhaps elk, browse on forbs and consume less grass than do bison (McCullough 1980). The absence of competition from the two other large ungulates in the Midwest, especially the elk, may be a factor contributing to the rapid expansion of the deer herd in this century, in addition to the loss of predators and habitat modification.

Conclusions

The ability of the white-tailed deer to thrive in disturbed and fragmented habitats, the removal of effective predator control, and, perhaps, the loss of competition from other large herbivores, resulted in rapid recovery of the deer herd in the Midwest from precariously low levels. Current population densities threaten the success of other species in many areas (DeCalestra 1994, McShea et al. 1995). In intensely-farmed regions in the Midwest, agricultural activities created conditions where food resources often are not a limiting resource. At the same time, wintering areas are limited to fragmented natural habitats that are heavily used by deer for forage and cover during the winter. Because deer obtain food resources from agricultural fields year-round, they can deplete resources in natural habitats beyond the point where deterioration of habitat would normally limit population growth. Under these conditions deer can affect competitive abilities of plant species and cause local extirpation of species.

In areas where old-growth forests occur as islands within recently cut and young forests, deer densities in fragmented old-growth forests are much higher than they were under historic conditions when young forests occurred as islands within large tracts of old-growth and virgin forests. Under conditions of high deer density, many dominant plant species of old-growth forests are unable to withstand intensive browsing and are eliminated or have their reproductive capacity greatly reduced.

Browse-sensitive herbaceous species and trees can recover when intensive browsing by white-tailed deer is eliminated. However, in fragmented habitats, deer browsing could extirpate or severely reduce sensitive populations. Trophic effects could impact insect pollinators and other herbivores dependent on these plant resources. Furthermore, in highly fragmented habitats interspersed within areas of unsuitable habitats, even with reduced deer densities, dispersal distances may prevent understory species lost to deer browsing from reestablishing themselves (Miller et al. 1992, Anderson and Katz 1993).

For most of this century, efforts of people concerned with managing deer herds focused on increasing deer densities by manipulating habitat and controlling hunter access to deer. It is only in the past decade or so that we have come to understand that the success of the deer herd has occurred at the expense of other natural resources. It is likely that we are just beginning to appreciate the full impact of what excessive deer numbers have done to many species in fragmented habitats.

While the focus of this chapter has been the midwestern United States, the negative influences of white-tailed deer in areas of fragmented habitats are common throughout most of the eastern United States (e.g., Robbins 1980, Miller et al. 1992, DeCalestra 1994, McShea et al. 1995). Concern related to excessive numbers of deer also extends to issues of public safety which include automobile collisions involving deer and transmission of Lyme disease (Porter et al. 1991). The white-tailed deer is remarkably well adapted to the human-altered environment. Without predation its high rate of reproduction allows populations to expand rapidly beyond what would be their natural limits. Consequently, active intervention by humans is necessary to ensure that negative impacts of deer on other species and ecosystems are mitigated.

The lessons learned from white-tailed deer management has application to other herbivores. These include elk, mule deer, and, perhaps, other species of large herbivores that evolved rapid rates of reproduction in response to predation and are adapted to edge habitats. Removal of predator control from these populations invites ecological disasters by permitting excessive resource consumption by single species to the detriment of whole communities of organisms. The stability of ecosystems supporting these large herbivores is dependent upon enlightened resource management that recognizes the ecological cost of emphasizing the resource needs of one or a few species. It is of interest that a growing portion of the public recognizes the negative impacts of removing predation, including hunting by humans, from large herbivore populations. However, they remain somewhat reluctant to support reintroduction of wolves into Yellowstone National Park and debate the value of mountain lions in California and elsewhere in the nation. It may be time for ecologists to add the benefit of large predators to the value of ecosystem services to society.

References

Adams, D.E., and R.C. Anderson. 1980. Species response to a moisture gradient in central Illinois forests. *American Journal of Botany* 67:381–392.

Alverson, W., D.S. Waller, and S.L. Solheim. 1988. Forests too deer: edge effects in northern Wisconsin. *Conservation Biology* 2:348–358.

Anderson, R.C. 1994. Height of white-flowered trillium (*Trillium grandiflorum*) as an index of deer browsing intensity. *Ecological Applications* 4:104–109.

Anderson, R.C., and O.L. Loucks. 1979. White-tail deer (*Odocoileus virginianus*) influence on structure and composition of *Tsuga canadensis* forests. *Journal of Applied Ecology* 16:855–861.

Anderson, R.C., and A.J. Katz. 1993. Recovery of browse-sensitive tree species following release from white-tailed (*Odocoileus virginianus*) Zimmerman browsing pressure. *Biological Conservation* 63:203–208.

Austin, P.J., Sucher L.A., Robbins C.T., and A.E. Hagerman. 1989. Tannin-binding proteins in saliva of deer and their absence in saliva of sheep and cattle. *Journal of Chemical Ecology* 15:1335–1347.]

Balgooyen, C., and D. Waller. 1995. The use of *Clintonia borealis* and other indicators to gauge impacts of white-tailed deer on plant communities in northern Wisconsin. *Natural Areas Journal* 15: 308–318.

Beals, E.G., and G. Cottam. 1960. Influence of deer on vegetation of the Apostle Island, Wisconsin. *Journal of Wildlife Management* 24:66–80.

Bersing, O. 1966. *A Century of Wisconsin Deer*, 2nd ed. Game Management Division, Wisconsin Conservation Department, Madison.

Canham, C.D., and O.L. Loucks. 1984. Catastrophic windthrow of the presettlement forest of Wisconsin. *Ecology* 65:803–809.

Case, D.J., and D.R. McCullough. 1987. The white-tailed deer of North Manitou Island. *Hilgardi* 55:1–57.

Clutton-Brock, T.H., and B.D. Albon. 1992. Trial and error in the highlands. *Nature* 358:11–12.

Curtis, J.T. 1959. *The Vegetation of Wisconsin*. University of Wisconsin Press, Madison.

Dahlberg, B.L., and R.C. Guettinger. 1956. *The White-Tailed Deer in Wisconsin*. Technical Wildlife Bulletin Number 14. Game Management Division, Wisconsin Conservation Department, Madison.

Dary, D.A. 1974. *The Buffalo Book*. The Swallow Press, Chicago, Ill.

DeCalestra, David S. 1994. Effect of white-tailed deer on songbirds within managed forests in Pennsylvania. *Journal of Wildlife Management* 58:711–718.

Englund, J.V., and W.J. Meyer. 1984. The impact of deer on 24 species of prairie forbs. In G. Clamber and R. Pebble, eds. *The Prairie Past, Present, and Future: Proceedings of the Ninth North American Prairie Conference*. Tri-College University Center For Environmental Studies, North Dakota State University, Fargo. 210–212.

Frelich, L.E., and C.G. Lorimer. 1985. Current and predicted long-term effect of deer browsing in hemlock forests in Michigan, USA. *Biological Conservation* 34:99–120.

Fritts, S.H., and L.N. Carbyn. 1995. Population viability, nature reserves, and the outlook for gray wolf conservation in North America. *Restoration Ecology* 3:26–38.

Girard, G.T., B.D. Anderson, and T.A. DeLaney. 1993. Managing conflicts with animal activists: white-tailed deer and Illinois Nature Preserves. *Natural Areas Journal* 13:10–17.

Guttenspergen, G. 1983. The minimum size for nature preserves: evidence from southeastern Wisconsin. *Natural Areas Journal* 3:38–46.

Habeck, J.R. 1960. Winter deer activity in the white cedar swamps of northern Wisconsin. *Ecology* 41:327–333.

Hett, J.M., and O.L. Loucks. 1976. Age structure models of balsam fir and eastern hemlock. *Journal of Ecology* 64:1029–1044.

Horsley, S.B., and B.A. Marquis. 1983. Interference by weeds and deer with Allegheny hardwood reproduction. *Canadian Journal of Forestry and Reclamation* 13:61–69.

Kelley, T.M. 1994. *Effect of White-Tailed Deer on the Understory Vegetation of an Oak-Hickory Forest and Growth of Trees in a White Pine Plantation*. Master's of Sciences thesis. Department of Biological Sciences. Illinois State University, Normal.

LaGory, M., K. LaGory, and D. Taylor. 1985. Winter browse availability and use by white-tailed deer in southeastern Indiana. *Journal of Wildlife Management* 49:120–124.

Larson, L., and G.K. Murdock. 1989. Small bison herd utilization of tallgrass prairie. In T. Bragg and J. Stubbendieck, eds. *Proceedings of the North American Prairie Conference, Prairie Pioneer: Ecology, History, and Culture*. University of Nebraska Printing, Lincoln. 243–245.

Leopold, A. 1943. Deer irruptions. *Transactions of the Wisconsin Academy of Science, Arts, and Letters* 35:351–366.

Leopold, A., L.K. Sowls, and D.L. Spencer. 1947. A survey of overpopulated deer ranges in the United States. *Journal of Wildlife Management* 11:162–177.

Martin, N.D. 1959. An analysis of forest succession of Algonquin Park, Ontario. *Ecological Monographs* 2:196–218.

McCaffery, K. 1986. On deer carrying capacity in northern Wisconsin. In R.J. Regan and S.R. Darling, compilers. *Transactions of the 22nd Northeast Deer Technical Committee.* Vermont Fish and Wildlife Department, Waterbury. 54–69.

McCullough, Y.B. 1980. *Niche Separation of Seven North American Ungulates on the National Bison Range, Montana.* Ph. D. dissertation, University of Michigan.

McFall, D. 1991. *A Directory of Illinois Nature Preserves.* Illinois Department of Conservation. Division of Natural Heritage. Springfield.

McShea, W.J., M.V. McDonald, E.S. Morton, R. Meier, and J.H. Rappole. 1995. Long-term trends in habitat selection by Kentucky warblers. *Auk* 112:375–381.

Miller, S.G., S.P. Bratton, J. Hadidian. 1992. Impacts of white-tailed deer on endangered and threatened vascular plants. *Natural Area Journal* 12:67–74.

Mladenoff, D.J., and F. Stearns 1993. Eastern hemlock regeneration and deer browsing in the northern Great Lakes region: a re-examination and model simulation. *Conservation Biology* 7:889–900.

Nixon, C.M., L.P. Hansen, P.A. Brewer, and J.E. Chelsvig. 1991. Ecology of white-tailed deer in an intensively farmed region of Illinois. *Wildlife Monographs* 118:1–77.

Pietsch, L.R. 1954. *White-tailed Deer Populations in Illinois.* Biological Survey Notes No. 43. Natural History Survey Division, Urbana.

Porter, W.F., R.W. Sage, and D.F. Behrend. 1991. Social organization in deer: implications for localized management. *Environmental Management* 15:809–814.

Risser, P.G. 1990. Landscape processes and the vegetation of the North American grassland. In S. Collins and L. Wallace, eds. Fire in the North American Prairie. University of Oklahoma Press, Norman, 133–146.

Robbins, C.S. 1980. Effect of forest fragmentation on breeding bird populations in the Piedmont of the Mid-Atlantic region. *Atlantic Naturalists* 33:131–136.

Robbins, C.S., J.R. Sauer, R.S. Greenberg, and S. Droege. 1989. Population declines in North American birds that migrate to the Neotropics. *Proceedings of the National Academy of Science (USA)* 86:7658–7662.

Robbins, C.T., T.A. Haney, A.E. Hagerman, O. Hjeljord, D.L. Baker, C.C. Schwartz, and W.W. Mautz. 1987. Role of tannins in defending plants against ruminants: reduction in protein availability. *Ecology* 68:98–107.

Ross, B.A., J.R. Bray, and W.H. Marshall. 1970. Effects of long-term deer exclusion on a *Pinus resinosa* forest in north-central Minnesota. *Ecology* 51:1089–1093.

Strole, T.A. 1988. *Influence of White-Tailed Deer (Odocoileus virginianus) Browsing on Successional Patterns and Woody Species Composition in Central Illinois Upland Forests.* Master's thesis, Illinois State University, Normal.

Strole, T.A. and R.C. Anderson. 1992. White-tailed deer browsing species preferences and implications for central Illinois forests. *Natural Areas Journal* 12:139–144.

Swift, E. 1948. *Wisconsin's Deer Damage Forest Reproduction Survey—Final Report.* Wisconsin Department of Conservation, Madison, WI. 347.

Tilghman, N. 1989. The impacts of white-tailed deer on forest regeneration in northwestern Pennsylvania. *Journal of Wildlife Management* 53:524–532.

Trefethen, J.B. 1975. *An American Crusade for Wildlife*. Winchester Press and the Boone and Crockett Club., Winchester, N.Y.

White, P., R.I. Miller, S.P. Bratton. 1983. Island biogeography and preserve design: preserving the vascular plants of Great Smoky Mountain National Park. *Natural Areas Journal* 3:4–13.

Witham, H.H., and J.M. Jones. 1987. *Chicago Urban Deer Study*. The Illinois Natural History Survey Reports. No. 265. Illinois Natural History Survey, Champaign.

Witham, J.H., and J.M. Jones. 1990. White-tailed deer abundance on metropolitan forest preserves during winter in northeastern Illinois. *Wildlife Society Bulletin* 18:13–16.

Witham, J.H., and J.M. Jones. 1992. *Biology, Ecology, and Management of Deer in the Chicago Metropolitan Area*. Final Report. Pittman-Robertson Project W-87-R. Center for Wildlife Ecology, Illinois Natural History Survey, Champaign.

7

Mammals of Illinois and the Midwest: Ecological and Conservation Issues for Human-Dominated Landscapes

Philip C. Mankin and Richard E. Warner
Department of Natural Resources and Environmental Sciences,
University of Illinois, 1102 S. Goodwin, Urbana, Illinois

In this chapter, we address how mammals have been affected by changes in midwestern landscapes over time, using Illinois as an example of extreme habitat disturbance. We will outline the key events which took place since the advent of European settlers, including an in-depth look at the last four decades, when land use changes have accelerated and anthropogenic disturbances have become even more dramatic.

This overview is particularly significant because many of the life history studies of mammals over the past century have focused on natural habitats. There has been little synthesis of how the highly disturbed environments of the Midwest have affected mammalian fauna, from the common extant species to those that have extirpated. As part of such a synthetic perspective, we focus on the historical reasons for the changes in composition of mammalian populations and in abundance of mammals.

Over much of the Midwest, agriculture has transformed the landscape to such an extent that, in many areas, it is impossible to detect what the original terrain looked like before the arrival of European settlers. Illinois has been the center of the storm for progressively intensive agricultural land use—a harbinger of change for the Corn Belt. The midwestern United States is a major agricultural center where 44% of the land area is devoted to crops (U.S. Department of Agriculture 1995). The amount of land devoted to row crops has more than doubled since the period of 1910–1950. Before 1950, corn and soybeans made up 17% of the farmland in the 12 north-central states, and by 1987 that figure had increased to 27% (U.S. Department of Commerce 1925, 1952, 1987). Some states such as Michigan, Wisconsin, and Minnesota have more natural habitat than Illinois, due partly to terrain and soil differences. Likewise, extreme western and southern Illinois have retained a higher degree of natural space than the rest of the state because topographic relief has prevented large-scale row crop planting.

The composition of bird and mammal communities is indicative of habitat changes, but when much of the natural environment has vanished, interpreting the impact of habitat on the vertebrate fauna is a difficult task. What are the historical reasons for the changes in composition of populations and abundance of wildlife? Why have some animals been able to survive and even prosper in spite of human influences and others not? In order to answer these questions, historical trends must first be analyzed and put into perspective with the current status of wildlife populations.

Much of the life history literature over the past century has focused on natural habitats. For a given animal, habitat is wherever it spends most of its time. In the Midwest, this can encompass woodlands, row crops, or barren fields. Even if there has not been enough time to adapt to changes in habitat in a long-term evolutionary sense, evidence indicates that behavioral adaptations are taking place (Henderson et al. 1985, Mankin 1993, Matthiae and Stearns 1981, Middleton and Merriam 1981, Nixon et al. 1991, Oxley et al. 1974, Wegner and Merriam 1990).

1800–1900

Around 1800 two-thirds of Illinois was a vast prairie interrupted occasionally by dendritic riparian areas. There were both dry (4.9 million ha) and wet (3.3 million ha) prairies (Havera 1985, Suloway and Hubbell 1994, Winsor 1975). Small northern portions of the state contained savannas, while the western and southern regions were mostly forested (Iverson et al. 1989). The wooded river banks were the first to be settled due to the prevalence of timber and animals (Hubert 1982).

In fact, the initial reduction in mammalian diversity had little to do with changes in the landscape. The first major impact on mammals was exploitation, for the purposes of economics (furs and hides), sustenance (meat), and control (competition and fear). In addition to providing food, the trapping of beaver *(Castor canadensis),* river otter *(Lutra canadensis),* muskrat *(Ondatra zibethicus),* and mink *(Mustela vison)* was a major source of income. Bison *(Bison bison)* also supplied hides and meat, but not to the extent that it did farther west on the Great Plains. Primarily economic interests led to the demise of the bison and elk *(Cervus elaphus)* by the early 19th century. Fear and perceived competition motivated pioneers to destroy mountain lion *(Felis concolor),* black bear *(Ursus americanus),* and gray wolf *(Canis lupus);* settlers saw the larger carnivores as competitors for game. The fisher *(Martes pennanti),* marten *(Martes americana),* porcupine *(Erethizon dorsatum),* wolverine *(Gulo gulo),* and lynx *(Felis lynx)* were believed to be present in Illinois (Hoffmeister 1989), and although they were not hunted or trapped extensively, the eventual destruction of their habitat ensured their extinction (Fig. 7.1).

By 1840, 50% of the presettlement forests were gone. With the invention of the steel plow in 1836, the conversion from prairie to cropland proceeded rapidly in the drier portions of the prairie (Iverson et al. 1989, Winsor 1975) (Fig. 7.2).

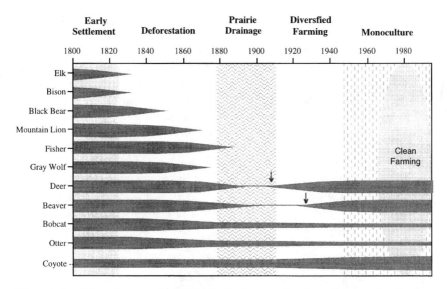

Figure 7.1. Selected mammals of Illinois, land use, and estimated times of extinction. Arrows mark periods of reintroductions.

From Hoffmeister 1989, Hubert 1982, Wood 1910; adapted from Wood 1910.

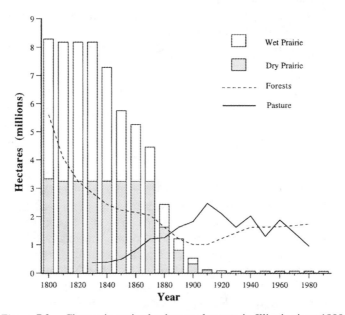

Figure 7.2. Change in major landscape elements in Illinois since 1800.

By 1870 most of the 4.9 million ha of more mesic dry prairie had been plowed to plant corn and wheat (Flagg 1875).

From 1870 to 1900 the remaining wet and marshy prairie areas in the state were nearly eliminated (Fig. 7.2). The advent of clay drainage tile systems, decreased rail transportation costs, and legislation to create drainage districts facilitated the demise of wet prairie (Anderson 1970, Winsor 1975). Drainage ditches were dug and many miles of naturally meandering streams were channelized. By about 1900, with the wetlands drained, the once vast prairie had been transformed into some of the most productive cropland in the world. Fencerows were established to graze livestock, bordering a vast patchwork of crops and pasture. The fencerows commonly provided a linear woody habitat that did not exist prior to agriculture.

As the prairie declined, primarily those species which could adapt to an agricultural environment prevailed. Moreover, removal of forests, which continued until about 1900, reduced the distribution and abundance of woodland mammals such as the bobcat *(Felis rufus)*, eastern chipmunk *(Tamias striatus)*, white-footed mouse *(Peromyscus leucopus)*, and tree squirrels.

1900–1950

The predominately rural human population of the first half of the 20th century no doubt controlled the abundance of most mammal species by habitat alteration and the taking of animals for a variety of reasons, including elimination of nuisance animals. Predator control was encouraged through bounties for species perceived as conflicting with various human interests (Hubert 1982). After game laws were strengthened in the early 1900s, the recovery of several threatened species of mammals might have been possible, had their habitats not been so dramatically altered.

Thus, the degradation of habitat was the second and most pervasive impact on mammalian fauna. By the early 1900s, the conversion from wilderness to agriculture had reached its peak (Fig. 7.2). Some land which had been cleared of forests was found to be unacceptable for profitable farming of crops and was allowed to revert to woodland, but with considerable grazing (U.S. Department of Commerce 1925). Through World War II, small diversified farms dominated the landscape, producing livestock and associated forage crops and cash grains.

Even with much of the land planted in crops, these small farms had extensive edge habitat such as fencerows and other field borders, and relatively undisturbed marginal areas. These characteristic farm mosaics, interspersed with woodland, allowed some mammals to prosper (Hoffmeister 1989, Matthiae and Stearns 1981). Species which benefitted the most were the coyote *(Canis latrans)*, raccoon *(Procyon lotor)*, woodchuck *(Marmota monax)*, opossum *(Didelphis virginiana)*, foxes, and rodents. Fencerows served as corridors and even refuges, especially for small edge-adapted species. The development of global grain markets was beginning by the end of this era.

1950–Present

The technological revolution in agriculture that began in the early 1900s accelerated after World War II. The landscape alterations that ensued had dramatic effects on mammals. For example, fall plowing was pervasive to help decrease insect populations, and larger, more powerful machinery allowed for the conversion of marginal areas to cropland, thus further reducing the remaining natural cover for all wildlife species. While machinery became more efficient, genetic research and the widespread application of herbicides, insecticides, and fertilizers greatly improved crop yields. Small grains such as wheat, oats, barley, and rye were being supplanted by soybeans and corn.

Of Illinois' 14.4 million ha, almost 81% is farmland (50% is row crops), less than 10% is forested, and the remaining landscape is urban, industrial, and transportation related (Neely and Heister 1987). From 1956 to 1989, the area in corn and soybeans increased 25% and 91%, respectively, while hay, small grains (oats and wheat), and noncrop acreages decreased 56%, 59%, and 50%, respectively (Fig. 7.3). Average county farm size increased 42% statewide. In 1964, only 29% of counties had an average farm size >100 ha, but after 23 years that percentage increased to 87%. These trends are important because the consolidation

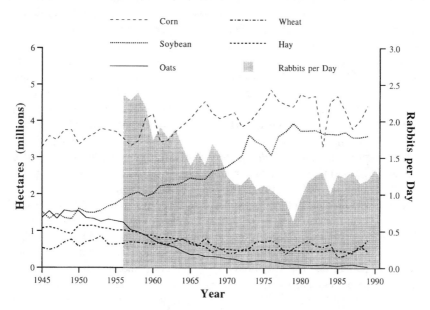

Figure 7.3. Acreages of selected crops in Illinois and the rabbit hunter harvest index.

of farms into relatively few larger farms brought a reduction in edge habitat, such as fencerows and windbreaks. In east-central Illinois, the most intensively farmed part of Illinois, 75% of a five-county region consists of row crops. The 37 natural areas designated by the Illinois Natural Areas Inventory (White 1978) make up only 0.17% of the five-county region, and excluding one area of 645 ha, the remaining 36 natural areas average 34 ha in size.

Generally, the effect of topographic relief is correlated negatively with row crop farming and positively with noncrop areas such as pasture and woodland (Iverson 1988). By 1980 only nine counties in Illinois had >25% of their land area in woodland (maximum of 55%), 48 counties contained 8–25% woodland, and the remaining 45 counties had <8% woodland. Even the heavily wooded counties have patches of timber of varying sizes and shapes resulting in high edge:interior ratios such that landscape patterns are heterogeneous.

Mammalian Responses to Land Use

The 12 north-central states have more than 100 species of mammals ranging in size from the black bear, elk, and moose *(Alces alces)* to the tiny pygmy shrew *(Sorex hoyi)* (Burt and Grossenheider 1976). Illinois, originally rich in prairie grasses and forests, was inhabited by as many as 83 species of mammals, including bison, black bear, mountain lion, and elk (Hoffmeister 1989). The only large mammal remaining in Illinois is a herbivore, the white-tailed deer *(Odocoileus virginianus)*. According to Hoffmeister (1989), there are at least 62 species of mammals in Illinois, of which seven are endangered and three are threatened. Over two-thirds of the mammals in the state are rat-sized or less (Hoffmeister 1989). At least 14 mammals have ranges which are restricted to certain geographical regions within Illinois. The swamp rabbit *(Sylvilagus aquaticus),* for example, is confined to the southern quarter of Illinois due to the drainage of floodplains, while the white-tailed jackrabbit *(Lepus townsendii)* is restricted to the northwestern sand prairie portion of the state (Hoffmeister 1989), although it has not been seen for more than a decade.

The eastern cottontail *(Sylvilagus floridanus)* in Illinois is a good example of a species responding to changing farm practices. Mankin (1993) reported that in recent decades wheat, noncrop land, and hay have been associated with the relative abundance of cottontails. Noncrop land includes all rural land not used for crops including wooded areas, pasture, riparian zones, and marginal areas. Those Illinois counties with more wheat and more noncrop land had the highest levels of cottontail abundance. Havera (1973) and Edwards et al. (1981) also found the annual harvest of cottontails by hunters to be correlated negatively with row crops and positively with grassland habitat (oats, hay, and brome). Storm and Shope (1989) found similar correlations for cottontails in southeastern Pennsylvania.

From the period 1956–69 to the period 1982–89, rabbit abundance decreased in all but one of the 102 Illinois counties, with an average decline of 41%. Although noncrop acreage declined, it continued to be more prevalent in western Illinois compared to the rest of the state. Thus, rabbit abundance declined less in that area, because the noncrop habitat was a stabilizing factor. The increase in corn and soybeans over recent decades has amplified the importance of noncrop land as rabbit habitat. It is no surprise that regions with more diverse habitat, including woodland with a variety of agricultural uses, can support higher populations than can less diverse regions.

Radio-tagged cottontails in east-central Illinois have been shown to adapt behaviorally to agricultural landscapes in surprising ways. Certainly, cottontails have adjusted to humans and urbanization, as seen by their presence in towns, but the structure of row crops and the absence of weed species in these fields would lead one to expect them to avoid row crops. On the contrary, the monitored cottontails spent roughly 75% of the time in row crops (Mankin 1993). As crops emerged, cottontails shifted their activities from farmsteads to corn, and then to soybeans as this crop began to provide concealment. The movement into row crops may be a response to predators. It is less likely that a rabbit will fall prey to coyotes, raptors, or domestic pets while hidden by corn or soybeans. Home ranges of cottontails in the intensively farmed study area were larger than those found in Wisconsin (43.3 ha vs 3.4 for males, 15.4 ha vs 1.3 for females) (Mankin 1993, Trent and Rongstad 1974).

Other species have shown interesting responses to agriculture as well. Two mammals now widespread in Illinois, the beaver and the white-tailed deer, recovered from near extirpation. These are examples of mammals that over many decades have come to tolerate humans and have adapted to highly fragmented landscapes. The beaver, nearly exterminated by 1900, was reintroduced in the 1930s and has made a successful comeback. Despite few trees for dam building, beavers in east-central Illinois have caused problems by using the few ecologically valued trees present to dam drainage streams. The white-tailed deer was also reintroduced in the early 1900s and their numbers have continually increased. In 1992, hunter harvest of deer was estimated at 127,341, compared to 46,531 ten years earlier.

Nixon et al. (1991) reported that deer adjusted their activities seasonally to make use of row crop cover during the summer, enabling them to use small woodlots and narrow riparian areas. They also found that deer use forage crops (alfalfa, wheat, and hay) in greater frequency than would be expected based on availability. Deer in east-central Illinois were considered to be in excellent condition (Nixon et al. 1991) as were the cottontails (Mankin 1993).

The coyote, a predator more abundant now than in the past, is common in the intensively farmed region of Illinois (Heske and Miller 1995, Hoffmeister 1989). As a predator, the coyote plays an important role in ecosystems and has also been of concern to livestock owners throughout the Midwest. In Kansas, for example, coyotes are the primary predator of livestock including poultry, swine, sheep, and cattle (Boggess et al. 1980).

Changes in woodland vegetation in Illinois as they have affected mammals is exemplified in the distribution and abundance of the gray squirrel *(Sciurus carolinensis).* The presence of the gray squirrel is strongly associated with the proportion of forested land with dense understory and an abundance of winter-storable foods, such as acorns, hickories, and walnuts (Nixon et al. 1978). Forests must be mature enough to provide reliable mast supplies and numerous cavities for nesting and escape. Thus, the renewal of trees on land unsuitable for intensive agricultural use can result in the maturation of forests and an increase in gray squirrels (Nixon and Hansen 1987, Nixon et al. 1978).

Today, much of the available habitat for Illinois mammals is different types of edge, and habitat alteration has blurred the concept of edge effect. In intensively farmed regions, classic edges between forests and prairie are far fewer than the edges between forests and crops or between different types of agricultural activities. Agricultural practices create sharp transitions between types of vegetation, resulting in ecotones of an abrupt nature, both spatially and temporally (di Castri and Hansen 1992). It can be said that an entirely new biome has been created by intensive agriculture—an extremely dynamic one. For wildlife populations, the present-day practice of harvesting crops in a matter of days or weeks is comparable to the destructive alterations of habitat which accompany many natural catastrophes. Although natural stochastic events of catastrophic nature have been occurring over evolutionary time, the regular and dramatic alteration of habitat by farming is unprecedented. Thus, rather than a habitat of choice, agriculture can become the only habitat available.

Through ongoing environmental education, predators are now generally viewed as an integral part of the ecosystem and are valued. But predators must have a prey base they can depend on over many years. Consequently, the landscape should also provide for species like rodents, ground squirrels, and rabbits in order for the predators to maintain their numbers. Predation is a major cause of bird nesting failure and mammals are an important component of those predators (Best 1978, Maxson and Oring 1978, Schranck 1972). The role of predation has been altered by changes in the landscape (Mankin and Warner 1992, Matthiae and Stearns 1981, Wilcove 1985) as can be seen from data on mammalian nest predators (Bowman and Harris 1980, Marini et al. 1995). For example, ecotones have been shown to have increased nest predation (Best and Stauffer 1980, Gates and Gysel 1978), and there is evidence that edge effects have affected the predator/prey systems in highly fragmented forests (Angelstam 1986, Best 1978, Heske 1995, Small and Hunter 1988) and grasslands (Dumke and Pils 1979, Johnson and Temple 1990).

At least seven species of Illinois mammals have expanded their range over the last 50 years (Getz et al. 1978, Gremillion-Smith 1985, Hoffmeister 1989, Klimstra and Roseberry 1969). The least weasel *(Mustela nivalis),* meadow vole

(Microtus pennsylvanicus), western harvest mouse *(Reithrodontomys megalotis),* and possibly the badger *(Taxidea taxus)* have expanded their ranges southward. The beaver, southeastern shrew *(Sorex longirostris),* and masked shrew *(Sorex cinereus)* have extended their ranges in other directions. It is difficult to conclude whether the expansion of these species was because of, or in spite of, modern agriculture. Also, the importance of corridors to achieve range or population expansion is probably highly variable among species and is poorly understood (Hobbs 1992).

Corridors and Linkages

Local extinctions can result from predation, disease, competition, hunting and trapping, or destruction of habitat. If a habitat is destroyed and the animals are not destroyed with it, then they must find refuge elsewhere. Their ability to survive the move to a suitable place is contingent upon several factors, such as mobility, risk from predation, distance to the nearest suitable habitat, and connectivity. Some mammals do not have the same ability as birds to quickly exploit a patchy environment, and the extent to which habitats are connected may be critical (Getz et al. 1978, Henderson et al. 1985, Henein and Merriam 1990, Wegner and Merriam 1990). These linkages can take the form of waterways, railroads, fencerows, and roadsides. Such corridors, to be truly useful, must link one habitat with another, but their impact on population dynamics has yet to be assessed.

The most promising of the corridors are the waterways and adjacent riparian zones. Illinois has over 41,800 km of flowing streams (Illinois Department of Energy 1994). Drainage ditches dug in the late 1800s and early 1900s increased the total waterway miles, but channelization reduced the length of some of the original streams. Approximately 32% of Illinois' stream length has been channelized, resulting in destruction of natural riparian habitat (Illinois Department of Energy 1994). Although 67% of the land along the streams in the major drainage basins has been classified as forest and mixed woody vegetation, it is limited to within 25 m on either side of the streams. The habitat type most closely associated with waterways in Illinois is bottomland forest, totaling 307,043 ha or 2.1% of the state (Suloway and Hubbell 1994). Stream corridors are among several landscape types targeted for the planning of a regional greenway network in northeastern Illinois connecting urban and rural environments (Northeastern Illinois Planning Commission 1992).

In 1995, active rail routes in Illinois totaled 12,700 km, declining from over 17,400 km in 1975 (Ill. Dept. Trans. 1976, 1996). Railroads are generally constructed on a raised bed allowing good drainage. Thus, railroads not only provide travel lanes, but also habitation for numerous small mammals, including the woodchuck. Franklin's ground squirrel *(Spermophilus franklinii),* long-tailed weasel *(Mustela frenata)*, eastern cottontail, pocket gopher *(Geomys bursarius)*, striped skunk *(Mephitis mephitis)*, mice, and voles. Predatory mammals are also attracted to these areas as potential food sources because of other wildlife fauna.

Although the railroad right-of-way width varies, there is approximately 2.7 ha of grassland per km along active rural rail lines. It is unknown how much grassland remains along the >4,700 km of abandoned railway. Where the terrain was favorable, old rail beds have often been plowed to expand agricultural land. The amount of abandoned rails which have reverted to a more natural state is unknown, but public and private organizations such as the Illinois Department of Natural Resources, the Nature Conservancy, Grand Prairie Friends, and Rails-to-Trails, Inc. have been working towards maintaining or acquiring some of the abandoned railways for the benefit of plants and animals.

Fencerows have been shown to provide important dispersal routes as well as areas for habitation (Wegner and Merriam 1979). Henderson et al. (1985) found fencerows to support breeding populations of chipmunks, which also used them for linkages between woodlots. The small mammal populations which support the larger carnivores in an agro-ecosystem depend heavily on fencerows. Wegner and Merriam (1990) found that the higher the intensity of farming, the more white-footed mice were found in fencerows.

We compared aerial photographs of Champaign County in east-central Illinois for 1954 and 1982 covering a ten square km agricultural area and calculated the change in total length of fencerows surrounding agricultural fields. Linear fence-row length went from 19.5 km to 3.8 km, a decrease of 80%. This occurred during the period of farm consolidation and expansion. An important consideration for fencerows (or any other corridor) as wildlife habitat is the question: what does it connect? Fencerows, more than the other types of corridors, are likely to fall into the category of dead ends. Some may act as linear islands of marginal vegetation which do not go anywhere (Hobbs 1992).

The least natural of the corridors are the roadsides, with their primary vegetation consisting of mowed introduced grasses. Illinois has over 154,500 km of rural roads, including interstate, federal and state highways, and county and township roads. Each type has its own characteristic roadside right-of-way distance, ranging from 91 m along interstates down to 12 m on township roads. Subtracting the combined surface area of the road lanes and shoulders, there is about 15,000 ha of grassland rights-of-way along interstate highways, 36,000 ha along state and federal highways, and more than 109,000 ha along county and township roads totaling more than 161,000 ha of linear grassland in Illinois.

Although roadside corridors are narrow, they should not be overlooked as potential avenues of travel for small mammals, as evidenced by roadkills (Leedy 1975). In areas where little natural vegetation exists, such as in the cash grain region of the Midwest, these ribbons of grassland may be partially responsible for range expansion. For example, the meadow vole, an important prey species of several raptors, snakes, and foxes, is believed to have expanded its range further southward through the use of the interstate highway system (Getz et al. 1978). Thirteen-lined ground squirrels *(Spermophilus tridecemlineatus)* make extensive use of short grasses and are prevalent along roadsides. Hawks, searching for these and other prey, can be seen along interstate highways.

The quality of the various corridors is highly variable, and therefore must be taken into account (Henein and Merriam 1990). However, wildlife managers face special challenges where there are few or no high-quality corridors, where the only linear habitat is a mowed roadside along intensively farmed fields, fencerows are far and few between, and fields are tilled close to the edges of streams. In addition, there is concern for the possibility of overselling the potential of corridors (Harrison 1992, Hobbs 1992, Simberloff and Cox 1987, Simberloff et al. 1992). In fact, corridors of all kinds have the potential to encourage mobility of undesirable and/or overabundant species as well as desirable ones. More research needs to be done in order to make informed decisions on preserving or creating corridors.

Mammals and Humans

Enhancing the diversity and abundance of mammals will likely result in increased contacts with people. Suburban sprawl has produced a positive effect on the abundance of raccoons, opossums, cottontails, deer, and thirteen-lined ground squirrels, to the delight of some and the dismay of others. Conflicts between mammals and humans are numerous: deer/vehicle collisions are common; cottontails, deer, and voles cause damage to ornamental plants, orchards, and tree farms; ground squirrels are a problem to golf courses and cemeteries; woodchuck burrows undermine structures; muskrats weaken earthen dams; and beavers flood property. The introduced black rat *(Rattus rattus),* Norway rat *(Rattus norvegicus),* and house mouse *(Mus musculus)* are of concern for health reasons, especially in urban areas.

Conover et al. (1995) estimated that in the U.S. each year about 75,000 people are injured or become ill because of wildlife-related incidents. Many of the human-wildlife conflicts have well-recognized economic implications, but one of the most important aspects of mammal distribution and abundance is the prevalence of disease (Telford and Spielman 1989). Mammals can be reservoirs or vectors for Lyme disease, distemper, tularemia, and rabies. In Illinois from 1971–1994, 38% of the skunks tested were positive for rabies, followed by cattle (8%), bats (6%), foxes (6%), horses (4%), cats (0.4%), dogs (0.4%), and raccoons (0.2%) (Langkop 1995).

Our concern for animals has also brought about ambivalent feelings toward management activities. Suburban homeowners like to have deer and cottontail nearby as part of living close to nature, but do not want them eating their gardens. Indeed, most of the loss of farmland in the last few decades has been the result of urban sprawl. This transformation from farmland to suburbia will likely increase the numbers of urban mammal pests like raccoon and deer. The frequent movement between urban and nonurban environments decreases the emphasis on physical boundaries. As noted for various flora and fauna (Davis and Glick 1978), less sensitive species can become dominant in urban ecosystems.

The domestic cat has also thrived because of humans and is an important predator, especially in rural environments. As shown by a radiotelemetry study in the intensively farmed area of east-central Illinois, free-ranging cats commonly killed rodents, rabbits, and other wildlife (Warner 1985). When not on farmsteads, 73% of the radiolocations of 11 rural cats were found to be in linear or edge habitat. The farmsteads in the study averaged 5.6 cats per farm residence. In Illinois, there were an estimated 1.5 million cats considered to be urban or house cats, but there may be 4 million free-ranging rural cats (Warner 1985). In 1995, an estimated 33% of U.S. residences had at least one cat for a total of 65 million cats (Pet Food Institute 1996).

Mammal Conservation Efforts

The effects of habitat changes on mammals are far from predictable and not well understood. Several possibilities exist for enhancing wildlife communities in fragmented landscapes: one is to provide large patches of suitable habitat, such as forests, prairies or wetlands, in close proximity to each other and the second is to create extensive corridors linking widely dispersed patches. The backbone of such a corridor system—the streams, railroads, and roadsides—is already in place. Windbreaks can serve as wildlife habitat and increase diversity in the agricultural regions. The value of fencerows and shelterbelts to both agriculture and wildlife has been reported by Bennett et al. (1994) and Swihart and Yahner (1982a, 1982b, 1983, 1984). Regardless of the target species, strong environmental programs (i.e., Roadsides for Wildlife, Private Land Wildlife Habitat Initiative, Pheasants Forever, Quail Unlimited, Ducks Unlimited, the Nature Conservancy) can increase the number of cooperators in habitat reclamation, but their impact on wildlife populations has not been adequately assessed.

The overriding concern of most landowners is not the restoration of the wilderness, but the economics of living and the fear of losing what one has worked hard to attain. Those landowners and agencies who are trying to establish agricultural systems which protect soil from wind and water erosion and provide riparian buffers to leach out harmful chemicals in our water supplies should be encouraged, as they will set the example for others. But we must recognize that these noble efforts will miss many important mammals and other wildlife species that require larger, more natural habitats. On two of the few relatively large grasslands in Illinois, Midewin National Tallgrass Prairie and Nachusa Grasslands, managers are exploring the opportunities that exist to reintroduce bison, and possibly elk, as part of their ecosystem management.

Emerging Concerns and Trends

Agricultural practices have been changing in recent years. Conservation tillage, including ridge till, mulch till, and no-till, is defined as leaving at least 30% of the crop residue on the soil after harvesting. Conservation tillage was conducted on 39% of Illinois farmland in 1995 (Conservation Technology Information Center 1995). The long-term effect of these cropping patterns on wildlife is unclear, but such cropland has encouraged avian nesting along with mammalian nest predators (Basore et al. 1986).

The recurring theme in most discussions of wildlife is the quality and quantity of habitat at all levels, including local, meta-, and mega-scales. Some mammals present in low numbers will take advantage of the slightest improvement in their local environment. If enough attention is devoted to the renewal of natural vegetation, mammals and other animals will likely find it, provided that distances from populated regions are not too far for dispersal. This is not to say that we should ignore opportunities to preserve or restore small, local patches which may be isolated by a sea of row crops. Such fragments may show little effect in the short-term, but could provide important benefits into the future as stepping stones along corridors. But realistically, regions of intensive agriculture are not going to be removed from food production to create large habitat reserves. As much as we may argue for preserving and restoring large reserves for conservation, in regions of extreme disturbance, numerous small patches (Quinn and Harrison 1988) and corridor linkages (Harris 1984) are going to be the gradual successes leading to biotic richness.

We tend to emphasize the lack of medium- and large-sized mammals in the agricultural landscape, but we need to begin not with the animals, but with the land itself. Even a landscape left undisturbed and unmanaged will support small herbivores and insectivores, including both birds and mammals. These will, in turn, attract avian and mammalian predators to the area. Given a modicum of habitat management, such an area can sustain a higher level of species richness and diversity, if this is our goal. We have seen that many species will readily adjust and adapt when given the opportunity. But once again, when this is near human development, conflicts will arise between nature and economic interests.

Thus, we can learn from the areas of extreme disturbance in Illinois. Preventing the further loss of suitable habitat is far more feasible than trying to recreate an ecosystem to replace the one which has emerged due to human disturbance. There is a need to continue monitoring these new ecotones and their wildlife in order to make decisions on conservation efforts.

Conclusion

Mammals are important for hunting and trapping, are vectors for diseases, and have complex predator/prey functions in midwestern ecosystems. Of increasing concern to society, they represent the wilderness of the past. With the loss of forests, prairies, and wetlands, mammals have had to adapt to radical changes in both their physical environment and the activities of humans from 1800 to the present. Many natural features present 200, 100, or just 50 years ago are now missing. Maintaining existing natural habitat is of prime importance for providing for the long-term viability of mammal populations.

A long-term perspective of the mammals in Illinois and surrounding regions brings forth several ecology- and conservation-related points, where anthropogenic disturbances abound. These include:

Relatively little attention has been paid to highly disturbed and fragmented landscapes compared with ecological studies of more natural habitats. Both areas of research are needed for determining changes in trends.

The most common management activities associated with mammals have been monitoring of abundance and regulation of exploitation. In addition, there are emerging efforts to curb overpopulation and intervene for imperiled species.

The effects of losing the large mammals, as predicted by ecological theory regarding keystone species and other community-level dynamics, are not clear. Perhaps these effects have been masked, in part, by the continued dramatic effects of human settlement and other disturbances. Nonetheless, predictions about how various species will fare in human-dominated landscapes, based primarily on their niches in natural landscapes, have often been short-sighted.

Corridor management for mammals should become a focus of research to determine both benefits and drawbacks. Both line (sufficient for movement only) and strip (sufficient for reproduction) corridors are potential habitats for mammals in the Midwest; however, for all but the smallest mammals, many key habitats today exist as relative degrees of edge.

The alteration of the intricate relationships between mammals and their environments increasingly has led to coping with extremely unstable environments and altered ecological linkages.

Even if there has not been enough evolutionary time to adapt to changes in habitat, there is evidence that behavioral adaptations are taking place for some species.

Having a vision for an ecologically sound future is essential, while we work with the reality of today, including conflicting public attitudes, limited funding, and fragmented landscapes. A shift from local to comprehensive regional approaches (Noss 1983) is slowly taking place. The relatively natural ecosystems, agro-ecosystems, and urban ecosystems of the Midwest each have unique elements, but they are interconnected, and interact in ways that conservationists are only beginning to acknowledge. Determining the patterns and complexity inherent in ecosystems is even more difficult where the land is so radically disturbed. The challenge of understanding this larger, intricate system lies in the continued development of relevant theories and research.

References

Anderson, R.C. 1970. Prairies in the prairie state. *Transactions of the Illinois State Academy of Science* 63:214–221.

Angelstam, P. 1986. Predation on ground-nesting birds' nests in relation to predator densities and edge habitat. *Oikos* 47:365–373.

Basore, N.S., L.B. Best, and J.B. Wooley. 1986. Bird nesting in Iowa no-tillage and tilled cropland. *Journal of Wildlife Management* 50:19–28.

Bennett, A.F., K. Henein, and G. Merriam. 1994. Corridor use and the elements of corridor quality: chipmunks and fencerows in a farmland mosaic. *Biological Conservation* 68:155–165.

Best, L.B. 1978. Field sparrow reproductive success and nesting ecology. *Auk* 95:9–22.

Best, L.B., and D.F. Stauffer. 1980. Factors affecting nesting success in riparian bird communities. *Condor* 82:149–158.

Boggess, E.K., F.R. Henderson, and C.W. Spaeth. 1980. Managing predator problems: practices and procedures for preventing and reducing livestock losses. Kansas State University Cooperative Extension Service Publication, C-620, New York.

Bowman, G.B., and L.D. Harris. 1980. Effect of spatial heterogeneity on ground-nest depredation. *Journal of Wildlife Management* 44:806–813.

Burt, W.H., and R.P. Grossenheider. 1976. *A Field Guide to the Mammals of America North of Mexico*. Peterson Field Guide Series 5. Houghton Mifflin Co., Boston, MA.

Conover, M.R., W.C. Pitt, K.K. Kessler, T.J. DuBow, and W.A. Sanborn. 1995. Review of human injuries, illnesses, and economic losses caused by wildlife in the United States. *Wildlife Society Bulletin* 23:407–414.

Conservation Technology Information Center, 1995. *National crop residue management survey. Executive summary.* West Lafayette, Indiana.

Davis, A.M., and T.F. Glick. 1978. Urban ecosystems and island biogeography. *Environmental Conservation* 5:299–304.

di Castri, F., and A.J. Hansen. 1992. The environment and development crises as determinants of landscape dynamics. In F. di Castri and A.J. Hansen, eds. *Landscape Boundaries: Consequences for Biotic Diversity and Ecological Flows.* Springer-Verlag, New York.

Dumke, R.T., and C.M. Pils. 1979. Renesting and dynamics of nest site selection by Wisconsin pheasants. *Journal of Wildlife Management* 43:705–716.

Edwards, W.R., S.P. Havera, R.F. Labisky, J.A. Ellis, and R.E. Warner. 1981. The abundance of cottontails in relation to agricultural land use in Illinois (U.S.A.) 1956–1978, with comments on mechanisms of regulation. In K. Meyers and C.D. MacInnes, eds. *Proceedings of the World Lagomorph Conference.* University of Guelph, Ontario, 761–798.

Flagg, W.C. 1875. The Agriculture of Illinois, 1683–1876. *Transactions of the Department of Agriculture of the State of Illinois* 8:287–308.

Gates, J.E., and L.W. Gysel. 1978. Avian nest dispersion and fledging success in field-forest ecotones. *Ecology* 59:871–883.

Getz, L.L., F.R. Cole, and D.L. Gates. 1978. Interstate roadsides as dispersal routes for *Microtus pennsylvanicus. Journal of Mammalogy* 59:208–212.

Gremillion-Smith, K. 1985. Range extension of the badger *(Taxidea taxus)* in southern Illinois. *Transactions of the Illinois Academy of Science* 78:111–114.

Harris, L.D. 1984. *The Fragmented Forest.* University of Chicago Press, Ill.

Harrison, R.L. 1992. Toward a theory of inter-refuge corridor design. *Conservation Biology* 6:293–295.

Havera, S.P. 1973. *The Relationship of Illinois Weather and Agriculture to the Eastern Cottontail Rabbit.* Illinois State Water Survey Technical Report. Champaign, Ill.

Havera, S.P. 1985. *Waterfowl of Illinois: Status and Management. Final Federal Aid Performance Report, 1980–1985.* Cooperative Waterfowl Research W-88-R. Submitted by Illinois Natural History Survey to Illinois Dept. of Conservation. Springfield, Ill.

Henderson, M.T., G. Merriam, and J. Wegner. 1985. Patchy environments and species survival: chipmunks in an agricultural mosaic. *Biological Conservation* 31:95–105.

Henein, K., and G. Merriam. 1990. The elements of connectivity where corridor quality is variable. *Landscape Ecology* 4:157–170.

Heske, E.J., and M. Miller. 1995. Coyotes in the cornfields. *Illinois Natural History Survey Reports* 334:1.

Heske, E.J. 1995. Mammalian abundances on forest-farm edges versus forest interiors in southern Illinois: is there an edge effect? *Journal of Mammalogy* 76:562–568.

Hobbs, R.J. 1992. The role of corridors in conservation: solution or bandwagon? *Trends in Ecology & Evolution* 7:389–392.

Hoffmeister, D.F. 1989. *Mammals of Illinois.* University of Illinois Press, Urbana.

Hubert, G.F., Jr. 1982. History of midwestern furbearer management and a look to the future. In G.C. Sanderson, ed. *Midwest Furbearer Management, Symposium, North Central Section, Central Mountains and Plains Section, and Kansas Chapter.* Wildlife Society, 175–191.

Illinois Department of Energy and Natural Resources. 1994. *The Changing Illinois Environment: Critical Trends.* vol. 3, *Ecological Resources.* Illinois Department of Energy and Natural Resources, Springfield.

Illinois Department of Transportation. 1976. 1975 Illinois railroad inventory. Illinois Department of Transportation, Bureau of Railroads. Springfield, Ill.

Illinois Department of Transportation. 1996. Fiscal Year 1997 proposed rail improvement program. Illinois Department of Transportation Bureau of Railroads. Springfield, Ill.

Iverson, L.R. 1988. Land-use changes in Illinois, USA: The influence of landscape attributes on current and historic land use. *Landscape Ecology* 2:45–61.

Iverson, L.R., R.L. Oliver, D.P. Tucker, P.G. Risser, C.D. Burnett, and R.G. Rayburn. 1989. The forest resources of Illinois: an atlas and analysis of spatial and temporal trends. Illinois Natural History Survey Special Publication 11. Champaign, Ill.

Johnson, R.G., and S.A. Temple. 1990. Nest predation and brood parasitism of tallgrass prairie birds. *Journal of Wildlife Management* 54:106–111.

Klimstra, W.D., and J.L. Roseberry. 1969. Additional observations on some southern Illinois mammals. *Transactions of the Illinois Academy of Science* 62:413–417.

Langkop, C.W. 1995. *Animal Rabies Surveillance—1994.* Memorandum. Illinois Department of Public Health. Springfield.

Leedy, D.L. 1975. *Highway-Wildlife Relationships.* vol. 1, *A State-of-the-Art Report.* Federal Highway Administration, Washington, D.C.

Mankin, P.C. 1993. *Agricultural land use and the eastern cottontail in Illinois.* Ph.D. thesis, University of Illinois, Urbana.

Mankin, P.C., and R.E. Warner. 1992. Vulnerability of ground nests to predation on an agricultural habitat island in east-central Illinois. *American Midland Naturalist* 128:281–291.

Marini, M.A., S.K. Robinson, and E.J. Heske. 1995. Edge effects on nest predation in the Shawnee National Forest, southern Illinois. *Biological Conservation* 74:203–213.

Matthiae, P.E., and F. Stearns. 1981. Mammals in forest islands in southeastern Wisconsin. In R.L. Burgess and D.M. Sharpe, eds. *Forest Dynamics in Man-Dominated Landscapes.* Springer-Verlag, New York, 55–56.

Maxson, S.J., and L.W. Oring. 1978. Mice as a source of egg loss among ground-nesting birds. *Auk* 95:582–584.

Middleton, J., and G. Merriam. 1981. Woodland mice in a farmland mosaic. *Journal of Applied Ecology* 18:703–710.

Neely, R.D., and C.G. Heister, compilers. 1987. *The Natural Resources of Illinois: Introduction and Guide.* Illinois Natural History Survey Special Publication 6. Champaign, Ill.

Nixon, C.M., and L.P. Hansen. 1987. *Managing Forests to Maintain Populations of Gray and Fox Squirrels.* Illinois Department of Conservation Technical Bulletin 5. Springfield.

Nixon, C.M., L.P. Hansen, P.A. Brewer, and J.E. Chelsvig. 1991. Ecology of white-tailed deer in an intensively farmed region of Illinois. *Wildlife Monographs* 118:1–77.

Nixon, C.M., S.P. Havera, and R.E. Greenberg. 1978. *Distribution and Abundance of Gray Squirrels in Illinois.* Illinois Natural History Survey Biological Notes 105. Champaign, Ill.

Northeastern Illinois Planning Commission. 1992. *Northeastern Illinois Regional Greenways Plan.* Chicago, Ill.

Noss, R.F. 1983. A regional landscape approach to maintain diversity. *Bioscience* 33:700–706.

Oxley, D.J., M.B. Fenton, and G.R. Carmody. 1974. The effects of roads on populations of small mammals. *Journal of Applied Ecology* 11:51–59.

Pet Food Institute. 1996. Pet Food Institute Fact Sheet. Pet Food Institute. Washington, D.C. 6 pp.

Quinn, J.F., and S.P. Harrison. 1988. Effects of fragmentation and isolation on species richness: evidence from biogeographic patterns. *Oecologia* 75:132–140.

Schranck, B.W. 1972. Waterfowl nest cover and some predation relationships. *Journal of Wildlife Management* 36:182–186.

Simberloff, D., and J. Cox. 1987. Consequences and costs of conservation corridors. *Conservation Biology* 1:63–71.

Simberloff, D., J.A. Farr, J. Cox, and D.W. Mehlman. 1992. Movement corridors: conservation bargains or poor investments? *Conservation Biology* 6:493–504.

Small, M.F., and M.L. Hunter. 1988. Forest fragmentation and avian nest predation in forested landscapes. *Oecologia* 76:62–64.

Storm, G.L., and W.K. Shope. 1989. Cottontail populations in changing farm/forest habitats. In J.C. Finley and M.C. Brittingham eds. *Timber Management and Its Effects on Wildlife, Proceedings of the 1989 Pennsylvania State Forest Resources Issues Conference.* Pennsylvania State University, University Park, 122–145.

Suloway, L., and M. Hubbell. 1994. *Wetland Resources of Illinois: An Analysis and Atlas.* Illinois Natural History Survey Special Publication 15. Champaign, Ill.

Swihart, R.K., and R.H. Yahner. 1982a. Habitat features influencing use of farmstead shelterbelts by the eastern cottontail *(Sylvilagus floridanus). American Midland Naturalist* 107:411–414.

———. 1982b. Eastern cottontail use of fragmented farmland habitat. *Acta Theriologica* 27:257–273.

———. 1983. Browse preferences of jackrabbits and cottontails for species used in shelterbelts plantings. *Journal of Forestry* 81:92–94.

———. 1984. Winter use of insular habitat patches by the eastern cottontail. *Acta Theriologica* 29:45–56.

Telford, S.R., III, and A. Spielman. 1989. Competence of a rabbit-feeding *Ixodes* (Acari: Ixodidae) as a vector of the Lyme disease spirochete. *Journal of Medical Entomology* 26:118–121.

Trent, T.T., and O.R. Rongstad. 1974. Home range and survival of cottontail rabbits in southwestern Wisconsin. *Journal of Wildlife Management* 49:340–346.

U.S. Department of Agriculture. 1995. *Natural Resources Conservation Service. Summary Report 1992.* National Resources Inventory, Washington, D.C.

U.S. Department of Commerce. 1925. *U.S. Census of Agriculture, 1925.* vol. II, *General Report on Field Crops and Vegetables.* Bureau of Census, Washington, D.C.

U.S. Department of Commerce. 1952. *U.S. Census of Agriculture, 1952.* vol. II, *General Report on Field Crops and Vegetables.* Bureau of Census, Washington, D.C.

U.S. Department of Commerce. 1987. *U.S. Census of Agriculture, 1987.* vol. II, *General Report on Field Crops and Vegetables.* Bureau of Census, Washington, D.C.

Warner, R.E. 1985. Demography and movements of free-ranging domestic cats in rural Illinois. *Journal of Wildlife Management* 49:340–346.

Wegner, J.F., and G. Merriam. 1979. Movements by birds and small mammals between a wood and adjoining farmland habitats. *Journal of Applied Ecology* 16:349–357.

Wegner, J., and G. Merriam. 1990. Use of spatial elements in a farmland mosaic by a woodland rodent. *Biological Conservation* 54:263–276.

White, J. 1978. *Illinois Natural Areas Inventory Technical Report.* vol. I, *Survey Methods and Results.* Illinois Natural Areas Inventory, Urbana.

Wilcove, D.S. 1985. Nest predation in forest tracts and the decline of migratory songbirds. *Ecology* 66:1211–1214.

Winsor, A.W. 1975. *Artificial Drainage of East-Central Illinois, 1820–1920.* Ph.D. thesis, University of Illinois, Urbana.

Wood, F.E. 1910. A study of the mammals of Champaign County, Illinois. *Bulletin of the Illinois State Laboratory of Natural History* 8:501–613.

8

Effectiveness of Small Nature Preserves for Breeding Birds

Scott K. Robinson, Jeffrey D. Brawn, and Jeffrey P. Hoover
Illinois Natural History Survey, 607 East Peabody Dr., Champaign, IL 61820

Introduction

The ecological effects of habitat fragmentation pose problems for birds breeding in small nature preserves. Negative effects of habitat fragmentation have been well documented in breeding birds of midwestern forests and grasslands (Robinson 1988, Robinson and Wilcove 1994, Herkert 1994, Robinson et al. 1995). Area sensitivity, the absence of birds from small tracts even when suitable habitat is present, is pronounced in midwestern grasslands (Herkert 1991) and forests (Bond 1957, Kendeigh 1982, Ambuel and Temple 1982, Hayden et al. 1985, Blake and Karr 1984, 1987). Freemark and Collins (1992) found that area sensitivity was more extreme in the isolated tracts of the Midwest than in the more closely spaced tracts of forest of eastern North America. Although there are few long-term censuses from midwestern fragmented habitats, available evidence suggests long-term declines in populations of many species in fragmented grasslands (Herkert et al. 1992) and eastern forests (Hagan 1993, Wilcove and Robinson 1990).

A frequently hypothesized cause of area sensitivity and local population declines of certain species within fragmented landscapes is reproductive failure (reviewed in Temple and Cary 1988, Askins et al. 1990, Wilcove and Robinson 1990, Faaborg et al. 1993, Robinson and Wilcove 1994). Fragmented forests are characterized by high levels of edge-related nest predation (Gates and Gysel 1978, Angelstom 1986), brood parasitism by brown-headed cowbirds *(Molothrus ater)* (Brittingham and Temple 1983), or both (Temple and Cary 1988, Robinson 1992, Johnson and Temple 1990, Robinson et al. 1995). Brood parasitism severely reduces nesting success because host species raise cowbird young in place of their own (Friedmann 1929, Rothstein 1975, May and Robinson 1985, Robinson et al. 1993, in press-a,b). In combination, high levels of parasitism and predation may drive local populations to extirpation in the absence of immigration (Temple and Cary 1988, Brawn and Robinson 1996).

Fragmentation-related problems with nesting success are particularly severe in chronically fragmented sections of the Midwest (Gibbs and Faaborg 1990, Robinson et al. 1995). Community-wide levels of brood parasitism in small Illinois woodlots (Robinson 1992, Robinson et al. in press-b) are among the highest documented. A study of geographical variation in parasitism levels of the wood thrush *(Hylocichla mustelina)* showed the highest intensity in the Midwest (Hoover and Brittingham 1993). In the Bariboo Hills of south-central Wisconsin, parasitism levels near edges averaged 50–80% (Brittingham and Temple 1983).

Demographic data suggest that populations of many forest-breeding species in severely fragmented landscapes may be *sinks* (*sensu* Pulliam 1988) that produce too few young to compensate for adult mortality (Robinson 1992, Brawn and Robinson 1996, Trine et al. in press). Rates of parasitism and predation are so much lower in more forested landscapes (>75%) that they may act as *sources* that produce a surplus of young able to recolonize small tracts in fragmented landscapes (Robinson et al. 1995, Thompson et al. in press). The persistence of nonreproducing populations in small fragments provides some of the best evidence to date that source-sink dynamics operate on a regional scale (Robinson 1992, Robinson et al. 1995, Brawn and Robinson 1996). Bird populations in small forest tracts in northern Missouri, Illinois, and southern Wisconsin may be maintained by immigrants from forested regions in the Missouri Ozarks, the Hoosier National Forest area of south-central Indiana, and in northern Wisconsin and Minnesota (Robinson et al. 1995), or even from outside the region.

In this chapter, we use Illinois as a case study to assess how effective nature preserves are in preserving the forest bird communities in a chronically fragmented landscape. We first examine their effectiveness in providing habitat for forest birds during the breeding season. In the second section, we use data on nesting success from six sites to explore reproductive success in relation to tract size and buffering from surrounding agriculture.

Study Areas

Our study sites consisted of 16 sites in 15 nature preserves in Illinois (Fig. 8.1). We censused bird populations in all 15 preserves and measured songbird nesting success in 6 of them (Table 8.1). Each site is a dedicated nature preserve (Herkert, Chapter 17, this volume). Although we have data from many other sites (Robinson et al. 1995, Brawn and Robinson 1994, 1996), we restrict our analyses here to nature preserves and evaluating their potential for conserving midwestern forest bird communities.

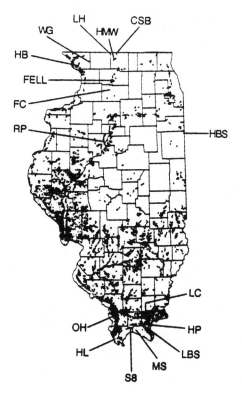

Figure 8.1. Locations of nature preserves where studies of avian communities were conducted. See text for abbreviations.

The 16 sites represent a wide range of forest types (Table 8.1) and geographical locations throughout Illinois (Fig. 8.1). Relative to Illinois forests in general (Iverson 1989) and to the nature preserve system as a whole, swamp forests (HL, MS, S8, LBS, parts of HP) are somewhat overrepresented and small barrens and glades are underrepresented (see Robinson 1994 for censuses of barrens and glades in southern Illinois). Otherwise, study tracts also include upland forests with and without steep ravines (HMW, CSNP, FC, WG, HB, FELL, OH, LC), floodplain forest (CSNP, HP), and savannas and burned tracts (HBS and RP). For the purposes of this paper, we split the Heron Pond/Little Black Slough Nature Preserve into two different sites, separated by 500–1000 m. The first, Heron Pond, consists primarily of mature floodplain oak forest with relatively closed-canopy cypress swamps and an open beaver pond. The second, Little Black Slough, consists mostly of very open-canopy tupelo-dominated swamp with standing water most years. These habitats are sufficiently different in structure to be treated separately.

The size of nature preserves ranged from 19–1410 acres and the tracts in which they were embedded ranged from 40–3500 acres (Table 8.1). Because tract sizes are often difficult to estimate in complex landscapes (Lord and Norton 1990), we also estimated the extent to which preserves were buffered from the surrounding agricultural fields. In this respect, tracts ranged from islands of forest completely surrounded by agriculture (HMW, HL) to those with limited buffering (LHNP, CSNP, FC, WG, S8, HBS) to those embedded in much more extensive forests (RP, FELL, OH, LBS, HP, LC).

The six sites for which we have data on nesting success also represent a wide range of habitat types including dry/savanna upland forest (RP), floodplain forest with some swamps (HP), and upland oak forest with (HB, OH, FELL) and without (WG) steep ravines. Because all of these sites are fairly large (>300 acres), we could not examine the effects of very small preserve size on nesting success.

Methods

Censuses

Birds were censused using the fixed-radius point-count method of Hutto et al. (1986). Observers walked predetermined routes through forest tracts and stopped every 150 m to conduct 6-minute point counts. During the census period, observers recorded every bird heard or seen. Points were censused 1–6 times per season depending upon the intensity of the study (all areas in which nesting success was quantified were censused at least 4 times per season). Censuses were conducted from 15 May to 30 June (southern sites) and from 20 May to 10 July (northern sites), 1989–1994. Many sites, however, were only censused during a single season (Table 8.1). For sites that were censused more than one year, we averaged data over years. Censuses occurred only during the morning (05:15–11:45) on days with little or no wind and no rain or water dripping from foliage after a recent rain (Ralph et al. 1993). Six-minute census periods were chosen (rather than five as recommended by Ralph et al. 1993) to maintain consistency with previous studies in Illinois (Robinson 1992) and because bird-rich habitats such as floodplain forests could not be censused adequately in 5 minutes (Robinson unpublished data). Censuses were conducted only by experienced observers who could identify all birds by voice. We could not control for potential observer biases because censuses were conducted by seven different observers and tracts were censused by different combinations of these observers. All observers were carefully trained to improve consistency of distance estimates.

We report only observations of birds heard singing within a 70-m fixed radius around the census point. This distance was chosen because circles of that radius do not overlap the areas associated with neighboring census points (located 150 m apart). We chose 70 m rather than 50 m (Ralph et al. 1993) to increase the number of detections in small tracts and in tracts that were censused only once per season. With the exception of the blue-gray gnatcatcher, all bird songs were

Table 8.1. Nature preserves included in this study.

Site	Code	Size[a] (acres)	Tract size[b]	Buffering[c]	Habitat types[d]	Years censused	No. censuses[e]	No. census points[f]	No. species detected
Hartley Memorial Woods	HMW	40	40	0	1	1994	1	5	32
Laona Heights	LHNP	19	100	1	1	1994	1	5	33
Colored Sands Bluff	CSNP	44	60+	1	2,3,1	1994	1	7	39
Franklin Creek	FC	96	225	1	1,3	1994	1	12	41
Horseshoe Lake	HL	220	220	0	4,3	1993	1	24	56
						1994	1	24	
Ward's Grove	WG	335	380	1	1	1992*	5	33	44
						1993*	5	33	
Hanover Bluff	HB	362	580	2	1	1992	5	28	50
						1993	1	28	
Mermet Swamp	MS	43	400	1	4,3	1993	1	24	56
Section 8	S8	300	700	2	4,3	1993	1	23	55
						1994	1	23	
Robinson Park	RP	152	400	2	1,2	1993	2	13	45
						1994*	4	15	
Hooper Branch	HBS	483	600	1–2	2	1993	1	14	50
						1994	1	22	
George B. Fell	FELL	686	850	2	1,3,(2)	1993	1	30	61
						1994*	4	24	
Ozark Hills	OH	222	2100	3–4	1	1990–92*	5	16	47
Little Black Slough	LBS	450	2500	3	3,4,(1)	1993	1	32	72
						1994	1	27	
Heron Pond	HP	1410	2500	3	3,4,(1)	1993*	5	50	78
						1993*	1	30	
						1994*	5	50	

continued

158

Table 8.1. Continued.

Site	Code	Size[a] (acres)	Tract size[b]	Buffering[c]	Habitat types[d]	Years censused	No. censuses[e]	No. census points[f]	No. species detected
Lusk Creek	LC	125	3000	3–4	1	1989	1	10	58
						1990	1	10	

[a]Size of the actual nature preserve.

[b]Size of the tract of similar habitat in which the nature preserve is embedded.

[c]0 = No buffer; completely surrounded by agriculture; 1 = Buffered on at least one side by at least a 100 m strip of similar habitat; 2 = Buffered from agricultural lands by at least 100 m of similar habitat on at least two sides; 3 = Buffered by at least 100 m of similar habitat on at least three sides; 4 = Buffered on all sides by similar habitat.

[d]1 = Upland dry-mesic forest; 2 = Upland dry, burned forest; 3 = Floodplain forest; 4 = Swamp forest. Habitat types listed in order of area covered.

[e]Number of times each census route was replicated within a season.

[f]Number of points censused during each visit; each census route listed separately.

*Nest searching conducted.

159

audible at least to 70 m (Robinson unpublished data). Each census route was designed to include the maximum number of census points that could be established 150 m apart and at least 50 m from an agricultural edge. Therefore, census points were not chosen at random. Any birds heard outside of the 70-m radius circles were recorded separately as "present" in these tracts. For small tracts, our estimates of rare and wide-ranging species and those that vocalize irregularly will be imprecise because only a few census points could be included. For small preserves embedded in larger tracts (e.g., LHNP, FC, MS, LC), we also included census points located in the same habitats within 50 m of the nature preserve boundaries. These additional census points included no species that were not also present within the nature preserve. Inclusion of these additional points, however, might have changed the relative abundances of some species, especially those with patchy distributions. For each nature preserve, we calculated the mean number of detections per census point per 70-m radius for each species.

To assess the effects of area on community structure we performed univariate and multiple regression analyses using size of the preserve, total tract size (see Table 8.1), or both as independent variables to explain variation in species richness or relative abundances. For species richness, we analyzed all species detected and then performed separate analyses on three subsets of the community: long-distance (or neotropical) migrants, short-distance migrants, and permanent residents. Associations between area (preserve and tract) and abundance were assessed on a species by species basis. We log transformed all variables prior to regression analyses.

To compare the bird communities in the 16 sites, we ordinated the communities in multivariate space using Principle Components Analysis (PCA). Average abundances of each species within each preserve were used as the input matrix. Factor scores (i.e., correlation of each species with each principle component) were derived after varimax rotation. To aid interpretation, we limited the PCA to three components.

Nesting Success

In the six intensive study sites (Table 8.1), teams of 4–10 observers searched for nests and determined their contents and fates. Each time a nest was located, its position was mapped and its contents were observed (including number of cowbird eggs). Nests were then monitored every 2–3 days until the young either were fledged or were destroyed by predators or storms. We quantified the frequency (proportion of nests parasitized) and intensity (cowbird eggs per parasitized nest) of brood parasitism (Robinson et al. 1995, in press-a) for all nests found in each nature preserve. Rates of nest predation were quantified by using the Mayfield (1975) index to calculate the daily percentage of nests lost to predators. Rates of nest predation at different distances from edges were compared statistically using Sauer and Williams' (1989) program CONTRAST. For sites with more than one year of data, we pooled all years together. Because of uncontrolled year effects and the limited number of sites, we made no statistical comparisons of nesting success among tracts. Within tracts, however, we compared frequency and intensity of parasitism and nest predation rates at different distances from edges of anthropogenic openings such as agricultural fields, recreational areas, and residential tracts. Distances were estimated from mapping the locations of nests and openings on topographic maps confirmed by aerial photographs.

Results

Community Composition

We observed 108 species at the 15 nature preserves (Table 8.2, Appendix A). Of the possible forest species that were not recorded, two are probably extirpated from Illinois (Swainson's warbler [which formerly nested in Heron pond] and Bachman's warbler), one (black-throated green warbler) nests in non-native pine

Table 8.2. Species with significant (P<0.10) correlations between abundance and area.

Species	Coefficient		Adjusted R²	Significance
Species positively correlated with area				
Pileated woodpecker	0.21	(P)[1]	0.33	0.015
Eastern tufted titmouse	0.01	(P)	0.30	0.012
Veery	0.01	(P)	0.32	0.03
Cedar waxwing	1.2	(P)	0.36	0.03
White-eyed vireo	0.01	(T)	0.59	0.001
Black-and-white warbler	0.002	(P)	0.20	0.048
Cerulean warbler	0.018	(P)	0.30	0.015
Kentucky warbler	0.009	(T)	0.63	0.004
Ovenbird	0.003	(T)	0.40	0.02
Louisiana waterthrush	0.003	(T)	0.83	0.001
Worm-eating warbler	0.0013	(T)	0.27	0.06
Rufous-sided towhee	0.009	(T)	0.13	0.091
Species negatively correlated with area				
Red-bellied woodpecker	−0.54	(P)	0.13	0.09
Great crested flycatcher	−0.50	(T)	0.20	0.044
Eastern phoebe	−0.46	(P)	0.40	0.015
Blue jay	−1.05	(T)	0.25	0.03
House wren	−0.002	(T)	0.14	0.082
European starling	−0.91	(P)	0.21	0.045
Indigo bunting	−0.003	(T)	0.20	0.043
Summer tanager	−0.009	(P)	0.27	0.046

[1]P = size of preserve, T = size of tract.

plantations, and five (long-eared owl, Swainson's hawk, Bewick's wren, Chuck-will's-widow, and Bachman's sparrow) occur in very open savannas or barrens that we did not census. Bewick's wrens formerly nested in barrens within the Heron Pond Nature Preserve (Vern Kleen, pers. comm. Nov. 1995).

Most forest birds were found in two or more of the nature preserves (Table 8.2). Only the yellow-bellied sapsucker (north only), ruffed grouse (reintroduced in the south and probably extinct as of 1993 [Robinson unpublished data]), prairie warbler, Canada warbler (north only), lark sparrow, and sharp-shinned hawk were recorded at just one site. With the exception of the state-endangered sharp-shinned hawk, all of these species either barely occur in Illinois or are mostly restricted to nonforest habitat (e.g., lark sparrow, prairie warbler).

Species restricted to far northern Illinois were found in several northern preserves (e.g., veery, least flycatcher), and those restricted to southern Illinois (e.g., black vulture, Mississippi kite) were found in several southern preserves. Pine warblers were found only in pine plantations along the edge of two southern nature preserves (Appendix A). Native populations, however, survive in the Pine Hills Ecological Area, a protected section of the Shawnee National Forest where shortleaf pines occur naturally (Robinson 1994).

Area Effects

We found clear area effects on avian species richness within the preserves. Species richness was significantly associated with area of the preserve (coefficient = 0.14, adjusted R^2 = .45; $F_{1,14}$ = 13.37; P < 0.001) and total tract size (coefficient = 0.14; adjusted R^2 = .51; $F_{1,14}$ = 16.73; P < 0.001). Stepwise regression, using preserve area and tract area as independent variables, indicated that total tract size was the better predictor of species richness. With tract size in the model, preserve size explained little residual variation.

Swamp and floodplain forests in southern Illinois consistently contained more species than comparably sized upland forest tracts, partly because of the addition of aquatic species and partly because of the addition of species that require open canopies (see below). The low species richness of the four smallest sites undoubtedly resulted in part from their low census intensity (one visit each). A single census in three swamps (HL, S8, and MS), however, yielded 52, 54, and 51 species, respectively. Burned upland forests (HBS and RP) had low species richness relative to tracts of comparable size. The richest upland-dominated tract (FELL) also contained a small section of floodplain forest.

Analysis of area effects on long-distance (neotropical) migrants, short-distance migrants, and permanent residents indicated that area was an important predictor of species richness within each group (Fig. 8.2). Neotropical migrants, however, were the most area sensitive; multiple regression revealed that nearly one-half the variation in neotropical migrant species richness was explained by the combined effects of tract area and preserve area (adjusted R^2 = .47; $F_{2,13}$ = 7.92; P

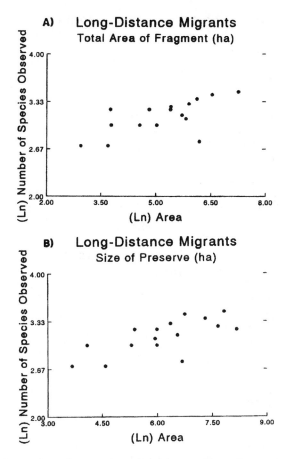

Figure 8.2. Scatterplots of area and species richness of long-distance (neotropical) migrants (a, b), short-distance migrants (c, d), and residents (e, f).

< 0.01) (Fig. 8.2a,b). Size of preserve explained only 5% of the residual variation after tract size was entered into the model. Interestingly, size of preserve was the only important predictor of species richness within the short-distance migrants (Adjusted R^2 = .32; $F_{1,14}$ = 7.92; P = 0.041) (Fig. 8.2c,d). For permanent residents, which were least sensitive to area, only tract size was significant (Adjusted R^2 = .24; $F_{1,14}$ = 5.81; P < 0.05) (Fig. 8.2e,f).

Overall, abundance per point (all species pooled) was not significantly associated with tract size (Adjusted R^2 = .001; $F_{2,13}$ = .10; P = 0.91), but area effects on the abundances of many species were pronounced (Table 8.2). Overall, abundance was significantly (P < 0.10) positively correlated with area for 12 species and negatively correlated with area for 8 species. Abundances of the remaining species were only weakly associated with area.

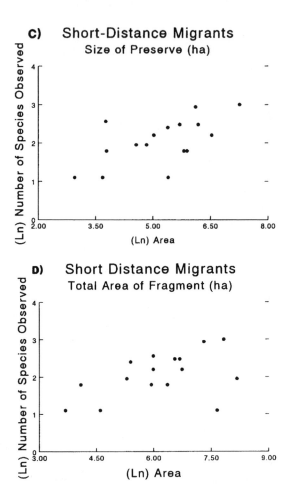

Figure 8.2. Continued.

Of the species with abundances positively correlated with tract size (Table 8.2), some were large-sized species (e.g., pileated woodpecker), some are known to be area-sensitive throughout their ranges (e.g., veery, Kentucky, and worm-eating warblers, ovenbird [Herkert 1995, Wenny et al. 1993]), and others were most abundant in more extensive disturbed shrublands found in the largest tracts (e.g., white-eyed vireo, black-and-white warbler, and rufous-sided towhee). Species that were less abundant in larger tracts included many permanent residents (e.g., red-bellied woodpecker) and some short-distance (e.g., northern flicker, see Appendix) and neotropical migrants (e.g., house wren, indigo bunting, and Baltimore oriole, see Table 8.2 and Appendix) that prefer habitat edges or open woodlands. Among forest-nesting neotropical migrants, only the great crested

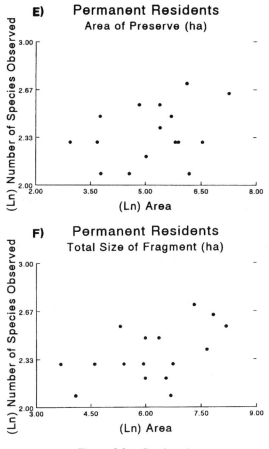

Figure 8.2. Continued.

flycatcher and summer tanager showed significant trends toward decreasing abundance with greater tract size, although the eastern wood-pewee, red-eyed vireo, and scarlet tanager showed nonsignificant trends (Appendix A). Abundances of parasitic cowbirds and nest predators such as blue jays, crows, and catbirds all decreased with area (Table 8.2, Appendix A).

Habitat Effects

Habitat effects on community structure were pronounced (Fig. 8.3). Swamp and floodplain forest (e.g., LBS, S8) were distinguished by the presence of aquatic species (e.g., green, great blue, and yellow-crowned night herons) and birds of open canopies (e.g., tree swallow, eastern bluebird, white-eyed vireo, yellow

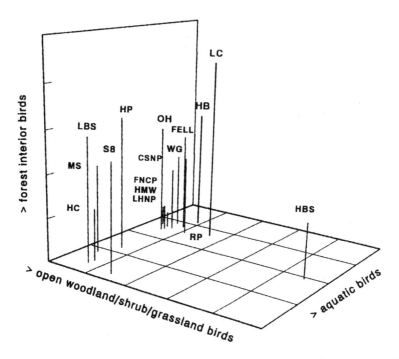

Figure 8.3. Ordination of 16 avian communities based on principal components analysis. See Table 1 for abbreviations.

warbler, song sparrow, red-winged blackbird, Mississippi kite, and American redstart). Of the forest species, only the red-shouldered hawk, brown creeper, and prothonotary warbler were restricted to floodplain forests.

Closed canopy upland forest communities (e.g., OH, FELL, WG, HB, LC, CSNP, FC, HMW, LHNP) tended to cluster together (Fig. 8.3). Only the worm-eating warbler, broad-winged hawk, ovenbird, and black-and-white warbler were confined to upland forests (Appendix A).

Hooper Branch Savanna (HBS) was distinct from the other communities (Fig. 8.3). With the exception of the solitary vireo, all of the species sampled at this site are more characteristic of grasslands (e.g., eastern meadowlark) and shrub-lands (e.g., lark and field sparrows, orchard oriole, northern bobwhite, mourning dove, and brown thrasher).

Some species had specific habitat requirements and their presence depended upon the composition and structure of the vegetation within nature preserves rather than just tract size and geographic location. Canada and blue-winged warblers were confined to fens (wet shrublands), although both are also found in human-disturbed early-successional habitats such as clear-cuts outside of nature preserves (Robinson unpublished data). Chestnut-sided warblers nested only along power line right-of-ways. Eastern phoebes were confined to cliffs and other exposed rocks. Swainson's warblers, when present in Illinois, were confined to canebreaks (Eddleman 1978). Some canebreaks still exist in Heron Pond/Little Black Slough Nature Preserve, but no Swainson's warblers have been recorded there since 1984 (Vern Kleen, pers. comm. Nov. 1995).

Many species were found in most sites, regardless of habitat, and therefore are insensitive to the composition and structure of the vegetation. The species found in all 15 sites include neotropical migrants (yellow-billed cuckoo, great crested flycatcher, eastern wood-pewee, red-eyed vireo, and indigo bunting), year-round residents (great horned owl, red-bellied, downy, and hairy woodpeckers, blue jay, eastern tufted titmouse, either black-capped or Carolina chickadee, white-breasted nuthatch, and northern cardinal), and a short-distance migrant (brown-headed cowbird). Other species found in at least 13 sites include the barred owl, ruby-throated hummingbird, red-headed woodpecker, blue-gray gnatcatcher, wood thrush, yellow-throated vireo, and scarlet tanager.

Birds of Open Forests

One of the most striking aspects of Appendix A is the large number of species that were found in wooded nature preserves, but usually are associated with such openland habitats as edges, shrublands, savannas, and barrens. Of the 108 species in Appendix A, 56 require at least some kind of disturbance in the canopy. Some arboreal species appear to require openings and/or widely scattered trees (e.g., red-headed woodpecker, eastern kingbird, cedar waxwing, solitary vireo, warbling vireo, American redstart, northern oriole, summer tanager [in northern Illinois], and American goldfinch). Shrublands that form in some openings attract black-billed cuckoos, house wrens, gray catbirds, white-eyed vireos, blue-winged, chestnut-sided, prairie, yellow, Canada, and hooded warblers, common yellowthroats, yellow-breasted chats, indigo buntings, rufous-sided towhees, song, lark, field, and chipping sparrows, red-winged blackbirds, orchard orioles, northern bobwhites, and brown thrashers. Possibly, these "natural" shrublands were the original habitat of these species, many of which are now abundant statewide in human-modified habitats (Graber and Graber 1963). Other species that require or benefit from at least some openings include Mississippi kite (Evans 1981), chuck-will's-widow, whip-poor-will, common nighthawk (for nesting), northern flicker, red-shouldered hawk (Bednarz and Dinsmore 1981), eastern phoebe, tree and northern rough-winged swallows, eastern bluebird, American robin, and purple martin. Maintaining these species will require managing to perpetuate the disturbances that create openings (see below).

Nest Parasitism and Predation

When censusing female cowbirds by their "rattle" vocalization (Robinson et al. 1993), there were no obvious area effects on abundance (Table 8.2). The ratios of female cowbird detections to host detections, a good index of parasitism intensity (Robinson et al. in press-a, Thompson et al. in press), varied greatly among sites (Fig. 8.4). The ratios were lowest in the largest tracts (HP/LBS, LC). Excluding the smallest tracts that included fewer than ten census points (Table 8.1) (HMW, LHNP, CSNP), there was a significant negative relationship between tract size and cowbird:host ratio. The two burned areas had high cowbird:host ratios (.14 and .11) relative to tract size, whereas floodplain/swamp tracts had relatively low ratios (Fig. 8.4).

Levels of nest predation and brood parasitism were high in all sites for most species (Tables 8.3, 8.4). Parasitism frequencies were generally high for species in all sites, but sample sizes precluded statistical significance. Wood thrushes, in particular, were heavily parasitized in all sites (see also Robinson 1994, Robinson and Wilcove 1994, Robinson et al. 1995, in press-a). Only the northern cardinal and indigo bunting showed a negative relationship between tract size and parasitism levels. Nest predation rates also showed little consistent variation with tract size. Wood thrush predation rates were significantly higher within 100 m of agricultural and residential edges in Hanover Bluff (2.6 ± 1.1, N = 229 vs. 5.8 ± 1.6, N = 225, $P < 0.05$), but not in Wards' Grove (agricultural edge only), Fell Nature Preserve (road edges), Ozark Hills (recreation area edges), or Heron Pond (<500 m and >500 m from agricultural openings) ($P > 0.10$ for all comparisons). We did not have enough nests <50 m from edges (Paton 1994) for statistical tests.

Parasitism levels were generally higher near edges, but the differences were

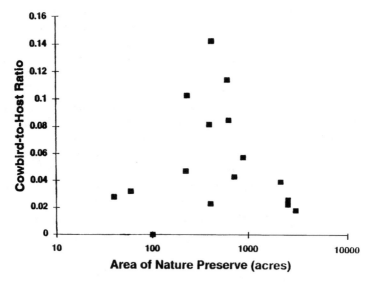

Figure 8.4. Scatterplot of relative abundance of brown-headed cowbirds and area of nature preserve.

Table 8.3. *Levels of brood parasitism for songbirds in Illinois nature preserves, 1990–1994.*

			Site			
			% Parasitized/(n)			
Species	WG	HB	RP	FELL	OH	HP
Tract Size	380	580	400	850	2100	2500
Eastern wood-pewee			0 (3)			
Acadian flycatcher	88.5 (96)			50 (8)	45.8 (24)	33.1 (169)
Wood thrush		82.6 (46)	100 (8)	50 (20)	80.0 (25)	90.6 (117)
Veery	100 (8)	100 (1)				66.7 (21)
White-eyed vireo						
Red-eyed vireo				100 (1)	50 (2)	
Prothonotary warbler						28.9 (38)
Cerulean warbler					50 (2)	
Kentucky warbler					16.7 (6)	33.3 (39)
Worm-eating warbler					42.9 (7)	
Ovenbird		100 (2)				
Louisiana waterthrush					0 (2)	40.0 (5)
American redstart				5.3 (19)		
Rose-breasted grosbeak	75 (4)	25 (12)		22.9 (9)		
Northern cardinal	60 (10)	80 (10)	70.0 (10)	33.3 (6)	27.3 (11)	13.3 (30)
Indigo bunting	66.7 (9)	60 (5)	75.0 (12)		40.0 (5)	59.4 (32)
Rufous-sided towhee		66.7 (3)		60 (5)		
Scarlet tanager		100 (1)		100 (1)		
Summer tanager					50 (2)	50 (2)

Table 8.4. Rates of daily nest predation for songbirds in Illinois nature preserves, 1990–1194.

Species Tract size	WG 380	HB 580	RP 400	FELL 800	OH 2100	HP 2500
				Site Mean +sd% (exposure days)[1]		
Eastern wood-pewee	—	—	0.0 (45)	—	0.0 (6)	—
Acadian flycatcher	2.8+0.4 (1439)	3.7+0.7 (741)	—	5.2+2.3 (96)	3.4+1.1 (292)	2.7+0.4 (1936)
Wood thrush	10.5+5.0 (38)	9.5+9.1 (11)	0.8+0.7 (126)	2.5+0.9 (309)	5.4+1.4 (280)	4.1+0.8 (634)
Veery	—	—	—	—	—	—
American robin	—	—	4.2+2.4 (71)	5.5+1.8 (163)	—	—
Grey catbird	5.3+3.0 (57)	3.6+3.6 (28)	—	2.7+1.0 (264)	—	—
Red-eyed vireo	—	—	—	10.0+9.5 (10)	—	—
White-eyed vireo	—	—	—	—	—	3.3+1.0 (306)
Prothonotary warbler	—	—	—	—	—	4.0+1.0 (402)
Kentucky warbler	—	—	—	—	4.7+3.2 (43)	3.5+0.9 (399)
Worm-eating warbler	—	—	—	—	2.5+2.5 (40)	—
Louisiana waterthrush	—	—	—	—	0.0 (24)	0.0 (64)
American redstart	5.5+3.1 (55)	—	—	3.5+1.1 (260)	—	—
Rose-breasted grosbeak	6.8+4.6 (30)	0.0 (14.5)	—	3.4+1.7 (118)	—	—
Northern cardinal	—	9.0+3.2 (78)	1.9+1.1 (162)	7.7+3.0 (78)	8.0+2.7 (101)	3.0+0.8 (395)
Indigo bunting	—	14.0+5.3 (43)	4.7+1.6 (170)	—	5.7+3.2 (53)	5.1+1.2 (336)
Rufous-sided towhee	0.0 (33)	—	—	5.1+3.5 (40)	—	—
Scarlet tanager	0.0 (16)	—	—	6.3+6.0 (16)	—	—
Summer tanager	—	—	—	—	—	6.8+4.7 (2)

[1]Calculated using the Mayfield (1975) index. A 2% daily predation rate translates to a 40% overall loss to predation assuming a 25-day nest cycle; daily predation rates translate to the following overall losses: 3% = 53%; 4% = 64%; 5% = 72%; 6% = 79%; 7% = 84%; 10% = 93%; 15% = 98%.

not significant ($P > 0.10$) for Ward's Grove (agricultural edges, <100 m vs. >100 m), Fell Nature Preserve (road edges, <100 m vs. >100 m), Hanover Bluff (agricultural and residential, <100 m vs. >100 m), and Ozark Hills (recreational areas, <100 m vs. >100 m). Wood thrushes in the eastern third of the Heron Pond area (200–700 m from agriculture) were parasitized significantly more often (97% of 65 nests vs. 79% of 52 nests, $X_2 = 6.4$, $P < 0.05$) than those in the central area, which were located 500–2000 m from agriculture. Similarly, Acadian flycatchers were parasitized significantly more often in the eastern section of Heron Pond (54.3% of 46 nests vs. 25.0% of 123 nests, $X_2 = 12.8$, $P < 0.01$). Acadian flycatchers were also parasitized significantly more often within 100 m of recreational areas than in the interior (>100 m) of Ozark Hills (75% of 8 nests vs. 31.3% of 16 nests, Fisher Exact Probability = 0.049). Sample sizes were too small (< 5 nests per category) for any other comparisons of edge-related differences in predation and parasitism.

Discussion

Problems of Poor Reproductive Performance

The Illinois Nature Preserve system appears to provide sufficient habitat to attract most, or perhaps all, of the forest birds native to Illinois (Appendix A). Populations of all but a few forest species were found in the sites censused, which represent only a small fraction (<10%) of the nature preserves in Illinois. Nevertheless, reproductive success of most species that we studied was very low due to high rates of nest predation (> 5% daily nest predation = 70–80% overall predation, see Table 8.4) and brood parasitism by cowbirds. Parasitism and predation rates were somewhat higher in small tracts and near forest edges, at least for some species. Edge and area effects on nest predation, however, were inconsistent among species, sites, and habitats, and even the interior of the largest tracts had low nesting success (see also Robinson and Wilcove 1994, Thompson et al. in press). These results suggest that most, if not all, of Illinois' nature preserves, even the largest ones, may not be providing the ecological conditions necessary for successful nesting.

In comparison with larger forest tracts in extensively forested sections of Missouri, Wisconsin and Indiana, rates of parasitism are extremely high in Illinois' nature preserves (Robinson et al. 1995, Thompson et al. in press). The typical rates of parasitism are 70–80% per species in small tracts in Illinois, compared with less than 10% in the heavily forested central Missouri Ozarks and less than 20% in the most forested sections of the Hoosier National Forest in Indiana (Robinson et al. 1995). In these areas, average forest tract size is 10,000–25,000 ha, and over 80% of the landscape is forested (Robinson et al. 1995). In Illinois, which has small tracts (< 2500 ha) and less than 50% forest cover in any county (Robinson et al. 1995, Iverson 1989), there may be no forest tracts outside the daily commuting range of cowbirds (Thompson in press). Given the reproductive costs of brood parasitism (Rothstein 1975, May and Robinson 1985, Robinson et al. in press-b), cowbird parasitism may be reducing the reproductive success below levels necessary for long-term population maintenance (Brawn and Robinson 1996, Trine et al. in press). Similarly, the generally high daily predation rates (4–10%) in Illinois' nature preserves exceed those in more forested landscapes (Robinson et al. 1995) and are much higher than the 2% daily loss rates considered typical of open-cup nesting passerines (Nice 1957, Ricklefs 1973). These problems are most severe for neotropical migratory songbirds, most of which build open-cup nests that are susceptible to cowbird parasitism and nest predators (Whitcomb et al. 1981, Finch 1991, Martin 1992, Li and Martin 1991). At least one cavity-nesting migrant, the prothonotary warbler, and several residents and short-distance migrants (e.g., northern cardinal, rufous-sided towhee) also experienced high levels of parasitism and predation (Tables 8.3, 8.4).

Problems with low reproductive success may be chronic in agricultural and urban landscapes dominated by nonforest uses where there are unlimited feeding opportunities for cowbirds (Thompson in press) and some nest predators (Marini et al. in press). Very small nature preserves (<200 acre) may have little potential for preserving viable forest songbird populations. The best strategy for managing reproductively viable songbird populations may be restoring large tracts rather than focusing on smaller, high-quality nature preserves. Nevertheless, there are many ways in which existing nature preserves can be managed to improve conditions and populations of forest birds. In this section we expand upon some of these strategies.

Edge Reduction and Type

Even though many forest birds depend upon disturbances that open the canopy (Noss 1991), some human-induced edges may act as ecological traps (sensu Gates and Gysel 1978) which attract birds but fail to provide conditions for successful nesting. Many edges are associated with high levels of brood parasitism (Gates and Gysel 1978, Chasko and Gates 1982, Brittingham and Temple 1983, Temple and Cary 1988) and nest predation (Andren et al. 1985, Johnson and Temple 1990, Moller 1989, Paton 1994, Ratti and Reese 1988, Sandström 1991). Edges also are associated with high populations of many nest predators including mammals (Bider 1968), snakes (Durner and Gates 1993, Withgott 1994), and corvids (Andren 1992, Angelstom 1986, Marini et al. in press). Adverse edge effects may be particularly severe at abrupt, human-maintained edges (Ratti and Reese 1988, Suarez et al. unpublished). At least some edge-dependent species may require more gradual, shrubby edges for successful nesting.

Edge effects, however, may vary in intensity among landscapes that differ in forest cover (Thompson et al. in press, Robinson et al. in press-a). In landscapes saturated by nest predators and cowbirds, parasitism and predation levels may remain high throughout a forest (Heske in press, Robinson and Wilcove 1994, Marini et al. in press). Edge contrast may not always affect nest predation rates (Yahner et al. 1989). Paton (1994) concluded that most adverse edge effects occur within 50 m of the edge, but he did not deal with brood parasitism. Gap-dependent species may also vary considerably in their nesting success in gaps created by logging (W.D. Robinson and S.K. Robinson unpublished data, Illinois Natural History Survey). The effects of edges on predation and parasitism levels in Illinois nature preserves vary among sites and species. Taken together, these studies suggest that reducing the negative impacts of edges will not be a simple task. Edge reduction may be beneficial in some landscapes but have little effect in others.

Tract Sizes

The debate over the size of reserves for effective conservation (single large versus several small) remains unresolved. Whether or not scientists advocate fewer, larger preserves or many smaller ones depends partly on which organism is considered (Noss and Harris 1986). Any reserve system, however, must contain at least a few large tracts to accommodate the needs of area-sensitive birds (Blake and Karr 1987, Herkert, Chapter 17, this volume) and to minimize losses to nest predation and parasitism. A network of small (<100 acre) reserves in the Midwest would lack many characteristic forest species (Bond 1957, Ambuel and Temple 1982, Kendeigh 1982, Blake 1986, Blake and Karr 1987). In Illinois, however, virtually all forest birds were found in medium-sized (200–1000 acre) tracts (Appendix A). Even all large raptors occupied tracts smaller than 500 acres and some (cooper's hawk and barred owl) nested in tracts smaller than 100 acres.

The higher species richness of large tracts results from several interrelated factors. First, large tracts generally contain several different habitats and well-developed systems of streams and ravines with birds of more mesic habitats (e.g., acadian flycatcher, Louisiana waterthrush). Second, they are large enough in diverse natural disturbances (e.g., blowdowns, flood damage, fires) and other openings (e.g., floodplain backwaters, fens) that create habitat for disturbance-dependent birds. Such natural disturbances may have been the original habitats of the edge/shrubland birds that originally adapted well to human-altered landscapes (Forbes 1908, Forbes and Gross 1922, Graber and Graber 1963, Noss 1991), many of which have recently begun to show rapid population declines (Hill and Hagan 1991, Askins 1993, Hagan 1993). A network of medium-sized sites, however, could preserve populations of the same species as those favored by large sites, as long as they were chosen to sample a variety of habitats, managed to promote conditions for disturbance-dependent birds, or both.

The Need for Larger Sites

Managing forest bird populations in chronically fragmented regions such as Illinois poses a difficult challenge. If the maintenance of many populations depends upon forested areas outside of Illinois (Robinson et al. 1995), then local management practices may have little effect on populations. In regions of high forest cover (>80%) and large tract sizes (>25,000 acre), cowbird feeding areas are scarce and there are few agricultural areas to augment predator populations (Robinson et al. 1995). To recreate these conditions in chronically fragmented landscapes would require restoration of large sites (at least 10,000 acres) that would contain a core of forest far from agricultural and residential openings. Maintaining forest bird populations in chronically fragmented landscapes therefore may depend upon a combination of restoration of large sites and conservation of source habitats in often-distant unfragmented landscapes. Migratory birds therefore require habitat conservation on a regional scale (i.e., the midwestern U.S.) as well as a local scale. For grassland and shrubland birds, however, Illinois may once have been a major source habitat for other parts of the Midwest. In the long run, species of these openland habitats may be of more concern to Illinois managers than forest birds. Perhaps these species should be the focus of management for birds on the smaller sites that represent the majority of the Illinois nature preserve system. The network of corridors, woodlots, and diverse agro-ecosystems recommended by Mankin and Warner (Chapter 7, this volume) might be ideal for both mammals and many open-country birds, which may be better adapted to withstand high parasitism and predation rates (Robinson et al. 1995).

Finally, we believe that nature preserves in Illinois offer important opportunities for monitoring communities and populations over time. By monitoring the abundances and reproductive success of birds (or other fauna) in preserves that span a large range of tract sizes and sample diverse habitats, we can learn much about the behavior of populations in fragmented landscapes and assess the effectiveness of management practices within the preserves. Managers often inquire whether a certain species or group of species will be preserved on areas under their jurisdiction. With long-term monitoring of abundances and population viability, we may be able to predict what species will be where and for how long.

Acknowledgments

We would like to thank our tireless, skilled, and dedicated field crews who gathered most of the data used in this paper, especially S. Bailey, R. Jack, J. Knapstein, R. Brumfield, L. Morse, C. Morse, B. Condon, S. Amundsen, J.W. Seets, K. Pfennig, and W.D. Robinson, J.W. Seets, E. Anderson, and T. Simpson provided logistical support for all phases of the work.

We also thank B. McFall and Randy Heidorn of the Nature Preserves Commission and A. Branhagen for permission to work in the many preserves we have studied. Funding was provided by the Illinois Departments of Energy and Natural Resources and Conservation (Divisions of Natural Heritage and Wildlife) (all sites), the National Fish and Wildlife Foundation (OH), the Illinois Chapter of The Nature Conservancy (RP, S8, HP/LBS, HL), the U.S. Fish and Wildlife Service (RP, S8, HP/LBS, HL), and Federal Aid (all northern sites).

References

Ambuel, B., and S.A. Temple. 1982. Area-dependent changes in the bird communities and vegetation of southern Wisconsin forest. *Ecology* 64:1057–1068.

Andren, H. 1992. Corvid density and nest predation in relation to forest fragmentation: a landscape perspective. *Ecology* 73:794–804.

Andren, H., P. Angelstom, E. Linström, and P. Widen. 1985. Differences in predation pressure in relation to habitat fragmentation: an experiment. *Oikos* 45:273–277.

Angelstom, P. 1986. Predation on ground-nesting birds' nests in relation to predator densities and habitat edge. *Oikos* 47:365–373.

Askins, R.A. 1993. Population trends in grassland, shrubland, and forest birds in eastern North America. In D.M. Power, ed. *Current Ornithology,* vol. 11. Plenum Press, New York, 1–34.

Askins, R.A., J.F. Lynch, and R. Greenberg. 1990. Population declines in migratory birds in eastern North America. In D.M. Power, ed. *Current Ornithology,* vol. 7. Plenum Press, New York, 1–58.

Bednarz, J.C., and J.J. Dinsmore. 1981. Status, habitat use, and management of red-shouldered hawks. *Journal of Wildlife Management* 45:236–241.

Bider, J.M. 1968. Animal activity in uncontrolled terrestrial communities as determined by a sand transect technique. *Ecological Monographs* 38:269–308.

Blake, J.G., and J.R. Karr. 1987. Breeding birds of isolated woodlots: area and habitat relationships. *Ecology* 68:1724–1734.

Blake, J.G. 1986. Species-area relationships of migrants in isolated woodlots in east-central Illinois. *Wilson Bulletin* 98:291–296.

Blake, J.G., and J.R. Karr. 1984. Species compositions of bird communities and the conservation benefit of large versus small forests. *Biological Conservation* 30:173–187.

Bond, R.R. 1957. Ecological distribution of breeding birds in the upland forests of southern Wisconsin. *Ecological Monographs* 27:351–384.

Brawn, J.D., and S.K. Robinson. 1994. Forest birds in Illinois: changes in abundances and breeding ecology. *Erigenia* 13:109–116.

Brawn, J.D., and S.K. Robinson. 1996. Source-sink population dynamics may complicate interpretation of long-term census data. *Ecology* 77:3–12.

Brittingham, M.C., and S.A. Temple. 1983. Have cowbirds caused forest songbirds to decline? *BioScience* 33:31–35.

Chasko, G.C., and J.E. Gates. 1982. Avian habitat suitability along a transmission-line corridor in an oak-hickory forest region. *Wildlife Monographs* 82:1–41.

Durner, G.M., and J.E. Gates. 1993. Spatial ecology of black rat snakes on Remington Farms, Maryland. *Journal of Wildlife Management* 57:812–826.

Eddleman, W.R. 1978. *Selection and Management of Swainson's Warbler Habitat.* M.S. thesis, University of Missouri, Columbia.

Evans, S.A. 1981. *Ecology and Behavior of the Mississippi Kite (Ictinia mississippiensis) in Southern Illinois.* M.S. thesis, Southern Illinois University, Carbondale.

Faaborg, J., M.C. Brittingham, T.M. Donovan, and J.G. Blake. 1993. Habitat fragmentation in the temperate zone: a perspective for managers. In D.M. Finch and P.W. Stangel, eds. *Status and Management of Neotropical Migratory Birds.* General Technical Report RM-229. U.S. Dept. of Agriculture, Forest Service. Rocky Mountain Forest and Range Experiment Station, Fort Collins, Colorado, 331–338.

Finch, D.M. 1991. *Population Ecology, Habitat Requirements, and Conservation of Neotropical Migratory Birds.* General Technical Report RM-205. U.S. Dept. of Agriculture, Forest Service. Rocky Mountain Forest and Range Experiment Station, Fort Collins, Colorado.

Forbes, S.A. 1908. The mid-summer bird life of Illinois: a statistical study. *American Naturalist* 42:505–519.

Forbes, S.A., and A.O. Gross. 1922. The numbers and local distribution in summer of Illinois land birds of the open country. *Bulletin of Illinois Natural History Survey* 14:187–218.

Freemark, K., and B. Collins. 1992. Landscape ecology of birds breeding in temperate forest fragments. In J.M. Hagan III and D.W. Johnston, eds. *Ecology and Conservation of Neotropical Migrants.* Smithsonian Institution Press, Washington, D.C., 443–454.

Friedmann, H. 1929. *The Cowbirds: A Study in the Biology of Social Parasitism.* C. Thomas, Springfield, Ill.

Gates, J.E., and L.W. Gysel. 1978. Avian nest dispersion and fledging success in field-forest ecotones. *Ecology* 59:871–883.

Gibbs, J.P., and F. Faaborg. 1990. Estimating the viability of ovenbird and Kentucky warbler populations in forest fragments. *Conservation Biology* 4:193–196.

Graber, R.R., and J.W. Graber. 1963. A comparative study of bird populations in Illinois, 1906–1909 and 1956–1958. *Illinois Natural History Survey Bulletin* 28:383–528.

Hagan, J.M., III. 1993. Decline of the Rufous-sided towhee in the eastern United States. *Auk* 110:863–874.

Hayden, T.J., J. Faaborg, and R.L. Clawson. 1985. Estimates of minimum area requirements for Missouri forest birds. *Transactions of the Missouri Academy of Science* 19:11–22.

Herkert, J.R. 1991. Prairie birds of Illinois: population response to two centuries of habitat change. *Illinois Natural History Survey Bulletin* 34:106–111.

Herkert, J.R. 1994. The effects of habitat fragmentation on midwestern grassland bird communities. *Ecological Applications* 4:461–471.

Herkert, J.R. 1995. Status and habitat area requirements of the veery in Illinois. *Auk* 112:794–797.

Herkert, J.R., R.E. Szafoni, V.M. Kleen, and J.E. Schwegman. 1992. *Habitat Establishment, Enhancement, and Management for Forest and Grassland Birds in Illinois.* Natural Heritage Technical Publication No. 1, Division of Natural Heritage, Illinois Department of Conservation, Springfield.

Heske, E.J. 1995. Mammal abundances on forest-farm edges versus interiors in southern Illinois: is there an edge effect? *Journal of Mammalogy* 76:562–568.

Hill, N.P., and J.M. Hagan III. 1991. Population trends of some northeastern North American landbirds: a half-century of data. *Wilson Bulletin* 103:165–182.

Hoover, J.P., and M.C. Brittingham. 1993. Regional variation in cowbird parasitism of wood thrushes. *Wilson Bulletin* 105:228–238.

Hutto, R.L., S.M. Pletschet, and P. Henricks. 1986. A fixed-radius point count method for nonbreeding and breeding season use. *Auk* 103:593–602.

Iverson, L.R. 1989. *Forest Resources of Illinois: An Atlas and Analysis of Spatial and Temporal Trends.* Illinois Natural History Survey Special Publication 11, Champaign.

Johnson, R.G., and S.A. Temple. 1990. Nest predation and brood parasitism of tallgrass prairie birds. *Journal of Wildlife Management* 54:106–111.

Kendeigh, S.C. 1982. *Bird Populations in East-Central Illinois: Fluctuations, Variations, and Development Over a Half-Century.* Illinois Biological Monograph No. 52. University of Illinois Press, Urbana.

Li, P., and T.E. Martin. 1991. Nest-site selection and nesting success of cavity-nesting birds in high-elevation forest drainages. *Auk* 108:405–418.

Lord, J.M. and D.A. Norton. 1990. Scale and the spatial concept of fragmentation. *Conservation Biology* 4:197–202.

Marini, M.A., S.K. Robinson, and E.J. Heske. 1995. Edge effects on nest predation in the Shawnee National Forest, southern Illinois. *Biological Conservation* 74:203–213.

Martin, T.E. 1992. Breeding productivity considerations: what are the appropriate habitat features for management. In J.M. Hagan III and D.W. Johnston, eds. *Ecology and Conservation of Neotropical Migrant Landbirds.* Smithsonian Institution Press, Washington, D.C., 455–473.

May, R.M., and S.K. Robinson. 1985. Population dynamics of avian brood parasitism. *American Naturalist* 126:475–494.

Mayfield, H. 1975. Suggestions for calculating nest success. *Wilson Bulletin* 87:456–466.

Moller, A.P. 1989. Nest site selection across field-woodland ecotones: the effect of nest predation. *Oikos* 56:240–246.

Nice, M.M. 1957. Nesting success in altricial birds. *Auk* 74:305–321.

Noss, R.F. 1991. Effects of edge and internal patchiness on avian habitat use in an old-growth Florida hammock. *Natural Areas Journal* 11:34–47.

Noss, R.F., and L.D. Harris. 1986. Nodes, networks and MUMS: preserving diversity at all scales. *Environmental Management* 10:299–309.

Paton, P.W.C. 1994. The effect of edge on avian nesting success: how strong is the evidence? *Conservation Biology* 8:17–26.

Pulliam, H.R. 1988. Sources, sinks, and population regulation. *American Naturalist* 132:652–661.

Ralph, C.J., G.R. Geupel, P. Pyle, T.E. Martin, and D.F. DeSante. 1993. *Handbook of Field Methods for Monitoring Landbirds.* General Technical Report PSW-GTR-144.

Forest Service, U.S. Dept. of Agriculture. Pacific Southwest Research Station, Albany, California.

Ratti, J.T., and K.P. Reese. 1988. Preliminary test of the ecological trap hypothesis. *Journal of Wildlife Management* 52:484–491.

Ricklefs, R.E. 1973. Fecundity, mortality, and avian demography. In D.S. Farner, ed. *Breeding Biology of Birds*. National Academy of Sciences, Washington, D.C., 336–434.

Robinson, S.K. 1988. Reappraisal of the costs and benefits of habitat heterogeneity for nongame wildlife. *Transactions of the North American Wildlife and Natural Resources Conference* 53:145–155.

Robinson, S.K. 1992. Population dynamics of breeding neotropical migrants in a fragmented Illinois landscape. In J.M. Hagan III and D.W. Johnston, eds. *Ecology and Conservation of Neotropical Migrant Landbirds*. Smithsonian Institution Press, Washington, D.C., 408–418.

Robinson, S.K. 1994. Bird communities of restored barrens and savannas of southern Illinois. *Proceedings of the North American Conference on Savannas and Barrens*. Illinois State University, Normal, 147–150.

Robinson, S.K., J.A. Grzybowski, S.I. Rothstein, M.C. Brittingham, L.J. Petit, and F.R. Thompson, III. 1993. Management implications of cowbird parasitism for neotropical migrant songbirds. In D.M. Finch and P.W. Stangel, eds. *Status and Management of Neotropical Migratory Birds*. General Technical Report RM229. U.S. Dept. of Agriculture. Forest Service, Rocky Mountain Forest and Range Experiment Station. Fort Collins, Colorado, 93–102.

Robinson, S.K., and D.S. Wilcove. 1994. Forest fragmentation in the temperate zone and its effects on migratory songbirds. *Bird Conservation International* 4:233–249.

Robinson, S.K., F.M. Thompson, III, T.M. Donovan, D.R. Whitehead, and J. Faaborg. 1995. Regional forest fragmentation and the nesting success of migratory birds. *Science* 267:1987–1990.

Robinson, S.K., J.P. Hoover, J.R. Herkert, and R. Jack. In press-a. Cowbird parasitism in a fragmented landscape: effects of tract size, habitat, and abundance of cowbirds and hosts. In T. Cook, S.K. Robinson, S.I. Rothstein, S.G. Sealy, and J.N.M. Smith, eds. *Ecology and Management of Cowbirds*. University of Texas Press, Austin.

Robinson, S.K., S.I. Rothstein, M.C. Brittingham, L.J. Petit, and J.A. Gryzbowski, Jr. In press-b. Ecology and behavior of cowbirds and their impact on host populations. In T.E. Martin and D.M. Finch, eds. *Ecology and Management of Neotropical Migrant Landbirds*. Oxford University Press, Oxford, England.

Rothstein, S.I. 1975. An experimental and teleonomic investigation of avian brood parasitism. *Condor* 77:250–271.

Sandström, U. 1991. Enhanced predation rates on cavity birds' nests at deciduous forest edges—an experimental study. *Ornis Fennica* 68:93–98.

Sauer, J.R., and B.K. Williams. 1989. Generalized procedures for testing hypotheses about survival or recovery rates. *Journal of Wildlife Management* 53:137–142

Suarez, A., K. Pfennig, and S.K. Robinson. In Press. Nesting success of a disturbance dependent songbird on different kinds of edges. *Conservation Biology*.

Temple, S.A., and J.R. Cary. 1988. Modeling dynamics of habitat-interior bird populations in fragmented landscapes. *Conservation Biology* 2:340–347.

Thompson, F.R., III. 1994. Temporal and spatial patterns of breeding brown-headed cowbirds in the midwestern United States. *Auk* 11:979–990.

Thompson, F.M., III, S.K. Robinson, T.M. Donovan, J. Faaborg, and D.R. Whitehead. In press. Biogeographic, landscape, and local factors affecting cowbird abundance and host parasitism levels. In T. Cook, S.K. Robinson, S.I. Rothstein, S.G. Sealy, and J.N.M. Smith, eds. *Ecology and Management of Cowbirds* ed. T. Cook, S.K. Robinson, S.I. Rothstein, S.G. Sealy, and J.N.M. Smith University of Texas Press, Austin.

Trine, C.L., W.D. Robinson, and S.K. Robinson. In press. Consequences of brown-headed cowbird parasitism for host population dynamics. In S.I. Rothstein and S.K. Robinson, eds. *Parasitic Birds and Their Hosts.* Oxford Univ. Press, Oxford, England.

Wenny, D.G., R.L. Clawson, S.L. Sheriff, and J. Faaborg. 1993. Population variation, habitat selection, and minimum area requirements of three forest-interior warblers in central Missouri. *Condor* 95:968–979.

Whitcomb, R.F., C.S. Robbins, J.F. Lynch, B.L. Whitcomb, K. Klimkiewicz and D. Bystrak. 1981. Effects of forest fragmentation on avifauna of the eastern deciduous forest. In R.L. Burgess and D.M. Sharpe, eds. *Forest Island Dynamics in Man-Dominated Landscapes.* Springer-Verlag, New York, 125–205.

Wilcove, D.S., and S.K. Robinson. 1990. The impact of forest fragmentation on bird communities in eastern North America. In A. Keast, ed. *Biogeography and Ecology of Forest Bird Communities.* SPB Academic Publishing, The Hague, the Netherlands, 319–331.

Withgott, J.H. 1994. *Behavior and Ecology of the Black Rat Snake (Elaphe o. obsoleta) and its Predation on Bird's Nests.* M.S. thesis, University of Arkansas.

Yahner, R.H., T.E. Morrell, and J.S. Rachael. 1989. Effects of edge contrast on depredation of artificial avian nests. *Journal of Wildlife Management* 53:1135–1138.

Appendix A. Relative abundances (number/10 70-m census points) of birds present in 16 nature preserves in Illinois (codes given in Table 1). Dashed cells represent nature preserves outside the range of a given species.

Species	Nature preserve															
	HMW	CBS	LH	HL	FC	WG	MS	RP	HB	HBS	S8	FELL	OH	LBS	HP	LC
Green-backed heron (Butorides striatus)	0.0	0.0	0.0	0.7	0.0	0.0	0.6	0.0	0.0	0.0	0.2	0.0	0.0	0.7	0.1	0.0
Great blue heron (Ardea herodias)	0.0	0.0	0.0	0.7	0.0	0.0	0.6	0.0	0.0	0.0	0.1	0.0	0.0	3.4	0.7	0.0
Sandhill crane (Grus canadensis)	0.0	0.0	0.0	0.0	0.0	0.0	0.0	0.0	0.0	0.0	0.0	0.0	0.0	0.0	0.0	0.0
Yellow-crowned night heron (Nyctanassa violacia)	0.0	0.0	0.0	0.0	0.0	0.0	0.1	0.0	0.0	0.0	0.5	0.0	0.0	0.1	0.1	0.0
Mallard (Anas platyrhynchos)	0.0	0.0	0.0	0.0	0.0	0.0	0.0	0.0	0.0	0.0	0.0	0.0	0.0	0.0	0.0	0.0
Wood duck (Aix sponsa)	0.0	0.1	0.1	0.9	0.0	0.0	0.1	0.0	0.0	0.0	0.2	0.0	0.0	0.9	0.1	0.0
Hooded merganser (Lophodytes cucullatus)	0.0	0.0	0.0	0.0	0.0	0.0	0.0	0.0	0.0	0.0	0.0	0.0	0.0	0.1	0.1	0.0
American woodcock (Philohela minor)	0.0	0.1	0.0	0.0	0.0	0.0	0.0	0.0	0.0	0.0	0.0	0.1	0.0	0.1	0.1	0.0
Turkey vulture (Cathartes aura)	0.1	0.1	0.1	0.1	0.1	0.1	0.1	0.1	0.1	0.1	0.1	0.1	0.1	0.1	0.1	0.1
Black vulture (Coragyps atratus)	—	—	—	0.0	—	—	0.0	—	—	0.0	0.0	—	0.0	0.1	0.1	0.0
Mississippi kite (Ictinia mississippiensis)	—	—	—	0.1	—	—	0.6	—	—	—	0.1	—	0.0	0.1	0.1	0.0
Sharp-shinned hawk (Accipiter striatus)	0.0	0.0	0.0	0.0	0.0	0.0	0.0	0.0	0.0	0.0	0.0	0.0	0.0	0.0	0.0	0.1
Cooper's hawk (Accipiter cooperii)	0.0	0.1	0.1	0.0	0.0	0.1	0.0	0.1	0.1	0.0	0.0	0.3	0.1	0.1	0.1	0.1
Red-shouldered hawk (Buteo lineatus)	0.0	0.0	0.0	0.0	0.0	0.0	0.6	0.0	0.0	0.0	0.2	0.0	0.0	0.3	0.1	0.0
Broad-winged hawk (Buteo platypterus)	0.0	0.0	0.0	0.0	0.0	0.2	0.0	0.0	0.1	0.0	0.0	0.1	0.1	0.1	0.0	0.1

continued

Appendix A. Continued.

	Nature preserve															
Species	HMW	CBS	LH	HL	FC	WG	MS	RP	HB	HBS	S8	FELL	OH	LBS	HP	LC
Red-tailed hawk (*Buteo jamaicensis*)	0.0	0.0	0.0	0.2	0.0	0.0	0.0	0.8	0.0	0.0	0.0	0.0	0.0	0.1	0.1	0.0
Swainson's hawk (*Buteo swainsoni*)	0.0	0.0	0.0	0.0	0.0	0.0	0.0	0.0	0.0	0.0	0.0	0.0	0.0	0.0	0.0	0.0
Ruffed grouse (*Bonasa umbellus*)	—	—	—	—	—	—	—	—	—	—	—	0.0	0.1	0.0	0.0	0.0
Northern bobwhite (*Colinus virginianus*)	0.0	0.0	0.0	0.0	0.0	0.0	0.0	0.0	0.0	3.8	0.0	0.0	0.0	0.0	0.1	1.0
Wild turkey (*Meleagris gallopavo*)	0.0	0.0	0.0	0.0	0.0	0.1	0.0	0.1	0.1	0.0	0.1	0.1	0.1	0.1	0.1	0.1
Mourning dove (*Zenaida macroura*)	0.0	0.0	0.0	0.1	0.0	0.0	0.1	0.5	0.0	4.4	0.0	0.0	0.0	0.1	0.1	0.1
Yellow-billed cuckoo (*Coccyzus americanus*)	0.1	0.1	0.1	3.5	0.8	1.8	5.6	0.8	0.3	0.0	4.9	0.3	1.7	1.2	3.7	1.0
Black-billed cuckoo (*Coccyzus erythrophthalmus*)	0.0	0.1	0.0	0.0	0.0	0.0	0.0	0.5	0.0	0.0	0.0	0.0	0.0	0.0	0.0	0.0
Long-eared owl (*Asio otus*)	0.0	0.0	0.0	0.0	0.0	0.0	0.0	0.0	0.0	0.0	0.0	0.0	0.0	0.0	0.0	0.0
Great-horned owl (*Bubo virginianus*)	0.1	0.1	0.1	0.1	0.1	0.1	0.1	0.1	0.1	0.1	0.1	0.1	0.1	0.1	0.1	0.1
Barred owl (*Strix varia*)	0.1	0.1	0.1	0.1	0.1	0.1	0.1	0.0	0.1	0.4	0.1	0.1	0.1	0.1	0.1	0.1
Eastern screech owl (*Otus asio*)	0.1	0.0	0.1	0.0	0.0	0.0	0.0	0.0	0.0	0.0	0.0	0.0	0.1	0.0	0.0	0.0
Chuck-will's-widow (*Caprimulgus carolinensis*)	—	—	—	0.0	—	—	0.0	0.0	—	0.0	0.0	0.0	0.0	0.0	0.0	0.0
Whip-poor-will (*Caprimulgus vociterus*)	0.0	0.1	0.0	0.0	0.1	0.1	0.1	0.1	0.1	0.1	0.1	0.1	0.1	0.1	0.1	0.1
Common nighthawk (*Chordeiles minor*)	0.1	0.1	0.1	0.1	0.1	0.1	0.1	0.1	0.1	0.1	0.1	0.1	0.1	0.1	0.1	0.1

continued

Appendix A. *Continued.*

Species	Nature preserve															
	HMW	CBS	LH	HL	FC	WG	MS	RP	HB	HBS	S8	FELL	OH	LBS	HP	LC
Chimney swift (Chaetura pelagica)	0.1	0.1	0.1	0.4	0.1	0.1	0.1	0.1	0.1	0.1	5.0	0.1	0.1	0.1	1.1	0.1
Ruby-throated hummingbird (Archilochus colubris)	0.1	1.4	2.5	3.1	0.1	0.1	0.6	0.0	0.7	0.0	1.2	0.7	1.4	4.4	1.5	0.1
Belted kingfisher (Megaceryle alcyon)	0.0	0.0	0.0	0.0	0.1	0.0	0.1	0.0	0.0	0.0	0.1	0.0	0.0	0.1	0.1	0.1
Red-bellied woodpecker (Melanerpes carolinus)	4.0	1.4	5.0	3.9	0.1	3.6	1.7	2.0	1.8	2.2	3.4	1.3	3.3	0.5	0.1	3.0
Northern flicker (Colaptes auratus)	2.0	0.1	2.5	1.3	0.1	1.0	0.1	1.3	0.0	1.1	0.3	0.4	0.0	2.4	0.2	0.1
Red-headed woodpecker (Melanerpes erethrocephalus)	0.0	2.9	2.5	8.9	0.8	0.0	0.6	1.1	0.2	4.2	3.6	0.2	0.0	6.0	1.0	1.0
Yellow-bellied sapsucker (Sphyrapicus varius)	0.0	0.0	0.0	—	0.0	0.0	—	—	0.1	—	—	0.0	—	—	—	—
Downy woodpecker (Picoides pubescens)	4.0	1.4	5.0	8.9	6.2	6.6	4.4	0.9	1.6	0.1	4.7	2.6	1.8	3.6	5.3	1.0
Hairy woodpecker (Picoides villosus)	2.0	1.4	0.1	1.3	0.1	1.6	0.1	0.4	0.3	0.0	1.2	0.4	0.9	2.1	0.8	1.0
Pileated woodpecker (Dryocopus pileatus)	0.0	0.0	0.0	0.2	0.0	0.1	0.1	0.5	0.2	0.0	0.7	0.1	1.4	0.9	1.1	0.1
Eastern kingbird (Tyrannus tyrannus)	0.0	0.0	0.0	0.0	0.0	0.0	0.0	0.0	0.0	0.0	0.0	0.0	0.0	0.0	0.1	0.0
Great crested flycatcher (Myiarchus crinitus)	6.0	4.3	2.5	3.7	2.3	3.0	3.9	2.8	1.8	1.3	4.6	2.7	3.5	3.9	2.8	1.0
Eastern wood-pewee (Contopus virens)	10.0	1.4	15.0	12.2	8.5	9.3	7.2	1.3	6.8	10.0	10.9	9.4	10.0	6.7	7.0	3.0

continued

Appendix A. *Continued.*

Species	Nature preserve															
	HMW	CBS	LH	HL	FC	WG	MS	RP	HB	HBS	S8	FELL	OH	LBS	HP	LC
Eastern phoebe (*Sayornis phoebe*)	0.0	0.1	0.1	0.0	0.1	0.0	0.0	0.0	0.1	0.0	0.0	0.1	0.1	0.9	0.0	3.0
Least flycatcher (*Empidonax minimus*)	0.0	0.0	0.0	—	0.1	0.0	—	0.0	0.0	0.0	0.0	1.0	—	—	—	—
Acadian flycatcher (*Empidonax virescens*)	0.0	0.0	0.0	18.5	10.0	0.4	11.7	0.8	0.3	0.0	16.6	3.8	10.8	15.1	23.6	2.0
Tree swallow (*Iridoprocne bicolor*)	0.0	0.0	0.0	0.0	0.0	0.0	0.1	0.0	0.0	0.0	0.0	0.0	0.0	0.1	0.1	0.0
Purple martin (*Progne subis*)	0.0	0.0	0.0	0.9	0.0	0.0	3.9	0.0	0.0	0.0	0.1	0.0	0.0	0.0	0.1	0.0
Northern rough-winged swallow (*Stelgidopteryx ruficollis*)	0.0	0.1	0.0	0.0	0.1	0.0	0.0	0.0	0.0	0.0	0.0	0.0	0.0	0.1	0.1	0.0
Blue jay (*Cyanocitta cristata*)	8.0	2.9	5.0	0.4	5.4	5.4	0.0	5.0	2.5	6.7	1.2	2.1	1.5	0.4	1.5	1.0
American crow (*Corvus brachyrhynchos*)	0.1	0.0	5.0	0.7	0.1	0.0	0.6	0.0	0.0	1.1	0.5	0.0	0.0	0.5	0.7	0.1
Fish crow (*Corvus ossifragus*)	0.0	0.0	0.0	0.7	0.0	0.0	0.6	0.0	0.0	0.0	0.0	0.0	0.0	0.5	0.1	0.0
Eastern tufted titmouse (*Parus bicolor*)	0.1	0.1	2.5	10.0	2.3	2.4	5.6	8.7	3.7	5.5	6.6	4.9	7.6	8.1	11.5	2.0
Black-capped chickadee (*Parus atricapillus*)	8.0	1.4	5.0	—	9.2	2.8	—	5.2	3.5	0.4	7.2	3.6	—	—	—	—
Carolina chickadee (*Parus carolinensis*)	—	—	—	9.1	—	—	3.3	—	—	—	6.0	—	1.6	3.5	5.6	1.0
Brown creeper (*Certhia familiaris*)	0.0	0.0	0.0	0.0	0.0	0.0	0.0	0.0	0.0	0.0	6.0	0.0	0.0	2.2	0.1	0.0
White-breasted nuthatch (*Sitta carolinensis*)	8.0	1.4	5.0	13.0	9.2	6.1	5.0	4.2	4.2	3.3	9.6	3.6	5.7	4.2	6.2	4.0
House wren (*Troglodytes aedon*)	10.0	1.4	15.0	0.0	10.8	10.0	0.0	0.0	0.2	0.0	0.0	0.7	0.0	0.0	0.0	0.0

continued

Appendix A. Continued.

Species	Nature preserve															
	HMW	CBS	LH	HL	FC	WG	MS	RP	HB	HBS	S8	FELL	OH	LBS	HP	LC
Carolina wren (*Thryothorus ludovicianus*)	0.0	0.0	0.0	6.7	0.0	0.1	1.7	0.0	0.1	0.0	6.0	0.1	1.6	5.0	4.8	1.0
Bewick's wren (*Thryomanes bewickii*)	0.0	0.0	0.0	0.0	0.0	0.0	0.0	0.0	0.0	0.0	0.0	0.0	0.0	0.0	0.0	0.0
Blue-grey gnatcatcher (*Polioptila caerulea*)	4.0	2.9	2.5	16.3	3.1	1.4	5.6	0.3	1.9	0.0	8.2	4.4	6.3	13.4	8.6	1.0
Eastern bluebird (*Sialia sialis*)	0.0	0.0	0.0	0.2	0.0	0.0	0.6	0.0	0.0	0.5	0.5	0.0	0.0	1.2	0.1	0.0
Wood thrush (*Hylocichla mustelina*)	4.0	1.4	0.0	0.4	2.3	8.5	2.8	1.3	3.8	0.0	1.5	3.0	3.7	0.3	3.8	3.0
Veery (*Catharus fuscescens*)	0.0	0.0	0.0	—	0.8	5.6	—	0.3	0.2	—	—	3.6	0.0	—	—	—
American robin (*Turdus migratorius*)	0.1	0.0	0.0	0.2	6.9	2.5	0.6	10.5	1.0	4.0	0.5	7.7	0.0	0.1	0.1	0.0
Gray catbird (*Dumetella carolinensis*)	0.0	1.4	2.5	0.0	2.3	2.8	0.1	0.0	0.1	2.0	0.3	3.5	0.0	0.3	0.4	0.0
Brown thrasher (*Toxostoma rufum*)	0.0	0.0	0.0	0.0	0.0	0.0	0.0	0.0	0.0	1.1	0.0	0.0	0.0	0.0	0.1	1.0
Cedar waxwing (*Bombycilla cedrorum*)	0.0	0.0	0.0	0.0	0.8	0.1	0.0	3.6	0.2	0.0	0.0	3.6	0.0	0.0	0.1	0.0
European starling (*Sturnus vulgaris*)	0.1	0.1	14.0	0.0	0.0	0.0	0.0	0.0	0.0	0.0	0.0	0.0	0.0	0.7	0.0	0.0
White-eyed vireo (*Vireo griseus*)	0.0	0.0	0.0	0.2	0.0	0.0	0.1	0.0	0.0	0.0	0.0	0.0	0.1	2.9	1.9	3.0
Yellow-throated vireo (*Vireo flavifrons*)	2.0	4.3	1.4	2.8	0.0	0.4	0.1	0.3	0.4	0.0	2.8	1.7	1.9	2.1	1.7	1.0
Solitary vireo (*Vireo solitarius*)	0.0	0.0	0.0	0.0	0.0	0.0	0.0	0.0	0.0	0.6	0.0	0.0	0.0	0.0	0.0	0.0
Red-eyed vireo (*Vireo olivaceus*)	4.0	11.5	12.5	4.8	11.5	5.5	1.1	4.1	8.8	1.1	4.2	9.2	9.8	4.3	4.5	3.0
Warbling vireo (*Vireo gilvus*)	0.0	0.0	0.0	0.0	0.0	0.0	0.0	0.0	0.0	0.0	0.0	0.1	0.0	0.0	0.0	0.0

continued

Appendix A. Continued.

Species	Nature preserve															
	HMW	CBS	LH	HL	FC	WG	MS	RP	HB	HBS	S8	FELL	OH	LBS	HP	LC
Prothonotary warbler (*Protonotaria citrea*)	0.0	0.0	0.0	4.6	0.0	0.0	2.8	0.0	0.0	0.0	6.6	0.1	0.0	9.3	5.6	0.0
Blue-winged warbler (*Vermivora pinus*)	0.0	0.0	0.0	0.0	0.0	0.0	0.0	0.0	0.1	0.0	0.0	0.1	0.0	0.0	0.0	0.0
Gold-winged warbler (*Vermivora chrysoptera*)	0.0	0.0	0.0	—	0.0	0.0	—	0.0	0.0	0.0	0.0	0.1	0.0	—	—	—
Northern parula (*Parula americana*)	—	—	—	3.3	—	—	0.0	1.0	—	0.0	1.9	—	1.5	7.5	5.2	2.0
Black and white warbler (*Mniotilta varia*)	0.0	0.0	0.0	0.0	0.8	0.0	0.0	0.0	0.0	0.0	0.0	0.3	0.1	0.0	0.1	1.0
Cerulean warbler (*Dendroica cerulea*)	0.0	0.0	0.0	0.0	0.0	0.0	0.0	0.5	0.3	0.0	0.0	4.2	0.3	0.7	1.6	0.0
Chestnut-sided warbler (*Dendroica pensylvanica*)	0.0	0.0	0.0	0.0	0.0	0.0	0.0	0.0	0.1	0.0	0.0	0.1	0.0	—	0.0	0.0
Black-throated green warbler (*Dendroica virens*)	0.0	0.0	0.0	0.0	0.0	0.0	0.0	0.0	0.0	0.0	0.0	0.0	0.0	0.0	0.0	0.0
Yellow-throated warbler (*Dendroica ominica*)	0.0	0.0	0.0	0.1	0.0	0.0	1.1	0.0	0.0	0.0	3.5	0.0	0.2	0.7	0.3	0.0
Prairie warbler (*Dendroica discolor*)	—	—	—	0.0	—	—	0.0	0.0	—	0.0	0.0	—	0.0	—	0.0	0.1
Pine warbler (*Dendroica pinus*)	—	—	—	0.0	—	—	0.0	—	—	0.0	0.0	—	0.1	0.0	0.0	0.1
Yellow warbler (*Dendroica petechia*)	0.0	0.0	0.0	0.0	0.0	0.0	0.0	0.0	0.0	0.1	0.0	0.1	0.0	0.0	0.0	0.0
Mourning warbler (*Oporornis philadelphia*)	0.0	0.0	0.0	0.0	0.0	0.0	0.0	0.0	0.0	0.0	0.0	0.0	0.0	0.0	0.0	0.0

continued

Appendix A. Continued.

Species	Nature preserve															
	HMW	CBS	LH	HL	FC	WG	MS	RP	HB	HBS	S8	FELL	OH	LBS	HP	LC
Kentucky warbler (*Oporornis formosus*)	0.0	0.0	0.0	1.1	0.0	0.1	0.6	0.0	0.1	0.0	2.7	1.8	2.5	0.5	3.8	3.0
Canada warbler (*Wilsonia caradensis*)	0.0	0.0	0.0	—	0.0	0.0	—	—	0.0	—	0.0	0.1	—	—	—	—
Hooded warbler (*Wilsonia citrina*)	0.0	0.0	0.0	0.0	0.0	0.2	0.0	0.0	0.0	0.3	0.3	0.1	0.0	0.0	0.0	0.1
Worm-eating warbler (*Helmitheros vermivorus*)	0.0	0.0	0.0	0.0	0.0	0.0	0.0	0.0	0.2	0.0	0.0	0.1	7.5	0.0	0.1	2.0
Swainson's warbler (*Limnothlypis swainsonii*)	—	—	—	0.0	—	—	0.0	—	—	0.0	0.0	—	0.0	0.0	0.1	0.0
Ovenbird (*Seiurus aurocapillus*)	0.0	0.1	0.0	0.0	0.8	3.9	0.0	0.3	6.3	0.0	0.2	3.6	1.3	0.0	0.1	14.0
Louisiana waterthrush (*Seiurus motacilla*)	0.0	0.0	0.0	0.1	0.0	0.0	0.0	0.0	0.2	0.0	0.2	0.0	0.8	0.8	0.6	1.0
Common yellowthroat (*geothlypis trichas*)	0.0	0.0	0.0	0.4	0.0	0.0	3.9	0.0	0.0	4.4	0.1	0.5	0.0	0.7	1.0	1.0
Yellow-breasted chat (*Icteria virens*)	0.0	0.0	0.0	0.0	0.0	0.0	2.2	0.0	0.0	0.0	0.0	0.0	0.0	0.0	0.1	1.0
American redstart (*Setophaga ruticilla*)	0.0	0.0	0.0	0.0	0.1	0.0	0.0	0.0	0.0	0.0	0.0	6.7	0.0	0.0	0.1	0.0
Rose-breasted grosbeak (*Pheucticus ludovicianus*)	8.0	0.1	2.5	—	0.0	4.5	—	1.8	1.0	0.0	0.0	11.0	—	—	0.1	—
Northern cardinal (*Cardinalis cardinalis*)	10.0	12.9	2.5	15.7	8.5	3.4	21.1	4.7	3.8	1.1	12.7	6.0	3.8	6.1	8.0	9.0
Blue grosbeak (*Guiraca caerulea*)	0.0	0.0	0.0	0.0	0.0	0.0	0.0	0.0	0.0	0.0	0.0	0.0	0.0	0.0	0.0	0.0

continued

Appendix A. *Continued.*

Species	Nature preserve															
	HMW	CBS	LH	HL	FC	WG	MS	RP	HB	HBS	S8	FELL	OH	LBS	HP	LC
Indigo bunting (*Passerina cyanea*)	18.6	4.3	12.5	8.7	1.5	4.4	16.1	6.2	1.0	8.9	2.8	3.7	0.2	2.0	3.2	1.0
Rufous-sided towhee (*Pipilo erythrophthalmus*)	0.0	0.1	0.0	0.0	0.0	1.1	1.7	0.0	0.7	6.3	0.0	3.4	0.1	0.7	0.1	6.0
Song sparrow (*Melospiza melodia*)	0.0	0.0	0.0	0.2	0.0	0.0	1.7	0.0	0.0	0.0	0.1	0.0	0.0	0.5	0.0	0.0
Bachman's sparrow (*Aimophila aestivalis*)	0.0	0.0	0.0	0.0	0.0	0.0	0.0	0.0	0.0	0.0	0.0	0.0	0.0	0.0	0.0	0.0
Lark sparrow (*Chondestes grammacus*)	0.0	0.0	0.0	0.0	0.0	0.0	0.0	0.0	0.0	0.5	0.0	0.0	0.0	0.0	0.0	0.0
Field sparrow (*Spizella pusilla*)	0.0	0.0	0.0	0.1	0.0	0.0	0.0	0.0	0.0	10.3	0.0	0.0	0.0	0.1	0.1	0.0
Chipping sparrow (*Spizella passerina*)	0.0	0.0	0.0	0.0	0.0	0.0	0.0	0.0	0.0	1.1	0.0	0.2	0.0	0.0	0.0	0.0
Swamp sparrow (*Melospiza georgiana*)	0.0	0.0	0.0	0.0	0.0	0.0	0.0	0.0	0.0	0.0	0.0	0.0	0.0	0.0	0.0	0.0
Eastern meadowlark (*Sturnella magna*)	0.0	0.0	0.0	0.0	0.0	0.0	0.0	0.0	0.0	1.1	0.0	0.0	0.0	0.0	0.0	0.0
Red-winged blackbird (*Agelaius phoeniceus*)	0.0	0.0	0.0	0.9	0.0	0.0	6.1	0.3	0.0	0.0	0.0	0.0	0.0	2.1	1.4	0.0
Brown-headed cowbird (*Molothrus ater*)	2.0	1.4	0.0	5.0	5.4	4.3	2.2	4.1	4.3	4.0	3.5	4.5	2.6	1.6	2.2	1.0
Common grackle (*Quiscalus quiscula*)	0.0	0.0	0.0	17.2	0.8	0.8	12.2	5.7	0.5	1.1	3.3	0.6	0.0	10.8	2.3	0.0
Orchard oriole (*Icterus spurius*)	0.0	0.0	0.0	0.1	0.0	0.0	0.0	0.0	0.0	3.3	0.0	0.0	0.0	0.1	0.0	0.0
Northern oriole (*Icterus galbula*)	8.0	0.0	2.5	0.4	0.0	2.1	0.1	2.2	0.0	1.1	0.0	2.2	0.0	0.0	0.0	0.0

continued

Appendix A. Continued.

								Nature preserve								
Species	HMW	CBS	LH	HL	FC	WG	MS	RP	HB	HBS	S8	FELL	OH	LBS	HP	LC
Scarlet tanager (*Piranga olivacea*)	10.0	4.3	0.0	0.2	3.8	5.2	0.0	1.8	2.5	1.0	0.0	3.8	3.7	0.5	1.1	3.0
Summer tanager (*Piranga rubra*)	0.0	0.0	0.0	1.5	0.0	0.0	0.6	0.8	0.1	3.3	1.0	0.0	1.9	0.4	0.5	3.0
Pine siskin (*Carduelis pinus*)	0.0	0.0	0.0	0.0	0.0	0.0	0.0	0.0	0.0	0.0	0.0	0.0	0.0	0.0	0.0	0.0
American goldfinch (*Carduelis tristis*)	0.0	0.0	0.0	9.8	1.3	0.0	11.7	3.9	0.0	1.1	4.4	0.0	0.0	0.5	2.3	0.0

9

Impacts of Fragmentation on Midwestern Aquatic Organisms

Lawrence M. Page, Mark Pyron, and Kevin S. Cummings
Illinois Natural History Survey, 607 E. Peabody Dr., Champaign, IL 61820

Introduction

Fragmentation has been identified as a major cause of declines in species diversity for many terrestrial ecosystems (reviewed by Saunders 1991). Much less empirical information is available on the effects of fragmentation on freshwater species and communities (Bradford et al. 1993, Townsend and Crowl 1991). Fragmentation in streams (i.e., a lack of connectivity between upstream and downstream populations) can be caused by many anthropogenic influences, but few studies have investigated the problem. In this review we present evidence that freshwater organisms are declining as a result of factors that lead, initially, to fragmentation and, ultimately, to extirpation of populations. Examples of stream modifications that cause fragmentation are described, followed by examples of management and restoration strategies that can mitigate the impact of fragmentation.

Diversity of Stream Organisms in the Midwest

The United States has the most diverse temperate-stream biota in the world. Fishes, mussels, and crayfishes, the organisms for which the most complete information is available, are all more diverse in the United States than they are in the temperate regions of Europe or Australia (Table 9.1). Within the United States, the greatest diversity in these groups is found in streams in the southern Appalachians. Although biological diversity in the Midwest is less than in montane areas, it is greater than in most temperate regions of the world. For example, Illinois has or had 188 native species of fishes, 79 native mussels, and 20 native crayfishes.

Declines in Stream Biodiversity

Recent declines in populations of stream-inhabiting species in the Midwest are well known and well documented. The best data are for Illinois, where two statewide surveys have been conducted on fishes (Forbes and Richardson 1908,

Table 9.1. Numbers of species in temperate regions of the world. From Bogan (1993), Hobbs (1988), Merrick and Schmida (1993), Page and Burr (1991), Smith (1992), Taylor et al. (1996), Williams et al. (1993).

	Fishes	Mussels	Crayfishes
United States	800	281	308
Europe	357	16	7
Australia	185	17	102

Smith 1979), one has been completed for crayfishes (Page 1985a), and one is nearing completion for mussels (Cummings in prep.). At the turn of the century, Forbes and Richardson (1908) found 187 native species of fishes reproducing in Illinois. When Smith completed his resurvey, only 179 native fishes were still reproducing in Illinois: 8 species (4% of the total) had been eliminated in the 70 years since the original survey (Smith 1979). Today, only 17 years after the publication of Smith's study, only 175 native fishes remain. Another 4 species have disappeared, for a total loss of 6% of the native fishes (Table 9.2). The factors that contributed to the loss of fishes continue to impact streams, and 23 more species (12%) of fishes are listed as endangered or threatened in Illinois (Illinois Endangered Species Protection Board, 1994).

The loss of mussels in Illinois has been even more dramatic. Of the 79 species for which historical records are available, 17 (22%) are extirpated, and another 24 (30%) are listed as endangered or threatened (Table 9.3) (Cummings and Mayer 1997). An astonishing 52% of the native species are gone or in imminent danger of disappearing. Of the 20 species of crayfishes native to Illinois, 1 (Cambarus robustus) is gone (5%), and 4 (20%) are listed as endangered or threatened.

The number of extirpated and endangered species appears enormous until it is compared to the loss of native landscape. It is estimated that less than 1% of the original landscape of Illinois remains in a natural state, as defined by criteria established for an inventory of Illinois natural areas (White 1978). As discussed elsewhere in this book, the landscape of Illinois and much of the Midwest has been transformed from predominantly prairie, savanna, wetlands, and forest, to mainly corn fields, soybean fields, and urban areas.

Table 9.2. Extirpated species of native Illinois fishes.

Species lost by 1979	Additional species lost by 1996
Ohio lamprey, Ichthyomyzon bdellium	Alligator gar, Atractosteus spatula
Blackfin cisco, Coregonus nigripinnis	Bigeye chub, Hybopsis amblops
Muskellunge, Esox masquinongy	Bluehead shiner, Pteronotropis hubbsi
Rosefin shiner, Lythrurus ardens	Northern madtom, Noturus stigmosus
Gilt darter, Percina evides	
Saddleback darter, Percina ouachitae	
Crystal darter, Crystallaria asprella	
Spoonhead sculpin, Cottus ricei	

Table 9.3. Extinct and extirpated species of native Illinois mussels (Unionidae).

Globally Extinct	
Epioblasma flexuosa (Rafinesque, 1820)	Leafshell
Epioblasma personata (Say, 1829)	Combshell
Epioblasma phillipsii (Conrad, 1835)	Conrad's riffleshell
Epioblasma propinqua (Lea 1857)	Tennessee riffleshell
Epioblasma sampsonii (Lea, 1861)	Wabash riffleshell
Epioblasma torulosa (Rafinesque, 1820)	Tubercled blossom
Extirpated from Illinois	
Fusconaia subrotunda (Lea, 1831)	Longsolid
Hemistena lata (Rafinesque, 1820)	Cracking pearlymussel
Plethobasus cicatricosus (Say, 1829)	White wartyback
Pleurobema plenum (Lea, 1840)	Rough pigtoe
Quadrula fragosa (Conrad, 1835)	Winged mapleleaf
Epioblasma obliquata (Rafinesque, 1820)	White catspaw
Epioblasma rangiana (Lea, 1838)	Northern riffleshell
Lampsilis abrupta (Say, 1831)	Pink mucket
Leptodea leptodon (Rafinesque, 1820)	Scaleshell
Obovaria retusa (Lamarck, 1819)	Ring pink
Villosa fabalis (Lea, 1831)	Rayed bean

With the pervasive transformation that has occurred in the landscape of the Midwest, it is surprising that not more species have disappeared. Why does Illinois still have most of the native aquatic species (>90% of the fishes and crayfishes, and nearly 80% of the mussels) if most of the original landscape has been modified? The percentage of extirpated species is small in relation to the pervasiveness of the landscape modifications because species presence is determined on a statewide basis, and many species survive in the state in very small populations. The larger the area under consideration, the greater is the likelihood that at least one population will be found. When we examine data on extirpation for smaller areas, we expect to find, on average, a larger loss of species than we find when we consider an area as large as Illinois. For example, the Embarras River drainage in east-central Illinois historically supported 43 species of freshwater mussels, but only 31 (72%) are extant. In the Saline River system in southeastern Illinois, only 39 of the 67 fishes (58%) known historically in the now badly polluted river system are still present.

The relatively low number of aquatic species extirpations for the entire state is misleading as an indicator of environmental condition. Many species persist in small populations that are widely separated from all other conspecific populations and, hence, are extremely vulnerable to extirpation. The diminution and isolation of populations caused by fragmentation of the landscape and concomitant loss of suitable habitats will likely lead to a dramatic increase in the number of extirpated species in the near future in Illinois. The 23 species of fishes (13% of the surviving native species), 24 species of mussels (39% of survivors), and

4 species of crayfishes (20% of survivors) that are listed as endangered or threatened are especially vulnerable.

The deleterious effect of fragmentation on aquatic organisms is demonstrated by the temporal distributions of Illinois minnows. Forbes and Richardson (1908) found the bigeye chub *(Hybopsis amblops)* to be common in eastern Illinois in the late 1800s. Populations of the bigeye chub disappeared in subsequent decades as land use changed and by the 1950s, the species persisted only in highly fragmented populations (Fig. 9.1). By the 1960s the species was gone (Smith 1979). Causes for the extirpation of the bigeye chub were clearly understood by Smith (1979: 78), who noted that "deposits of fine silt over substrates that were once sand and gravel eliminated the habitat of the species. Other alterations of streams and their watersheds and local fish kills hastened the disappearance of this chub, and ultimately there were no sources for recruitment left." The black-nose shiner *(Notropis heterolepis)* once occurred statewide but by the middle of this century it had been reduced to a few populations in northern Illinois (Fig. 9.2). Although still extant, the blacknose shiner is affected by at least some of the same forms of degradation as was the bigeye chub, and it continues to decline in abundance.

The few remaining isolated populations of the blacknose shiner and many other aquatic species are highly vulnerable to extirpation. Prior to its isolation, a population can rebound from local extirpation through recruitment of individuals from nearby populations (Detenbeck et al. 1992). As long as environmental conditions are suitable, immigration will occur and the population will become reestablished (Bayley and Osborne 1993). For example, a population adversely affected by an extraordinary flood or drought can reconstitute in a short period of time through dispersal from other populations; in contrast, isolated or semi-isolated populations have no chance of becoming reestablished because there is no source of immigrants, or because immigration occurs too infrequently to maintain populations constantly exposed to degradation.

The impact of fragmentation may be even more detrimental to stream organisms with more complex life cycles, such as mussels, than it is to fishes. Mussels that inhabit eastern Northern America have a larva (a glochidium) that is an obligatory parasite, primarily on fishes, resulting in strong correlations between mussel and fish distributions (Watters 1992). Stream degradation can affect a mussel species directly, just as it affects a fish, or it can affect the mussel indirectly by harming or eliminating its host. Without the host to complete its life cycle, the mussel is doomed to extirpation. The large loss of mussels in the Midwest is likely due to the synergistic effects of stream degradation and loss of fish hosts (Cummings & Mayer 1992, Bogan 1993, Neves 1993, Williams et al. 1993).

The large number of populations of aquatic organisms persisting only in isola-tion suggests that many more will soon disappear. A mussel on the brink of extirpation in Illinois is the snuffbox *(Epioblasma triquetra)* (Fig. 9.3). Histori-cally, the species had a statewide distribution; today, it persists only in a short

Figure 9.1. Pre-1950 (open circles) and post-1950 (black dots) distribution of the bigeye chub *(Hybopsis amblops).*

From Forbes and Richardson (1908), Smith (1979).

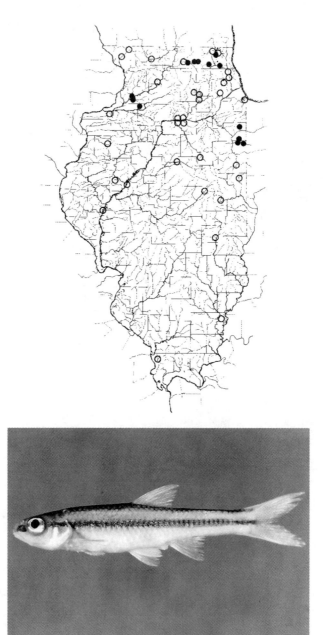

Figure 9.2.   Pre-1950 (open circles) and post-1950 (blackdots) distribution of the black-nose shiner *(Notropis heterolepis)* in Illinois.

From Forbes and Richardson (1908), Smith (1979).

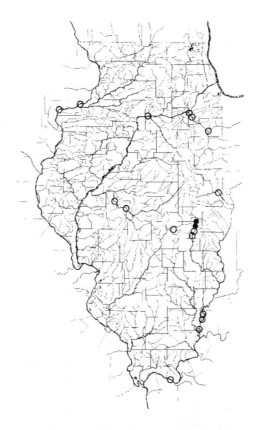

Figure 9.3. Pre-1970 (open circles) and post-1970 (black dots) distribution of the snuffbox mussel *(Epioblasma triquetra).*

From Cummings (in prep.).

segment of the Embarras River. A harmful event, such as a drought or pesticide runoff, could eliminate the sole surviving Illinois population. Although the snuff-box population in Illinois is small, it appears to be self-sustaining. Other mussel species (i.e., fanshell) *(Cyprogenia stegaria)* and orange-foot pimpleback *(Pletho-basus cooperianus)* are not reproducing and are likely to be extirpated from Illinois at the end of the current generation.

The above examples of the impact of fragmentation on stream organisms are midwestern, with data coming from Illinois. However, fragmentation caused by landscape modification and stream degradation is occurring throughout the United States and the rest of the developed world. Unless corrective measures are taken, the large number of species persisting only in fragmented landscapes soon will translate into an extraordinarily high number of species extinctions. Species extinctions lead to changes in food webs and other ecosystem functions which can have negative effects on other species, including those that are valuable sport and commercial species, and the process of extinction can accelerate.

Stream Habitat Fragmentation: Landscape Change and Stream Modification

Stream ecosystems are fragmented by landscape changes that render stream habitats unsuitable for aquatic organisms and by in-stream modifications that eliminate stream habitats. Smith (1971) ranked the causes of extirpation or decline in fish species in Illinois as follows: siltation (as the primary factor responsible for the loss of 2, and decimation of 14, species), drainage of bottomland lakes, swamps, and prairie marshes (0, 13), desiccation during drought (0, 12), species introductions (2, 7), pollution (2, 5), impoundments (0, 4), and increased water temperatures (0, 1). All of these factors render habitats unsuitable for many aquatic species throughout the Midwest, cause extirpations, and lead to the isolation of populations.

Other chapters in this book discuss landscape modifications that negatively affect terrestrial organisms; many of these activities also have led to major changes in stream environments. For example, streams in the Midwest naturally have wooded floodplains (Fig. 9.4) which are extremely important in maintaining a healthy aquatic environment. The vegetation on a floodplain shades the stream and prevents abnormally high water temperatures during the summer, stabilizes the stream bank and reduces erosion, and acts as a filter which removes topsoil and pesticides which would otherwise reach the stream as water drains from croplands. During periods of high water, vegetated floodplains provide feeding and spawning areas for many species of aquatic organisms and nurseries for developing larvae. When floodplains are converted to crop production (Fig. 9.5), as they have been throughout much of the Midwest, they no longer provide these benefits to aquatic organisms.

Figure 9.4. A natural stream with flowing water and a clean rocky substrate that provides living space for a great variety of species and spawning habitat for fishes. One of the primary causes of the decline in species diversity in streams in the Midwest is the accumulation of fine sediments over natural rocky substrates.

The tiling of land for agriculture is another major landscape change that has negatively impacted streams. As Forbes and Richardson noted almost 100 years ago (Forbes and Richardson 1908) in their description of the Sangamon River, a typical midwestern stream: "Formerly the flow of the river was more or less regular. This was due to the fact that the portion of the basin lying within the Shelbyville moraine was filled with swamps which absorbed the water as it fell and then gave it forth very gradually. Now, however, a very complete system of tile drainage carries off the water very quickly, and so leaves the river subject to low stages for a large part of the year." Land that once drained slowly drains quickly once it is tiled. Rapid drainage of land increases the pulse of a flood and increases the intensity and duration of low-flow once the water has moved downstream. These artificially extreme fluctuations in water levels subject stream organisms to environmental conditions to which they are not adapted and can lead to the extirpation of populations.

Siltation

Siltation, increased water temperatures, and desiccation follow the removal of riparian vegetation and the tiling of fields as land is prepared for agriculture.

Figure 9.5. Trees are being removed along this small tributary, presumably to enhance drainage of the surrounding cropland. Once the trees are removed there will be nothing to prevent topsoil and pesticides applied to the land from washing into the stream.

The excessive siltation associated with the removal of floodplain vegetation is among the most damaging forms of stream pollution in the Midwest. The clean rock and gravel substrates that normally characterize riffles and other stream habitats with fast-flowing water (Fig. 9.4) provide living space for many species of aquatic insects and other invertebrates (Hynes 1970), and important spawning habitat for many species of fishes (Balon 1975, Page 1985b). The complex nature of rocky substrates provides excellent cover from predators. This cover is important for invertebrates and small fishes that have no defense against predators other than hiding, and is important to fishes in providing places for hiding eggs. The deposition of silt covers the rocks and fills in spaces among rocks, leaving no place for small organisms to hide or to deposit their eggs.

Silt can also cover the leaves of aquatic plants and, if sufficient to prevent gas exchange or photosynthesis, will cause the plants to die. The reduction of plant life in a stream has a cascading negative impact on the stream ecosystem. Many animals, in particular insect larvae and fishes, use the plants as places to hide and forage. Some fishes use plants to hide from predators; others use plants as sites from which to ambush prey. As plants are eliminated, populations of insects and fishes are reduced or eliminated because they have fewer places to live. Fish populations are also reduced because the insects that they normally feed on are less common. Some fishes, e.g., the pugnose shiner *(Notropis anogenus)* and pugnose minnow *(Opsopoeodus emiliae),* are particularly susceptible to the loss of plants because they are morphologically adapted to feed on insects that live on plants and are unable to survive by feeding elsewhere. These two fishes persist in the Midwest only in highly isolated populations (Smith 1979, Becker 1983).

In addition to covering the substrate, silt increases turbidity, making it more difficult for species that rely on sight to find one another for spawning, to find food, and to complete other necessary aspects of their life histories. Large-eyed fishes that rely on sight have been among those most negatively impacted. The bigeye chub *(Hybopsis amblops)* disappeared from Illinois in the 1960s; the bigeye shiner *(Notropis boops)* persists only in isolated populations (Smith 1979). The devastating effect of siltation on aquatic species results from the combination of its deposition over natural substrates and increased turbidity.

Increased Water Temperatures

The impact of increased water temperatures resulting from the loss of riparian vegetation and reduced water flow during warm seasons is difficult to separate from the effects of siltation and other factors that occur concomitantly. However, throughout the Midwest increased water temperatures per se are probably especially harmful to cool-water species such as northern pike *(Esox lucius)* and native trout *(Salvelinus* species), and species dependent on springs and spring-fed streams, such as the southern redbelly dace *(Phoxinus erythrogaster)* (Smith 1971) and many species of amphipods, isopods and crayfishes (Page 1974, 1985a).

Stream Desiccation

As discussed above, stream desiccation is thought to be primarily an effect of the artificially extreme fluctuations in water levels that follow the tiling of fields for agriculture. The rapid drainage of surrounding land increases the intensity and prolongs the duration of low-flow once the water has moved downstream. A drought that historically would have decreased the flow in a stream can now lead to a dry stream bed. During the drought of 1988, the upper 50 miles of the Sangamon River streambed were dry in late summer for a period of several weeks (Page pers. obs.); obviously this eliminated, at least temporarily, virtually all of the aquatic species that had been present. Complete drying of the upper Sangamon River may never have occurred prior to tiling of the drainage basin.

Irrigation, although not nearly as extensive in the Midwest as it is in the West (Moyle and Williams 1990), will exacerbate the problem of stream desiccation in the Midwest if it increases. As more water is removed from aquifers to supply agriculture and urban use, less will remain in streams.

Drainage of Bottomland Lakes

Floodplains of large rivers normally have low areas that fill with water during floods and survive year-round as shallow lakes. These lakes provide primary habitat for a wide variety of plants and animals. Because they naturally have luxuriant plant growth, they are important feeding areas for waterfowl, and they provide spawning areas, nurseries for larvae, and overwintering refugia for fishes.

Unfortunately, most of the bottomland lakes in the Midwest have been drained to create cropland, and those that remain have become shallow and barren because of the tremendous silt loads deposited in them each year during periods of high water. The shallow muddy lakes no longer support the plant life that was fundamental to successful completion of the life cycles of many aquatic species. Several species that persist only in isolated areas are those that depend on bottomland lakes or other vegetated bodies of standing water for their survival, e.g., spotted sunfish *(Lepomis punctatus)*, bantam sunfish *(Lepomis symmetricus)*, and the crayfish *Orconectes lancifer*.

Introduction of Non-Native Species

Several recent reviews discussed the causes of fish introductions and their impacts on biological communities (Moyle 1976, Welcomme 1988, Crowl et al. 1992). The impacts of introduced fishes identified by Moyle et al. (1986) were competition, predation, inhibition of reproduction, environmental modification, transfer of parasites and diseases, and hybridization.

Flecker and Townsend (1994) noted that introductions into communities lacking the invading guild are most likely to cause community-level effects. For example, introductions of trout, which feed heavily on insects, into North American streams where other trout occur result in population changes in native trout and other salmonids, but introductions of trout into streams lacking large insectivores are likely to result in more extensive community-level effects. Ecosystem changes from introduced species are difficult to measure; however, Moyle (1976) described several examples of a single species of fish disrupting normal ecosystem function.

In the Midwest, the most spectacular results of introduced species have been changes in the biological communities of the Great Lakes. The arrival of the sea lamprey *(Petromyzon marinus)* in the 1940s was followed by precipitous declines in, among other species, the commercially important lake trout *(Salvelinus namaycush)* and whitefishes *(Coregonus* species). Subsequent introductions, some of which were accidental, e.g., the alewife *(Alosa pseudoharengus)* and white perch *(Morone americanus)*, and some of which were deliberate, e.g., the rainbow smelt *(Osmerus mordax)* and coho salmon *(Oncorhynchus kisutch)*, have led to further declines in native species. Fishes introduced into midwestern streams have included Eurasian carps (e.g., carp *[Cyprinus carpio]* and grass carp *[Ctenopharyngodon idella]*) that are known to significantly alter aquatic communities by feeding on or uprooting plants.

Freshwater mussels and crayfishes have been seriously impacted in the Midwest in recent decades by exotic invaders, most notably the zebra mussel *(Dreissena polymorpha*) and the rusty crayfish *(Orconectes rusticus)*. Nalepa (1994) documented the severe decline in native mussels due to the invasion of zebra mussels in Lake St. Clair over a six-year period. He found that mussel densities declined from 2.4 m^{-2} in 1986 to 0 m^{-2} in 1992 in areas heavily infested with zebra mussels. The rusty crayfish, introduced through its use as fishing bait, is rapidly spreading through parts of the Midwest and displacing native crayfishes (Taylor and Redmer 1996).

Pollution

Neves and Angermeier (1990) cite examples of chemical spills resulting in the deaths of large numbers of fishes and invertebrates. They found that, although most fishes and invertebrates are able to recolonize because the impact is localized, mollusks have a more difficult time doing so because of their limited dispersal abilities.

Baker (1922) examined the effects of sewage and manufacturing wastes on the molluscan fauna of the Vermilion River in east-central Illinois in 1918–1920. He found that sewage pollution had killed almost all aquatic life in the Salt Fork Vermilion River for a distance of 14 miles below the city of Urbana and created unfavorable conditions for a distance of 20 miles.

Point sources of pollution include industrial wastes and domestic sewage. In the Midwest considerable progress has been made in identifying and eliminating point sources of pollution, and water quality has improved as a result (Jackson and Davis 1994). Nonpoint sources are now a larger problem than are point sources, and include siltation, as discussed above, and agricultural pesticides that reach streams following the removal of floodplain vegetation. Because of the pervasive nature of agriculture in the Midwest, some form of pollution has affected a large percentage of streams. The impact on the stream varies with the type and intensity of pollution and the tolerance of the species present.

Impoundments and River Regulation

Impounding a stream converts it into a standing body of water that lacks the riffles, runs, pools, and other habitats that stream-inhabiting organisms require. Most stream species are eliminated from the inundated area, and upstream and downstream populations become isolated from one another. There are many examples of fishes being extirpated from a stream by an impoundment, and even more examples of extirpations that have occurred as a result of multiple effects that include impoundments (Miller et al. 1989).

Freshwater mussels seem to be particularly susceptible to loss of habitat caused by the creation of impoundments (Bates 1962, Suloway et al. 1981, Williams et al. 1992, Parmalee and Hughes 1993). While some mussels may be able to survive in the lentic habitat created by an impoundment, many of these populations are functionally sterile and will eventually die out (Williams 1969). An example of the loss of mussels in an impounded stream is the fauna of the Little Tennessee

River, where only 6 of the 50 mussels once found in the river can now be found in Tellico Lake (Parmalee and Hughes 1993).

Dams also block migrations of fishes that, in many species, are necessary for reproduction (Fig. 9.6) (Holden 1979). The loss of migratory fishes from a stream ecosystem can lead to the loss of mussels using the migratory fishes as glochidial hosts and other species important to the ecosystem. Other adverse effects caused by impoundments are increased parasitism, low temperature, oxygen sags, increased water pressure, and siltation (Fuller 1974). Diverse mussel beds are often found below dams where highly oxygenated water and a stable substrate provide excellent habitat for mussels. However, dams that utilize a hypolimnetic discharge release cold, unoxygenated waters which can eliminate mussel populations for a considerable distance below the dam.

How water is released from a reservoir determines the impact on downstream habitats. The temperature and dissolved oxygen of release water depend on whether water is released from upper or lower levels behind the dam. Cold

Figure 9.6. Dams can block migrations of fishes that, in many species, are necessary for reproduction.

hypolimnial release water was identified years ago as a cause of fish extirpations (Spence and Hynes 1971). The release regime determines water levels and flow fluctuations downstream. "Flow regulation by dams disrupts the downstream river system's natural disturbance regimes" (Ward and Stanford 1995). Longitudinal and lateral connectivity that are necessary for transmission of nutrients, silt, and allochthonous materials are lost with river regulation (Welcomme 1995). The release regime also affects the channel hydrology, which impacts organisms inhabiting downstream reaches (Ward and Stanford 1995).

River regulation not only affects biota within the river but also along the entire floodplain. Riparian tree species that are closely tied to the hydrological regime do not recruit without normal flow regimes, resulting in replacement with late successional community species (Ward and Stanford 1995). Stable channel conditions resulting from river regulation are leading to a decline in prairie rivers of North America.

Most reservoirs may not be old enough to have caused genetic differentiation (although see Hansen et al. 1993), or populations might be sufficiently large above and below stream sections that are isolated by dams that genetic drift might not be apparent (Berg and Gall 1988). King et al. (1985) found genetic differences between populations of *Cyprinella lutrensis* collected at different distances from a dam on the Brazos River, Texas. The variation corresponded with differences in temperature tolerance, with one-third of the variation attributable to stream regulation effects.

Channelization

Channelization is the straightening of a stream to enhance drainage of the surrounding land. The straightening converts the diversity of habitats in a stream to one continuous straight channel (Fig. 9.7) that supports few species (Shields et al. 1995). Reduced fish numbers and biomass were found after channelization and construction of weirs in streams in Indiana (Karr and Gorman 1975).

Because of their sedentary nature mussels are particularly susceptible to the effects of channelization. In a mussel survey of the Kankakee, Yellow, and Iroquois rivers in Indiana and Illinois, Wilson and Clark (1912: 34) noted that the rivers had a "very rich and varied mussel fauna throughout their entire lengths, except in those portions which have been artificially dredged." They further stated that dredging "annihilates" the fauna and creates conditions which are unsuitable for new populations to reestablish themselves. They noted that portions of the basin that had been dredged 15–20 years ago showed no signs of recolonization even though there were many mussels in nearby tributaries.

Detection of Fragmentation Prior to Extinction

Genetic monitoring of isolated populations is necessary for conservation of fisheries (Ryman 1991) and of fishes in general (Bruton 1995), and for detection of

Figure 9.7. A channelized stream. Channelization converts the diversity of habitats in a natural stream to a continuous straight channel that supports far fewer species than were there originally.

fragmented populations. Meffe and Vrijenhoek (1988) described a model for examining the population structure of fishes that results from varying degrees of the connectivity of streams. Their model is intended to describe population structure in streams that are dewatered, resulting in reduced gene flow between isolated populations. However, it appears to be useful for detecting effects of any natural or anthropogenic causes of population fragmentation. The model generates a hierarchical population structure of genetically defined groups in isolated populations.

Shuter (1990) suggested that population monitoring of smaller fish species can provide early evidence of environmental degradation. Small fishes are usually lower in a food web, often depend on sensitive invertebrate species, and respond more rapidly to stresses (Shuter 1990). An alternative to population monitoring is the detection of fluctuating asymmetry among individuals in a population to identify environmental stress (Leary and Allendorf 1989). We suggest that in addition to genetic monitoring programs, mark-recapture studies are badly needed to understand normal movements of fishes and other aquatic organisms and, hence, the impacts of stream habitat fragmentation.

Management Strategies

Fragmentation of habitats and the resulting local extinctions have been studied extensively for certain groups of terrestrial organisms (see other chapters), but similar studies of aquatic organisms are nearly nonexistent. Little information is available on the magnitude of fragmentation in aquatic ecosystems or its impact on aquatic organisms.

Management strategies for aquatic ecosystems must consider the entire watershed. Attempting to correct problems locally, without consideration of upstream activities and downstream implications, will result in partial and probably temporary improvement at best. Management directed at improving in-stream conditions must be linked to proper management of the surrounding terrestrial landscape.

Reserves, areas where biotic communities are more or less intact and are managed to protect their natural characteristics, are mostly designed around terrestrial communities. In the Midwest, biological reserves tend to be small and rarely, if ever, protect an entire watershed. A new concept being developed in Illinois is the recognition and management of *macrosites,* areas that are large and contain the best remaining biological resources. Although use of the land for recreation, agriculture, and other consumptive activities will continue, management will strive to reverse whatever forms of degradation have affected the area. Macrosites are being selected on a watershed basis, and therefore streams included in the area will be offered protection from harmful activities.

The National Wild and Scenic Rivers Act, passed into law in 1968, recognizes that certain streams have "outstandingly remarkable" value and should be protected from development. The Act provides protection against dams and other forms of development on rivers, and also sets aside a quarter-mile riparian corridor in which development on public lands is restricted. Although affording important protection to some of the most outstanding rivers in the United States, the Act does not control watershed activities; streams federally designated as wild and scenic can still be degraded. The most important impact of the Act may be that it recognizes the inherent value of streams and provides a national policy for their protection.

Correction of some factors that have led to stream habitat fragmentation in past decades is relatively easy. Important initiatives that society has taken and seems to be in favor of continuing include building sewage treatment plants and avoiding the construction of mainstream impoundments when possible. Other initiatives, such as stopping the removal of riparian vegetation, cessation of stream channelization and dredging, and the drainage of bottomland lakes, require more public education and governmental action including, perhaps, providing better incentives to landowners. Assuming that pollution will be held at current levels or reduced, nothing will be more beneficial to the biota of midwestern streams than to have natural riparian vegetation restored. Siltation, desiccation, and elevated temperatures would all be reduced to acceptable levels if streams were lined with native plants that shaded the stream, stabilized the banks, and filtered sediment and chemicals from runoff before they reached the stream. A promising method of protecting riparian vegetation without government ownership is the establishment of conservation easements, where a private landowner or organization agrees to restrict or prohibit land uses deemed detrimental to the property's conservation value in exchange for tax relief (Roth 1994).

Most introductions of exotic fishes have been done in an effort to improve sport or commercial fishing, and usually government agencies have been responsible for the introductions. We now know that non-native species alter ecosystems, and the long-term effect of any introduction is likely to be negative rather than positive. No new introductions should be allowed in any waters. Additional legislation is needed to prevent accidental introductions from ballast water and other sources.

Restoration of Stream Habitats

Much information is now available on stream hydrodynamics, habitat preferences of aquatic species, and which habitats or stream reaches support the highest species diversity in a given region. Given the opportunity, streams will restore themselves. Often the best approach to restoration may be to encourage restoration of the native vegetation of the drainage basin, in particular the riparian zone, correct any additional pollution problems, and let the stream return to natural conditions. Over time, even channelized ditches will begin to meander (Fig. 9.8) and develop the riffle and pool habitats that are necessary for restoration of normal stream biodiversity.

A more activist approach to stream restoration, i.e., adding structures that imitate natural stream habitats, has been successful in a number of restoration projects (Newbury and Gaboury 1993). The fish and invertebrate fauna in channelized streams has been shown to be improved by the addition of weirs or structures that increase pool habitat (Borchardt 1993, Shields et al. 1995). Other recommendations for fish habitat improvements are described by Poddubny and Galat (1995), including construction of islands, diking, and restoration and preservation of preferred habitats in the main channel. Restoration of streams requires imitating the hydraulic habitat units of that geologic region to produce habitat heterogeneity of pool, riffle, and run development (Rabeni and Jacobson 1993). However, modifications for habitat improvement such as in-channel structures require knowledge of the resulting hydrological changes to the channel to avoid creating more damage (Rosgen 1994).

Restoration efforts in large river systems begin with restoring the natural flooding regime to allow connectivity between the floodplains and the river. Lands adjacent to large rivers that are not farmed on an annual basis and yet are protected from floods by federal levees should be allowed to flood. Organic matter and woody debris should be restored to provide habitat for species dependent on such materials for food and living space (Hesse and Sheets 1993).

For existing dams, management plans need to be developed that more closely

Figure 9.8. Left alone, this channelized ditch has begun to meander and develop the riffle and pool habitats that are necessary for restoration of normal stream biodiversity. If the native vegetation of the riparian zone returns and any existing pollution problems are eliminated, the stream will return to more natural conditions.

mimic natural disturbance regimes of rivers (Ward and Stanford 1995). Plans should call for releasing water that is not too cold or hot, is not anoxic, and that allows downstream flow characteristics that allow survival and reproduction of stream species. The amount, duration, and frequency of releases should mimic the original river or a nearby reference river (Gippel and Stewardson 1995). Bayley (1991) suggested that natural, predictable flood pulses result in increased fish diversity, which results in increased production and is an important step in restoring the natural hydrological regime of a river. The reestablishment of connectivity between river channels and their floodplains is becoming a recognized component of restoration (Ward and Stanford 1995). Unnecessary dams often should be removed, although care needs to be taken that the release of silt, and toxins in the silt, which have built up behind the dam is done in a way that will not damage downstream habitats.

In the Midwest, an example of a river restoration project is that on the upper Mississippi River. Theiling (1995) details current habitat rehabilitation on the upper Mississippi River which is designed to restore side channels and backwaters from sedimentation. Various techniques have been used including island construction, notching existing wing dikes, alternative bank revetments (to prevent channel movement) that create artificial backwaters, and bendway weirs that prevent deposition from filling in the main channel. Theiling (1995) suggests that these are necessary but are limited due to the small areas they affect. Infrequent, planned drawdowns to expose backwater and channel border sediments will allow vegetation to become established in wetland management areas and transform backwater and channel border habitats as they are flooded.

Additional restoration measures that have met with success include cleaning lakes and streams by limiting effluents, stopping management agencies' promotion of exotic species, and decreasing reservoir construction by examining real costs and benefits. Protection of streams at the ecosystem level by including all processes and habitats is essential to preserving the remaining aquatic biota (Franklin 1993).

Acknowledgments

We appreciate the help of Christopher A. Taylor and Donald W. Webb who read and improved the manuscript. Chris Taylor also provided information on the numbers of crayfishes in different parts of the world. Maurice Kottelat provided an estimate of the number of fishes in temperate Eurasia. Thanks to Christine A. Mayer for help in preparing the figures.

References

Baker, F.C. 1922. The molluscan fauna of the Big Vermilion River, Illinois: with special reference to its modification as the result of pollution by sewage and manufacturing wastes. *Illinois Biological Monographs* 7(2):105–224.

Balon, E.K. 1975. Reproductive guilds of fishes: a proposal and definition. *Journal of the Fisheries Research Board of Canada* 32:821–864.

Bates, J.M. 1962. The impact of impoundment on the mussel fauna of Kentucky Reservoir, Tennessee River. *American Midland Naturalist* 68(1):232–236.

Bayley, P.B. 1991. The flood pulse advantage and the restoration of river-floodplain systems. *Regulated Rivers* 6:75–86.

Bayley, P.B., and L.L. Osborne. 1993. Natural rehabilitation of stream fish populations in an Illinois catchment. *Freshwater Biology* 29:295–300.

Becker, G.C. 1983. *Fishes of Wisconsin.* University of Wisconsin Press. Madison, WI.

Berg, W.J., and G.A.E. Gall. 1988. Gene flow and genetic differentiation among California coastal rainbow trout populations. *Canadian Journal of Fisheries and Aquatic Sciences* 45:122–131.

Bogan, A.E. 1993. Freshwater bivalve extinctions *(Mollusca: Unionoida):* a search for causes. *American Zoologist* 33:599–609.

Borchardt, D. 1993. Effects of flow and refugia on drift loss of benthic macroinvertebrates: implications for habitat restoration in lowland streams. *Freshwater Biology* 29:221–227.

Bradford, D.F., F. Tabatabai, and D.M. Graber. 1993. Isolation of remaining populations of the native frog, *Rana muscosa,* by introduced fishes in Sequoia and Kings Canyon National Parks, California. *Conservation Biology* 7:882–888.

Bruton, M.N. 1995. Have fishes had their chips?: the dilemma of threatened fishes. *Environmental Biology of Fishes* 43:1–27.

Crowl, T.A., C.A. Townsend, and A.R. McIntosh. 1992. The impact of introduced brown and rainbow trout on native fish: the case of Australasia. *Reviews in Fish Biology and Fisheries* 2:217–241.

Cummings, K.S., and C.A. Mayer. 1992. *Field Guide to Freshwater Mussels of the Midwest.* Illinois Natural History Survey Manual 5. Champaign, Ill.

Cummings, K.S., and C.A. Mayer. 1997. The status of the freshwater mussel *(Unionacea)* fauna in Illinois. In *Conservation and Management of Freshwater Mussels II: Initiatives for the Future: Proceedings of a UMRCC Symposium, 16–18 October 1995, St. Louis, Missouri.* Upper Mississippi River Conservation Committee, Rock Island, Ill.

Detenbeck, N.E., P.W. DeVore, G.J. Niemi, and A. Lima. 1992. Recovery of temperate-stream fish communities from disturbance: a review of case studies and synthesis of theory. *Environmental Management* 16:33–53.

Flecker, A.S., and C.R. Townsend. 1994. Community-wide consequences of trout introduction in New Zealand streams. *Ecological Applications* 4:798–807.

Forbes, S.A., and R.E. Richardson. 1908. *The Fishes of Illinois.* Illinois State Laboratory of Natural History. Champaign, Ill.

Franklin, J.F. 1993. Preserving biodiversity: species, ecosystems, or landscapes? *Ecological Applications* 3:202–205.

Fuller, S.L.H. 1974. Clams and mussels *(Mollusca: Bivalvia).* In C.W. Hart, Jr. and S.L.H. Fuller eds. *Pollution Ecology of Freshwater Invertebrates.* Academic Press, New York, 215–273.

Gippel, C.J., and M.J. Stewardson. 1995. Development of an environmental flow management strategy for the Thomason River, Victoria, Australia. *Regulated Rivers* 10:121–135.

Hansen, M.M., V. Loeschcke, G. Rasmussen, and V. Simonsen. 1993. Genetic differentiation among Danish brown trout *(Salmo trutta)* populations. *Hereditas* 118:177–185.

Hesse, L.W., and W. Sheets. 1993. The Missouri River hydrosystem. *Fisheries* 18:5–14.

Hobbs, H.H., Jr. 1988. Crayfish distribution, adaptive radiation and evolution. In D.M. Holdich and R.S. Lowery eds. *Freshwater Crayfish: Biology, Management, and Exploitation.* Croom Helm, London, 52–82.

Holden, P.B. 1979. Ecology of riverine fishes in regulated stream systems with emphasis on the Colorado River. In J.V. Ward and J.A. Stanford eds. *The Ecology of Regulated Streams.* Plenum Press, New York, 57–74.

Hynes, H.B.N. 1970. *The Ecology of Running Waters.* Liverpool University Press, Liverpool.

Illinois Endangered Species Protection Board. 1994. *Checklist of Endangered and Threatened Animals and Plants of Illinois.* Illinois Endangered Species Protection Board. Springfield, Ill.

Jackson, S., and W. Davis. 1994. Meeting the goal of biological integrity in water-resource programs in U.S. Environmental Protection Agency. *Journal of the North American Benthological Society* 13:592–597.

Karr, J.R., and O.W. Gorman. 1975. Effects of land treatment on the aquatic environment. In *Non-Point Source Pollution Seminar: Section 108(a) Demonstration Projects.* U.S. Environmental Protection Agency, Office of the Great Lakes Coordinator, Chicago, Ill., EPA-905/9-75-007, 120–130.

King, T.L., E.G. Zimmerman, and T.L. Beitinger. 1985. Concordant variation in thermal tolerance and allozymes of the red shiner, *Notropis lutrensis,* inhabiting tailwater sections of the Brazos River, Texas. *Environmental Biology of Fishes* 13:49–57.

Leary, R.F., and F.W. Allendorf. 1989. Fluctuating asymmetry as an indicator of stress: implications for conservation biology. *Trends in Research in Ecology and Evolution* 4:214–217.

Meffe, G.K., and R.C. Vrijenhoek. 1988. Conservation genetics in the management of desert fishes. *Conservation Biology* 2:157–169.

Merrick, J.R. and G.E. Schmida. 1993. *Australian Freshwater Fishes.* Griffen Press Limited, Netley, South Australia.

Miller, R.R., J.D. Williams, and J.E. Williams. 1989. Extinctions of North American fishes during the past century. *Fisheries* 14:22–38.

Moyle, P.B. 1976. Fish introductions in California: history and impact on native fishes. *Biological Conservation* 9:101–118.

Moyle, P.B., H.W. Li, and B.A. Barton. 1986. The Frankenstein effect: impact of introduced fishes on native fishes in North America. In R.H. Stroud ed. *Fish Culture in Fisheries Management.* American Fisheries Society, Bethesda, Md., 415–426.

Moyle, P.B., and J.E. Williams. 1990. Biodiversity loss in the temperate zone: Decline of native fish fauna of California. *Conservation Biology* 4:275–283.

Nalepa, T.F. 1994. Decline of native unionid bivalves in Lake St. Clair after infestation by the zebra mussel, *Dreissena polymorpha. Canadian Journal of Fisheries and Aquatic Sciences* 51:2227–2233.

Neves, R.J. 1993. A state-of-the-Unionids address. In K.S. Cummings, A.C. Buchanan, and L.M. Koch eds. *Conservation and Management of Freshwater Mussels. Proceedings of a UMRCC Symposium, 12–14 October 1992, St. Louis, Missouri.* Upper Mississippi River Conservation Committee, Rock Island, Ill., 1–9.

Neves, R.J., and P.L. Angermeier. 1990. Habitat alteration and its effects on native fishes in the upper Tennessee River system, east-central U.S.A. *Journal of Fish Biology* 37(Supplement A):45–52.

Newbury, R.W., and M.N. Gaboury. 1993. *Stream Analysis and Fish Habitat Design— A Field Manual.* Newbury Hydraulics Ltd., Gibsons, British Columbia.

Page, L.M. 1974. Aquatic *Malacostraca* recorded from Illinois, with notes on their distributions and habitats within the state. *Transactions of the Illinois State Academy of Science* 67:89–104.

Page, L.M. 1985a. The crayfishes and shrimps *(Decapoda)* of Illinois. *Illinois Natural History Survey Bulletin* 33:335–448.

Page, L.M. 1985b. Evolution of reproductive behaviors in percid fishes. *Illinois Natural History Survey Bulletin* 33:275–295.

Page, L.M., and B.M. Burr. 1991. *A Field Guide to Freshwater Fishes.* Houghton Mifflin, Boston.

Parmalee, P.W., and M.H. Hughes. 1993. Freshwater mussels *(Mollusca: Pelecypoda: Unionidae)* of Tellico Lake: twelve years after impoundment of the Little Tennessee River. *Annals of the Carnegie Museum* 62(1):81–93.

Poddubny, A.G , and D.L. Galat. 1995. Habitat associations of Upper Volga River fishes: effects of reservoirs. *Regulated Rivers* 11:67–84.

Rabeni, C.F., and R.B. Jacobson. 1993. The importance of fluvial hydraulics to fish-habitat restoration in low-gradient alluvial streams. *Freshwater Biology* 29:211–220.

Rosgen, D.L. 1994. A classification of natural rivers. *Catena* 22:169–199.

Roth, J. 1994. Conservation easements and their use in Illinois. *Illinois Steward* 3:3–5.

Ryman, N. 1991. Conservation genetics considerations in fishery management. *Journal of Fish Biology* 39(Supplement A):211–224.

Saunders, D.A. 1991. Biological consequences of ecosystem fragmentation: a review. *Conservation Biology* 5:18–32.

Shields, F.D., Jr., S.S. Knight, and C.M. Cooper. 1995. Incised stream physical habitat restoration with stone weirs. *Regulated Rivers* 10:181–198.

Shuter, B.J. 1990. Population-level indicators of stress. *American Fisheries Society Symposium* 8:145–166.

Smith, B.J. 1992. *Zoological Catalogue of Australia,* vol. 8. *Non-Marine Mollusca.* Australian Government Publishing Service, Canberra.

Smith, P.W. 1971. *Illinois Streams: A Classification Based on Their Fishes and an Analysis of Factors Responsible for Disappearance of Native Species.* Illinois Natural History Survey Biological Notes No. 76. Champaign, Ill.

Smith, P.W. 1979. *The Fishes of Illinois.* University of Illinois Press, Urbana.

Spence, J.A., and H.B.N. Hynes. 1971. Differences in fish populations upstream and downstream of a mainstream impoundment. *Canadian Journal of Fisheries and Aquatic Sciences* 28:45–46.

Suloway, L., J.J. Suloway, and E.E. Herricks. 1981. Changes in the freshwater mussel *(Mollusca: Pelecypoda: Unionidae)* fauna of the Kaskaskia River, Illinois, with emphasis on the effects of impoundment. *Transactions of the Illinois State Academy of Science* 74(1/2):79–90.

Taylor, C.A. and M. Redmer. 1996. The dispersal of the crayfish *Orconectes rusticus* in Illinois, with notes on species displacement and habitat preference. *Journal of Crustacean Biology* 16:547–551.

Taylor, C.A., M.L., Warren, Jr., J.F. Fitzpatrick, Jr., H.H. Hobbs III, R.F. Jezerinac, W.L. Pflieger, and H.W. Robison. 1996. Conservation status of crayfishes of the United States and Canada. *Fisheries* 21:25–38.

Theiling, C.H. 1995. Habitat rehabilitation on the upper Mississippi River. *Regulated Rivers* 11:227–238.

Townsend, C.R. and T.A. Crowl. 1991. Fragmented population structure in a native New Zealand fish: an effect of introduced trout? *Oikos* 61:347–354.

Ward, J.V., and J.A. Stanford. 1995. Ecological connectivity in alluvial river ecosystems and its disruption by flow regulation. *Regulated Rivers* 11:105–119.

Watters, G.T. 1992. Unionids, fishes, and the species area curve. *Journal of Biogeography* 19:481–490.

Welcomme, R.L. 1988. International introductions of inland aquatic species. *FAO Fisheries Technical Paper* 294:1–318.

Welcomme, R.L. 1995. Relationships between fisheries and the integrity of river systems. *Regulated Rivers* 11:121–136.

White, J. 1978. *Illinois Natural Areas Inventory Technical Report.* Illinois Natural Areas Inventory, Urbana.

Williams, J.C. 1969. *Mussel Fishery Investigations, Tennessee, Ohio, and Green rivers. Final Report.* Kentucky Department of Fish and Wildlife Resources, Frankfort, Kentucky.

Williams, J.D., S.L.H. Fuller, and R. Grace. 1992. Effects of impoundments on freshwater mussels *(Mollusca: Bivalvia: Unionidae)* in the main channel of the Black Warrior and Tombigbee rivers in western Alabama. *Bulletin of the Alabama Museum of Natural History* 13:1–10.

Williams, J.D., M.L. Warren, Jr., K.S. Cummings, J.L. Harris, and R.J. Neves. 1993. Conservation status of freshwater mussels of the United States and Canada. *Fisheries* 18:6–22.

Wilson, C.B., and H.W. Clark. 1912. The mussel fauna of the Kankakee basin. *Report and Special Papers of the U.S. Fish Commission.* [Issued separately as U.S. Bureau of Fisheries Document 758]. 1911:1–52.

10

Midwestern Fire Management: Prescribing a Natural Process in an Unnatural Landscape

Mark W. Schwartz
Center for Population Biology, University of California-Davis, Davis, CA 95616

Sharon M. Hermann
Tall Timbers Research Station, P.O. Box 678, Rt. 1, Tallahassee, FL 32312

> A mountain of flame, thirty feet high, and of unknown length, moving onward, roaring like "many waters"—in a gentle, stately movement, and unbroken front—then impelled by a gust of wind, suddenly breaks itself to pieces, here and there shooting ahead, whirling itself high in the air—all becomes noise, and strife, and uproar, and disorder.
>
> —Amos Parker, 1835, from *Trip to the West and Texas*

Introduction

In this chapter we review the philosophy and use of prescribed fire in the fragmented landscape of the Midwest. Forty years ago most resource management agencies viewed fire as a destructive force to be suppressed at all costs (reviewed by Pyne 1982). Over time, and with increasing knowledge and experience, there has been a shift in attitude. Many scientists and land stewards now understand that fire was once an important component of many natural landscapes and today, prescribed burning is a vital tool for land management. Fire is now frequently studied for its ecological effects (e.g., Kozlowski and Ahlgren 1974; Higgins et al. 1989a,b; Warren et al. 1987; Collins and Wallace 1990; Robbins and Myers 1992). Modern textbooks describing the ecology of North American ecosystems include discussions on the significance of fire in almost every biome (e.g., Barbour et al. 1980, Barbour and Billings 1988). In particular, there is strong evidence to indicate that habitats with a grass-dominated ground cover were maintained by frequent, often low-intensity, fires prior to European settlement (e.g. Barbour et al. 1980, Christensen 1988, Sims 1988). Without fire, the vegetation of prairies, oak savannas, and shortleaf pine barrens changes dramatically (Anderson 1972, Gleason 1913, Haney and Apfelbaum 1990).

Today the debate generally focuses on when and how fire should be prescribed and not whether fire ought to be used as a management tool (but see Swengel 1996). Within this context, the practical application of fire continues to evolve. Burn frequency, intensity, and timing have become central issues in the management of biodiversity in natural habitats. To relate these components of fire regimes to various objectives of land management activities, we must first develop an understanding of the ecological basis for burning and the historical context of fire in the Midwest.

We begin with an overview of our current understanding of general fire effects and a summary of pre-European settlement fire along the midwestern prairie-forest border and then summarize relevant research on fire effects in the various habitat types. We do not attempt to duplicate the information on fire in specific habitats addressed elsewhere in this text, but to target broad landscape patterns. We focus primarily on vegetation because it has been well studied and because many effects on animals are related to vegetation composition and structure (Niemi and Probst 1990). Further, there is little specific information available on faunal groups that may be most sensitive to the effects of fire such as insects (Swengel 1996, Warren et al. 1987) and native vertebrates (Vogl and Beck 1970, Hill and Platt 1975, Herkert 1994).

Following discussions on ecology and history, we address the philosophy of prescribed fire, logistical constraints on managed burns, and potential management alternatives. We stress the importance of establishing specific management goals. Simply stated, sites should not be burned just for the sake of engaging in the activity. Further, we argue that attempting to replicate a natural disturbance regime is not automatically the appropriate model for a prescribed fire program. Several considerations, including a lack of specific historical knowledge, current land use, recent vegetation change, and global atmospheric change, make it impossible to restore a completely natural fire regime.

Finally, we assert that establishing a presettlement historic fire regime may not accomplish desired conservation goals. There is no guarantee that the species composition and habitat structure that developed with fire under past conditions would be restored from a degraded state under current climate and habitat patchiness conditions. As an alternative to traditional fire management, we outline the fundamental considerations required to enact a prescriptive fire program that targets specific management objectives. These considerations include identifying management objectives, prescribing fire to achieve these objectives, and monitoring success in order to implement an adaptive management strategy.

It is difficult to use fire to restore and maintain natural communities in severely altered landscapes. The highly fragmented Midwest is an excellent region in which to address this challenge.

Fire and the Historical Landscape

General Effects of Fire

In the absence of fire many communities exhibit rapid transitions (Robertson et al., Chapter 3, Fralish, Chapter 11, this volume). In other words, fire may act more as a stabilizing force than as a disturbance that promotes succession. In prairies and oak savannas, fire has been demonstrated to suppress or eliminate invading species. This is true for populations of native species, especially trees (e.g., Haney and Apfelbaum 1990) that may expand from nearby, less fire-prone habitats (Vogl 1974) or shrubs that may aggressively spread vegetatively (e.g., Hutchinson 1992). Burns may also be useful in eradicating exotic species (e.g., Zedler and Loucks 1969).

Nonetheless, many (e.g., Pickett and White 1985, Collins 1990) define fire as an agent of disturbance. The issue seems to revolve partially around how one assesses stability in grasslands (Collins 1995). Although in prairies and savannas fires do not typically kill established (adult) perennial native plant species (Collins 1995), they may change species abundances, percent cover, and/or biomass productivity of vegetation. Burns cause shifts in other aspects of prairie ecology; they remove litter and may alter growth rates and flowering attributes (Pemble et al. 1981). The direction and magnitude of these fire effects, however, vary among species, years, and sites (Glenn-Lewin et al. 1990).

The impact of fire is dependent on many factors; one of the most important is fuel (i.e., vegetation) type. The Midwest prior to European settlement has been characterized as a simple mixture of two basic habitat types: prairie and forest (e.g., Barbour et al. 1980). In reality, the Midwest was a complex of various types of prairies (Robertson et al., Chapter 3), open forest savannas (Taft, Chapter 2), woodlands (Ebinger, Chapter 1), and wetlands (Havera and Suloway, Chapter 4). Plant species composition defines fuel types, which burn differently under various conditions (Wright and Bailey 1982). Fuel production and flammability influence the fire regimes associated with each habitat. Basic components of a fire regime include frequency, season, and intensity (Robbins and Myers 1992). Obviously these factors are part of a feedback loop that influences what vegetation will regrow following a fire.

As in the case of prairie fires, savanna and woodland fires typically result in little mortality to mature trees. Fires in these habitats, however, can have strong influences on forest structure by limiting recruitment among trees and reducing understory cover (e.g., Schwartz and Heim, 1996). When fires were suppressed in the late 19th and early 20th centuries, the relatively open midwestern forests quickly filled in and began shifting toward dominance by shade-tolerant mesophytic trees such as sugar maple (Gleason 1913, Cottam 1949, Fralish, Chapter 11). In open-canopy forests a lack of fire results in increased cover in the tree stratum and decreased understory cover and diversity (Taft, Chapter 2).

Fire effects in other habitats are less well known. Although there seems to be little doubt that midwestern wetlands burned periodically, there are few descriptions of these fires. There is also little research on community-level response. Fire in wetlands removes accumulated litter and, at times, peat. Plants with roots in substrate that is burned or heated may be killed; individuals with roots lower than the fire-consumed substrate may resprout. Vogl (1967) summarized past fire management in Wisconsin wetlands and Higgins et al. (1989a) reviewed literature on the response to fire of six prairie wetland plant species. More recently, Johnson and Knapp (1995) studied the role of fire in prairie cordgrass-(*Spartina pectinata*) dominated wetlands in Kansas.

Fires in the shortleaf pine barrens of southern Illinois are also not well documented. Anderson (1972), however, outlined a scenario that he suggested as the likely result of fire suppression in the Shawnee National Forest. He postulated that shortleaf pine was disappearing from the region because shading prohibited successful establishment. A recently implemented managed fire program in these habitats is seeking to redress this management issue.

Studies of the effects of prairie fire on insect groups summarized by order or family suggest varying responses to fire that are somewhat predictable (e.g., Warren et al 1987). Below-ground arthropods, as a rule, respond positively to fire (Lussenhop 1972; 1976; James 1982, 1988; Seastedt 1984a,b). Similarly, most vagile insects respond favorably to fire within a short time period after a burn (e.g., Cancelado and Yonke 1970, Nagel 1973, Van Amburg et al. 1981). What is less clear is how those species that are not vagile, or in non-vagile stages (eggs or larvae) at the time of fire, and are remnant-dependent (*sensu* Panzer et al. 1995) respond to fire. These species are probably the most vulnerable to the effects of fire (Panzer et al. 1995) and it has been argued that fire may reduce the abundance and diversity of these prairie-dependent insects (Opler 1981, Stannard 1984, Panzer 1988, Swengel 1996). Determining the responses of potentially vulnerable, habitat-dependent insect species remains a primary research need in the study of fire ecology in midwestern habitats.

Fire in the Pre-European Midwestern Landscape

Fire, being common and notable, was highlighted in many early accounts of the Midwest; it made a great impression on explorers and settlers alike (McClain and Elzinga 1994, White 1995). Unfortunately, there was little attempt to understand the ecological significance of fire and the narratives tended to deal with the most sensational aspects of this phenomenon (cf. Bakeless 1961). Consequently, we must use caution when interpreting this information. Today we are not greatly concerned about how close a fire came to the ears of a horse (although this might give some indication of intensity), or whether fires outran cows (although this says something about rate of spread). There is, instead, an interest in reconstructing specific attributes of presettlement fire. The most useful historical reconstructions would include information from which to determine sources of ignition (i.e., natural or anthropogenic), fire frequency, seasonality (e.g., dormant or growing season), and ecological impacts.

It may be impossible in the Midwest to ascertain past fire frequencies based on hard evidence in the same way that past fire frequencies have been determined for conifer-dominated areas (e.g., Agee 1993). In the forests of the western United

States for example, tree ages, growth rings, and fire-scars help document the intervals between fires. The successful use of fire scars in determining past burn regimes requires the presence of trees, a condition lacking in the Midwest as a result of logging of virtually all old-growth forests. Further, little information can be gleaned from charcoal deposits. Clark (1989) discusses the limitation of charcoal analysis, pointing out that it can be used to determine the importance of fire for broad spatial and temporal scales, but cannot resolve individual fires that occur more frequently than once every 30–50 years. Thus charcoal deposits have had little successful use in the Midwest.

Despite the lack of quantifiable evidence, early accounts indicate that fire was a widespread and pervasive force in midwestern habitats. Anecdotal reports from early settlers suggest that fire in tallgrass prairie had a nearly annual return interval (White 1995); Native Americans frequently ignited fires (McClain and Elzinga 1994); anthropogenic fires occurred predominantly in the fall (McClain and Elzinga 1994); and when fires were suppressed, both prairies and forests changed rapidly (McClain and Elzinga 1994, White 1995). In general, fires appear to have recurred in most prairie habitats nearly annually, and in savanna and open woodlands on the order of every 5–15 years (Trabaud et al. 1993).

Only a small fraction of the original midwestern landscape remains in high-quality patches of native vegetation (Klopatek et al. 1979). What is left of natural habitats has been fragmented into small pieces (e.g., White 1978, Sharpe et al. 1987, Iverson and Schwartz 1994, Robertson and Schwartz 1994). Finally, the composition within these remnant natural communities often differs substantially from presettlement times (e.g., Taft, Chapter 2, Fralish, Chapter 11). These changes include differences in dominant species and biomass production (Fralish, Chapter 11), which may translate to differences in fuel loads that alter fire behavior and make achieving prescribed fire objectives difficult.

Ignition Sources of Wildlife

We can identify two primary sources of fire in the pre-European Midwest: human and lightning. It has been suggested that fires from these sources might each have resulted in different outcomes. Possible differences in fire effects could relate to differences in season of ignition and/or frequency.

Humans have occupied the Midwest since shortly after the glaciers retreated some 14,000 B.P. (Pielou 1991). From accounts of European colonists, we know that Native Americans used fire as a tool for habitat management and to assist with hunting (McClain and Elzinga 1994). Some authors have attributed virtually all fires of the region to human ignitions and have asserted that without human-ignited fires, the prairie peninsula and associated oak savannas would not exist (Pyne 1982). There is, however, documentation of lightning-ignited burns in midwestern prairies (Rowe 1969, Vogl 1974, Westover 1976). The implications of fires set by Native Americans depend largely on the likelihood of fire in the absence of anthropogenic ignitions. The definition of *naturalness* depends on the necessarily arbitrary cutoff we use for defining when human fire ignition was "natural" versus "anthropogenic."

While it would be desirable to know the relative frequency of anthropogenic versus lightning-ignited fires, attempts to estimate a fire interval based on lightning ignitions may be misleading. Anthropogenic fires influenced fuel loads and altered natural fire frequency (e.g., potentially maintaining the tallgrass prairie in Illinois during the cool post-Hypsithermal period from 5000 B.P. to the present (Robertson et al., Chapter 3)). Modern land-use changes, likewise, alter the probability of ignitions (e.g., recently plowed fields will not ignite if struck). In addition, we have no way to estimate when Native Americans began using fire as a management tool. The climate prior to any North American human habitation (~12,000 B.P.), was sufficiently different from current conditions that it would not provide an appropriate analog for recent fire regimes. Similar arguments apply to midwestern oak-hickory forests, savannas, and wetlands. The question of whether we view the presence of tallgrass prairie, savanna, and oak-hickory woodlands east of the Mississippi River as natural or as an anthropogenic artifact is largely academic and probably unanswerable.

Season of Fire

Currently there is debate regarding the appropriate season for prescribed fire in various fire-dependent habitats (e.g., Robbins and Myers 1992). Most modern prescribed fire in the Midwest has been conducted prior to the onset of the growing season. These spring burns tend to be mild when compared to summer fires; soil moisture levels are often high and ambient temperatures are cool. The appeal of spring fire is that fire management risks are minimized while the number of potential burn days is maximized (Schwegman 1984). Many resource agency personnel, however, recommend management burns during autumn (John Schwegman, personal communication, July 1994).

Higgins et al. (1989b) defined high-risk fires in the northern Great Plains as those occurring when wind speeds were greater than 32 km/hr, relative humidity was less than 20%, and air temperatures were greater than 35° C. These conditions occur most often from July through September, leaving most low-risk (good) controlled burn days in the spring and late fall. The probability of ignition is one component needed to estimate a fire return interval. The likelihood of spread, or amount of area burned, is the other. As noted above, the time of year that has the most "good" prescribed burn days is the season when fires, once ignited, might have naturally had a relatively low probability of spread. The severity of fires on good burn days is also likely to be lower than that created by prescribed fire conducted on high risk burn days.

These differences between modern and presettlement fires may result in different fire effects. For example, cooler fires often produce less top kill of shrubs and may consume less leaf litter. There is, however, little quantified research designed to evaluate the impact of season-of-burn in prairies (but see Gibson 1989). Streng et al. (1993) summarized problems of season-of-burn studies in another grass-dominated ground cover. Their review provided a thorough discussion of experimental design challenges related to this type of research. They also provided evidence that, in some grass-dominated habitats, cool-season fires, when applied under specific conditions, may be as intense as warm-season burns.

In contrast to modern, managed fires, Higgins (1984, 1986) and Rowe (1969) determined that lightning-ignited fires in the northern shortgrass prairie regions of the Dakotas occurred during summer and fall. Higgins (1984, 1986) reported that 73% of almost 300 lightning-ignited fires in the grasslands of North Dakota and pine savannas of Montana and South Dakota occurred in July and August. The rest were in April–June and September. Bragg (1982), studying the incidence of thunderstorm days and lightning-caused fires in Nebraska, determined that late-summer lightning-ignited fires were probably common in tallgrass prairies.

Indian-set fires were reported from every month of the year except January (Higgins 1986). Higgins' (1986) review of early accounts indicated Indian fires in two periods, March–May and June–November, with peaks in April and October. Similarly, McClain and Elzinga (1994) documented that most presettlement midwestern woodland and prairie fires occurred in September and October.

The management implications of season-of-fire are complex. Hover and Bragg (1981) stated that the time of a management activity was more important in determining the response than was the type of activity (fire versus mowing). Bragg (1982) observed fuel moisture content to be lowest in March and April, with similar levels of post-fire burn residue after early spring (March and April) and late fall (October and November) fires. Thus, there is a higher fuel consumption rate in autumn fires owing to the higher biomass in fall fires (Bragg 1982). Similarly, seasonal differences in weather may strongly influence fire behavior (Cheney et al. 1983).

Towne and Owensby (1984) pointed out that many studies on fire in prairies have not addressed the importance of the timing of fires. Their results on annual fires applied at different times to a suite of grasses indicated that only three weeks difference in the timing of burns could result in dramatically different responses by the vegetation. This implies that researchers who present information on treatments as a broad season category (spring, summer, fall) have not provided sufficient description of their methods. Exact dates, plus weather information and time since last burn, should always be included in reports of the results of fire research.

In contrast to Towne and Owensby's (1984) work on grasses, Biondini et al. (1989) focused on forbs and reported that treatment seasons of fire alone were not sufficient to initiate changes in plant populations. They stressed the importance of considering vegetation patch size and landscape scale when evaluating season-of-burn results.

Howe (1994a,b;1995) has added another dimension to this problem by asserting that the life history attributes of prairie species, especially responses to fire, suggest that their evolutionary history is associated with summer burns. Howe (1994a,b;1995), using experimental summer fires in a prairie restoration, observed a decrease in warm-season grasses and an associated increase in forbs as a result of summer fire. In this case summer fire increased richness and diversity in plastic species. Howe's result is attributed to the fact that the bulk of prairie plant diversity is in forbs, while the majority of the biomass is in warm-season grasses. Following this argument, Howe (1994a,b; 1995) recommended summer fire, when possible, in order to maximize diversity. The initial plant diversity in Howe's study, however, was far below that of a remnant native prairie for the region, making it difficult to apply this result in diverse native-prairie stands.

Fire Frequency

As shown above, we have little way of knowing presettlement fire frequencies. Annual burns have been applied in some management programs and have been the basis for research projects (e.g., Gibson 1989, Towne and Owensby 1984). Towne and Owensby (1984) indicated that "annual late-spring burns, even in dry years was not detrimental to herbage production, species composition, or total basal cover in tallgrass prairie (p. 392)." They documented shifts in species composition, however, indicating that some species were favored over others. Other authors have suggested that impacts of fire periodicity are mediated by interactions with grazing (Vinton and Hartnett 1992) as well as climate and soil type (Gibson and Hulbert 1987).

Fire in a Dynamic Landscape

The origin of tallgrass prairie east of the Mississippi River, in the prairie peninsula, is relatively recent (Robertson et al., Chapter 3). The mechanism suggested for this recent establishment is a warm and dry period from approximately 8000 B.P. to 5000 B.P. (Anderson 1982, Axelrod 1985). A subsequent cool and wet period led to a slight recession of the eastern prairie, but prairie has persisted across much of its maximum extent.

Gleason (1910, 1912) was one of the first biologists to recognize the significance of fire in structuring the prairie-forest border. The prevailing winds in the Midwest are west (Gleason 1913) or southwest (Chapman and Miller 1924). Early authors (Gleason 1913, Chapman and Miller 1924, Transeau 1935) observed that water provided protection from grassland fires and that meant that trees would tend to survive on the protected or eastern side of rivers, streams, or ponds. Gleason (1913) described "isolated prairie groves in central Illinois" (p. 173) as "uniformly situated on the eastern side of prairie sloughs." He noted that the "location of forests throughout central and northern Illinois, and also the adjacent states, is closely correlated with prairie fires." (p. 173) In a similar vein, Grimm (1983) studied the prairie-forest border in Minnesota and concluded that the patchiness in prairie and forest near the ecotone of these biomes is largely a result of topography and fire breaks provided by small lakes and glacial moraines. Grimm (1983) suggested that habitat types in specific areas were often a matter of precedence. That is, once established, frequent fire maintains the prairie. In contrast, forest fuels are less flammable and hold moisture better. Once forested habitat is established, fire intrusion is reduced and prairie species are excluded.

In addition to describing the role of fire in determining the landscape positions of forests, Gleason also wrote about other important fire effects. He noted prairie species that were found within a forest margin (Gleason 1910) and suggested that this introgression was the result of fire burning into a shrub zone at the edge of the forest (Gleason 1913). Gleason (1913) also noted that edges of forests were "an almost impenetrable thicket of several shrub species (p. 174)."

Those studying modern plant community patterns tend to view the prairie-forest ecotone as dynamic (e.g., Taft, Chapter 2; Fralish, Chapter 11). Prescribing fire for management of a landscape that is constantly in flux as a result of fire-generated dynamics is far different than prescribing fire to maintain static ecotonal habitats. Management for dynamic communities requires a large matrix of interacting communities that are allowed to shift. In contrast, those studying forest history treat the prairie-forest border as relatively stable and a function of natural firebreaks such as streams or topographical relief.

It has been recommended that regional conservation include sites that are large enough to contain patches of habitat in all stages of recovery from ecological disturbance regimes (Pickett and Thompson 1978, Noss and Cooperrider 1994). Conservation of a dynamic mosaic of habitat types poses a particular problem in the Midwest, where natural habitat remnants tend to be small (Schwartz and van Mantgem, Chapter 16). Originally the region was a complex of varying vegetation types: most are now all but gone. For example, by the early part of the 20th century, almost 90% of Illinois was already taken up by farms, and three-quarters of this area was tilled (Chapman and Miller 1924). Currently less than 1% of the original tallgrass prairie east of the Mississippi River remains (Robertson et al., Chapter 3). Forest area is, likewise, reduced to a small fraction of its original abundance (Klopatek et al 1979, Iverson and Schwartz 1994).

As a result of habitat loss, transition zones (ecotones) between natural habitats are often nonexistent; most natural habitats, particularly prairies, abut agricultural, residential, or industrial lands. The specific nature of the prairie-forest border was largely determined by the interaction between fire and the landscape (Bowles et al. 1994). The role of midwestern savanna, as an edaphically controlled vegetation type or a manifestation of the ecotone between forest and prairie, is problematic (Taft, Chapter 2). Very few examples of savanna remain that provide models for community composition (Apfelbaum and Haney 1991; Packard 1991, 1993). Similarly, we are just beginning to understand the role of fire in maintaining natural oak woodlands in the Midwest (Lorimer 1987, Abrams 1992). We are still far from understanding the effects of fire moving across a prairie-forest edge. Further, there are few sites in which we can do the experiments from which to obtain critical information.

To summarize, we are not very much better informed regarding the role of fire in maintaining a dynamic, versus a steady-state, prairie-forest ecotone than we were nearly 100 years ago. Similarly, our understanding of how early humans used fire in the pre-European landscape remains imprecise. Our understanding of what the vegetation would have been like in the absence of anthropogenic fire is nonexistent. While we have improved our ability to predict the outcome of specific fire-management prescriptions, we have not resolved a clear directive of what ought to be the target of natural-lands management: there is relatively little information available that would help make specific recommendations regarding the model for ecosystem-based management.

Ecosystem Management and Fire

The Resiliency of Intact Habitats

A central tenet of ecosystem-based management emphasizes the value of managing for the maintenance of natural processes; a self-sustaining native habitat is the goal of ecosystem-based management. The simplified ideal is that once natural processes are in place, species composition and habitat structure will revert to presettlement analogues. The implication is that management activities beyond routine maintenance, such as continued prescribed fire, will not be required. In other words, nature is expected to right itself and be self-perpetuating once appropriate processes are re-instituted. While occasionally enunciated as a goal in various agencies, the experience of land managers often varies from this idea. Numerous environmental changes (e.g., global increases in CO_2 concentration and rates of nitrogen deposition (Wedin and Tilman 1993), the lack of large grazers or top predators (Mankin and Warner, Chapter 7), or the presence of non-indigenous species (Luken, Chapter 5)) have inexorably changed the natural system. Setting a fire does not guarantee the re-creation of an original ecosystem process. The breadth and magnitude of extrinsic forces provide reason to doubt the efficacy of management via replication of historic fire regimes to reproduce historic community structure.

Management Constraints

Most of the natural variation in the scale, intensity, and patchiness of presettlement fire can not be re-created in the Midwest of today owing to habitat alteration and fragmentation. As a safety precaution, prescribed burns are typically not set during drought or under high-wind conditions. Woodland fires are typically set under conditions that would minimize the likelihood of canopy tree mortality.

Similarly, very low intensity, very high-intensity, and/or patchy burns may have been more common under a natural fire regime. Managed fires tend to be prescribed for weather conditions that maximize the chance of a complete burn. Site managers are often interested in extirpating problematic non-indigenous plant species, or woody invaders, from a site using fire (e.g., Nuzzo 1991; Schwartz and Heim, 1996), and strive to burn when the weather will facilitate a complete burn. Night fires, with relatively cool temperatures and high humidity, are also typically not used as a management tool. Yet historical records suggest that night fires occurred (McClain and Elzinga 1994). It would be unfair to claim that extreme fire events are not encountered with prescribed fire; managed fires often vary from the expectations of the prescriptions (James Heim, personal communication, June 1993). Safety precautions and immediate burn objectives, however, often direct fire management plans toward intermediate fire intensities. Variation in the fire interval is also likely to be lower under management, as people tend to schedule fires at regular intervals. In summary, both high- and low-extreme effects of natural burns are not likely to be planned through prescribed fire management.

In addition to concerns related to fire intensity and interval, managers must also consider issues linked to altered fuel loads and fuel types (that is, fuel loads composed of different species mixtures). Vegetation changes as a site is subjected to fire suppression. Short-term fire suppression may lead to increased fuel volume. Long-term fire suppression is often associated with the invasion of species that are neither adapted to, or tolerant of, fire. The resulting fuel is often less pyrogenic than the original vegetation. Thus, when fire is reintroduced after a period of suppression the outcome may vary from expectations.

In summary, there are several reasons why it is unlikely that the goal of restoring natural fire regimes could ever be attained. (1) We have a limited ability to understand actual prehistoric fire regimes. (2) The way we view Native American burning (natural or not) is unresolvable. (3) We have almost no information on the actual range of variability of natural fire conditions. (4) Natural fires were undoubtedly landscape-level processes, and we now burn in discrete management units that are typically not at the landscape scale and, in chronically fragmented regions, are typically quite small. (5) Alternative concerns (e.g., public safety, non-indigenous species control, or workload scheduling) often drive decisions with respect to fire weather and fire conditions for controlled burning and restrict the variety of conditions of burning relative to natural fires.

Possible Alternatives to Prescribed Fire

Mowing (clipping), sometimes in conjunction with raking (haying), has been applied to prairies in lieu of or in addition to fire (e.g. Gibson 1989, Old 1969, Swengel 1996). Some workers contend that mowing is preferable to fire management on prairies. Although haying has been studied from a range-management point of view, there are only a few studies that permit quantified comparison of the ecological outcomes of mowing and fire. Old (1969) determined that the production of flowering stalks was, on average, enhanced with burning as compared to mowing treatment. Gibson (1989) reported that mowing permitted annual and biennial plants (predominantly non-indigenous species) to become established and that fire depressed this group. This is an important negative result for any conservation effort.

Mowing may produce a short-term response that mimics the results of prescribed fire, but there appear to be ecological responses that clipping can not replicate. This is an important concern for long-term management of a site. Swengel (1966) monitored butterfly abundance over a short time period on mowed sites and compared the results to those of burned areas. Her conclusions are surprising in that she found the five butterfly species she categorized as prairie specialists to have the highest population numbers on mowed sites. Owing to small sample sizes, short response intervals after mowing, little mention of standardized conditions (e.g., site size) between treatments, and no information on past land use of research areas, the veracity of this data remains unclear. Nonetheless, the data suggest the need for further study with a long-term, controlled experimental design. What is clear is that the use of mowing for short-term enhancement of a suite of species may result in an altered and perhaps unsuitable habitat over the long term.

Fire Management Goals

If we discard the notion of restoring a wholly natural disturbance process as a realistic management goal, then what should be our management objective, and does this include the use of prescribed fire? Schwartz (1994) suggests three alternative conservation management objectives: (1) species preservation (to minimize loss of biodiversity); (2) maintenance of community structure (to re-create approximations of historical community descriptions); or (3) maintenance of ecological processes (to preserve the ecological and evolutionary context for species in their environments). While management activities may work toward simultaneously achieving all three conservation objectives, land managers must be aware that prioritizing these goals is essential, as these objectives may suggest different management strategies (Schwartz 1994). With respect to midwestern habitats, all three proposed conservation objectives can include the use of prescribed fire. These different goals, however, may suggest different fire regimes.

Season and Frequency of Fire

One strategy for fire management has been to rely on historical estimates of fire to approximate natural fire season and frequency as the target of management efforts. This management by tradition approach may succeed, but requires a cautionary note: the fire effect, and not the fire itself, is the management objective.

Desired fire effects may range from enhancing targeted native species populations to reconstructing vegetation structure and perceived natural distributions of species abundances to minimizing the abundance of non-indigenous species. With a clear view of discrete management objectives, however, one is able to target the fire management for the particular goal. For example, eliminating non-indigenous species is often best accomplished through frequent, intense burns that exceed natural fire frequency.

Much of the current discussion over appropriate fire management focuses on the season (timing) of fires (McClain and Elzinga 1994; Howe 1994a,b). Howe (1994a,b; 1995) expressed concern that the current use of fire in tallgrass prairie management promotes the dominance of some species (especially C_4, late-flowering grasses) at the expense of others (especially early-flowering forbs). Howe (1994b) has challenged the common conservation management goal of managing assemblages of species to reflect presettlement conditions and has recommended the use of summer fire in prairie restorations. Howe argued that the common community structure objective would be supported if natural communities were tightly linked, co-evolved, integrated systems (e.g., communities as super-organisms—Clements 1936). The majority of ecological studies, however, suggest that plant communities are more accurately described as loose aggregates of species assembled in space and time (Gleason 1926).

Howe (1994b) proposes species preservation as the primary conservation land management objective. Howe's data suggest, at least for prairie reconstructions, that summer fire increases species richness and evens the distribution of abundances in prairie plants by decreasing the abundance of a few strongly dominant warm-season grasses. According to Pimm (1991), the surest predictor of local extinction is few and small populations. Using Howe's results, the best way to simultaneously minimize the probability of population loss for the largest number of species would be to increase species richness and increase the uniformity of abundances with summer fire. This management strategy is complicated by typically high summer fuel moisture making it hard to conduct summer fires in the Midwest. Nonetheless, if our primary conservation goal is to reduce local extinction of prairie plants, then burning during dry summers may be a good strategy. We still need much evidence showing whether this is the appropriate decision for prairie remnants with respect to prairie fauna (Howe 1994b).

Making a Plan

There are many resources available to aid land managers in prescribing burns. Of special significance is the federal "RX" series of fire courses. These are often conducted by agencies (e.g., the U.S. Fish and Wildlife Service, Bureau of Land Management, and U.S. Forest Service) as well as The Nature Conservancy. Many states have, or are developing, certification programs for prescribed burners; these are usually associated with the state's Division of Forestry. The *Fire*

Management Manual developed by The Nature Conservancy (1991) is especially helpful and provides appropriate forms and guidelines for developing and implementing a fire plan.

Following the lead of Howe (1994, p. 700) we agree that the goal of fire management "should be to develop scientific rationales for restoration and conservation, rather than to rely on unexamined convention." We urge readers to use ten steps in order to decide if fire management is warranted and from which to base the writing of a fire management plan (Table 10-1). First, clearly state the management objectives for the site whether they are biological (e.g., endangered species management) or not (fuel reduction and safety, enhancement of recreational opportunities, etc). Although we cannot determine a perfect reconstruction of original burn regimes, we can state that many species and habitats of pre-European settlement midwestern communities are dependent on fire. If mowing and/or herbicide use were to totally replace prescribed burning, many species and perhaps even habitat integrity would eventually be lost.

Second, identify the alternative management strategies that may accomplish the stated objectives. Here one must identify whether there are alternatives to fire (grazing, mowing, herbicide treatments) that could accomplish any site objectives. Treating one set of management goals with activities other than fire (e.g., spraying to control non-indigenous plants, or cutting of woody invaders in a grassland) may be combined with burning or free the use of fire to be directed primarily toward a management objective more uniquely suited for its use. Third, if fire is indicated, review the relevant fire research. A site newly planted with a handful of species may support a very different fuel type and/or load than an intact site. Individual plant mortality and/or species extirpation are likely to be affected by fuel condition. Recent site fire history (month and year of previous burns) should be known. Even though time of burn is expressed as a season (winter, spring, summer, fall), it does not provide enough information to evaluate the treatment (see Streng et al. 1993 for a discussion of this issue related to the southeastern U.S.).

Fourth, if fire is recommended, then prioritize the management objectives to be accomplished with fire. Fire often results in multiple habitat changes, such as the reduction of invasive plants species (either non-indigenous or off-site native species) or site modification (litter removal may alter soil pH, temperature and/or light level—e.g., Wright and Bailey 1982). Fifth, identify potential negative impacts of the proposed fire management regime and list activities that could moderate these negative effects. Sixth, prepare a fire management schedule, asking whether there is sufficient variability in the proposed plan and if there are contingencies for unplanned events, such as a drought, that can be incorporated into the plan. Seventh, devise a monitoring schedule for evaluating the impact of the management. Eighth, begin implementation of the plan. Ninth, evaluate the results of the initial management program. Tenth, revise the management plan according to results obtained. Careful planning, thorough evaluation, and

Table 10.1. Ten steps toward constructing and using a fire management plan.

1. Clearly state and prioritize management objectives. For example:
   a) enhance or maintain a target (threatened, endangered, or game) species
   b) rehabilitate degraded habitat
   c) depress non-indigenous species
   d) maintain biological diversity
   e) restore a habitat to a historically documented model
   f) enhance habitat quality for wildlife
   h) reduce fuel

2. Identify alternative management strategies that may accomplish the stated objectives:
   a) fire
   b) physical / mechanical control of vegetation
   c) herbicides
   d) biocontrol

3. If fire is recommended, then evaluate and describe the target site.
   a) Is the site a remnant or a planting?
   b) What is the management history?
   c) Is the primary objective to maintain or to change the site?
   d) What is the recent burn history?
   e) What was the date of the most recent burn?
   f) What was the fire weather and local soil moisture conditions?
   g) What sites represent the best analogues to the target site in terms of fire management?
   h) What is known of historic fire regime in this natural community?
   i) What is known of the effects of varying season, frequency or intensity of fire in this habitat?

4. Re-evaluate and prioritize positive management objectives of proposed fire management (as in no. 1).

5. Identify potential negative impacts of the fire management regime proposed. For example:
   a) incidental negative impact on native species
   b) landowner relations
   c) conflict with recreation, hunting or other activities
   d) negative impacts of smoke and smoke management
   e) manpower limitations to conduct managed fire

6. Write a fire management plan.[1]
   a) Draft a schedule.
   b) Review and ask whether there is sufficient variability in the proposed fire plan.
   c) List contingencies for unplanned events, such as a drought.
   d) Propose a time period when to expect certain results of fire management.

7. Devise a monitoring plan to evaluate success and failure.

8. Begin implementation of the plan.

9. Evaluate the results of the initial management program.
   a) Were the fires accomplished as planned?
   b) Did the fires accomplish the stated objectives?
   c) Was the incidental negative different than expected?

10. Revise the management plan (steps 1–7) according to results obtained.

[1]Several guides, such as The Nature Conservancy's *Fire Management Guide* (1991), exist to help with the practical aspects of planning for safe managed fire, including obtaining required permits.

meticulous documentation will allow the results of one management plan to be used to further our basic understanding of fire management and will provide background to assist in the development of other management plans.

References

Abrams, M.D. 1992. Fire and the development of oak forests. *Bioscience* 42:346–353.

Agee, J.K. 1993. *Fire Ecology of Pacific Northwest Forests.* Island Press, Washington, D.C.

Anderson, R.C. 1972. Prairie history, management and restoration in Southern Illinois. In J.H. Zimmerman, ed. *Midwest Prairie Conference Proceedings* 2:15–21.

Anderson, R.C. 1982. An evolutionary model summarizing the roles of fire, climate, and grazing animals in the origin and maintenance of grasslands: an end paper. In J.R. Estes, R.J. Tyrl, and J.N. Brunken, eds. *Grasses and Grasslands.* University of Oklahoma Press, Norman, 297–308.

Apfelbaum, S., and A. Haney. 1991. Management of degraded oak savanna remnants in the upper Midwest: preliminary results from three years of study. In G.V. Burger, J.E. Ebinger, and G.S. Wilhelm, eds. *Proceedings of the Oak Woods Management Symposium,* Eastern Illinois University, 81–89.

Axelrod, D.I. 1985. Rise of the grassland biome, central North America. *The Botanical Review* 51(2):163–201.

Bakeless, J. 1961. *America as Seen by its First Explorers.* Dover, New York.

Barbour, M.G., and W.D. Billings, ed. 1988. *North American Terrestrial Vegetation.* Cambridge University Press, Cambridge.

Barbour, M.G., J.H. Burk, and W.D. Pitts. 1980. *Terrestrial Plant Ecology.* Benjamin-Cummings, Redwood City, Calif.

Biondini, M.E., A.A. Steuter, and C.E. Grygiel. 1989. Seasonal fire effects on the diversity patterns, spatial distribution and community structure of forbs in the Northern Mixed Prairie, USA. *Vegetatio* 85:21–31.

Bowles, M.L., M.D. Hutchison and J.L. McBride. 1994. Landscape pattern and structure of oak savanna, woodland and barrens in northeastern Illinois at the time of European settlement. In J.S. Fralish, R.C. Anderson, J.E. Ebinger and R. Szafoni, eds., *Proceedings of the North American Conference on Barrens and Savannas.* Illinois State University, Normal, 65–74.

Bragg, T.B. 1982. Seasonal variations in fuel and fuel consumption by fires in a bluestem prairie. *Ecology* 63(1):7–11.

Cancelado, R., and T.R. Yonke. 1970. Effect of fire on prairie insect populations. *Journal of the Kansas Entomological Society* 43:274–281.

Chapman, H.H., and R.B. Miller. 1924. *Bulletin: Second Report on a Forest Survey of Illinois, The Economics of Forestry in the State.* Natural History Survey, Urbana, Ill.

Cheney, N.P., J.S. Gould, and W.R. Catchpole. 1993. The influence of fuel, weather, and fire shape variables on fire-spread in grasslands. *International Journal of Wildland Fire* 3(1):31–44.

Christensen, N.L. 1988. Vegetation of the Southeastern Coastal Plain. In M.G. Barbour and W.D. Billings, eds. *North American Terrestrial Vegetation.* Cambridge University Press, New York, 317–363.

Clark, J.S. 1989. Ecological disturbance as a renewal process: theory and application to fire history. *Oikos* 56:17–30.

Clements, F.E. 1936. Nature and structure of the climax. *Journal of Ecology* 24:552–584.

Collins, S.L. 1990. Introduction: fire as a natural disturbance in tallgrass prairie ecosystems. In S.L. Collins and L.L. Wallace, eds. *Fire in North American Tallgrass Prairie.* University of Oklahoma Press, Norman, 3–7.

Collins, S.L. 1995. The measurement of stability in grasslands. *Tree* 10(3):95–96.

Collins, S.L., and L.L. Wallace, eds. 1990. *Fire in North American Tallgrass Prairie.* University of Oklahoma Press, Norman.

Cottam, G. 1949. The phytosociology of an oak woods in southwestern Wisconsin. *Ecology* 30:271–287.

Gibson, D.J. 1989. Hulbert's study of factors effecting botanical composition of tallgrass prairie. *Proceedings of the North American Prairie Conference* 11:115–133.

Gibson, D.J., and L.C. Hulbert. 1987. Effects of fire, topography and year-to-year climate variation on species composition in tallgrass prairie. *Vegetatio* 72:175–185.

Gleason, H.A. 1910. The vegetation of the inland sand deposits of Illinois. *Illinois State Laboratory of Natural History Bulletin* 9:23–174.

Gleason, H.A. 1912. An isolated prairie grove and its phytogeographical significance. *Botanical Gazette* 53:38–49.

Gleason, H.A. 1913. The relation of forest distribution and prairie fires in the middle west. *Torreya* 13(8):173–181.

Gleason, H.A. 1926. The individualistic concept of the plant association. *Bulletin of the Torrey Botanical Club* 53:7–26.

Glenn-Lewin, D.C., L.A. Johnson, T.W. Jurik, A. Akey, M. Leoschke, and T. Rosberg. 1990. Fire in central North American grasslands: vegetative reproduction, seed germination, and seedling establishment. In S.L. Collins and L.L. Wallace, eds. *Fire in North American Tallgrass Prairie.* University of Oklahoma Press, Norman, 28–45.

Grimm, E.C. 1983. Chronology and dynamics of vegetation change in the prairie-woodland region of southern Minnesota, USA. *New Phytologist* 93:311–350.

Haney, A., and S.I. Apfelbaum. 1990. Structure and dynamics of midwest oak savannas. In J.M. Sweeney, ed. *Management of Dynamic Ecosystems.* The Wildlife Society, West Lafayette, Ind., 19–30.

Herkert, J.R. 1994. Breeding bird communities of midwestern prairie fragments: the effects of prescribed burning and habitat-area. *Natural Areas Journal* 14:128–135.

Higgins, K.F. 1984. Lightning fires in North Dakota grasslands and in pine-savannah lands of South Dakota and Montana. *Journal of Range Management* 37(2):100–103.

Higgins, K.F. 1986. *Interpretation and Compendium of Historical Fire Accounts in the Northern Great Plains.* U.S. Fish and Wildlife Service Resource Publication 161.

Higgins, K.F., A.D. Kruse, and J.L. Piehl. 1989a. *Effects of Fire in the Northern Great Plains.* U.S. Fish and Wildlife Service Publication EC 761.

Higgins, K.F., A.D. Kruse, and J.L. Piehl. 1989b. *Prescribed Burning Guidelines in the Northern Great Plains.* U.S. Fish and Wildlife Service and Cooperative Extension Service Publication EC760. South Dakota State University, U.S. Department of Agriculture.

Hill, G.R., and W.J. Platt. 1975. Some effects of fire upon a tall grass prairie plant community in northwestern Iowa. In M.K. Wali, ed. *Prairie: A Multiple View.* University of North Dakota Press, Grand Forks, 103–113.

Hover, E.I. and T.B. Bragg. 1981. Effects of season of burning and mowing on an eastern Nebraska *Stipa-Andropogon* prairie. American Midland Naturalist 105:13–18.

Howe, H.F. 1994a. Response of early- and late-flowering plants to fire season in experimental prairies. *Ecological Applications* 4(1):121–133.

Howe, H.F. 1994b. Managing species diversity in tallgrass prairie: assumptions and implications. *Conservation Biology* 8(3):691–704.

Howe, H.F. 1995. Succession and fire season in experimental prairie plantings. *Ecology* 76(6):1917–1925.

Hutchinson, M. 1992. Vegetation management guidelines: smooth sumac (*Rhus glabra* L.). *Natural Areas Journal* 12:158.

Iverson, L.R., and M.W. Schwartz. 1994. Forests. In *The Changing Illinois Environment: Critical Trends.* Technical Report, vol. 3. Illinois Department of Energy and Natural Resources, Springfield, 33-66. ILENR/RE-EA-94/05.

James, S.W. 1982. Effects of fire and soil type on earthworm populations in a tallgrass prairie. *Pedobiologia* 24:37–40.

James, S.W. 1988. The post-fire environment and earthworm populations in a tallgrass prairie. *Ecology* 69:476–483.

Johnson, S.R., and A.K. Knapp. 1995. The influence of fire on Spartina pectinata wetland communities in a northeastern Kansas tallgrass prairie. *Canadian Journal of Botany* 73:84–90.

Klopatek, J.M., R.J. Olson, C.J. Emerson, and J.L. Joness. 1979. Land-use conflicts with natural vegetation in the United States. *Environmental Conservation* 6:191–199.

Kozlowski, T.T., and C.E. Ahlgren, eds. 1974. *Fire and Ecosystems.* Academic Press, New York.

Lorimer, C.G. 1987. The role of fire in the perpetuation of oak forests. In *8th Northern Illinois Prairie Workshop Proceedings,* 59–76. The Forest Pressure District, Will County, Ill.

Lussenhop, J.F. 1972. Distribution and phenology of a prairie soil arthropod population. In J.H. Zimmerman, ed. *Proceedings of the Second Midwest Prairie Conference* 2:60–72.

Lussenhop, J.F. 1976. Soil arthropod response to prairie burning. *Ecology* 57:88–98.

McClain, W.E., and S.L. Elzinga. 1994. The occurrence of prairie and forest fires in Illinois and other midwestern states, 1679 to 1854. *Erigenia* 13:79–90.

Nagel, H.G. 1973. Effect of spring prairie burning on herbivorous and non-herbivorous arthropod populations. *Journal of the Kansas Entomological Society* 46:485–496.

Niemi, G.J., and J.R. Probst. 1990. Wildlife and Fire in the Upper Midwest. In J.M. Sweeney, ed. *Management of Dynamic Ecosystems.* The Wildlife Society, West Lafayette, Ind., 31–46.

Noss, R.F., and A.Y. Cooperrider. 1994. *Saving Nature's Legacy: Protecting and Restoring Biodiversity.* Island Press, Washington, D.C.

Nuzzo, V.A. 1991. Experimental control of garlic mustard [*Alliaria petiolata* (Bieb.) Cavara & Grande] in northern Illinois using fire, herbicide and cutting. *Natural Areas Journal* 11:158–167.

Old, S.M. 1969. Microclimate, fire and plant production in an Illinois prairie. *Ecological Monographs* 39:355–384.

Opler, P.A. 1981. Management of prairie habitats for insect conservation. *Journal of the Natural Areas Association* 1:3–6.

Packard, S. 1991. Rediscovering the tallgrass savanna of Illinois. In G.V. Burger, J.E. Ebinger, and G.S. Wilhelm, *Proceedings of the Oak Woods Management Symposium.* Eastern Illinois University, Charleston, 55–66.

Packard, S. 1993. Restoring oak ecosystems. *Restoration and Management Notes* 11:5–16.

Panzer, R. 1988. Managing prairie remnants for insect conservation. *Natural Areas Journal* 8(2):83–90.

Panzer, R., D. Stillwaugh, R. Gnaedinger, and G. Derkovitz. 1995. Prevalence of remnant dependence among the prairie- and savanna-inhabiting insects of the Chicago region. *Natural Areas Journal* 15(2):101–116.

Pemble, R.H., G.L. Van Amburg, and Lyle Mattson. 1981. Intraspecific variation in flowering activity following a spring burn on a northwestern Minnesota prairie. Ohio Biological Survey, *Biological Notes* 15:235–239.

Pickett, S.T.A., and J.N. Thompson. 1978. Patch dynamics and the design of nature reserves. *Biological Conservation* 13:27–37.

Pickett, S.T.A., and P.S. White, eds. 1985. *The Ecology of Natural Disturbance and Patch Dynamics.* Academic Press, New York.

Pielou, E.C. 1991. *After the Ice Age: The Return of Life to Glaciated North America.* University of Chicago Press, Chicago.

Pimm, S.L. 1991. *The balance of nature?: Ecological Issues in the Conservation of Species and Communities.* University of Chicago Press, Chicago.

Pyne, S.J. 1982. *Fire in America: A Cultural History of Wildlife and Rural Fire.* Princeton University Press, Princeton, N.J.

Robbins, L.E., and R.L. Myers. 1992. *Seasonal Effects of Prescribed Burning in Florida: A Review.* Tall Timbers, Tallahassee, FL., miscellaneous publication no. 8.

Robertson, K.R., and M.W. Schwartz. 1994. Prairies. In *The Changing Illinois Environment: Critical Trends.* Technical Report of the Critical Trends Assessment Project. Vol. 3: Ecological Resources. Illinois Department of Energy and Natural Resources, Springfield, 1–32. ILENR/RE-EA-94/05.

Rowe, J.W. 1969. Lightning fires in Saskatchewan grassland. *Canadian Field Naturalist* 83:317–324.

Schwartz, M.W. 1994. Conflicting goals for conserving biodiversity: issues of scale and value. *Natural Areas Journal* 14:213–216.

Schwartz, M.W., and J. Heim. 1996. The effects of prescribed fire on degraded forest vegetation. *Natural Areas Journal* 16:184–191.

Schwegman, J. 1984. Prescribed burning in the autumn for community management in nature preserves and natural areas on Illinois Department of Conservation lands. The Sixth Northern Illinois Prairie workshop, McHenry College Crystal Lake.

Seastedt, T.R. 1984a. Belowground macroarthropods of annually burned and unburned tallgrass prairie. *American Midland Naturalist* 111:405–408.

Seastedt, T.R. 1984b. Microarthropods of burned and unburned tallgrass prairie. *Journal of the Kansas Entomological Society* 57:468–476.

Sharpe, D.M., G.R. Guntenspergen, C.P. Dunn, L.A. Leitner, and F. Stearns. 1987. Vegetation dynamics in a southern Wisconsin agricultural landscape. In M.G. Turner, ed. *Landscape Heterogeneity and Disturbance.* Springer-Verlag, New York, 137–155.

Sims, P.L. 1988. Grasslands. In M.G. Barbour and W.D. Billings, eds. *North American Terrestrial Vegetation.* Cambridge University Press, New York, 266–286.

Stannard, L.J. 1984. On the origin and maintenance of La Grande Prairie of Illinois. *Erigenia* 1984:31–36.

Streng, D.R., J.S. Glitzenstein, and W.J. Platt. 1993. Evaluating effects of season of burn in longleaf pine forests: a critical literature review and some results from an ongoing long-term study. In S.M. Hermann, ed. *Proceedings of the 18th Tall Timbers Fire Ecology Conference* 18:227–263.

Swengel, A.B. 1996. Effects of fire and hay management on abundance of prairie butterflies. *Biological Conservation* 76:73–85.

The Nature Conservancy. 1991. *Fire Management Manual.* The Nature Conservancy, Arlington, Va.

Towne, G., and C. Owensby. 1984. Long-term effects of annual burning at different dates in ungrazed Kansas tallgrass prairie. *Journal of Range Management* 37:392–397.

Trabaud, L.V., N.L. Christensen, and A.M. Gill. 1993. Historical biogeography of fire in temperate and Mediterranean ecosystems. In P.J. Crutzen and J.G. Goldhammer, eds. *Fire in the Environment: The Ecological, Atmospheric, and Climatic Importance of Vegetation Fires.* John Wiley & Sons, Chichester, 277–295.

Transeau, E. 1935. The prairie peninsula. *Ecology* 16:424–427.

Van Amburg, G.L., J.A. Swaby, and R.H. Pemble. 1981. Response of arthropods to a spring burn of a tallgrass prairie in northwestern Minnesota. Ohio Biological Survey, *Biological Notes* 15:240–243.

Vinton, M.A., and D.C. Hartnett. 1992. Effects of bison grazing on *Andropogon gerardii* and *Panicum virgatum* in burned and unburned tallgrass prairie. *Oecologia* 90:374–382.

Vogl, R.J. 1967. Controlled burning for wildlife in Wisconsin. *Proceedings of the 6th Tall Timbers Fire Ecology Conference* 6:47–96.

Vogl, R.J. 1974. Effects of fire on grasslands. In T.T. Kozlowski, ed. *Fire and Ecosystems.* Academic Press, San Diego, Calif., 139–194.

Vogl, R.J., and A.M. Beck. 1970. Response of white-tailed deer to a Wisconsin wildfire. *American Midland Naturalist* 84:270–273.

Warren, S.D., C.J. Scifres, and P.D. Teel. 1987. Response of grassland arthropods to burning: a review. *Agriculture, Ecosystems & Environment* 19:105–130.

Wedin, D., and D. Tilman. 1993. Competition among grasses along a nitrogen gradient— intial conditions and mechanisms of competition. *Ecological Monographs* 63:199–229.

Westover, D.E. 1976. *Nebraska Wildfires.* Department of Forestry, University of Nebraska, Lincoln.

White, J. 1978. *Illinois Natural Areas Inventory Technical Report.* Vol. I. *Survey Methods and Results.* Illinois Natural Areas Inventory, Urbana.

White, J. 1995. Unpublished manuscript about fire in early Illinois. Ecological Services, Urbana, Ill.

Wright, H.A., and A.W. Bailey. 1982. *Fire Ecology.* John Wiley & Sons, New York.

Zedler, J., and O.L. Loucks. 1969. Differential burning response of *Poa pratensis* fields and *Andropogon scoparius* in central Wisconsin. *American Midland Naturalist* 81:341–352.

11

Community Succession, Diversity, and Disturbance in the Central Hardwood Forest

James S. Fralish
Departments of Forestry and Plant Biology, Southern Illinois University,
Carbondale, IL 62901

Introduction

During the past two decades, ecologists have voiced increasing concern over the problem of maintaining forest ecosystem integrity and sustainability, not only locally and regionally but also nationally. This concern has grown concurrent with the hard database that has provided new information on succession, stability, and biodiversity. In the central hardwood region, the process of forest succession is characterized by *natural fragmentation* of the oak-hickory forest overstory as canopy gaps are filled with stems of other hardwood species. The loss of oak and hickory over time will have a major impact on the entire ecosystem because they impart a unique structure and function to the forest community. These species are considered *keystone species,* which Bond (1994) defines as those that should be conserved because they have a disproportionate effect on the persistence of other species. Oak- and hickory-dominated forests not only produce mast but create environmental conditions required by a variety of understory plants as well as mammals, birds, and insects not found in other forest types. The impact of forest habitat loss on mammals is well known, but our understanding of the impact of fragmentation (i.e., caused by agriculture) on neotropical migrant songbird and cowbird populations is relatively recent (Thompson and Fritzell 1990, Terborgh 1992, Thompson et al. 1992, Martin 1993). Less well studied is the impact of succession on shrub and herbaceous plants. These strata produce seed and support a myriad of insect species that constitute the food supply of many songbirds (Martin et al. 1951). A relatively new concept is that many common herbaceous plants depend on the oak-forest environment and are strongly negatively impacted by succession to shade-tolerant species.

The objectives of this chapter are to examine community succession in upland forests and describe the influence of disturbance (historical events) and succession on forest community composition and diversity. Examples will be drawn from several distinct natural regions within Illinois, Kentucky, and Tennessee as representative of the central hardwood forest ecosystem.

Forest Community Concepts

Community Succession

Succession (henceforth referred to as succession or forest succession) is the systematic replacement of a forest community composed of relatively shade-intolerant species by a community composed of more shade-tolerant species (Fralish 1988a). The sequence of events leading to the successional process occurs most often on soil of high water-holding capacity when the canopy of a forest community near the successional endpoint (climax or compositionally stable) is partially removed or eliminated by disturbance. With high light intensity at the forest floor, seedlings of *pioneer species* (also called shade-intolerant, light-demanding, or early successional species) may invade and grow to dominate the new community. As the pioneer forest progresses toward maturity, seedlings of shade-tolerant species found in the original forest re-establish and create a dense, shaded understory. Since the pioneer species usually are shade intolerant, or at most shade intermediate, their seedlings cannot grow and develop in the moderate to heavy shade, while shade-tolerant species flourish and grow into the overstory to dominate the community. The pioneer species eventually disappear with death of the old overstory trees. On dry sites, the invasion process may be so slow that continuous regrowth of stems of the original forest species creates a compositionally stable forest. Peet and Loucks (1977) noted a much protracted successional sequence on sandy soils in southern Wisconsin.

Succession is occurring in all forested regions of North America. In each region, shade-tolerant species are invading and replacing stands composed of either shade-intolerant or shade-intermediate *disturbance dependent* species (Burns and Honkala 1990a, 1990b). These species include Douglas fir (*Pseudotsuga menziesii,* coastal form), giant sequoia (*Sequoiadendron giganteum*), quaking aspen (*Populus tremuloides*), bigtooth aspen (*P. grandidentata,* white birch (*Betula papyrifera*), lodgepole pine (*Pinus contorta*), red pine (*P. resinosa*), and white pine (*P. strobus*). In the eastern and southeastern United States, shortleaf pine (*P. echinata*), loblolly pine (*P. taeda*), slash pine (*P. elliottii*), and longleaf pine (*P. palustris*) are being replaced by scrub oak.

On deep, moist soil in the central hardwood forest, sugar maple (*Acer saccharum*), American beech (*Fagus grandifolia*), white ash (*Fraxinus americana*), red maple (*A. rubrum*), red elm (*Ulmus rubra*), American elm (*U. americana*), American basswood (*Tilia americana*), bitternut hickory (*Carya cordiformis*), black walnut (*Juglans nigra*), hackberry (*Celtis occidentalis*), and Ohio buckeye (*Aesculus glabra*) are invading oak-hickory forest (Figure 11.1). Conversion of oak-hickory stands to these species (henceforth referred to as *mesophytes* or *mesophytic species*) has been reported for Pennsylvania (Abrams 1992, Downs and Abrams 1991), Ohio (McCarthy and Wistendahl 1988, Cho and Boerner 1995), Indiana (Parker et al. 1985, Ward and Parker 1989), Kentucky and Tennessee (Kettler 1990, Fralish and Crooks 1989), Michigan (Host et al. 1987), Hammitt and Barnes 1989), Wisconsin (Menges and Loucks 1984), Missouri (Nigh et al. 1985a, 1985b; Richards et al. 1995), Iowa (Countryman and Miller 1989), and as far west as Kansas (Abrams 1986).

A similar replacement pattern in oak-hickory forest has been reported in northern Illinois (Wilhelm 1991), central Illinois (Adams and Anderson 1980, Ebinger 1986, Edgington 1991, Landes and Ebinger 1991), and southern Illinois (Fralish et al. 1991, McArdle 1991, Shotola et al. 1992, Schildt 1995). The seriousness of the problem is reflected by Iverson et al. (1989), who reported that between 1962 and 1985, the amount of commercial oak-hickory forest land declined 14% (980,000 ha to 840,300 ha) while the amount of maple-beech increased by 4,119% (10,290 ha to 434,200 ha).

Stability

In the absence of a major alteration in soil or site condition, stand composition will stabilize when the shade and drought tolerances of species in the understory match that of the overstory species. Subsequently, when large trees die they are replaced by smaller stems of the same species or by another species which has similar tolerances. In the latter situation for example, the understory of a white oak (*Quercus alba*) stand on a xeric-mesic south slope may be dominated by black oak (*Q. velutina*) seedlings. With death or removal of the white oak, black oak may become the overstory dominant, but shade tolerances of the two species are nearly equal, and oak would continue to occupy the site (Fralish 1988a). The problem of stability may be accentuated in a stand of mixed mesophytes where a large number of species may cause moderate variation in composition from overstory to understory while general shade tolerance for each stratum remains relatively constant.

Soil and site conditions largely influence the point in time at which successional processes cease and community composition becomes stable. If soil is continuously moist through the growing season (mesic site) because of depth or favorable location on a north slope or in a drainage or cove (Downs 1976), the stand will progress to mesophytic species (Fralish 1988a). These forests tend to be extremely stable because of their shade tolerance and because their dense, deep upper crowns create a heavy shade that excludes shade-intolerant (early successional) and intermediate shade-tolerant (midsuccessional) species.

Limited soil resources, specifically soil water, may terminate the succession process or so protract it that succession appears terminated (Peet and Loucks 1977). For example, shade-intermediate white and black oak form stable stands on southeast to west slopes (xeric-mesic sites) where a soil drought period prevents invasion of mesophytes. Stable post oak stands occur on southwest slopes where the soil is thin and rocky, and several soil drought periods prevent invasion by white and black oak. On sandstone outcrops in southern Illinois, soil drought is extreme, and the stable redcedar woodlands are unlikely to be replaced by oak (Fralish 1988a, Downs 1976).

Species Richness

The simplest and most widely applied concept of diversity is that of species number, also called species richness, although equability is also a component (Peet 1974). High species richness has been considered an important characteristic of stands, communities, and ecosystems. According to Horn (1974), the concept that high richness imparts stability to a community, originally attributed to MacArthur (1955), was refuted by May (1973), but has been reiterated by Tilman and Downing (1994). Horn (1974, 30) states that the one nearly universal axiom of diversity is " . . . the diversity [species richness] of the climax [compositionally stable] community must be lower than that of some preceding [successional] stage." Logically, during the process of succession from a community of relatively shade-intolerant tree species to one of shade-tolerant species, the transition stage will contain tree species of both communities and have a higher number of species than either the earlier pioneer or final climax community (Figure 11.1).

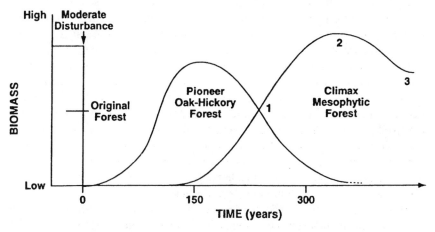

Figure 11.1. Stand succession and development of the compositionally stable forest following a major disturbance on a mesic site in the central hardwood region. Time zero represents the point at which development began, after either (1) fire was removed from presettlement forest or (2) cutting and fire were removed the original forest, followed by protection of the forest to the present time. The steepness of the left one-half of the curves indicates a faster growth rate for oak and hickory compared to sugar maple (mesophytes), and the height of the curves indicates the maximum stand biomass developed by the community. The developmental phases of the climax forest are (1) aggrading, (2) mature, and (3) old-growth (after Bormann and Likens 1994). Total biomass and species richness are greatest in the area of the curve between phases 1 and 2 (150–300 years) where species from both communities are present. In this area, large old oak and hickory trees extend above the general canopy level of dense mesophytes.

In the central states, the transition stand of oak and hickory species intermixed with developing mesophytes may contain as many as 30 to 35 tree species, but individual stands of oak-hickory or mixed mesophytes may contain up to 20 species.

Odum (1975, 55) states that "it does not necessarily follow that diversity in itself produces stability." Moreover, based on the level of species richness in transition forest, it can be argued that high diversity is an indication of instability. This concept can be expanded to recovering old field communities where there is an exceptionally high number of grass, forb, herb, and woody species. However, for most ecosystems, the relationship between species richness, successional stage, and environment has not been completely defined.

Disturbance

Disturbance is an integral part of the forest ecosystem environment and an important ecological process (Turner and Dale 1991). White and Pickett (1985, 7) define disturbance as ". . . any relatively discrete event in time that disrupts ecosystem, community, or population structure and changes resources, substrate availability, or the physical environment." This definition approaches the concept from both the neutral (normal environmental fluctuations) and negative (destruction events) aspect. Conversely, Bormann and Likens (1994) suggest that forest disturbance is a relatively positive event that initiates a series of complex feedback processes that ultimately return the ecosystem to its original state. These processes include (1) a reduction of light interception and its redistribution to the forest floor to stimulate seedling and sapling growth, (2) an increase in soil water within the profile due to reduction of evapotranspiration, and (3) increased soil nutrient availability due to increased decomposition resulting from high soil-surface temperatures. With these readily available resources, the disturbed forest may quickly become a dense vegetative mass that not only protects the soil but stores nutrients and reduces their concentration in stream water.

Absence of disturbance may be considered a disruption of normal ecosystem function in many temperate ecosystems that have evolved with and depend upon some type of disturbance, primarily fire, for their continued existence. Odum et al. (1987, 123) states that "the artificial suppression of natural disturbance can often lead to a variety of side effects, ranging from alterations in geomorphology to significant changes in ecological productivity and community structure and structural properties at the landscape level of organization." White (1979) further indicates that these changes are frequently unanticipated and detrimental (see Odum et al. 1987).

One negative impact from the artificial suppression of natural disturbance, particularly fire, is that disturbance-dependent species ultimately are eliminated by succession. Thus, ecologists and resource managers now use fire to stabilize community composition and structure as part of the restoration or maintenance of common as well as rare communities and endangered species. The primary impact of light to moderate prescribed fire is not on the forest overstory but on understory composition, where fire controls invading species of less desirable seedlings and saplings that grow to replace the overstory trees. A generally accepted belief supported by the original land survey records of 1806–7 is that fire was common and the forests of southern Illinois were more open than the present forest. Timber harvesting, grazing, and fire continued to be common disturbance elements from the mid-1800s into the mid-1930s. Telford (1926) reported numerous concurrent fires and extensively burned woods in southern Illinois. These prevented the development of a mesophytic forest by eliminating large trees as a seed source and/or preventing the establishment and growth of seedlings. Near total protection was initiated in the 1930s when the United States Forest Service purchased abandoned farm and adjacent forested lands, and statewide fire prevention programs were developed. The present large number of seedlings, saplings, and small trees (DBH < 15 cm) of mesophytes and associated species such as dogwood (*Cornus florida*), ironwood (*Ostrya virginiana*), and pawpaw (*Asimina triloba*) can be traced to the absence of disturbance that began 60 years ago: many stems have grown into seed-bearing trees that accelerate the successional process.

Light to moderate frequent fire (natural or prescribed) also controls stand structure. The character of the forests in the early 1800s was a direct result of frequent fire. In the Missouri Ozarks, the fire return period for post oak savanna varied from 2.8 to 4.3 years between 1740 and 1850 but increased to as high as 24 years after 1850. This resulted in a profound change in mosaic pattern and tree density of the Ozark forest-prairie ecotone (Guyette and Cutter 1991; Cutter and Guyette 1994). Citing Schoolcraft (1821), Schroeder (1967, 15) reported that early travelers from Kentucky and Tennessee were impressed by the openness of the Ozark woods and were led to emphasize the barrenness of ridgetops and uplands: "Our route this day has been over barrens and prairies, with occasional forests and oak, the soil poor, and covered with grass, with very little under-brush." Streyermark (1959) also supported the idea that the present closed forests of the Missouri Ozarks have been greatly modified from those of the early 19th century. In southern Illinois, Fralish et al. (1991) reported that presettlement forest was considerably more open than the present forest.

In the Ozarks, the absence of fire also permits redcedar expansion, which parallels the problem of sugar maple invasion. Although both are fire intolerant, sugar maple is a climax species on mesic sites, and redcedar is known to invade xeric sites and degrade barrens, glades, and grasslands while forming a stable community. The absence of fire is cited as the chief cause for this rapid expansion (Beilman and Brenner 1951, Hall 1955). The species has been reported as climax in sandstone outcrop communities in the Shawnee Hills (Fralish 1988a).

Many of our present forests have developed after a moderate to severe disturbance such as wildfire, extensive windthrow or crown breakage, severe insect attack, or timber harvesting. These factors open the forest floor to sunlight, which increases surface temperatures and seed germination of shade-intolerant species (Bazzaz 1979), thus increasing the potential for invasion of early successional (e.g., pine and redcedar) and midsuccessional species (oak and hickory), thus increasing diversity. Also in disturbed areas, high soil-nitrate levels in the spring may stimulate germination and early growth of early successional species (Vitousek and Reiners 1975). At the extreme, repeated severe disturbances may degrade the soil and reduce diversity as well as forest growth and productivity.

The Central Hardwood Forest Community

The tristate area of southern Illinois, western Kentucky, and western Tennessee is located near the center of the central hardwood forest (Figure 11.2) described by Clark (1976). In the southern one-third of Illinois are four natural regions (divisions, *sensu* Schwegman 1973), each in a different physiographic province: Southern Till Plain (East Central Lowlands), Shawnee Hills (Shawnee Hills section of the Interior Low Plateau), Illinois Ozark Hills (Ozark Plateau), and Coastal Plain (Gulf Coastal Plain; Fenneman 1938). A fifth region, Land between the Lakes (LBL) in Kentucky and Tennessee, is located at the interface of the Eastern Highland Rim/Pennyroyal section of the Interior Low Plateau (Smalley 1980) and the Mississippi Embayment Section of the Gulf Coastal Plain (Braun 1964). Geology, soil, topography, elevation and microclimate, and community composition, succession, and fragmentation pattern vary from division to division, but collectively, they appear to be representative of other ecosystems within the central hardwood region. Superimposed on vegetation patterns created by environmental constraints operating within each region are variations created by different combinations of fire, agriculture, grazing, and timber harvesting.

Southern Till Plain Region

This region, extending from the prairie peninsula region of central Illinois to the Shawnee Hills region, is the southernmost extension of glaciation in Illinois. The soils developed under both forest and prairie vegetation. Because of the gently to moderately rolling topography, absence of a major river acting as a firebreak, and relatively low annual precipitation, fire probably moved rapidly, frequently, and relatively unrestricted through the region (Table 11.1). One important source of fire may have been the extensive Native American settlements in the Mississippi River east bank floodplain near Cahokia. The Grand Prairie region to the north, where precipitation is lower (United States Department of Agriculture 1941) and where fires were common, may have been an important location from which fire moved into the region. An analysis of witness tree data from the original land survey records indicated that presettlement vegetation of the region ranged from

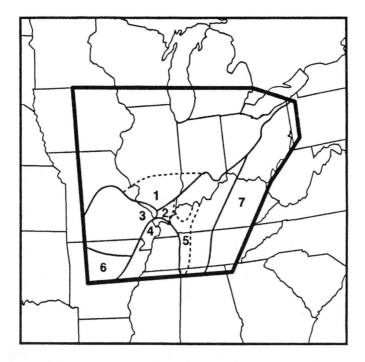

1. **Central Lowland Province–Southern Till Plain**
2. **Interior Low Plateau Province–Shawnee Hills**
3. **Ozark Plateau Province**
4. **Gulf Coastal Plain Plateau**
5. **Interior Low Plateau Province–Western Highland Rim and Pennyroyal**
6. **Ouachita Province**
7. **Appalachian Provinces**

Figure 11.2. Physiographic provinces and natural regions of the central hardwood forest region.

open oak forest to oak savanna to prairie (Anderson and Anderson 1975). It appears that the forest here was highly fragmented by prairie before settlement in the mid-1800s.

Two concurrent events, development of agriculture and elimination of fire, had a major effect on forest communities. Because of relatively extensive level areas, most of the forest land was cleared for farming. Today, the forests of the Till Plain region are highly fragmented and found primarily as small farm woodlots or in small areas of state forest or parks. The fragmentation pattern is similar to that of much of Illinois (Iverson et al. 1989), southern Wisconsin (Sharpe et al. 1987; Dunn and Stearns 1993), and Ohio (Simpson et al. 1994).

Table 11.1. *Summary of land history, present conditions and forest communities in five natural divisions of the central hardwood forest. Regions follow Schwegman (1973), and physiographic provinces follow Fenneman (1938).*

Region/ physiographic province	Forest ecosystem conditions					
	Geographic location	Fragmentation history	Geologic conditions	Site environment	Community types	Successional status
Southern Till Plain/East Central Lowlands.	Grand Prairie province to north and west a fire source.	Agriculture; forest fragmented into isolated woodlots (islands).	Glaciated; glacial till capped by 1–3 m loess.	A) Xeric soil; level land surfaces; pan B) Xeric-mesic, gently rolling topography	A) Post oak flatwoods. B) White and black oak.	A) Indefinitely stable. B) Successional but isolation slows invasion rate.
Shawnee Hills/ Interior Low Plateau.	Somewhat protected on west by Mississippi River floodplain. Till Plain to north a fire source.	Old farm fields on Shawnee National Forest planted to pine; large areas of private inholdings/ fields.	Massive Mississippian sandstone and some interbedded limestone; generally capped by 2–5 m loess.	A) Rock Outcrops; 15 cm loess. B) Xeric southeast to southwest slopes; fragipan soils. C) Mesic north slopes and stream terraces.	A) Redcedar glades. B) Post, white, and black oak. C1) White oak. C2) Sugar maple and American Beech.	A) Extremely stable. B) Generally stable. C1) Successional to maple and beech. C2) Stable.
Illinois Ozark Hills/Ozark Plateau.	Strongly protected by the Mississippi River to the west.	Large blocks of forest; topography generally too steep for farming.	Limestone bedrock capped with 1–10 m loess; some rock outcrops.	A) Southwest rocky slopes. B) Mississippi bluffs. C) All slopes, narrow deep valleys; deep soil.	A) Post oak. B) Shortleaf pine. C) White, black, and northern red oak.	A) Stable. B) Successional to oak. C) Successional to maple and beech.
Coastal Plain/Gulf Coastal Plain.	Protected on west and south by Mississippi and Ohio River floodplains. Shawnee Hills to north no possible source of fire.	Extensively farmed; woodlots scattered.	Unconsolidated ocean sediments capped with 3–6 m loess; extensive wetland intermixed with upland.	A) Scattered sandstone hills. B) Other sites mesic, with high water-holding capacity.	A) Post oak. B1) White oak, northern red oak. B2) Sweetgum, cherrybark oak.	A) Stable. B1) Successional to maple and beech. B2) Successional to mesophytes.
Land between the Lakes/Interior Low Plateau.	Peninsula protected by Lake Barkley and Kentucky Lake.	Forest cleared for charcoal in mid-1800s. Regrowth to a continuous block of forest.	Unconsolidated sediments of Gulf Coastal Plain interfaced with bedrock of Interior Low Plateau.	A) Gravel. B) Loess w/fragipan. C) Mixed material; most slopes w/elev. > 140 m. D) Loess; most slopes w/ elev. < 140 m. E) Deep loess; loess over limestone.	A) Chestnut oak. B) Post oak. C1) Shortleaf pine. C2) White and black oak. D) White and black oak. E) Sugar maple and American beech.	A) Stable. B) Stable. C1) Successional to oak. C2) Presently stable. D) Successional to maple and beech. E) Stable.

Remaining forest stands are composed of post oak or white and black oak. Before 1800, the post oak "flatwoods" community covered approximately 2.25 million ha (Taft et al. 1995). At present, stands of this community are relatively rare because the level topography (< 2% slope), if not the soil, is ideal for agriculture. Wynoose is the major soil type (Fehrenbacher et al. 1984). It has a clayey (30–50% clay) strongly compacted (bulk density = 1.6–1.7 g/cc) horizon beginning at about a 15 cm depth and continuing downward a meter or more (Katerere 1979). Tree roots have the difficulty of first surviving an extended period of soil saturation in spring because the level land surface does not readily drain and the fragipan restricts percolation, and second surviving the summer drought when soil moisture drops below 5% (Fralish, unpublished data). In Posen Woods Nature Preserve, two habitat types based on differences in drainage have been identified (Fralish 1988b). Post oak is the primary species that tolerates extremes in soil conditions, probably because its roots penetrate the pan to a depth of nearly a meter while white and black oak roots remain in a shallow zone at the surface. Only a limited number of high-quality, post oak flatwood remnants with their associated shrub and herb layer remain in the region, and a few remain in Indiana (Menges et al. 1987).

Stands dominated by white and black oak are common within the Southern Till Plain but also are isolated by agricultural land (Katerere 1979). The stands are located on Ava soil found in shallow drainages or on gentle slopes. This soil has a deep fragipan, is relatively well drained, and is easily penetrated by tree roots. At the time of Katerere's study, sugar maple and other mesophytes had invaded only about 50% of the white and black oak dominated woodlots, usually as saplings or small trees in stands on slopes adjacent to the larger drainages. In other stands, succession to sugar maple was relatively slow because as "islands" within a matrix of agricultural land, they were effectively isolated from a maple seed source. These islands remain vulnerable to elimination at the whim of the landowner and continue to be converted to agriculture at a slow rate.

Shawnee Hills Region

The Shawnee Hills is a 400,000 ha unglaciated east-west escarpment bisecting southern Illinois. Elevation ranges from approximately 110 m above sea level (ASL) where the region interfaces with the Till Plain on the north to a general level of 160 to 210 m ASL, with a few hills extending above 240 m. The underlying sandstone (with interbedded limestone) bedrock is covered by a 2 to 5 m loess deposit that varies locally in thickness from 15 cm in soil lenses on rock outcrops to nearly 3 m in stream terraces. Deep deposits of loess occur on broad ridgetops, nearly all of which have been farmed.

Analysis of witness tree data from the 1806–7 original land survey records indicates that the presettlement forest was dominated by white and black oak on south, ridgetop, high north, low, and alluvial sites (Table 11.2; Crooks 1988,

Fralish et al. 1991). Post oak was the dominant species of rocky southwest sites. Sugar maple importance value was less than 4%, and all mesophytes combined had less than 27% importance, even on the mesic low and alluvial sites. It appears that in pre-European settlement time, fire and possibly bison played a major role in preventing the development of mesophytic forest. An important source of fire may have been the Till Plain region of forest and prairie directly to the north.

In forest stands disturbed 60 to 70 years ago by timber harvesting, fire, or grazing, importance values for the major species in communities across the six site types were strongly similar to those for presettlement forest (Harty 1978). For five of six site types, similarity values were high, varying from 55% to 78%, except for stands on south sites where a marginal similarity of 45% occurred. Stands are considered extremely similar for values above 55% (Fralish et al. 1991). Post oak remained the major dominant on southwest rocky sites, while white and black oak dominated south, ridgetop, high north, and low site types. Sugar maple and other mesophytes dominated only alluvial sites. Based on this comparison, it appears that until the 1930s, the level of forest anthropocentric disturbance was as severe or at least had the same effect as natural disturbance in presettlement forest communities.

Compositionally stable forest stands on rocky southwest, south, and ridgetop sites were similar to those of presettlement forest; for these stands, similarity ranged from 58 to 84%. However, on high north and all low slopes and terraces, similarity varied between 22 and 30%, indicating substantially dissimilar species composition (Fralish et al. 1991) because the presettlement oak-hickory forest was held in the subclimax condition while the present old-growth forest progressed to mesophytes in the absence of fire.

The five leading dominant species in old-growth forest (Table 11.2) were distributed according to soil depth and available water-holding capacity, aspect, and slope position (Chambers 1972; Cerretti 1975; Fralish 1976, 1988a; Fralish et al. 1978). Eastern redcedar was the major species on rock outcrops and cliff edges, while post oak communities were common on shallow rocky soil of southwest slopes. White oak with some black oak and hickory dominated deeper soil on the southeast to southwest and west slopes. Stands of northern red oak were positioned on north-slope sites near the top of the hills, but there was some indication that they were successional. Sugar maple and associated mesophytes stands were found on the mid to low north slopes and stream terrace sites. These two site types are ideal for mesophytes because they remain moist throughout the growing season (Downs 1976).

A comparison of presettlement, disturbed, and stable forest stands indicates that in the absence of disturbance, the present oak-hickory stands on mesic sites eventually will be replaced by mesophytes but stands on xeric south slopes and more hot rocky sites are stable and will remain oak-hickory. Moreover, old-growth forests on xeric sites are an acceptable representation of presettlement forest (Fralish et al. 1991). A further comparison of disturbed/successional stands

Table 11.2.   *Importance values for major species and for xerophytic and mesophytic species groups in presettlement, second-growth (successional), and compositionally stable mature forest communities on six site types in the Illinois Shawnee Hills. Relative basal area is used as importance value for trees in presettlement and present forest. Data from Fralish et al. (1991).*

Species	Site Type					
	Rocky south	South[1]	Ridgetop	North[1]	Low	Alluvial
A Presettlement forest						
Q. stellata	76.3	4.8	3.8			
Q. velutina	2.3	4.9	32.8	18.7	25.6	2.4
Q. alba	3.4	81.0	45.3	65.4	38.5	27.4
Q. rubra		3.0		2.9	2.5	11.7
Xerophytes[2]	96.9	98.0	88.0	91.1	71.5	44.4
L. tulipifera			5.6	1.2	8.9	10.5
F. grandifolia					0.2	0.5
A. saccharum		0.5			2.6	3.4
Mesophytes[3]	3.1	2.0	7.4	4.3	18.4	26.5
B. Successional forest overstory						
Q. stellata	58.6	18.0	6.0			
Q. velutina	1.1	21.7	17.2	16.5	13.0	
Q. alba	5.9	29.9	53.1	47.9	21.3	27.4
Q. rubra		1.3	2.4	6.1	21.8	6.8
Xerophytes[2]	98.0	98.4	97.9	89.9	75.3	20.2
L. tulipifera			5.6		2.5	17.2
F. grandifolia					0.4	5.3
A. saccharum		0.5		1.8	13.5	31.6
Mesophytes[3]	2.0	1.2	2.1	5.5	18.2	60.9
C. Compositionally stable forest						
Q. stellata	39.5	12.2	11.0			
Q. velutina	7.8	10.0	12.0	5.9	0.8	
Q. alba	13.2	56.9	54.0	9.3	0.9	
Q. rubra		1.4	3.0	31.4	7.5	
Xerophytes[2]	99.6	97.5	96.0	76.8	22.3	18.8
L. tulipifera				1.9	4.1	6.3
F. grandifolia				2.5	9.4	13.0
A. saccharum			1.0	6.5	43.9	51.2
Mesophytes[3]	0.4	0.8	2.5	18.0	64.8	76.4

[1]Mid to high slope position

[2]Xerophytic species include *Quercus alba, Q. stellata, Q. muhlenbergii, Q. coccinea, Q. falcata, Q. marilandica, Q. rubra, Q. velutina, Carya glabra-ovalis, C. ovata, C. texana, C. tomentosa, Juniperus virginiana,* and *Ulmus alata.*

[3]Mesophytic species include *Acer saccharum, A. rubrum, Fagus grandifolia, Juglans nigra, Liriodendron tulipifera, Nyssa sylvatica, Fraxinus* spp., *Ulmus americana, U. rubra,* and *Cornus florida.*

and compositionally stable (climax) stands indicates that on mesic sites, richness is higher in disturbed/successional communities. On the high north, low, and terrace site types, the number of species was equal or greater in disturbed forest.

Although a sizable portion of forest land is owned by the U.S. Forest Service (Shawnee National Forest), fragmentation is high. Most ridgetops and other land areas were in agriculture until the mid-1930s, when many farms were abandoned. Open land purchased by the Forest Service was planted to shortleaf pine (*P. echinata*) to reduce soil erosion, but these plantations also reduced fragmentation. However, considerable land in private ownership remains open and interspersed with national forest land, making the Shawnee National Forest possibly the most fragmented national forest. This fragmentation has had a strong negative impact on neotropical migrant birds. Research data indicate that there is not a healthy breeding population due to nest parasitism by the brown-head cowbird, and the number of young produced each year is well below any reasonable replacement level. It appears that the present population is subsidized by excess birds from the Missouri Ozarks and the Appalachian Mountains (research by Scott Robinson cited by Terborgh 1992). Robinson et al. (1995) and Brawn and Robinson (1996) provide additional information on the problem of source-sink population dispersal in Illinois forests.

Illinois Ozark Hills Region

The Ozark Hills region in southwestern Illinois is characterized by mature dissected (steep and hilly) topography underlain by cherry limestone that outcrops at higher elevations. The drainages are relatively deep, narrow, and moist. Loess once covered the entire land area, but erosion has frequently exposed a cherty soil on steep slopes, and near the shoulder of ridges, bedrock often appears. A 10 m thick loess cap makes the ridgetops more mesic than the side slopes, where the soils have developed in a thin layer of loess and weathered bedrock. The most xeric sites are on the exposed slope created by 100 m high bluffs overlooking the Mississippi River floodplain to the west.

Alexander County, representative of the region, was extensively logged from approximately 1880 to 1920 (Miller and Fuller 1922), and fire was relatively common into the 1920s (Miller 1920). Fire-scarred trees, the remains of barbed-wire fencing, and an immature forest structure indicate a history of fire, grazing, and logging that continued on private land possibly into the 1940s (Bagienski 1979). Large sections of property purchased by the U.S. Forest Service in the 1930s for development of the Shawnee National Forest have been protected since that time (60 years). Fragmentation is less a problem here than in the Till Plain, Shawnee Hills, or Coastal Plain; rather, the forest continues to close and increase in density. Forest succession away from oak-hickory is a serious problem.

Witness tree data from the 1806–7 land survey records were used to estimate species importance, presettlement community patterns, and long-term succession on each of six site types (McArdle 1991). Under an apparently moderated fire regime due to protection of the Mississippi River as the west boundary, the presettlement forest on the drier high southwest, south, ridgetop, and mid-high north sites was dominated by white oak, with black oak and American beech as secondary species (Table 11.3). On the mesic low and alluvial sites, the importance of oak progressively decreased while the importance of sugar maple, beech, and other mesophytic species increased.

Compared to presettlement forest, oak importance increased in the present forest overstory on five of six site types. This increase is consistent with a higher level of disturbance associated with postsettlement timber harvesting, fire, and grazing that occurred into the 1920s and 1930s. With the Mississippi River and the presence of deep mesic coves acting as natural firebreaks against presettlement fire, the level of disturbance apparently was greater after settlement. However, with the general absence of fire during the past 60 years, it appears that understory sugar maple, with a present relative density of 35 to 60% on all site types, eventually will form an overstory monoculture across most of the region.

Brennan (1983) arrived at a similar conclusion for six of seven identified community types in the Ozark Hills. In nearly all black, white, and northern red oak stands, regardless of aspect and slope position, the understory density of mesophytes exceeded, sometimes by double or triple, that of oak and hickory. Succession also was occurring in stands dominated by shortleaf pine located on the xeric 100 m high bluffs and slopes overlooking the Mississippi River floodplain.

Table 11.3.   Importance values for xerophytic[1] and mesophytic[2] species groups in presettlement, present, and projected forest communities on six site types in the Illinois Ozark Hills. Relative basal area is used as importance value for trees in presettlement and present forest. Relative density is used as importance value for the present forest understory of seedlings and saplings. Data from McArdle (1991).

	Southwest	South	Ridgetop	North	Low	Alluvial
A. Presettlement forest						
Xerophytes	75.5	67.7	76.6	65.0	29.9	13.4
Mesophytes	19.7	26.4	27.0	27.9	59.4	63.6
B. Present forest overstory						
Xerophytes	78.2	73.4	87.7	39.7	47.3	18.1
Mesophytes	12.1	15.8	6.0	51.0	42.1	23.5
C. Present forest understory						
Xerophytes	39.1	29.8	29.5	14.9	19.5	15.4
Mesophytes	49.1	59.3	33.9	83.2	62.1	61.5

[1]Xerophytic species include *Quercus alba, Q. stellata, Q. muhlenbergii, Q. velutina, Q. rubra, Q. coccinea, Q. falcata, Q. prinus, Carya glabra-ovallis, C. ovata, C. texana,* and *U. alata.*

[2]Mesophytic species include *Acer saccharum, A. rubrum, Fagus grandifolia, Ulmus rubra, U. americana, Fraxinus* spp., *Juglans nigra, Liriodendron tulipifera, Magnolia acuminata, Nyssa sylvatica,* and *Cornus florida.*

Shortleaf pine dominated in the 9 to 25 cm and 25 to 50 cm DBH stem classes, but black, white, and blackjack oak, and pignut and black hickory dominated the seedling and sapling strata. Recently the Forest Service began a program of prescribed burning to control the development of oak and hickory while creating conditions favorable to the development of shortleaf pine. Postfire observations indicated the presence of young shortleaf seedlings soon after the fire, but the massive number of new oak and hickory sprouts quickly overtopped and killed them. Repeated fire may be a necessity; a single prescribed fire is probably more detrimental than no fire because of the strong sprouting response after burning (Bagienski 1979, Presmyk 1987). A single fire in a pine stand with an understory of oak and hickory may effectively accelerate the rate of succession to the latter because of increased density from sprouting. Only the post oak community located on thin, cherty soils of southwest-facing slopes appeared stable because all species of the overstory were strongly represented in the understory.

Coastal Plain Region

The unglaciated Coastal Plain in the southern tip of Illinois is the northernmost extension of the Gulf Coastal Plain physiographic province (Fenneman 1938). The underlying Cretaceous rock is covered by a thick deposit of unconsolidated sand, clay, and gravel of Gulf Coastal Plain origin. Overlying the Coastal Plain material is 3 m to 6 m deep loess. The topography varies from gently rolling hills on uplands to flat, poorly drained bottomland. Elevation varies from 83 to 114 m ASL, with a few outcroppings of the Shawnee Hills geologic system extending higher.

Schildt (1995) found that the presettlement (1806–7) forest communities were strongly dominated by oak and hickory on the drier southwest, south ridgetop, and high north slopes (IV = 69.0–89.1; Table 11.4) as they were in the Shawnee Hills presettlement forest. However, because of the lower elevation and the predominance of moist sites where uplands grade into lowlands, there was a stronger component of sugar maple and other mesophytes. The importance of mesophytes nearly equaled that of oak and hickory on the low (north and south) site type and they dominated the alluvial site. The adjacent Mississippi and Ohio Rivers and internally interspersed bottomland areas apparently functioned as natural firebreaks, thus permitting the development of mesophytic stands that became a seed source for invasion of upland sites after wildfires were eliminated in the 1930s.

Unlike the Shawnee and Ozark Hills regions, most of the land in the Coastal Plain has remained in private ownership, resulting in extensive clearing of forest land for agriculture. Fire and heavy logging in the late 1800s were responsible for establishment of the older and widely scattered existing stands from which tree, seedling, and sapling data were collected. Selective logging has reduced the amount of oak on all site types. With removal of oak, individual hickory

Table 11.4.   Importance values for oak[1] (*Quercus* spp.), hickories[2] (*Carya* spp.), and mesophytic[3] species groups in presettlement forest, and present forest overstory and understory on six site types in the Coastal Plain region. Relative basal area is used as importance value for trees in presettlement and present forest. Relative density is used as importance value for the present forest understory of seedlings and saplings. Data from Schildt (1995).

	Southwest	South	Ridgetop	North	Low	Alluvial
A. Presettlement forest						
Oak	67.1	64.7	80.6	67.8	32.8	22.5
Hickory	1.9	4.3	8.5	8.8	3.6	0.8
Mesophytes	12.0	20.6	1.7	11.2	33.2	50.7
B. Present forest overstory						
Oak	60.0	55.9	56.4	34.1	30.1	34.7
Hickory	19.4	11.5	11.5	26.7	19.3	6.4
Mesophytes	16.9	24.4	26.2	31.8	28.8	32.1
C. Present forest understory						
Oak	18.6	12.6	9.4	4.5	7.9	3.1
Hickory	7.0	10.9	3.8	5.6	8.5	10.7
Mesophytes	50.8	43.3	44.6	63.4	64.8	65.7

[1]Oak includes *Quercus alba, Q. stellata, Q. velutina,* and *Q. rubra.*

[2]Hickory includes *Carya glabra-ovallis, C. ovata, C. texana, C. tomentosa,* and *C. cordiformis.*

[3]Mesophytic species include *Acer saccharum, A. rubrum, Fagus grandifolia, Ulmus rubra, U. americana, Fraxinus* spp., *Juglans cinerea, Juglans nigra, Liriodendron tulipifera, Nyssa sylvatica, Tilia americana,* and *Cornus florida.*

stems had more soil, water, and light resources available for increased growth, and large, mature hickory trees were encountered in many stands. Compared with presettlement forest, there is an increase in importance of mesophytes in the present overstory on the four driest site types, with sugar maple being the major species (IV = 7.0–25.8; Table 11.4).

Compared with the present overstory, there is a major decrease in the understory oak and hickory component that is matched by a major increase in the mesophytic component dominated by sugar maple (IV = 30.0–52.0; Table 11.4). If left undisturbed, the mesophytic seedlings and saplings in the present forest understory will ultimately develop to dominate the overstory and eliminate the oak and hickory component.

Land between the Lakes

Land between the Lakes (LBL) is a 68,800 ha forested peninsula between Kentucky Lake and Lake Barley. LBL is approximately 11.5 km wide and 60 km long and its entire length is bisected by the Tennessee Ridge (Thach and Doyle 1988). Elevation ranges from approximately 110 m ASL at lake level to approximately 299 m on the ridge. Upland soil types have formed in weathered Mississippina limestone, white and brown Cretaceous gravel layers, and a thin layer of loess (United States Department of Agriculture 1953, 1981; Fralish and Crooks 1988, 1989; Harris 1988).

Historic descriptions indicate that the presettlement forest was maintained in a relatively open condition by fire, bison, and other natural events (Franklin 1994). In the early to mid-1800s, the original forest was severely disturbed by iron smelting. There were nine iron furnaces and numerous kilns that supplied charcoal for smelting. Near each kiln, the land was denuded as forest was cleared for several miles in all directions. Mining, cattle grazing, wildfires, timber harvesting for moonshine stills, railroad ties, and lumber (Henry 1975, Wallace 1988, Franklin 1994) were continuing disturbances until the land became Tennessee Valley Authority (TVA) property in 1964.

At present, LBL is 95% forested (Groton et al. 1988) and the continuous forest landscape shows little fragmentation. A variety of mature and nearly mature oak-hickory communities dominate the landscape, but a few stands of shortleaf pine, sugar maple, and American beech are present (Franklin 1990; Kettler 1990; Fralish and Crooks 1988, 1989). Several coenoclines (Figure 11.3) were developed to examine the distribution of species in compositionally stable stands on xeric, xeric-mesic, and mesic sites (Franklin 1990, Fralish et al. 1993, Franklin et al. 1993). The most xeric site condition is found on the Cretaceous gravel (Saffell soil type, 35–70% loose stone and conglomerate) that supports the chestnut oak forest community (Figure 11.3a). Several other oak species and sourwood (*Oxydendrum arboreum*) are common components (Figure 11.3b) because they also tolerate low available soil water. These chestnut oak stands are extremely stable (climax). Tree growth is relatively slow, and the openness of the stands gives the appearance of a barren; many stands have attained old-growth age (150+ years).

Where loessal soil containing a fragipan (Lax soil type) exists on southwest-facing slopes, compositionally stable stands of post, blackjack, black, southern red, and scarlet oak have developed, although some individual chestnut oak trees may be intermixed. The Lax soil type limits root penetration because of the shallow (40–50 cm deep) fragipan which effectively reduces available soil water.

Compositionally stable white oak stands dominate the xeric-mesic sites of southeast, south, southwest, and west aspects at middle to high slope positions and at higher elevations (> 140 m ASL). On these sites, the soil is less rocky than that supporting chestnut oak and deeper than the soil of post oak sites; however, the south slopes are too dry for invasion by mesophytes. On north slopes and alluvial sites at low elevation, only a few stands of American beech or sugar maple were found because these community types were generally eliminated by past fire and other disturbances.

Community successional patterns were found to vary with the site environment (Kettler 1990). Shortleaf pine stands on the Tennessee Ridge are being replaced by chestnut oak, post, blackjack, and scarlet oak on xeric sites, and by white and

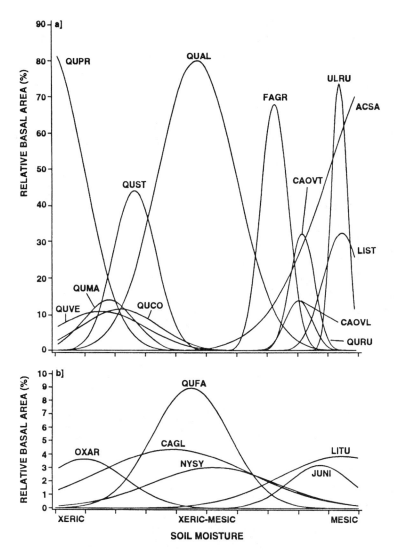

Figure 11.3. Coenocline (vegetational continuum) developed from ordination of 64 compositionally stable stands at Land between the Lakes. The distributions for major species (importance value > 10) are shown in Figure a and distributions for minor species in Figure b. Species scientific names for acronyms are: QUPR, *Quercus prinus;* QUST, *Q. stellata;* QUVE, *Q. velutina;* QUMA, *Q. marilandica;* QUCO, *Q. coccinea;* QUFA, *Q. falcata;* QUAL, *Q. alba;* FAGR, *Fagus grandifolia;* ULRU, *Ulmus rubra;* ACSA, *Acer saccharum;* CAOVT, *Carya ovata;* CAOVL, *C. ovalis;* QURU, *Q. rubra;* LIST, *Liquidambar styraciflua;* LITU, *Liriodendron tulipifera;* CATO, *C. tomentosa;* OXAR, *Oxydendrum arboreum;* NYSY, *Nyssa sylvatica;* JUNI, *Juglans nigra.* After Fralish et al. (1993).

black oak on xeric-mesic sites (compare Figure 11.4a with Figure 11.3a); (Schibig and Chester 1988, Kettler 1990). Mixed oak stands on these high xeric sites (> 140 m) were cleared when Fort Henry was built in the early 1860s. The presence of fire scars within the rings of recently cut oak stumps shows the occurrence of fire during this period. Increment cores indicate that there were at least one or two 40- to 60-year-old pine trees present in each study stand to provide seed for development of the present extensive shortleaf pine.

The numerous white and black oak stands at all elevations and on all aspects

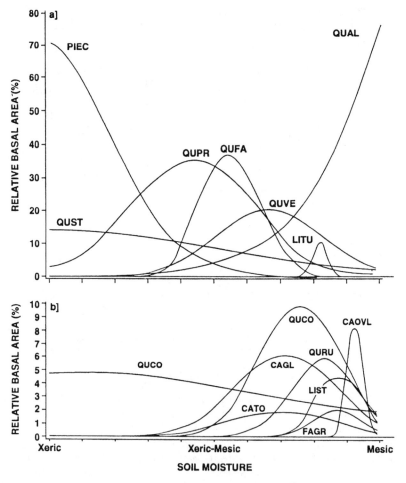

Figure 11.4. Coenocline (vegetational continuum) developed from ordination of 73 successional stands at Land between the Lakes. The distributions for major species (importance value > 10) are shown in Figure a and distributions for minor species in Figure b. See Figure 11.3 for species names. After Fralish et al. (1993).

date from the extensive land clearing of the mid-1800s and later. These stands are located below the ridgetops on mesic northwest, north, northeast, and east slopes above 140 m. On nearly all sites below 140 m these white and black oak stands are successional (Figure 11.4a) to sugar maple and American beech (Figure 11.3a). The lower the elevation, the more extensive and rapid the invasion process. Disturbance such as clearcutting without fire on mesic sites immediately converts the stand to sugar maple or red elm. (Fralish and Snyder 1993, Snyder 1995). Although widely scattered, chestnut oak stands on xeric-mesic sites are being replaced by white and black oak, and on more mesic sites by sugar maple and other mesophytes.

Rate of Community Composition Change

An estimate on the forest succession rate since protection began in the 1930s is available from two sources. One source is analysis of data from permanent plots established in the 1920s and 1930s and remeasured at periodic intervals. Data on composition change in a forest stand on a mesic site at the Kaskaskia Experimental Forest (Shawnee Hills region) has been reported by Schlesinger (1976, 1989) and Fralish (1988a, 1994; Figure 11.5). The stand received a moderately heavy timber cut about 1890 and again about 1910, and probably was burned. When the plots were established and measured in 1935, basal area was 19.8 m²/ha. Several species of oak as well as hickory, yellow-poplar (*Liriodendron tulipifera*), and sassafras (*Sassafras albidum*) dominated the overstory (DBN > 10 cm). Oak and hickory were also important in the sapling (DBH 4–10 cm) and seedling strata (stems < 10 cm DBH; Figure 11.5a). Basal area increased to 31.1 m²/ ha in 1973 and became relatively constant at 32.0 m²/ha in 1978 and 30.2 m²/ha in 1983, suggesting a state of maximum biomass and complete canopy closure. By 1983, 10 years after full development of the overstory canopy, oak and hickory had nearly disappeared from the seedling and sapling strata, and sugar maple, white ash, and red elm dominated the seedling, sapling, and small tree (10–28 cm DBH) strata (Figure 11.5b). Given another 50 years with no major disturbances, this stand originally dominated by oak-hickory probably will have been replaced by one dominated by mesophytes.

   In other studies of protected forest, Brownfield Woods in central Illinois has been repeatedly measured since 1925 (Miceli et al. 1977). Recently, Edgington (1991) reported that canopy gaps from the death of oak and American elm have been filled with stems of sugar maple, American basswood, red elm, and Ohio buckeye. In particular, sugar maple increased in importance from 36.8 to 50.0%. Similar changes have been reported for Davis-Purdue Research Forest in Indiana, where permanent plots were established in 1926 (Parker et al. 1985, Parker and Sherwood 1986, Ward and Parker 1989).

   The second source of information is from predictive models. Helmig (1997)

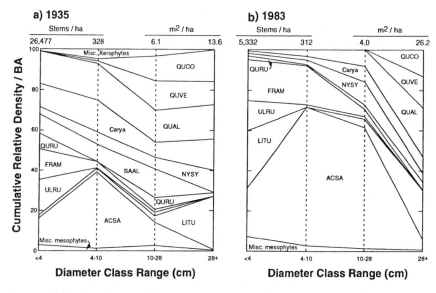

Figure 11.5. Stand composition/structure diagrams for a 0.8 ha plot on the Kaskaskia Experiment Forest in the Shawnee Hills region. Data for Figure a were collected in 1935 at the time of plot establishment; Figure b is based on the 1983 remeasurement data. Cumulative values are based on density for the < 4 cm and 4–10 cm DBH classes and on basal area in the larger size classes. Miscellaneous xerophytes include *Juniperus virginiana, Quercus falcata, Diospyros virginiana,* and *Morus rubra.* Miscellaneous mesophytes include *Prunus serotina, Fagus grandifolia, Carya cordiformis, Juglans nigra, Ulmus americana,* and *Acer negundo.*

integrated stand data from forested section and quarter-section corners in the Ozark Hills (McArdle 1991) with data from specific site types (south slope, ridgetop, north slope, terrace) within Ozark Hills Nature Preserve of Trail of Tears State Forest. The data indicated strong successional trends from oak and hickory toward sugar maple and associated mesophytes on all site types. Subsequently, average density and growth rates for seedlings, saplings, and trees were used in a stand table projection model (see Husch et al. 1972, Avery and Burkhart 1994) to predict the time at which the basal area of mesophytes would exceed that of oak and hickory. Basal area was used as the index because it directly reflects biomass level (Fralish 1994). The model incorporated data on ingrowth, growth rate, and mortality by species. Total stand basal area was constrained to 35 m²/ha because this is the maximum possible value in the central deciduous forest (Held and Winstead 1975, Fralish 1994). Projections indicated that the basal area of mesophytes will exceed that of oak and hickory in 2054, only 58 years hence. At that time the oak-hickory ecosystem will be naturally but highly fragmented as a result of succession. Mesophytes will have developed beyond the point at which restoration and maintenance of oak and hickory dominated stands is likely to be either economically or ecologically feasible except where they remain on the driest sites. The Ozark Hills oak-hickory forest will have become scattered trees in a matrix of maple-beech. A similar pattern of equal extent will be repeated in the Coastal Plain and on mesic sites in the Shawnee Hills and at Land between the Lakes. Only the forests of the Till Plain region are likely to be unaffected.

Protection, Species Richness, and Productivity

The elimination of natural disturbance such as fire has several distinct negative impacts on species richness and site productivity. A number of these effects result directly from the process of succession.

Loss of Black Oak Species

The death of "black oak" trees in post and white oak stands has been documented at LBL (Kentucky and Tennessee) and in Illinois. At LBL, data from the 1976 and 1986 remeasurement of permanent plots indicated that high mortality occurred in the "black oak" group (black; blackjack [*Quercus marilandica*], scarlet, southern red oak, and northern red oak) while species of the "white oak" (white oak, post oak, and chestnut oak) and hickory had relatively low mortality (Groton et al. 1988). Approximately 70% of the stems alive in 1988 were oak with only 20% of these in the black oak group, but approximately 45% of total mortality was black oak (Wellbaum 1989). On permanent plots at Kaskaskia Experimental Forest in southern Illinois, mortality of scarlet, black, and northern red oak was higher than that of white oak, with the mortality level of scarlet twice that of black oak (Schlesinger 1989).

A comparison of 10- to 12-year-old clearcut oak stands at Land between the Lakes indicates that species of the black oak group have a collective average importance of 20 to 31% (Snyder 1995); however, in many stands, the density was double or triple that of the white oak group or hickory, suggesting that the black oak group remains an important component of young stands. The importance of black oak in clearcut stands equals that of the overstory component (Groton et al. 1988).

The loss of black oak species (blackjack, southern red, black, and scarlet) from post oak dominated stands on xeric sites or from stands of mixed white oak and black oak on xeric-mesic sites is the beginning of a general loss of biodiversity; species richness (number) decreases concurrently with purification (reduced equitability) as post oak or white oak assumes greater dominance. The largest trees (70–100 cm DBH) of the shorter lived (150–175 years) "black oak" species are being phased out while trees of the longer lived (300–350 years) white oak remain. Individuals of "black oak" reach physiological maturity and the end of their life span at about 150 to 170 years. At 125 to 150 years or earlier for some species such as scarlet oak, trees begin to show the typical signs of old age: heart rot (center of stem decayed or hollow), presence of large dead branches, patches of dead bark, large broken branches and/or tops, reduced number of leaves (thin crown), and a weak root system (frequent wind-thrown trees). The relatively high density and increased competition in the forest stands in addition to the drought and insect attacks of the 1980s may have reduced tree vigor, which subsequently resulted in increased mortality due to secondary causal agents such as Hypoxylon canker.

Loss of White Oak and Hickory

On mesic sites, succession is a two-stage process. Subsequent to the loss of the black oak species group on moist sites, white oak (specifically *Quercus alba*) and hickory (life expectancy of 200–350 years) will be replaced by the more long-lived (450–500 years) sugar maple and American beech (Figure 11.1). Depending on regional environmental conditions, the effect will be to create "islands" of the remaining white oak and post oak stands on xeric and xeric-mesic sites (Shawnee Hills, LBL) or to completely blanket the landscape with a near monoculture of sugar maple or American beech (Illinois Ozark Hills, Illinois Coastal Plain). Because of the predominance of oak at LBL, the diversity of community types across the landscape will increase with the addition of mesophytes, but succession will negatively impact the herb stratum.

Loss of Herbaceous Plants

The present high density of seedlings, saplings, and small trees of mesophytic species invading oak-hickory forest has a major effect on the herbaceous layer. Data collected from Trail of Tears State Forest in the Ozark Hills indicates that as photosynthetically active radiation (PAR) decreases and the amount of ground litter increases, there is a major decrease in the number of herbaceous species (Table 11.5). Species richness increased 200% from an average of 10 species/ 10 m^2 in a forest composed of oak and hickory with a closed canopy of smaller sugar maple trees (DBH 10–20 cm) to an average of 31.5 species/10 m^2 in open stands dominated by black oak, white oak, and hickory without maple, or in

Table 11.5. The relationship between number of species, photosynthetically active radiation (PAR), and litter weight under four forest canopy/community types on southeast, south, and southwest slopes in the Illinois Ozark Hills region.

	Canopy/community type			
	Closed oak/maple	Closed black oak	Open black oak	Open post oak
Par (umol $m^{-2}s^{-1}$)	8.85	51.7	138.4	233.8
Litter weight (kg/m^2)	1.10	0.97	0.66	0.75
Species/10 m^2	10.0	25.0	31.5	31.5

stands dominated by post oak. There appears to be little difference in species richness between the open black/white and post oak stands, although post oak occurs on drier sites and has considerably higher PAR levels. Compared with stands without a seedling/sapling stratum, a mesophytic understory of intermediate density present in black/white oak stands reduces the number of species from 31.5 to 25 species/10 m^2. In dense sugar maple dominated forest of the Ozark Hills region, few seedlings or herbs can be observed. Wilhelm (1991) also reported a decrease in the number of summer and fall flowering species between 1925 and 1988, and related this decrease to the increase in sugar maple importance in the tree canopy.

The amount of PAR reaching the herbaceous layer and the amount of litter on the forest floor is a function of crown and stand density. The single canopy layer and relatively thin crowns of the shade intolerant/intermediate (light-demanding) oak and hickory species permits considerable light penetration so that the midcrown leaves obtain sunlight for photosynthesis. Leaves and branches at the lowest levels on the main stem are usually dead because of insufficient sunlight. The uppermost oak leaves in tree crowns are highly dissected so that light easily penetrates to the lowest leaves, which have small sinuses and high leaf area for intercepting light. Similarly, the uppermost leaflets of hickory tend to be the smallest on the tree. This adaptive geometry of trees (Horn 1971) permits light penetration through the canopy and increases photosynthesis not only in lower leaves but also in herbaceous plants on the forest floor. Furthermore, shade-intolerant trees cannot be closely packed because too much sunlight is intercepted and dieback occurs. As observed in nearly all white and black oak stands, the crowns in the upper canopy seldom touch, and in stands dominated by the shade-intolerant post oak, the space between crowns is considerably greater.

Conversely, extremely shade-tolerant species such as sugar maple and American beech have a high stem density, overlapping crowns, and thick crowns of multiple leaf layers because lower branches remain alive. These characteristics produce a high leaf biomass. In autumn, the leaves create a thick (3–5 cm deep) litter layer that often remains throughout the growing season and smothers the new growth of herbaceous plants. The litter appears to be of sufficient thickness that new seedlings will not survive because the extending radical cannot reach mineral soil and water before desiccation occurs. Bazzaz (1979) describes other relationships.

Although the invasion of mesophytes reduces the number of oak forest herbs, the herbaceous layer of maple-beech dominated communities has high species richness in some regions (Curtis 1959) and some mesic sites in the central hardwood forest (Jones 1974, Harty 1978). Small stems of sugar maple, American beech, and other mesophytes indicate the advance of this forest, but the gap between time of elimination of oak-hickory forest herbs and time of invasion of mesophytic forest herbs may be 50 to 100 years or longer and may not occur on more xeric sites. During this gap, insect populations are likely to be reduced and soil surface erosion increased, depending on seedling density. These aspects of herb importance should be the thrust of future research.

Loss of Shortleaf Pine

Shortleaf pine is a high light-demanding (extremely shade-intolerant) species that survives under a fire regime that maintains an open condition for light penetration and seedling establishment. When protected from fire, pine is rapidly replaced by oak on all sites and landscape diversity is reduced.

Reduced Mast/Productivity

Succession impacts stand productivity by reducing the amount of mast (nuts, acorns) produced for wildlife as oak and hickory are replaced by mesophytes. While beech is a mast producer, the soft tissues of maple seed quickly decompose if the seed does not germinate.

The rate of productivity also decreases because oak and hickory trees in a high light environment (direct sunlight on the crowns) grow faster than maple and beech. The physiological basis for the growth differential between these two groups is reviewed by Kramer and Kozlowski (1979), Hale and Orcutt (1987), and Kozlowski et al. (1991).

However, there is an interesting paradox regarding the rate of growth and rate of succession. It would be reasonable to expect that stands of slow-growing oak and hickory on xeric and xeric-mesic sites should be easily replaced by faster growing invading species, while their high growth rate on mesic sites would permit the development of a compositionally stable community. The reverse situation actually occurs. The lack of soil moisture that results in slow growth on xeric sites also prevents succession to other species. High soil moisture on mesic sites permits a rapid growth rate but creates an environment suitable for development of a community dominated by shade-tolerant mesophytes. In terms of resource management, the most productive oak and hickory stands are being replaced by slower growing mesophytic species, while the least productive stands remain intact.

Concluding Remarks

In recent years, new attitudes developed jointly with new available scientific information have directed forest management away from timber production and toward other forest ecosystem values, such as preservation of rare or endangered species, development of old-growth characteristics, and maintenance of species diversity at the level thought to be present in presettlement communities (ca. 1800). Unfortunately, it is too often believed that total protection will permit the forest to maintain or restore these values. This belief possibly would be correct if oak and hickory were shade-tolerant species, but they are not and thus their response is similar to other disturbance-dependent pioneer species and community types. Loss of these dominant keystone species through succession may result in loss of herbs, insects, and possibly birds.

Disturbance plays an important role in ecosystem development. Fire, in particular, reduces invasion of mesophytes in oak stands. With a less dense overstory, white and black oak stands can be maintained to old growth with a full complement of understory herbs. Conversely, the extremely dense, multilayered mesophytic forest is viewed by many as the epitome of old growth (primeval forest), yet according to early land survey records, it was rare to nonexistent in most areas of the central hardwood forest.

Acknowledgments

The research was supported by the Department of Forestry, Southern Illinois University, Carbondale, McIntire-Stennis Cooperative Forest Research, and the Center for Field Biology, Austin Peay State University, Clarksville, Tennessee. The author acknowledges the Tennessee Valley Authority (Land between the Lakes), Illinois Department of Conservation, Nature Preserves Commission, and U.S. Forest Service (Shawnee National Forest) for kindly permitting the use of land under their jurisdiction for data collection and study. Dr. Philip A. Robertson played a major role in the analysis of some data sets. Dr. Kathleen B. Fralish and Dave D. Close provided a valuable review of the manuscript.

References

Abrams, M.D. 1986. Historical development of gallery forests in northeast Kansas. *Vegatatio* 65:29–37.

Abrams, M.D. 1992. Fire and the development of oak forests. *BioScience* 42:346–53.

Adams, D., and R.C. Anderson. 1980. Species response to a moisture gradient in central Illinois. *American Journal of Botany* 67:381–92.

Anderson, R.C., and M.R. Anderson. 1975. The presettlement vegetation of Williamson County, Illinois. *Castanea* 40:345–63.

Avery, E.T., and H.E. Burkhart. 1994. *Forest Measurements.* 4th ed. McGraw-Hill, New York.

Bagienski, F.F. 1979. The effect of a prescribed spring fire on four hill prairies in the Ozark region of southern Illinois. M.S. thesis. Southern Illinois University, Carbondale.

Bazzaz, F.A. 1979. The physiological ecology of plant succession. In R.F. Johnston, P.W. Frank, and C.D. Michener, eds. *Annual Review of Ecology and Systematics,* Vol. 10. Annual Reviews, Palo Alto, Calif., 351–71.

Beilman, A.P., and L.G. Brenner. 1951. Changing forest flora of the Ozarks. *Annals of the Missouri Botanical Garden* 38:283–91.

Bond, W.J. 1994. Keystone species. In E.D. Schulze, and H.A. Mooney, eds. *Biodiversity and Ecosystem Function.* Springer-Verlag, New York, 237–53.

Bormann, F.H., and G.E. Lichens. 1994. *Pattern and Process in a Forested Ecosystem,* Springer-Verlag, New York.

Braun, E.L. 1964. *Deciduous Forests of Eastern North America.* Hafner Press, New York.

Brawn, J.D., and S.K. Robinson. 1996. Source-sink population dynamics may complicate the interpretation of long-term census data. *Ecology* 77:3–12.

Brennan, M.E. 1983. *Site Characteristics for Major Tree Species in the Ozark Region of Southern Illinois.* M.S. thesis, Southern Illinois University, Carbondale.

Burns, R.M., and B.H. Honkala. 1990a. *Silvics of North America: Conifers.* Vol. 1, U.S. Forest Service, Agric. Handbk 654.

Burns, R.M., and B.H. Honkala. 1990b. *Silvics of North America: Hardwoods.* Vol. 2. U.S. Forest Service, Agric. Handbk 654.

Cerretti, D.S. 1975. *Vegetation and Soil-Site Relationships for the Shawnee Hills Region, Southern Illinois.* M.S. thesis, Southern Illinois University, Carbondale.

Chambers, J.L. 1972. *The Compositional Gradient for Undisturbed Upland Forests in Southern Illinois.* M.S. thesis, Southern Illinois University, Carbondale.

Cho, D.S., and R.E.J. Boerner. 1995. Dendrochronological analysis of the canopy history of two old-growth forests. *Vegatatio* 120:173–83.

Clark, F.B. 1976. The central hardwood forest. In J.S. Fralish, G.T. Weaver, and R.C. Schlesinger, eds. *Proceedings of the First Central Hardwood Forest Conference.* Southern Illinois University, Carbondale, 1–9.

Countryman, D.W., and H.R. Miller. 1989. Investment analysis of upland oak stands with sugar maple understories: management for oak vs. conversion to sugar maple in Iowa and Missouri. *Northern Journal of Applied Forestry* 6:165–69.

Crooks, F.B. 1988. *Comparison of Presettlement and Old Growth Forest Communities in the Shawnee Hills, Illinois.* M.S. thesis. Southern Illinois University, Carbondale.

Curtis, J.T. 1959. The Vegetation of Wisconsin: An Ordination of Plant Communities. University of Wisconsin Press, Madison.

Cutter, B.E., and R.P. Guyette. 1994. Fire frequency on an oak-hickory ridgetop in the Missouri Ozarks. *American Midland Naturalist* 132:393–98.

Downs, J.A., and M.D. Abrams. 1991. Composition and structure of an old-growth versus a second-growth white oak forest in southwestern Pennsylvania. In L.H. McCormick and K.W. Gottschalk, eds. *Proceedings of the Eighth Central Hardwood Forest Conference.* General Technical Report NC-148. U.S. Forest Service, Northeastern Forest Experiment Station, Radnor, Pa. 207–23.

Downs, J.M. 1976. *Soil Water Regimes for Undisturbed Forest Communities in the Shawnee Hills, Southern Illinois.* M.S. thesis. Southern Illinois University, Carbondale.

Dunn, C.P., and Stearns, F. 1993. Landscape ecology in Wisconsin: 1830–1990. In J.S. Fralish, R.P. McIntosh, and O.L. Loucks, eds. *John T. Curtis: Fifty Years of Wisconsin Plant Ecology.* Wisconsin Academy of Science, Arts and Letters, Madison, 197–216.

Ebinger, J.E. 1986. Sugar maple, a management problem in Illinois forests? *Transactions of the Illinois State Academy of Science* 79:25–30.

Edgington, J.M. 1991. Brownfield Woods. Illinois: present composition and changes in community structure. *Transactions of the Illinois State Academy of Science* 84:95–112.

Fehrenbacker, J.B., J.D. Alexander, I.J. Jansen, R.G. Darmody, R.A. Pope, and M.A. Flock. 1984. *Soils of Illinois.* Bulletin 778. University of Illinois, Champaign.

Fenneman, N.M. 1938. *Physiography of Eastern United States.* McGraw-Hill, New York.

Fralish, J.S. 1976. Forest site-community relationships in the Shawnee Hills region, southern Illinois. In J.S. Fralish, G.T. Weaver, and R.C. Schlesinger, eds. *Proceedings of the First Central Hardwood Conference,* Southern Illinois University, Carbondale, 65–87.

Fralish, J.S. 1988a. Predicting potential stand composition from site characteristics in the Shawnee Hills forest of Illinois. *American Midland Naturalist* 120:79–101.

Fralish, J.S. 1988b. Diameter-height-biomass relationships for Quercus and Carya in Posen Woods Nature Preserve. *Transactions of the Illinois State Academy of Science* 81:31–38.

Fralish, J.S. 1994. The effect of site environment on forest productivity in the Illinois Shawnee Hills. *Ecological Applications* 4:134–43.

Fralish, J.S., and F.B. Crooks. 1988. Forest communities of the Kentucky portion of Land Between The Lakes: A preliminary assessment. In D.H. Snyder, ed. *Proceedings of the First Annual Symposium on the Natural History of Lower Tennessee and Cumberland River Valleys.* Center for Field Biology, Austin Peay State University, Clarkesville, Tenn., 164–75.

Fralish, J.S., and F.B. Crooks. 1989. Forest composition, environment and dynamics of Land Between The Lakes in northwest middle Tennessee. *Journal of the Tennessee Academy of Science* 64:107–11.

Fralish, J.S., F.B. Crooks, J.L. Chambers, and F.M. Harty. 1991. Comparison of presettlement, second-growth and old-growth forest on six site types in the Illinois Shawnee Hills. *American Midland Naturalist* 125:294–309.

Fralish, J.S., S.C. Franklin, P.A. Robertson, S.M. Kettler, and F.B. Crooks. 1993. An ordination of compositionally stable and unstable forest communities at Land Between The Lakes, Kentucky and Tennessee. In J.S. Fralish, R.P. McIntosh, and O.L. Loucks, eds. *John T. Curtis: Fifty Years of Wisconsin Plant Ecology.* Wisconsin Academy of Science. Arts and Letters, Madison, 247–67.

Fralish, J.S., S.M. Jones, R.K. O'Dell, and J.L. Chambers. 1978. The effect of soil moisture on site productivity and forest composition in the Shawnee Hills of southern Illinois. In W.E. Balmer, ed. *Proceedings of the Soil Moisture-Site Productivity Symposium.* U.S. Forest Service, Atlanta. 263–85.

Fralish, J.S., and P.R. Snyder. 1993. Forest regrowth in 10–12 years old clearcuts at Land Between The Lakes, Kentucky and Tennessee. In S.W. Hamilton, E.W. Chester, and A.F. Scott, eds. *Proceedings of the Fifth Annual Symposium on Natural History of Lower Tennessee and Cumberland River Valleys,* Center for Field Biology, Austin Peay State University, Clarksville, Tenn., 179–94.

Franklin, S.B. 1990. *The Effect of Soil and Topography on Forest Community Composition at Land Between The Lakes KY and TN.* M.S. thesis, Southern Illinois University, Carbondale.

Franklin, S.B. 1994. Late Pleistocene and Holocene vegetation history of Land Between The Lakes, Kentucky and Tennessee. *Transactions of the Kentucky Academy of Science* 55:6–19.

Franklin, S.B., P.A. Robertson, J.S. Fralish, and S.M. Kettler. 1993. Overstory vegetation and successional trends of Land Between The Lakes, U.S.A. *Journal of Vegetation Science* 4:1–12.

Groton, E.S., R.J. Field, and B.P. Pullin. 1988. *Land Between The Lakes Forest and Wildlife Resources: Twenty Year Trends.* Tennessee Valley Authority, Norris, Tenn.

Guyette, R.P., and B.E. Cutter. 1991. Tree-ring analysis of fire history of a post oak savanna in the Missouri Ozarks. *Natural Areas Journal* 11:93–99.

Hale, M.G., and D.M. Orcutt. 1987. *The Physiology of Plants Under Stress.* John Wiley & Sons. New York.

Hall, M.T. 1955. Comparison of juniper populations on an Ozark glade and old fields. *Annals of the Missouri Botanical Garden* 62:171–94.

Hammitt, W.E., and B.V. Barnes. 1989. Composition and structure of an old-growth oak-hickory forest in southern Michigan over 20 years. In G. Rink, and C.A. Budelsky, eds. *Proceedings of the Seventh Central Hardwood Forest Conference*, General Technical Report NC-132. U.S. Forest Service, St. Paul, Minn., 247–53.

Harris, S.E., Jr. 1988. Summary review of geology of Land Between The Lakes, Kentucky and Tennessee. In D.H. Snyder, ed., *Proceedings of the First Annual Symposium on the Natural History of Lower Tennessee and Cumberland River Valleys.* Austin Peay State University, Clarksville, Tenn., 26–83.

Harty, F.M. 1978. *Tree and Herb Species Distribution, and Herbaceous Vegetation as an Indicator of Site Quality for Disturbed Upland Forest Stands in the Greater Shawnee Hills of Southern Illinois.* M.S. thesis, Southern Illinois University, Carbondale.

Held, M.E. and J.E. Winstead. 1975. Basal area and climax status in mesic forest systems. *Annals of Botany* 19:1147–48.

Helmig, L.M. 1997. *Predicting the threshold time of conversion from Quercus-Carya to mesophytic forest in the Illinois Ozark Hills,* M.S. thesis, Southern Illinois University, Carbondale.

Henry, J.M. 1975. *The Land Between the Rivers.* Austin Peay State University, Clarksville, Tenn., and Tennessee Valley Authority.

Horn, H.S. 1971. *The Adaptive Geometry of Trees.* Princeton University Press, Princeton, NJ.

Horn, H.S. 1974. The ecology of secondary succession. In R.F. Johnston, P.W. Frank, and C.D. Michener, eds. *Annual Review of Ecology and Systematics.* Vol. 5. Annual Reviews, Palo Alto, Calif., 25–37.

Host, G.E., K.S. Pregitzer, D.W. Ramm, J.B. Hart, and D.T. Cleland. 1987. Landform-mediated differences in successional pathways among upland forest ecosystems in northwestern lower Michigan. *Forest Science* 33:455–57.

Husch, B., C.I. Miller, and T.W. Beers. 1972. *Forest Mensuration,* 2nd ed. Ronald Press, New York.

Iverson, L.R., R.L. Oliver, D.P. Tucker, P.G. Risser, C.D. Burnett, and R.G. Rayburn. 1989. *The forest resources of Illinois: An Atlas and Analysis of Spatial and Temporal Trends.* Special Publication 11. Illinois Natural History Survey, Champaign.

Jones, S.M. 1974. *Herbaceous Vegetation as an Indicator of Site Quality and Potential Stand Composition for Upland Forest in Southern Illinois,* M.S. thesis, Department of Forestry, Southern Illinois University, Carbondale.

Katerere, Y.M.S. 1979. *The Influence of Site Characteristics on Forest Stand Composition and Basal Area in the Southern Till Plain Division of Illinois.* M.S. thesis, Southern Illinois University, Carbondale.

Kettler, S.M. 1990. *The Effect of Soil and Topography on Forest Successional Patterns at Land Between The Lakes, KY and TN.* M.S. thesis, Southern Illinois University, Carbondale.

Kramer, P.J., and T.T. Kozlowski, 1979. *Physiology of Woody Plants.* Academic Press, New York.

Kozlowski, T.T., J.P. Kramer, and S.G. Pallardy. 1991. *The Physiological Ecology of Woody Plants.* Academic Press, New York.

Landes, J.S., and J.E. Ebinger. 1991. Woody understory of Barber Woods, Edgar County, Illinois. *Erigenia* 11:18–26.

MacArthur, R.H. 1955. Fluctuations of animal populations and a measure of community stability. *Ecology* 36:533–36.

Martin, A.C. 1951. *American Wildlife and Plants: A Guide to Wildlife Food Habits.* Dover Publications, New York.

Martin, A.C., H.S. Zim and A.L. Nelson. 1993. Nest predation and nest sites. BioScience. 43:523–32.

May, R.M. 1973. *Stability and Complexity in Model Ecosystems.* Princeton University Press, Princeton, NJ.

McArdle, T.G. 1991. *Comparison of Presettlement and Present Forest Communities by Site Type in the Illinois Ozark Hills.* M.S. thesis, Southern Illinois University, Carbondale.

McCarthy, B.C., and W.A. Wistendahl. 1988. Hickory (*Carya* spp.) distribution and replacement in a second-growth oak hickory forest of southeastern Ohio. *American Midland Naturalist* 119:156–64.

Menges, E.S., and O.L. Loucks. 1984. Modeling a disease-caused patch disturbance: Oak wilt in the midwestern United States. *Ecology* 65:487–98.

Menges, E.S., R.W. Dolan, and D.J. McGrath. 1987. *Vegetation, Environment, and Fire in a Post Oak Flatwoods/Barrens Association in Southwestern Indiana.* HRI Report no. 98. Holcomb Research Institute. Butler University, Indianapolis.

Miceli, J.C., G.L. Rolfe, D.R. Pelz, and J.M. Edgington. 1977. Brownfield Woods. Illinois: Woody vegetation changes since 1960. *American Midland Naturalist* 98:469–76.

Miller, R.B. 1920. *Fire Prevention in Illinois.* Forestry Circular no. 2. Illinois Natural History Survey, Springfield.

Miller, R.B., and G.D. Fuller. 1922. Forest conditions in Alexander County, Illinois. *Transactions of the Illinois Academy of Science* 14:92–108.

Nigh, T.A., S.G. Pallardy, and H.E. Garrett. 1985a. Sugar maple-environmental relationships in the River Hills and central Ozark Mountains of Missouri. *American Midland Naturalist* 114:235–51.

Nigh, T.A., S.G. Pallardy, and H.E. Garrett. 1985b. Changes in upland oak-hickory forests of central Missouri. In J.O. Dawson and K.A. Majerus, eds. *Proceedings of the Fifth Central Hardwood Forest Conference.* University of Illinois. Urbana. 170–77.

Odum, E.P. 1975. *Ecology: The Link Between the Natural and Social Sciences.* 2nd ed. Holt, Rinehart and Winston, New York.

Odum, W.E., T.J. Smith, III, and R. Dolan. 1987. Suppression of natural disturbance: Long term ecological change on the Outer Banks of North Carolina. In M.G. Turner, ed. *Landscape Heterogeneity and Disturbance.* Ecological Studies 64. Springer-Verlag, New York.

Parker, G.R., and P.T. Sherwood. 1986. Gap phase dynamics of a mature Indiana forest. *Ecology* 95:217–23.

Parker, G.R., D.J. Leopold, and J.K. Eichenberger. 1985. Tree dynamics in an old-growth, deciduous forest. *Forest Ecology and Management,* 11:31–57.

Peet, R.K. 1974. The measurement of species diversity. In R.F. Johnston, P.W. Frank, and C.D. Michener, eds. *Annual Review of Ecology and Systematics.* Vol. 5. Annual Reviews, Palo Alto, Calif., 285–307.

Peet, R.K., and O.L. Loucks. 1977. A gradient analysis of southern Wisconsin Forests. *Ecology* 58:485–99.

Presmyk, C.J. 1987. *The Effect of a Wildlife and Clearcutting on Woody Species Regeneration in a Southern Illinois Ozark Hills Forest.* M.S. thesis. Southern Illinois University, Carbondale.

Richards, R.H., S.R. Shifley, A.J. Rebertus, and S.J. Chaplin. 1995. Characteristics and dynamics of an upland Missouri old-growth stand. In K.W. Gottschalk and L.C. Fosbroke, eds. *Proceedings of the Tenth Central Hardwood Forest Conference.* General Technical Report NE-197. U.S. Forest Service, Radnor, Pa., 11–22.

Robinson, S.K., F.R. Thompson, III., T.M. Donovan, D.R. Whitehead, and J. Faaborg. 1995. Regional forest fragmentation and the nesting success of migratory birds. *Science* 267:1987–90.

Schibig, J., and E.W. Chester. 1988. Vegetational and floristic characterization of a mixed hardwoods-shortleaf pine stand in Stewart County, Tennessee. *Journal of the Tennessee Academy of Science* 63:83–88.

Schildt, A.L. 1995. *A Study of Presettlement, Present, and Future Forest in the Coastal Plain Region of Southern Illinois.* M.S. thesis, Southern Illinois University, Carbondale.

Schlesinger, R.C. 1976. Hard maples increasing in an upland forest stand. In J.S. Fralish, G.T. Weaver, and R.C. Schlesinger, eds. *Proceedings of the First Central Hardwood Conference.* Southern Illinois University, Carbondale, 177–85.

Schlesinger, R.C. 1989. Dynamics of the sugar maple component of a white oak-yellow-poplar community. In G. Rink and C.A. Budelsky, eds. *Proceedings of the Seventh Central Hardwood Forest Conference.* General Technical Report NC-132. U.S. Forest Service, St. Paul, Minn., 262–66.

Schoolcraft, H.R. 1821. *Tour onto the Interior of Missouri in the Years 1818 and 1819.* Phillips, London.

Schroeder, W.A. 1967. *The Eastern Ozarks.* Special Publication no. 13. National Council for Geographic Education, Illinois State University, Normal.

Schwegman, J. 1973. *Natural Divisions of Illinois.* Illinois Nature Preserves Commission, Rockford.

Sharpe, D.M., G.R. Guntenspergen, C.P. Dunn, L.A. Leitner, and F. Stearns. 1987. Vegetation dynamics in a southern Wisconsin Agricultural Landscape. In M.G. Turner, ed. *Landscape Heterogeneity and Disturbance.* Springer-Verlag, New York, 137–55.

Shotola, S.J., G.T. Weaver, P.A. Robertson, and W.C. Ashby. 1992. Sugar maple invasion in an old-growth oak-hickory forest in southwestern Illinois. *American Midland Naturalist* 127:125–38.

Simpson, J.W., R.E. Boerner, M.N. DeMers, L.A. Berns, F.J. Artigas, and A. Silva. 1994. Forty-eight years of landscape change on two continuous Ohio landscapes. *Landscape Ecology* 9:261–70.

Smalley, G.W. 1980. Classification and evaluation of forest sites on the Western Highland Rim and Pennyroyal. General Technical Report SO-30. U.S. Forest Service. New Orleans.

Steyermark, J.A. 1959. *Vegetational History of the Ozark Forest.* University of Missouri, Columbia.

Snyder, P.R. 1995. *Forest Regrowth in 10–12 Year Old Clearcuts at Land Between The Lakes, Kentucky and Tennessee.* M.S. thesis, Southern Illinois University, Carbondale.

Taft, J.B., M.W. Schwartz, and R.P. Loy. 1995. Vegetation ecology of flatwoods on the Illinoisan Till Plain. *Journal of Vegetation Science* 6:647–666.

Telford, C.J. 1926. *Third Report on a Forest Survey of Illinois.* Illinois Natural History Survey Bulletin no. 16, 1–102.

Terborgh, J. 1992. Why American songbirds are vanishing. *Scientific American* May:98–104.

Thach, E.E., and L.M. Doyle. 1988. *Natural Resources Management, an Integral Part of Intensive Multiple Use: Land Between The Lakes, a Case History.* Tennessee Valley Authority, Golden Pond, Ky.

Thompson, F.R., III. W.D. Dijak, T.G. Kulowiec, and D.A. Hamilton. 1992. Breeding bird populations in Missouri Ozark forests with and without clearcutting. *Journal of Wildlife Management* 56:23–30.

Thompson, F.R., III, and E.K. Fritzell. 1990. *Bird Densities and Diversity in Clearcut and Mature Oak Hickory Forest.* Research Paper NC-293. U.S. Forest Service, St. Paul, Minn.

Tilman, D. and J.A. Downing. 1994. Biodiversity and stability in grasslands. *Nature* 367:363–365.

Turner, M.G., and V.H. Dale. 1991. Modeling landscape disturbance. In M.G. Turner and R.H. Gardner, eds. *Quantitative Methods in Landscape Ecology.* Springer-Verlag, New York, 323–351.

United States Department of Agriculture. 1941. *Yearbook of Agriculture: Climate and Man.* Washington, D.C.

United States Department of Agriculture. 1953. *Soil Survey of Stewart County, Tennessee.* Soil Conservation Service, Washington, D.C.

United States Department of Agriculture. 1981. *Soil Survey of Lyon and Trigg Counties. Kentucky.* Soil Conservation Service, Washington, D.C.

Vitousek, P.M., and W.A. Reiners. 1975. Ecosystem succession and nutrient retention: a hypothesis. *BioScience* 25:376–81.

Ward, S.J., and G.R. Parker. 1989. Spatial dispersion of woody regeneration in an old-growth forest. *Ecology* 70:1279–85.

Wallace, B.J. 1988. History of Land Between The Lakes. In D.H. Snyder, ed. *Proceedings of the First Annual Symposium on the Natural History of Lower Tennessee and Cumberland River Valleys.* Austin Peay State University, Clarksville, Tenn., 84–144.

Wellbaum, E.M. 1989. *Site, Stand and Tree Characteristics Associated with Oak Decline and Mortality.* M.S. thesis, Southern Illinois University, Carbondale.

White, P.S. 1979. Pattern, process and natural disturbance in vegetation. *Botanical Review* 45:229–99.

White, P.S., and S.T.A. Pickett. 1985. Natural disturbance and patch dynamics: an introduction. In S.T.A. Pickett, and P.S. White, eds. *The Ecology of Natural Disturbance and Patch Dynamics.* Academic Press, New York, 3–13.

Wilhelm, G.S. 1991. Implications of changes in floristic composition of the Morton Arboretum's East Woods. In G.V. Burger, J.E. Ebinger and G.S. Wilhelm, eds., *Proceedings of the Oak Woods Management Workshop.* Eastern Illinois University, Charleston, 31–48.

12

The Biogeography of and Habitat Loss on Hill Prairies

Mark W. Schwartz, Kenneth R. Robertson, Brian K. Dunphy,
Jeffrey W. Olson, and Ann Marie Trame
Illinois Natural History Survey, 607 E. Peabody Drive, Champaign, IL 61820

Introduction

According to Evers (1955) the term *hill prairie* was first used by A.G. Vestal in the 1940s during his ecology classes and seminars at the University of Illinois. Hill prairies, as defined by Vestal, are islandlike prairie openings occurring on steep slopes, typically river bluffs, that are (or were) otherwise forested. Hill prairies have also been called *bluff prairies, goat prairies,* and *prairie openings* (Robertson et al. 1995). The distribution of hill prairies extends from the upper Mississippi River Basin, in central Minnesota (Olson 1989) and Wisconsin (Shimek 1924), to southern Illinois (Evers 1955), and in Missouri (Steyermark 1963), Iowa (Cooper and Hunt 1982, White and Glenn-Lewin 1984), and parts of South Dakota (Novacek 1985) primarily along the Missouri River. Four basic types of hill prairies are recognized based on soil substrate: (1) loess, (2) sand, (3) glacial drift, and (4) gravel hill prairies. The research described here focuses on loess hill prairies within Illinois. Loess hill prairies are the most frequent type within Illinois and occur along the Mississippi River, the Illinois River from its junction with the Mississippi River to Putnam County, and along with the Sangamon River in Cass, Menard, and Mason Counties (Evers 1955, Kilburn and Warren 1963). Glacial drift hill prairies occur in Coles and Vermilion Counties of east central Illinois (Reeves et al. 1978, Ebinger 1981). Before European settlement, it is likely that hill prairies never formed large continuous segments in Illinois but were fragmented by ravines that dissect the river bluffs and slopes, and delimited on the upland sides by forest. Hill prairies typically occupy southwest-facing portions of steep slopes where some combination of hot summer sun, dry prevailing winds, droughty soils, and periodic fire precludes forest vegetation (Evers 1955, Reeves et al. 1978). The flora of these insularized xeric habitats is a combination of typical tallgrass prairie species, species disjunct from the western plains region (e.g., *Asclepias stenophylla, Carex heliophila, Mirabilis hirsuto, Opuntia macrorhiza*), and hill prairie endemics. The habitat is dominated by grasses such as little bluestem (*Schizachyrium scoparium*), side oats grama (*Bouteloua curtipendula*), and big bluestem (*Andropogon gerardii*) (Anderson 1972, Kilburn and Ford 1963). Characteristic forbs on hill prairies include green milkweed (*Asclepias viridiflora*), false boneset (*Kuhnia eupatoriodes*), wild flax (*Linum sulcatum*), fringed puccoon (*Lithospermum incisum*), pale beardstongue (*Penstemon pallidus*), scurf-pea (*Psoralea tenuiflora*), leadplant (*Amorpha canescens*), showy goldenrod (*Solidago speciosa*), sky-blue aster (*Aster-azureus*), purple prairie clover (*Dalea purpureum*), heath aster (*A. ericoides*), and narrow-leaved bluets (*Hedyostis nigricans;* White 1978, McClain and Anderson 1990, Evers 1955). Frequent woody invaders are rough leaf dogwood (*Cornus drummondii*), white ash (*Fraxinus americana*), sumacs (*Rhus glabra, R. aromatica*), American elm (*Ulmus americana*), oaks (*Quercus* spp.) and maples (*Acer* spp.); McClain and Anderson 1990). Among these, rough leaf dogwood may pose the biggest threat because it is clonal, produces abundant fruit that is well dispersed by birds, reduces fuel flammability of hill prairies, and shades out prairie plants (Mutel 1989).

Because of their relative inaccessibility, hill prairies have rarely been cleared for crop production. Thus, in Illinois a higher proportion of original hill prairie remains than most other prairie types, leaving hill prairies as some of the best remnants of the prairie biome that dominated Illinois for 8,000 years prior to European settlement (King 1981). Only 127 of the 446 hill prairie sites examined during field work for the Illinois Natural Areas Inventory, encompassing about 161 ha., were of high quality (Nÿboer 1981). Most remaining hill prairies are severely degraded as a result of grazing pressure (Nÿboer 1981). Since that time, 2 additional sites have been added to the inventory list, bringing the total to 129. Under present climate conditions, and in the absence of fire, it appears that hill prairies are readily invaded by trees (Kilburn and Warren 1963, McClain 1983). Light to moderate grazing may retard the process of woody invasion of hill prairies, while overgrazing often degrades prairie communities. While loss of hill prairies probably dates to the time of European settlement, the lack of fire management and diminution of grazing in Illinois during the latter half of the 20th century have resulted in rapid secondary succession that has accelerated the rate of hill prairie conversion. Several reports have suggested that the remaining high-quality sites are being lost at an alarming rate (White 1978, McClain 1983, Voigt 1983, Werner 1994). In a study of five hill prairies in Pere Marquette State Park in Jersey County, McClain (1983) compared aerial photographs of the area taken in 1937 and 1974 and calculated that 62% of the prairie area had been converted to forest during that 37-year interval.

This chapter focuses on conservation concerns regarding hill prairies by addressing four specific questions. First, what is the rate of loss of hill prairies? We broaden the assessment of rates of habitat loss using 15 Illinois hill prairies to discern whether the rate of habitat loss found at Pere Marquette State Park (McClain 1983) is a general phenomenon. Second, to what extent do small hill prairies contribute to the conservation of biodiversity? We use floristic data to examine species-area relationships on hill prairies to discern the minimum size of hill prairies that contain a full complement of the hill prairie flora. Third, to what is extent is the flora of hill prairies unique to these habitats? We compare the flora of 33 hill prairies to that of 45 black soil, sand, and gravel prairies to delineate the portion of flora that is particular to hill prairies. Fourth, are hill prairie specialist species negatively associated with small hill prairies? We assess the potential sensitivity of hill prairie specialists to habitat loss based on the frequency of their occurrence in small hill prairies compared with large hill prairies. Together, the answers to these questions allow us to assess whether hill prairies remain viable habitats for the conservation of biodiversity.

Methods

Rates of Habitat Loss

To assess rates of change in the area we chose one large (39.2 ha), eight medium sized (1.7–7.2 ha), and six small (< 0.5 ha) hill prairies for use in this study (Figure 12.1). Through this selection we tried to examine sites that were representative of

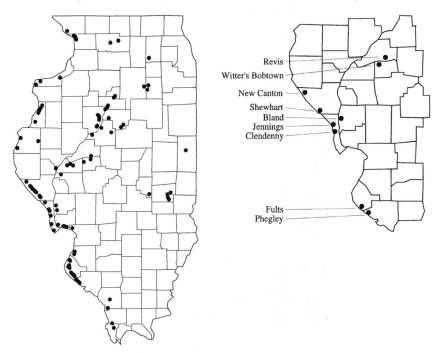

Figure 12.1. Areas identified on the Illinois Natural Areas Inventory with hill prairie components as of November 1994 (left) and the locations of the nine larger hill prairies sampled in this study (right).

the sizes of hill prairies available within Illinois (Figure 12.2). For small sites (< 0.5 ha), we estimate the amount of habitat loss from the 1950s to present using field reconnaissance. Area estimates from the 1950s are based on site visits by R. A. Evers (field notes on file at the Illinois Natural History Survey herbarium). Field crews measured the size of sites in 1993. Field crews gathering modern estimates were unbiased by not being informed of the 1950s size estimate before the site visit.

To investigate the rate of loss in area of the nine medium and large hill prairies, we used aerial photographs spanning 1938 to 1988. We digitized the aerial extent of each of the nine hill prairies at three to five time periods into a geographical information system (GIS—ARC/INFO version 6.0). All patches of hill prairie within each site at each time were summed to derive a site area. Forest was defined as any patch of trees consisting of two or more adjacent canopy-sized trees. Isolated trees within hill prairies were, by definition, a part of the hill prairie community.

Aerial photographs were obtained from the archives of the University of Illinois Map Library. Photographs before 1988 were taken at a 1:20,000 scale by the U.S. Department of Agriculture Soil Conservation Service. The 1988 photo series, taken at a 1:40,000 scale by the Mark Hurd Company, had lower resolution than previous series. While the 1988 series resulted in a generally lower root mean

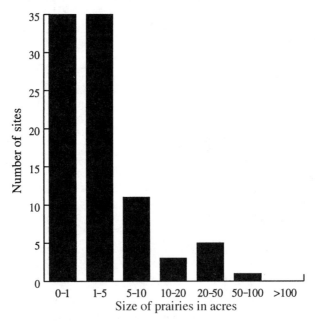

Figure 12.2. Number of grade A and B hill prairies, by acreage categories, as identified by the Illinois Natural Areas Inventory (White 1978).

square error estimate during the digitization process (Robertson and Schwartz 1994), the actual error is likely to be higher in these photos as a result of lower resolution and a decreased ability to photo-interpret fine detail in habitat boundaries. Our results, however, show a consistent rate of habitat loss through 1988, suggesting that the poorer resolution did not systematically bias our results. The 1988 coverage for one site (Bobtown Hill Prairie) was partially obscured by late afternoon shadows, making community delineation very difficult. We eliminated this 1988 photo from our analysis and estimated current habitat size through field observation.

Besides summarizing changes in area and the number of patches for each study site, we address the issue of the relative amount of edge to center in each site. The perimeter-to-area (p/a) ratio is used to assess the relative amount of edge across which woody species invasion may occur. This value is predicted to be related to how fast areas may be invaded, all other factors being equal. A simple geometric relationship is expected in the p/a ratio over time if the area is decreasing. To determine if the p/a ratio is increasing at rates faster than expected for these shrinking habitat patches, we use a p/a ratio index. This index is a measure of the p/a ratio relative to a circle of equal size. Since a circle has the minimum p/a ratio of any two-dimensional shape, this index will always be greater than 1.0. There is no maximum to the p/a ratio index; higher values indicate a more complex shape with increasing amounts of edge for a given area. We also consider the relationship between the perimeter length and the square root of area as a unitless measure of the p/a relationship.

Biogeographical Patterns

Between 1950 and 1975 Dr. R. Evers of the Illinois Natural History Survey studied the floristic composition of over 75 hill prairies. Species lists for 36 of these sites were previously published (Evers 1955); all of Evers' species lists are on file at the Illinois Natural History Survey (INHS) herbarium. To construct a species-area curve we used a suite of 43 hill prairies that Evers visited at least on six occasions, compiling a thorough species list, and for which a size was estimated at the time of the initial floristic survey. The Illinois prairie flora was then compared among prairie types using the published species lists for (1) 36 hill prairie sites (Evers 1955), (2) 29 prairies on silt loam soils (Betz and Lamp 1989), and (3) 16 sand prairies (Betz and Lamp 1992). To assess the floristic similarity between prairie types, species were categorized as absent, infrequent, or frequent within each prairie type. Frequent species were defined as those occurring in 3 or more sites of a given prairie type. A three-way log-linear model was used to test for nonrandom association of species. Overall significant results of this test would confirm a nonrandom pattern of similarity in the flora among the various prairie types. In other words, the test would confirm that species that are frequent on one type of prairie are more likely to be frequent in other prairie types. The degree of failure to confirm the model indicates the level of support for the hypothesis that the flora of the three prairie types are sampling-independent suites of species. To examine biogeographical patterns more specifically we used nonparametric regression (Kendall's tau) to compare species frequencies between prairie types and assess the relationship of hill prairies to other prairie types.

We estimate the potential consequence of habitat loss in hill prairies with respect to the conservation of biological diversity (by species loss) through two tests. The first test uses a simulation to compare the actual and expected distributions of infrequent species (with two or fewer occurrences) on hill prairies of varying size. In this test we assume that the probability of occurrence of infrequent species is proportional to site size. These tests utilize methodologies developed by Simberloff and Gotelli (1984) where each site is a bucket (BS) into which balls (species) are randomly assigned. The size (S) of the buckets are proportional to the size of the actual remnant. Each species (N) has a discrete number of occurrences (i), or balls (N_i). We randomly tossed balls into buckets under two constraints: (1) the probability of a ball falling into any bucket is proportional to bucket size and (2) two like balls (samples of the same species) are not allowed to fall into the same bucket (site). The simulation was repeated 300 times to derive an expected value for the number of species in sites (balls in buckets) in differing sizes. We then use a Kilomogorov-Smirnov test to test for deviations from expected as we accumulate species from the smallest to largest sites. We used three different criteria for these tests. First we examined the distribution of the 156 infrequently (1–2 occurrences) sampled native species on hill prairies of different size. We repeated this test, restricting our consideration to 98 species classified by Mohlenbrock (1986) as occurring on grasslands or prairies. Finally, we tested 68 species that were infrequent on hill prairies and also infrequent on the silt-loam and sand-gravel prairies (< 3 occurrences on either silt-loam or sand-gravel prairie types). The identities of the species used in these tests are presented in Appendix A. In a second observational experiment we compared the observed frequencies of the 39 most frequently sampled species (13 or more occurrences) on sites divided into small (< 0.5 ha), medium (0.5–1.5 ha), and large (1.5–7.7 ha) categories to expected distributions using a chi-square test. We use this test to examine the flora of hill prairies to detect association of common species to sites of a particular size.

Results

Rate of Habitat Loss

Over the approximately 50-year study interval, medium and large hill prairies were reduced in size by an average of 63.0% (range 36.7% to 82.5%—Figure 12.3. Table 12.1). For Revis Hill Prairie, the largest site in our study, the data show a 55.6% decrease in size from 15.85 ha in 1939 to 7.03 ha in 1988 (Figure

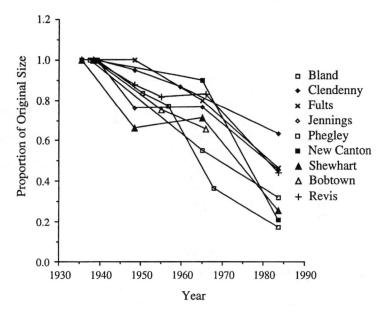

Figure 12.3. The change in sizes of nine Illinois hill prairies between about 1940 and 1988, expressed as a proportion of the size measured in the earliest aerial photograph (see Table 12.1).

12.3). McClain and Anderson (1990) use a larger region of the Revis hill prairie site and observe a 65% loss (70 ha in 1939 to 24 ha in 1978) over nearly the same period. A relatively modest rate of loss on Bobtown prairie may be partially a result of burning and brush clearing during the 1980s (W. McClain, Illinois Department of Natural Resources, personal communication). Community loss on medium and large sizes does not indicate a relationship between the size of a site and rate of community loss. Small sites, in contrast, averaged 72% loss, exceeding the average rates of loss for medium and large sites (Table 12.1). Examples of 1940 to 1988 decrease in area are presented for the Bland and Phegley hill prairies (Figure 12.4). In addition to losing significant area, our results show that hill prairies are becoming more fragmented. Two-thirds of sites had increased the number of patches of hill prairie at some point during the study interval (Robertson and Schwartz 1994, Robertson et al. 1995). In the case of New Canton and Phegley, the number of patches is currently decreasing as small isolated units are lost (Robertson and Schwartz 1994, Robertson et al. 1995).

The p/a ratio shows an average increase of over 100% during the study interval (Figure 12.5a). Thus, not only are our hill prairies declining from woody invasion at an alarming rate, but the propensity for woody invasion is accelerating because of an increased ratio of edge to center of the habitat. As any two-dimensional object shrinks in size the ratio of edge to center will increase. The p/a ratio index

Table 12.1. Hill prairie sites studied for loss of area during the period of approximately 1940 to 1990.

A. Medium and large hill prairie sites

Site	County	1940		1988		% net change	
		Size	P/A	Size	P/A	Area	P/A
Bland	Greene	2.04	0.035	0.65	0.121	−68.1%	345%
Clendenny	Calhoun	3.97	0.057	2.52	0.081	−36.7%	141%
Fults	Monroe	7.20	0.063	3.35	0.117	−53.4%	187%
Jennings	Calhoun	2.16	0.108	0.99	0.151	−54.2%	140%
New Canton	Pike	1.71	0.094	0.32	0.125	−78.8%	132%
Phegley	Randolph	2.65	0.054	0.46	0.191	−82.5%	351%
Shewhart	Pike	3.10	0.067	0.79	0.157	−74.6%	236%
Bobtown[1]	Menard	1.99	0.030	1.31	0.042	−34.2%	140%
Revis	Mason	39.2	0.041	17.4	0.081	−55.6%	198%

B. Small hill prairie sites

Site	County	1950 Size	1993 Size	% net change
Hidden Lake	Adams	0.081	0.041	−50%
Fall Creek	Adams	0.138	0.020	−85.5%
Ursa	Adams	0.358	0.011	−96.9%
Rock Creek	Adams	0.440	0.006	−98.7%
Homan	Adams	0.488	0.000	−100%
Parker Heights	Adams	0.163	0.163	0%

[1]Missing data in 1988.

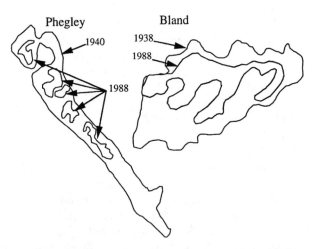

Figure 12.4. A graphical depiction of the areas of Phegley (left) and Bland (right) hill prairies in 1940 (outer lines) and 1988 (inner lines).

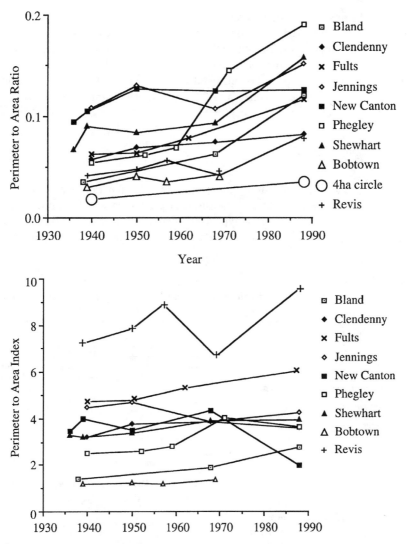

Figure 12.5. The change in perimeter-to-area ratio (left) for nine Illinois hill prairies between about 1940 and 1988. For reference, the change in the perimeter-to-area ratio for a circle that is halved in size is plotted between the 1940 and 1988 markers. The change in perimeter-to-area ratio index (right) is the perimeter-to-area ratio divided by the perimeter-to-area ratio for a circle of the same area, and is a measure of the complexity of shape of each hill prairie.

assesses the amount of edge present in a hill prairie patch relative to a circle of equal area. The observed p/a ratio index does not increase over the study interval at most sites (Figure 12.5b), although the p/a ratio index was higher in 1988 than at the beginning of the series in seven of the nine sites. Clendenny, one of the two sites where the p/a ratio index ended lower than it began, is an exception in that it lost numerous patches by 1988. Before 1988, this site also had an increasing p/a ratio index (Table 12.1).

Biogeographical Patterns

The species composition of hill prairies appears to be generally similar to other eastern tallgrass prairie types as demonstrated by the three-way log-linear model, relating frequency on one prairie type to frequency on other prairie types (Table 12.2). There are, however, notable differences in the vegetation. In particular,

Table 12.2. Three-way log-linear model tests of the correlation of the frequency of plants on hill prairies (33) versus silt-loam (29) and sand-gravel (19) prairies. Rare is defined as species sampled two or fewer times within each prairie type.

A. Species **absent** from silt-loam prairies

| | | Hill prairies | | | |
		Absent	Rare	Common	Total
Sand-gravel prairies	**Absent**	0	113	71	184
	Rare	44	9	11	64
	Common	15	7	13	35
	Total	59	129	95	283

B. Species **rare** on silt-loam prairies

| | | Hill prairies | | | |
		Absent	Rare	Common	Total
Sand-gravel prairies	**Absent**	19	6	4	29
	Rare	16	0	3	19
	Common	6	3	3	12
	Total	41	9	10	60

C. Species **common** on silt-loam prairies

| | | Hill prairies | | | |
		Absent	Rare	Common	Total
Sand-gravel prairies	**Absent**	9	3	6	18
	Rare	14	4	4	22
	Common	22	12	51	85
	Total	45	19	61	125

Chi-square = 2.55, degrees of freedom = 6, p = 0.863

Bouteloua curtipendula and *Kuhnia eupatorioides* are common on hill prairies, but not on other prairie types. In general, the correlation of species frequencies between hill prairies and sand-gravel prairies is stronger than the correlation between hill prairie and silt-loam prairies (Figure 12.6). Further, the species-area relationships for plants on hill prairies suggest that exceedingly small

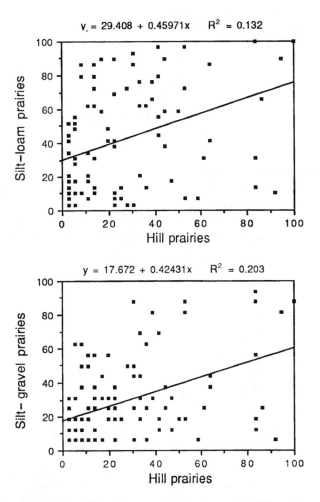

Figure 12.6. Scatter plots of the frequency of species on (A) hill prairies versus silt-loam prairies, (B) hill prairies versus sand-gravel prairies, and (C) sand-gravel prairies versus silt-loam prairies. The strength of the positive relationship reflects the degree to which these different habitat types (as identified by their authors) sample the same suite of species at the similar frequencies.

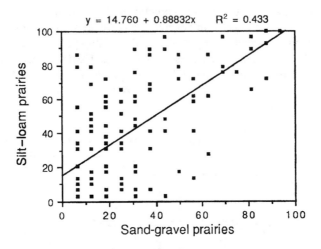

Figure 12.6. Continued.

sites capture biological diversity as well as larger sites (Figure 12.7). We have no information about whether the community structure of these small sites resembles larger sites.

Our analysis of the association between infrequently sampled plants on hill prairies and site size shows that small sites contain more infrequent species

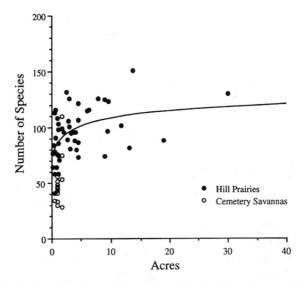

Figure 12.7. Number of plant species censused in prairie remnants of various sizes demonstrating that diversity of prairies increases with size. Data from Evers (unpublished data on file at the Illinois Natural History Survey), and Betz and Lamp (1989, 1992).

than we would expect based on their size under the model that plants randomly sampled the environment with respect to the site size (Figure 12.8). Further, this pattern is consistent across the three definitions of frequency we tested. The positive deviation between observed and expected numbers of species begins with sites as small as 0.3 ha (the sixth smallest site). Finally, the chi-square test for association of common species with site size was not significant ($X^2 = 35.7$, df = 1, p > .995), indicating that common plants, similarly, are present on small sites.

Discussion

The results of this study suggest that hill prairies have, on average, been more than halved in size since 1940. This estimate includes only those sites that have remained hill prairies during this period and is thus a conservative estimate of the total rate of habitat loss. There is a natural propensity for habitat patches to increase in the amount of edge as the total size declines. Hill prairies are shown to be no exception to this rule; however, most sites increased the amount of edge relative to a uniform shape of the size during each sample period, indicating increasing complexity of habitat patch shape. This increasing amount of edge is an important trend because if habitat encroachment is a diffusive process where invasion is most rapid along the ecotone between forest and prairie, then increasing the relative amount of this ecotone should increase the future rates of decline in this habitat.

The results of this study point to the single clear trend toward loss of naturally rare hill prairie communities in Illinois. The Illinois Department of Natural Resources is currently taking measures to protect hill prairie sites through active fire management and woody vegetation removal (Schwegman, personal communication). These measures, however, may be inadequate. Of the nine sites studied, only Revis and Fults have a history of fire management since the 1970s. Sites acquired by the state of Illinois, such as Revis, and managed to maintain hill prairies have still declined in size since the 1970s. This continued habitat loss may be a result of long intervals between fire treatments on these habitats, allowing woody species to resprout. There is much debate on the natural fire frequency for hill prairies: our best estimate is that the fire return interval is probably less than five years (W. McClain, Illinois Department of Natural Resources, personal communication). When combating advanced recruitment of woody invaders, managed fire frequencies may need to far exceed natural levels until woody invasion is suppressed.

It comes as something of a comfort to conservation biologists, however, that biogeographical analyses reveal that even very small hill prairie sites are likely to retain a large complement of hill prairie flora. Species of highest conservation concern are oversampled, relative to expectations, on small sites. The observation

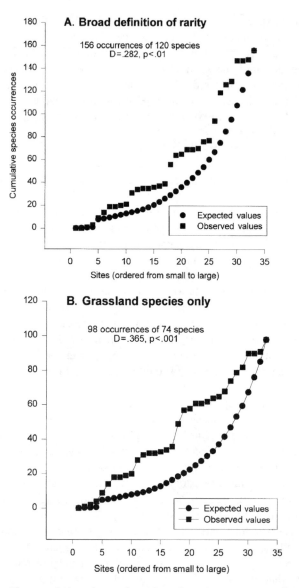

Figure 12.8. The cumulative observed number of species occurrences for rare species found when sampling from progressively larger hill prairie sites (data from Evers, 1955–1972) compared to the expected distribution of species occurrences on these sites using three definitions of "rare": (A) all 156 species that occur one or two times on the 36 hill prairies sampled, (B) the 98 species that fit the above criteria and are listed by Mohlenbrock (1986) as prairie species, and (C) the 68 species that fit the prior two criteria and that were rare on other prairie types as sampled by Betz and Lamp (1989, 1992).

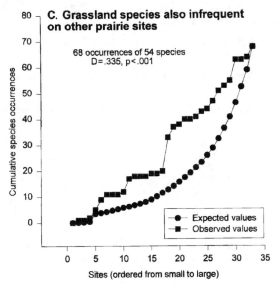

Figure 12.8. Continued.

that prairie plants have persisted into the late 20th century on exceedingly small sites is not new (e.g., Simberloff and Gotelli 1984). The question remains whether these high levels of diversity can be maintained through time.

Acknowledgements

The authors wish to thank William E. McClain and John Schwegman of the Division of Natural Heritage, Illinois Department of Natural Resources, for giving freely of their experiences with hill prairies. This project was part of a larger study to investigate critical trends in Illinois, funded by the Illinois Department of Energy and Natural Resources.

References

Anderson, R.C. 1972. Prairie history, management, and restoration. In J. Zimmerman, ed. *Proceedings of the Second Midwestern Prairie Conference*. Madison, Wisconsin, 15–21.

Betz, R.F., and H.F. Lamp. 1989. Species composition of old settler silt-loam cemetery prairies. In T.B. Braggs, and J. Stubbendieck, eds. *Proceedings of the Eleventh North American Prairie Conference, Prairie Pioneers: Ecology, History and Culture*. University of Nebraska, Lincoln, 33–39.

Betz, B.F., and H.P Lamp. 1992. Species composition of old settler savanna and sand prairie cemeteries in northern Illinois and northwestern Indiana. In D.A. Smith, and

C.A. Jacobs, eds. *Proceedings of the Twelfth North American Prairie Conference.* University of Northern Iowa, Cedar Falls, 39–87.

Cooper, T.C., and N.S. Hunt. 1982. *Iowa's Natural Heritage.* Iowa Natural Heritage Foundation and Iowa Academy of Science, Des Moines.

Ebinger, J.E. 1981. Vegetation of glacial drift hill prairies in east-central Illinois. *Castanea* 46:115–121.

Evers, R.A. 1955. Hill prairies of Illinois. *Illinois Natural History Survey Bulletin* 26:368–446.

Kliburn, P.D. and C.D. Ford, Jr. 1963. Frequency distribution of hill prairie plants. Transactions of the Illinois State Academy of Science 56:94–97.

Kilburn, P.D., and D.K. Warren. 1963. Vegetation-soil relationships in hill prairies. *Transactions of the Illinois State Academy of Science* 56:142–145.

King, J.E. 1981. Late Quaternary vegetational history of Illinois. Ecological Monographs 51:43–62.

McClain, W.E. 1983. Photodocumentation of the loss of hill prairie within Pere Marquette State Park. Jersey County Illinois. *Transactions of the Illinois State Academy of Science* 76:343–346.

McClain, W.E., and E.A. Anderson. 1990. Loss of hill prairie through woody plant invasion at Pere Marquette State Park. Jersey County, Illinois. *Natural Areas Journal* 10:69–75.

Mohlenbrock, R.H. 1986. *Guide to the Vascular Flora of Illinois.* Revised and enlarged edition. Southern Illinois University Press, Carbondale.

Mutel, C.F. 1989. *Fragile Giants, A Natural History of the Loess Hills.* University of Iowa Press.

Novacek, J.M. 1985. The loess hills of western Iowa: a problem in phytogeography. *Proceedings of the Iowa Academy of Science* 92:213–219.

Nÿboer, R.W. 1981. Grazing as a factor in the decline of Illinois hill prairies. In R.L. Stuckey and K.J. Reese, eds. The prairie peninsula in the "shadow" of Transeau: Proceedings of the Sixth North American Prairie Conference. *Ohio Biological Survey Biological Notes,* 15.

Olson, J.W. 1989. *The Hill Prairies of Goodhue, Wabasha, and Winona Counties.* Undergraduate Research Opportunities Program, University of Minnesota.

Reeves, J.T., U.G. Zimmerman, and J.E. Ebinger. 1978. Microclimatic and soil differences between hill prairies and adjacent forests in east-central Illinois. *Transactions of the Illinois State Academy of Science* 71:156–164.

Robertson, K.R., and M.W. Schwartz. 1994. Prairies. Chapter 7 in *Critical Trends of Illinois.* Illinois Department of Energy and Natural Resources, Springfield.

Robertson, K.R., M.W. Schwartz, J.W. Olson, B.K. Dunphy, and H.D. Clarke. 1995. 50 years of change in Illinois Hill Prairies. *Erigenia* 14:41–52.

Shimek, B. 1924. The prairie of the Mississippi River bluffs. *Iowa Academy of Science Proceedings* 31:205–212.

Simberloff, D., and N. Gotelli. 1983. Refuge design and ecological theory: Lessons for prairie and forest conservation. *Proceedings of the Eight North American Prairie Conference.* Department of Biology, Western Michigan University, Kalamazoo.

Steyermark, J.A. 1963. *Flora of Missouri.* Iowa State University Press, Ames.

Voigt, J.W. 1983. Death of a hill prairie. *Illinois Audubon Bulletin* 207:14–18.

Werner, W.E., Jr. 1994. Vegetative dynamics of the forest/prairie interface at Cole Creek Hill Prairie. Proceedings of the Illinois Forest Conference. *Erigenia* 13:63–64.

White, J. 1978. Illinois Natural Areas Inventory technical report, vol. 1. *Survey Methods and Results.* Illinois Natural Areas Survey, Urbana.

White, J.A., and D.C. Glenn-Lewin. 1984. Regional and local variation in tallgrass prairie remnants of Iowa and eastern Nebraska. *Vegetatio* 57:65–78.

Appendix A

List of infrequently sampled species on Illinois hill prairies used to test for association with sites of varying size. Test number indicates the level of restriction on consideration in the test. Species labelled for test one were only used in the most general test of all native dry woodland or grassland species. Test 2 species were used both in test 1 and in a more restrictive test that included only species characterized as occurring in grassland habitats. Test 3 species were similar to those used in test 1 but were also characterized as having been sampled two or fewer times in 45 other prairies in Illinois. Sites are as follows: Block House— BH; Bielema—BI; Bluff Springs—BS; Bunker—BU; Cave Creek—CC; Clendenny—CL; Devil's Backbone—DB; El Rancho—ER; Fountain Bluff—FB; Fults—FT; Government Rock—GR; Hidden Lake—HL; Homan—HO; Menonemie Station—MS; Mud Creek—MC; North Eldred—NE; Northeast Meredosa—NM; Pere Marquette—PM; Phegley—PH; Principia—PR; Rock Creek— RC; Renault—RE; Revis—RV; Sampson—SA; Sessions—SE; South New Canton—SH; South Palisades—SO; Seehorn-Payson—SP; Swarnes—SW; Stotz— SZ; Ursa—UR; Vahmeyer—VA; Walnut Creek—WC. Site locations and complete species lists are presented in Evers (1955).

Species	Test	Sites		Species	Test	Sites	
Acalypha gracilens	3	FB		*Carex umbellata*	3	RV	
Acer negundo	1	FT		*Carya ovalis*	1	CL	FT
Acer saccharum	1	PH		*Carya texana*	1	AS	PH
Agoseris cuspidata	3	RV		*Cassia nicitans*	3	SH	FB
Agrostis hyemalis	3	FB		*Cerastrum nutans*	1	VA	FB
Andropogon virginicus	3	FB		*Chaerophyllum procumbens*	1	CL	
Androsace occidentalis	2	DB		*Cheilanthes feei*	3	CL	
Arabis hirsuta var.	3	CL		*Cheilanthes lanosa*	1	CC	
adpressipilis				*Chenopodium leptophylum*	2	HO	
Aristida intermedia	3	DB		*Coreopsis tripteris*	1	CL	
Aristida longestpica	3	DB		*Corydolis aurea* var.	3	VA	
Aristida oligantha	3	SP		*occidentalis*			
Asclepias tuberosa	2	GR		*Corylus americana*	1	CL	
Aster anomalus	3	FT		*Crataegus mollis*	1	CL	
Aster linariifolius	3	NM	BU	*Croton capitarus*	3	PR	
Aster sagittifolius	1	CL	PH	*Croton glandulosus*	3	BS	BH
Aster turbinellus	3	FB		*Cuphea petiolata*	3	CL	
Astragalus canadensis	2	VA	PR	*Cuscuta gronovii*	1	CL	
Astragalus distortus	3	SP		*Desmanthus illinoensis*	3	PM	PR
Carex muhlenbergii	1	FB		*Desmodium canadense*	2	ER	
Campanula rotundifolia	3	BI		*Desmodium glabellum*	1	CL	FT
Carex flaccosperma	3	FB		*Desmodium paniculatum*	1	PH	
Carex gravida	2	BS	RC	*Diodia teres*	3	PH	SZ
Carex meadii	2	CC		*Dodecatheon meadia*	2	RV	
Carex pensylvanica	2	DB	NM	*Draba cuneifolia*	3	FT	

Species	Test	Sites		Species	Test	Sites	
Equisetum hyemale	2	ER	BU	*Myosotis verna*	1	FT	FB
Eragrostis capillaris	1	FB		*Nothoscordum bivalve*	3	GR	CC
Erigeron divaricatus	1	SP		*Ostrya virginana*	1	SA	
Euphorbia glyptosperma	3	DB		*Panicum capillare*	3	BS	RV
Euphorbia obtusata	1	FT		*Panicum dichotomum*	3	FB	
Fraxinus americana	1	HP	CL	*Panicum virgatum*	2	SP	
Galactia volubilis	1	GR	CC	*Parthenocissus*	1	PH	
Galium aparine	1	CL	SA	*quinquefolia*			
Galium virgatum	3	FT		*Pellaea atropurpurea*	3	GR	CC
Gerardia tenuifolia	1	CL	FT	*Physalis pubescens*	3	BS	
Gleditsia triacanthos	1	PH		*Plantago rugelii*	1	PR	
Helianthus hirsutus	3	PH		*Platanus occidentalis*	1	CL	PH
Helianthus mollis	2	CL		*Polygala incarnata*	3	NM	
Helianthus occidentalis	2	CL		*Polygonum tenue*	3	FB	
Helianthus tuberosus	3	RV		*Potentilla simplex*	2	ST	
Heliopsis helianthoides	2	RV	BH	*Quercus marilandica*	1	CL	
Heliotropium tenellum	3	FT		*Quercus muehlenbergii*	1	CL	PH
Heuchera americana var.	1	PH	FT	*Ranunculus fascicularis*	3	DB	
hirsuticaulis				*Rhus radicans*	1	PH	
Hordeum pusillum	3	PH		*Rosa setigera*	1	SA	
Houstonia longifolia	2	VA	FB	*Rubus flagellaris*	1	PH	
Ilex decidua	1	SA	PH	*Sabatia angularis*	3	SE	
Juglans nigra	1	CL	FT	*Salvia azurea*	3	CC	
Juncus dudleyi	3	FB		*Scutellaria ovata*	1	VA	
Juncus interior	3	ST		*Silphium terebinthinaceum*	2	VA	CC
Lechea stricta	3	VA		*Stylosanthes biflora*	3	SA	FB
Lepidium virginicum	3	FT	BS	*Taenidia integerrima*	3	CC	
Leptoloma cognatum	2	HL	DB	*Teucrium canadense*	3	FT	
Lespedeza hirta	1	PH		*Tradescantia virginiana*	3	FB	GR
Lespedeza simulata	3	FT	RE	*Triosteum perfoliatum*	1	RV	
Lespedeza stuevei	1	FT		*Ulmus rubra*	1	CL	PH
Liatris scabra	3	FB	CC	*Veronica peregrina*	3	FB	
Lithospermum croceum	2	SP	NE	*Viburnum prunifolium*	1	CL	
Melica nitens	3	FT		*Viola pedata*	2	DB	GR
Monarda punctata	3	WC		*Vitis aestivalis*	3	CL	SA
Muhlenbergia frondosa	1	CL		*Vitis cinerea*	1	FT	
Muhlenbergia racemosa	3	ER		*Vitis riparia*	1	CL	
Muhlenbergia schreberi	1	RV		*Zizia aurea*	2	CC	

13

Fragmentation and the Role of Seed Banks in Promoting Persistence in Isolated Populations of *Collinsia verna*

Susan Kalisz
Department of Biological Sciences, University of Pittsburgh, Pittsburgh, PA 15260

Lisa Horth
Department of Biological Sciences, Florida State University, Tallahassee FL 32306

Mark A. McPeek
Department of Biological Sciences, Dartmouth College, Hanover, NH 03755

Introduction

Plant species that inhabit environments characterized by environmental stochasticity and/or catastrophe have evolved two common bet-hedging strategies: one based on seed dispersal attributes and one on dormancy attributes, which lead to the formation of a soil seed bank. The environmental conditions that select for the evolution of spatial versus temporal dispersal will depend on both the magnitude of the environmental variance and the spatial array of suitable habitat patches. In species that normally are connected as a metapopulation, repeated local extinction occurs, and recolonization of the available habitat patches is accomplished by seed dispersal. In a metapopulation structure, individuals are distributed among a series of subpopulations that are connected to one another by dispersal. The number of individuals in each subpopulation fluctuates according to local demogrpahic conditions, and subpopulations can fluctuate largely independently. These fluctuations in numbers of individuals may periodically extirpate a subpopulation, but persistence of a species in such a subpopulation is enhanced because dispersing individuals from other subpopulations can recolonize an extirpated area. Thus metapopulation structure and function enhances the regional persistence of species in spatially and temporally variable environments (Hanski and Gilpin 1991). Spatiotemporal variability in subpopulation size and persistence probability favors the evolution of high dispersal rates among subpopulations (Gadgil 1971, Cohen and Levin 1991, den Boer 1987, McPeek and Holt 1992).

High dispersal rates will enhance the persistence of the entire metapopulation by increasing the recolonization rate of extinct subpopulations (Hanski and Gilpin 1991, den Boer 1987, McPeek and Holt 1992, Ebenhard 1991, Verboom and Lankester 1991, Hanski 1991). However, if the distance among subpopulations exceeds the dispersal capacity of the organism and the probability of successful recolonization is low, the evolution of dormancy will be favored.

Habitat fragmentation can be expected to alter population function in two ways. First, for typical continuously distributed species populations, fragmentation will convert a continuous distribution into a subdivided population that may superficially resemble a metapopulation. The ability of such populations to function in a metapopulation framework will depend on the prior dispersal attributes of the species and/or the rate at which increased dispersal ability can evolve. Second, for species in which metapopulation function is the norm, habitat fragmentation can disrupt metapopulation structure and magnify the effects of processes that reduce the likelihood of species persistence (McCauley 1993, Holsinger 1993). In either case, the degrading effects of fragmentation on habitat quality (Meffe and Carroll 1994) can be expected to exacerbate the magnitude and frequency of environmental variability experienced by a subpopulation. This will directly enhance the likelihood of subpopulation extinction because of environmental variability (Hanski 1991), and because subpopulations will be small in size more frequently, this will also enhance the likelihood of extinction through demographic stochasticity (Shaffer 1981, McCauley 1993, Holsinger 1993). Simultaneously, as fragmentation increases the degree of subpopulation isolation, there will be a concomitant decrease in the likelihood that a subpopulation will be reestablished after extirpation (McCauley 1993, Holsinger 1993, De Mauro, 1993). The likelihood of reestablishment is lessened because fragmentation can increase the distances between subpopulations, which will decrease the chances that dispersers will successfully locate another subpopulation. Also, upon fragmentation, dispersers may be forced to travel across inhospitable territory to reach a suitable habitat, which could significantly decrease the survival probability of dispersers during movement. Thus, fragmentation can enhance the detrimental effects of environmental variability and reduce the ability of metapopulation structure to prevent local and regional extinction. The role of population size, isolation, and persistence for 52 plant species in 143 sites along the Dutch Rhine River system was investigated between 1956 and 1988 (Ouburg 1993). For some species, extinction was related only to population size; for others it was related only to isolation. However, for some species, extinction and recolonization were found to be affected by isolation, suggesting that those species had been connected as a metapopulation. Thus, fragmentation that results in isolation can totally uncouple species within habitat remnants from their metapopulation functions.

If fragmentation magnifies the effects of environmental variability and makes dispersal among subpopulations within a metapopulation more difficult and risky, the evolution of other bet-hedging strategies (Seger and Brockmann 1987, Philippi and Seger 1989, Philippi 1993) may be favored. One alternative bet-hedging strategy against environmental variability is the development of a pool of dormant propagules. Dormancy, like dispersal, evolves to maximize geometric mean fitness in a variable environment. The fraction of individuals entering the dormant pool in a population should evolve to increase as environmental variability increases (Cohen 1966, 1967). Seed banks are commonly considered a bet-hedging strategy of many short-lived plants to counteract the detrimental effects of an unpredictable environment (Cohen 1966, 1967; Venable and Lawlor 1980; Westoby 1981; Ellner 1985a, 1985b; Venable 1985; Brown and Venable 1986; Silvertown 1988). Seed banks are formed because some seeds produced in a given year germinate immediately, but other seeds delay germination until subsequent years. In annual plants, the fraction of seeds that delay germination is expected to evolve in response to the regime of temporal unpredictability in adult fitness (Cohen 1966, 1967; Ellner 1985a, 1985b). Germination of seeds from the seed bank each year should buffer fluctuations in population size, especially in years when the adult population size is small. Consequently, this reduces the likelihood of extinction by increasing the number of breeding adults in the population each year (MacDonald and Watkinson 1981). Seed banks are especially important because they can reestablish a population of breeding adults after catastrophic events (Kalisz and McPeek 1993, Del Castillo 1994). In isolated habitat fragments, the decrease in number of successful migrants or the total loss of migrants will increase the demographic value of temporal dispersal as well. An expected demographic consequence of this evolution is that population persistence should increase as the fraction of dormant individuals increases. Therefore, increased habitat fragmentation for populations connected as metapopulations may change the importance of spatial versus temporal dispersal. Fragmentation and isolation may lead to the evolution of increased dormancy within the subpopulations of a metapopulation and a loss of spatial dispersal.

A number of authors have considered the joint evolution of dormancy and dispersal in plant populations (Kuno 1981, Klinkhamer et al. 1987, Cohen and Levin 1991); as dispersal becomes more costly, the fitness consequences of averaging across space become more dire, and maximizing long-term geometric mean fitness becomes increasingly dependent on the dormant fraction in the population. Consequently, for populations connected as a metapopulation, fragmentation should result in the evolution of decreased dispersal rates among the subpopulations and increased dormancy within subpopulations. This will be especially true if the magnitude of environmental variability within subpopulations is large enough to result in complete reproductive failure in some years, thus causing immediate extinction without dormancy or age structure to maintain the population.

In this paper we consider the demographic consequences of evolved dormancy in simulation models of field data from a native annual plant, *Collinsia verna*. As discussed below, *C. verna* populations are presumed to have originally been connected as metapopulations, but habitat fragmentation has completely isolated these patches in the Midwest. A previous model using multiyear data from a natural population has shown that *Collinsia*'s short-lived seed bank can significantly prolong population persistence in a temporally variable environment (Kalisz and McPeek 1992, 1993). That analysis incorporated the variability in the population data for two years and permitted population size to grow without bounds if the population persisted. Since performing that analysis we have observed one occurrence of complete reproductive failure in the population from which the demographic data were taken. In this paper we first briefly present the ecological and evolutionary role of dormancy with habitat fragmentation. Second, we describe the case study and the catastrophic event that took place in one study population, and we incorporate demographic catastrophes into the projection matrix model along with density dependence operating in the adult phase of the life cycle of *C. verna*. We also examine how increasing age structure in this population, by increasing the length of time a seed can remain in the seed bank, affects the persistence of populations in a temporally variable environment with periodic reproductive catastrophes.

Ecological and Evolutionary Role of Dormancy in Fragmented Habitats

Temporal environmental variability can have profound detrimental consequences for populations, and these consequences are expected to increase in magnitude in fragmented habitats. However, temporal variability should also impose selection pressures favoring adaptations that may mitigate these detrimental demographic and genetic consequences of variable environments. Increasing temporal environmental stochasticity in fragmented habitats may mean an increase in the selective pressure for such adaptations. These adaptations generally fall under the rubric of *bet-hedging strategies* (Seger and Brockmann 1987, Philippi and Seger 1989, Philippi 1993). Bet-hedging strategies include dispersal of individuals among populations (Gadgil 1971, den Boer 1987, McPeek 1989, Cohen and Levin 1991, McPeek and Holt 1992), diapause in insects (Dingle 1978), dormancy of seeds, eggs, or spores (Levins 1969, Schneller 1988, Hairston and De Stasio 1988, DeStasio 1989, Leck et al. 1989, Reese 1994), long-lived gametophytes (Schneller et al. 1990), resting stages in algae (Binder and Anderson 1990), and iteroparity (Chesson 1983, 1984, 1985; Huntly and Chesson 1989). Bet-hedging phenotypes can be favored by selection when fitness varies temporally (Cohen 1966, Seger and Brockmann 1987, Philippi and Seger 1989) and can actually maintain genetic variation in populations with overlapping generations under fluctuating selection (Ellner and Hairston 1994).

Dormancy is successful in variable environments because it spreads the reproductive effort of a population over many years by generating greater age structure in the population. This reduces the variability in fitness among years in the face of temporal environmental variability and consequently increases the long-term geometric mean fitness (Philippi and Seger 1989). With habitat fragmentation and isolation of populations, the ecological and evolutionary importance of dormancy can be expected to increase for species whose regional persistence relies on metapopulation function. Increasing distances among populations as a result of fragmentation could result in a shift in the relative importance of spatial and temporal dispersal. If a population is part of a metapopulation and that metastructure is diminished through fragmentation and isolation, then migrants sent out of the home population have zero fitness because they will disperse into unsuitable habitat. This mortality of migrants could represent strong selection against long-distance dispersal among subpopulations. It has been shown that increasing the amount of dormancy results in a lowering of the optimal dispersal distance (Levin et al. 1984). Data supporting the balance of spatial dispersal and dormancy is found for *Carduus,* where "old" populations have decreased frequency of genotypes with long-distance dispersing seeds. This loss of dispersal among populations results in an increased fitness value of local dispersal or dormancy (Oliviere et al. 1990). Given random catastrophes, temporal dispersal is a population's only source of numerical and genetic restoration if residing in isolated fragments.

Seed banks should also mitigate many of the genetic consequences of temporally variable environments, fragmentation, and isolation. By damping fluctuations in population size, seed banks increase annual effective population sizes, which will reduce the rate of loss of alleles through genetic drift. Seed banks may also serve as a "genetic repository," which can restore allelic variation to the adult population (Templeton and Levin 1979, Brown and Venable 1986). Furthermore, Ellner and Hairston (1994) have shown that temporally varying selection can promote the maintenance of genetic variation in age-structured populations, such as annual plants with a seed bank. However, direct empirical evidence of seed banks as genetic repositories is scant, but supportive, of this function. Epling et al. (1960) and Gottlieb (1974) demonstrated relative constancy of allele frequencies in two different annual plant populations over 15 and 4 years respectively, and attributed the allele constancy to the presence of a seed bank in each case. A few studies have demonstrated that different alleles are present in the seed bank relative to the adults in the population; thus the seed bank increased population-level genetic variance (Bennington et al. 1991, Vavrek et al. 1991, Tonsor et al. 1993). Seed bank was an important factor in numerically restoring patchily distributed populations of *Phacelia dubia* and for maintaining genetic variation in the population following an extreme population size bottleneck (Del Castillo 1994). Similarly, a large shift in the timing of diapausing egg production was observed in a population of copepods following the extirpation of predatory fish from the pond (Hairston and De Stasio 1988). The rapid shift in timing of egg production resulted from the introduction of genetic variation from the persistent egg bank in the sediment. Not only can the seed bank restore genetic variation, it has also been suggested as a source of genetic novelty (Levin

1990). If mutations occur at a higher rate or accumulate in the seed bank, then seed banks may serve a further evolutionary function of increasing the rate of introduction of new mutations into the population compared with populations without seed banks.

Given that populations may be restored both genetically and numerically through dormancy, the fitness value of seed banks can be expected to increase for plant populations that are experiencing habitat degradation, fragmentation, and/or isolation. Our case study of *Collinsia verna* addresses the ability of the seed bank to restore numerically one study population that exists in an isolated forest fragment and experiences temporal variability in conditions affecting survivorship and reproduction.

Case study: Demographic Stability of an Isolated *Collinsia verna* Population

Natural History

Collinsia verna (Scrophulariaceae), blue-eyed Mary, is a winter annual that grows in floodplains and mesic woods often containing rivers or streams. Typical of winter annuals, seeds of *C. verna* germinate in the autumn, overwinter as small plants, flower with the spring ephemeral flora, and set seed and die by the beginning of June. The species range extends from New York west to lower Michigan and Iowa, and south to Missouri, Arkansas, Kentucky, and West Virginia (Rickett 1966). Given its habitat preference for floodplain forests it is likely that before European settlement of North America, *C. verna* occurred as vast populations or metapopulations following creek beds and river courses. The rich soil and proximity to fresh water found in the habitats of *C. verna* also define desirable habitat for farming. Today, forest fragments containing *C. verna* are usually embedded in a matrix of agricultural fields and pastures that in recent years may have become more developed. In addition, it is likely that habitat fragmentation has significantly reduced population sizes relative to historical numbers. The extremes of population size range from a patch of 7 plants to an estimated 20,000,000 (Greenlee and Rai 1986, S. Kalisz, personal observation, Paul Wegman, West Penn Conservancy, personal communication, January 1996). Seed dispersal in *C. verna* has both a spatial and a temporal component. Primary dispersal of the seeds is passive; the capsules split open and the seed falls to the ground in the vicinity of the parent plant. However, it is has been suggested that the seeds may float and could be carried long distances by water of creeks or streams following storm events or flooding (F. Swink, personal communication). If a substantial number of seeds disperse by water, their movement could be important both in the colonization/recolonization of new habitat patches within a local area and in long-distance migration events, possibly connecting regional metapopulations. Data on water-mediated dispersal is lacking for this species, and most present-day populations are isolated. Thus the land-use patterns in the species range described above have rendered nearly all present-day populations of *C. verna* closed with respect to immigration and emigration, functionally unable to receive or send dispersing migrants as seed. Currently, only a few large populations still exist in West Virginia and Pennsylvania; most populations are both small and separated by large distances or geographical features (Greenlee et al. 1984, personal observation), that preclude seed dispersal among them. In such isolated populations, any seeds that disperse out of the population have zero fitness because they are dispersing into unsuitable habitat. This change in the patterning of suitable habitat for *C. verna* can be expected to shift or has already shifted the selective importance of dormancy within populations; a shift from a reliance on spatial dispersal for recolonization of populations following local extinction (metapopulation function) to a reliance on temporal dispersal (seed dormancy) for recolonization can be expected for this species.

Temporal dispersal has been well documented for *C. verna* (Kalisz 1991, Thiede and Kalisz, unpublished data). *Collinsia verna* seeds in the soil can remain dormant and viable in the field for at least four years before germinating (Kalisz 1991). All populations examined for the presence of a soil seed bank to date have a dormant fraction (Thiede and Kalisz, unpublished data). In demographic projection matrix analyses, the presence of dormant seeds in the seed bank in this species produces age structure that has been shown to influence long-term population dynamics positively under temporally variable environments (Kalisz and McPeek 1992) and to reduce the likelihood of extinction (MacDonald and Watkinson 1981). Dormancy in *C. verna* has a significant genetic component (Thiede 1996). In addition, maternal plant families from the same populations studied by Thiede and Kalisz differ significantly in the proportion of seeds they produced that remained dormant (Kalisz and Thiede, unpublished data). This variation among maternal sibships means that dormancy has significant broad sense heritability. Genetic variation in dormancy in this species would mean that further evolution of this trait is possible.

Collinsia verna maintains relatively high levels of neutral genetic variation within populations. Greenlee and Rai (1986) examined genetic variation in electrophoretic loci within 12 populations of this species in Illinois, Indiana, and Kentucky. Despite small population sizes and total isolation of the populations, the authors found high values of mean heterozygosity per locus (0.33–0.43) and percent polymorphic loci (86–100%). As has been seen in other studies (Leberg 1992, Linhart and Premoli 1994), there was no relationship between population size and heterozygosity. There are two possible explanations for the observed results. First, although it has been assumed that *C. verna* is a self-pollinating species, a high level of outcrossing could help explain the higher than expected levels of heterozygosity. A recent study of the selfing rate in three populations of *C. verna* over four years revealed that this species is moderately to highly outcrossing (Holtsford et al., manuscript). Outcrossing rates among individual populations ranged from 0.63 to 0.93, with relatively consistent outcrossing rates within populations among years (Holtsford et al., manuscript). If *C. verna* as a species is indeed outcrossing, then mating system could explain the high average heterozygosity found by Greenlee and Rai (1986). An additional explanation for the high percentage of polymorphic loci present in all 12 populations observed by Greenlee and Rai (1986) could be storage of alleles in the seed bank (Templeton and Levin 1979) or the accumulation of mutations in stored seeds (Levin 1990). The seed banks of other species have been shown to contain rare alleles and are postulated to contribute to the maintenance of alleles within populations (Bennington et al. 1991, Vavrek et al. 1991, Tonsor et al. 1993, Del Castillo 1994).

Finally, field populations of *C. verna* experience extreme environmental stochasticity that affects population growth rates. For example, in two consecutive years in one Illinois population located in the Raccoon Grove Forest Preserve of Will County, the population growth rate, lambda, was 1.81 and 0.41, respectively (Kalisz and McPeek 1992). Since adult population sizes during those two years were estimated as greater than one million each year, environmental stochasticity is the likely cause of this fourfold difference. In addition, random catastrophes can further change the population dynamics and may be very important in determining persistence of populations (Gabriel and Burger 1992; Lande 1993; Mangel and Tier 1993a, 1994). The north branch of Rock Creek flows through the Raccoon Grove Forest Preserve (see Greenlee et al. 1984 for a detailed site description). During the 1992–1993 field season, a flood occurred at that site, which caused the mortality of all plants and therefore no seed input in the spring of 1993. Stream flow gauges located on streams of similar order to that of Rock Creek that are also in the Kankakee River watershed recorded new record high water levels between autumn 1992 and spring 1993 (Table 13.1). These high waters undoubtedly carried both seedlings and soil containing the seed bank downstream into habitats in which they have no chance of survival. Because there are no upstream populations of *C. verna,* the probability of migrants seeds arriving from upstream locations into Raccoon Grove is also zero. Because we did not directly

Table 13.1. Stream gauge readings for three nearby creeks of similar order in the Kankakee River watershed taken during 1992–1993 indicate record high water levels during this time. The Raccoon Grove study population is on the north branch of Rock Creek, which has no gauging stations on its length. X = Exceeds long-term monthly mean; X* = New high monthly mean record.

Station	J	F	M	A	M	J	J	A	S	O	N	D	J	F	M	A	M	J	J
	1992												1993						
Thorn Creek	X									X	X		X*		X	X			X*
Deer Creek										X	X		X*		X	X	X*		
Hickory Creek			X							X	X		X		X	X		X	X
Kankakee River										X	X	X	X	X	X	X	X	X	X

observe the record floods in 1992, they may not be the only explanation for the total lack of plants at the site in the spring of 1993. The fact remains, however, that an event or series of events occurred between the spring of 1992 (when we had found millions of plants bearing seeds) and the spring of 1993 that resulted in a flowering population size of zero. Therefore seedling emergence following the 1992 catastrophe could only be from the seed bank. The likelihood of recovery and persistence, or decline and extinction, of the Raccoon Grove population will be a function of its ability to recover numerically and genetically through the seed bank when faced with environmental and demographic stochasticity and random catastrophes.

Environmental Stochasticity: Simulations with Collinsia verna *Field Data*

Environmental stochasticity as described above for *C. verna* is a ubiquitous feature of natural populations (Tuljapurkar 1989) that can reduce populations to such low numbers that recovery is unlikely without a bet-hedging strategy such as a seed bank. Unfortunately, long-term demographic data from natural populations documenting fluctuations in size and especially extinction dynamics are rare in the literature. Simulations provide a method for exploring the potential demographic outcomes for species of concern even when only incomplete data regarding long-term demography are present (Menges 1990). This simulation technique has been used previously to investigate the extent to which the seed bank can buffer populations of *C. verna* from extinction in the face of highly variable environments (Kalisz and McPeek 1993).

Two years of field demographic data on adults and seeds in the seed bank that were collected at the Raccoon Grove Forest Preserve of Will County near the town of Monee, Illinois, (Kalisz 1991) were used in the simulations (Kalisz and McPeek 1993) to investigate the extent to which the presence of the seed bank improved persistence of that population given the natural environmental stochasticity. Previous bootstrapped matrix projection analyses of that data (Kalisz and McPeek 1992) indicated that one year had a positive r indicating rapid population growth and one year had a negative r indicating population decline. Accordingly, these years were categorized as "good" (Lambda = 1.80) and "poor" (lambda = 0.41) for population growth, respectively. The *C. verna* population on the flood-plain at Raccoon Grove was visited regularly between 1981 and 1992, and a large adult population was present each spring. Therefore, it is likely that the quantified differences in lambda between years can be attributed to environmental stochasticity, not demographic stochasticity (*sensu* Tuljapurkar 1989). In the previous simulations (Kalisz and McPeek 1993), both the frequency of good and poor years (10% to 90% good) and a range of autocorrelations among years (−0.9 to +0.9) were simulated. No density dependence survival of adult stages was imposed. Two sets of simulations were conducted: one that excluded the seed bank from the matrix and one that included the seed bank.

The results of those simulations over all parameters showed that a higher percentage of the populations persisted when the seed bank was included in the model compared with the simulations without the seed bank. In addition, when the frequency of good years was 50% or less for all autocorrelation levels tested, populations that eventually went extinct persisted longer and had somewhat larger values of r when the seed bank was included in the model compared with the no-seed-bank model. The time to extinction was longest in the simulations in which the environment was most unpredictable (50% good years, 0 autocorrelation). Thus the seed bank was shown to have a positive effect on the population dynamics of *C. verna* given the quantified range of field environments. Those results highlight the potential importance of temporal dispersal for populations experiencing environmental stochasticity.

Random Catastrophes and Population Persistence: Simulations

Here we extend the simulations of Kalisz and McPeek (1993) to examine the roles age-structured seed banks and random catastrophe play in the rate of population extinction for the same *C. verna* population data. We use the same two consecutive years of field data as were used previously and again assigned "quality" to the two years as follows: one in which r was greater than zero (lambda = 1.80) was categorized as "good," and one in which r was less than zero (lambda = 0.41) was categorized as "poor." Figures 13.1a and 13.1b illustrate the demographic quality of the two years with respect to population size when a run of only good years or only poor years is simulated. Simulation of a series of poor years (13.1a) results in rapid extinction of the population, even with an initial population size of 50,000 adults and 350,000 seeds in the seed bank. Simulation of a run of good years (13.1b) shows the population reaching its carrying capacity within 10 years and persisting indefinitely. It is doubtful that field populations experience such runs of good luck or misfortune. However, habitat degradation following fragmentation may result in runs of a higher frequency of poor years. In Figure 13.2 we illustrate a simulation of 50% good/50% poor years. This simulated population went extinct in 50 years with dramatic fluctuations in the size of the adult population (100 individuals to 50,000 individuals) as well as the seed bank (10,000 to 330,000) before declining to zero. In addition to natural environmental stochasticity evident in the two years quantified, the population at Raccoon Grove has experienced complete failure to survive and reproduce in the 1992–1993 growing season. Figure 13.3 illustrates the effect of a single catastrophe year in a run of only good years. In this simulation, the population recovers quickly to its precatastrophe numbers, restored by temporal dispersal from the seed bank.

The series of simulations presented below are similar to those done by Kalisz and McPeek (1993) with the following changes: we varied the frequencies of good and poor years (0.1, 0.3, 0.5, 0.7, and 0.9) but only ran the analyses with no autocorrelation among year types. We introduced density dependence of adults

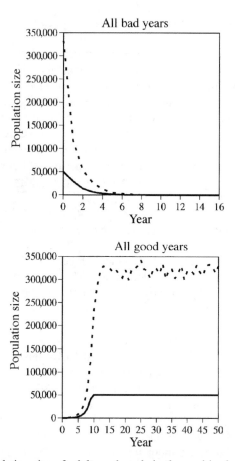

Figure 13.1. Population size of adults and seeds in the seed bank using demographic projections of all "poor" years (lambda = 0.41) or all "good" years (lambda = 1.8) years. Data are from two years of field data from a natural population of *Collinsia verna*. Solid line represents the adults; dotted line represents the seeds in the seed bank. A. Population declines to extinction within six years because the seed bank is depleted by a run of poor years. B. With only "good" years, within ten years the population increases to its carrying capacity of adults (50,000), with substantial increases in the seed bank. There is no carrying capacity imposed on the seed bank.

into the system (carrying capacity). Population size for the adult plants was capped at 50,000 individuals, while the number of seeds in the seed bank was allowed to vary freely. Seeds persisted in the seed bank up to three years, with no possibility of continued dormancy beyond that. Finally, we included catastrophe years (0 adult survival = 0 seed production by adults) in the simulations with possible frequencies of 0, 0.005, 0.01, 0.05, and 0.1.

For each regime of good and poor years, we performed 50 replicate simulations

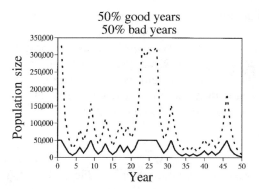

Figure 13.2. Example of fluctuations in population size due to a variation in year quality. This simulation was run with 50% good/50% bad years and no autocorrelation among years. Solid line represents the adults; dotted line represents the seeds in the seed bank. This simulation ended in extinction at 50 years.

of 1,000 iterations/replicate (years/replicate). For each iteration, the initial year type (good or poor) is chosen at random. A bootstrapped sample of the original data for the year type was made and the population transition matrix constructed from the bootstrapped samples according to the methods of Kalisz and McPeek (1992). The transition matrix was then multiplied by the initial vector of stage/age abundances [$N_0 = 100$ adults] to determine the vector of stage/age abundances in the next year. The next year type was determined, a new bootstrapped matrix was constructed for that year type, and the process was repeated. See McPeek and Kalisz (1993) for a detailed description of the matrix bootstrapping methods. A population was considered extinct when there were no individuals left in any age class. Varying the starting conditions from 10 to 10,000 individuals was found to have no effect on the outcome.

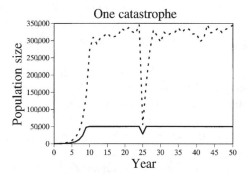

Figure 13.3. The effect of a single catastrophe resulting in no seed production in year 25 in a run of only "good" years. Under these simulated conditions, the population recovers to its precatastrophe size in two years.

The population descriptors we recorded during each simulation were percent extinctions, expressed as the fraction of the 50 replicated runs that went extinct for each simulated distribution of year types and catastrophes; the year in which each population went extinct; the average years of extinction for populations that went extinct over the 50 replicated runs; population size in year 1000 for those populations that persisted the entire run; and average population size for those populations that persisted over the 50 replicated runs.

Simulation Results

When the frequency of good years was less than 50%, all runs went extinct for all frequencies of complete reproductive failure (Figure 13.4, top three panels), and these extinctions occurred rapidly (Figure 13.5, top three panels). For all frequencies of complete reproductive failure, the 0.1 good years simulations went extinct in less than 10 years, the 0.3 good years simulations went extinct in less than 20 years and all 0.5 good years simulations went extinct in less than 75 years (Figure 13.5). Thus in an environment in which the "good" years are less than or equal to 50% with random catastrophes, the three–to five–year seed bank of *C. verna* cannot restore populations size, and extinction is always the outcome.

When the frequency of good years was 70% or 90%, the seed bank prevented extinction under some frequencies of catastrophe (Figure 13.4, bottom two panels). When the frequency of good years was 70%, all populations persisted in both the no-catastrophes runs and in those with catastrophe frequency of 0.005. Only 2 of 50 runs failed to persist in the 0.01 catastrophe frequency. However, all populations went extinct when the catastrophe frequency was 0.1. Similarly, when the frequency of good years was 90%, no extinctions occurred with 0.005, and 0.05 catastrophe frequency; only 1 run in 50 went extinct at the 0.01 catastrophe level; and 20% of the simulations went extinct when the catastrophe frequency was 0.1. Those populations that did go extinct in the 70% good years (the 0.01, 0.05, and 0.1 catastrophe levels) and the 90% good years (the 0.01 and 0.1 catastrophe levels; Figure 13.4, bottom two panels), persisted significantly longer when compared with the rapid extinctions experienced in the simulations with 10% to 50% good years (Figure 13.5, compare top three panels to bottom two panels).

For populations that did persist until the end of the simulations (only in 70% and 90% good years), the frequency of catastrophe substantially altered both the number of adults and the number of seeds in the seed bank (Figure 13.6). When catastrophic years are less than one in ten with a 70% good year frequency, populations persist but the number of adults is depressed relative to the carrying capacity. When catastrophic years are one in ten, even with a 90% good year frequency population size of the adults is diminished to well below the carrying capacity (50,000; Figure 13.6), and the number of seeds in the seed bank is nearly halved. Extinction of the population occurred under all but the most restricted conditions.

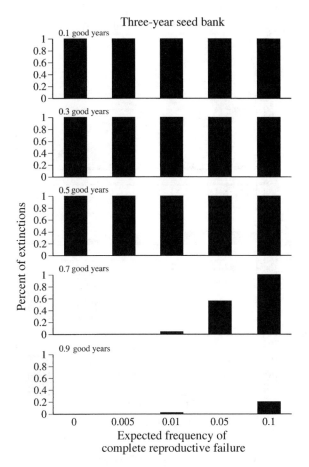

Figure 13.4. Histogram of the percent of extinctions for 50 runs/simulations for a range of expected frequencies of complete reproductive failure (catastrophe). Five frequencies of "good" years were simulated. All runs go extinct when the frequency of good years is less than or equal to 50%. Percent of extinctions is low for 70% and 90% good years but increases significantly with increasing catastrophe frequency.

The three-year seed bank quantified for the Raccoon Grove population is not sufficient to restore the population numerically under most simulated conditions. However, the demographic simulations performed here do not allow an evolutionary response within the population to occur as a result of either the fragmentation or the catastrophe. In all populations of *C. verna* studied to date, it is known that maternal families differ significantly in the extent to which their offspring remain in the seed bank (Kalisz and Thiede, unpublished data) and that this dormancy is heritable (Thiede 1996). Therefore, an evolutionary response to selection for dormancy could occur in this species. Since all immediately germi-

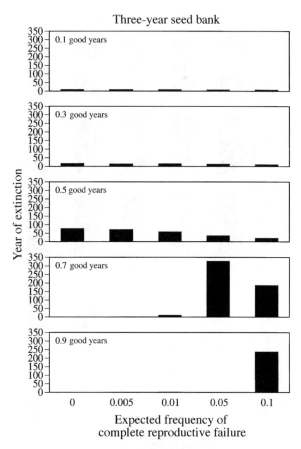

Figure 13.5. Histogram of the average year of extinctions for 50 runs/simulations for a range of expected frequencies of complete reproductive failure (catastrophe). Five frequencies of "good" years were simulated. All runs go extinct quickly when the frequency of good years is less than or equal to 50%. In general, populations that do go extinct persist longer when the fraction of good years was 70% and 90%.

nating seeds died as a result of the 1992–1993 catastrophe and the population is in an isolated forest fragment, emergence of seedlings in the autumn of 1993 in Raccoon Grove could only have been from seeds that had the propensity to remain dormant at least one year in the seed bank. Thus, this catastrophe imposed a significant natural selection event, favoring those individuals that were dormant. This catastrophe can be regarded as truncation selection for dormancy. Truncation selection can shift the mean value of a heritable trait expressed in the population by several standard deviations within one generation (Falconer 1989). Thus, given the genetic basis for dormancy in this species and the likely strong selection favoring dormant individuals, it is possible that the average length of seed dor-

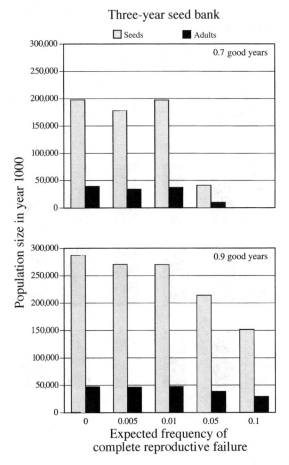

Figure 13.6. Histogram of the average population size for those populations which persisted 1,000 years. Numbers of seeds in the seed bank (hatched bars) and adults (solid bars) are presented for the range of expected frequencies of complete reproductive failure (catastrophe) for 70% and 90% "good" years. Results from 70% good year runs show that the population of adults does not reach its density-dependent limit, even with no catastrophes, and the number of dormant seeds is reduced substantially when compared to the 90% good years runs.

mancy in this population has increased as a result of the 1993 catastrophe. To examine the potential for altering the demographic outcome for this Illinois population through an evolved response in the length of seed dormancy, we repeated the simulations described above using a matrix that extended the persistence of the seed bank from three years to six years. Therefore, the stage/age classes in the model include seeds 1, 2, 3, 4, 5, and 6 years old and adult plants

1, 2, 3, 4, 5, 6, and 7 years old. Plants age as a function of their time spent in the seed bank before emergence.

Simulations Including the Evolved Seed Bank

The presence of a seed bank of six years' duration did not affect the percentage of extinctions when frequencies of good years were 0.5 or less (compare Figures 13.4 and 13.7, top three panels); all populations in those simulations eventually

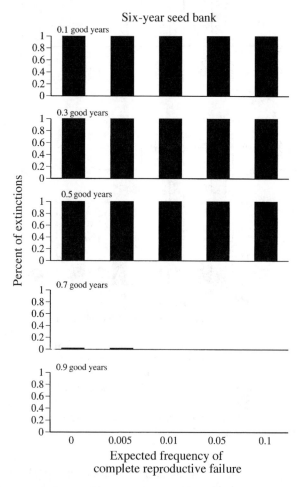

Figure 13.7. Histogram of the percent of extinctions for 50 runs/simulations for a range of expected frequencies of complete reproductive failure (catastrophe) with a six-year seed bank. Five frequencies of "good" years were simulated. All runs go extinct when the frequency of good years is less than or equal to 50%. Percent of extinctions is negligible for 70% good years and zero for 90% good years.

went extinct. There was also no change in year of extinction for the 0.1 and 0.3 good year frequencies with increase in seed bank duration. However, the increased duration of the seed bank did substantially increase the length of time a population persisted before going extinct under some simulated conditions (compare Figures 13.5 and 13.8). For the 0.5 good years simulations, the six-year seed bank resulted in a doubling of the persistence time for all catastrophe conditions. Populations persisted up to 150 years in the 50% good years simulations.

However, the increase in seed bank duration had a significant positive effect

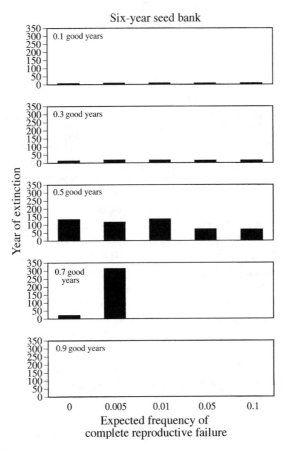

Figure 13.8. Histogram of the average year of extinctions for 50 runs/simulations for a range of expected frequencies of complete reproductive failure (catastrophe) with a six-year seed bank. Five frequencies of "good" years were simulated. All runs go extinct quickly when the frequency of good years is less than or equal to 30%. Persistence time is doubled for 50% good year run relative to three-year seed bank runs (Figure 13.5). Only two populations in the 70% good year simulations went extinct and no populations went extinct in the 90% good year simulations.

on the demographic outcomes when good years were more frequent than 50%. Simulations with 0.7 and 0.9 good year frequencies examined over all catastrophe levels experienced only two and zero extinctions, respectively (compare Figures 13.4 and 13.7, bottom two panels, to see the effect of the increased dormancy). The increased duration of the seed bank positively influenced both the number of simulated populations persisting (Figure 13.7) and the number of individuals in both the seed and adult stages at higher catastrophe frequencies (compare Figures 13.6 and 13.9 at catastrophe levels 0.05 and 0.1).

Prospects for *Collinsia verna* at Raccoon Grove

Population Persistence

Two types of data collected before 1992 indicate that the Raccoon Grove Forest Preserve population of *C. verna* has been severely reduced in size by the 1993 catastrophe (Kalisz et al., manuscript). First, natural seedling densities prior to the catastrophe were 925 and 1,006 seedlings per m^2 for 1982–1983 and 1983–1984, respectively (Kalisz 1991). Second, experimental exclusion of seed input into the study plots in 1982 allowed the estimation of number of seeds that would naturally emerge from the seed bank. On average, 356 seedlings per m^2 emerged in those seed input exclusion plots. In sharp contrast, the average density of seedlings emerging in the fall after the catastrophe was only 16 seedlings per m^2 in our study plots. Flood water undoubtedly washed away both plants and significant amounts of topsoil containing the seed bank.

Besides low total numbers of plants emerging from the seed bank, population size was decremented by low survival of the plants. Those that did emerge had an average probability of survival to reproduction similar to that of the "poor" year quantified in the demographic analyses (Kalisz and McPeek 1992; 19% survival in good year versus 12% survival in poor year and 13% survival postcatastrophe). Diminished population sizes may create conditions in which the influence of demographic stochasticity may be manifested for this population.

In general, the likelihood of extinction for small populations is expected to be higher than that for large populations (Gabriel and Burger 1992, Holsinger 1993, Meefe and Carroll 1994). For single, isolated populations, Lande (1993) has shown that if long-run population growth rate is positive and populations are of modest size, long-term persistence is possible even in the face of random catastrophes. However, Mangel and Tier (1993a, 1993b, 1994) stress the likelihood of extinctions for most populations, regardless of size. Unfortunately, there is no theoretical generality that can be made regarding populations facing environmental stochasticity and/or random catastrophes.

Based on our simulations, we believe that the population at Raccoon Grove will probably go extinct. It should be stressed that these simulations are based on three years of field data: one "good," one "poor," and one catastrophic. The

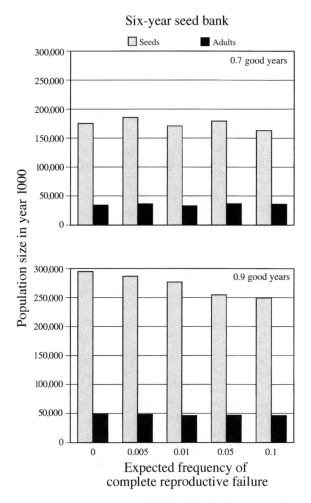

Figure 13.9. Histogram of the average population size for those populations that persisted 1,000 years with a six-year seed bank. Numbers of seeds in the seed bank (hatched bars) and adults (solid bars) are presented for the range of expected frequencies of complete reproductive failure (catastrophe) for 70% and 90% "good" years. Compared with the three-year seed bank simulations (Figure 3.7), populations maintain higher densities of both seeds and adults.

actual frequencies of relatively good, poor, or catastrophic years are not known for this population nor is it known if the actual range of year types is even broader than that which has been quantified. Knowledge of the actual distribution of temporal variation including data on catastrophes are rarely collected (but see Menges 1990, 1992). However, this type of long-term data that examines the range of environmental stochasticity experienced by single populations is invaluable for understanding factors influencing population persistence.

Changes in Mating

While persistence or extinction of this population remains unclear, other significant changes in the ecology of the population at the Raccoon Grove Forest Preserve have been documented postcatastrophe (Kalisz et al., manuscript). Decrease in population size associated with fragmentation or random catastrophes as described above for *C. verna* can have fundamental ecological consequences for plants. Because many flowering plants are dependent on pollen vectors for cross-fertilization, and because floral density is expected to be directly related to pollinator visitation rates per flower (Rathcke 1983), populations with low numbers are likely to experience significantly lower pollinator visitation rates, potentially resulting in low numbers of seeds produced and/or an increase in self-pollination. Between 1990 and 1994, a study was conducted at Raccoon Grove and two other *C. verna* populations to estimate variation in outcrossing rates among populations and years (Holtsford et al., manuscript). Data precatastrophe at Raccoon Grove indicated a high level of outcrossing, $t = 0.98$ in 1990 and $t = 0.92$ in 1992. Postcatastrophe, all the plants that survived to reproduce in 1994 were derived from dormant seeds in the seed bank. In that year the outcrossing rate was severely decremented: $t = 0.67$ in 1994. One explanation for the 20% to 30% increase in the selfing rate could be a decrease in pollinator visitation rates as a function of low plant density, a case of the Allee effect. An alternative, but not mutually exclusive, explanation is that the selfing rate increased as a correlated response to selection for dormancy. If floral traits that confer a higher selfing rate are genetically correlated to traits that confer dormancy, an increase in selfing rate could have occurred as a correlated response to selection for increased dormancy. It is interesting to note that there were no changes in the allele frequencies for the isozymes used to estimate the outcrossing rate (Holtsford, manuscript), suggesting that allele frequencies in the population before the catastrophe were maintained in the seed bank.

The broader implications for plant populations in forest fragments are great. Plants in small populations could experience the loss of a whole spectrum of coevolved interactions (Oleson and Jain 1994), such that fragmentation and isolation could result in the "coordinated extinctions of mutualists" for plant populations and associated animals. If mutualistic relationships erode due to changes in availability of suitable habitat for pollinators, seed dispersers, and other associated species upon fragmentation, population and community-level relationships including nonmutualists such as herbivores or granivores could also be lost. This kind of cascading degradation and local extinction of a species association has been documented in a fragmented *Phragmites* habitat (Tscharntke 1992).

Conclusions

When fragmentation is extreme and populations are isolated, metapopulation function can be completely eroded. Dispersal or migration distances among habitat patches may exceed dispersal capacity such that the probability of reaching a suitable habitat for colonization is effectively zero. This is especially true for organisms like plants that are sessile and those that rely on external vectors to achieve dispersal into new habitat. This isolation makes populations more vulnerable to extinction regardless of population size. Even large isolated populations may fail to persist due to the effects of environmental stochasticity or random catastrophe if the long-run growth rate of the population is negative (Lande 1993). For this case study with *C. verna,* it is likely that changes in the landscape-level connectivity of populations (metapopulations) after European settlement along with environmental changes that accompany fragmentation (both in the mean and variance of environmental quality) have altered the selective importance of traits, especially those associated with spatial dispersal versus temporal dispersal (dormancy) for this species. Future persistence of this population depends on the ability of the seed bank to restore the population numerically and genetically and the potential for the further evolution of long-term dormancy.

Habitat fragmentation is a ubiquitous secondary outcome of land development practices in the Midwest and beyond. The breakdown of metapopulation function through fragmentation or complete isolation of subpopulations of species previously functioning in a metapopulation context is likely to be a common outcome of development. In general, species whose metapopulation functions are impacted by isolation can be expected to experience selective pressures for alternative bet-hedging strategies instead of relying on dispersal. The evolutionary plausibility of evolving a bet-hedging strategy that enhances fitness and thus population persistence depends on the interaction of demographic and evolutionary factors. These factors include population size, magnitude of the environmental change, and the degree of genetic variation for selected traits (Lynch and Lande 1993, Gomulkiewicz and Holt (1995). However, overall extinction probabilities remain high for isolated populations. Clearly, important considerations in the conservation of any metapopulation species will be the retention of physical features that retain or enhance metapopulation function. Size and configuration of the preserve are core variables. It is obvious that larger areas of land are more likely to contain multiple subpopulations than are small areas. Perhaps the best plan for the conservation of metapopulation species is to conserve now, because recovery plans with reintroduced species rarely succeed.

Acknowledgments

We thank Sally A. McConkey, PE of the Illinois State Water Survey, for stream-reading data and two reviewers whose comments improved this chapter. This work is funded by an NSF grant to S. Kalisz and M. A. McPeek.

References

Bennington, C.C., J.B. McGraw, and M.C. Vavrek. 1991. Ecological genetic variation in seed banks. II. Phenotypic and genetic differences between young and old subpopulations of *Luzula parviflora. Journal of Ecology* 79:627–643.

Binder, B.J., and D.M. Anderson. 1990. Biochemical composition and metabolic activity of *Scrippsiella trochoidea* (*Dinophyceae*) resting cysts. *Journal of Phycology,* 26:289–298.

Brown, J.S., and D.L. Venable. 1986. Evolutionary ecology of seed-bank annuals in temporally varying environments. *American Naturalist* 127(1):31–47.

Chesson, P.L. 1983. Coexistence of competitors in a stochastic environment: the storage effect. In H.I. Freedman, and C. Strobeck, eds. *Population Biology.* Lecture Notes in Biomathematics no. 52, Springer-Verlag, Berlin, 188–198.

Chesson, P.L. 1984. The storage effect in stochastic population models. In S.A. Levin, and T.G. Hallum, eds. *Mathematical Ecology.* Lecture Notes in Biomathematics no. 54. Springer-Verlag, Berlin, 76–89.

Chesson, P.L. 1985. Coexistence of competitors in spatially and temporally varying environments: A look at the combined effects of different sorts of variability. *Theoretical Population Biology* 28:263–287.

Cohen, D. 1966. Optimizing reproduction in a randomly varying environment. *Journal of Theoretical Biology* 12:119–129.

Cohen, D. 1967. Optimizing reproduction in a randomly varying environment when a correlation exists between the conditions at the time a choice has to be made and the subsequent outcome. *Journal of Theoretical Biology* 16:1–14.

Cohen, D., and S.A. Levin. 1991. Dispersal in patchy environments: The effects of temporal and spatial structure. *Theoretical Population Biology* 39:63–99.

De Mauro, M.M. 1993. Relationship of breeding system to rarity in the lakeside daisy (*Hymenoxys acaulis* var. *glabra*). *Conservation Biology* 7:542–550.

Del Castillo, R.F. 1994. Factors influencing the genetic structure of *Phacelia dubia,* a species with a seed bank and large fluctuations in population size. *Heredity* 72:446–458.

den Boer, P.J. 1987. Spreading the risk and stabilization of animal numbers. *Acta Biotheoretica* 18:165–194.

DeStasio, B.T. 1989. The seed bank of a freshwater crustacean: copepodology for the plant ecologist. *Ecology* 70:1377–1389.

Dingle, H. 1978. Migration and diapause in tropical, temperate, and island milkweed bugs. In H. Dingle, ed. *Evolution of Insect Migration and Diapause.* Springer, New York.

Edenhard, T. 1991. Colonization in metapopulations: A review of theory and observations. *Biological Journal of the Linnean Society* 42:105–121.

Ellner, S. 1985a. ESS germination strategies in randomly varying environments. I. Logistic-type models. *Theoretical Population Biology* 28:50–79.

Ellner, S. 1985b. ESS germination strategies in randomly varying environments. II. Reciprocal yield-law models. *Theoretical Population Biology* 28:80–116.

Ellner, S., and N.G. Hairston. 1994. Role of overlapping generations in maintaining genetic variation in a fluctuating environment. *American Naturalist* 143:403–417.

Epling, C., H. Lewis, and F.M. Ball. 1960. The breeding group and seed storage: A study in population dynamics. *Evolution* 14:238–255.

Falconer, D.S. 1989. *Introduction to Quantitative Genetics*. 3rd ed. Longman, New York.

Gabriel, W., and R. Burger. 1992. Survival of small populations under demographic stochasticity. *Theoretical Population Biology* 41:44–71.

Gadgil, M. 1971. Dispersal: population consequences and evolution. *Ecology* 52:253–261.

Gomulkiewicz, R., and R.D. Holt. 1995. When does evolution by natural selection prevent extinction? *Evolution* 49(1):201–207.

Gottlieb, L.D. 1974. Genetic stability in a peripheral isolate of *Stephanomeria exigua* spp. *coronaria* that fluctuates in population size. *Genetics* 76:551–556.

Greenlee, J.K., and K.S. Rai. 1986. Population differentiation in *Collinsia verna*. Nuttal (Scrophulariaceae): A multifaceted approach. *Genetica* 71:51–61.

Greenlee, J.K., K.S. Rai, and A.D. Floyd. 1984. Intraspecific variation in nuclear DNA content in *Collinsia verna* Nutt. (Scrophulariaceae). *Heredity* 52:235–242.

Hairston, N.G., Jr. and B.T. De Stasio, Jr. 1988. Rate of evolution slowed by a dormant propagule pool. *Nature* 336:239–242.

Hanski, I., and M. Gilpin. 1991. Metapopulation dynamics: Brief history and conceptual domain. *Biological Journal of the Linnean Society* 42:3–16.

Hanski, I. 1991. Single species metapopulation dynamics: concepts, models and observations. *Biological Journal of the Linnean Society* 42:17–38.

Holsinger, K.S. 1993. The evolutionary dynamics of fragmented plant populations. In P.M. Kareiva, J.G. Kingsolver, and R.B. Huey, eds. *Biotic Interactions and Global Change*. Sinauer Associates, Sunderland, Mass., 198–216.

Huntly, N., and P.L. Chesson. 1989. Short-term instabilities and long-term community dynamics. *Trends in Ecology and Evolution* 4:293–298.

Kalisz, S. 1991. Experimental determination of seed bank age structure in the winter annual *Collinsia verna*. *Ecology* 72(2):575–585.

Kalisz, S., and M.A. McPeek. 1992. Demography of an age structured annual: Resampled projection matrices, elasticity analyses and seed bank effects. *Ecology* 73:1082–1093.

Kalisz, S., and M.A. McPeek. 1993. Extinction dynamics, population growth and seed banks. An example using an age-structured annual. *Oecologia* 95:314–320.

Klinkhamer, P.G.L., T.J. DeJong, J.A. Metz, and J.Val. 1987. Life history tactics of annual organisms: The joint effects of dispersal and delayed germination. *Theoretical Population Biology* 32:127–156.

Kuno, E. 1981. Dispersal and the persistence of populations in unstable habitats: A theoretical note. *Oecologia* (Berlin) 49:123–126.

Lande, R. 1993. Risks of population extinction from demographic and environmental stochasticity and random catastrophes. *American Naturalist* 142:911–927.

Leberg, P.L. 1992. Effects of population bottlenecks on genetic diversity as measured by allozyme electrophoresis. *Evolution* 46(2):477–494.

Leck, M.A., V.T. Parker, and R.L. Simpson. 1989. *Ecology of Soil Seed Banks.* Academic Press, San Diego, 462.

Levin, D.A. 1990. The seed bank as a source of genetic novelty in plants. *American Naturalist* 135:563–572.

Levin, S.A., Cohen, D., and Hastings, A. 1984. Dispersal strategies in patchy environments. *Theoretical Population Biology* 26:165–191.

Levins, R. 1969. Dormancy as an adaptive strategy. *Symposia of the Society for Experimental Biology* 23:1–10.

Linhart, Y.B., and A.C. Premoli. 1994. Genetic variation in central and disjunct populations of *Lilium parryi. Canadian Journal of Botany* 72:79–85.

Lynch, M., and R.S. Lande. 1993. Evolution and extinction in response to environmental change. In P.M. Kareiva, J.G. Kingsolver, and R.B. Huey, eds. *Biotic Interactions and Global Change.* Sinauer Associates, Sunderland, Mass., 234–250.

McCauley, D.E. 1993. Genetic consequences of extinction and recolonization in fragmented habitats. In P.M. Kareiva, J.G. Kingsolver, and R.B. Huey, eds. *Biotic Interactions and Global Change.* Sinauer Associates, Sunderland, Mass., 217–233.

MacDonald, N., and A.R. Watkinson. 1981. Models of an annual plant population with a seed bank. *Journal of Theoretical Biology* 93:643–653.

McPeek, M.A. 1989. Differential dispersal tendencies among Enallagma damselflies (*Odonata: Coenagrionidae*) inhabiting different habitats. *Oikos* 56:187–195.

McPeek, M.A., and R.D. Holt. 1992. The evolution of dispersal in spatially and temporally varying environments. *American Naturalist* 140:1010–1027.

Mangel, M., and C. Tier. 1993a. Dynamics of metapopulations with demographic stochasticity and environmental catastrophes. *Theoretical Population Biology* 44:1–31.

Mangel, M., and C. Tier. 1993b. A simple direct method for finding persistence times of populations and application to conservation problems. *Proceedings of the National Academy of Science of the United States of America* 90:1083–1086.

Mangel, M., and C. Tier. 1994. Four facts every conservation biologist should know about persistence. *Ecology* 75:607–614.

Meffe, G.K., and C.R. Carroll. 1994. *Principles of Conservation Biology.* Sinauer Associates, Sunderland, Mass.

Menges, E.S. 1990. Population viability analysis for an endangered plant. *Conservation Biology* 4:52–62.

Menges, E.S. 1992. Stochastic modeling of extinction in plant populations. In P.L. Fiedler, and S.K. Jain, eds. *Conservation biology: the theory and practice of nature conservation, preservation and management.* Chapman and Hall, New York, 253–276.

Olesen, J.M., and S.K. Jain. 1994. D: Fragmented plant populations and their lost interactions. In V. Loeschcke, J. Tomiuk and S.K. Jain eds. *Conservation Genetics.* Birkhauser Verlag, Basel, 417–426.

Oliviere, I., D. Couvet, and P.H. Gouyon. 1990. The genetics of transient populations: Research at the metapopulation level. *Trends in Ecology and Evolution* 5(7):207–210.

Ouburg, N.J. 1993. Isolation, population size and extinction—the classical and metapopulational approach applied to vascular plants along the Dutch Rhine-system. *Oikos* 66:298–308.

Phillipi, T. 1993. Bet-hedging germination of desert annuals: Beyond the first year. *American Naturalist* 142:474–487.

Philippi, T., and J. Seger. 1989. Hedging one's evolutionary bets, revisited. *Trends in Ecology and Evolution* 4:41–44.

Rathcke, B. 1983. Competition and facilitation among plants for pollination. In L. Real, ed. *Pollination Biology*. Academic Press, Orlando, 305–329.

Reese, M. 1994. Delayed germination of seeds: A look at the effects of adult longevity, the timing of reproduction and population age/stage structure. *American Naturalist* 144:43–64.

Ricket, W.H. 1966. *Wild Flowers of the United States*. Vol. 1. Part 2. McGraw-Hill, New York, 401–402.

Schneller, J.J. 1988. Spore bank. Dark germination and gender determination in *Athyrium* and *Dryopteris:* Results and implications for population biology of pteridophyta. *Botanica Helvetica* 98:77–86.

Schneller, J.J., C.H. Haufler, and T.A. Ranker. 1990. Antheridiogen and natural gametophyte populations. *American Fern Journal* 80:143–152.

Seger, J., and H.J. Brockmann. 1987. What is bet hedging? *Oxford Surveys in Evolutionary Biology* 4:182–211.

Shaffer, M.L. 1981. Minimum population sizes for species conservation. *BioScience* 31:131–134.

Silvertown, J. 1988. The demographic and evolutionary consequences of seed dormancy. In A.J. Davy, M.J. Hutchings, and A.R. Watkinson, eds. *Plant Population Ecology*. Blackwell Scientific Publications, Oxford.

Templeton, A.R., and D.A. Levin. 1979. Evolutionary consequences of seed pools. *American Naturalist* 114:232–249.

Thiede, D.A. 1996. *An Empirical Examination of Evolutionary Models of Maternal Effects*. Ph.D. thesis. Michigan State University.

Tonsor, S.J., S. Kalisz, J. Fisher, and T.P. Holtsford. 1993. A life-history based study of population genetic structure: Seed bank to adults in *Plantago lanceolata. Evolution* 47:833–843.

Tscharntke, T. 1992. Fragmentation of Phragmites habitats, minimum viable population size, habitat suitability, and local extinction of moths, midges, flies, aphids, and birds. *Conservation Biology* 6(4):530–535.

Tuljapurkar, S.D. 1989. An uncertain life: Demography in random environments. *Theoretical Population Biology* 35:227–294.

Vavrek, M.C., J.B. McGraw and C.C. Bennington. 1991. Ecological genetic variation in seed banks. III. Phenotypic and genetic differences between young and old seed populations of *Carex bigelowii. Journal of Ecology* 79:645–662.

Venable, D.L. 1985. The evolutionary ecology of seed heteromorphism. *American Naturalist* 126:577–595.

Venable, D.L., and L. Lawlor. 1980. Delayed germination and escape in desert annuals: Escape in space and time. *Oecologia* 46:272–282.

Verboom, J., and K. Lankester. 1991. Linking local and regional dynamics in stochastic metapopulation models. *Biological Journal of the Linnean Society* 42:39–55.

Westoby, M. 1981. How diversified seed germination behavior is selected. *American Naturalist* 118:882–885.

14

Effects of Livestock Grazing on Forest Habitats

Ann Dennis
USDA Forest Service, Pacific Southwest Research Station, Berkeley, CA.
94701

Introduction

The presettlement landscape of the Midwest was a mosaic of prairie, woodland and savanna (Ebinger, Chapter 1, and Robertson et al., Chapter 2, this volume). Today, row crops and pasture dominate this landscape, and native vegetation occurs mostly as woodland along streams or on terrain too steep to plow. Although some remnants of native vegetation are protected in parks or nature preserves, these mostly occur as small and scattered islands. Although protected areas are central to strategies for protecting rare species and communities, a large land base is required to maintain regional biotas, ecological dynamics, and potential for range adjustment and evolution. (Noss and Cooperrider 1994). In the Midwest this land base of natural habitats is privately owned. For example, small, privately owned woodlands (including farm woodlands) account for about 70% of all land remaining in native vegetation in Illinois (Neely and Heister 1987, Iverson 1989). For this reason, privately owned woodlands, including those used for grazing, are a major element in long-term conservation in the Midwest, and farm activities that affect woodland habitat function deserve specific attention.

In the Midwest, farm woodlands were traditionally used as shelter for livestock as part of a farming operation that combined crop and livestock production. Since the 1960s, confined hog production and specialized cattle feeding has grown rapidly. As a result, on-farm livestock feeding has declined substantially and has, in some regions, ceased to be a typical element of farm operations. Production of calves for sale to off-farm feedlots, on the other hand, has not declined and remains an important element in many Midwestern farm operations. Decline in on-farm livestock feeding has resulted in a cessation of woodland use in many farm operations. Calf production, on the other hand, has resulted in continued grazing of pastures that include woodland areas. Efforts to remove marginal cropland from production has, in fact, increased forest land cover in much of the Midwest (e.g., Hahn 1987). Livestock use of woodlands continues to be a major type of agricultural use affecting Midwestern woodland habitats. Owing to differences in farm operations, however, the current use of woodlands differs from that prevalent in the past. In general, current grazing is less intensive and involves relatively more cattle and fewer pigs.

It is well known that livestock use can have severe adverse effects on woodlands as habitat for native species (McQuilkin and Scholten 1989, Flood et al. 1977). Several specific matters of concern have been identified. Heavy use by livestock can cause diverse assemblages of understory plants to be replaced by ubiquitous weedy species (Diller 1937, Marks 1942, Steinbrenner 1951). Grazing can also reduce structural diversity of understory vegetation, resulting in lower habitat quality for many woodland-dependent vertebrates and reduced species richness for the site as a whole (Day 1930, Dambach 1944). Livestock use can cause increased soil erosion, which, in turn, damages aquatic habitats and reduces site productivity (Johnson 1952). Further, livestock use can cause destruction of the woodland itself by severely injuring mature trees and eliminating seedlings and saplings (DenUyl and Day 1939).

In the early 1930s there was a major effort to draw attention to the problem of livestock damage to woodland resources. Drawing on photographs and data from woodlands showing different levels of livestock damage, Day and DenUyl (1932) described woodland degradation by livestock use as a series of discrete stages of decline and death. Day and DenUyl explicitly pointed out that their intention was to illustrate the problems associated with intensive production involving feeding of harvested forages. This distinction was lost, however, as their stage theory was widely applied in the subsequent decades in both the popular and technical literature (e.g., Diller 1937, Chandler 1940, Dambach 1944, Steinbrenner 1951). Embedded in this body of research on livestock effects in forests of the Midwest is the implicit assumption that differences in condition between grazed sites are due primarily to time since initiation of livestock use, rather than to differences in management practices.

In trying to understand the implications of varied grazing management practices, Day and DenUyl's stage theory provides little information on the link between specific grazing practices and ecological impacts in current farm woodlands. In fact, by portraying the impacts of the most intensive types of livestock use as the inevitable result of any type of livestock use, this literature has supported a persistent misperception on the part of land managers that deforestation is less destructive of ecological values than continued grazing of hardwood stands (e.g., Ahlgren et al. 1946, Guise 1950, Reeves 1989). This misperception can only contribute to further fragmentation and loss of woodland habitats. If we are to assess the actual and potential role of grazed farm woodlands in the broader picture of habitat conservation, we need information that allows us to distinguish implications of different management practices.

This study is a survey that looks broadly at several kinds of impacts cattle have on woodland habitats in order to identify differences associated with contrasting pasture-based cattle production management practices. The purpose was to identify the most pressing issues and lay the groundwork for further investigation.

The central focus was an analysis of floristic differences associated with contrasting grazing management practices within the study area. I use this preliminary assessment to address the implications of farm woodland management for conservation of floristic diversity at a local scale. My purpose is not to assess the impacts of management practices on undisturbed vegetation, given that virtually all woodlands in this region have had major impacts from livestock use in the past. Instead, this study examines the implication of alternative practices for native plant species on sites with histories of disturbance typical of farm woodlands in the region.

Setting

Historical and geographic setting are important elements in evaluating particular patterns of habitat maintenance or loss. In southern Illinois, where this study was conducted, conversion of native vegetation to cropland has been less complete than in other parts of the Midwest corn belt. Here, cattle and forage crop production are major components of the local agricultural economy, and woodland remnants interfinger with open pasture and cropland on hilly terrain. The farm woodlands in this region are for the most part remnants of oak-hickory forest, a common forest type in much of Illinois and Missouri, northern Arkansas, western Tennessee and Kentucky, and southern Indiana and Ohio (Kuchler 1966). Species characteristic of this community, although showing varying degrees of site specificity at a fine scale, tend to be widely distributed geographically. The flora is diverse but contains few endemic species compared with other regions (Gentry 1986). As a consequence, in spite of drastic loss of habitat in the last 150 years, few species losses have occurred at a regional scale. At smaller scales, however, species losses have been dramatic, especially for species that are least tolerant of the types of ecological change associated with settlement and agriculture, as well as for species restricted to the kinds of sites that are most in demand as cropland. Each loss of a local population represents to some degree a loss of local adaptations. Cumulatively, these losses add up to substantial loss of genetic resources and substantial threats to long-term viability of species (Ledig 1993).

Major changes in ecological factors have occurred within the life span of the trees that form the current overstory dominants in forests of this region. Fire, both naturally occurring and set by humans, was an important element in the ecology of these woodlands until the present century. Logging in the 1800s has also had a major influence on the overstory composition we see today. The native fauna of forest habitats in this region once included forest bison *(Bison bison)* and elk *(Cervus canadensis),* but their grazing impacts were undoubtedly quite different from those of the domestic livestock that have replaced them. Whitetail deer *(Odocoileus virginianus)* are still present, though populations have undergone major fluctuations in this century (Anderson, chapter 6, this volume). The system under examination here is not a static one, but one that is responding to major changes in a number of important ecological factors.

Farms in this region are typically moderate-sized single-family operations. Many farms emphasize cattle production and devote the majority of land to forage crops and pasture, but also produce corn and other crops. In this region, the prevalent type of cattle husbandry involves maintenance of stable herds of mature cows, with a few bulls, for the purpose of producing a regular crop of calves each spring. Calves are sold following weaning in fall. Cattle are typically kept on pastures year-round, although they are fed supplemental feeds during winter and other periods when forage growth is slow. Pastures have typically been cleared of trees and planted with introduced forage species, but some wooded areas are retained. Cattle graze the woodland understory vegetation, but because woodlands are typically small and have very low production compared to open portions of the pasture, they make a negligible contribution to forage resources. The main economic function of woodlands in this system is shelter. Access to shade in woodlands alleviates health problems and poor weight gains during the hottest summer months. Shelter is also important in preventing loss of calves during severe storms that occasionally occur during early spring.

In this area, farmers distinguish two major types of pasture use. "Summer" pastures are used during times of active forage growth, typically from April to November. Animals are typically moved among several summer pastures over the course of the season. Number of animals and duration of use in a given summer pasture is limited by the forage available, so intensity of use in associated woodlands depends largely on proportion of woodland to open pasture area within the fenced unit. Considerably more area is in summer pasture than in other pasture types. "Winter" pastures are used when animals are receiving supplemental feed, usually during winter but occasionally during other times of year. Number of livestock per unit area is typically much higher than on summer pastures. Winter pastures differ from feeding paddocks, however, because both grazing and harvested feeds contribute to animal maintenance and animal numbers are regulated to protect productivity of forage plants.

In ordinary practice, cattle are sometimes kept off a summer pasture until after harvest of a hay crop, usually late June or July. Use during the rest of the season follows the normal pattern for summer pastures. This deferment of use typically occurs on different pastures in successive years but is occasionally repeated on the same pasture for several years. Repeated deferment is of particular interest because of its resemblance to practices designed to promote vegetation recovery on rangelands. I have designated this regime "deferred" use and included it as a third treatment type in this study.

Study Design

This study was carried out at Dixon Springs Agricultural Center in southeastern Illinois, located on lands of the Shawnee National Forest and operated by the

University of Illinois. The agricultural center lands are intermixed with other National Forest lands and privately owned farms over an area of about 60 km² of moderately rolling terrain. Pastures used in this study are managed to maintain herds of Hereford and Angus cows and calves used in veterinary research with staff hired locally and using pasture management practices typical of local farms.

This site was selected because it has a relatively large number of pastures with conditions needed to make the comparisons of interest. These conditions include (1) well-documented, consistent use histories, (2) grazing regimes typical of farms in the region, and (3) woodlands areas of at least 1 ha included within pasture units. Because the contrasts among different grazing regimes was of primary interest and the scale of this preliminary survey necessarily small, it was desirable to reduce other sources of variation by limiting the study to upland, midslope sites with closed-canopy, predominately oak-history (*Quercus* spp.-*Carya* spp.) overstories. All pastures within the Dixon Springs Agricultural Center that met these conditions were identified. Of qualifying pastures I randomly selected two winter pastures and two summer pastures. Deferred pastures were so designated if they had been ungrazed for each of the three preceding years. Only two deferred pastures met the selection criteria, so both were selected for the study. Using the same site criteria, I also selected two "ungrazed" woodland areas that had formerly been part of summer pastures but had been fenced to exclude grazing at least 15 years before the study. Characteristics of these eight pasture units are described in Table 14.1.

Conditions in the winter and summer pastures are intended to represent outcomes of typical local grazing management practices. The deferred pastures represent a variation on local practice that is of particular interest as discussed above. Ungrazed woodlands represent the outcome of grazing removal as a management alternative and are in no way intended to represent baseline or pristine condition of the grazed woodlands. Feeding paddocks, fenced units in which animals are maintained on harvested feeds rather than grazed forage, were not included in this study.

Within woodland portions of each pasture included in the study, two random points were selected. From each point a line transect 50 m in length was laid out along a randomly chosen compass bearing. The area within 5 m of the canopy boundary was excluded from sampling. Point and bearing choices that placed a transect within the excluded area were rejected. A complete inventory was conducted of species present on a belt 1 m wide centered on the transect line. These belts were examined in May and again in September to ensure that both early- and late-developing species were included in the list. In addition, along each transect line 100 point observations were made to (1) estimate vegetation cover and vertical structure by species, and (2) estimate extent of bare soil, leaf litter, and woody debris. I estimated litter depths from 10 point observations on each transect. At the September sampling data, all tree seedlings (individuals less than 2 cm basal diameter) within the 100 m by 1 m belt were inventories by species.

Table 14.1. Characteristics of the pastures sampled.

Grazing regime	Ungrazed		Winter		Summer		Deferred	
Stocking density	None		Heavy		Moderate		Moderate	
Pasture ID	A	B	C	D	E	F	G	H
Season of use	None	None	Dec–Apr	Dec–Apr	Apr–Nov	Apr–Nov	July–Nov	Jun–Aug
Years of similar use	13	16	20+	20+	20+	20+	3	3
Pasture area (ha)	4	4	12	22	29	23	14	19
Aspect	SW	SW	S-SW	E-SE	NW	S-SE	SW	E
Percent wooded	100%	100%	25%	10%	10%	10%	10%	15%
Part of contiguous woodland area larger than 10 ha?	Yes	No	Yes	No	No	Yes	Yes	No
Comments	Formerly part of adjacent pastures. No vegetation management activities since grazing exclusion.		Cattle are concentrated on these pastures when supplemental feeding is needed, primarily in winter. Occasionally grazed at other times. Pasture D used Sept–Apr for past three years.		Use adjusted to forage availability; cattle usually taken on and off several times during active forage growth. Occasionally mowed for hay.		Grazing is withheld until midseason. Nonwooded portion of pasture G is mowed for hay before being grazed, whereas pasture H is not mowed. Previously under summer use.	

To inventory saplings and mature trees and to assess rate of injury to stems and roots, a 12 m wide belt was laid out centered on the same transect line. Each tree with basal diameter of more than 2 cm within this broader belt was measured and scored for stem injury, root exposure, injury to exposed roots, and apparent overall health.

The approach adopted for analyzing species inventory data was designed to distinguish impacts on species vulnerable to local loss from impacts on species that are likely to persist in local landscapes in spite of loss or deterioration of woodland habitats. The full list from this inventory included over 200 species. To proceed with analysis of differences between species lists associated with different types of grazing use, each native species was classified according to its degree of specificity to intact native vegetation, specificity to forest habitats, and site specificity or rarity within forests. This approach is an adaptation of methods suggested by Swink and Wilhelm (1979). Strict decision rules were applied to distribution descriptions from a regional flora (Mohlenbrock and Voight 1959) to assign the species to one of seven categories (Table 14.2).

Species with distributions that include nonwoodland areas disturbed by agriculture and other human activities (categories 2 and 3) are relatively unlikely to suffer from habitat loss in this landscape. At the other extreme, uncommon species that only occur in specialized habitats within woodlands (category 7) are most vulnerable to loss, although species in categories 5 and 6 also depend on maintenance of suitable woodland habitats. Persistence of species in category 4 does not depend entirely on woodland conditions, although with little other natural vegetation, woodlands may be their primary habitat in this landscape. Introduced species were put in a separate category since conservation issues for this group are quite different from those relating to native species.

Variation in number and category distribution of understory species, in number and size-class distribution of trees, and frequency of injury and mortality was

Table 14.2.   Seven categories of plant species habitat specificity designations.

Description	Example from Mohlenbrock and Voigt (1959)
1. Introduced	"*Festuca pratensis* . . . Native of Europe."
2. Primarily on artificially disturbed sites	"*Geranium carolinianum* . . . a common species of waste ground."
3. In two or more native plant communities as well as on artificially disturbed sites	"*Oxalis violacea* . . . found on dry sandstone bluffs, in moist woods, or in waste ground."
4. In two or more plant communities but not typical of recently disturbed sites	"*Hedeoma pulegioides* . . . common in dry fields or dry woodlands."
5. Woodlands only, common	"*Trillium recurvatum* . . . common in woods of southern Illinois."
6. Woodlands only, common but ecologically specialized	"*Arisaema dracontium* . . . common in moist woods."
7. Woodlands only, occasional	"*Hypericum prolificum* . . . occasional in woods along streams . . ."

partitioned among types of grazing use and between pastures using log likelihood ratio methods (Sokal and Rohlf, 1981). These methods, designed for analysis of attribute and frequency data, use log-linear models in a manner parallel to the use of linear models with continuous variables in analysis of variance. Deviations of observed from expected values for individual cells were analyzed after converting cell chi-square values to standard normal deviates. Litter depths were analyzed by nested analysis of variance, with Ryan-Einot-Gabriel-Welsh multiple F test comparison of means (SAS Institute, 1985).

In a survey of this kind, where baseline data is not available and management practices under comparison were not randomly assigned to the units sampled, it is important to examine both historical factors and patterns of variation in important site factors to detect potential sources of bias that would influence interpretation of results. Although on the whole one would expect aspect and topography to influence assignments to winter and summer use, examination of pasture layouts at the Dixon Springs Agricultural Center did not reveal a pattern of this kind. Interviews with management personnel suggests that assignments were made primarily for logistical reasons unrelated to condition or site characteristics within woodland portions of these pastures. Site factors (e.g., species composition, canopy closure of overstory trees, proximity to large woodland tracts, slope, and aspect) are known to affect understory vegetation characteristics of interest here. As criteria for inclusion in the study, all sites were of moderate slope, topographically midslope, and had closed canopies of trees dominated by oaks and hickories in the larger size classes. Other important site characteristics varied among sites (Table 14.1, Appendix B). Distribution of variation among sites is of primary importance in understanding the potential for confusing grazing effects with effects due to site differences. If sites in the same treatment category are similar to each other but different from the other sites in one or more important site characteristics, the influence of the treatment is not distinguishable from influence of the site factors. On the other hand, if sites in the same treatment category differ as much from each other as they do from the rest of the sites under comparison in particular site characteristics, then the influence of those site factors is unlikely to be confused with the treatment effect. Instead, the influence of those factors will tend to add variation unexplained by treatments and make it less likely that significant differences due to treatment will be observed. Proximity to large woodland tracts, a factor that may be important in species richness, was well distributed with no sites under the same grazing treatment similar in this attribute. Variation in aspect was fairly well distributed, except that the two ungrazed sites differed less from each other than sites under other types of use.

Overstory tree composition is an important site factor as an influence on characteristics of the understory environment and as an indicator of site conditions that may affect other vegetation characteristics. Summary data on species composition and size-class distribution of overstory trees is shown in Appendix B. Analysis of variation in size-class distribution is reasonably well distributed among sites, although both winter-use sites are at the low end in total number of stems per ha. On all sites, the larger trees were mostly oaks and hickorys, but the relative abundance of the two genera as well as the abundance of individual oak and hickory species varied widely. On the whole this variation was well distributed, with no pattern of similarity between sites under the same grazing treatment. Other tree species formed minor components of the larger size classes, but were varyingly abundant as small trees. Sugar maple *(Acer sacharrum)* was abundant in the subcanopy in one of the sites under winter-, summer-, and ungrazed-used regimes, but absent on both deferred sites. Given issues concerning the effects of sugar maple invasion on woodland understories, this pattern will merit attention in interpretation of results.

Results and Discussion

Plant Diversity

Results showed that the number of species (species richness) was approximately the same under all types of use except deferred, where species richness was substantially higher (Table 14.3, Appendix A). Adding ecological rankings to the analysis indicates that there were major differences among all of these use types not revealed by total species numbers. Introduced and native ruderal species were most abundant in winter-use woodlands. Ungrazed sites, in contrast, contained many species that are restricted to woodlands and only a few ruderal

Table 14.3. Species richness of understory vegetation by ecological category, in woodlands under contrasting grazing regimes. Species lists were compiled from two inventories (May and September) of two plots (0.01 ha) in each woodland.

Grazing regime	Pasture ID	Number of species by ecological category[a]								Total species
		1	2	3	4	5	6	7	Ucl	
Ungrazed	A	3	5	7	10	15	12	1	4	57
	B	2	3	10	13	11	11	0	4	54
Winter	C	6	12	7	10	9	9	0	3	56
	D	16	12	10	8	10	3	0	5	64
Summer	E	11	8	7	10	7	6	3	3	55
	F	9	6	9	12	16	9	2	2	65
Deferred	G	5	7	15	25	17	14	1	6	90
	H	6	4	10	16	21	12	3	3	75

[a]Ecological categories (see text)

Note: Column headings are as follows: 1—introduced; 2—primarily on disturbed sites, native; 3—in two or more vegetation types, including disturbed sites; 4—in two or more vegetation types but not typical of disturbed sites; 5—woodlands only, common and unspecialized; 6—woodlands only, common but environmentally restricted; 7—woodlands only, occasional; and Ucl—unclassified; ecological characteristics unknown or specimen not identified to species.

Table 14.4. *Composition of understory vegetation and number of species represented by life form for woodlands under contrasting grazing regimes. Values are average percent cover and cumulative number of species for all plots in each grazing category.*

Life form	Ungrazed		Winter		Summer		Deferred	
	Cover	#spp.	Cover	#spp.	Cover	#spp.	Cover	#spp.
Forbs	10	34	26	53	29	47	19	62
Graminoids	<1	16	4	17	13	17	5	29
Vines	<1	7	<1	6	2	5	20	9
Shrubs	18	7	<1	2	9	3	31	7
Seedling trees	2	20	<1	11	<1	15	3	2

species. Woodlands under summer use had intermediate numbers of both ruderal species and species restricted to woodlands. Woodlands under deferred use had relatively few introduced and ruderal species, but they had more species in all the other ecological categories than the other sites. Sites with abundant sugar maple did not differ consistently in species richness from similarly treated sites without sugar maple but did tend to have slightly fewer ruderal species and slightly more species of woodlands (Table 14.3, Appendix B). Both the small magnitude and the direction of this association suggest that absence of sugar maple on both deferred sites is unlikely to have contributed to the contrasts between deferred use and other use types discussed above.

I observed little correspondence between abundance and species richness for individual life forms (Table 14.4). Conditions on summer-grazed sites were apparently favorable for graminoid growth, but these sites were not rich in graminoid species. Vines were a negligible component of vegetation on the ungrazed sites in terms of aerial cover, but these sites had almost as many vine species as the deferred sites where vines were quite abundant.

A central purpose of this survey was to make a preliminary analysis of the contribution of each of these use types to maintenance of floristic diversity at the landscape level. Examining where the lists do and do not overlap sheds some light on this question. Table 14.5 shows numbers of species that occurred only

Table 14.5. *Number of species unique to samples from a single grazing regime. Ecological categories are pooled to reduce the number of cells with small values.*

	Ungrazed	Winter	Summer	Deferred
Disturbance specialists (categories 1 and 2)	2	16	4	3
Generalists (categories 3 and 4)	4	5	3	14
Woodland specialists (categories 5, 6, and 7)	7	3	9	21
Total	13	24	16	38

on the species lists from a single use type, here called unique species. This table was constructed by combining species lists from individual plots to form a single list for each type of grazing use, then deleting species that occurred on more than one list. Almost all the species on the resulting list were, in fact, unique to sample plots from a single pasture of the two under similar grazing use (Appendix A). Presence on this sample-based list does not imply that the species was entirely absent on other sites.

Statistical analysis of both total numbers of unique species and the distribution of unique species among ecological ranks shows that variation attributable to differences among grazing types far outweighs other sources of variation in the model (Table 14.6). Winter and deferred woodlands stand out has having more unique species than either ungrazed or summer woodlands (Table 14.5). There are more unique species on the deferred list than on the winter list, but even more striking is the difference in distribution of species among ecological categories. Two-thirds of the species unique to winter sites were introduced and ruderal. The majority of the species unique to deferred sites were woodland natives, and most of the rest were characteristic of native plant communities. The species unique to winter sites were nearly all broadleaf herbs and graminoids, mostly annuals. The large majority of species unique to deferred sites were also broadleaf herbs and graminoids, but mostly perennial species. The list of species unique to the deferred sites also included a few woody species. There is no strong contrast in rank distributions between ungrazed and summer sites. It is worth noting, however, that species unique to summer sites were almost all herbaceous dicots, but species unique to ungrazed sites were mostly woody species (Appendix A).

The high number of unique species on the winter sites exaggerates their

Table 14.6. Summary of statistical analyses for vegetation characteristics. Total variation is partitioned into contributions associated with contrasting grazing regimes, and between pastures under similar grazing regimes.

| | Source of variation | | | | | | | | |
| | Grazing regimes | | | Between pastures | | | Total | | |
	G^a	df	p	G	df	p	G	df	p
Distribution of species among ecological categories	38.6	12	0.000	14.5	16	0.562	53.0	28	0.003
Total number of understory species	13.1	3	0.004	2.8	4	0.592	16.0	7	0.025
Distribution of unique species among ecological categories	29.2	6	0.000						
Total number of unique species	15.7	3	0.001						

[a]Likelihood ration chi-square, after Sokal and Rohlf (1981). G distribution approximately as chi-square. P values shown here are from the chi-square distribution.

contribution to maintenance of species diversity in the landscape, because the majority of these species also occur in the open, disturbed habitats that are increasingly abundant in the local area. Although woodland-dependent species are present on these sites, no woodland natives appear dependent on conditions these sites provide. On the other hand, each of the other use types appears to contribute uniquely to support of a recognizable group of species dependent on woodland environments.

Persistence of Forest Cover

The scenario of forest destruction by livestock rested on the plausible assumption that cattle hasten mortality of existing canopy trees by injuring stems and roots, at the same time preventing regeneration by eliminating seedlings and saplings (Day and DenUyl 1932). Evidence that this occurs is easy to find in the Illinois landscape, but it is equally easy to observe that the magnitude of damage in grazed woodlands varies widely. Forest destruction is clearly not the simple function of time it was portrayed to be, as we see from the continued existence of woodlands that have been grazed for many decades. My study included a survey of tree injury, health, and reproduction to identify questions pertinent to a better understanding of relationships between grazing management and maintenance of the forest overstory.

Tree Injury

In the woodlands included in this study, severe injury to tree stems was low overall, though perhaps somewhat elevated in the woodlands under winter use (Table 14.7). Many of the through-bark injuries recorded were probably not due to livestock damage. Partially healed holes from long-dead basal sprouts, not readily distinguishable from other partially healed wounds at the base of stems, and damage to saplings from deer rubbing their antlers were common. These were major sources of through-bark injuries and affected trees under all types of use, including ungrazed. Superficial stem injuries, on the other hand, were

Table 14.7. Stem injury rates (percent) for trees under contrasting grazing regimes. Based on inventories of two 605 m^2 plots in each of two pasture woodlands for each grazing regime. Includes all individuals over 10 cm DBH.

Grazing regime	n	No injuries	Superficial injuries and/or bark smoothing	Through-bark wounds
Ungrazed	108	89	3	8
Winter	92	18	74	8
Summer	135	30	68	2
Deferred	114	55	44	1
Overall	449	48	47	4

clearly much more common in woodlands used by cattle than on ungrazed sites and increased progressively with overall intensity of use. Rates of stem injury in saplings were roughly the same as for trees except that winter sites had somewhat higher rates of injury. A few trees in woodlands under winter use had large, severe wounds from rubbing by cattle. Although bark smoothing was very common on all the other grazed sites, rubbing intensity apparently was not enough to cause wounds of this type. Higher stocking rates on the winter pastures, along with the propensity of fed cattle to spend more time in woods, may account for this difference. It is possible that there is a threshold above which rubbing injury rates are quite high, a threshold that is not reached under the types of use examined here. Such a threshold would explain the very high rates of stem injury in small, isolated tree stands within large pastures and in paddocks where large numbers of cattle are kept on feed.

The picture for root injury is quite different and more complex. Although rate of root exposure increased progressively with higher use levels, rates of injury to exposed roots were similarly low on both ungrazed and deferred sites (Table 14.8). These low rates contrast with high rates of injury in woodlands under both winter and summer use. Root exposure and injury rates were considerably lower in saplings than in trees over 10 cm DBH, with 31% of saplings showing some degree of exposure or injury in contrast to 82% for trees. It is of interest to note apparent differences among tree species in both rate of root exposure and rate of injury to exposed roots (Table 14.9). Across all grazing regimes, hickories had relatively low rates of root exposure and low rates of injury to roots that were exposed. White ash *(Fraxinus americana)*, at the other extreme, had a relatively high rate of root exposure and a high rate of injury to roots that were exposed. Oaks had high rates of root exposure but intermediate rates of injury or exposed roots. Differences in root architecture, more pronounced as trees mature, seems to be an important factor in vulnerability to root exposure and visible damage. Season of livestock use appears to be important here also. Similarity in rates of exposure and injury between winter and summer use may reflect increased sensitively to damage in late winter and early spring. The effect is quite striking and deserves further attention.

Rates of mortality and obvious decline in vigor were low overall and association

Table 14.8. Root exposure and injury rates (percent) for trees under contrasting grazing regimes. Based on inventories of two 605 m² plots in each of two pasture woodlands for each grazing regime. Includes all individuals over 10 cm DBH.

Grazing regime	n	No exposure	Exposure, no injury	Exposed and injured
Ungrazed	108	23	73	4
Winter	92	5	38	57
Summer	135	17	36	47
Deferred	114	22	67	11
Overall	449	17	53	29

Table 14.9. Species differences in root exposure and injury rates (percent). Based on inventories of two 605 m² plots in each of eight pasture woodlands. Includes all individuals over 10 cm DBH.

Species	n	No exposure	Exposure, no injury	Exposed and injured
Carya spp.	120	32	56	12
Quercus spp.	132	15	54	31
Acer saccharum	98	9	59	32
Ulmus spp.	30	13	50	37
Fraxinus americanus	33	6	39	55

Carya spp.: *Carya cordiformis* (Wang.) K. Koch, *C. ovalis* (Wang.) Sarg., *C. ovata* (Mill.) K. Koch, *C. tomentosa* (Poir.) Nutt.

Quercus spp.: *Quercus alba* L., *Q. imbricaria* Michx., *Q. palustris* Muenchh., *Q. prinoides* Willd. var. *acuminata* (Michx.) Gl., *Q. rubra* L., *Q. stellata* Wangh., *Q. velutina* Lam.

Ulmus spp.: *Ulmus alata* Michx., *U. americana* L., *U. rubra* Muhl.

with differences in grazing regimes were not significant (Table 14.10, Table 14.12). Analysis of association between individual tree health status and visible injury to roots did not show a positive relationship between injury and decline.

Seedling and Sapling Populations

Tree seedling and sapling density varied significantly among types of grazing use, although there was also significant variation between pastures under the same type as use (Table 14.11, Table 14.12). Seedlings densities were similar on all sites except those under winter use, where density was lower. Density of small saplings (DBH less than 3 cm) was low on both winter and summer sites, intermediate on sites with deferred use, and highest on ungrazed sites. In the larger sapling classes, differences in grazing regime accounted for progressively less of the variation among sites sampled. Since individuals in these size classes could easily be over 20 years old (Fowells 1965, Merritt 1980), the specific management practices under which they were established are unknown.

Black cherry *(Prunus serotina)*, although rare or absent as a canopy species, was relatively abundant in seedling populations of most sites, a pattern not

Table 14.10. Health status of trees under contrasting grazing regimes. Based on inventories of two 605 m² plots in each of two pasture woodlands for each grazing regime. Includes all individuals over 10 cm DBH.

Grazing regime	n	Good	Poor	Dead
Ungrazed	108	95	2	3
Winter	92	85	8	8
Summer	135	86	6	8
Deferred	114	90	4	6
Overall	449	89	5	6

Table 14.11.   Numbers of seedlings (basal diameter <2 cm) and saplings (basal diameter >2 cm and <10 cm diameter at breast height) in woodlands under contrasting grazing regimes. For seedlings, estimates are from inventories of two 50 m^2 plots. For saplings, estimates are from inventories of two 605 m^2 plots. All values are expressed as stems per ha.

Grazing regime	Pasture	Seedlings	<3.0 cm	3.0–0.65 cm	6.6–10.0 cm
Ungrazed	A	7,500	450	150	50
	B	10,800	1470	350	90
Winter	C	1,400	40	70	40
	D	1,900	0	80	160
Summer	E	13,700	30	10	70
	F	10,000	0	120	80
Deferred	G	11,700	140	210	220
	H	4,600	440	80	90

unexpected in this species with fruits dispersed by birds (Appendix B). Hackberry *(Celtis occidentalis),* also bird dispersed, was present as seedlings on sites where it was rare or absent as a canopy species. Other species, such as sugar maple and individual oak and hickory species, were present in seedling populations only on sites where they were also present as mature trees.

Table 14.12.   Summary of statistical analyses for tree injury and health status and seedling and sapling population data. Total variation is partitioned into contributions associated with contrasting grazing regimes, and between pastures under similar grazing regimes.

	Source of variation								
	Grazing regimes			Between pastures			Total		
	G^1	df	p	G	df	p	G	df	p
Seedlings[2]	184.3	3	0.000	44.2	4	0.000	228.9	7	0.000
Saplings[2]:									
<3.0 cm DBH	441.2	3	0.000	101.8	4	0.000	543.0	7	0.000
3.0–6.5 cm DBH	35.8	3	0.000	31.0	4	0.000	66.8	7	0.000
6.6–10.0 cm DBH	5.0	3	0.172	8.3	4	0.081	13.3	7	0.065
Stem injury[3]	178.2	6	0.000	33.2	8	0.000	211.4	14	0.000
Root injury[4]	121.9	6	0.000	29.8	8	0.000	151.8	14	0.000
Health status[5]	9.0	6	0.172	19.8	8	0.011	28.9	14	0.011

[1] G is distributed approximately as a chi-square likelihood ratio, after Sokal and Rohlf (1981). P-values are from the chi-square distribution.

[2] From Table 7.

[3] From Table 8.

[4] From Table 9.

[5] From Table 11.

Although representation of the many individual tree species was variable among tree stands sampled, some patterns in seedling populations that may be related to grazing use can be distinguished in the more widespread species and genera (Appendix B). Hickory, oak, and maple seedlings were most abundant on ungrazed sites. Elm, ash, and cherry had highest densities under summer or deferred use. Only three sites had substantial numbers of small saplings, both of the ungrazed sites and one of the deferred sites. On one of the ungrazed sites (pasture A), sugar maple was the only species with abundant small saplings. The other ungrazed site (pasture B) had a large number of cherry and elm saplings. The deferred site (pasture H) had large numbers of elm saplings and a scattering of other species. Oak saplings of the smaller size classes were rare or absent on all sites.

Wildlife Habitat

Woodland size, isolation, and position relative to other habitat elements are important factors in habitat use for many vertebrates dependent on woodland environments. Consequently, conditions within a woodland patch may have less explanatory value for presence, absence, or species richness of particular vertebrate groups than is the case with plants. Nevertheless, understory vegetation characteristics are often an important element in the complex picture of habitat requirements for individual species. Birds have received particular attention in past discussion of negative effects of livestock on woodland wildlife (Day 1930, Dambach 1944) as well as in recent discussion of fragmentation effects (e.g., Robinson et al., chapter 8, this volume). Vertical structure of vegetation is an important habitat variable for many woodland bird species, affecting both nesting and feeding substrates (Blake and Karr 1987, Kahl et al. 1985, Martin 1988). Extent of herbaceous vegetation and litter depth may be important factors in small mammal habitat use and in abundance and diversity of litter and soil macroinvertebrates (Dambach 1944). We evaluated vertical structure of vegetation and litter depths to determine if differences among grazing management practices are of a magnitude likely to affect vertebrate habitat use substantially.

Ungrazed woodlands had little herbaceous vegetation and moderate development of a shrub stratum (Table 14.4). These were the only sites with a subcanopy tree stratum, consisting mostly of sugar maple and black cherry saplings. The winter sites had well-developed cover of broadleaf herbs in spring but little other understory vegetation. Summer sites were similar but with considerably more cover of grasses and sedges and some development of shrubs. The deferred sites had well-developed strata of shrubs and vines and intermediate cover of herbaceous vegetation.

Table 14.13 shows vegetation cover in height strata up to 4 m. Cover near the ground decreased markedly between May and September on all sites, whether they were grazed or not during this period, due largely to senescence of the

Table 14.13. Vertical structure of understory vegetation in woodlands under contrasting grazing regimes. Extent of vegetation (percent cover) in half-meter strata[a] was sampled in May and in September. Because cover above 1 m differed little between dates, only September values are shown for those strata.

Grazing regime	<0.5 m May	<0.5 m Sept	0.5–1.0 m May	0.5–1.0 m Sept	1.0–1.5 m Sept	1.5–2.0 m Sept	2.0–4.0 m Sept
Ungrazed	28	14	10	10	12	14	19
Winter	29	6	0	0	0	0	0
Summer	46	22	6	8	3	1	0
Deferred	62	35	28	17	9	2	0

[a]The four 0.5 m strata between 2 m and 4 m are pooled.

annual and early-season forb component. On the winter sites, where more persistent vegetation components were absent, this meant virtually complete disappearance of understory vegetation.

Differences in vegetation structure between grazed and ungrazed sites are clearly of a magnitude likely to affect habitat quality for birds, especially those that nest or forage in strata between 1 m and the overstory canopy. Differences between contrasting grazing regimes were also substantial, possibly of a magnitude that would affect habitat use or quality for birds that nest or forage near the ground.

Litter depth averaged 7 cm on ungrazed sites, differing significantly (at p = 0.05) from the 3 cm average depth we found on winter sites. Litter depths on summer and deferred sites were intermediate at 4 cm and 5 cm respectively. In comparing adjacent grazed and ungrazed maple woodlands. Dambach (1944) found that variation in litter depth accounted for much of the variation among his sample plots in populations of invertebrates and small mammals, organisms that can in turn affect seedling establishment of trees and other understory plants (Fowells 1965). Litter characteristics also affect nutrient regimes and other attributes of environment known to influence germination and establishment of plants (Facelli and Pickett 1991, Minckler and Jensen 1959). Although the magnitude of differences observed here does not appear large, further study of the relationships between specific attributes of grazing regimes and litter dynamics would be warranted.

Management Implications

Results of this survey suggest that removing cattle from pasture woodlands, a practice that has been strenuously advocated by public agencies, is not without merit as a means of increasing the range of habitats available for native plant species. Here, ungrazed woodlands appear to provide conditions for growth and development of a number of species that do not grow successfully in grazed areas, especially woody species. These results suggest that if applied to all woodlands in this landscape, however, grazing exclusion could result in reduction of habitat for a large number of understory herbaceous plants. This outcome may be mediated through companion management actions that promote understory vegetation growth.

The dynamics of seedling and sapling populations in woodland understory is an important factor affecting habitat for plants, animals, and persistence of the forest canopy itself. Results here suggest that there are major differences in the way grazing regimes affect tree reproduction, and that individual tree species respond differently to grazing impacts. This topic clearly deserves further research attention.

This survey was limited to a relatively small set of pastures in a limited geographic area. The results clearly suggest, however, that impacts of extensive, pasture-based livestock production systems differ substantially from impacts of intensive uses associated with feeding harvested forages. In particular these grazing impacts may be substantially less detrimental to the continued support for forest plant species diversity. Thus, the potential value of grazed farm woodlands in the broader picture of habitat conservation should not be dismissed without further attention. Day and DenUyl's concern in 1932 was that livestock feeding was replacing extensive livestock grazing, bringing ecological disaster to farm woodland resources. Our concern today is that as extensive grazing practices return, the implications of these changes be adequately recognized.

References

Ahlgren, M.L., M.L. Wall, R.J. Muckenhirn, and J.M. Sund. 1946. Yields of forage from woodland pastures on sloping land in southern Wisconsin. *Journal of Forestry* 44:709–711.

Blake, J.G., and J.R. Karr. 1987. Breeding birds of isolated woodlots: Area and habitat relationships. *Ecology* 68:1724–1734.

Chandler, R.F. 1940. The influence of grazing upon certain soil and climate conditions in farm woodlands. *Journal of the American Society of Agronomy* 32:216–230.

Dambach, C.A. 1944. A ten-year ecological study of adjoining grazed and ungrazed woodlots in north-eastern Ohio. *Ecological Monographs* 14:257–270.

Day, R.K. 1930. Grazing out the birds. *American Forests* 36:555–557, 594.

Day, R.K., and D. DenUyl. 1932. *The Natural Regeneration of Farm Woods following the Exclusion of Livestock.* Purdue University Agricultural Experiment Station Bulletin no. 368.

DenUyl, D., and R.D. Day. 1939. *Woodland Livestock Carrying Capacities and Grazing Injury Studies.* Purdue University Agricultural Experiment Station Bulletin no. 391.

Facelli, J.M., and S.T.A. Pickett. 1991. Plant litter: its dynamics and effects on plant community structure. *Botanical Review* 57:1–32.

Flood, B.S., M.E. Sangster, R.D. Sparrowe, and T.S. Baskett. 1977. A handbook for habitat evaluation procedures. Resource Publication 132. U.S. Fish and Wildlife Service, Washington, D.C.

Fowells, H.A. 1965. *Silvics of Forest trees of the United States.* Agriculture Handbook no. 271. U.S. Forest Service, Washington, D.C.

Gentry, A.H. 1986. Endemism in tropical and temperate plant communities. In M.E. Soulé, ed. *Conservation Biology: The Science of Scarcity and Diversity.* Sinauer Press, Sunderland, Mass, 153–181.

Guise, C.H. 1950. *The Management of Farm Woodlands.* McGraw-Hill, New York.

Hahn 1987. *Illinois Forest Statistics, 1985.* U.S. Forest Service Resource Bulletin NC-103. St. Paul, Minn.

Iverson, L.R. 1989. Forest resources of Illinois: an atlas and analysis of spatial and temporal trends. Illinois Department of Energy and Natural Resources, Illinois Natural History Survey Special Publication 11, Champaign, Ill., 73.

Johnson, E.A. 1952. Effects of farm woodland grazing on watershed values in the southern Appalachian Mountains. *Journal of Forestry* 50:109–113.

Kahl, R.B., T.S. Baskett, J.A. Ellis, and J.N. Burroughs. 1985. *Characteristics of Summer Habitats of Selected Nongame Birds in Missouri.* University of Missouri-Columbia Agricultural Experiment Station Research Bulletin 1056.

Kuchler, A.W. 1966. Potential natural vegetation. National Atlas Sheet 90. U.S. Geological Survey, Washington, D.C.

Ledig, F.T. 1993. Secret extinctions: the loss of genetic diversity in forest ecosystems. In M.A. Fenger et al., eds. *Our Living Legacy: Proceeding of a Symposium on Biological Diversity.* Royal British Columbia Museum, Victoria, B.C.

Marks, J.B. 1942. Land use and plant succession in Coon Valley, Wisconsin. *Ecological Monographs* 12:114–133.

Martin, T.E. 1988. Habitat and area effects on forest bird assemblages: Is nest predation an influence? *Ecology* 69:74–84.

McQuilkin, R.A., and H. Scholten. 1989. Grazing in Central Hardwood Forests. In F.B. Clark and J.G. Hutchinson, eds. Central Hardwood Notes. North Central Forest Experiment Station, St. Paul, Minnesota, Loose-leaf.

Merritt, C. 1980. The central region. In J.W. Barrett, ed. *Regional silviculture of the United States.* John Wiley & Sons, New York, 107–143.

Merz, R.W., and S.G. Boyce. 1956. Age of oak "seedlings." *Journal of Forestry* 54:774–775.

Minckler, L.S., and C.E. Jensen. 1959. Reproduction of upland central hardwoods as affected by cutting, topography, and litter depth. *Journal of Forestry* 57:424–428.

Mohlenbrock, R.H. 1986. *Guide to the Vascular Flora of Illinois.* Southern Illinois University Press, Carbondale.

Mohlenbrock, R.H., and J.W. Voight. 1959. *Flora of Southern Illinois.* Southern Illinois University Press, Carbondale.

Neely, R.D., and C.G. Heister. 1987. The natural resources of Illinois: introduction and guide. Illinois Natural History Survey Special Publication 6.

Noss, R.F., and A.Y. Cooperrider. 1994. *Saving Nature's Legacy: Protecting and Restoring Biodiversity.* Island Press, Washington, D.C.

Reeves, T. 1989. To kill a forest, fill it with livestock. *Ohio Farmer* 284:10.

SAS Institute Inc. 1985. *SAS User's Guide: Statistics.* Version 5 edition. SAS Institute Inc., Cary, North Carolina.

Sokal, R.R., and F.J. Rohlf. 1981. *Biometry.* 2nd edition. W.H. Freeman, San Francisco.

Steinbrenner, E.C. 1951. Effect of grazing on floristic composition and soil properties in southern Wisconsin. *Journal of Forestry* 49:906–910.

Swink, F., and G. Wilhelm. 1979. *Plants of the Chicago region.* Morton Arboretum, Lisle, Illinois.

Appendix A

Species occurrence in woodlands under different types of grazing use

Table A1. Cumulative species lists from May and September inventories. In cases where species determination was uncertain, category assignments were made only if all likely species belonged to the same group. Each grazing use type was represented by two woodlands. In each woodland, two 50 m × 1 m plots were sampled (sampled area = 0.01 ha per woodland). Nomenclature follows Mohlenbrock (1986).

***—occurred in sample plots on both woodlands, mean cover >5%
+++—occurred in sample plots on both woodlands, mean cover = 2–5%
xxx—occurred in sample plots on both woodlands, mean cover <2%
xx—occurred on both sample plots in one woodland only
x—occurred in one plot

Ecological categories are the following (see text):

1— introduced; 2—primarily on disturbed sites, native; 3—in two or more vegetation types, including disturbed sites; 4—in two or more vegetation types, but not typical of disturbed sites; 5—woodlands only, common and unspecialized; 6—woodlands only common but environmentally restricted; 7—woodlands only, occasional; and blank—ecological characteristics unknown or specimen not identified to species

Use types are the following (see text): UG—ungrazed; W—winter; S—summer; D—deferred

Species	Ecological category	Use type			
		UG	W	S	D
Forbs					
Acalypha gracilens Gray	4	xxx	xxx	+++	xxx
Acalypha rhomboidea Raf.	3	x	xxx		
Allium vineale L.	1	xx		+++	xxx
Ambrosia artemisiifolia L.	2	x	xxx	xx	
Ambrosia trifida L.	2	xx	xxx		
Amphicarpa bracteata (L.) Fern	6			x	xx
Arisaema dracontium (L.) Schott	6	xx	x	x	xx
Arisaema triphyllum (L.) Schott	6	xx	x		x
Aster simplex Willd.	4			x	xxx
Aster sp. (patens Ait./other)		x			xx
Callitriche terrestris Raf.	3	x	xxx		
Cardamine parviflora L. var. *arenicola* (Britt.) O.E. Schultz	4	xxx		x	xxx
Chenopodium album L.	1	x	xxx	xx	
Claytonia virginica L.	5	xx	xxx	x	
Convolvulus arvensis L.	1	x		x	xxx
Corydalis flavula (Raf.) DC	6	xx	xx	xx	
Cunila origanoides (L.) Britt.	6	xx			x
Dentaria laciniata Muhl.	6	xx		x	xx
Erigeron annuus (L.) Pers.	2		x	x	
Erigeron philadelphicus L.	2		x	x	

Species	Ecological category	Use type			
		UG	W	S	D
Eupatorium rugosum Houtt.	3	x	xxx		xxx
Galium aparine L.	3	xxx	x	xxx	+++
Galium circaezans Michx.	6	xxx		xxx	xx
Galium triflorum Michx.	5			x	xxx
Geranium carolinianum L.	2	x	xx	x	xx
Geum canadense Jacq.	5		xxx		x
Heliotropium indicum L.	1		x	x	xx
Hydrophyllum macrophyllum Nutt.	7			x	xx
Impatiens sp. (*capensis* Meerb./*pallida* Nutt.)	4	xxx	***	+++	xxx
Krigia dandelion (L.) Nutt.	3	x		x	xxx
Lactuca floridana (L.) Gaertn.	5		xxx		x
Myosotis sp. (*macrosperma* Engelm./*verna* Nutt.)			x	xxx	xxx
Oxalis dillenii Jacq.	2		xx		xx
Oxalis stricta L.	2		x		x
Oxalis violacea L.	3	xxx		x	xxx
Parthenocissus quinquefolia (L.) Planch.	4	***	xx	xxx	xxx
Phlox divaricata L. ssp. *laphamii* (Wood) Wherry	4		x		xx
Phytolacca americana L.	2		xxx	xx	x
Podophyllum peltatum L.	5	xxx		xxx	xx
Polygonum punctatum Ell.	2		xx	xxx	
Pycnanthemum tenuifolium Schrad.	4	x		x	x
Ranunculus abortivus L.	2	x	xxx	x	xx
Sanguinaria canadensis L.	6	xx	x		
Sanicula sp. (*gregaria* Bickn./*canadensis* L.)		xxx	xxx	xxx	xxx
Solidago canadensis L.	4		x	xx	x
Stellaria media (L.) Vill.	1	x	xxx	xxx	x
Trifolium repens L.	1		xx	xxx	
Trillium recurvatum Beck.	5	x			xx
Triodanis perfoliata (L.) Nieuwl.	2	xxx	xxx	xxx	x
Vicia dasycarpa Ten.	1		x	x	
Viola sp. (*pratincola* Greene/other)		xxx	xxx	x	xxx
Penstemon pallidus Small	4	x			
Amaranthus sp.	1	x[a]			
Arctium minus Bernh.	1	x			
Bidens bipinnata L.	2	xx			
Capsella bursa-pastoris (L.) Medic.	1	xx			
Cardamine pensylvanica Muhl.	4	x			
Chenopodium ambrosioides L.	2	xx			
Commelina communis L.	1	x			
Conyza canadensis (L.) Cronq.	1	xx			
Erigeron pulchellus Michx.	6	x			
Glechoma hederacea L. var. *micrantha* Moricand	1	x			
Pilea pumila (L.) Gray	3	x			
Plantago lanceolata L.	1	x			
Plantago rugelii Dcne.	2	xxx			

Species	Ecological category	Use type UG	W	S	D
Polygonum virginianum L.	5		x		
Trifolium pratense L.	1		x		
Urtica dioica L.	1		xx		
Verbena hastata L.	3		x		
Veronica peregrina L.	2		xxx		
Acalypha virginica L.	3			x	
Barbarea vulgaris R.Br.	1			x	
Chenopodium desiccatum A. Nels. var. *leptophylloides* (Murr.) Wahl	2			xx	
Parietaria pensylvanica Muhl.	5			xxx	
Polygonatum biflorum (Walt.) Ell.	6			*x*	
Silene stellata (L.) Ait.f.	5			xx	
Solanum carolinense L.	1			x	
Solidago flexicaulis L.	7			x	
Verbesina sp. (*helianthoides* Michx./*alternifolia* (L.) Britt.)	6			x	
Viola rafinesquii Greene	1			xx	
Agrimonia parviflora Ait.	3				x
Agrimonia sp. (*rostellata* Wallr./*pubescens* Wallr.)	5				x
Antennaria neglecta Greene	4				x
Antennaria plantaginifolia (L.) Richards	4				xx
Aristolochia serpentaria L.	6				x
Dioscorea villosa L.	5				x
Euphorbia corollata L.	3				xx
Hedeoma pulegioides (L.) Pers.	4				xx
Helianthus divaricatus L.	6				xx
Helianthus hirsutus Raf.	2				xx
Helianthus rigidus (Cass.) Desf.	4				x
Hypoxis hirsuta (L.) Coville	4				x
Krigia sp. (*biflora* (Walt.) Blake)					x
Manfreda virginica (L.) Rose	4				x
Paronychia fastigiata (Raf.) Fern.	3				x
Penstemon hirsutus (L.) Willd.	4				xx
Porteranthus stipulatus (Muhl.) Britt.	6				xx
Potentilla simplex Michx.	3				x
Prenanthes altissima L.	5				x
Ranunculus micranthus Nutt.	5				x
Salvia lyrata L.	6				x
Solidago ulmifolia Muhl.	5				xx
Viola pubescens Ait. var. *eriocarpa* (Schwein.) Russell	6				x
Viola triloba Schwein.	6				xx
Total, forb species		**34**	**53**	**47**	**62**

Ferns

Species	Ecological category	UG	W	S	D
Asplenium platyneuron (L.) Oakes	5	xx	x		xxx
Botrychium dissectum Spring. var. *obliquum* (Muhl.) Clute	5			x	

Species	Ecological category	Use type			
		UG	W	S	D
Cystopteris protrusa (Weatherby) Blasd.	4		xx		xx
Polystichum acrostichoides (Michx.) Schot	5				x
Total, fern species		**1**	**2**	**1**	**3**

Graminoids

Species	Ecological category	UG	W	S	D
Carex amphibola Steud.	7	x		x	x
Carex artitecta Mack.	5	xxx	x	xxx	xxx
Carex blanda Dewey	5	xxx	xxx	xxx	xx
Carex bushii Mack.	4	xx			xx
Carex glaucodea Tuckerm.	5		x	xx	xx
Carex grisea Wahlenb.	5		xxx	xxx	xxx
Carex hirsutella Mack.	4	xx			xxx
Carex hirtifolia Mack.	7			x	xx
Carex jamesii Schwein.	6	x		+++	x
Dactylis glomerata L.	1		x	xx	
Danthonia spicata (L.) Roem. & Schultes	5	x		x	xx
Dichanthelium boscii (Poir.) Gould & Clark	5	xxx		xx	xxx
Dichanthelium villosissimum (Nash.) Freckm.	4	x		xx	x
Elymus villosus Muhl.	4		x	x	xx
Elymus virginicus L.	2	x		xxx	x
Festuca pratensis Huds.	1		xx	xx	x
Leersia virginica Willd.	5	x	xxx		
Muhlenbergia schreberi J.F. Gmel.	3	x	xxx	xxx	xx
Poa pratensis L.	1		x	xxx	
Poa sylvestris Gray	6		x		xx
Poa undet. (*sylvestris* Gray/*pratensis* L.)		xxx			xx[b]
Dichanthelium acuminatum (Sw.) Gould & Clark	4	x			
Dichanthelium commutatum (Schult.) Gould	6	x			
Dichanthelium commutatum (Schult.) Gould	6	x			
Sphenopholis nitida (Biehler) Scribn.	5	x			
Elymus canadensis L.	4		xx		
Dichanthelium microcarpon (Muhl.) Mohlenbr.	4		x		
Juncus tenuis Willd.	2		x		
Paspalum sp.			x		
Poa annua L.	1		x		
Setaria sp. (*glauca* (L.) Beauv./*viridis* (L.) Beauv.)	1		xxx		
Glyceria striata (Lam.) Hitchcock	4			xxx	
Agrostis alba L.	1				x
Arundinaria gigantea (Walt.) Chapm.	4				xx
Brachyelytrum erectum (Schreb.) Beauv.	5				x
Carex retroflexa Muhl.	6				x
Festuca obtusa Biehler	6				xx
Poa compressa L.	2				x
Sphenopholis obtusata (Michx.) Scrib	5				x
Sphenopholis undet. (*nitida/obtusata*)	5				xx[a,b]
Total, graminoid species		**16**	**17**	**17**	**24**

Species	Ecological category	Use type UG	W	S	D
Vines					
Campsis radicans (L.) Seem.	2		x	xx	xxx
Lonicera japonica Thunb.	1	x		x	***
Rubus allegheniensis Porter	3	x	xx		xxx
Smilax glauca Walt.	5	x	x	x	x
Smilax hispida Muhl.	4		x		x
Toxicodendron radicans (L.) Kuntze	3	x	xxx	xxx	xxx
Vitis riparia Michx.	6	xxx	xx		xx
Rosa carolina L.	2	x			
Vitis vulpina L.	3	x			
Passiflora lutea L. var. *glabriflora* Fern.	5			x	
Smilax rotundifolia L.	4				xx
Vitis aestivalis Michx.	4				x
Total, vine species		**7**	**6**	**5**	**9**
Shrubs					
Crataegus sp.	5	x			x
Euonymus atropurpurea Jacq.	5	xx			xx
Prunus sp. (*americana* Marsh./*hortulana* Bailey/*virginiana* L.)	4	xxx			xxx
Rosa multiflora Thunb.	1		x	+++	xx[c]
Sambucus canadensis L.	4			x	x
Symphoricarpos orbiculatus Moench	4	***	xxx	***	***
Amelanchier arborea (Michx.f.) Fern.	6	x			
Asimina triloba (L.) Dunal.	5	x			
Cornus florida L.	5	xx			
Hypericum prolificum L.	7				x
Total, shrub species		**7**	**2**	**3**	**7**
Seedling and sapling trees					
Acer saccharum Marsh.	6	***	xxx	xx	
Carya cordiformis (Wang.) K.Koch	5	xx			x
Carya glabra (Mill.) Sweet	6	xxx		x	xxx
Carya sp. (*ovata* (Mill.) K. Koch/*ovalis* (Wang.) Sarg.)	6	xxx	xxx	xxx	xx
Carya texana Buckl.	6		x		x
Celtis occidentalis L.	3	xxx	xx	xxx	xxx
Fraxinus americana L.	4	xxx	xxx	xxx	xxx
Juniperus virginiana L.	4		xx	x	xxx
Morus rubra L.	4	xx			x
Nyssa sylvatica Marsh.	6	x			xxx
Prunus serotina Ehrh.	3	***	x	xxx	xxx
Quercus alba L.	5	xxx		xxx	xx
Quercus imbricaria Michx.	4	x	x	x	xx
Quercus marilandica Muenchh.	6	x			x

Species	Ecological category	Use type			
		UG	W	S	D
Quercus rubra L.	5	xx	xx		x
Quercus velutina Lam.	5	xx		x	x
Ulmus alata Michx.	3	xx[c]	xx	xxx	xxx
Ulmus rubra Muhl.	5	xx		x	xxx
Acer rubrum L.	4	xxx			
Carya tomentosa (Poir.) Nutt.	6	xxx			
Diospryos virginiana L.	2	xx			
Ostrya virginiana (Mill.) K.Koch	5	xx			
Gleditsia triacanthos L.	5		x		
Quercus palustris Muenchh.	6			x	
Sassafras albidum (Nutt.) Nees	3			x	
Tilia americana L.	7			x	
Carya laciniosa (Michx.) Loud	6				xx
Juglans nigra L.	5				x
Quercus stellata Wangh.	6				x
Quercus prinoides Willd. var. *acuminata* (Michx.) Gl.	5				x
Total, seedling and sapling tree species		**20**	**11**	**15**	**21**
Total, all species		**85**	**91**	**88**	**126**

[a]not included in summary of unique species (Table 2)

[b]not included in species count for this grazing type

[c]abundant on one pasture, absent on the other.

Appendix B

Overstory characteristics of sampled woodlands. Estimates of stems per hectare are based on inventories of two 605 m^2 plots in each pasture, and include all trees 10 cm DBH and larger.

Table B1. Species composition

Grazing regime	Pasture ID	Carya spp.	Quercus spp.	Acer saccharum	Fraxinus americana	Ulmus spp.	Celtis occidentalis	Other[a]
Ungrazed	A	41	25	421	33	0	0	17
	B	83	256	0	0	8	0	8
Winter	C	66	25	198	0	8	33	49
	D	50	157	50	33	74	0	17
Summer	E	124	223	0	74	41	0	25
	F	364	66	132	8	33	0	25
Deferred	G	91	298	0	74	41	0	8
	H	165	41	0	50	50	107	17

[a]*Cornus florida* L., *Diospyros virginiana* L., *Gleditsia triacanthos* L., *Juglans nigra* L., *Juniperus virginiana* L., *Nyssa sylvatica* Marsh., *Ostrya virginiana* (Mill.) K.Koch, *Platanus occidentalis* L., *Sassafras albidum* (Nutt.) Nees

Table B2.   Size distribution and stem basal area

Grazing regime	Pasture ID	Stems per hectare by diameter class (cm DBH)						Basal area (m^2ha^{-1})
		10–20	20–30	30–40	40–50	>50	Total	
Ungrazed	A	231	165	107	8	25	537	27
	B	140	91	91	33	0	355	19
Winter	C	107	116	91	50	17	380	28
	D	207	66	50	17	41	380	25
Summer	E	165	132	91	74	25	488	37
	F	347	215	33	33	0	628	23
Deferred	G	322	132	25	33	0	512	19
	H	182	107	58	66	17	430	27

Analysis of variation in distribution of overstory trees among diameter classes:

Source	G^a	df	p
Grazing regimes	15.9	9	0.069
Between pastures	32.6	12	0.001
Total	48.5	21	0.001

[a]Likehood ratio chi-square, after Sokal and Rohlf (1981). G is distributed approximately as chi-square. P values shown here are from the chi-square distribution.

Table B3.   Species composition of seedling and sapling populations in woodlands under contrasting grazing regimes. Estimates of stems per hectare are based on inventories of two plots in each pasture. Plot size was 50 m² for seedlings inventories, 605 m² for sapling inventories.

Grazing Regime	Size Classa (cm DBH)	Stems per ha								
		Carya spp.	*Querc.* spp.	*Acer sacc.*	*Frax. amer.*	*Ulmus* spp.	*Prunus ser.*	*Celtis occi.*	Otherb	Total
Ungrazed	Seedlings	1,500	2,100	1,400	1,250	700	1,250	200	750	9,150
	Sp < 3 cm	33	0	178	54	248	248	58	140	959
	Sp < 3–6.5 cm	4	4	62	4	136	4	12	21	248
	Sp < 6.6–10 cm	33	8	29	0	0	0	0	0	70
Winter	Seedlings	200	250	100	550	150	200	100	100	1,650
	Sp < 3 cm	0	0	12	0	0	0	4	4	21
	Sp < 3–6.5 cm	33	4	4	4	0	0	16	17	79
	Sp < 6.6–10 cm	33	12	4	0	33	0	17	0	99
Summer	Seedlings	900	550	300	6,700	750	2,050	250	350	11,850
	Sp < 3 cm	0	0	0	0	0	0	0	17	17
	Sp < 3–6.5 cm	4	0	4	4	50	0	0	4	66
	Sp < 6.6–10 cm	29	0	17	17	12	0	0	0	74
Deferred	Seedlings	150	700	0	2,000	3,200	1,350	600	150	8,150
	Sp < 3 cm	21	4	0	29	116	12	33	74	289
	Sp < 3–6.5 cm	70	16	0	21	25	0	8	4	145
	Sp < 6.6–10 cm	54	25	0	41	8	0	4	21	133

aSeedlings are individuals with basal diameter less than 2 cm. Saplings (Sp) are individuals with basal diameter greater than 2 cm and DBH less than 10 cm.

bIncludes: *Acer negundo* L., *Acer rubrum* L., *Asimina triloba* (L.) Dunal., *Cercis canadensis* L., *Cornus florida* L., *Crataegus* sp., *Diospyros virginiana* L., *Gleditsia triacanthos* L., *Juglans nigra* L., *Juniperus virginiana* L., *Morus rubra* L., *Nyssa sylvatica* Marsh., *Ostrya virginiana* (Mill.) K.Koch, *Platanus occidentalis* L., *Sassafras albidum* (Nutt.) Nees, *Prunus* sp., *Tilia americana* L.

Species and groups are as follows:

Carya spp.	*Carya cordiformis* (Wang.) K.Koch, *C. ovalis* (Wang.) Sarg., *C. ovata* (Mill.) K.Koch, *C. tomentosa* (Poir.) Nutt.
Querc. spp.	*Quercus alba* L., *Q. imbricaria* Michx., *Q. palustris* Muenchh., *Q. prinoides* Willd. var. *acuminata* (Michx.) Gl., *Q. rubra* L., *Q. stellata* Wangh., *Q. velutina* Lam.
Acer sacc.	*Acer saccharum* Marsh.
Frax. amer.	*Fraxinus americana* L.
Ulmus spp.	*Ulmus alata* Michx., *U. americana* L., *U. rubra* Muhl.
Prunus ser.	*Prunus serotina* Ehrh.
Celtis occi.	*Celtis occidentalis* L.

PART III

Conservation Strategies in Action

15

Terrestrial Nature Reserve Design at the Urban/Rural Interface

Craig L. Shafer
George Wright Society, P.O. Box 65, Hancock, MI 49930

Introduction

Wisconsin had 28 nature reserves five years after the Wisconsin State Board for the Preservation of Scientific Areas was created in 1951. Iltis (1956) remarked that "time is running out," indicating that 280 or even 500 reserves were needed. By 1993, Wisconsin had a remarkable 276 dedicated nature reserves. However, for much of the Midwest and other parts of the United States, time is running out in spite of some remarkable achievements (Figures 15.1–15.2). Awareness is increasing that terrestrial conservation efforts in some parts of the United States must by necessity be on small pieces of habitat, supporting small populations of species (e.g., Mitchell et al. 1990). Small reserves are important in areas where landscape alteration is very high *and* very low (Shafer 1995).

The effects of people on any landscape can be either dramatic or subtle where human populations are dense (McDonnell and Pickett 1993). In California, documentation of the loss of biodiversity (e.g., Jensen et al. 1993) has resulted in endorsement of new planning approaches by the highest state government officials. Perhaps because urbanization is moving closer to our rural and wilderness areas, this interface is receiving more attention in research (e.g., McDonnell and Pickett 1990). Urbanization, with its accompanying loss of native habitat and creation of new habitat, has been correlated with a decreasing number of bird species, increasing avian biomass, and increasing dominance of a few species (Emlen 1974, Beissinger and Osborne 1982).

Urban areas, however, are not necessarily a death knell for all wildlife. In fact, many opportunities for wildlife habitat or corridors in urban/suburban areas, like golf courses, are overlooked. (Terman 1994). Red foxes in Great Britain use railroad corridors to travel in and out of towns and cities (Kolb 1985, cited in Adams 1994), and Adams indicates that white-tailed deer, coyotes, and raccoons are thriving in some U.S. urban areas. Their presence may cause concern when deer browse on home shrubbery and gardens, coyotes attack pets, and raccoons

Figure 15.1. A 48-acre virgin beech-maple forest in Indiana. The tree is a 68-inch DBH Shumard's red oak.

Photo taken 1973, courtesy U.S. National Park Service

transmit disease or raid home garbage cans. Gill and Bonnett (1973) document how many species occur in London and Los Angeles. "The wolves, mountain lions, bears, salmon, and oysters that were part of Manhattan are gone, but the red fox, opossum (a new resident), flying squirrel, gray squirrel, muskrat, raccoon, several species of bats, and a host of birds remain" (Ehrenfeld 1972, 182–183).

European Precursors

Westhoff (1970) categorized landscapes as natural (undisturbed—no longer present in western and central Europe), *subnatural* (human influenced but still related to the potential natural vegetation), *seminatural* (sites now very different from the potential natural vegetation such as heathlands and moors, undrained/mowed/leveled dry pastures and hayfields, hedges, coppices, or older coastal dunes), and *cultivated* (e.g., a bean field). Seminatural landscapes predominated in western and central Europe from the Middle Ages until the end of the 19th century. Westhoff maintains that human influence during this time was more positive than negative. His explanation for this claim is that land management amplified and stabilized biotic variation. Land management methods stayed the same for centuries, people did not travel far from home, and their operations were gradual and

Figure 15.2. A 330-acre remnant tallgrass prairie near the eastern margin of Indiana's "Prairie Peninsula."

Photo taken 1973, courtesy U.S. National Park Service

of small scale. van der Maarel (1975) gives the distribution of plant species in the Netherlands by degree of naturalness: 20% near natural (e.g., woodlands, bogs, dunes), 60% seminatural (e.g., hay meadows, grazed salt marshes, coppices), and 20% agricultural and suburban. van der Maarel claims many plant species are tied to, or have an advantage in, seminatural environments. Similarly, Erhardt and Thomas (1991) claim a large percentage of British butterflies are confined to human-made niches, like secondary grassland created or maintained by agricultural practices.

Although Native Americans affected the North American landscape before Europeans arrived (Denevan 1992), their influence was much less profound compared with what Europe experienced. Much of the U.S. Midwest resembles the seminatural landscape that predominated in Europe for centuries. Europeans tried to devise conservation strategies for their countries accordingly. We have much to learn from this European example as parts of our country are modified to less wilderness characteristics (see Green 1981). Although we should focus much of our efforts on *remnant ecosystems/natural islands,* other classifications with more urban affinities also harbor some native biota, e.g., urban savanna, mowed/grassland, urban/forest plantation, rail-highway/grassland, and so forth (Brady et al. 1979).

Remnant Persistence

Statistics about how much is left of a particular biotic community are common and depressing. For ecosystems whose spatial extent has declined by more than 98% in the United States, the greatest losses are from grassland, savanna, and barrens (Noss et al. 1995). Only about 2% of California's interior wetlands remain. Some of these communities were not widespread to begin with; for example, vernal pools covered only 1% of the state and 80% are gone (Barbour and Whitworth 1994). Leopold (1949) long ago pointed out that some of the best examples of prairie communities are remnants found along railroad rights-of-way. Betz (1977) explains that many tiny tracts can still be found along fenced railroads, along farmers' creeks, in hay meadows, in cemeteries, and in some suburban areas. Some states, such as Minnesota, have gone to great lengths to inventory their highways for remnant prairies (see Harrington 1994). In southern Saskatchewan, less than 1% of the grasslands ecoregion is in highly protected reserves (Gauthier and Patino 1995). Less than 202 ha of intact oak savanna remain in Wisconsin, which is less than 0.01% of the original 5.5 million acres in the state (Department of Natural Resources 1995). A 1985 inventory of the entire Midwest revealed that only 0.02% of this plant community is left (Henderson and Epstein 1995). These intact remnants (prairie and savanna) are almost exclusively found on marginal soil types (with the exception of railroad rights-of-way).

The most important woodlands in England and Wales—the species-rich "ancient" tracts that have persisted since the Middle Ages—were recently better quantified by Spencer and Kirby (1992). They found that those woodlands still covered a remarkable 2.6% of the land surface, with 83% of the sites under 20 ha. They calculate that 7% of the ancient tracts were lost in the last 50 years. Such detailed baseline information is necessary in setting conservation priorities in human-dominated landscapes. Some British biotic communities are also very rare. For example, 0.1% of the peat fens in eastern England, such as Wicken Fen, remain undrained. The swallowtail butterfly *Papilio machaon* was lost from Wicken Fen in 1952, leaving only one other population in Great Britain. Studies have focused on why reintroductions have not yet worked, presumably because of food plant availability (Harvey and Meredith 1981).

The 140,000 km² Western Australian wheatbelt once had 41,000 km² of woodland, but only 1,000 km² remain. The Australian government designated 639 forest patches as reserves, and thousands of other privately owned patches are scattered throughout the region. It represents an enormous test case in potential cooperation with private landowners to preserve patches and decrease patch isolation. Many species have already been lost as a result of fragmentation, but positive action rather than resignation may permit others to persist (Saunders and Hobbs 1989).

At times native biotic communities can display surprising resiliency, and their persistence is known only after detailed inventory. For example, the Canterbury Plains in New Zealand was assumed to have lost many of its native biotic communities after 100 years of deforestation. In spite of its apparent continuous expanse of farmland and urban areas, a closer look revealed that many of these communities still survived (Molloy 1971). The Crown purchased 2 to 3 ha tracts of vegetation types that once covered approximately 100,000 to 200,000 ha. The best remaining examples of some vegetation types included 526, 16, and 3 ha tracts.

Remnants As Refugia

Species and Area

The theory of island biogeography (MacArthur and Wilson 1963, 1967) has been equated with the beginning of conservation biology (Simberloff 1988). The theory served as a foundation for thinking about nature reserve design in the 1970s and later. The empirical basis supporting such use is slim, and respect for the theory's conservation usefulness has declined (Shafer 1990, Formann 1995). "The inability of ecological theory to predict precisely future population sizes, the rate at which a fauna will collapse following insularization of its habitat, or the response of an ecosystem to a complex series of insults does not necessarily represent failure of the theory . . . . The problem of balancing precision against generality is much more difficult for ecological theoreticians than it is for theoretical physicists" (Ehrlich 1989, 315). Complete agreement in the scientific community about the theory's empirical foundation does not exist even today (Rosenzweig 1995). However, most would agree that much more autecological information is needed for specific reserve design prescriptions. McCoy (1983) pointed out that the minimum area needed by a suite of butterfly species can only be determined by detailed autecological study, and area alone may not be the most important factor.

The species-area relationship (see Williamson 1988), one component of the theory of island biogeography, may have relevance to conservation practice in some situations (see Shafer 1990 for detractors). That species increase with area is well known, with very rare exceptions (e.g., Dunn and Loehle [1988] for plants). Birds are one of the best studied groups in this regard. The number of rural studies that found that bird species increased with woodlot size is substantial: Freemark and Merriam (1986) outside Ottawa, Canada; Opdam et al. (1985) in the Netherlands; Lynch and Whigham (1984) on Maryland's coastal plain; Woolhouse (1985) in Great Britain; Ambuel and Temple (1983) for southern Wisconsin; and Kitchener et al. (1982) for western Australia. For more urban areas, habitat size has been shown to determine species number for birds (Gavareski 1976, Tilghman 1987, Vizyova 1986), for reptiles and amphibians (Dickman 1987, Vizyova 1986), and for small mammals (Matthiae and Stearns 1981).

Small but Not Vacant

That small, urban parks could play a role as nature reserves has often been ignored in our focus on recreational/psychological values (e.g., Seymour 1969), but this is changing (e.g., Spirn 1984, Gilbert 1991, Adams 1994, Platt et al. 1994). Dickman (1987), based on species-area relationships in the city of Oxford, thought mammal species (excluding deer) could be maintained in a system of small 0.65+ ha habitat patches and amphibians and reptiles in 0.55+ ha patches with permanent water. Because there was no temporal dimension to the study, presence may not necessarily mean persistence.

Based on a survey of 72 remnant grasslands in the Chicago area between 1982 and 1994 and other information, Panzer et al. (1995) concluded that around 25% of the insect species are remnant dependent. One small English garden contained 21 of the 70 known butterfly species in Britain (Owen 1978, cited in Adams 1994). However, more than one patch may be needed to ensure their survival (Hanski and Thomas 1994). One square foot of Pacific Northwest old-growth forest soil and litter can yield 200 to 250 species of invertebrates (Moldenke and Lattin 1990).

Some authors have concluded that suburban and urban parks are unsuccessful as avifaunal reserves due to small size, isolation, and vulnerability to human impacts (e.g., Lynch and Whitcomb 1978). An ongoing study of 225 forest fragments in Prince Georges County, Maryland, including some urban tracts, has a minimum size cutoff of 0.5 ha (Robbins, personal communication). Some birds will nest in the smallest tracts, often "suburban" species (Robbins et al. 1989a). In their literature review, Adams and Dove (1989) made predictions for expected species number as a function of habitat size—they thought some woodland and chaparral birds would be present in 1 ha remnants. Such remnants can provide habitat to produce some birds, which is different from providing viable habitat by themselves. Sometimes a small remnant can be the last refuge for a plant or invertebrate species (Shafer 1995). Ehnström and Waldén (1986, cited in Hansson 1992) describe a 5 ha old oak forest in Sweden that is the last refuge for some species of rare beetles.

Population Viability

The persistence of *minimum viable populations* (MVP) has been defined as hinging on genetic, demographic, and environmental stochasticities, and natural catastrophe (Shaffer 1981), although the term MVP was in use earlier (e.g., Frankel 1970). Early on, very rough generalizations emerged about how large a population needed to be to persist for a certain length of time. For example, it was proposed that a mean of 2,000 vertebrates (give or take one order of magnitude) was needed for a 95% expectation of population persistence for 200 years (Soulè 1987b). Soulè and Simberloff (1986, 32) state: "Thus, not only is there no magic number, there is no magic protocol. Intuition, common sense and judicious use of available data are still the state of the art." Thomas (1990) proposed to move Soulè's (1987b) well-known generalization of "low thousands" to a mean of 2,000 to 10,000 (Note: Soulè [1987b] also used the terms "few thousand" or "several thousand.") Lande (1995, 789) argues for an effective population size of 5,000 "to maintain normal levels of potentially adaptive genetic variance in quantitative characters under a balance between mutation and random genetic drift" (*see also* Culotta 1995). A *population viability analysis* or PVA (Gilpin and Soulè 1986), reviewed in detail by Boyce (1992) and Ballou et al. (1995), is far better than relying on any generalizations. As Holsinger (1995) pointed out, only a few endangered species are likely to receive a complete population viability analysis because of the enormous data-gathering work required. Such best-data scenarios will still not allow fine predictions about needed population size. Why is this?

Genetics is presumed the least important component of MVP, and catastrophe the most important (Shaffer 1987). Since catastrophe is so difficult to account for, long-term predictions by PVA are still in the realm of guesswork (Barrow-clough 1992). Additionally, the deterministic human dimension (e.g., human population density, development and pollution, or exotic species and climate change) could overshadow any so-called stochastic events in traditional PVA. Demographic stochasticity was claimed to be more important than genetics (Lande 1988). Similarly, Brakefield (1991) maintains that an insect population size that minimizes ecological extinction (providing effective population size does not go below several hundred individuals and longer-term evolutionary potential is not taken into account) should automatically take care of genetic variation. Nunney and Campbell (1993), in contrast, maintain that genetic and demographic concerns dictate a similar population size threshold. Regardless, we can still be fairly confident that the upper threshold will be dictated by catastrophe.

The Nature Conservancy concluded that 1,678 United States plant taxa (8.4%) are known from five or fewer locations or less than 1,000 individuals (Falk 1991). In spite of the pressing need, addressing MVP for plants is more recent (Menges 1990). Menges suggested that minimum island size may not be important for plants but metapopulation considerations will be. Weaver and Kellman (1981) concluded that area and isolation did not explain tree species persistence or loss in ten Ontario woodlots. Ouborg's (1993) data from the Dutch Rhine caused him to conclude that metapopulation structure, the negative effect of isolation, and population size was important for some plant species. Widén and Svensson (1992) assume that self-fertilizing annual plants that are selected for inbreeding may not be harmed genetically by habitat fragmentation but outbreeding perennials could be. However, they conclude that present empirical knowledge about genetic diversity and population size in plants is still insufficient to confidently devise strategies to thwart habitat fragmentation. Inbreeding depression in plants has been invoked as a cause of poor survival (Menges 1991, Waller 1993). Schemske et al. (1994) found that the primary cause of endangerment for all but 1 of 98 U.S. plant species listed as threatened or endangered by the U.S. Fish and Wildlife Service was human activity. Most ultimate causes of animal extinction today are probably anthropogenic, although the proximate cause (i.e., reason the last individuals die) could be genetic, demographic, by catastrophe, or through direct human action like collecting or hunting (Simberloff 1986b).

Caughley (1994) contrasted the small population versus declining population paradigms, arguing that the latter has received much less attention but is more germane to conservation. Unless these two things are combined in PVA, the factors probably most significant to a population's survival will be ignored. The National Research Council (1995) concluded that all PVAs are limited by data and methods; that most PVAs vary only some important influences, resulting in casual estimates; and that single factor PVAs will underestimate extinction threats. Because "formal population viability analyses are complex and are impossible to conduct on a routine basis" (Ruggiero et al. 1994, 371), these authors recommended a shortcut to allow managers to do some impact assessment. PVA should be made more available and digestible to managers, with or without shortcuts. Better yet, we need to focus on the real driving factors in any PVA, which requires transdisciplinary approaches. The traditional approach at PVA may be more comfortable to biologists (e.g., Remmert 1994) but is not a depiction of the real world. (Note: There is further debate on these points in the August 1995 issue of *Conservation Biology*.)

Metapopulations

The term *metapopulation* is usually attributed to Levins (1968, vi): "any real population [that] is a population of local populations which are established by colonists, survive for a while, send out migrants, and eventually disappear," although Simberloff (1988) pointed out a form of the idea that arose earlier. The rough metapopulation idea involves a set of geographically distinct populations together comprising a larger population. These subpopulations occasionally receive immigrants amongst one another; there can be a "winking" on and off (local extinction) of subpopulations; but the overall metapopulation persists (see Gilpin and Hanski 1991, Wilson 1992). Conservationists have used the metapopulation model as rationale for preserving multiple-habitat patches or reserves, presuming some species are adapted to this population structure. Some others have used it as a reason why it is acceptable to give up some local populations! The degree to which this model has been supported by field data hinges on the rigidity of model definition (see Shafer 1995). However, the idea that some species now exist in small patches is not arguable. For example, Hanski (1994) indicates that the Finland butterfly *Melitaea cinxia* lives in a series of 50 small patches, most under 1 ha.

The important underlying conservation assumption is that one habitat or reserve is not enough if we want to simulate a population's natural metapopulation structure. Bank voles showed a pattern of recolonization following local patch extinction. Extinctions were most likely in woodlots under 0.5 ha, and their abundance decreased as distance increased from woods of more than 25 ha (van Apeldoorn et al. 1992). Even an enormous population of small organisms is not necessarily safe on a small habitat patch. Tscharntke (1992) concluded that populations of 180,000 adult moths *Archanara geminipuncta* cannot persist on 2 ha *Phragmites* nature reserves without nearby reservoir populations. However, most questions about reserve size, numbers, and distance between habitat patches for invertebrates remains a mystery due to lack of dispersal data (Thomas and Morris 1995).

After three decades of research on the bay checkerspot butterfly *(Euphydryas editha bayensis),* the modeling of Murphy et al. (1990) permitted a reserve design conclusion: small, low-quality, serpentine grassland patches within seven miles of the largest reservoir patch could be as important, or more important, to the survival of the metapopulation than larger, higher-quality patches at greater distances. Computer simulation modeling conducted by Fahrig et al. (1983) led to the following conclusions: links between habitat patches are important and there is a minimum number of patches needing connection.

The metapopulation concept involves *replicates* of habitat. However, the early recognition that more than one reserve is desirable was not tied to metapopulation theory (e.g., Specht et al. 1974) but to intuitive common sense. The replication message became intertwined and perhaps obscured with the academic Single Large Or Several Small controversy (abbreviated SLOSS) that began in 1976 (Simberloff and Abele 1976). The early SLOSS debate centered around whether it is more desirable to have *(but not necessarily retain over a long period)* species in one large reserve or in a number of smaller reserves whose total area equals that of the single large one. Whether one large reserve is better than several small reserves was raised earlier (e.g., Bourliere 1962, 66) but not as a scientific hypothesis. The advantages of replication, irrespective of SLOSS, was occasionally pointed out (e.g., Soulè and Simberloff 1986; Shafer 1990, 1994, 1995). The mean size of scientific areas in Wisconsin (18.8 ha) is smaller than the 50 ha typically affected by individual tornados (Guntenspergen 1983).

Lessons from the Temperate Zone

Moore (1962, 390) implied that a biotic community has a minimum size—"The smallest viable size of a habitat is the smallest which supports a viable population of its weakest species." There have been efforts for some time to gauge it from species-area relationships (e.g., Vestal 1949). However, Usher's (1986) review led him to claim that minimum biotic community size is yet to be determined for any community. This claim has not stopped scientists from providing their best judgements for biotic communities, however defined or demarcated. For example, plant diversity declined with heathland fragment size in Dorset, England (Webb and Vermaat 1990), and the authors recommended 55 ha for maximum heathland plant representation. Levenson (1981) estimated a 4 to 5 ha undisturbed tract was needed to secure the future of all plants characteristic of a southern Wisconsin mesic beech-maple forest and 7 to 8 ha was needed for a dry mesic oak forest. The reason was that below this size the invasion rate by edge-adapted, shade-intolerant tree species was too high. Another biotic edge effect is nest predation. Species like cowbirds are severely decreasing the survival of neotropical migrant birds, no longer protected in deep interior forests because of habitat fragmentation (Wilcove 1985). Woodlot edges are also created by human impacts (Matlack 1993). Some think edge effects encompass a plethora of human encroachments on national parks (e.g., National Park Service 1980), but many might best be called matrix effects. Schonewald-Cox and Bayless (1986) proposed an all-encompassing boundary effects model. The intuitive assumption that human impacts would be greater in small tracts arose earlier (Wright et al. 1933, 43).

Mader (1984) indicates that very small tracts (less than 0.5 ha) in West Germany should be disregarded because they are all edge and no core. This does not mean, however, that they have no biological value to conservation. Although very small reserves might not allow long-term persistence for certain species, particularly large mammals, many other species use them and some small species may be able to persist in them (Figure 15.3). Small tracts have other values too (Shafer 1995), like education, science, habitat to facilitate dispersal, and providing propogules for restoration.

Really small tracts (e.g., 0.1 ha of vegetation) "do not reveal any fundamental

HOW SMALL A RESERVE?

Arctic National Wildlife Refuge, Alaska	7,804,819 ha
Everglades National Park + Big Cypress National Preserve, Florida	796,809 ha
Shenandoah National Park, Virginia	79,055 ha
Congaree Swamp National Monument, South Carolina	6,126 ha
Muir Woods National Monument, California	224 ha
Davis-Purdue Experimental Forest, Indiana	21 ha
Weston Cemetery Prairie, Illinois	2 ha

Figure 15.3. Each U.S. protected area is approximately one-tenth the size the one listed above it.

diversity properties of the places or the taxa being sampled" (Rosenzweig 1995, 279). In other words, there is some data to suggest the typical species-area plot is *not* found below some area threshold—not surprising as biotic communities on such small tracts will not be unaltered representative examples of pristine species assemblages.

Lessons from the Tropics

The decline of neotropical migrant songbirds in North America is well known. What is influencing this trend the most—forest tract size for spring breeding in North America versus deforestation in the tropics where they spend the winter— is not yet known (Robbins et al. 1989b). Some neotropical migrant bird species need forest tracts of at least 3,000 ha to breed in North America (Robbins et al. 1989a). However, we should not overlook that some forest-dependent neotropical migrant songbirds do survive the winter on the Yucatan Peninsula in small patches of trees in an agricultural landscape (Greenberg 1989). Patches with eight small trees (ungrazed) and ten small trees (grazed) gave three times more sightings than patches with fewer trees. Schelhaus and Greenberg (1993) provide a good compendium and analysis of tropical literature, some of which I will use here.

Lovejoy et al. (1984) found that Amazon butterflies with uniform distributions needed 10 ha tracts of tropical forest for representative communities but that butterflies with patchy distributions needed 100 ha tracts. Klein (1989) found that dung and carrion beetle communities in the Brazilian Amazon had fewer species as forest patch size decreased—100 ha, 10 ha, and 1 ha. Lovejoy (1987) indicates that the howler monkey *Alouatta seniculus* was able to persist and reproduce in all of their 10 ha isolated Brazilian rainforest patches, though many other monkey species were quickly lost. Lovejoy et al. (1986) reported that tree mortality (over 10 cm DBH) in isolated 1 and 10 ha tropical forest fragments was almost twice as high as in continuous forest. Laurence (1991) believed a tropical forest reserve that is too small may end up preserving species that could have survived outside of the reserves anyway.

A species can be found in a fragment long after its population is presumably too low to persist (Janzen 1988). Some scientists have recorded low extinctions in some tropical forests (e.g., Brown and Brown 1992), though massive extinctions are predicted by species-area relationships (e.g., Simberloff 1986a). There can be a long lag effect. The remaining species could be doomed because the species loss period following deforestation is not immediate. Science journalists (e.g., Mann 1991) might stress that continued species presence over the short term may not invalidate some species-area extinction predictions. On the other hand, these doomed species could form the nucleus of a species salvage effort.

One Danger of Guidelines—Biotic Community Size

The provision of guidelines to planners on how small a tract is too small for a population is useful, if based on thorough research. Guidelines are much more difficult for *communities*. In most cases, we simply do not know how many species and what species a small remnant will preserve. We presume that some plants and insects will fare better than medium-sized mammals and area-sensitive birds. The umbrella-species approach at gauging needed reserve size assumes that the area required to protect viable populations of large vertebrates like bears will automatically be large enough to protect other species with small home ranges (Wilcox 1984, Shafer 1995). Unfortunately, it tells us nothing about the space requirements of smaller species in the biotic community. The umbrella species may have been lost from the region long ago or the isolated remnant has become so small as to make such an approach pointless.

Misuse of size guidelines is a danger. Size guidelines do not mean sites below this size should be abandoned, serving no purpose for a "flagship" species, other species, or for science or education (Shafer 1995). Size is only one consideration. Habitat management, connectivity, replication, and buffering will also greatly influence the perpetuity of species in a habitat patch or reserve.

Value of Dispersal Corridors

Corridors have captured the attention of scientists (e.g., Saunders and Hobbs 1991), elicited guidance to planners (e.g., Smith and Hellmund 1993), and generated grassroots action to create greenways (e.g., Little 1989, Flink and Searns 1993). The pros and cons of corridors are discussed in Noss (1987) and elsewhere. I will highlight here some research that is particularly germane to very human-dominated landscapes.

Studies in the actual use of any corridor by a species is still meager (Simberloff et al. 1992). Based on painstaking research, fencerows in farmland near Ottawa, Canada, appear to allow the dispersal of chipmunks and white-footed mice, allowing populations in isolated woodlots to persist (Wegner and Merriam 1979, Fahrig and Merriam 1985, Henderson et al. 1985). However, looking at fifteen 1 to 25 ha Ottawa farmland woodlots varying from 300 to 500 meters apart, Middleton and Merriam (1983) concluded that only 7 of 86 taxa (trees, herbs, squirrels, or invertebrates) reflected any isolation influence. Most of these species may be adapted to medium-distance movement. Hence, one has to be cautious about making "island" assumptions based only on casual landscape observation. Some species may need corridors but others may not. Soulè et al. (1988) observed some California chaparral bird species occupying 1 to 10 ha ribbons of habitat and then presumed that the ribbons were needed for dispersal between larger tracts.

There are certainly documented barriers to dispersal. Mader (1984) found that some species of beetles rarely cross highways in West Germany, but mice, far more able to navigate this distance, rarely cross either. Eversham and Telfer (1994), however, argue roadside verges in the Netherlands are used by carabid beetles not as corridors but as refugia. Klein (1989) found a 100 m gap in Brazilian rainforest would affect the movement of dung and carrion-feeding beetles. Volant species presumably will be less affected by isolation, but some are poor dispersers. For example, one butterfly species *(Mellicta athalia)* rarely moves between boreal forest gaps of 1 km (Warren 1987). Knaapen et al. (1992) estimated that butterflies would have much more difficulty traversing a built-up landscape (residential, commercial, or industrial, especially with less than 5% forest cover) in the Netherlands than would deer, squirrels, or forest birds. Dispersal is important for the survival of arthropods (der Boer 1990) and barriers do exist (Mader et al. 1990).

Moon (1990) described koalas moving from one park sanctuary to another through open paddocks. These paddocks contained sparsely distributed trees as much as 300 m apart. The koalas commonly used individuals of the tree *Eucalyptus tereticornis* 14 to 18 m in height for movement, suggesting tree plantings might be feasible to enhance corridor appeal for koalas in degraded areas.

Elton (1958, 156–158), discussing the virtues of hedgerows, remarked "I cannot think of any ecological system in Britain that so clearly has all the virtues inherent in the conservation of variety. . . . They form, as it were, a connective tissue binding together the separate organs of the landscape." We need to know the habitat needs of a species to complete its life cycle before we conclude a particular habitat linkage means the difference between extinction and perpetuity. Preferably, research should come first to ascertain whether corridors would be useful for a particular species, and if so, what its dimensions should be (Simberloff et al. 1992, Hobbs 1993). However, that is a luxury often not available in places like San Diego County, California (Mann and Plummer 1995). In lieu of good data, perhaps the best advice is to maintain habitat connectivity until we know more. Elton may have agreed with this logic. Once connectivity is gone, it is very difficult to re-create. England lost roughly a quarter of its hedgerows—96,000 miles—from 1945 to 1985. A further study gave a decline of 53,000 miles between 1984 and 1990 (Bryson 1993).

Whyte (1968, 389–399) said, "The most pressing need now is to weave together a host of seemingly disparate elements—an experimental farm, a private golf course, a local park, the spaces of a cluster subdivision, the edge of a new freeway right-of-way." His reasons were not based on conservation biology but because this linearity created more "visual space" for humans to see. His idea is nevertheless valid for animal movement. Isolation may have some pluses—for example, restricting exotic species, limiting transfer of disease, and denying entry of domestic predators like cats and dogs (Simberloff and Cox 1987)—but the greater danger lies in not being able to re-create natural landscape connections (Noss 1987).

Reserve Design

More Science

Reserve design guidelines for terrestrial ecosystems, reportedly derived from island biogeography theory, were soon advocated for incorporation in the planning process of nature reserves (Balser et al. 1981). Based on a study of chaparral fragments in San Diego, California, Soulè (1991) concluded that at least three of Diamond's (1975) general reserve design guidelines would be applicable to this urbanized setting as well: large is better than small, single large is better than several small (SLOSS), and corridors are better than no connection.

Wildlife conservation efforts in urban areas must proceed based on available scientific guidance, often inadequate in providing explicit directions to planners (Adams and Leedy 1987, 1991). Although they are not a substitute for detailed information on a particular species of concern, Shafer (1994) nevertheless proposed some updated graphic nature reserve design guidance (Figure 15.4). These

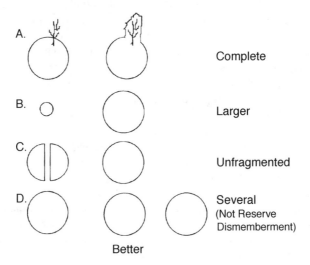

Figure 15.4. The option on the right is proposed as better than the one on the left. See text for discussion.

From Shafer 1994, reprinted with permission of Elsevier Science, Amsterdam

A. Complete watersheds, migratory routes, feeding grounds are preferable inside reserves.
B. Larger is better than smaller, especially for wide-ranging large mammals.
C. Unfragmented is better than fragmented.
D. Several reserves (e.g., two reserves, each 1,000 km², instead of one 1,000 km² reserve) are better because replication guards against catastrophe and human exploitation, and may capture more endemic or patchily distributed species. This is not a recommendation for reserve dismemberment.

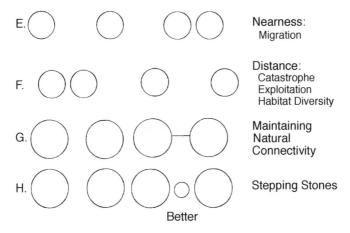

Figure 15.4. Continued.

E. Nearness is better than being father apart because it facilitates migration to a sister reserve, providing the landscape is traversable by the species.

F. A greater distance may be better, however, to reduce the effects of catastrophe, disease, and human exploitation; increase the likelihood of more habitat heterogeneity and thus more species; and enhance the possibility of more intraspecific genetic variation.

G. Maintaining existing natural connectivity/usable corridors is a far better alternative than no connection.

H. Small stepping-stone reserves, if used, are better than none at all.

guidelines are a mix of very broad ideas, but are real-world oriented. Most are also germane to densely populated regions.

There may be no single answer about what a minimum viable population is for a species, and hence there is no consensus on the best reserve design (Nunney and Campbell 1993). McCoy (1983) concluded that minimum area and best-choice options for remaining habitat patches can only be determined from detailed information about species natural history and the patches themselves, not from simple species-area equation calculations. Since local extinction of fragmented populations is common, an understanding of a particular species' dispersal characteristics is essential if the most optimal patches for future reserves are to be sought from the pool of remaining patches (Fahrig and Merriam 1994). I think Wright (1990) correctly indicated that general reserve design guidelines derived from model populations are potentially useful only when detailed information on a species' requirements are unavailable.

Bennett (1990) concludes that forest fragmentation in southwestern Victoria, Australia, leads to four recommendations for mammalian conservation: a regional perspective, maintenance of substantial total area of forest, maintenance and enhancement of forest continuity, and protection and promotion of faunal habitat. The broad generalities of needing large tracts of habitat, avoiding fragmentation,

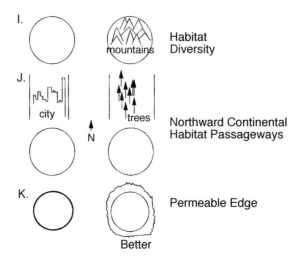

Figure 15.4. Continued.

I. Higher within-habitat heterogeneity (e.g., mountains, lakes) should allow for more species due to more habitat. The elevational diversity that mountains provide is also helpful in thwarting climate change.

J. Continental habitat passageways may be vital for overcoming climate change, especially toward higher latitude.

K. A permeable edge encourages animal movement across a park boundary. Edge abruptness, width, vertical structure, and natural discontinuities influence permeability (Forman and Moore 1992).

and maintaining connectivity were later made by Shafer (1990) and Wilcove and Murphy (1991). These ideas are indeed simple (see Soberon 1992) but their adoption could have a profound positive effect.

Other Realities

Kelly and Rotenberry (1993, 85) said, "In regions that are undergoing rapid urbanization, such as much of Southern California, the question of preplanning the establishment of reserves of sufficient size and configuration to maintain population or community viability is often moot because of high land values and the extent of pre-existing habitat fragmentation." They nevertheless argue for a scientific framework for buffer zone establishment; otherwise the reserves will be "gradually eroded away by external forces." Vast reserves in some parts of California may now be precluded, but networks of smaller ones are not.

San Diego County has initiated one of the most detailed nature reserve design planning efforts in the country, which could serve as a template elsewhere (City of San Diego 1995, Boucher 1995). Gap analysis has been applied to a 235,387 ha area in the southwest portion of the county, identifying core reserves, linkages, and available buffer zones. The analysis involved 15 layers of GIS design information (including land ownership and projected land use) and four proposed reserve

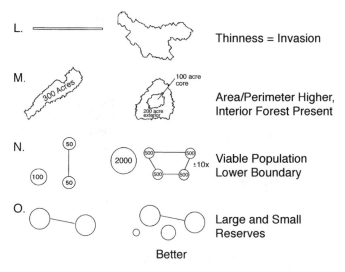

Figure 15.4. Continued.

L. Very thin reserves (e.g., roughly 200–500 m) can encourage invasion by avian predators or weedy species.

M. Similarly, reserves with no or too little core interior forest may lack area required for some U.S. neotropical migrant birds. Theory and some modeling also suggest higher area-perimeter ratios may be better for buffering some external influences and facilitating animal movement across boundaries.

N. A thoughtful guess at the lower limit for minimum viable population size (Soulè 1987b) is better than assumed nonviable ones. However, be forewarned that "there is no single 'magic number' that has universal validity" (Soulè 1987a). This is not a recommendation for reserve dismemberment but for reserve connection as needed. Note: some (e.g., Lande 1995) would argue this lower limit should be upped tenfold.

O. Small reserves can provide a useful purpose for some species in any reserve system.

design options (Stallcup, personal communication). Observers await its potential adoption in an extremely urbanized and fast-growing region of the country. Reid and Murphy (1995) and Manson (1994) discuss similar efforts in other California counties.

An ongoing effort in Wisconsin, led by The Nature Conservancy, is a good example of reserve planning for multiple small nature reserves within a specific regional landscape. The landscape design for Baraboo Hills, Wisconsin, consists of a plethora of small fragments and buffer zones, connected by other habitat or corridors. The results of this planning effort, and others like it, is not yet known.

Falk (1992, 398) said "The daily practice of conservation is as different from the world of theory and scholarly research as is the blackboard at a military academy from the battlefield. As every conservationist knows, decisions in the field are as likely to be influenced by real-estate transactions, land use, the economics of resource extraction, state and federal taxation, political expediency,

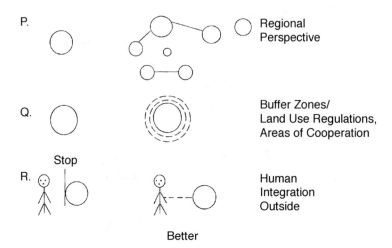

P.

Regional
Perspective

Q.

Buffer Zones/
Land Use Regulations,
Areas of Cooperation

Stop

R.

Human
Integration
Outside

Better

Figure 15.4. Continued.

P. A regional perspective rather than a local perspective is crucial in preserving reserve biota.
Q. Buffer zones/land use regulations or areas of cooperative planning outside reserve boundaries are crucial to minimizing human impacts.
R. Human population outside the reserve must be socially and economically integrated into a reserve management plan so the park boundaries are not viewed as an abrupt wall or the park considered an island. Application of social sciences, e.g., Q and R, not just application of ecological theory, is among the foremost nature reserve planning challenges.

and the vagaries of public opinion as they are by careful planning grounded in sound conservation biology." The economic, political, and legal considerations gain importance when one is looking at regional landscapes (Shafer 1994).

The issue is therefore not just one of science. The social, economic, and political circumstances must be dealt with (Frankel 1974) or scientific guidance may become irrelevant (Shafer 1990, 1994, in press). Many other factors come into play, such as funding, accessibility, land cost, level of protection, owner attitude, adjacent landowner sympathy toward regional planning, and proximity to large urban areas. Goldsmith (1991) indicated reserve selection criteria for London includes public access, aesthetic appeal, proximity to urban communities, and degree of open-space deficiency.

Role of Nonreserves

Seminatural areas, as we have seen, can contribute to the conservation of biological diversity. In the San Diego County plan, more than just strict nature reserves are being sought. Nearly three-quarters of the remaining coastal sage scrub is on private land. Planners are treating the entire existing landscape as a de facto reserve system. Besides the buffer zones and corridors essential for the strict reserves, homes on large lots can also be a asset (Reid and Murphy 1995). Elsewhere in the United States, some urban parks, county fishing reservoirs, certain resorts, and even golf courses might be assets. We need to think of habitat wherever it occurs, not just in terms of reserves. The agricultural landscape has often been proposed as an alternative approach for biological diversity conservation (e.g., Green 1989), adopted in much of Europe, in part by default. Far more species exist in agricultural/forestry and other human-dominated ecosystems, covering 95% of the terrestrial environment, than in protected reserves (Pimental et al. 1992). In British urban areas, railway embankments, ancient forts, old quarries, gardens, and "wasteland" can provide habitat for some species (Gilbert 1991). In eastern Denmark, a primary function of small *biotopes* is to mark the boundaries of fields and estates. These boundary markers also provide habitat, and permission is required from authorities to disturb some of them. A gross categorization of biotopes include hedges, roadside verges, drainage ditches, small brooks, bogs, marl pits, natural ponds, thickets, and prehistoric barrows (Agger and Brandt 1988).

Insects Are Important

Insect ecology was once studied with the sole aim of potential control (e.g., Price 1984), but a new subdiscipline (i.e., conservation biology of insects) has emerged (Samways 1994). Insect conservation does matter (e.g., Kim 1993), in large part because they constitute 55% of the world's 1.4 million named organisms (Wilson 1992). Insects have been called the "little things that run the world" (Wilson 1987, 344) because of the vital role they play in ecosystem function.

Thomas and Morris (1995) think terrestrial invertebrate extinction rates in Britain have matched or exceeded those of vertebrates or vascular plants during the present century. There are success stories; Thomas (1991) provides accounts of endangered British butterfly populations recovering on small, isolated reserves with proper management. However, the rate of butterfly extinction in Europe is depressing in spite of valiant efforts (Warren 1992).

Looking again at California, the El Segundo blue butterfly *(Euphilotes battoides allyni)* resides on less than 1% of its original geographic range, which once extended about 36 miles along the shore of Santa Monica Bay, from Marine Del Ray to San Pedro. Its survival is closely tied with the Seacliff buckwheat plant. As of 1986, it survived on only two dune remnants—122 ha and 0.6 ha. Chevron, the owner of the 0.6 ha remnant, fenced off this area in 1975 and made it a butterfly sanctuary. Weed removal and outplanting of buckwheat on Chevron's remnant dune habitat occurred in 1983, 1984, and 1986. From 1977 to 1984, the estimated population declined by 70%, but 1985 and 1986 censuses indicated a slowing of this trend. Assuming this was a cause-effect relationship, a recommendation was made to continue outplanting buckwheat and clearing weeds. This was all for the perpetuation of a very small (0.6 ha) but critical piece of habitat for an endangered butterfly species (Arnold and Goins 1987). For their examples in California and elsewhere, see Beatley (1994).

Insect conservation can benefit other species. Launer and Murphy (1994) showed that if all central California serpentine grassland fragments containing the bay checkerspot butterfly *(Euphydryas editha bayensis)* were set aside, about 98% of the native spring flowering plants would receive some protection. The largest number of invertebrate extinctions and candidates for federal listing in the United States is in Hawaii and California (Hafernik 1992). California and Hawaii have the highest number of imperiled species (i.e., 600 or more) in the United States (Stein 1996). Hawaii is, however, our country's extinction capital—two-thirds of all extinct plants and animals come from this one state (Vitousek et al. 1987).

Remnant Restoration

Habitat restoration around habitat fragments can sometimes be accomplished by just allowing natural revegetation to proceed. For example, New York's Onondaga County had only 8% of its area in forest islands in 1930. However, forest cover increased by 40% by 1980, surrounding many older forest islands with younger 50-year-old trees (Nyland et al. 1986). Mladenoff et al. (1994, 752) proposed a design model for harvested Wisconsin forest that incorporates an "old-growth restoration zone surrounding old-growth patches to buffer and enhance forest-interior habitat and link nearby old-growth remnants. A larger secondary zone is delineated for uneven-aged forest management." The important point is that there may be opportunities to enhance remnant viability by allowing succession to proceed outside its boundaries and thereby expand its effective size or connect it to another fragment.

At a much larger scale, Alverson et al. (1994) proposed the creation of *diversity maintenance areas* (DMAs). The center of these idealized DMAs would consist of old-growth remnants. These centers would provide the building blocks for regeneration of large unfragmented tracts of late successional forests adjacent to them. The overall goal is to create mature, wild, old-growth forests and their natural ecological processes and disturbance regimes. The focus of Alverson and colleagues is primarily U.S. Forest Service lands, especially in Wisconsin, but they indicate the idea is applicable elsewhere.

True restoration can take a long time (e.g., hundreds to thousands of years). Tropical lowland dry forest can take 150 years to recover from timber harvest, and tropical lowland wet forest can take 1,000 years (Opler et al. 1977, cited in Reid and Miller 1989). Young successional forest inside or outside a fragment may increase the viability of a fragment in a much shorter time.

Private Initiative

Establishing vast reserves often requires the help of governments, but perhaps less so for smaller parcels. Prime (1992, 11) relates a situation in India, one of the world's most densely populated countries. Historically, between Indian villages three types of reserves were common: forest sanctuaries (raksha), dense forest (ghana), and planted single-species sacred groves (e.g., mango). The forest sanctuaries were off limits to the Hindu people, but the dense forest could be used to collect dry wood, forest produce, and a small amount of green timber. These one- to ten-acre tracts were cared for by the village communities, because they depended on it for their livelihood and they had a tradition of respect for nature. The standard of protection reportedly often exceeded that of current huge government-operated reserves. In the United States, Henry David Thoreau in 1859 thought each town should have "a primitive forest of five hundred or a thousand acres where a stick should never be cut for fuel, a common possession forever" (cited in Udall 1963, 173). Many small reserves are protected by a plethora of private organizations in the United States without the help of government (catalogued in The Nature Conservancy 1982). Throughout the world, private initiative in setting aside reserves is impressive (Alderman 1994).

In 1966, the U.S. Congress held hearings on senate bill S. 2282, a sweeping proposal for a nationwide effort at ecological survey and research. It was an early partial vision of what transpired in 1993—the creation of the U.S. National Biological Survey (later National Biological Service, and still later the Biological arm of the U.S. Geological survey). The role of this organization encompasses some of the need identified in 1966. The potential role it can potentially play is large (National Research Council 1993). The first Natural Heritage Program was created in 1974 under the leadership of The Nature Conservancy (TNC), now expanded to all 50 states, Latin America, and Canada, another example of private initiative at its best. Small tracts were often the focus of early TNC inventories, and some current gap analysis efforts also now consider them (Scott et al. 1993).

U.S. Midwest

It can be argued the U.S. Midwest is a success story in setting aside small remnant tracts. One can always bemoan biotic losses, but it is important to look back at the status of the small protected area enterprise here only 50 years ago. Progress was the result of commitment by thousands of individuals. Reserve location here was the result of an early but still very useful form of gap analysis. Reserve design was based primarily on academic and amateur field notes, common sense, and intuition.

Science-based management can accomplish much, but some problems stem from initial reserve size and layout. In highly urbanized regions, options to create new preserves or improve existing ones may be limited. It can be done, however, using sympathetic landowners, easements, or land purchases. Many states and private conservation organizations already have done this and can continue to do so. Monitoring is needed to gauge preservation success (Drayton and Primack 1996).

Ultimately, reserve design hinges on the value society places on preserving small natural areas. In other words, do we prefer a potentially higher quality of life amidst some native species, or a higher standard of living amidst landscape blight? One recent and able attempt to better educate Wisconsin natural resources personnel (Department of Natural Resources 1995) should be extended to other states. Other such attempts have surfaced (e.g., Nigh et al. 1992). State and federal natural resources personnel, from the maintenance staff to the politically appointed senior executives, need some basic information about what biological diversity means if they are to be effective land stewards in the next century.

An oversimplification of Leopold's (1949) famous land ethic is that humans should treat the outdoors as they would their home. If only this simple but profound idea were adopted as a personal and national principle by the general public, top officials, and politicians. Until then, only proactive foresight will help retain more species and biotic communities in highly impacted landscapes, sometimes their only remaining potential sanctuary.

Acknowledgements

I want to thank Frank Panek, Ron Hiebert, Mark Schwartz, and Phil van Mantgem for helpful comments on the draft manuscript. I am also grateful to the scientists who educated their audience, including this author, about small population viability during a June 1995 workshop at the Society for Conservation Biology meetings in Fort Collins, Colorado. The views expressed here are my own and do not reflect those of any organization.

References

Adams, L.W., and D.L. Leedy, eds. 1987. *Integrating Man and Nature in the Metropolitan Environment.* National Institute for Urban Wildlife, Columbia, Md.

———. 1991. *Wildlife Conservation in Metropolitan Environments.* National Institute for Urban Wildlife, Columbia, Md.

Adams, L.W., and L.E. Dove. 1989. *Wildlife Reserves and Corridors in the Urban Environment.* National Institute for Urban Wildlife, Columbia, Md.

Adams, L.W. 1994. *Urban Wildlife Habitats: A Landscape Perspective.* University of Minnesota Press, Minneapolis.

Agger, P., and J. Brandt. 1988. Dynamics of small biotopes in Danish agricultural landscapes. *Landscape Ecology* 1:227–240.

Alderman, C.L. 1994. The economics and the role of privately-owned lands used for nature tourism, education, and conversation. In M. Munasinghe, and J. McNeely, eds. *Protected Area Economies and Policy: Linking Conservation and Sustainable Development.* World Bank, Washington, D.C., 273–317.

Alverson, W., W. Kuhlmann, and D.W. Waller. 1994. *Wild Forests: Conservation Biology and Public Policy.* Island Press, Washington, D.C.

Ambuel, B., and S.A. Temple. Area-dependent changes in the bird communities and vegetation of southern Wisconsin forests. *Ecology* 64:1057–1068.

Arnold, R.A., and A.E. Goins. 1987. Habitat enhancement techniques for the El Segundo blue butterfly: An urban endangered species. In L.W. Adams, and D.L. Leedy, eds. *Integrating Man and Nature in the Metropolitan Environment.* National Institute for Urban Wildlife, Columbia, Md., 173–181.

Ballou, J., M. Gilpin, and T. Foose, eds. 1995. *Population Management for Survival and Recovery: Analytical Methods and Strategies in Small Population Survival and Recovery.* Columbia University Press, New York.

Balser, D., A. Bielak, G. De Boer, T. Tobias, G. Adindu, and R.S. Dorney. 1981. Nature reserve designation in a cultural landscape, incorporating island biogeography theory. *Landscape and Urban Planning* 8:329–347.

Barbour, M.G., and V. Whitworth. 1994. California's living landscape. *Fremontia* 22:3–13.

Barrowclough, G.F. 1992. Systematics, biodiversity, and conservation biology. In N. Eldridge, ed. *Systematics, Ecology, and the Biodiversity Crisis.* Columbia University Press, New York, 121–142.

Beatley, T. 1994. *Habitat Conservation Planning: Endangered Species and Urban Growth.* University of Texas Press, Austin.

Beissinger, S.R., and D.R. Osborne. 1982. Effects of urbanization on avian community organization. *Condor* 84:75–83.

Bennett, A.F. 1990. Land use, forest fragmentation and the mammalian fauna at Naringal, South-western Victoria. *Australian Wildlife Research* 17:325–347.

Betz, R.F. 1977. What is a prairie? *Nature Conservancy News* 27:9–13.

Boucher, N. 1995. Species of the sprawl. *Wilderness* 58:11–24.

Bourliere, F. 1962. Science in the parks in the tropics. In A.B. Adams, ed. *First World Conference on National Parks.* National Park Service, Department of the Interior, Washington, D.C., 63–68.

Boyce, M. 1992. Population viability analysis. *Annual Review of Ecology and Systematics* 23:481–506.

Brady, R.F, T. Tobias, P.F.J. Eagles, R. Ohrner, J. Micak, B. Veale, and R.S. Dorney. 1979. A typology for the urban ecosystem and it relationship to larger biogeographic landscape units. *Urban Ecology* 4:11–28.

Brakefield, P.M. 1991. Genetics and the conservation of invertebrates. In I.F. Spellerberg, F.B. Goldsmith, and M.G. Morris, eds. *The Scientific Management of Temperate Communities for Conservation.* Blackwell Scientific Publications, Oxford, 45–79.

Brown, K.S., and G.G. Brown. 1992. Habitat alteration and species loss in Brazilian forests. In T.C. Whitmore and J.A. Sayer, eds. *Tropical Deforestation and Species Extinction.* Chapman and Hall, London, 119–142.

Bryson, B. 1993. Britain's hedgerows. *National Geographic* 184:94–117.

Caughley, G. 1994. Directions in conservation biology. *Journal of Animal Ecology* 63:215–244.

City of San Diego. 1995. *Multiple Species Conservation Program: MSCP Plan Executive Summary.* Draft mimeo. City of San Diego, San Diego, Calif.

Culotta, E. 1995. Minimum population grows larger. *Science* 270:31–32.

Denevan, W.M. 1992. The pristine myth: The landscape of the Americas in 1492. *Annals of the Association of American Geographers* 82:369–385.

Department of Natural Resources. 1995. *Wisconsin's Biodiversity as a Management Issue: A Report to Department of Natural Resources Managers.* Department of Natural Resources, Madison, Wis.

der Boer, P.J. 1990. The survival value of dispersal in terrestrial arthropods. *Biological Conservation* 54:175–192.

Diamond, J.M. 1975. The island dilemma: Lessons of modern biogeographic studies for the design of natural reserves. *Biological Conservation* 7:129–146.

Dickman, C.R. 1987. Habitat fragmentation and vertebrate species richness in an urban environment. *Journal of Applied Ecology* 24:337–351.

Drayton, B., and R.B. Primack. 1996. Plant species lost in an isolated conservation area in metropolitan Boston from 1894 to 1993. *Conservation Biology* 10:30–39.

Dunn, C.D., and C. Loehle. 1988. Species-area parameter estimation testing the null model of lack of relationship. *Journal of Biogeography* 15:721–728.

Ehnström, B., and H.W. Waldén. 1986. *Faunavard i Skogsbruket, Del 2, Den lägre Faunan.* Skogsstyrelsen, Jönköping.

Ehrenfeld, D.W. 1972. *Conserving Life on Earth.* Oxford University Press, New York.

Ehrlich, P.R. 1989. Discussion: Ecology and resources management—Is ecological theory any good in practice? In J. Roughgarden, R.M. May and S. Levin, eds. *Perspectives in Ecological Theory.* Princeton University Press, Princeton, N.J., 306–318.

Elton, C.S. 1958. *The Ecology of Invasions by Animals and Plants.* Chapman and Hall, London.

Emlen, J.T. 1974. An urban bird community in Tucson, Arizona: Derivation, structure, regulation. *Condor* 76:184–197.

Erhardt, A., and J.A. Thomas. 1991. Lepidoptera as indicators of change in the semi-natural grasslands of lowland and upland Europe. In N.M. Collins, and J.A. Thomas, eds. *The Conservation of Insects and Their Habitats.* Academic Press, London, 213–236.

Eversham, B., and M.G. Telfer. 1994. Conservation value of roadside verges for stenotopic heathland Carabidae: Corridors or refugia? *Biodiversity and Conservation* 3:538–545.

Fahrig, L., L.P. Lefkovitch, and H.G. Merriam. 1983. Population stability in a patchy environment. In W.K. Lauenroth, G.V. Skogerboe, and M. Flug, eds. *Analysis of*

Ecological Systems: State-of-the-Art in Ecological Modeling. Elsevier, Amsterdam, 61–67.

Fahrig, L., and G. Merriam. 1985. Habitat patch connectivity and population survival. *Ecology* 66:1762–1768.

———. 1994. Conservation of fragmented populations. *Conservation Biology* 8:50–59.

Falk, D.A. 1991. Joining biological and economic models for conserving plant genetic diversity. In D.A. Falk, and K.E. Holsinger, eds. *Genetics and Conservation of Rare Plants.* Oxford University Press, New York, 209–223.

———. 1992. From conservation biology to conservation practice: Strategies for protecting plant diversity. In P.L. Fielder, and S.K. Jain, eds. *Conservation Biology: The Theory and Practice of Nature Conservation Preservation and Management.* Chapman and Hall, London, 397–431.

Flink, C.A., and R.M. Searns, eds. 1993. *Greenways: A Guide to Planning Design and Development.* Island Press, Washington, D.C.

Forman, R.T.T. 1995. *Land Mosaics: The Ecology of Landscapes and Regions.* Cambridge, London.

Forman, R.T.T. and P.N. Moore. 1992. Theoretical foundations for understanding boundaries in landscape mosaics. In A.J. Hansen, and F. di Castri, eds. *Landscape Boundaries: Ecological Studies 92.* Springer-Verlag, New York, 236–258.

Frankel, O.H. 1970. Variation—the essence of life. Sir William Macleay memorial lecture. *Proceedings of the Linnean Society of New South Wales* 95:158–169.

———. 1974. Genetic conservation: our evolutionary responsibility. *Genetics* 78:53–65.

Freemark, K.E., and H.G. Merriam. 1986. Importance of area and habitat heterogeneity to bird assemblages in temperate forest fragments. *Biological Conservation* 36:115–141.

Gauthier, D.A., and L. Patino. 1995. Protected area planning in fragmented, data-poor regions: Examples of the Saskatchewan grasslands. In T.B. Herman, S. Bondrup-Nielson, J.H. Willison, and N.W.P. Munro, eds. *Ecosystem Monitoring and Protected Areas.* Science and Management of Protected Areas Association, Acadia University, Wolfville, Nova Scotia, 537–547.

Gavareski, C.A. 1976. Relation of park size and vegetation to urban bird populations in Seattle, Washington. *Condor* 78:375–382.

Gilbert, O.L. 1991. *The Ecology of Urban Habitats.* Chapman and Hall, New York.

Gill, D., and P. Bonnett. 1973. *Nature in the Urban Landscape: A Study of City Ecosystems.* York Press, Baltimore, Md.

Gilpin, M.E., and I. Hanski, eds. 1991. *Metapopulation Dynamics: Empirical and Theoretical Investigations.* Academic Press, New York.

Gilpin, M.E., and M.E. Soulè. 1986. Minimum viable populations: Processes of species extinction. In M.E. Soulè, ed. *Conservation Biology: The Science of Scarcity and Diversity.* Sinauer Associates, Sunderland, Mass., 19–34.

Goldsmith, F.B. 1991. The selection of protected areas. In I.F. Spellerberg, F.G. Goldsmith, and M.G. Morris, eds. *The Scientific Management of Temperate Communities for Conservation.* Blackwell Scientific Publications, Oxford, 273–291.

Green, B. 1981. *Countryside Conservation: The Protection and Management of Amenity Ecosystems*. George Allen & Unwin, London.

————. 1989. Conservation in cultural landscapes. In D. Western, and M. Pearl, eds. *Conservation for the Twenty-First Century*. Oxford University Press, New York, 182–198.

Greenberg, R. 1989. Forest migrants in non-forest habitats on the Yucatan Peninsula. In J.M. Hagan III, and D.W. Johnston, eds. *Ecology and Conservation of Neotropical Migrant Songbirds*. Smithsonian Institution Press, Washington, D.C., 273–286.

Guntenspergen, G. 1983. The minimum size for nature preserves: evidence from southeastern Wisconsin forests. *Natural Areas Journal* 3:38–46.

Hafernik, J.E. 1992. Threats to invertebrate biodiversity: Implications for conservation strategies. In P.L. Fielder, and S.K. Jain, eds. *Conservation Biology: The Theory and Practice of Nature Conservation Preservation and Management*. Chapman and Hall, London, 171–195.

Hanski, I. 1994. Patch-occupancy dynamics in fragmented landscapes. *TREE* 9:131–135.

Hanski, I., and C.D. Thomas. 1994. Metapopulation dynamics and conservation: A spatially explicit model applied to butterflies. *Biological Conservation* 68:167–180.

Hansson, L., ed. 1992. *The Ecological Principles of Nature Conservation: Applications in Temperate and Boreal Environments*. Elsevier Applied Science, Amsterdam.

Harrington, J.A. 1994. Roadside landscapes: prairie species take hold in Midwest rights-of-way. *Restoration & Management Notes* 12:8–15.

Harvey, H.J., and T.C. Meredith. 1981. Ecological studies of *Peucedanum palustre* and their implications for conservation management at Wicken Fen, Cambridgeshire. In H. Synge, ed. *The Biological Aspects of Rare Plant Conservation*. John Wiley and Sons, Chichester, England, 365–378.

Henderson, M.T., G. Merriam, and J. Wegner. 1985. Patchy environments and species survival: Chipmunks in an agricultural mosaic. *Biological Conservation* 31:95–105.

Henderson, R.A., and E.J. Epstein. 1995. Oak savannas in Wisconsin. In E.T. LaRoe, G.S. Farris, C.E. Puckett, P.D. Doran, and M.J. Mac, eds. *Our Living Resources: A Report to the Nation on the Distribution, Abundance, and Health of U.S. Plants, Animals, and Ecosystems*. U.S. Government Printing Office, Washington, D.C., 230–232.

Hobbs, R.J. 1993. The role of corridors in conservation: Solution or bandwagon? *TREE* 389–392.

Holsinger, K.E. 1995. Population biology for policy makers. *BioScience Supplement 1995*: S10–S20.

Iltis, H. 1959. We need many more scientific areas. *Wisconsin Conservation Bulletin* 24:13–18.

Janzen, D.H. 1988. Management of habitat fragments in a tropical dry forest: Growth. *Annals of the Missouri Botanical Garden* 75:105–116.

Jensen, D.B., M.S. Horn, and J. Harte. 1993. *In Our Hands: A Strategy for Conserving California's Biological Diversity*. University of California Press, Berkeley.

Kelly, P.A., and Rotenberry, J.T. 1993. Buffer zones for ecological reserves in California: Replacing guesswork with science. In J.E. Kelly, ed. *Interface between Ecology and Land Development in California.* Southern California Academy of Sciences, Los Angeles, 85–92.

Kim, K.C. 1993. Biodiversity, conservation and inventory: Why insects matter. *Biodiversity and Conservation* 2:191–214.

Kitchener, D.J., J. Bell, and B.G. Muir. 1982. Birds in Western Australian Wheatbelt reserves—Implications for conservation. *Biological Conservation* 22:127–163.

Klein, B.C. 1989. Effects of forest fragmentation on dung and carrion beetle communities in central Amazonia. *Ecology* 70:1715–1725.

Knaapen, J.P., M. Scheffer, and B. Harmes. 1992. Estimating habitat isolation in landscape planning. *Landscape and Urban Planning* 23:1–16.

Kolb, H.H. 1985. Habitat use by foxes in Edinburgh. *Terre Vie* 139–143.

Lande, R. 1988. Genetics and demography in biological conservation. *Science* 241:1455–1460.

———. 1995. Mutation and conservation. *Conservation Biology* 9:782–791.

Launer, A.E., and D.D. Murphy. 1994. Umbrella species and the conservation of habitat fragments: A case of a threatened butterfly and a vanishing grassland ecosystem. *Biological Conservation* 69:145–153.

Laurence, W.F. 1991. Edge effects in tropical forest fragments: Application of a model for the design of nature reserves. *Biological Conservation* 57:205–219.

Leopold, A.S. 1949. *A Sand County Almanac: And Sketches Here and There.* Oxford University Press, New York.

Levenson, J.B. 1981. Woodlots as biogeographic islands in southeastern Wisconsin. In R.L. Burgess, and D.M. Sharpe, eds. *Forest Island Dynamics in Man-Dominated Landscapes.* Springer-Verlag, New York, 13–39.

Levins, R. 1968. *Evolution in Changing Environments: Some Theoretical Explorations.* Princeton University Press, Princeton, New Jersey.

Little, C.A. 1989. *Greenways for America.* Johns Hopkins University Press, Baltimore, Md.

Lovejoy, T.E., J.M. Rankin, R.O. Bierregaard, Jr., K.S. Brown, Jr., L.H. Emmons, and M. Van de Voort. 1984. Ecosystem decay of Amazon forest remnants. In M.H. Nitecki, ed. *Extinctions.* University of Chicago Press, Chicago, 295–325.

Lovejoy, T.E. 1987. National Parks: How big is big enough? In R. Hermann, and T.B. Craig, eds. *Conference on Science in National Parks, Volume I: The Fourth Triennial Conference on Research in the National Parks and Equivalent Reserves.* The George Wright Society, Hancock, Michigan, and U.S. National Park Service, Washington, D.C., 49–58.

Lovejoy, T.E., R.O. Bierregaard, Jr., A.B. Rylands, J.R. Malcolm, C.E. Quintela, L.H. Harper, K.S. Brown, Jr., A.H. Powell, G.V.N. Powell, H.O.R. Schubart, and M.B. Hays. 1986. In M.E. Soulè, ed. *Conservation Biology: The Science of Scarcity and Diversity.* Sinauer Associates, Sunderland, Mass., 257–285.

Lynch, J.F., and D.F. Whigham. 1984. Effects of forest fragmentation on breeding bird communities in Maryland, USA. *Biological Conservation* 28:287–324.

Lynch, J.F., and R.F. Whitcomb. 1978. Effects of the insularization of the eastern deciduous forest on avifaunal diversity and turnover. In A. Marmelstein, ed. *Classification, Inventory and Analysis of Fish and Wildlife Habitat: Proceedings of a National Symposium, Phoenix, Arizona, January 24–27, 1977.* U.S. Fish and Wildlife Service, Department of the Interior, Washington, D.C., 461–489.

MacArthur, R.H., and E.O. Wilson. 1963. An equilibrium theory of insular zoogeography. *Evolution* 17:373–387.

———. 1967. *The Theory of Island Biogeography.* Princeton University Press, Princeton, N.J.

Mader, H.J. 1984. Animal habitat isolation by roads and agricultural fields. *Biological Conservation* 29:81–96.

Mader, H.J., C. Schell, and P. Kornacker. 1990. Linear barriers to arthropod movement in the landscape. *Biological Conservation* 54:209–222.

Mann, C.C. 1991. Extinction: Are ecologists crying wolf? *Science* 253:736–738.

Mann, C.C., and M.L. Plummer. 1995. Are wildlife corridors the right path? *Science* 270:1428–1430.

Manson, C. 1994. Natural communities conservation planning: California's new ecosystem approach to biodiversity. *Environmental Law* 24:603–615.

Matlack, G.R. 1993. Sociological edge effects: Spatial distribution of human impact in suburban forest fragments. *Environmental Management* 17:829–835.

Matthiae, P.E., and F. Stearns. 1981. Mammals in forest islands in southeastern Wisconsin. In R.L. Burgess, and D.M. Sharpe, eds. *Forest Island Dynamics in Man-Dominated Landscapes.* Springer-Verlag, New York, 55–66.

McCoy, E.D. 1983. The application of island-biogeographic theory to patches of habitat: How much land is enough? *Biological Conservation* 25:53–61.

McDonnell, M.J., and S.T.A. Pickett. 1990. Ecosystem structure and function along urban-rural gradients: An unexploited opportunity for ecology. *Ecology* 71:1231–1237.

McDonnell, M.J., and Pickett, S.T.A., eds. 1993. *Humans as Components of Ecosystems: The Ecology of Subtle Human Effects and Populated Areas.* Springer-Verlag, New York.

Menges, E.S. 1990. The application of minimum viable population theory to plants. In D.A. Falk, and K.E. Holsinger, eds. *Genetics and Conservation of Rare Plants.* Oxford University Press, New York, 45–61.

———. 1991. Seed germination percentage increases with population size in a fragmented prairie species. *Conservation Biology* 5:158–164.

Middleton, J., and G. Merriam. 1983. Distribution of woodland species in farmland woods. *Journal of Applied Ecology* 20:625–644.

Mitchell, R.S., C.J. Sheviak, and D.J. Leopold, eds. 1990. *Ecosystem Management: Rare Species and Significant Habitats.* New York State Museum, Albany, New York.

Mladenoff, D.J., M.A. White, T.R. Crow, and J. Pastor. 1994. Applying principles of landscape design and management to integrate old-growth forest enhancement and commodity use. *Conservation Biology* 8:752–762.

Moldenke, R.A., and J.D. Lattin. 1990. Dispersal characteristics of old-growth soil arthropods. *Northwest Environmental Journal* 6:408–409.

Molloy, B.P.J. 1971. Possibilities and problems for nature conservation in a closely settled area. *Proceedings of the New Zealand Ecological Society* 18:25–37.

Moon, C. 1990. Koala corridors: A case study from Lismore. In D. Lunney, C.A. Uquhart, and P. Reed, eds. *Koala Summit: Managing Koalas in New South Wales. Proceedings of the Koala Summit held at the University of Sydney 7–8 November 1988.* NSW National Parks and Wildlife Service, Hurtsville, NSW, Australia, 87–92.

Moore, N.W. 1962. The heaths of Dorset and their conservation. *Journal of Ecology* 50:369–391.

Murphy, D.D., K.E. Freas, and S.B. Weiss. 1990. An environment-metapopulation approach to population viability analysis for a threatened invertebrate. *Conservation Biology* 4:41–51.

National Park Service. 1980. *State of the Parks—1980: A Report to the Congress.* National Park Service, Department of the Interior, Washington, D.C.

National Research Council. 1993. *A Biological Survey for the Nation.* National Academy Press, Washington, D.C.

———. 1995. *Science and the Endangered Species Act.* National Academy Press, Washington, D.C.

Nigh, T.A., W.L. Pflieger, P.L. Redfearn, Jr., W.A. Schroeder, A.R. Templeton, and F.R. Thompson III. 1992. *The Biodiversity of Missouri: Definitions, Status, and Recommendations for its Conservation.* Conservation Commission of the State of Missouri, Jefferson City.

Nilsson, S.G. 1992. Forests in the temperate-boreal transition-natural and man-made features. In L. Hansson, ed. *Ecological Principles of Nature Conservation: Applications in Temperate and Boreal Environments.* Elsevier, London, 373–393.

Noss, R.F. 1987. Corridors in real landscapes: A reply to Simberloff and Cox. *Conservation Biology* 1:159–164.

Noss, R.F., E.T. LaRoe, III, and M.S. Scott. 1995. *Endangered Ecosystems of the United States: A Preliminary Assessment of Loss and Degradation.* National Biological Survey, Department of the Interior, Washington, D.C.

Nunney, L., and K.A. Campbell. 1993. Assessing minimum viable population size: Demography meets population genetics. *TREE* 8:234–239.

Nyland, R.D., W.C. Zipperer, and D.B. Hill. 1986. The development of forest islands in exurban central New York state. *Landscape and Urban Planning* 13:111–123.

Opdam, P., G. Rijsdijk, and F. Hustings. 1985. Bird communities in small woods in an agricultural landscape: Effects of area and isolation. *Biological Conservation* 34:333–352.

Opler, P.A., H.G. Baker, and G.W. Frankie. 1977. Recovery of tropical lowland forest ecosystems. In J. Cairns, Jr., K.L. Dickson, and E.E. Herricks, eds. *Recovery and Restoration of Damaged Ecosystems.* University of Virginia Press, Charlottesville, 379–421.

Ouborg, N.J. 1993. Isolation, population size and extinction: The classical and metapopulation approaches applied to vascular plants along the Dutch Rhine-system. *Oikos* 66:298–308.

Owen, D.F. 1978. Insect diversity in an English suburban garden. In G.W. Frankie, and C.S. Koehler, eds. *Perspectives in Urban Entomology.* Academic Press, New York, 13–29.

Panzer, R., D. Stillwaugh, R. Gnaedinger, and G. Derkovitz. 1995. Prevalence of remnant dependence among the prairie- and savanna-inhabiting insects of the Chicago region. *Natural Areas Journal* 15:101–116.

Pimental, D., U. Stachow, D.A. Takacs, H.W. Brubaker, A.R. Dumas, J.J. Meaney, J.A.S. O'Neil, D.E. Onsi, and D.B. Corzilius. 1992. Conserving biological diversity in agricultural/forestry systems. *BioScience* 42:354–362.

Platt, R.H., R.A. Rowntree, and P.C. Muick, eds. *The Ecological City.* University of Massachusetts, Amherst.

Price, P.W. 1984. *Insect Ecology.* John Wiley & Sons, New York.

Prime, R. 1992. *Hinduism and Ecology: Seeds of Truth.* Cassell, London.

Reid, W.V., and K.R. Miller. 1989. *Keeping Options Alive: The Scientific Basis for Conserving Biodiversity.* World Resources Institute, Washington, D.C.

Reid, T.S., and D.D. Murphy. 1995. Providing a regional context for local conservation action. *BioScience Supplement 1995:* S84–S90.

Remmert, H., ed. 1994. *Minimum Animal Populations.* Springer-Verlag, New York.

Robbins, C.S., D.K. Dawson, and B.A. Dowell. 1989a. Habitat area requirements of breeding forest birds in the Middle Atlantic States. *Wildlife Monographs* 103:1–34.

Robbins, C.S., J.R. Sauer, R.S. Greenberg, and S. Droege. 1989b. Population declines in North American birds that migrate. *Proceedings of the National Academy of Science of the United States of America* 86:7658–7662.

Rosenzweig, M.L. 1995. *Species Diversity in Space and Time.* Cambridge University Press, Cambridge.

Ruggiero, L.F., G.D. Hayward, and J.R. Squires. 1994. Viability analysis in biological evaluations: Concepts of population viability analysis, biological population, and ecological scale. *Conservation Biology* 8:364–372.

Samways, M.F. 1994. *Insect Conservation Biology.* Chapman and Hall, London.

Saunders, D., and R. Hobbs. 1989. Corridors for conservation. *New Scientist* 121:63–68.

Saunders, D.A., and R.J. Hobbs, eds. 1991. *Nature Conservation: The Role of Corridors.* Surrey Beatty and Sons, Chipping Norton, NSW, Australia.

Schelhas, J., and R. Greenberg. 1993. *Forest Patches in the Tropical Landscape and the Conservation of Migratory Birds. Migratory Bird Conservation Policy Paper No. 1.* Smithsonian Migratory Bird Center, National Zoological Park, Washington, D.C.

Schemske, D.W., B.C. Husband, M.H. Ruckelhaus, C. Goodwillie, I.M. Parker, and J.G. Bishop. 1994. Evaluating approaches to the conservation of rare and endangered plants. *Ecology* 75:584–606.

Schonewald-Cox, C.M., and J.W. Bayless. 1986. The boundary model: A geographical analysis of design and conservation of nature reserves. *Biological Conservation* 38:305–322.

Scott, J.M., F. Davis, B. Csuti, R. Noss, B. Butterfield, C. Groves, H. Anderson, S. Caicco, F. D'Erchia, T.C. Edwards, Jr., J.G. Ulliman and R.G. Wright. 1993. Gap analysis: A geographical approach to protection of biological diversity. *Wildlife Monographs* 123:1–41.

Seymour, W.N., Jr., ed. 1969. *Small Urban Spaces.* New York University Press, New York.

Shafer, C.L. 1990. *Island Theory and Conservation Practice.* Smithsonian Institution Press, Washington, D.C.

———. 1994. Beyond park boundaries. In E.A. Cook, and H.N. van Lier, eds. *Landscape Planning and Ecological Networks.* Elsevier, Amsterdam, 201–223.

———. 1995. Values and shortcomings of small reserves. *BioScience* 45:80–88.

———. Selecting and designing nature reserves on islands. *Boletin Do Museu Municipal Do Funchal* (in press).

Shaffer, M.L. 1981. Minimum population sizes for species conservation. *BioScience* 31:131–134.

———. 1987. Minimum viable populations: Coping with uncertainty. In M. Soulè, ed. *Viable Populations for Conservation.* Cambridge University Press, Cambridge, 69–86.

Simberloff, D.S., and L.G. Abele. 1976. Island biogeography theory and conservation practice. *Science* 191:285–286.

Simberloff, D., and J. Cox. 1987. Consequences and costs of conservation corridors. *Conservation Biology* 1:63–71.

Simberloff, D.F. 1986a. Are we on the verge of mass extinction in tropical rain forests? In D.K. Elliott, ed. *Dynamics of Extinction.* John Wiley and Sons, New York, 165–180.

———. 1986b. The proximate causes of extinction. In D.M. Raup, and D. Jablonski, eds. *Patterns and Processes in the History of Life.* Springer-Verlag, Berlin, 259–276.

———. 1988. The contribution of population and community ecology to conservation biology. *Annual Review of Ecology and Systematics* 19:473–511.

Simberloff, D.S., J. Farr, J. Cox, and D. Mehlman. 1992. Movement corridors: Conservation bargains or poor investments. *Conservation Biology* 6:493–504.

Smith, D.S., and P.C. Hellmund, eds. 1993. *Ecology of Greenways.* University of Minnesota Press, Minneapolis.

Soberon, J.M. 1992. Island biogeography and conservation practice. *Conservation Biology* 1:161.

Soulè, M.E. 1987a. Introduction. In M.W. Soulè, ed. *Viable Populations for Conservation.* Cambridge University Press, Cambridge, 1–10.

———. 1987b. Where do we go from here? In M.E. Soulè, ed. *Viable Populations for Conservation.* Cambridge University Press, Cambridge, 175–183.

———. 1991. Land use planning and wildlife maintenance: Guidelines for conserving wildlife in an urban landscape. *Journal of the American Planning Association* 57:313–323.

Soulè, M.E., and D.F. Simberloff. 1986. What do genetics and ecology tell us about the design of nature reserves? *Biological Conservation* 35:19–40.

Soulè, M.E., D.T. Bolger, A.C. Alberts, J. Wright, M. Sorice, and M.S. Hill. 1988. Reconstructed dynamics of rapid extinctions of chaparral-requiring birds in urban habitat islands. *Conservation Biology* 2:75–92.

Specht, R.L., E.M. Roe, and V.H. Boughton. 1974. Conservation of major plant communities in Australia and Papua-New Guinea. *Australian Journal of Botany Supplemental Series* 7:1–667.

Spencer, J.W., and K.J. Kirby. 1992. An inventory of ancient woodland for England and Wales. *Biological Conservation* 62:77–93.

Spirn, A.W. 1984. *The Granite Garden: Urban Nature and Human Design.* Basic Books, New York.

Stein, B.A. 1996. Putting nature on the map. *Nature Conservancy* 46:25–27.

Terman, M.R. 1994. The promise of natural links. *Golf Course Management* December: 52–59.

The Nature Conservancy. 1982. *Preserving Our Natural Heritage Volume III: Private, Academic, and Local Government Activities.* National Park Service, Department of the Interior, Washington, D.C.

Thomas, C.D. 1990. What do real population dynamics tell us about minimum viable population sizes? *Conservation Biology* 4:324–327.

Thomas, J.A. 1991. Rare species conservation: Case studies of European butterflies. In I.F. Spellerberg, F.B. Goldsmith, and M.G. Morris, eds. *The Scientific Management of Temperate Communities for Conservation.* Blackwell Scientific Publications, Oxford, 149–197.

Thomas, J.A., and M.G. Morris. 1995. Rates and patterns of extinction among British invertebrates. In J.H. Lawton, and R.M. May, eds. *Extinction Rates.* Oxford University Press, Oxford, 111–130.

Tilghman, N.G. 1987. Characteristics of urban woodlands affecting breeding bird diversity and abundance. *Landscape and Urban Planning* 14:481–495.

Tscharntke, T. 1992. Fragmentation of *Phragmites* habitats, minimum viable population size, habitat suitability, and local extinction of moths, midges, flies, aphids, and birds. *Conservation Biology* 6:530–536.

Udall, S.T. 1963. *The Quiet Crisis.* Avon Books, New York.

Usher, M.B. 1986. Wildlife conservation evaluation: Attributes, criteria and values. In M.B. Usher, ed. *Wildlife Conservation Evaluation.* Chapman and Hall, London, 3–44.

van Apeldoorn, R.C., W.T. Oostenbrink, A. van Winden, and F.F. van der Zee. 1992. Effects of habitat fragmentation on the bank vole, *Clethrionomys glareolus,* in agricultural landscape. *Oikos* 65:265–274.

van der Maarel. 1975. Man-made ecosystems in environmental management and planning. In W.H. van Dobben, and R.H. Lowe-McConnell, eds. *Unifying Concepts in Ecology.* Dr. W. Junk B.V. Publishers, The Hague, 263–274.

Vestal, A.G. 1949. *Minimum Areas for Different Vegetations: Their Determination from Species-Area Curves.* University of Illinois Press, Urbana.

Vitousek, P.M., L.L. Loope, and C.P. Stone. 1987. Introduced species in Hawaii: Biological effects and opportunities for ecological research. *TREE* 2:224–227.

Vizyova, A. 1986. Urban woodlots as islands for land vertebrates: A preliminary attempt on estimating the barrier effects of structural units. *Ecology (CSSR)* 5:407–419.

Waller, D.M. 1993. The statics and dynamics of mating system evolution. In N. Thornhill, ed. *The Natural History of Inbreeding and Outbreeding.* University of Chicago Press, Chicago, 97–117.

Warren, M.S. 1987. The ecology and conservation of the heath fritillary butterfly, *Mellicta athalia,* III. Population dynamics and the effect of habitat management. *Journal of Applied Ecology* 24:499–513.

Warren, M.S. 1992. The conservation of British butterflies. In R.L.H. Dennis, ed. *The Ecology of Butterflies in Britain.* Oxford University Press, Oxford, 246–274.

Weaver, M., and M. Kellman. 1981. The effects of forest fragmentation on woodlot tree biotas in Southern Ontario. *Journal of Biogeography* 8:199–210.

Webb, N.R., and A.H. Vermaat. 1990. Changes in vegetational diversity on remnant heathland fragments. *Biological Conservation* 53:253–264.

Wegner, J.F., and G. Merriam. 1979. Movements of birds and small mammals between a wood and adjoining farmland habitats. *Journal of Applied Ecology* 16:349–357.

Westhoff, V. 1970. New criteria for nature reserves. *New Scientist* 46:108–113.

Whyte, W.H. 1968. *The Last Landscape.* Anchor Books, Garden City, N.Y.

Widén, B., and L. Svensson. 1992. Conservation of genetic variation in plants—the importance of population size and gene flow. In L. Hansson, ed. *Ecological Principles of Nature Conservation: Applications in Temperate and Boreal Environments.* Elsevier, London, 113–161.

Wilcove, D.S. 1985. Nest predation in forest tracts and the decline of migratory songbirds. *Ecology* 66:1211–1214.

Wilcove, D., and D. Murphy. 1991. The spotted owl controversy and conservation biology. *Conservation Biology* 5:261–262.

Wilcox, B.A. 1984. In situ conservation of genetic resources: Determinants of minimum area requirements. In J.A. McNeely, and K.R. Miller, eds. *National Parks, Conservation, and Development: The Role of Protected Areas in Sustaining Society.* Smithsonian Institution Press, Washington, D.C., 639–647.

Williamson, M. 1988. Relationship of species number to area, distance, and other variables. In A.A. Myers, and P.S. Giller, eds. *Analytical Biogeography.* Chapman and Hall, London, 91–115.

Wilson, E.O. 1987. The little things that run the world (the importance and conservation of invertebrates). *Conservation Biology* 1:344–345.

———. 1992. *The Diversity of Life.* Belknap Press of Harvard University Press, Cambridge, Mass.

Woolhouse, M.E.J. 1985. The theory and practice of the species-area effect applied to breeding birds of British woods. *Biological Conservation* 27:315–332.

Wright, G.M., J.S. Dixon, and B.H. Thompson. 1933. *Fauna of the National Parks: A Preliminary Survey of Faunal Relations in National Parks.* Fauna Series No. 1. U.S. Government Printing Office, Washington, D.C.

Wright, S.J. 1990. Conservation in a variable environment: the optimal size of reserves. In B. Shorrocks, and I.R. Swingerland, eds. *Living in a Patchy Environment.* Oxford University Press, Oxford, 187–195.

16

The Value of Small Preserves in Chronically Fragmented Landscapes

Mark W. Schwartz
Center for Population Biology, University of California–Davis, Davis, CA 95616

Phillip J. van Mantgem
Graduate Group in Ecology, University of California–Davis, Davis, CA 95616

Introduction

The 1990s has ushered in a transition among conservation practitioners from focusing on maximizing quality in preserve acquisition to a "bigger is better" philosophy. This change seems to be driven both by the difficulty in managing many small preserves and an urge to incorporate the concepts of biological sustainability on a regional scale. *Bioreserves, bioregions, biosphere reserves,* and *sustainable development areas* are the popular conservation terms for the 1990s. Noss and Cooperrider (1994, 142) assert that the "old model of isolated parks has failed. Unless it contains many millions of acres, no reserve can maintain its biodiversity for long." Similarly, Pickett and Thompson (1978, 34) define a minimum dynamic area for preserves the "smallest area with a natural disturbance regime which maintains internal recolonization sources." A variety of authors who have focused on large-scale wilderness preserves have made estimates, based primarily on personal experience, to suggest that anywhere between 25% and 75% of a region must be dedicated to the maintenance of biodiversity to succeed over the long term (sources reviewed in Noss and Cooperrider 1994, 167–172). Within this context, Noss and Cooperrider (1994, 172) refer to U.S. Forest Service Research and Natural Areas with sizes under 1,000 ha as "tiny."

These estimates pose a serious constraint within the Midwest, where a 1,000 ha preserve appears very large, and "tiny" is generally restricted to sites less than 2 ha in size. If permanently securing biotic diversity requires the millions of acres envisioned by Pickett and Thompson (1978) or Noss and Cooperrider (1994), then it appears that it is not possible to create a viable reserve system across most of the eastern United States. The Wildlands Project (1992) delineated potential wilderness as roadless areas larger than 20,000 ha in the eastern United

States. Using this criterion the Wildlands Project found the entire Midwest region to be devoid of large potential wilderness areas. In fact, no sites were identified in 21 of the 37 states east of the Rocky Mountains. Because current reasoning leads us to believe that only large reserves can maintain viable populations of the natural biota, it becomes relevant to question whether it is justifiable to expend limited conservation resources on incomplete ecological systems that are potentially unsustainable. This question bears directly on conservation efforts in the Midwest, where present-day natural habitats are fragmented and occupy only a fraction of their original area (e.g., less than $\frac{1}{100}$ of 1% of native tallgrass prairie communities can still be found in Illinois, Robertson and Schwartz 1994).

While we agree that large reserves and wilderness areas are key components in the maintenance of biodiversity, in this chapter we forward the idea that small preserves (<10 ha), even in the most highly fragmented regions, have critical roles to play in conservation programs. The purpose of this discussion is to provide a balance to the growing belief that we ought to focus exclusively on large-scale conservation projects. We will demonstrate that the real potential for the Midwest to contribute to both conservation and our understanding of conservation biology may lie in its many small preserves. A portion of this argument relies on our scientific understanding of conservation. The remainder of the argument is based on the premise that for conservation to be effective on a global scale, we must engage the largest possible proportion of the general public to take an active role in conservation.

Conservation Objectives: Are Incomplete Ecosystems Acceptable Conservation Projects?

Lacking large tracts of unspoiled wilderness, virtually all Midwestern preserves represent incomplete ecosystems. While ecosystem-based management may represent a logical approach to protecting total biodiversity (Grumbine 1994, Beattie 1995), it remains unclear whether preserving incomplete ecosystems is worthwhile in terms of conservation. The answer to this question will ultimately hinge on the specific conservation goals for each project. Suitable goals range from saving species (often under the auspices of the U.S. Endangered Species Act) to conserving landscape and ecosystem functions (e.g., Costanza et al. 1992). Conservation values and goals are primarily cultural (Norton 1994) and determined at a regional level, because typically most of the funding for conservation originates within the state in which it will be spent. Therefore, it is in reference to apparent Midwestern conservation objectives that the value of small sites and incomplete ecological systems must be judged.

The Midwest, like any area within the United States, has opportunities and obstacles to conservation that are unique to the region. Although few states have produced explicit plans for the conservation of biotic resources, one can nonetheless get a sense of what are considered to be central objectives by examining the information used to make decisions on preserve acquisition and site management. In Illinois, for example, the Natural Areas Inventory identifies sites for potential acquisition and ranks them by community type (White 1978). These sites are of conservation value because they possess relatively intact communities and not, as a rule, because of the occurrences of endangered species. A rationale for this approach may be that the Midwest has few species that are globally threatened (e.g., Robertson et al., Chapter 3, this volume). Site acquisition that stresses intact communities over species or ecosystems is illustrated by conservation history in Illinois. This state began obtaining relatively large sites of high overall quality in the 1970s but began to procure small sites at a faster rate through the 1980s (Figure 16.1). Wisconsin has followed similar goals with respect to site acquisition (Stearns and Matthiae, Chapter 19, this volume). In talking to Midwestern preserve managers or reading preserve management plans, one is repeatedly confronted with the premise that the proper objective is to restore or maintain sites that best reflect the community structure of the presettlement habitat—a community-level attribute. Thus, acquiring representatives of natural communities appears to be the primary functional conservation goal in the Midwest. Capturing populations of threatened and endangered species, as well as a representative coverage of all native biota, is a secondary goal. Maintaining ecosystem function or ecosystem health (*sensu* Costanza et al. 1992) appears to be a goal primarily restricted to wetland systems.

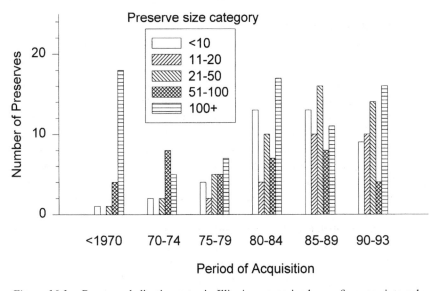

Figure 16.1. Preserve dedication rates in Illinois summarized over five-year intervals, classified by preserve size (acres).

Data from the Illinois Nature Preserves Commission

From a biological standpoint, community-level conservation is useful as a vehicle to simultaneously support native species, genetic diversity, and the biological interactions that provides the raw materials for natural selection and evolution. Small preserves, however, are unlikely to support large predators and grazers (e.g., timber wolves [*Canis lupus*] and bison [*Bison bison*]). Although the macrofauna comprise only a fraction of the total species richness, numbers of individuals, and biomass (Ricklefs 1979, 784), their absence potentially creates two distinct problems—one ecological, the other sociological. In terms of food web dynamics, it is possible that the missing macrofauna may leave gaps in trophic linkages. Yet, disrupting cascading effects caused by the removal of "keystone" predation or herbivory is highly unlikely in complex terrestrial systems (Strong 1992). With respect to cultivating public appeal and support for small preserves, the absence of "charismatic megafauna" may prove to be a serious obstacle. The popular emphasis on flagship species, however, may be changing. In his bestselling book on biodiversity, *The Diversity of Life*, E.O. Wilson (1992, 113) has argued that if all insect life disappeared, "humanity could probably not last more than a few months." This sentiment is beginning to take hold in mainstream thinking, evidenced by the establishment of small preserves specifically for the protection of native butterflies around the San Francisco Bay (Arnold 1985) and new books emerging focused on insect conservation (Gaston et al. 1993). Preserving incomplete communities does not necessarily negate the efficacy of conservation under the operational rules of conservation in the Midwest.

Science and Small Preserves

Preserve Design

The question of how well the extremes of preserve size, small and large, accomplish Midwestern conservation goals remains. Much of the scientific literature that pertains uniquely to the conservation of biological diversity has focused on issues related to the size and arrangement of preserves (e.g., Soulé and Simberloff 1986, Shafer chapter 15, this volume). Preserve design goals were formalized with five simple rules, the first two of which refer to the assertion that bigger preserves, all other things being equal, are better (IUCN 1980). During the 1980s a debate developed around how best to capture and maintain regional diversity (SLOSS—Single Large versus Several Small preserves, Soule and Simberloff 1986). The maintenance of biodiversity issue currently revolves around two simple observations. First, larger sites support larger and more stable populations (e.g., Pimm 1991). Second, partially isolated populations (metapopulations) on networks of small sites buffer species from chance extinctions through local catastrophe (models reviewed by Pimm 1991). Much remains to be learned about actual extinction probabilities, movement rates between sites, population stability, and balancing population size and subdivision to minimize extinction probabilities. In the meantime conservation managers are saddled with uncertainty regarding the proper emphasis to place on large versus small preserves.

Within the Midwest, the tiny 2 ha nature preserves have, historically, been assumed to contribute to the conservation of broadscale biodiversity. It is clear, however, that we cannot conserve the full suite of biodiversity on small habitat fragments regardless of habitat quality. Bison cannot, for example, be restored on a 10 ha preserve. Large sites provide habitat for species with area requirements that cannot be met in small sites (e.g., Herkert 1994a, 1994b). Very small prairie sites provide habitat for as many prairie plants as the largest high-quality sites (Schwartz et al., Chapter 12, this volume), but may lack the area required to maintain these populations through time. Alternately, numerous small sites capture diversity, and hence species interactions amongst the broadest array of species, better than few large sites (e.g., Simberloff and Gotelli 1984, Schwartz et al., Chapter 12, this volume).

While large reserves have many benefits, they are not immune to negative influences often highlighted in the discussions of small preserves. External effects such as pollution and poaching are well documented on large and small preserves alike (Janzen 1986, Shafer 1994). While buffer zones can be created to alleviate edge effects in large preserves, this can only be done at considerable expense (Polasky 1994, Shafer 1994). Large preserves are valued primarily because they supply refuges for wide-ranging carnivores; the associated fauna and plant species on these refuges are often given secondary consideration at best. Typically it is believed that small, uncharismatic species will be protected in large preserves (i.e., the idea of umbrella species). Omitting explicit goals for the protection of these species, however, can easily result in gaps in their protection (Shafer 1995). Due to the high cost of creating (see below) and managing large preserves, the actual increase in total biodiversity gained in establishing large reserves may not represent the best return on the investment of conservation dollars.

Large areas set aside for conservation undoubtedly have merit, but small preserves still have much to offer in terms of biodiversity. Surveys of Wisconsin prairies have shown that there are typically over 200 vascular plant species per community type even in highly fragmented communities (Curtis 1959). Surprisingly, small populations of native Great Plains plants along railroad rights-of-way and in pioneer cemeteries have been resistant to extinction, particularly when fire has been used to keep the invasion of exotic plants in check (although the consequences of inbreeding and the loss of native pollinators may have unforeseen future effects). In addition, many small replicate reserves may conserve a large variety of local ecotypes. Recently, a survey of the 32 ha Wolf Road Prairie in urban Chicago found approximately 250 plant species, 2 amphibians, 3 reptiles, 30 birds, and 8 mammals (Shafer 1995). This diversity has been maintained through 100 years of fire suppression and isolation within the urban Chicago region. The biological value of small preserves, it seems, may have been seriously underestimated.

One of the arguments in favor of well-connected, large preserves is that large populations tend to resist stochastic events that may drive a population to extinction (Noss and Cooperrider 1994). The idea that preserves require physical connectivity to maintain healthy populations may be overstated in the literature (Harris 1984, Noss and Cooperrider 1994). While corridors may enhance migration between sites, it is equally true that corridors are often low-quality habitat and may serve as a pathway for diseases and the invasion of exotic species (Simberloff et al. 1992). Other than isolation and small population size, the creation of numerous replicate reserves has no appreciable drawbacks (Shafer 1995). While models of population viability have shown that larger populations are less likely to go locally extinct (Menges 1992), subdivided populations may buffer species from extinction (Hanski 1994). Although metapopulation behavior (where subpopulations become extinct and are colonized from surrounding sub-populations) is a growing area of research, our ability to assess its importance in reserve design remains far from resolved.

Preserve Quality, Size, and the Need for Restoration

For land managers in the continental United States, the SLOSS debate is largely academic; in a very real sense the choice between large and small preserves does not exist. The issue of preserve design was developed under a conceptual model in which habitat destruction is ongoing and one has the opportunity to choose among an array of potential preserve sites. The application of this literature is limited in regions where habitat loss is already severe. The more pertinent question in the Midwest is whether it is more effective to invest in expanding and/ or connecting existing reserves through habitat restoration or in acquiring and maintaining additional separate areas of the highest possible quality.

Small areas (< 10 ha) are generally of conservation interest because they are high-quality remnants. Conversely, in chronically fragmented habitats large sites are often already degraded. In the Midwest, large sites (> 200 ha) under consideration for acquisition usually require significant habitat restoration. If large preserves are the target of conservation efforts, it can be argued that we should focus on restoring diversity into large sites. Unfortunately, the history of restoring diversity in grassland, forest, or wetland systems has been checkered (e.g., Robertson et al., Chapter 3, this volume). After nearly 20 years of work, habitat restorations remain relatively depauperate in comparison to intact remnants (R. Panzer, Northeastern Illinois University, unpublished data). Experience with over 50 years of prairie restoration at the University of Wisconsin, Madison arboretum demonstrates that even with sufficient time, resources, and scientific knowledge, the successful restoration of relatively well-understood communities is by no means assured (Cottam 1987). Our knowledge of the systems that we attempt to replace is not sufficient to achieve successful results reliably. As an alternative to the reintroduction of entire communities, the preservation of small parcels of intact populations will often be more logically suited for maintenance populations of rare or threatened species.

The critical point that gets lost in the search for clear, singular, general answers is that the science cannot guarantee the right position on the issue of preserve size and connectivity. The optimal preserve design for a region is contextual. The answers to current questions about developing a preserve system will only become apparent in the distant future. Both large and small preserves have a role in the conservation of biological diversity in the Midwest and elsewhere. We suggest that a combination of large and small sites be employed to conserve biological diversity. To undervalue small sites in terms of their potential for maintaining biological diversity would squander an important resource for conservation.

Can We Conserve Biodiversity on a Small Proportion of the Total Land Mass?

As conservation biology grew into a fledgling scientific discipline, one of the central questions perceived to be under its sole domain was that of how to design nature preserves to best capture and sustain biological diversity. A more recent question has focused on whether small or isolated populations are viable (e.g., Soule 1987, Menges 1992). Noss and Cooperrider (1994), indirectly, pose another question that ought to be central to the field of conservation biology: how small a proportion of the total land mass of a region is required to conserve regional biodiversity—a minimum natural habitat area analysis. The risk in chronically fragmented regions is that they may fall below the minimum requirement.

The current trend toward focusing on larger blocks of natural habitats as nature preserves has been fueled by four specific, although somewhat related, developments in conservation biology. First, we are recognizing that the job of saving biodiversity species by species is just too big. Thus, the global trend over the past several years has been to focus on large-scale conservation projects that provide the potential to accomplish numerous conservation goals in a single conservation action. Second, an interest in providing habitat for those species, such as the grizzly bear (*Ursa horribilis*) and timber wolf, that would otherwise be unable to cope in a fragmented world has increased the sizes of preserve units. Third, an interest in preserving "wilderness" has focused on large, undisturbed tracts of natural habitats. Finally, the development of landscape ecology as an academic pursuit (e.g., Turner and Gardner 1990, Forman 1995) has fueled an interest in a systems approach to conservation that, by definition, incorporates large land areas. During the past decade we have seen conservation projects increase in scale from species to communities and landscapes, and shift in emphasis from patches of the highest possible quality habitat to sustainable bioreserves of the largest possible size.

Noss and Cooperrider (1994) urge us to "think big" in pursuing large-scale regional conservation programs. Remarkably, given the high degree of habitat fragmentation, the Midwest is participating in this large-scale bioreserve conservation movement. With recent acquisitions of large sites like the Nachusa Grasslands, the Cache River, and other bioreserve programs, the Midwestern states are doing remarkably well in protecting relatively large bioreserves. This recent shift, however, has left small conservation organizations and the private landowner on the periphery of the perceived conservation mainstream. Bioreserve projects, being expensive and management intensive, are largely the domain of state and federal agencies. New tools and new approaches are required to address the question of how small or how isolated preserves can be and still adequately preserve biological diversity. There are no ready answers to these questions, but restricting our attention to public lands is not sufficient. We must count on the participation of private landowners to contribute to conservation of biological diversity. Personal responsibility for biological diversity on privately owned lands is a required component of conservation. The following sections will discuss the humanistic aspects of conservation on fragmented landscapes.

Accessibility of Small Preserves

Several critical attributes of small versus large preserves are independent of science. As an example, we must enlist the broadscale support of humanity to succeed at global conservation. An effective way to implement this is to engage people personally in the act of saving naturalness (i.e., stewardship) within what people view as their neighborhood. Providing people the opportunity to take an active relationship with their natural environment is probably the fastest route in developing the land ethic envisioned by Aldo Leopold (1949). Local participation makes it possible for a wide spectrum of the public to appreciate not only the benefits of, but also their obligations to, the natural landscape. Through an understanding of what it takes to preserve the biotic community in their regions, people come to see the value, and cost, of preserving nature globally. Extending traditional ethics beyond the human community to encompass the natural landscape is a likely route to success in conserving the stability, integrity, and beauty of our natural areas.

One of the negative attributes of small preserves is that stewardship of preserves is not additive by area. Numerous small sites require far more stewardship than a single preserve of area equal to the aggregate of the small sites. A positive side to the stewardship burden of small preserves is that everyone who has the desire to take primary responsibility for a management project has the opportunity. There are numerous sites in chronically fragmented regions in need of saving: stewardship efforts needed, restoration projects waiting to happen, educational opportunities being missed. With numerous small preserves, the Midwest has a great need for volunteers to help manage biological diversity. It is no coincidence that the Midwestern states have some of the largest volunteer stewardship networks in the country. We all have the opportunity to develop a personal sense of responsibility to the land and actively participate in stewardship of biodiversity. With many small preserves, one of them is usually close to home. In contrast, large reserves frequently require a professional staff as well as a degree of isolation from human populations. While we enjoy large sites, and they also require volunteer assistance, it often takes substantially more effort for the private citizen to develop a personal relationship with large preserves.

An interest in nature seems to be what compels most people to be sympathetic toward conservation. Nobody advocates environmental degradation as a goal; people are uniformly in favor of a healthy environment (Norton 1994). Where we differ is in regard to the cost we are willing to bear to preserve a healthy environment. Arguments for conservation often invoke the undiscovered potential economic benefits of native species or balanced ecosystems. While these arguments may sway economists, we believe that they are too intangible for most people. What garners support for conservation efforts is to focus attention on the quality of the local environment and educate people on how they can help it improve. As the bumper sticker reads: think globally, act locally.

To build a conservation constituency we need to provide opportunities for participating in the management of native species and natural lands. A large network of small sites afford us the best opportunity to develop this connection to natural areas among the broadest spectrum of people. Further, it is the caring and nurturing of local biotic resources that often drives our concern for more global conservation issues. To accomplish global conservation goals we first need to get many people personally involved in their local environment. It would be an unmitigated disaster if all humanity felt the need to hike the arctic tundra to exercise their appreciation of nature. We would, however, like all humanity to embrace the goal of conserving that arctic tundra.

In a recent essay, Robert Putnam (1995) described how participation in social groups has declined during the past 50 years. Every major social organization that requires people to spend time together is declining in size. Organizations that have grown over the past 25 years are characterized by no social participation by most of the membership, and a professional staff hired to perform tasks seen as desirable by the membership (e.g., Sierra Club, The Nature Conservancy). Americans are spending less time talking to other people, less time socially engaged within our communities. We trust those to whom we send our checks to represent our interests appropriately. Putnam (1995) links the decline in social connectedness of Americans to a decline in participation in the democratic process. Putnam's assertion is that (1) when people get together they talk; (2) when people talk, the conversation drifts to shared concerns; and (3) when people talk about shared concerns, they are more likely to participate actively in tending to the shared concerns of the group through volunteerism. With reduced social activity, comes reduced participation in local government, school parent-teacher associations, and even bowling leagues (Putnam 1995). By analogy, the more people actively and communally participating in the conservation of biological diversity, the greater importance these conservation goals hold in society, and the greater influence conservation concerns will take in the political process. Facilitating the ability of individuals to participate in a meaningful project relating to the conservation of their environment ought to be a primary goal of conservation. This goal is currently being accomplished by a multitude of watershed protection groups, stream monitoring associations, and small conservation organizations springing up across the country (Kerr et al. 1994)—a grassroots movement. These are people who are tending to their immediate environment and have the resources to finance and manage small preserves.

Flexibility in Management Options on Small Preserves

Conservation biology is, at best, an inexact science that attempts to advise on a broad array of appropriate conservation objectives. While we do not have all the answers, large suites of small preserves provide the opportunity to remain flexible and experimental with preserve management. An obvious outcome of having many small nature preserves is that individual preserve management plans must be written for each preserve. This difficult process of articulating specific conservation goals is the first step in establishing standards to measure success of conservation actions. The process of delineating goals is difficult, in part, because there is a patchwork of views encompassed by the term "conservation." Goals under the rubric of conservation can, in certain circumstances, be in conflict with one another (Hobbs and Huenneke 1992, Schwartz 1994). In addition, this patchwork of values and goals is continually changing. For example, creating forest openings and feed plots for deer was a primary conservation management activity just 30 years ago (Anderson, chapter 6, this volume), but is rarely endorsed as conservation at present. Further, management strategies to achieve specific objectives are not always clear. Uncertainty regarding the best means to achieve conservation objectives, as well as variation in objectives, is a compelling argument in support of establishing smaller replicate preserves rather than few large preserves. This is the core idea behind *adaptive management* (Holling 1995), in which we acknowledge our ignorance concerning ecological systems and pursue a variety of management options in the attempt to observe which strategy works best.

An example of how strongly people currently disagree about conservation goals can be found in our motivation to conserve. Do we support conserving natural habitats for human use and enjoyment, or as refuges for native species irrespective of utility? How do we value those species whose existence we are endangering and manage the risk of extinction? What cost do we assign actions that impair the abilities of natural habitats to persist? There is no single right reason for conservation, and conservationists carry divergent opinions on these issues (e.g., Norton 1991, 1994). The debate over appropriate conservation motivation, and hence management actions, is by no means new. In this country the debate dates back to the very inception of our conservation structures, pitting "wise use" Aggregationists (e.g., Gifford Pinchot) against the Moralists (e.g., John Muir) *sensu* Norton (1991). Today, we describe differences between "conservationists" and "preservationists" (Norton 1991).

There is a broad spectrum of valid philosophical approaches and value systems encompassed under the rubric of conservation. Yet individual site management is most effective under one plan with one conservation ethic. National forests, which explicitly attempt to maintain a balance between divergent land uses and concerns, provide an example of the inevitable failure of trying to accommodate everyone's interests within one management plan. The acrimonious debates and numerous court cases involving nearly every national forest management plan speak for themselves. In contrast, the large number of small Midwestern preserves can accommodate differing views without generating the rancor created by trying to meld multiple philosophical underpinnings in the management of a single parcel of public land. It is this variation in conservation ethics that threatens many of our bioreserves and sustainable development partnerships; the divergent objectives of the congregation may, ultimately, be incompatible (but see Norton 1991).

An example of where we seem to agree in principal, but not always in practice, is with respect to exotic species. The level of concern over exotic species varies from native species purists to the horticultural industry's steadfast objection to restricting the import or sale of exotic plants. Most citizens would probably agree that conservation efforts ought to strive for managing assemblages of species that are representative of the natural world. This would entail excluding, to the best of our ability, invasive nonindigenous species. While there is a consensus that obvious pest species should be eliminated (e.g., Gypsy moth *Porthetria dispar*, zebra mussel *Dreissena polymorhpha*, purple loosestrife *Lythrum salicaria* L.), there appear to be a greater number of species where no such agreement exists. Indeed, our commitment to eliminating exotic species can get very muddled even within the context of natural areas (e.g., Luken 1994, Schwartz and Randall 1995).

Consider the ring-necked pheasant (*Phasianus colchicus*). Should we create appropriate natural habitats to increase pheasant populations to satisfy hunters, or should we try to eliminate this species to facilitate the recovery of the nearly extinct native prairie chicken (Westemeier and Edwards 1987)? Our response to this conflict depends on our view of acceptable conservation efforts. The conservation organization Pheasants Forever is dedicated to enhancing populations of this nonindigenous game bird. While prairie enthusiasts do not generally agree with their restoration techniques, Pheasants Forever is currently as active as any organization in preserving and restoring native grasslands in the Midwest. Having a multitude of small sites affords us the flexibility to differ in opinions about how we treat natural area preservation and act in accordance with those beliefs.

Translating these differences of opinion into a preserve system, we can meet our cultural need for open space in many ways. Some satisfy their needs through hunting or fishing. Others seek to view the expansive openness of a large tract of natural habitat to imagine the splendor of the pristine American wilderness. Others still prefer the details of the prairie, the small intricacies of the forest— the spiders, butterflies, birds, and squirrels. A small patch of woods close to home often ideally suits this latter need.

In this spirit, a debate remains about what constitutes a prairie. Is a prairie defined by its complement of herbivores, requiring the presence of bison? Are large, low-diversity grasslands prairies? How dominant can woody invaders or exotic species be in grasslands before we stop calling a site a prairie? Illinois Natural Heritage biologists have a system of assigning quality grades to prairies (White 1978). This subjective grade assignment to sites is fairly consistent and predictable. In contrast, how we assign grades to prairies in our own hearts and minds is undoubtedly variable. The Wolf Road Prairie in Chicago provides an excellent example. A 32 ha grassland site was passed by for development during the 1930s because of a complex set of legal problems. By the 1960s the site was well within the urbanized metropolitan area. The prairie, due to lack of management, was badly degraded from a formerly pristine site but still retained significant biotic resources and potential for recovery. Under the threat of development, a private citizens group (Save the Prairie Society) began to acquire the more than 100 deeds that comprised the site. In 1993 the Wolf Road Prairie was dedicated as the 230th nature preserve on the 30th anniversary of the Illinois Nature Preserves Commission. While the site is now of only moderate biological quality, it is widely recognized as one of the most important additions to the Nature Preserve System in Illinois because it (1) represents the culmination of a huge private conservation effort, (2) provides an excellent site for prairie recovery efforts, and (3) is readily accessible to several million people. While the habitat quality of Wolf Road Prairie may not be particularly impressive, one is awed by the spectacle of such wildness persisting within an urban setting.

Are Private Landowners Willing to Be Stewards of Biological Diversity, and with What Constraints?

The Midwest enjoys a remarkable legacy of ecological thought, natural history study, and conservation action. This legacy has developed around aggressive acquisition programs that targeted the highest quality sites and incorporated them into networks of nature preserves. For example, the Illinois Nature Preserves Commission began in 1963 to formulate the structure for a diverse array of dedicated nature preserves that had grown to more than 230 sites by 1994 (Herkert, Chapter 17 this volume). A primary concern of governmental bodies, however, must be whether they are able to manage the resource. From a management perspective, it appears that a few large sites enjoy a considerable advantage over numerous small sites. This observation is not lost on state agencies acquiring natural habitats. Ownership of Illinois Nature Preserves is split amongst the state (97 preserves), various municipal bodies (such as Chicago region county forest preserve districts, these are governmental bodies, 95 preserves), and private individuals and organizations (44 preserves). These entities, however, do not all own the same types of nature preserves. Nearly 88% of state-owned nature preserves are greater than 20 acres in size, 75% of municipally owned nature preserves are greater than 20 acres, while only 32% of privately held nature preserves are greater than 20 acres in size (Figure 16.2). Though individually small in size, one cannot disregard the importance of the private landowner; only one-third of the total landmass in the United States is in federal ownership (Shafer 1994). Small nature preserves are the forte of the private conservation effort. Indeed, the privately owned and managed Heron Lake preserve in Minnesota has provided a model for wetland conservation in the region (Rich Beilfuss, personal communication). The predominant forest owners in Illinois are private individuals who, on average, own about 20 acres and value their land predomi-

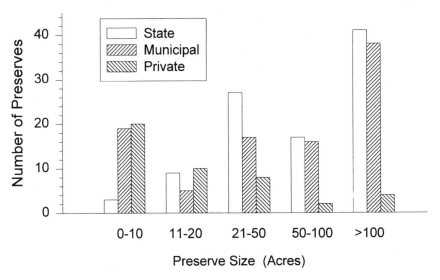

Figure 16.2.   Illinois preserve ownership categories.

Data from the Illinois Nature Preserves Commission

nantly for wildlife habitat and preservation (Iverson et al. 1989). We need to foster these private conservation activities by encouraging the establishment of small preserves.

Conclusions

In Illinois, the rate of acquisition of small sites by state, municipal, and private owners peaked in the years 1985–89 (McFall 1991). The job of acquiring small remnants in Illinois is not complete. This slowing of small-site acquisition may indicate that the private sector, which assumes primary management responsibility of these small preserves, is saturated. A more likely explanation is that those in Illinois, like those in other states, are concentrating efforts on larger scale projects. This shift in emphasis forces us to determine whether small sites are failing as nature preserves. Yet current evidence does not suggest that biological diversity is being lost on small sites. Remarkably small prairie sites appear to be as diverse as large prairies (Robertson and Schwartz 1994). Thus, we appear to be focusing on larger, lower-quality sites for reasons other than the failure of small sites. We contend that many of the big bioreserve projects are popular not because of scientific or management arguments but because we envision large sites as satisfying a wide variety of conservation objectives—both biological and recreational. Unfortunately, these large sites seem destined to fall short of expectations because our diverse goals for these sites are not always compatible. There are, of course, good reasons for acquiring large preserves (Robinson et al Chapter 8, Herkert Chapter 17, this volume), but failure of small sites to contribute to the conservation goals of maintaining biodiversity is not one of them. In contrast, an abundance of small sites provides the unique opportunity to experiment with varying management strategies for differing conservation objectives. Further, small sites in urbanized areas provides arguably the best opportunity for engaging human resources in conservation. We argue that this ought to be a principal goal of biological conservation in chronically fragmented regions.

References

Arnold, A.A. 1985. Private and government-funded conservation programs for endangered insects in California. *Natural Areas Journal*. 5:28–39.

Beattie, M. 1995. A broader view. *Endangered Species Bulletin*. 20:4–5.

Costanza, R.B. G. Norton and B.D. Haskell. 1992. *Ecosystem health: New Goals for Environmental Management*. Island Press, Washington, D.C.

Cottam, G. 1987. Community dynamics on an artificial prairie. In W.R. Jordan, M.E. Gilpin and J.D. Aber, eds. *Restoration Ecology*. Cambridge University Press, Cambridge, U.K., 257–290.

Curtis, J.T. 1959. *The Vegetation of Wisconsin*. University of Wisconsin Press, Madison.

Forman, R.T.T. 1995. Land Mosaics: The ecology of landscapes and regions. Cambridge University Press, Cambridge.

Gaston, K.J., T.R. New, and M.J. Samways, eds. 1993. *Perspectives on Insect Conservation*. Intercept Ltd, Andover, U.K.

Grumbine, R.E. 1994. What is ecosystem management? *Conservation Biology* 8:27–38.

Hanski, I. 1994. Patch occupancy dynamics in fragmented landscapes. *Trends in Ecology and Evolution* 9:131–135.

Harris, L.D. 1984. *The Fragmented Forest: Island Biogeography Theory and the Preservation of Biotic Diversity*. University of Chicago Press, Chicago.

Herkert, J.R. 1994a. Breeding bird communities of midwestern prairie fragments: The effects of prescribed burning and habitat-area. *Natural Areas Journal* 14:128–135.

Herkert, J.R. 1994b. The effects of habitat fragmentation on Midwestern grassland bird communities. *Ecological Applications* 4:461–471.

Hobbs, R.J., and L.F. Huenneke. 1992. Disturbance, diversity and invasion: Implications for conservation. *Conservation Biology* 6:324–337.

Holling, C.S. 1995. What Barriers? What Bridges? In L.H. Gunderson, C.S. Holling, and S.S. Light, eds. *Barriers and Bridges to the Renewal of Ecosystems and Institutions*. Columbia University Press, New York.

IUCN (International Union for the Conservation of Nature and Natural Resources). 1980. World Conservation Strategy. Gland, Switzerland.

Iverson, L.R., R.L. Oliver, D.P. Tucker, P.G. Risser, C.D. Burnett, and R.G. Rayburn. 1989. *The Forest Resources of Illinois: An Atlas of Spatial and Temporal Trends*. Illinois Natural History Survey special publication 11. Champaign.

Janzen, D.H. 1986. The eternal external threat. In M.E. Soule, ed. *Conservation Biology*. Sinauer Associates, Sunderland, Mass.

Kerr, M., E. Ely, V. Lee, and A. Desbonnet. 1994. *National Directory of Volunteer Environmental Programs* 4th ed. U.S. Environmental Protection Agency, Rhode Island Sea Grant. EPA 841-B-94-001. Narragansett, R.I.

Leopold, A. 1949. *A Sand County Almanac*. Oxford University Press, New York.

Luken, J.O. 1994. Valuing plants in natural areas. *Natural Areas Journal* 14:295–299.

McFall, D, ed. 1991. A Directory of Illinois Nature Preserves. Illinois Department of Conservation, Division of Natural Heritage, Springfield.

Menges, E.S. 1992. Stochastic modeling of extinction in plant populations. In P.F. Fielder, and S.K. Jain, eds. *Conservation Biology: The Theory and Practice of Nature Conservation, Preservation and Management*. Chapman and Hall, New York.

Norton, B.G. 1991. *Toward Unity among Environmentalists*. Oxford University Press, New York.

Norton, B.G. 1994. On what we should save: The role of culture in determining conservation targets. In P.L. Forey, C.J. Humphries, and R.I. Vane-Wright, eds. *Systematics and Conservation Evaluations*. Oxford Science Publications, Clarendon Press, Oxford.

Noss, R.F., and A.Y. Cooperrider. 1994. *Saving Nature's Legacy: Protecting and Restoring Biodiversity*. Island Press, Washington, D.C.

Pickett, S.T.A., and J.N. Thompson. 1978. Patch dynamics and the design of nature reserves. *Biological Conservation* 13:27–37.

Pimm, S.L. 1991. *The Balance of Nature? : Ecological Issues in the Conservation of Species and Communities*. University of Chicago Press. Chicago.

Polasky, S. 1994. What role for economic considerations in species conservation policy? *Endangered Species Update* 11(11):1–4.

Putnam, R.D. 1995. Bowling alone: America's declining social capital. *Journal of Democracy* 6:65–78.

Robertson, K.R., and M.W. Schwartz. 1994. Prairie. In *The Changing Illinois Environment: Critical Trends*. Technical Report of the Critical Trends Assessment Project. Vol. 3: Ecological Resources. Illinois Department of Energy and Natural Resources, Springfield, 1–32.

Ricklefs, R.E. 1979. *Ecology*. 2nd en. Chiron Press, New York.

Schwartz, M.W. 1994. Conflicting goals for conserving biodiversity: Issues of scale and value. *Natural Areas Journal* 14:213–216.

Schwartz, M.W., and J.M. Randall. 1995. Valuing natural areas and controlling nonindigenous plants. *Natural Areas Journal* 15:98–100.

Shafer, C.L. 1994. Beyond park boundries. In E.A. Cook, and H.N. van Lier, eds. *Landscape Planning and Ecological Networks*. Elsevier, Amsterdam.

Shafer, C.L. 1995. Values and shortcomings of small preserves. *Bioscience* 45:80–87.

Simberloff, D.S., and N.J. Gotelli. 1984. Effects of insularization on plant species richness in the prairie-forest ecotone. *Biological Conservation* 29:27–46.

Simberloff, D., J.A. Farr, J. Cox, and D.W. Mehlman. 1992. Movement corridors— conservation bargains or poor investments. *Conservation Biology* 4:493–504.

Soule, M.E., and D. Simberloff. 1986. What do genetics and ecology tell us about the design of nature reserves? *Biological Conservation* 35:19–40.

Soule, M.E. 1987. *Viable Populations for Conservation*. Cambridge University Press, Cambridge.

Strong, D.R. 1992. Are trophic cascades all wet? Differentiation and donor-control in speciose ecosystems. *Ecology* 73(3):747–754.

Turner, M.G., and R.H. Gardner. 1990. *Quantitative Methods in Landscape Ecology*. Ecological Studies, vol. 82. Springer-Verlag, New York.

Westemeier, R.L., and W.R. Edwards. 1987. Prairie-chickens: Survival in the Midwest. In H. Kallman, C.P. Agee, W.R. Goforth, and J.P. Linduska, eds. *Restoring America's Wildlife*. U.S. Fish and Wildlife Service, Washington, D.C., 119–131.

White, J. 1978. Illinois Natural Areas Inventory technical report, vol. 1. *Survey Methods and Results*. Illinois Department of Conservation. Springfield.

Wildlands Project. 1992. Largest remaining roadless areas in the continental United States. Map. *Wild Earth* (Special Issue), 44–45.

Wilson, E.O. 1992. *The Diversity of Life*. W.W. Norton, New York.

17

Nature Preserves, Natural Areas, and the Conservation of Endangered and Threatened Species in Illinois

James R. Herkert
Illinois Endangered Species Protection Board, 524 South Second Street, Springfield, IL 62701

Introduction

One of the big questions in conservation biology is how to design effective conservation programs in highly fragmented landscapes where little natural habitat remains. To direct limited resources in these landscapes, a solid framework for conservation efforts is needed. Illinois provides a good case study because much of its natural landscape was cleared early. By 1900, more than 97% of the state's prairies and roughly 75% of the state's original forests had been lost (Graber and Graber 1963). Today, Illinois remains one of the most intensively disturbed landscapes in the eastern United States (O'Neill et al. 1988). Illinois also has an extensive history of early biological study and cataloging (e.g., Kennicott 1855; Ulffers 1855; Forbs 1876; Ridgway 1889, 1895; Needham and Hart 1901; Forbs and Richardson 1908; Garman 1917). Therefore, there is a large historical database on which to evaluate the effectiveness of modern conservation actions and programs. Yet despite the high degree of disturbance in the state, Illinois has lost surprisingly few species (see review by Post 1991). This may be due in part to the fact that Illinois has an extensive network of legally protected preserves. Primack (1993) has suggested that establishing legally designated protected areas is one of the most critical steps in protecting biological communities. Additionally, Illinois has a tradition of assertive conservation action by groups such as Friends of Our Native Landscapes, the Natural Land Institute, The Nature Conservancy, the Illinois Nature Preserves Commission, the Illinois Endangered Species Protection Board, and the Illinois Department of Natural Resources (formerly the Department of Conservation). It is therefore a good place to examine the effects of a well-organized, focused conservation effort. Because of its relatively long history of conservation programs (Schwartz 1994), Illinois may be able to provide a template for conservation in other highly fragmented landscapes.

In Illinois the framework under which the protection of the state's rare species and communities is usually placed deals with legislatively established programs that focus on the protection and conservation of natural areas and endangered and threatened species. In this chapter I first provide an overview of significant events in the history and development of natural area and endangered species protection and conservation in Illinois. Second, I discuss the current status of natural area and endangered species protection in Illinois, specifically focusing on what is protected within the current network of legally protected nature preserves. And third, I conclude with a discussion of some of the major issues about the conservation and management of endangered and threatened species and natural areas in a network of isolated nature preserves in highly fragmented landscapes such as Illinois.

Establishment of the Illinois Nature Preserves System As a Means of Protecting Natural Areas

The Illinois Nature Preserves System was established in 1963 by the Illinois General Assembly with the passage of the Natural Areas Preservation Act. With the passage of this legislation, Illinois became the first state in the nation to establish a formal program of legal protection of natural areas (Schwartz 1994). Once dedicated, nature preserves receive maximum protection against future changes in land use (McFall and Karnes 1995). The Natural Areas Preservation Act declares that all preserves must be put to their highest, best, and most important use for the public benefit (McFall and Karnes 1995).

A major objective of the Illinois Nature Preserves System is to preserve adequate examples of all significant types of natural features occurring in the state (Illinois Nature Preserves Commission 1972). Natural features include land-forms and geologic formations, soils, streams and lakes, terrestrial and aquatic communities of plants and animals, and archaeological sites. To distinguish the natural features of Illinois for the purpose of providing a framework for the nature preserves system, a systematic arrangement of natural geographic division of Illinois was devised (Illinois Nature Preserves Commission 1972, Schwegman 1973). The natural division classification system divided the state into 14 regions called natural divisions and 33 subregions called sections (Schwegman 1973). The natural divisions and sections were differentiated on the basis of topography, glacial history, bedrock, soils, and distribution of flora and fauna (Schwegman 1973). The natural divisions of the state have provided the basic classification scheme for natural features to be included into the nature preserves system (Illinois Nature Preserves Commission 1972). One of the original goals of the nature preserves system in Illinois was to include at least one representative from each of the distinctive natural features within each division in the system.

Preservation of habitats of rare or endangered species was also an important objective in the establishment of the nature preserves system (Illinois Nature Preserves Commission 1972). Although protecting "high quality" areas would presumably also benefit rare and endangered species, it was recognized early on that important areas for rare and endangered species did not necessarily have to be in an undisturbed condition.

Wilderness remnants also qualified by statute for inclusion in the nature preserves system (Illinois Nature Preserves Commission 1973). "Wilderness" was defined as a physiological effect on the observer in contrast to "natural area," which referred to the physical condition of the land (Illinois Nature Preserves Commission 1973). Some areas could be natural in the sense of having a high-quality relic community but be of limited wilderness value because of their proximity to the sights and sounds of civilization (Illinois Nature Preserves Commission 1972). Large areas of lesser quality may be more remote but worthy of protection because of their aesthetic value and because these areas can provide important habitat for area-sensitive species.

Illinois Natural Areas Inventory

The completion of the Illinois Natural Areas Inventory (White 1978) was a milestone in the state's continuing efforts to protect natural areas (Illinois Department of Conservation et al. 1980). The inventory thoroughly documented where Illinois' remaining natural areas were, who owned them, and whether or not they were protected (Illinois Department of Conservation et al. 1980). The natural areas inventory also identified important habitats for endangered and threatened species, and outstanding geologic features. Another benefit of the Illinois Natural Areas Inventory was that it established an ecological community classification system for Illinois that provided the basis for more detailed conservation planning than had previously been possible (Don McFall, Illinois Nature Preserves Commission, personal comm.). One of the more sobering findings of the Illinois Natural Areas Inventory was that by 1978 only $7/100$ of 1% of the land in Illinois still reflected the natural conditions before settlement. Only 610 high-quality community remnants were identified in this effort, totaling just 10,414 hectares (Illinois Department of Conservation et al. 1980). The inventory also found that only about one in five of these areas could be regarded as preserved in 1978 (Illinois Department of Conservation et al. 1980).

Natural Areas Plan

Although the Illinois Natural Areas Inventory did a good job at identifying locations of the significant natural communities in the state, it had not allowed for their protection. This was made clear in the months following the completion of the inventory, when it was recognized that between autumn 1978 and spring

1980 the state had lost three additional prairies and seven high-quality forests, while portions of 21 other natural areas had been destroyed (Illinois Department of Conservation et al. 1980). As a means of following up the natural areas inventory, the Natural Areas Plan was developed. The Natural Areas Plan was a document that outlined the intention of the Illinois Nature Preserves Commission, the Illinois Department of Conservation, and the Illinois Endangered Species Protection Board to act on the needs revealed by the Illinois Natural Areas Inventory (Illinois Department of Conservation et al. 1980). The primary focus of this joint venture was to present a plan of action for the preservation and protection of significant natural areas in the state. Additionally, the plan outlined the need for proper management of the state's remaining natural areas and the need to assess the ownership and preservation status of the state's natural areas.

History and Development of Endangered and Threatened Species Conservation in Illinois

The identification and protection of endangered and threatened species in Illinois appears to have also had its roots with the development of the Illinois Nature Preserves Commission, because protecting the habitats of rare and endangered species was one of the original objectives outlined in the establishment of the nature preserves system (Illinois Nature Preserves Commission 1973). It was not until the early 1970s, however, when the first lists of rare, endangered, and extirpated species were developed for Illinois. In 1971, George (1971) published a list of vanished and endangered birds of Illinois as an outgrowth of the 1970 annual meeting of the Illinois Audubon Society. George's list identified 27 species of birds considered to be at risk of extirpation as breeding species in the state and identified an additional 16 species of birds that were considered to have been extirpated as breeding species in Illinois. In 1972, the Illinois Nature Preserves Commission approved a preliminary list of 121 rare and endangered vertebrates (Illinois Nature Preserves Commission 1973), which included 38 endangered, 83 rare and, 14 possibly extirpated vertebrate species.

Also in 1972, the Illinois General Assembly passed the Illinois Endangered Species Protection Act, providing legal protection for endangered species and creating the first official list of Illinois endangered species. However, when the Illinois Endangered Species Protection Act was passed it did little more than allow for the listing of which species were endangered and prohibit certain activities regarding those species (Illinois Endangered Species Protection Board 1990). Consequently, initial endangered species actives in Illinois were primarily involved in enforcement and permitting actions involving possession of endangered species (Illinois Endangered Species Protection Board 1990). The initial Illinois act was primarily focused on nationally and internationally endangered animals, and dealt with zoos, circus animals, and animal products such as coats and shoes (Illinois Endangered Species Protection Board 1990). Accordingly,

Illinois' first official list of endangered species included only exotic species such as tigers, leopards, cheetahs, crocodiles, jaguars, polar bears, and ocelots. Soon after the establishment of the initial endangered species legislation in Illinois, attention began to shift toward the protection of wild populations of species native to Illinois.

In 1974 another unofficial list of endangered, threatened, vulnerable, rare, and restricted vertebrate animals and vascular plants was produced as a cooperative effort of the Illinois Department of Conservation, Illinois Natural History Survey, Illinois State Museum, and the Illinois Endangered Species Protection Board. The first official lists of endangered and threatened native species, however, were not developed until the emergence of the Illinois Endangered Species Project, which was initiated in 1977 by the Natural Land Institute. The Endangered Species Project was formulated to determine which native vertebrate and vascular plant species were threatened with extirpation in Illinois. Following the compilation of preliminary information on potential species, a series of workshops were held in conjunction with the concurrent Illinois Natural Areas Inventory Project to discuss the status of each species among the group of assembled experts. The subsequent lists were then determined by a consensus of experts and forwarded to the Illinois Endangered Species Protection Board for action. The board held public hearings about the proposed lists and, following review, adopted a list of 72 endangered and threatened vertebrates and 364 endangered and threatened plants (Bowles 1981).

It was not until 1977 that the ability to list plants was added to the act. However, plants could only be listed as endangered or threatened, and initially were not provided any of the protection given to animals until additional amendments were made to the act in 1985. Also in 1985, the act was amended to clearly identify invertebrates in the definition of "animals" protected by the act. Previously only invertebrates on the federal list were included on the Illinois list.

The initial lists of native Illinois endangered and threatened species remained essentially unchanged for nearly 10 years until 1988–1989, when the list underwent its first major revision. Amendments added to the Illinois Endangered Species Protection Act in 1985 included a provision that called for the review and revision of the state list of endangered and threatened species no less than once every five years. A second major revision of the state list was completed in 1994 (Herkert 1994). Currently, the state list of endangered and threatened species includes 511 species, comprising 363 species of plants, 49 species of invertebrates, and 99 species of vertebrates.

Illinois Nature Preserves System and the Conservation of Natural Areas and Endangered and Threatened Species: Where Are We Now?

The Illinois Nature Preserves System currently includes 236 preserves and over 13,000 ha (McFall and Karnes 1995). Illinois Nature Preserves include lands that are owned by public agencies, private conservation organizations, private individuals and families, and corporations. Roughly 10% of all dedicated Illinois Nature Preserves are owned by private individuals or families (Don McFall, personal communication). Illinois Nature Preserves represent less than 1% of the total land area in the state of Illinois. Nevertheless, the nature preserves system includes representatives of 269 (53%) of the state's 511 endangered and threatened species. This list of endangered and threatened species includes 196 species of plants, 52 species of vertebrates, and 21 species of invertebrates. The nature preserves system is also home to 56 of the state's endangered and threatened species that are known to occur in the state only in dedicated Illinois Nature Preserves. An additional 75 endangered or threatened species have more than 50% of their known occurrences in the state in dedicated nature preserves. Therefore, fully 25% of the state's endangered and threatened species are either restricted to nature preserves or have a majority of their state population in this system. Clearly the Illinois Nature Preserves System plays a vital role in the conservation of the state's endangered and threatened species. Although this list is impressive, 213 endangered and threatened species are not currently known to occur in the system, including 91 species known from only a single location in the state. Of these more than one-third are primarily associated with aquatic habitats, a habitat that has not been easily captured in the Illinois Nature Preserves System, largely because of confusing state water laws.

One of the major goals originally developed for the Illinois Nature Preserves System was to include at least one representative from each of the distinctive natural features within each division in the system. This goal has been nearly achieved (Don McFall, personal communication).

In Illinois there are presently 97 recognized high-quality community types, of which 79 (roughly 81%) are presently included in the nature preserves system in Illinois. An additional seven high-quality community types not included in the Illinois Nature Preserves System are protected by designation as Federal Research Natural Areas or U.S. Forest Service Natural Areas and are afforded comparable protection. In 1978 only one in five natural areas in the state could be considered to be protected (Illinois Department of Conservation et al. 1980). In 1995 more than one in three natural areas was considered to be protected on the basis of inclusion in the nature preserves system. If the Illinois Natural Areas Inventory sites afforded comparable protection by the federal government are included in this total, then fully 43% of all natural areas in the state could be considered to be protected.

After Preservation Then What: Conservation and Management of Remnant Preserves in Fragmented Landscapes

Increasing human-caused stress to natural areas has led to the widespread realization that providing legal protection to natural areas is not, by itself, sufficient to ensure the protection of the ecological integrity of these areas (Pyle 1980, White and Bratton 1980, Janzen 1986, Schwartz 1994). Frequently the greater conservation challenge is in maintaining these areas against the onslaught of potential threats to the character of these natural remnants (Pyle 1980, Schwartz 1994). This is especially true for small remnants in highly fragmented areas that require manipulative management to retain or restore the conditions for which the reserve was set aside (Pyle 1980). Factors such as natural and human disturbances, manipulation of fire regimes, succession, imbalance of animal populations (i.e., absence of key predators, overabundance of large herbivores), protection from invasive exotic plants and animals, population and genetic change of rare species, altered hydrology, and increased visitor pressure are all serious threats to small reserves that require almost constant attention from land managers (Pyle 1980, White and Bratton 1980). As preserve size becomes smaller, external influences may play a greater role in these remnants than do internal influences (Saunders et al. 1991). As a result, there is a strong need to develop an integrated approach to landscape management that places conservation reserves in the context of the overall landscape (Saunders et al. 1991). Even large preserves are not immune to external threats to natural areas or to the rare species populations they possess (Janzen 1983, 1986; White 1987). Because these external factors exert such a strong influence on small and, occasionally, large reserves, management efforts must be directed toward the landscape mosaic and not solely on the reserves (Saunders et al. 1991, Wiens 1994). The Illinois Department of Conservation, Illinois Nature Preserves Commission, and Illinois Endangered Species Protection Board have recognized this and have begun to incorporate system-based landscape-scale considerations into resource conservation planning (e.g., Illinois Department of Conservation 1994).

Although most conservation biologists recognize the need for large, connected, multiple populations in some sort of landscape network to adequately ensure population persistence (e.g., Mann and Plumer 1993), small reserves may be the only feasible alternative for natural communities that have become extremely rare or for those in highly fragmented landscapes (Shafer 1995). In highly fragmented landscapes, habitat protection of small remnants is the important first step toward successful restoration, providing a base around which future restoration efforts can be focused. Small reserves are also important in terms of providing a critical template to guide restoration activity. Moreover, small areas may be very effective for conserving sessile species such as plants (e.g., Lesica and Allendorf 1992).

Although big areas are usually preferred to smaller ones, not all species will be captured by big reserves. For example, big reserves focused on providing habitat for large, wide-ranging species may not adequately protect the habitats of rare invertebrates and plants (e.g., Hafernik 1992). Additionally, large reserves focused on protecting high-diversity areas may also lack many rare species (Prendergast et al. 1993). Even the smallest prairie remnants can contain populations of rare prairie-restricted insects (e.g., Panzer 1988, Panzer et al. 1995) and many small native prairie patches still contain relatively high numbers of native prairie plants (e.g., Betz and Lamp 1981). Small remnants may also contribute significantly to regional floral and faunal diversity. For example, two-thirds of the native plant species in the Chicago area are essentially limited in distribution to natural areas (Wilhelm and Ladd 1988).

Need for Large Reserves

While a series of small reserves can provide protection for some rare and endangered species, many other species will require the protection of large areas to ensure population persistence in highly fragmented landscapes. For some species considered endangered in Illinois, such as the northern harrier, grasslands (or grassland complexes) as large as 800 ha may be required to maintain nesting populations (Sweet 1991). Presently very few grasslands or grassland complexes of this size are available in the state. The establishment and protection of large grassland complexes would also benefit a number of other endangered, area-sensitive grassland birds such as Henslow's sparrows, upland sandpipers, and short-eared owls (Herkert 1991, 1992). Large wide-ranging mammals such as the state-threatened bobcat have very large home ranges, often encompassing forest areas as large as 12 km^2 (e.g., Schwartz and Schwartz 1959, Jackson 1961), and also may require the conservation of extensive tracts. Additionally, several forest birds require large areas for nesting (e.g., Robbins et al. 1989) including the state-endangered red-shouldered hawk (e.g., Bednarz and Dinsmore 1982) and the state-threatened veery (e.g., Herkert 1995). Very large forest areas also may be required to maintain productive populations of forest birds because regional studies have documented high rates of nest losses in highly and even some moderately fragmented landscapes (Robinson et al. 1995). Restorations such as the 24,000 ha Cache River Restoration Project of the Illinois Department of Natural Resources, U.S. Fish and Wildlife Service, and The Nature Conservancy, and the establishment of the U.S. Forest Service's 7,600 ha Midewin National Tallgrass Prairie in northeastern Illinois are exemplary examples of the large-scale restoration efforts that will provide substantial conservation benefits for some of the state's rarer area-sensitive species.

Summary

Over the last 30 years the Illinois Nature Preserves System has come to encompass a vast representation of Illinois' significant natural features. These preserves provide critical habitat for many rare and declining species in the state and provide important long-term protection for high-quality natural community remnants. As a result, the Illinois Nature Preserves System plays a prominent role in efforts to preserve the state's biological diversity. Aquatic organisms and species requiring large habitat blocks may require additional conservation attention, however, because capturing the habitat requirements of these two groups of species has been difficult to accomplish under the current conservation system in Illinois.

Providing legal protection for natural areas is only the first step in securing the long-term protection of these precious areas. An equally important need in many cases is a sustained commitment for long-term stewardship and management of these sites to counteract the many potential degrading influences that are present in highly fragmented landscapes. Because most nature preserves are generally of small size, they are frequently inextricably linked to their surroundings. Their integrity is thus somewhat dependent on the integrity of their surroundings. Focusing conservation and management efforts solely on internal factors is another threat to the persistence and integrity of small remnant preserves in highly fragmented areas.

Providing legal protection for endangered and threatened species is usually only the first step toward successful recovery. While habitat destruction may be the most important initial threat to most plant and animals populations (e.g., Terbororgh and Winter 1980), removal of this initial threat is frequently not sufficient to ensure the recovery of the small populations that remain, particularly in small remnants. This is especially true if the total area needed for population persistence is not encompassed in the preserve (Newmark 1987). Once a population becomes small, its persistence can remain threatened even after the initial cause of endangerment has been alleviated (Belovsky et al. 1994). In many situations active and occasionally intense management will be necessary to ensure long-term persistence for these beleaguered populations (Belovsky et al. 1994). Proactive recovery efforts will be needed before these populations may be regarded as secure in a long-term perspective.

References

Belovsky, G.E., J.A. Bissonette, R.D. Dueser, T.C. Edwards, Jr., C.M. Luecke, M.E. Ritchie, J.B. Slade, and F.H. Wagner. 1994. Management of small populations: Concepts affecting the recovery of endangered species. *Wildlife Society Bulletin* 22:307–316.

Bednarz, J.C., and J.J. Dinsmore. 1982. Nest-sites and habitat of red-shouldered and red-tailed hawks in Iowa. *Wilson Bulletin* 94:31–45.

Betz, R.F., and H.F. Lamp 1981. The species composition of old settler cemetery prairies in northern Illinois and Indiana. *Proceedings of the North American Prairie Conference* 6:267.

Bowles, M.L. 1981. Introduction: the endangered species project. In M.L. Bowles, V.E. Diersing, J.E. Ebinger, and H.C. Schultz, eds. *Endangered and Threatened Species of Illinois: Status and Distribution.* Illinois Department of Conservation, Springfield, 1–2.

Forbs, S.A. 1876. List of Illinois crustacea, with descriptions of new species. *Illinois Museum of Natural History Bulletin* 1:3–25.

Forbs, S.A., and R.E. Richardson. 1908. *The Fishes of Illinois.* Illinois State Laboratory of Natural History, Danville.

Garman, P. 1917. The Zygoptera, or damsel-flies, of Illinois. *Illinois Natural History Survey Bulletin* 12:411–587.

George, W.G. 1971. Vanished and endangered birds of Illinois: A new "black list" and "red list." *Illinois Audubon Bulletin* 158:2–11.

Graber, R.R., and J.W. Graber. 1963. A comparative study of bird populations in Illinois, 1906–1909 and 1956–1958. *Illinois Natural History Survey Bulletin* 28:383–529.

Hafernik, J.E. 1992. Threats to invertebrate biodiversity: Implications for conservation strategies. In P.L. Fiedler, and S.K. Jain, eds. *Conservation Biology: The Theory and Practice of Nature Conservation Preservation and Management.* Chapman and Hall, London, 171–195.

Herkert, J.R. 1991. Prairie birds of Illinois: Population response to two centuries of habitat change. *Illinois Natural History Survey Bulletin* 34:393–399.

Herkert, J.R., ed. 1992. *Endangered and Threatened Species of Illinois: Status and Distribution, Part 2—Animals.* Illinois Endangered Species Protection Board, Springfield.

Herkert, J.R. 1994. *Endangered and Threatened Species of Illinois: Status and Distribution, Volume 3—1994 Changes to the Illinois List of Endangered and Threatened Species.* Illinois Endangered Species Protection Board, Springfield.

Herkert, J.R. 1995. Status and habitat-area requirements of the veery in Illinois. *Auk* 112:794–797.

Illinois Department of Conservation, Illinois Nature Preserves Commission, and Illinois Endangered Species Protection Board. 1980. *The Illinois Natural Areas Plan.* Illinois Department of Conservation, Springfield.

Illinois Department of Conservation. 1994. *A Strategic Plan for the Illinois Department of Conservation.* Illinois Department of Conservation, Springfield.

Illinois Endangered Species Protection Board. 1990. *1990 Transition Document.* Illinois Endangered Species Protection Board, Springfield.

Illinois Nature Preserves Commission. 1972. *Comprehensive Plan for the Illinois Nature Preserves System, Part 1: Guidelines.* Illinois Nature Preserves Commission, Rockford.

Illinois Nature Preserves Commission. 1973. *Illinois Nature Preserves: Two-Year Report 1971–1972.* Illinois Nature Preserves Commission, Springfield.

Jackson, H.H.T. 1961. *Mammals of Wisconsin.* University of Wisconsin Press, Madison.

Janzen, D.H. 1983. No park is an island: Increase in interference from outside as park size decreases. *Oikos* 41:402–410.

Janzen, D.H. 1986. The eternal external threat. In M.E. Soule, ed. *Conservation Biology: The Science of Scarcity and Diversity.* Sinauer Associates, Sunderland, Mass., 286–303.

Kennicott, R. 1855. A catalogue of animals observed in Cook County, Illinois. *Illinois State Agricultural Society Transactions for 1853–1854* 1:577–595.

Lesica, P., and F.W. Allendorf. 1992. Are small populations of plants worth preserving. *Conservation Biology* 6:135–139.

Mann, C.C., and M.L. Plumer. 1993. The high cost of biodiversity. *Science* 260:1868–1871.

McFall, D., and J. Karnes, eds. 1995. *A directory of Illinois Nature Preserves*, vol. 1. Illinois Department of Natural Resources, Springfield.

Needham, J.G., and C.A. Hart. 1901. The dragonflies (Odonata) of Illinois with descriptions of the immature stages. Part I. Petaluridae, Aeschnidae, and Gomphidae. *Illinois Natural History Survey Bulletin* 6:1–94.

Newmark, W.D. 1987. A land-bridge island perspective on mammalian extinctions in western North American parks. *Nature* 325:430–432.

O'Neill, R.V., J.R. Krummel, R.H. Gardner, G. Sugihara, B. Jackson, D.L. DeAngelis, B.T. Milne, M.G. Turner, B. Zygmunt, S.W. Christensen, V.H. Dale, and R.L. Graham. 1988. Indices of landscape pattern. *Landscape Ecology* 1:153–162.

Panzer, R. 1988. Managing prairie remnants for insect conservation. *Natural Areas Journal* 8:83–90.

Panzer, R., D. Stillwaugh, R. Gnaedinger, and G. Derkovitz. 1995. Prevalence of remnant dependence among the prairie- and savanna-inhabiting insects of the Chicago region. *Natural Areas Journal* 15:1001–116.

Post, S.L. 1991. Native Illinois species and related bibliography. *Illinois Natural History Survey Bulletin* 34:463–475.

Prendergast, J.R., R.M. Quinn, J.H. Lawton, B.C. Eversham, and D.W. Gibbons. 1993. Rare species, the coincidence of diversity hotspots and conservation strategies. *Nature* 365:335–337.

Primack, R.B. 1993. *Essentials of Conservation Biology*. Sinauer Associates, Sunderland, Mass.

Pyle, R.M. 1980. Management of nature reserves. In M.E. Soule, and B.A. Wilcox, eds. *Conservation Biology: An Evolutionary-Ecological Perspective*. Sinauer Associates, Sunderland, Mass.

Ridgway, R. 1889. *The Ornithology of Illinois*. Vol I. Illinois State Laboratory of Natural History, Champaign.

Ridgway, R. 1895. *The Ornithology of Illinois*. Vol II. Illinois State Laboratory of Natural History, Champaign.

Robbins, C.S., D.K. Dawson, and B.A. Dowell. 1989. Habitat area requirements of breeding forest birds of the middle Atlantic states. *Wildlife Monographs* 103:34.

Robinson, S.K., F.R. Thompson, III, T.M. Donovan, D.R. Whitehead, and J. Faaborg. 1995. Regional forest fragmentation and nesting success of migratory birds. *Science* 267:1987–1990.

Saunders, D.A., R.J. Hobbs, and C.R. Margules. 1991. Biological consequences of ecosystem fragmentation: A review. *Conservation Biology* 5:18–32.

Schwartz, C.W., and E.R. Schwartz. 1959. *The Wild Mammals of Missouri*. University of Missouri Press and Missouri Conservation Commission. Columbia.

Schwartz, M.W. 1994. Illinois' nature preserves a positive look toward the future. *The Illinois Steward* 3:3–7.

Schwegman, J.E. 1973. *Comprehensive Plan for the Illinois Nature Preserves System. Part 2: The Natural Divisions of Illinois*. Illinois Nature Preserves Commission, Springfield.

Shafer, C.L. 1995. Values and shortcomings of small reserves. *BioScience* 45:80–88.

Sweet, M.J. 1991. Kites and northern harrier. In *Proceedings of the Midwest Raptor Management Symposium and Workshop*. National Wildlife Federation, Washington, D.C., 32–41.

Terbororgh, J., and B. Winter. 1980. Some causes of extinction. In M.E. Soule, and B.A. Wilcox eds. *Conservation Biology: An Evolutionary-Ecological Perspective*. Sinauer Associates, Sunderland, Mass., 119–134.

Ulffers, H.A. 1855. Mollusca of southern Illinois *Illinois State Agricultural Society Transactions for 1853–1854* 1:610–612.

White, J. 1978. Illinois Natural Areas Inventory technical report, vol. 1. *Survey Methods and Results*. Illinois Department of Conservation, Springfield.

White, P.S. 1987. Natural disturbance, patch dynamics, and landscape pattern in natural areas. *Natural Areas Journal* 7:14–22.

White, P.S., and S.P. Bratton. 1980. After preservation: Philosophical and practical problems of change. *Biological Conservation* 18:241–255.

Wiens, J.A. 1994. Habitat fragmentation: Island *v* landscape perspectives on bird conservation. *Ibis* 137:S97–S104.

Wilhelm, G., and D. Ladd. 1988. Natural areas assessment in the Chicago region. *Transactions of the North American Wildlife and Natural Resources Conference* 53:361–375.

18

An Aid to Conservation Strategy in Illinois: The Critical Trends Assessment Project

Tom Heavisides and Bob Lieberman
Illinois Department of Natural Resources, 524 S. Second St, Springfield, IL 62701

Introduction

Circa 1992 a series of satellites orbiting the earth captured images of the spectural reflectance covering 36 million acres of a geopolitically sculptured place called Illinois. After sophisticated computer processing, these images show that 80% of the landscape is agricultural, primarily row crops such as, corn, soybeans, and small grains. Forested and wooded land covers 11% of the state, and wetlands cover a little more than 3%. Chicago, the third largest city in the country, and other urban and built-up land covers a little less than 3½% of the state. Open water, the last land cover classification, covers slightly less than 1½% of the Illinois landscape.

This is the modern landscape. What was it like before European colonization? Although the methods of land surveillance were not as high tech as satellite imagery, the United States General Land Office did survey the state between 1807 and 1844. The land cover would paint an Illinois landscape of mostly prairie (61%), with some forest (38%) and wetlands (25%; Iverson, et al. 1989, Suloway and Hubbell 1994) (percentages do not sum to 100% because the definitions of three habitat types vary among studies and overlap).

The differences in data collection are astounding. The historical estimates are based on data from hand-drawn maps, surveyed over more than 35 years. Surveyors collected the data by traveling across the state by canoe, horseback, or foot. Recent estimates used satellites orbiting the earth as part of a commercial reconnaissance mission, taking "snapshots" for applications ranging from weather forecasting to military intelligence (with sensitive computer photoimagery devices). For land cover mapping, the data are processed by a computerized geographic information system. The pre-European based estimate of "nature" presents a complex interaction of forest, wetland, and prairie landscape. The modern landscape is a much simpler mosaic. The difference in nature is not because of technological improvements that produce sharper outlines. Instead, the conclusion is that Illinois has changed.

Environmental Paradigm Shift

The current Illinois landscape is the result of trading nature for agriculture, cities, roads and suburban development. The debate over whether changes in landscape are good or bad requires one to supplement the data with value judgments.

Today's complex environmental issues are often stalled because they are framed by people's value judgments. The environmental problems of 20 or so years ago were certainly more apparent as to cause and effect. It was a visible smoke stack that caused the air to be dirty or a discharge pipe that killed the fish in the river. Presented with the evidence, we framed our response accordingly. Also, the solutions could be directed at other parties, and "we" seldom had to bear the cost of the solutions directly. As noted in the United States Environmental Protection Agency's Comparative Risk Report, when environmental problems are straightforward the nation does a good job of addressing them. When the problems are more complex—because myriad sources are involved, because we do not understand the cause and effect (i.e., latency of cancer), or because effects are incremental—the nation has not been as successful.

Thus, the changing nature of environmental issues requires us to rethink how we approach a satisfactory resolution of the problem. We must accept a *paradigm shift*. A *paradigm* is a framework of understanding accepted by a large part of a particular professional community. The environmental paradigm consists of the set of values, theories, methodologies, tools, and techniques that are employed by professionals in the environmental field. With the accumulation of a significant body of knowledge or information that is contradictory to, or unexplained by, the accepted paradigm, a paradigm shift occurs (Cortner and Moote 1994).

The literature has spawned many new conceptual phrases about emerging environmental paradigm(s). The more popular ones include *cumulative environmental change, multimedia pollution prevention, sustainable development, ecosystem management, watershed planning,* and *natural resource accounting.* While it is beyond this chapter to explore each of these paradigms, they all have similar characteristics. They aim to be proactive rather than reactive to problems, to employ better science through a multidisciplinary analysis, and to pursue a more collaborative effort involving both public and private interests in decision making. The intuitive basis of these paradigms is that natural resource stewardship and economic vitality are interdependent. How to establish a framework to value the economic tradeoffs with nonmonetized ecological values is at the core of many of these paradigms and, while much is still left to value judgments, data and science can assist with informing those judgments.

Environmental problems are frequently gridlocked but not because there is a shortage of scientific information. A vast amount of environmental data has been collected, but it is seldom placed in a context that policy makers and the public can use for decisions. Hence, the public and policy makers cannot grasp the overall view of the ecological situation (Brink 1991). Many environmental issues are contentious; determining priorities and accepting sacrifices are difficult. Policy makers do not necessarily wait for scientists to complete their analyses. As a result policy is often framed by "environmental crisis." Scientists are often frustrated and confused by the apparent impatience or disinterest policy makers show toward their analyses. Addressing this dilemma requires a new cooperation, a new pact between scientists and policy makers. Policy makers need to integrate science into policy decisions. Scientists need to produce information that is useful and understandable to policy makers.

It was with this premise in mind, applying the best science to understand environmental issues and inform the policy process, that the Illinois Critical Trends Assessment Project (CTAP) was founded. By "informing the policy process" we mean that data is collected in a scientifically valid manner and converted into information that can be understood. This information is then presented to the public and policy makers in a context that is relatively free of value judgments.

Paradigm Shift and Illinois' Institutional Response

"If we could first know where we are and whither we are tending,
we could better judge what we do and how to do it . . . " Abraham Lincoln

Shortly after being sworn in (1990), the new governor of Illinois fulfilled his campaign promise and hired an environmental advocate. The advocate embarked on three major initiatives, which, intentionally or not, looked to define more clearly the new environmental paradigm. Her three initiatives were the Governor's Water Resources and Land Task Force, the Conservation Congress, and the development of the state of the state environment report. Because our involvement was with the latter, that is the emphasis of this chapter.

The lead agency assigned to the state of the environment report was the now-defunct Department of Energy and Natural Resources (DENR). The department was recently reorganized into another department as part of an institutional attempt at integrating science and policy. The DENR was the state's nonregulatory research and information department and home to the Geological, Natural History, and Water Surveys and the Hazardous Waste Research Division. Besides the science members, the intradepartment team included members from DENR's Office of Research and Planning. DENR also worked with the environmental advocate to form an interdepartmental working group that assisted with inventory and interpretation of environmental (pollution), ecological, and economic data.

At the onset of the conceptual work, project staff were involved in discussions with USEPA's policy office. The USEPA had recently released its Unfinished Business report. The purpose of this USEPA effort was to define environmental priorities better and hence reallocate its resources. USEPA's Science Advisory Board critiqued their Unfinished Business (renamed Comparative Risk) project and recommended that a source receptor model be developed to organize data better and deal with priority setting. The model (USEPA 1990) was adopted by CTAP.

The source receptor model was used to organize the data and allow researchers a way to think about the data relative to environmental issues. The model organized the world into sources of environmental stress and receptors of environmental stress. Environmental processes were also included in the conceptual model as a link between sources and receptors. This third component allowed researchers to address the empirical data collected on climate, stream hydrology, and other environmental processes that did not neatly fit into source or receptor categories.

The sources were defined as human activities that affect environmental and ecological condition: manufacturing, urban dynamics, transportation, resource extraction, electricity generation and transmission, and waste systems. Receptors included forests, agro-ecosystems, streams and rivers, lakes, prairies and savannas, wetlands, and human populations. All in all, the data and trends are presented in a summary report and seven technical volumes. The integrative summary discusses Illinois' past and present relative to ecological and economic change. The report was widely distributed in both hard copy and electronic copy on an electronic bulletin board and the World Wide Web (http:// dnr.state.il.us).

The report presented several significant findings relative to changes in the biodiversity of the state. Although none of the findings were previously unknown, their presentation in a single document emphasized the significance of the cumulative impacts. The net verdict is that the simplification of the landscape is the result of an economic transformation that began in the last century. What we in Illinois think of as "nature" has been gone for years. However, over the last 20 or 25 years some parts of the environment have improved. These improvements have been measured largely by chemical parameters. Measurements of ecological changes are not as encouraging.

The analysis was able to pinpoint specific areas that need to be addressed. For example, forest fragmentation has reduced the ability of Illinois forests to maintain biological integrity, and exotic species invasions of Illinois forest are increasing in severity and scope. In the past century, one in seven native fish species in Lake Michigan was either extirpated or suffered severe population crashes. Again, exotics have assumed the roles of major predators and major forage species. Of the state's prairie remnants four of five are smaller than ten acres and one in three is smaller than one acre—too small to function as self-sustaining ecosystems. Long-term records of mussel populations for four rivers in east central Illinois reveal large reductions in numbers of all species over the last 40 years, apparently as suitable habitat was lost to siltation and other changes.

From these species, the report arrived at three metaconclusions: (1) the emission and discharge of regulated pollutants over the past 20 years has declined, in some cases dramatically; (2) existing data suggest that the condition of natural ecosystems in Illinois is rapidly declining as a result of fragmentation and continual stress; and (3) data designed to monitor compliance with environmental regulations or the status of individual species are not sufficient to assess ecosystem health statewide.

CTAP II: The Next Step

The next step of CTAP was to construct a framework for addressing the latter two conclusions. First off, CTAP was not alone in reporting the lack of systematic effort to collect ecosystem data. Every one of the aforementioned paradigms highlights the overwhelming requirement for better information collection and use to address today's environmental issues. As noted by the General Accounting Office (GAO), understanding ecosystems and the tradeoffs between ecological and socioeconomic considerations has been hindered by noncomparable and insufficient data—whose limitations stem from uncoordinated, incomplete collection efforts. Further, the GAO found that different missions and planning requirements, statutorily rooted in the federal and state environmental management framework, hamper interagency coordination and data collection (USGAO 1994).

There are several good examples of organizations who are trying to integrate data collection efforts. These include Kentucky's state of the state environment reports, USEPA's Environmental Monitoring and Assessment Program (EMAP), and the establishment of the National Biological Survey within the U.S. Department of Interior.

Both government officials and scientists have noted that it will be necessary to collect and link large volumes of scientific data about ecosystem structures, components, processes, and functions at several geographic scales. This effort must be matched in a consistent manner with the collection and organization of socioeconomic data to identify relevant relationships between human activities and ecological conditions/trends. It is clear that new technologies such as geographical information systems (GIS) have begun playing an important role. Additional data is needed to better understand and communicate the value of ecological systems. Without this data to support the dialogue concerning tradeoffs among ecological and socioeconomic values, decisions will continue to be ad hoc and produce less-than-satisfactory results.

The goals of the second phase of the Critical Trends Assessment Project (CTAP II) are tied to the metaconclusion that suggests we need to do a better job monitoring the condition of Illinois' ecosystems. The goal is to develop an ongoing process to (1) identify and assess the extent and condition of Illinois ecosystems, (2) monitor or measure changes in extent and condition of ecosystems and, (3) provide useful, scientifically valid information for environmental policy.

Several tools began to be developed during this second phase to address the aforementioned goals. These tools include citizen involvement for citizen-scientist monitoring programs, development of ecological indicators, and use of satellite,

GIS, and network technologies to map changes and link data and people. Each of the tools are introduced below and discussed in detail later.

Citizen-Scientist Monitoring

People across Illinois are looking for practical and useful ways to become involved in protecting their environment. We are harnessing their interests and energy by organizing individuals, community groups, and high school and college science classes into a network of volunteer "citizen-scientists" who will help collect ecosystem indicator data. This component is nicknamed Eco Watch. The rationale for using citizens are twofold: (1) the task of sampling the state of Illinois is too large to be done entirely by professional biologists and (2) fiscal resources are limited. Citizen volunteers will work with scientists to collect scientifically valid ecological data and at the same time increase their awareness of environmental problems and scientific approaches to solving them.

Ecosystem Indicators

To assess the condition of our economic system, we look at economic indicators—housing starts, tax revenues, gross national product, etc. Scientists are developing similar indicators for ecological systems so that we may systematically and scientifically determine their overall condition. These indicators will give a picture of the condition of an ecosystem and will be developed so they can be collected by citizens volunteers. The first phase of CTAP developed a statewide baseline inventory of economic and ecological data, almost exclusively research and regulatory data. The indicator data will supplement the research and regulatory data.

Technology

To grapple with the quantity of data that will be collected for the trends assessments, we will rely on GIS and computer networks. Geographic information systems allow vast amounts of data to be stored, analyzed, and presented in a relatively short time. They are at the core of the data management effort. Another technology tool that is being used to assess ecosystems is satellite imagery data. These data map the changing spatial contours of ecosystems, with a surface resolution of areas as little as 10 m by 10 m. This effort will help define the extent of ecosystems and establish a baseline from which changes in extent can be measured. The computer network will allow information and data to flow quickly and inexpensively among the different users, for their different interest as well as for the statewide trends report.

Citizen Monitoring—RiverWatch

Although the concept of citizen monitoring is not new, to conduct it on a systematic statewide basis demands close coordination and higher standards for the participants. River and stream ecosystems, for several reasons, were selected as the pilot to test the citizen monitoring program. Several citizen groups were already involved in local stream protection efforts, hence the citizen monitoring program established a partnership with the Illinois River Watch Network. The Illinois River Watch Network (IRWN) is a statewide affiliation of organizations and individuals dedicated to protecting the state's rivers and streams. The network's citizen-scientist monitoring is supervised by DNR planning staff and Natural History Survey scientists.

Another reason streams and rivers were selected as the pilot is that there are established monitoring procedures (indicators) that have been tested and used by environmental professionals. The indicators selected for the River Watch Network are benthic macroinvertebrates, including aquatic insects (such as mayflies, stoneflies, caddisflies, midges, and beetles), snails, worms, freshwater clams, mussels, and crayfish. The purpose of this project was to test whether volunteers could collect scientifically valid data and whether scientists would be comfortable with the data that volunteers collected.

In spring 1994, River Watch completed a pilot training session that tested the effectiveness of proposed sampling and assessment methods. Staff from the Illinois State Water Survey and the Illinois Environmental Protection Agency were instructors. This session helped to refine the stream monitoring protocols described in River Watch's Volunteer Stream Monitoring Manual. Since January 1995, more than 500 citizen scientists have monitored 97 streams at 104 sites. The network has also participated in numerous stream cleanups, with 850 volunteers removing more than 20 tons of garbage from Illinois streams. Although results are preliminary, it appears the stream monitoring protocol is ideally suited for citizen-scientists.

Indicators—ForestWatch

Not all ecosystems have readily available, off-the-shelf sets of indicators for volunteers to use. Forest ecosystems were selected as a test to develop "new" indicator protocols. The task of developing forest indicators was assigned to scientists at the Natural History Survey. To design monitoring protocols for citizens required scientists to think in terms of limited capital and ample but relatively unskilled labor. This task is contrary to their training and experience— monitoring exercises are capital intensive and conducted with small numbers of highly skilled personnel. Survey scientists completed a draft manual for Forest-Watch in summer 1995. Current plans are to "employ" high school science classes to test and refine the protocol. Eventually, science classes throughout the state will be part of the citizen-monitoring effort. The use of science classes allows students to (a) participate in an interactive learning exercise, and (b) collect data to be used in state of the environment reports.

The forest protocol consists of two phases: establishing transects in the forest stand and monitoring that site annually. The monitoring protocol includes survey-ing for non-native species, evaluating vegetative complexity, surveying for rep-tiles, surveying for disturbance of sensitive plant species, and evaluating canopy condition. Efforts to refine the forest protocol and develop protocols for prairies and wetlands should be completed by the summer of 1996. The selection of monitoring sites will be developed in the next phase of CTAP.

Technology—Communications/Data

The third component of CTAP II includes several technology tools. The first is communications. An electronic bulletin board system, Econet, is helping statewide RiverWatch organizations communicate with one another as well as with the central coordinating office. A DNR web site contains CTAP information and, in the future, volunteer monitors will be able to upload their data to this site.

One of the more exciting ventures involving GIS technology is converting satellite imagery to map land cover at a regional and statewide level. Actually, the GIS converts this imagery into more than a map; it transforms it into a database that can be used for a variety of applications. As noted in the introduction in this chapter, CTAP developed a statewide land cover database at 1:100,000 scale. An atlas containing a county-by-county summary of the land cover catego-ries, accompanied by a CD of the statewide land cover, will be released in the spring of 1996. This endeavor was expensive and time consuming but provided baseline data, a committment seldom financed exclusively at the state level. The opportunity now exists for analysis of future land cover change.

The next step in CTAP is to adjust the scale of analysis from statewide to regional. The impetus of the regional initiative is linked to the other governors' advocate projects, the Water Resources and Land Task Force, and the Conserva-tion Congress. During this phase of CTAP, scientific information will be combined with efforts to preserve or restore ecosystems.

Resource-Rich Areas

The policy response to these three governor-sponsored initiatives was the Conser-vation 2000 (C2000) legislation. (Indirectly these initiatives also led to the subse-quent integration of several natural resource agencies.) This piece of Illinois conservation legislation created a six-year, $100 million funding mechanism to protect and enhance Illinois' natural resources. The guiding paradigm of this legislation is ecosystem-based management. Using an ecosystem-based manage-ment approach, the state will promote protection of large, sustainable ecosystems (termed ecosystem partnerships) in partnership with private interests.

Ecosystem-based management advanced out of concern for the decline in biodiversity. Unfortunately, it means different things to different people. A litera-ture review on the subject presented this definition: "Ecosystem management integrates scientific knowledge of ecological relationships within a complex socio-political and values framework toward the general goal of protecting native ecosystem integrity over the long term." (Grumbine 1994, 31) As noted in the definition, ecosystem-based management has as one of its requisites integration of scientific knowledge. It is the goal of the next phase of CTAP to provide ecosystem-based information for ecosystem-based management.

Through the Governor's Natural Resources Coordinating Council (an initiative of the Water Resources and Land Task Force), Illinois has adopted the following as its working ecosystem-based management definition: "Ecosystem-based management [is] stewardship of our natural resources to enhance the functional integrity of large, complex environmental units called ecosystems and their physical and biological components. Ecosystem-based management is an active process that emphasizes the maintenance of biological diversity, of natural relationships among species, and of dynamic processes that contribute to ecosystem sustainability." (Loren Nevling, Chief, Illinois Natural History Survey, personal communication, Dec. 1994) Ecosystem management emphasizes resource conditions and long-term resource sustainability as a much-expanded concept beyond the traditional land and water management paradigm of sustained yield.

The C2000 ecosystem management approach is directed at influencing landowner behavior (public and private) in and around ecosystem partnerships. Ecosystem partnerships typically are "built" or established around tracts of publicly owned land (parks and preserves). The ecosystem partnership program goal is to establish a process to focus state, federal, and private efforts toward improving ecological and economic conditions through a collaborative planning and decision-making process. In Illinois, managing large-scale ecosystems requires the program to follow a collaborative approach because most land is privately owned. The C2000 program involves four major steps: inventory and assessment, cooperative planning, restoration and enhancement work, and stewardship and monitoring.

CTAP supports these four steps by providing a scientific and empirical framework. Further, the CTAP II tools are being used to support the informational needs of ecosystem management. The next CTAP phase of this merged CTAP/ C2000 program consists of three major directives—inventoring resource-rich areas, assessing regions contiguous to ecosystem partnerships (regional assessments), and developing long-term monitoring plans for the regions.

The C2000 legislation identified four initial ecosystem partnerships. The scientists at the state's Natural History, Geological, and Water Surveys are working in conjunction with DNR planning staff to develop a inventory of additional sites. Using watersheds as the primary unit of analysis, and working on a GIS, scientists incorporated ecological databases as attributes for each watershed. A set of criteria was developed and used to evaluate or screen the state for areas, referred to as resource-rich sites. The resource-rich areas then become candidates for ecosystem partnerships. Final selection of ecosystem partnerships will use this statewide inventory of resource-rich areas and include other factors, such as recreational potential, socioeconomic impacts, etc.

Natural History Survey scientists have provided preliminary criteria to be used to define the resource richness of individual watersheds: (1) percent of area in forest; (2) percent in rural grassland or pasture; (3) percent of wetland area as determined by Natural Wetland Inventory presence; (4) the number of natural areas of significant features; (5) the length of Biologically Significant Streams (Illinois classification); and (6) areas of public ownership. A final map of resource-rich areas and a discussion of the ranking scheme is scheduled to be published and distributed to the general public and interested groups by the summer of 1996. As noted by the land cover map, the soils, climate, and topography of Illinois, has resulted in roughly 80% of the state being farmed. Scientist's preliminary findings on the statewide inventory indicated that most remaining resource-rich areas are located in river bottomlands, essentially the land that could not be economically farmed. This is not to say that a small patch of hill prairie cannot be found in Illinois; it is just that these patches are too small to be recognized at the scale used by the inventory.

As mentioned, the C2000 legislation designated four areas as ecosystem partnerships. One will convert roughly 19,000 acres into tallgrass prairie. To continue with the principal intent of CTAP—to inform the policy process—regional assessments have begun on several of the proposed sites. These regional assessments are technical reports consisting of data on abiotic and biotic resources as well as socioeconomic data. In addition to the tabular data in support of this regional assessment, scientists have prepared land cover maps derived from satellite imagery at a scale of 1:24,000. The technical data and accompanying maps will be integrated into an executive summary and be available on the region's website.

The purpose of these regional assessments is to provide the cooperative planning step with an appraisal of the area's abiotic, biotic, and socioeconomic resources. This assessment simply presents to the citizens the status of their region. To supplement this picture of the current resource condition, a historical-ecological template of the region will be developed from presettlement inventories and maps. The historical template presents what was, the current assessment presents what is, and the cooperative planning process develops future scenarios that will facilitate and guide restoration or stewardship efforts. Again, the role of CTAP is to provide the context for local resource goals and decisions. This is not a minor role in Illinois because Illinois' ecosystems often are not self-sustaining and thus require extensive management (exogenous support).

The ability to measure the outcomes of future landscape scenarios is being addressed by the development of regional long-term monitoring plans. Survey scientist and planning staff are designing a monitoring plan to identify the data to be collected by scientists, land managers, and citizens. Each monitoring plan is tailored to specific regions and the subsequent goals of the region. The monitoring plan incorporates the lessons and tools that have been developed as part of CTAP II.

Ecosystem management recognizes that humans both influence and are influenced by ecological patterns and processes. Human values therefore play a dominant role in ecosystem management goals, regardless of the role of scientific knowledge. Linking the context of regional assessment to followup monitoring is strategic since local decisions tend to focus on narrow provincial concerns and often will discount the broader social value of biodiversity (Grumbine 1994).

Epilogue

One does not have to go far to find evidence of distrust of government; people are skeptical of its intention. The discussion of ecosystem management, however, began in areas with large federal landholdings; the western national parks are the model. Public landownership is clearly not the case in Illinois. The state does not possess the financial or political capital to acquire and set aside large tracts of land as nature preserves. On the other hand, people care about their land and the environmental amenities it can bring. The ecosystem partnership process simply hopes to link public and private efforts to preserve or restore ecological amenities and thereby begin reversing the downward trend in biodiversity.

References

Brink, B.T. 1991. The AMOEBA approach as a useful tool for establishing sustainable development? In O. Kuik, and H. Verbruggen, eds. *In Search of Indicators of Sustainable Development*. Kluwer Academic Publishers, Dordrecht, Netherlands.

Cortner, H.J., and M.A. Moote. 1994. Trends and issues in land and water resources management: Setting the agenda for change. *Environmental Management* 18:167–173.

Grumbine, R.E. 1994. What is ecosystem management? *Conservation Biology* 8:27–38.

Iverson, L., R.L. Oliver, D.P. Tucker, P.G. Risser, C.D. Burnett, and R.G. Rayburn. 1989. *Forest Resources of Illinois: An Atlas and Analysis of Spatial and Temporal Trends*. Illinois Natural History Survey, Champaign.

Suloway, L., and M. Hubbell. 1994. *Wetland Resources of Illinois*. Illinois Natural History Survey, Champaign.

United States General Accounting Office. 1994. *Ecosystem Management Additional Actions Needed to Adequately Test a Promising Approach*. USGAO. Washington, DC.

United States Environmental Protection Agency. 1990. *Environmental Monitoring and Assessment Program: Ecological Indicators*. USEPA, Washington, D.C.

19

History of Natural Areas Programs in Wisconsin

Forest Stearns
University of Wisconsin-Milwaukee, Emeritus; Forestry Science Laboratory,
5985 Highway K, Rhinelander, WI 54501

Paul Matthiae
Bureau of Endangered Resources, Wisconsin Department of Natural
Resources, Box 7921, Madison, WI 53707

Introduction

For many readers the words *conservation* and *Wisconsin* bring to mind Aldo
Leopold's *Sand County Almanac* (Leopold 1949), John Curtis's *Vegetation of
Wisconsin* (Curtis 1959), or John Muir's stories of his childhood (Muir 1965),
as well as places such as the Baraboo Hills, the Chiwaukee Prairie, or the prairie
restorations at the Madison Arboretum. While these names and features may
represent some of the best known ventures in natural area conservation in Wisconsin, the state has a long-standing effort in conservation that extends throughout
the 20th century (Loucks 1968, Stearns and Germain 1991). Although scientific
concerns and financial support have often changed during this period, the commitment has remained strong. The evolution of Wisconsin's habitat preservation
and restoration programs provides a guide for conservation in regions where
natural habitats are scarce. In this chapter we (1) describe the biological and
environmental context of the state and the forces that gave rise to its biota, (2)
describe the progress of natural area protection and stewardship in Wisconsin,
and (3) look to the future and examine how strategic planning, state/private
cooperation, and government policies may influence natural area conservation
into the 21st century.

Biological Context

Glacial ice covered much of Wisconsin and the Middle West 18,000 years B.P.
Only southwestern Wisconsin, adjacent Minnesota, and major portions of west
central Wisconsin were free of ice (Clayton et al. 1992). As the ice and cold
retreated, a fresh land surface was left to be populated by the plants and animals
that had survived under less rigorous conditions distant from the ice front. Repopu-

lation of glaciated regions with flora and fauna took time, with each species arriving at its own rate (Davis 1981, Davis et al. 1986). As glacial activity diminished, the warmer, moist period 14,000 to 12,000 B.P. enabled tamarack (*Larix laricina*) and spruce (*Picea* spp.) from the Great Plains to enter Wisconsin (Delcourt and Delcourt 1987). As this warming continued, pines (*Pinus* spp.), oaks (*Quercus* spp.), and other trees replaced spruce. As the climate became drier and even warmer the vegetation continued to change so that by 7000 B.P. prairie and savanna had advanced across southern Wisconsin and large areas of adjoining states. A gradual shift back toward a cooler and somewhat wetter climate began about 3500 B.P. (Delcourt and Delcourt 1987). This change provided conditions suitable to support forest vegetation. Early European settlers found a complex array of vegetation types that included forest, savannas, and prairies (Curtis 1959). Much prairie and savanna remained at the time of European settlement, with associated sedge meadows and open marshlands. Oak forest and patches of southern hardwood forest were present in areas protected from the frequent fires that had kept the savanna open and the grassland treeless. In southern and western Wisconsin much of the land supported a patchwork of forest and wetland communities embedded in a grassland and savanna matrix.

Impacts of Human Occupancy

Native Americans have been present in some parts of Wisconsin during most of the postglacial period (Green et al. 1986). The first brief occupation was dated at about 11,000 B.P. Numbers increased after 6000 B.P., when camps became more numerous and widely distributed. Several Archaic cultures succeeded each other and persisted until about 1000 B.C. These people subsisted primarily as hunters, fishers, and gatherers, and their camps were located throughout the state. Depending on local resources, these early native humans moved, or died out, in hard times. Some probably used fire to assist in hunting. Beginning about 1000 B.C. to 500 B.C. the Woodland cultures began to appear and remained until A.D. 1000 or A.D. 1200. These groups depended on hunting, fishing, and extensive use of native plants, although some practiced primitive agriculture. Extensive agriculture was a later development, starting about A.D. 1000 when large fields were associated with permanent villages. Native American use of fire to maintain an open landscape for ease in travel, for hunting, and to maintain game habitat (Curtis 1956, McClain and Elzinga 1994) was a major reason for the persistence of grassland, savanna, and oak woodland, as well as sedge meadow, in southern and western Wisconsin.

The early European explorers, trappers, traders, and missionaries likely had only transient and minor impact on the patchy landscape. Most of the critical locations had already been occupied by the Native Americans (Dorney 1981). When European settlers reached southeastern Wisconsin in the early years of the last century, they found sizable Native American settlements, often with large fields. In the early and mid-1800s, several treaties were consummated in which the Native American tribes transferred title for large tracts of land to the federal government and the tribes moved or were forced to move.

The Federal Land Office Survey for Wisconsin began in 1832, at the point where the Illinois state line intersects the 4th Principal Meridian (Onsrud 1979). The survey proceeded northward and eastward. Initially township lines were established, soon followed by division of each township into 36 sections. In southeastern Wisconsin most of this work was completed by 1836 so that land could be opened for purchase. Settlement, both rural and urban, occurred rapidly. By 1854 most of the southern half of Wisconsin had been surveyed, and much of it had already been transferred into private hands.

Initially settlers cleared a portion of the better (or more easily worked) land for crops. Wood from the clearing and adjacent forest was used for cabins, barns, and fuel. Later, plank roads, small settlements, and the rapidly expanding larger towns claimed much timber. Fragmentation of open prairie, savanna, and forest increased drastically as agriculture expanded (Schafer 1927). During the later half of the century abundant white pine (*Pinus strobus*) from the northern forests became available, providing some opportunity for farm woodlots and forested swamps to recover. The expansion of agriculture reduced and soon eliminated the fires that had maintained the prairie and savanna. Woodlots were often grazed or eliminated.

As the human population spread northward in the 1850s and 1860s, lumbering accelerated, beginning the destruction of the northern forest. Many forest stands in the southern and western portions of the state were also harvested. These factors, combined with the loss of fire, increased agriculture, and human population growth, put heavy pressure on the natural vegetation and wildlife of the state. During the mid-1800s, while the population of southern Wisconsin was growing rapidly, there was little concern for species or habitat preservation. Game was still fairly abundant, although most large mammals, both predators and herbivores, had been extirpated by 1850. Loss of the predators was not a matter of general concern and was usually viewed as a positive change.

Conservation Concerns and Programs

Alarm of the Citizenry

The Wisconsin population in the mid-19th century included physicians and engineers, some of whom were also naturalists. These early naturalists spent much effort in listing and studying species distributions. As logging accelerated in the 1860s a few key individuals became alarmed. *Report on the Disastrous Effects of the Destruction of Forest Trees* (Lapham et al. 1867) called for preservation and criticized the voracious lumber industry. Their warnings went essentially unheeded, as did those of Cheney (1894). In 1876 a farmer in central Wisconsin had established a white pine plantation using wild seedlings (Wisconsin Magazine, June 1944), but no other attempts at restoration were made until the state established a nursery at Trout Lake in 1911 and created the Star Lake Plantation in 1913 (Association of State Foresters 1968, Forest History Association of Wisconsin 1982).

A solid step toward natural area preservation occurred in 1937 when the Ridges Sanctuary Corporation was formed with support from Albert Fuller, curator of botany at the Milwaukee Public Museum (MPM). Fuller was an expert on native orchids, and the Ridges area along Lake Michigan in Door County supported a variety of orchid species. A donation of 40 acres from the state of Wisconsin, and another 40 acres from a private citizen served as the initial land base for a successful, privately supported, natural area. The Ridges property now includes over 1,000 acres, and the group has about 3,200 members.

State Government Programs

By the 1930s many Wisconsin citizens were becoming concerned about the loss of native vegetation. In 1938 Albert Fuller and N. Roeder from the Milwaukee Public Museum and E. Gilbert, Norman Fassett, and Aldo Leopold from the University of Wisconsin (UW), joined by Madison attorney George Sieker, developed a plan to conserve wildflowers as a natural resource (Stearns and Germain 1991). One approach was to convince communities to set aside land to enhance their surroundings to benefit the local tourist economy. A botanical survey by the State Planning Board brought considerable public awareness. In 1945 the Wisconsin Conservation Commission approved a motion by Aldo Leopold, then a commission member, that established a Natural Areas Committee. That group was directed to begin to obtain, either by purchase or gift, botanical areas of special value. Committee members were Norman Fassett (UW, botany), Albert Fuller (MPM), and Fred Wilson (Wisconsin Conservation Department).

A budget of $5,000 was allocated for the fiscal year. By the late 1940s three areas—Cedar Grove, a hawk migration site; Parfrey's Glen, an area heavily used for teaching; and the Cedarburg Bog near Milwaukee—had become the property of the Wisconsin Conservation Department (WCD). The Parks and Forests Division of WCD was given responsibility for management and the state forester, C. L. Harrington, questioned how the areas should be managed. As he said, "I was a forester and forestry meant harvest. There was no conception of the idea of using and studying the natural processes in vegetation, especially forest, as a means for guiding conservation" (Stearns and Germain 1991, 1). After a meeting with UW scientists he agreed that these areas should be called scientific areas and said that he would need a scientific committee with legal authority to advise the WCD on preservation and management.

A proposal for legislation was prepared by J. Hickey (UW, wildlife management) and was presented to the chairman of the State Senate Committee on Conservation. It was enacted promptly in 1951. Membership of this new state board was representative of the major interest groups and set the pattern for future membership. Members included C.L. Harrington (state forester for WCD), G.E. Watson (Department of Public Instruction), J.T. Curtis (botany, UW Madison), Alvin Throne (biology, Milwaukee State Teachers College), A.M. Fuller (MPM), and Carl Welty (zoologist, Beloit College), appointed by the Wisconsin Academy of Sciences, Arts, and Letters (WASAL) to represent private colleges (Stearns and Germain 1991).

The board worked rapidly and by the end of 1952 had designated 16 scientific areas. Work continued so that 32 areas were listed in the spring of 1961 (Stearns and Germain 1991). Fuller reported in the board's annual report that "Most of these areas were established on state-owned lands such as state parks, state forests, public hunting grounds and roadside parks. There are still many state-owned lands that should be set aside. . . . There are many privately held lands that should (also) be set side. These lands should be procured by public agencies and dedicated as scientific areas." He also noted that the board had recommended that there be at least 300 scientific areas dedicated by 1980 and that "it is desirable that a number of each type (Curtis vegetation types, 2) be preserved in various localities of the state" (State Board for the Preservation of Scientific Areas 1961, 2). This direction established the pattern of acquisition followed by the board for the next 20 years.

Shortly after the board's inception the program began to slow down. This was due to a combination of the facts that many of the best state lands were already designated and the board was operating without adequate funds and with no staff. Grant Cottam, board chairman in 1963, suggested action to obtain " . . . as complete a set of the terrestrial biotic communities as possible . . . a similar set of aquatic communities . . . species preserves, geologic sites, . . . (and) archaeologic sites." He also noted the need for formal administrative procedures and WCD support, including provision for a budget and staff, and suggested that a natural areas section might be included in the WCD Parks and Forest Division (State Board for the Preservation of Scientific Areas 1963, 1).

In 1965 a committee of the Wisconsin Academy of Sciences, Arts, and Letters, chaired by John Thomson (1965, 7–8), reported to the governor on the needs for natural areas, their uses, and how the program was administered. The committee made several strong recommendations including the need for state funds to support the program and to provide staff. Specifically the committee recommended that " . . . the State Board for the Preservation of Scientific Areas be supported in its inventory of all possible sites . . . " and that "the ideal situation would be to have in each county of the state a representative of each habitat which occurred in that county." In addition the committee suggested three categories of natural areas: (1) recreational and educational areas, (2) natural history areas, and (3) scientific areas. Different objectives and management criteria would apply to each category. They also noted the importance of permanent protection for the areas that were designated, the need to keep the state board as an independent body, and the critical need for funds and staff assistance (Thomson 1965). The state budget that was approved in 1965 provided staff and funds for the program. Clifford Germain was hired as the first full-time staff member in 1966.

The Wisconsin state government was reorganized by the Kellet Bill in 1967. Under the new organization, the Wisconsin Conservation Department became the Wisconsin Department of Natural Resources (WDNR). At the same time procedures for all advisory boards were formalized and the state board became the Scientific Areas Preservation Council (SAPC). The representative from the DPI who had been dropped from the board in 1957 was returned to SAPC membership. In a related matter an assistant attorney general was named as public intervenor, and the legislation specified that copies of all requests for waterway alteration permits were to be provided to both the intervenor and the SAPC. The purposes for this action were to provide the intervenor with the ecological expertise found in the council and to extend the council's function of preservation. During the 1950s and 1960s the Scientific Area System grew steadily and the concept became established state policy.

Modern Era of Private and Public Cooperation Begins

The Wisconsin Chapter of the Nature Conservancy (WCTNC) was formed in 1960, and cooperation between the chapter and the SAPC developed rapidly, providing a major catalyst for acquisition. The ability of the WCTNC to act rapidly in a purchase was particularly helpful.

In the late 1960s it was already clear to the SAPC that more and larger areas were needed to provide adequate species habitat and space for recreation and educational functions. In 1973 the Wisconsin Natural Resources Board appointed a Wild Resources Advisory Council (WRAC). The WRAC was particularly successful in designating Wild and Wilderness Areas, Wild Lakes, and Public Use Natural Areas in the northern part of the state. However, the WRAC was disbanded in 1985, and many of its responsibilities were turned over to the WDNR Scientific Areas Program and the SAPC.

In 1975 the SAPC established a Community Relations Advisory Committee to study council operations so as to improve effectiveness. Recommendations included increasing council membership from 6 to 11 to permit greater participation by members in SAPC committees and establishing a standard of two three-year appointments, with an understanding that SAPC members would be provided at least two days per month for council activities by the appointing organization. Legislation increasing SAPC membership, enacted in 1976, provided for the addition of two members from the UW System, two appointed by the Wisconsin Academy of Sciences, Arts, and Letters and one additional member from the WDNR.

Among other activities, in 1976 the SAPC cosponsored preparation of WDNR Bulletin 92, *Endangered and Threatened Vascular Plants in Wisconsin*, with collaboration of the UW-Madison Herbarium (Tans 1976). A breeding bird census for scientific areas had been started in 1971 by members of the Wisconsin Society for Ornithology with the support of the SAPC and the WDNR. This census continues to the present providing valuable data.

In 1977 the WDNR issued a technical bulletin on preserving native diversity using Wisconsin's scientific areas (Germain et al. 1977). This bulletin was widely read and used by scientists and educators. It provided the rational and techniques for preservation, described the recent activities of the program and provided other useful information. Included were brief descriptions of the 139 natural areas then in the system. This bulletin has been out of print for many years and despite its proven value, funding has not been available to issue a revised version.

For several years the council had felt the need for a long-range plan to guide future activity. Council activity had focused primarily on acquisition of sites, driven in part by inventory data indicating that potential areas, especially in southern Wisconsin, were disappearing rapidly. In addition, the flood of WDNR master plans for various state-owned properties was diminishing, resulting in reduced opportunity for new sites. On the other hand, with 184 designated sites in the state system, the need for baseline information, stewardship activity (management), stronger protection, and greater research and educational use on existing sites was obvious.

After several years of work, SAPC and the Department of Natural Resources established a strategic plan for the state's natural lands (SAPC 1983). The strategic plan recommended a shift in emphasis to place more effort on protection and management of areas, renovation of some communities, and attempts to "capitalize on opportunities provided by scientific areas for more research and educational use." Implementation of the plan was to include obtaining baseline data on both grassland and forested areas. Increased effort was to be placed on management and education.

Progress faltered when funding grew limited in the early 1990s, in part a result of other needs associated with the overall program of the WDNR Bureau of Endangered Resources. Currently (1996) management activity is limited to about one-third of its 1992 level. Since 1993 little progress has been made in obtaining baseline data. Complete data are now available for only eight to ten grassland areas and perhaps eight forested areas (WDNR 1995).

During the 1970s the WCTNC gained much strength and increased cooperation with the state Scientific Areas Program. The chapter had named its first full time staff member in 1978 and began gradually to increase staff. With impetus from the national office of The Nature Conservancy, development of a Wisconsin Natural Heritage Inventory Program was a major objective. Both the SAPC and the WDNR staff had long believed that stronger legislation was needed to protect designated scientific areas, a need with which the Wisconsin Chapter concurred.

Legislation was enacted in 1985 that provided funds to manage natural areas, changed the name of the SAPC to the Natural Areas Preservation Council (NAPC) and specified its functions, and provided definitions and procedures for permanent natural area dedication. This legislation also established a Wisconsin Natural Heritage Inventory Program within the WDNR, a Natural Heritage Match Grant Program, and a stronger system for designation and permanent protection of state natural areas.

This legislation resulted from joint action led by Clifford Messenger of TNC, supported by other conservation groups and legislators and backed by the governor. To partially alleviate funding problems the legislature in 1989 passed the Stewardship 2000 Program (effective in 1990) that allocated $250 million over the following ten years to purchase land for certain WDNR programs, including $1.5 million for state natural areas. Another $500,000 was made available through the Heritage Match Grant Fund, which permits grants in the form of cash, land, and legal dedication from both nonprofit conservation organizations and private individuals to be matched with stewardship funds for the acquisition of state natural areas. Funds for management and related functions, however, remain far from adequate to accomplish the work needed.

Several other approaches to funding have been used. A Stewardship Program Challenge Grant requested by the Bureau of Endangered Resources was approved by the legislature. This matches each dollar contributed to the Endangered Resources Fund (a state income tax check-off program) with state funds up to $500,000. The Natural Areas Program receives a portion of this fund, which then must support the entire Bureau of Endangered Resources. In approving this fund the legislature specified that the bureau would no longer receive direct program support from the general fund. The most recent attempt to provide additional funding for the Bureau of Endangered Resources was the establishment of an endangered resources vanity license plate. This approach was a successful fundraiser in its first year (1995). Contributions to the income tax check-off program, however, had begun to decline.

During the late 1980s the NAPC focused on developing policy guidelines relating to management issues. These efforts included preparing policy guidelines (Table 19.1), developing rationale for larger areas, and evaluating the role of

Table 19.1. Six policy guidelines relative to Wisconsin Natural Areas issued by the Wisconsin Natural Areas Preservation Council between 1987 and 1991.

Year	Policy guideline
1987	Acquisition and management of forested natural areas.
1987	Augmenting populations of rare, endangered, and threatened plant species.
1988	Use of pesticides on state natural areas.
1988	Landscape scale natural areas.
1989	Control of wild fire on state natural areas (in cooperation with forestry).
1991	Collecting seed on state natural areas.

geological and archeological areas. During this period, cooperative efforts with the WCTNC continued on several major ecosystem conservation initiatives, including Quincy Bluff, Mink River, Lulu Lake, Spread Eagle Barrens and the Baraboo Hills. Also in the early 1980s the council saw the need to determine boundaries of the natural regions of the state. A map produced by F. Hole and C. Germain (1994) permitted classification of the diverse landscape of the state and has since been included in broader land classification efforts.

In the late 1980s the WCTNC shifted preservation strategy, along with NAPC and the WDNR Natural Areas Program, to emphasize larger reserves and ecosystem preservation rather than species-oriented projects. The WCTNC has continued long-standing programs for fee acquisition, site registration, and conservation easements to protect small natural areas but has become more selective about the projects that it pursues.

During the late 1980s and early 1990s the WCTNC has grown rapidly in staff and financial resources and is blessed with many volunteers, many of whom serve in the stewardship program. Management activities have been extensive and range from prescribed burns to surveys of rare butterfly species. The WCTNC has developed an ambitious program, including components similar to those outlined in the NAPC 1983 Strategic Plan, e.g., education and the stimulation of ecological research. The impressive recent growth in WCTNC capability is fortuitous, coming at a time when the WDNR budget has been reduced, limiting state-funded acquisition activities.

During the late 1980s and early 1990s the WDNR staff and the NAPC invested considerable effort working with federal agencies to establish protected natural areas in the Apostle Islands National Lakeshore, Fort McCoy, and the Chequamegon and Nicolet National Forests. Cooperation with local governments, the WCTNC, and other private groups continued, and resulted in designation of many new natural areas.

The rapid spread of several exotic plant species (i.e., purple loosestrife [*Lythrum salicaria*], glossy and smooth buckthorn [*Rhamnus frangula, R. cathartica*], honeysuckle [*Lonicera* spp.], leafy spurge [*Euphorbia esula*], spotted knapweed [*Centaurea maculosa*], and garlic mustard [*Alliaria petiolata*]) has already created difficult and expensive problems for established areas and has diverted some attention from long-range management and restoration objectives. Movement of gypsy moth (*Lymantria dispar*) across Lake Michigan into several counties in eastern Wisconsin now presents a major challenge to natural area managers, foresters, and anyone else concerned with natural or cultivated vegetation. Major components of ecological communities may be lost as the moth becomes established and continues to spread.

Prairie restoration has been hampered by the lack of adequate seed from local sources. This need resulted in the development of a Native Plant Seed Farm Program to facilitate restoration of grass and savanna systems. The program has been slow to start but is now about to become operational and will produce native ecotypes of prairie species.

Conservation into the 21st Century

The Wisconsin program continues to face political challenges to accomplishing its task of protecting natural resources within the state. An ongoing reorganization of the WDNR may impact the State Natural Areas Program through the loss or transfer of knowledgeable staff. The network that has been established for monitoring the condition of natural areas may also become less efficient with decentralization of the field staff. Other interests in the state continue to attempt to obtain exemptions to the rules protecting natural areas.

The original master planning process resulted in identification and designation of a number of natural areas on state-owned properties. Initial master planning of state-owned lands is now largely completed with most units having gone through at least one cycle (SAPC 1983, WDNR 1995). Revision of older master plans will soon begin, a process that will require planners to consider land management from a regional perspective. This will likely result in a few additional designations of state-owned land as natural areas. Any major additions in number or size of natural areas, however, will probably result from cooperative projects developed with other agencies and with the private sector. Recent discussions have identified possible natural area designation projects on county forests (13 counties have expressed interest). In the future there will be a greater role for nonprofit conservation groups in addition to the WCTNC. Many such groups have formed in recent years, including various land trusts such as the Door County Land Trustees, an umbrella group named Gathering Waters, and specific interest groups such as Trout Unlimited, Ducks Unlimited, and the Wisconsin Prairie Enthusiasts.

As time passes, the WDNR Natural Areas Program, the NAPC, and similarly the WCTNC will become even more involved in management activities, public education, and stimulating conservation research, as envisioned in the SAPC 1983 Strategic Plan. Concurrently the WCTNC will emphasize development of its landscape scale projects and the completion of current major ecosystem initiatives. The WCTNC is also continuing an international effort with Nicaragua. A new national program is being launched to better connect sites in various biogeographical regions of the United States.

Overview

The Wisconsin Natural Areas System now includes over 316 areas covering 110,000 acres. Virtually all of the Curtis vegetation types are represented at least once. Many other key components (e.g., aquatic, archeological, and geological sites, and species-specific habitats) are also included within the program. Many of these categories, however, are represented in only one or two locations and should be replicated in other natural divisions of the state. Since 1951, development of the natural (scientific) areas system has passed through several stages. It began with designation of a few critical areas, primarily on state-owned lands, largely in the southern portion of the state. As time passed it became obvious that potential tracts, particularly near urban areas, needed to be located and preserved before they were engulfed by development. The first natural resources inventory was conducted in Dane County in 1969. Acquisition accelerated as tracts were located. Early in the program site acquisition priority was usually based on site availability. The first thought was to obtain critical areas while they were still available. When the statewide inventory was completed in the early 1980s, it had located 700 sites deemed of statewide significance.

As WDNR staff and the Scientific Areas Preservation Council considered the 184 areas already designated by 1984, they recognized growing problems and began to shift program emphasis to stewardship and other matters such as more effective legal protection for areas. The addition of new areas, however, has continued through an increase in cooperative efforts with federal agencies, The Nature Conservancy, and other nonprofit groups. During the 1980s it became clear that larger areas (500 acres and more) were needed to meet species protection needs, to permit more effective management, and to mitigate potential local catastrophic events. Research during this period was beginning to document the impact of habitat fragmentation. Even larger areas of 10,000 to 100,000 acres are now being considered essential for landscape planning. In the last few years effort has been directed more toward obtaining large areas incorporating several components of the local landscape. Likewise, increasing concern over the loss of many animals and plants has placed greater emphasis on areas that can support most components of their presettlement biotic diversity. Biodiversity and ecosystem management have been accepted as vital in Wisconsin land planning and will remain major factors in the growing cooperative effort as the natural areas movement faces the future.

References

Cheney, L.S. 1894. Is forest culture in Wisconsin desirable? *Transactions Wisconsin State Historical Society* 24:163–170.

Clayton, L., J. Attig, D. Mickelson, and M. Johnson. 1992. *Glaciation of Wisconsin*. Educational Series 36. Geological and Natural History Survey, University of Wisconsin Extension, Madison.

Curtis, J.T. 1956. The modifications of mid-latitude grasslands and forests by man. In W.L. Thomas, ed. *Man's Role in Changing the Face of the Earth*. University of Chicago Press, Chicago, 721–36.

Curtis, J.T. 1959. *The Vegetation of Wisconsin*, University of Wisconsin Press, Madison.

Davis, M.B. 1981. Quaternary history and the stability of forest communities. In D.C. West, and H.H. Shugart, eds. *Forest Succession*. Springer-Verlag, New York.

Davis, M.B., K.D. Woods, S.L. Webb, and R.P. Futyma. 1986. Dispersal versus climate: Expansion of *Fagus* and *Tsuga* unto the Upper Great Lakes region. *Vegetatio* 67:93–103.

Delcourt, P.A., and H.A. Delcourt. 1987. *Long-Term Forest Dynamics of the Temperate Zone: A Case Study of Late-Quaternary Forests in Eastern North America*. Ecological Studies, vol. 63. Springer-Verlag, New York.

Dorney, J. 1981. The impact of Native Americans on presettlement vegetation in southeastern Wisconsin. *Transactions of the Wisconsin Academy of Sciences, Arts, and Letters* 69:26–36.

Forest History Association of Wisconsin. 1982. *A Chronology of "Firsts" in Wisconsin Forest History*. Education Leaflet #1. Forest History Association of Wisconsin, Wausau.

Germain, C., W. Tans, and R. Read. 1977. *Wisconsin Scientific Areas—1977. Preserving Native Diversity*. Technical Bulletin no. 102. Wisconsin Department of Natural Resources, Madison.

Green, W., J.B. Stoltman, and A.B. Kehoe, eds. 1986. *Introduction to Wisconsin Archeology*. Historic Preservation Division, State Historical Society and Wisconsin Archeological Survey. The Wisconsin Archeologist (Special Issue), vol. 67.

Hole, F.D., and C.E. Germain. 1994. *Natural Divisions of Wisconsin*. Wisconsin Department of Natural Resources, Madison.

Lapham, I., J.C. Knapp, and H. Crocker. 1867. *Report on the Disastrous Effects of the Destruction of Forest Trees*. Attwood and Rublee, State Printers, Madison.

Leopold, A. 1949. *A Sand County Almanac*. Oxford University Press, Oxford.

Loucks, O.L. 1968. Scientific areas in Wisconsin: Fifteen years in review. *BioScience* 18:396–398.

McClain, W.E., and S.L. Elzinga. 1994. The occurrence of prairie and forest fires in Illinois and other Midwestern states, 1679 to 1854. *Erigenia* 13:79–90.

Muir, J. 1965. *The Story of My Boyhood and Youth*. University of Wisconsin Press, Madison.

Onsrud, H.J. 1979. A manual for resurvey of public land survey corners and sectionalized subdivision boundaries within the State of Wisconsin. M.S. thesis. University of Wisconsin-Madison.

Schafer, J. 1927. *Four Wisconsin Counties—Prairie and Forest*. Wisconsin Domesday Book. General Studies vol. II. State Historical Society of Wisconsin, Madison.

Scientific Areas Preservation Council (SAPC) and Scientific and Natural Areas Section, BER, Department of Natural Resources. 1983. *Scientific Areas Long-Range Plan*. Wisconsin Department of Natural Resources, Madison.

State Board for the Preservation of Scientific Areas. 1961. *Annual Report*. A. Fuller, chair. Department of Natural Resources, Madison, Wis.

State Board for the Preservation of Scientific Areas. 1963. *Annual Report*. G. Cottam, chair. Department of Natural Resources, Madison, Wis.

Stearns, F., and C. Germain. 1991. Natural Areas Preservation Council: A brief history and record of activity. Natural Areas Preservation Council. Madison, Wis. Mimeographed.

Tans, W. 1976. *Endangered and Threatened Vascular Plants in Wisconsin*. Technical Bulletin no. 92. Wisconsin Department of Natural Resources, Madison.

Thomson, J., chair. 1965. *Natural Areas Use and Management*. Report to the Governor. Wisconsin Academy of Sciences, Arts, and Letters, Madison.

WDNR (Wisconsin Department of Natural Resources). 1995. *Wisconsin's Biodiversity as a Management Issue: A Report to Department of Natural Resources Managers*. Wisconsin Department of Natural Resources, Madison.

Index